PHILOSOPHY
AND THE
MODERN WORLD

PHILOSOPHY
AND THE
MODERN WORLD

by

ALBERT WILLIAM LEVI

INDIANA UNIVERSITY PRESS
BLOOMINGTON

ACKNOWLEDGMENTS

For permission to reprint passages as epigraphs to the various chapters, I am indebted to the following: for Thomas Mann, *The Magic Mountain* (Chapters I, VIII) to Alfred A. Knopf, Inc.; for Marcel Proust, *Remembrance of Things Past* (*The Past Recaptured*) (Chapter III) to Random House, Inc.; for W. B. Yeats, *Collected Poems* (Chapter IV) to The Macmillan Co.; for W. H. Auden, *Collected Poems* (Chapter V) to Random House, Inc.; for Wallace Stevens, *The Collected Poems of Wallace Stevens* (Chapters V, IX) to Alfred A. Knopf, Inc.; for Ezra Pound, *The Cantos of Ezra Pound* (Chapter VI) to New Directions; for Albert Camus, *The Rebel* (Chapter X) to Alfred A. Knopf, Inc.

Acknowledgments for other works quoted will be found in the Notes.

To Michael
(*whose life, for the most part, coincides
with the writing of this book*)
and

To His Grandparents
*living and
dead*

Preface

The present book, as the title indicates, is an attempt to study the chief philosophical ideas which have been produced by, and in turn have influenced, the modern mind. "Ideas," said Auguste Comte, "rule the world, or throw it into chaos." Here are the conceptions, brilliantly originated, deeply pondered, carefully elaborated, which are the ruling notions lying behind our contemporary civilization. Whether they are primarily the agencies of order, or of destruction, lies with the judgment of the future.

These ideas illuminate both the intellect and the spirit of the West. For ideas are at once theories and alternatives, ideals and programs. They express not only the facts of our perception, but our hierarchies of importance and our sense of the worth of life. In figures like Freud, Lenin, Dewey, and Sartre, this is clear upon the surface, but I think it holds no less for the mentality of logic and exact science. I have, therefore, ventured to speak of the inspiration of Russell and Carnap as the "passion" for logic, and of the specialist aims of Moore and Wittgenstein as the "lure" of the part. If this is paradoxical, it is not meant to be invidious.

The area of my concern is limited. It stretches in space from Chicago to Moscow, and in time from the publication of Bergson's *Time and Free Will* in 1889 to the publication of Wittgenstein's *Philosophical Investigations* in 1954. But two qualifications must be added. First, I have not meant to be chronologically exact. Second, for reasons detailed in the first chapter, my conception of "philosophical ideas" is broader and more catholic than what the Europeans call *"reine Philosophie."* For those who are interested in present-day philosophical "schools of thought," Chapters VIII-XI detail the insights respectively of contemporary Pragmatism, Positivism, Existentialism, and Linguistic Analysis. Concerning those who are pure philosophers, but whose work overflows the narrow classification of the schools, there are the chapters on Bergson and Whitehead. But even beyond this, there is an area of the contemporary history of ideas which, although not technically, is indeed in

vii

actuality "philosophical" in the deepest sense of that word. The image of man provided by Freud and his followers, the image of society provided by Lenin and Veblen, the image of history provided by Spengler and Toynbee, and the image of physical nature provided by Einstein and Planck, haunt the background of contemporary mentality even when they do not actively enter into its professional practices and its dreams of social reform. Their details and their meaning I have tried to provide in Chapters IV-VII.

I suppose that in a certain sense *Philosophy and the Modern World* is a species of intellectual history. But in that case it is "Platonic" rather than "Aristotelian" history, for it attempts not merely exposition and description, but also interpretation and understanding. For this reason I believe it to be essentially philosophical. If it is not sufficiently critical for some tastes, this is because I agree with Whitehead that philosophy in the larger view "is not—or, at least, should not be—a ferocious debate between irritable professors . . . but . . . a survey of possibilities." The two ideas which have dominated my thinking are that philosophy in the modern world can be viewed as "varieties of contemporary intellectual experience," and that the root problem which it has inherited from the eighteenth and nineteenth centuries is that of rationality and the irrational. These ideas are developed in my two introductory chapters.

Every author perhaps owes his readers two species of candor: as to the audience for which he hopes, and as to his method and his bias. *Philosophy and the Modern World* has, no doubt, an ambitious subject matter. Its scope may be too large, but it represents my conviction that somewhere in this age of philosophical specialization and limited topics, there must be a place for a comprehensive treatment of the ideological foundations of contemporary civilization. At any rate, it is my own attempt to work through, and to make sense out of, the winds of doctrine of today. This conviction has also, no doubt, influenced my notion as to the ideal reader. I have written for my colleagues and my students of course, but *Philosophy and the Modern World*, although, I hope, scholarly and exact, is yet not technical. I have had in mind primarily that intelligent and generally educated kind of audience which in France in the eighteenth century read with enthusiasm Newton's *Principia* and the *Essays* of David Hume; which in the early decades of this century flocked to hear Henri Bergson's lectures in the great lecture hall of the Collège de France, and which listened to Whitehead deliver the Lowell Lectures in Boston in 1925. For, in the end, the assemblage of philosophical ideas is far more than a specialist study. It is the mirror of our type of civilization, and should be of interest to all those to whom our civilization is a matter of concern.

But how honestly to view the total contemporary philosophical scene without pleading a special metaphysical case? Most of us have, I fancy, at one time or another read Descartes' *Meditations* with a certain uneasiness, if not actual offense. For a man of mature years to pretend to strip everything from his mind except what he cannot doubt! To assert that with years of learning, experience, and mathematical skill behind him, he can in an instant forget it all and convert his consciousness into a blank slate! And to pass off this sorry subterfuge as philosophy! Fine fakery indeed! But later we come to see that Descartes was not deceiving himself; nor is he trying to deceive us. His doubt is not *real* doubt, it is a technical device: a fiction useful for the exhibition of his epistemological theory. Then, entering into this philosophical "as if" (assuming this "willing suspension of disbelief for the moment" which constitutes philosophic faith), we follow his argument, perhaps even to be convinced by it.

How to be impartial about the whole sweep of contemporary philosophic opinion? My dilemma is not un-Cartesian. My purpose is also practical, and my device analogous to his. Let me call it *methodological innocence*. As Descartes pretended in good faith that he could clear his mind, so I have pretended that I could treat all points of view fairly, not dismissing them, or distorting them, but permitting each to speak his own language and to display his virtues along with his inevitable defects. For I have not spent the last three years of my life with the noble intention of constantly "exhibiting the flaw." All of the thinkers here, from Bergson to Whitehead, are, in my opinion, great and important minds. Otherwise I should not have seen fit to include them.

But the bias behind the fiction? Even in Descartes the method occasionally betrays itself. The doubt comes apart at the seams to reveal the more dogmatic stuff underneath. Here too, I am afraid, from time to time, the innocence wears thin, and displays the preferences, judgments, and biases of original sin. I would not wish to dissemble (if I could) that I prefer Spengler to Toynbee; that although I deeply admire Russell and particularly the high seriousness of Carnap, their way is not mine; that although I respect Moore and Wittgenstein, I think that theirs is finally a blind alley. I have a special filial feeling for Freud. I am moved by the simple honesty of almost everything which Einstein has written. I have learned much from Sartre and Jaspers, although I am repelled by the *sang froid* of the first and the *schwerblütigkeit* of the second. Both Lenin and Veblen are interesting to me for their originality, but unattractive in their social solutions. I began as a Bergsonian, but my great and abiding love is Whitehead, and I now tend to see the former as a somewhat fossilized ancestor of the latter. I think that the figures toward whom I am most ambivalent are Dewey and Russell. There are long stretches of the former which are so dull that it is difficult to believe that they can be true, and short passages of the latter which are so clever that it is difficult not to suspect that they must be false. I tend to find each particularly sympathetic where they agree with the final outcome of Whitehead—for example, Russell's revolt against dualism, and Dewey's emphasis upon immediate experience and the interconnectedness of the world. Further lapses from impartiality the reader, I am sure, will have little difficulty in finding for himself.

Philosophy and the Modern World was begun in the summer of 1955 on a research grant from the Graduate School of Washington University, and completed on a similar grant in the summer of 1958. Thus the round of my indebtedness has come full circle. From October 1956 to September 1957 I was in residence at the University of Chicago. A fellowship from the Committee to Advance Original Work in Philosophy of the Western Division of the American Philosophical Association, and an invitation from the Department of Philosophy of the University, permitted me to write and do further research with only a nominal teaching load, giving seminars in the subjects on which I was working. I wish here again to offer my thanks to Dean Lewis Hahn of the Graduate School at Washington University, and to Professor Charner Perry, Chairman of the Department of Philosophy at the University of Chicago, for their unfailing sympathy and help in matters connected with the writing of this book.

Since *Philosophy and the Modern World* has been conceived and produced as an organic enterprise and not as a collection of essays, I have resisted the temptation to publish parts of it separately. But certain sections have been presented orally as experiments in "work in progress." "The Attack on Civilization" and "Rank and the Revisionists" from Chapter V have been read to the Departmental Seminar, and "The Theory of Violence" from Chapter VI to the Social Philosophy Seminar at the University of Chicago. "The Positivistic Avalanche" from Chapter IX has been read to the Philosophy Colloquium, and "Language and Communication" from Chapter XI to the Language and Literature Club at Washington University. The discussion which these produced was always valuable and enlightening to me.

A few of my colleagues at Chicago and at Washington have read separate chapters: Charner Perry and Alan Gewirth Chapter V, Abram Harris Chapter VI, Henry Mehlberg Chapter VII, and Leo Litwak Chapters V and X. I wish to thank them for criticism and encouragement, although they have no responsibility for shortcomings which the chapters possess.

To Miss Shelley Abelson, Secretary to the Department of Philosophy at Chicago, to Miss Maggie Mellies and Miss Helen Holman of Washington University, and to Fraulein Mary Pirrer of Graz, Austria, my thanks for secretarial help painstakingly and excellently accomplished.

To the publishers of the various works quoted in the text, specific acknowledgment will be made in the Notes.

ALBERT WILLIAM LEVI

Vienna, August 31, 1958

Contents

PART I

THE PROBLEMS

I

Multiplicity and Division

The point at which you go wrong is in your estimation of the things of the mind, in general. You obviously think they are too feeble to engender conflicts and passions comparable for sternness with those real life brings forth, the only issue of which can be the appeal to force. *All' incontro!* The abstract, the refined-upon, the ideal is at the same time the absolute—it is sternness itself; it contains within it more possibilities of deep and radical hatred, of unconditional and irreconcilable hostility, than any relation of social life can.

THOMAS MANN, *The Magic Mountain*

1. PERSONAL FRAGMENTATION

All of Western culture—today as in the time of the Periclean Greeks—is haunted by the recollection of a previous golden age. For Plato it was the age of the lost island of Atlantis. For us it is a particular segment of the Judeo-Christian myth. And ours is not (as many have supposed) a yearning for the naive felicity of Eden, innocent, and therefore for Western man without meaning, but rather for that brief moment of the generations of Noah beyond the flood when mankind lived together in solidarity and peace. Its essence is forever distilled in the magnificent opening words of the eleventh chapter of *Genesis*—"And the whole earth was of one language, and of one speech."

The moment was short-lived. Human solidarity, the community of speech, was not accepted humbly as the greatest of gifts; it was boldly exploited in the service of human pride. It was therefore destroyed. The common language was confounded and the people were scattered abroad upon the face of the earth.

The story is, of course, fanciful, compounded out of the wisdom and imagination of some Hebrew seer or scribe living some time between the thousandth and the seven hundredth year before the birth of Christ, but it is symbolic of the tragedy of modern man. For we too, like the sons of Noah, have been deprived of a common language and a common mode of intellectual discourse. What has been the nature of this deprivation? And to what is it due?

One of the deepest needs of the human person is for security. To feel secure in the pursuit of a calling through the knowledge that one uniquely performs a task and is irreplaceable, to feel secure within the

3

family in the knowledge that one loves and is loved according to a stable model of affection, to feel secure within the order of society by a clear recognition of one's station and its duties as fixed, and of one's historic place in the continuity of the generations, are the greatest satisfactions of the individual man. Such security is his only safe anchorage in the turbulent stream of time.

Corresponding to this need in the world of society and human relations is the need for security in the domain of the intellectual life. Here too there are hazards and uncertainties which men have sought to overcome. Here too are contingencies of existence and brute facts which must be ordered, stabilized, and understood. This is the *raison d'être* of scientific theories, systems of philosophy, and the great religions. To meet the daily problems of the mental life as they arise, to live so to speak from hand to mouth in the domain of ideas is not enough. Man's innate anxiety will not permit it. Out of his profound self-distrust he has been forced to become intellectually inventive.

Back of it all lies a stubborn human propensity for asking questions and demanding answers. Moreover, man is not content with *answers* but only with *the answer*. Out of this deep psychological need for intellectual security has come the philosophical search for unchangeable truth and the religious search for the immutable. These are but comradely rivals in the human quest for certainty.

But where in the modern world is this intellectual security to be found? Where is that body of established truth which not only charts the structure of the natural world but also fixes without question man's place within it? Where are those standards accepted universally and without dissent which define the human situation and set a limit to human aspiration? There is a conviction that they are not to be found, and the psychological result is a hollowness of the personality—a sense of emptiness and paralysis which only a contemporary poet of the sensitivity of T. S. Eliot can capture:[1]

> We are the hollow men
> We are the stuffed men.
> Leaning together
> Headpiece filled with straw. Alas!
> Our dried voices, when
> We whisper together
> Are quiet and meaningless
> As wind in dry grass
> Or rat's feet over broken glass
> In our dry cellar

Shape without form, shade without colour,
Paralyzed force, gesture without motion. . . .

There is in the climate of the modern world a sense of impending disaster, a rootlessness of the person, a pervasive tenseness which points to certainties dissolved and emotional centers displaced. It is not accidental that the two most novel philosophic positions of the time—Logical Empiricism and Existentialism—should contribute to this massive effect—the one by narrowing the region of authentic knowledge to a point where it is no longer adequate to the breadth of human concern, the other elevating into ontological principles the human emotions of care, anxiety, anguish, abandonment, and despair.

Clearly, the sense of integration has been lost. "More keenly than ever," says Nicholas Berdyaev, "I feel that night and shadow are descending on the world, just as was the case at the beginning of the Middle Ages, before the mediaeval Renaissance." The faith in a real future has been destroyed. "No one knows," says Ortega y Gasset, "toward what center human things are going to gravitate in the near future and hence the life of the world has become scandalously provisional." The consciousness of belonging to a great human enterprise seems to be withering away. "The insecure human being," says Karl Jaspers, "gives our epoch its physiognomy."

It was not always so. In other times the unity of the fabric of life was more clearly evident. Western man looks back with longing to two great periods of cultural synthesis—the secular millennium of the Athenian city state and the other-worldly paradise of the Middle Ages. From the outbreak of the Ionian revolt against Persia to the death of Socrates was one hundred years of unsurpassed cultural splendor. Whoever reads a Socratic dialogue, listens to a comedy of Aristophanes, or looks at a sculpture of Myron feels the truth of these words of Alfred Zimmern:[2]

The greatest legacy which the Greeks have left to the afterworld is their City State patriotism. The City State was the center and inspiration of all their most characteristic achievements, culminating in the great outpouring of literature and art and practical energy, of great men and great deeds in fifth-century Athens. The world has seen nothing comparable to it either before or since. When the Sovereign City passed away in the fourth century before Christ, the emotions and affections which it had kindled and fed passed away too, and it needs an effort of imagination in the modern man to recapture not them but their shadow.

The security of the intellectual life in fifth-century Athens derived from the function which it performed within the framework of civic affairs. "We differ from other states," says the Pericles of Thucydides, "in regarding the man who holds aloof from public responsibility not as unambitious but as useless." Socrates put to death by his fellow citizens or Euripides dying in exile could still look back upon a life of civic criticism and find it meaningful and important. For these men were "the indispensable opposition." When the intellectual life is indispensable to the social community or the political commonwealth, its security is beyond question.

The political state can be either the wielder of irresponsible power or the agency of humanization. In Periclean Athens it was the agency of humanization. Aristotle, writing when the Greek commonwealth was already in process of decay, but mirroring its deepest aspirations, could still call man *par excellence* a "city-dwelling animal." The life of the city was the basic frame of reference of Greek thought.

The other great cultural synthesis—that of mediaeval Europe from the tenth to the fourteenth century—was not primarily political but religious. Its spirit has been finely summarized by Maurice DeWulf:[3]

Christian dogma and Christian ethics permeated the whole human fabric, no activity being exempted from their influence. They endued with a certain supernatural sanction the life of individuals, families and peoples, who were all on a pilgrimage toward the heavenly home. Christianity gave a spirit of consecration to the workers in guilds, to the profession of arms, to ateliers of painters and of sculptors, to the builders of cathedrals, to cloister-schools and universities.

The remarkable character of this mediaeval synthesis lies in the achievement of a unity of intellectual life based upon a unity of social structure. The magnificent achievement of the scholastic philosophy of the thirteenth century is but the symptom of a deeper sociological integration.[4]

Far from being an anachronism, this remarkable fact of universal agreement in the West satisfies the profound aspirations of the time. For, there was one system of education for princes, lords and clerks; one sacred and learned language, the Latin; one code of morals; one ritual; one hierarchy, the Church; one faith and one common western interest against heathendom and against Islam; one community on earth and in heaven, the community of the saints; and also one system of feudal habits for the whole West.

It is a great temptation for a later age, and particularly one which has lost its own sense of unity and integration, to romanticize and overemphasize the unity and integration of its predecessors. Yet it is difficult to survey the philosophical tradition of western Europe from Saint Augustine to William of Ockham without a certain nostalgia for its unity of basic outlook. To be sure there are differences between the temperament of a Saint Anselm and a Peter Abelard, between the philosophic methods of Saint Thomas Aquinas and Saint Bonaventura, but behind the differences all these men speak a common language. Their endeavors are informed by a common purpose, they share a common vocabulary, and they are the joint heirs of the Greek and Christian tradition. The unity of mediaeval philosophy is a unity of men who are willing to stake their intellectual existence upon five basic texts—*The Old Testament, The New Testament,* the canon of Aristotle, a handful of Platonic dialogues, and the writings of Saint Augustine.

This matter of basic texts is of some importance. It is of the essence of intellectual integration that the number of books from which an age draws its inspiration shall be limited. This is one of the presuppositions which guarantees that any tradition shall be authoritative. And it is partly in these terms that we are to understand the intellectual crisis of the modern consciousness. For ours is the problem of a bewildering multiplicity. How many books may a man read and take seriously without losing his central orientation? This is the intellectual problem of the modern world stated in the language of a textual tradition.

In pointing to the cultural unity of the Athenian city state and of the Middle Ages it is significant to remember that each of these periods is predicated upon a philosophical doctrine about the nature of the human person. The Greeks understood this nature as reflecting the necessities of political life, of the natural relations existing between man and man. Mediaeval men understood this nature in terms of the quest of the individual soul for salvation, a quest which implies that the brotherhood of man is naturally deducible from the universal fatherhood of God. But, viewed from within, Greek naturalism and mediaeval supernaturalism have much in common as they describe human personality. Boethius, at once the last man of the classical world and the first of the scholastics, speaks both for the pagan philosopher Aristotle who is behind him and for the Angelic Doctor Saint Thomas Aquinas who is to come when he says *"persona est rationalis naturae individua substantia"*—the person is an individual being with a rational nature.

We are not primarily concerned with the content of Boethius' definition, which emphasizes human rationality. What is important is that both the ancient and the mediaeval world possess a picture of the human individual *which is not in doubt.* For almost two thousand years of history Western man seems to have known what his own nature is.

But sometime between the fourteenth and the seventeenth century (between the time of Nicholas of Cusa and of Descartes) this ceases to be true. The change can be stated in a somewhat different way. In distinguishing between ancient and mediaeval philosophy on the one hand, and modern philosophy beginning with Bacon or Descartes on the other, it has sometimes been asserted that the former was primarily metaphysical while the latter has been more and more epistemological. The ancient and mediaeval thinkers were concerned with "things." The moderns have been more concerned with "how things are known." To the Greeks man's nature presented no particular problems; but the world of nature and its genesis was a source of constant preoccupation and of doubt. To a discriminating reader Greek ethics (the *Nicomachean Ethics* or Plato's *Republic* perhaps) seems almost *descriptive* in its assurance, while Greek physics and Greek cosmology (the *Physics* or the *Timaeus*) have a tentative and *speculative* character.

From the time of the European Renaissance this situation has been reversed. Throughout the seventeenth century—"the century of genius" as Whitehead calls it—from the time of Kepler and Galileo to the time of Newton, Huygens, and Leibniz the world of physical nature was being made secure. The spatial relations of matter were given mathematical values; physical process was brought under such control that physics could be conceived as a demonstrative science. Therefore Newton's *Principia* is written on the geometrical model of Euclid's *Elements*.[5]

But at the very moment when the success of the science of the physical world is most assured, the status of the human mind through which that science had been obtained begins to be in doubt. It is not only Immanuel Kant who asks in his *Critique of Pure Reason*, How is the science of nature possible? What is the character of that human understanding which gives us physical science? All of the philosophers from Bacon to Hegel, and particularly those British thinkers following in the wake of Newton—Locke, Berkeley, and Hume—take as their fundamental point of departure this very question. Because the mind is the agency of natural understanding, its nature has become the center of the philosophical battleground. "But what, then, am I?" asks Descartes. "A thinking thing, it has been said. But what is a thinking thing?"

How does modern philosophy answer this question of Descartes? What stand does it take upon the crucial issue of personal identity?

The most characteristic answer, and indeed the most decisive answer, since it stems from the analytical method of modern empirical science, is that of David Hume. He says:[6]

... I may venture to affirm of the rest of mankind, that they are nothing but a bundle or collection of different perceptions, which succeed each other with an inconceivable rapidity, and we are in a perpetual flux and movement. Our eyes cannot turn in their sockets without varying our perceptions. Our thought is still more variable than our sight; and all our other senses and faculties contribute to this change; nor is there any single power of the soul, which remains unalterably the same, perhaps for one moment. The mind is a kind of theatre, where several perceptions successively make their appearance; pass, re-pass, glide away, and mingle in an infinite variety of postures and situations. There is properly no *simplicity* in it at one time, nor *identity* in different; whatever natural propension we may have to imagine that simplicity and identity.

For the Greeks, man possesses the unity of his rational nature; for the mediaevals the unity of his God-given soul. But if Hume is right and the mind is merely "a bundle of different perceptions," then the Renaissance break with the world which preceded it is complete, and the absolute unity of the human person is the fiction of a deluded consciousness. In finding human consciousness to consist in separate mental states detached from one another and from any discernible agency binding them together, Hume expressed once and for all the crisis of contemporary intellectual life—the fragmentation of the thinking subject.

Kant's response to Hume on this point is well known. After showing that Cartesian modes of thought are inadequate to the empirical challenge, he asserts that if one conceives the self as a transcendental idea rather than as an object of experience, then it may be taken as a regulative principle for the ordering of all natural knowledge, and we shall make connections between phenomena *as if* our mind were a simple substance, existing permanently, and with personal identity. Whether this fictionalism is adequate to the epistemological problem is highly debatable, but in the moral realm it is certainly open to the most serious question. Is it the case that our assessment of our own characters—our own feeling that we are centers of moral decision, that we are responsible for our deepest moral choices, that our personalities develop and mature, that our sense of life deepens and expands—is it the case that these evidences of internal sense hang upon a merely fictional unity of the human self? And what is the psychological consequence of the belief that any self exhibits a merely "fictional" unity?

Within the modern context, reference to the solution of Kant must seem a little quaint. For a problem which in the eighteenth century centered around the nature of perception has in our own time been cloaked in sociological and psychological dress. But Hume was prophetic. For the fragmentation of consciousness which he asserts in opposition to that "natural propension" we may have to imagine the simplicity and identity of our selves now recurs in the form of a real perplexity and doubt as to whether the multiple social responses of the empirical self spring from a ground that has any other unity than its physical organism publicly locatable in space and time. The most illuminating illustrations of this perplexity in modern fiction occur in the work of Pirandello. Let us listen for a moment to Moscarda, the hero of his novel. He is arguing with a friend:[7]

Very good. But what does it all mean? That actions like forms determine my and your reality? But how? Why? That actions are a prison no one can deny. But even if this is as far as you care to go in your assertions, see to it that you do not contradict me when I state and maintain that they are not only a prison but the most unjust sort of one that could be imagined.

I should think that I had proved it by now. I know Tizio and in accordance with the knowledge that I have of him, I attribute to him a reality. But you also know Tizio and the one that you know is not the one I know. Each of us knows him after his own fashion and after that fashion confers upon him a reality. Even to himself Tizio has as many realities as there are individuals among us who know him. Which is equivalent to saying that Tizio is really one individual with me, another with you, and still another to a third and fourth while he himself preserves the illusion that he is one to all. But the unfortunate thing is this. Suppose that we perform an action. We believe in all good faith that we have thrown ourselves wholly into that act. We soon perceive however that it was not so—that the act on the contrary was simply that of one of the many persons that we are capable of being. I mean to say we find that the whole of ourselves was not in the act and that it would be a terrible injustice to judge us by that act alone, to keep us strung up on that peg as in a pillory for the whole of our existence. "But I am also this one and that one and the other one" we start frantically shouting.

So many alas, so very many persons who remain quite outside that act and had nothing or very little to do with it. What is more, that one who committed the act, that momentary reality which we were, disappears altogether shortly afterward and as evidence of this, the memory of the act remains with us (if it remains at all) as an inexplicable and anguish-ridden dream. Another self, ten other selves, all the others that we are capable of being, rise up in us one by one to ask how we could ever have done such a thing. And we are at a loss for an explanation.

This is the ghost of Hume in modern dress. Of course, you may say that it is only fiction and not philosophy, or that the Moscarda of Pirandello's novel is obviously going mad, but this does not give much comfort. Mythical or mad, the theory of the self which Moscarda puts forward is none other than that standby of pragmatism, the social behaviorism of George Herbert Mead.

It is good pragmatic strategy to deny the relevance of rational psychology in favor of a developmental account of empirical selfhood. More than that, it is in accord with the temper of Western culture since Darwin and in opposition to the elegant formal categories of the eighteenth century. But it can be seriously questioned whether Mead's brilliant account of the social genesis of the self is any more successful than Kant's in establishing the essential unity of the human person.

In a transitional or fragmented society the competition between conflicting social expectations becomes internalized as a conflict between social roles, and the harassed individual under the unbearable weight of the social pressures echoes Pirandello's perplexity: "Who am I really? Am I one person? Am I nobody? Am I a hundred thousand different persons?"

Despite my belief that the pragmatic account of the genesis of the self is inadequate, it is impossible in the twentieth century to dispense with the category of the social as given prominence by Mead and Dewey. For if not in the great works of the pragmatic movement, then at least in the basic texts of the sociological sciences we are compelled to admit the power of sociality. It has now become a commonplace of social science that the character structure of individuals is a socially conditioned organization of drives and satisfactions, and that the components of personality are learned in the process of socialization. Since the chief agencies of socialization are systems of child training, and since these are relatively uniform within any social order, it follows that there should be an observable correlation between the form of any society and the structure of the characters which it produces.[8]

The most brilliant and persuasive reading of this correlation as it pertains to Western man since the Middle Ages has been provided by David Riesman.[9] The thesis is beautifully and classically simple. In the history of Western civilization there have been three stages of the economic process: handicraft production, early industrialization emphasizing work and productivity, late industrialization emphasizing leisure and consumption. Correlative are three types of character formation: the tradition-directed individual of the Middle Ages, the inner-directed individual of Europe from the seventeenth through the nineteenth

century, the other-directed individual of the middle classes of contemporary America. Under a system of tradition-direction, the behavior
of the individual is minutely controlled through kinship regulations,
ritual, routine, and religion. Man is fixed in a tight web of recognized
values, and the necessity of free choice is at a minimum. Under a
system of inner-direction, tradition has broken down, and individuals
must be able to live in an age of mobility and expansion but through
guidance from within, that is, through a system of motivation im-
planted by the parents and directed toward clear goals. Such individuals,
however vulnerable to their own sense of guilt, are easily capable of
withstanding the alien social pressures. The inner-directed type is easily
produced in the atmosphere of Puritanism, an individual strongly re-
liant upon the morality of conscience, relentlessly guided by an inner
drive. Kant was such a man. Although coming a century later, Mill was
also. And strangely enough, so was Sigmund Freud—not in his theory,
but in his own personality.

The type of selfhood known as other-directed—that which characterizes a culture in which there is much leisure and a high standard of
consumption—is very different. It is a type which is perhaps shallower,
friendlier, more uncertain of itself and its values, infinitely more demanding of approval from its surroundings. With the other-directed
type his contemporaries are the source of his values—whether directly
through friends or more indirectly through the mass media of communication. He strives constantly to please them and to be like them. He
achieves behavioral conformity through exceptional sensitivity to the
acts and wishes of others. His primary motivation is the insatiable force
of the psychological need for approval.

I think it is clear that if the Riesman thesis is valid, and we are in
an age of massive other-direction, then the contemporary crisis in the
philosophical theory of the self is paralleled by an actual crisis in the
state of contemporary personality. For if others are the sources of our
values, if these are not identified with the deepest promptings of the
self, then we are in grave danger of discovering one day that we are
mere accumulations of the debris around us, quite without authentic
selfhood. Here is one of the most tragic exemplifications of this that I
know—the words of the brilliant novelist F. Scott Fitzgerald a few
years before he died:[10]

After a long time I came to these conclusions just as I write them here:

(1) That I had done very little thinking save within the problems of my
    craft. For twenty years a certain man had been my intellectual con-
    science. That was Edmund Wilson.

(2) That another man represented my sense of the "good life" although I saw him once in a decade and since then he might have been hung. He is in the fur business in the Northwest and wouldn't like his name set down here. But in difficult situations I have tried to think what *he* would have thought, how *he* would have acted.

(3) That a third contemporary had been an artistic conscience to me. I had not imitated his infectious style, because my own style such as it was was formed before he published anything but there was an awful pull toward him when I was on a spot.

(4) That a fourth man had come to dictate my relations with other people when these relations were successful: how to do, what to say, how to make people at least momentarily happy. This always confused me and made me want to go out and get drunk, but this man had seen the game, analyzed it and beaten it and his word was good enough for me.

(5) That my political conscience had scarcely existed for ten years save as an element of irony in my stuff. When I became again concerned with the system I should function under, it was a man much younger than myself who brought it to me with a mixture of passion and fresh air.

So there was not an "I" any more—not a basis on which I could organize my self respect—save my limitless capacity for toil that it seemed I possessed no more. It was strange to have no self—to be like a little boy left alone in a big house, who knew that now he could do anything he wanted to do but found that there was nothing that he wanted to do.

It is a testimonial which could have been written for one of his characters by Pirandello, and shows that no perplexity of selfhood which appears upon the modern stage exaggerates the perplexity of real life.

2. SOCIAL FRAGMENTATION

The crisis precipitated by Hume's answer to Descartes was a philosophical crisis, an affair of the mind only. But it is deeply symbolic of the wider and more pervasive cultural crisis which confronts our age. For the modern world is faced not only with a fragmentation which has invaded the sources of personality, but with a cultural fragmentation as well.

From the moment when the mediaeval synthesis began to fall into decay, from the fourteenth and fifteenth centuries onward, traditional society likewise entered into a period of disintegration. The rise of the towns in Europe, the emergence of national states and cultures, the Lutheran Reformation, the spread of technology and economic motive throughout the industrial revolution, the revolt of the middle classes in France, the tremendous increase of population and public education in the last three hundred years, have shattered the unity of mediaeval culture into a thousand fragments. Today we are witnessing the last stages of "the Balkanization of life."

In what way has this fragmentation come about? To what characteristics of our society is it due? The two crucial elements in the life of Western man for the past two hundred years have been the growth of modern science and the industrialization of all areas of human life. Indeed, these elements have been interconnected in their effects upon modern society. Industrialization as represented in that continuing process spoken of as the industrial revolution is directly dependent upon the application of the methods and the discoveries of modern science to the ends of industrial production. And the requirements of large-scale production have in turn stimulated the development of scientific research in order that its fruits might be industrially applied. But the most striking fact is that both the requirements of large-scale production and the inherent tendency of an advancing natural science contain the seeds of social fragmentation.

Large-scale production is based upon a specialization of the machine process and upon the efficiency derivable from a highly developed division of labor. This means that industrial society tends to become broken up into classes of workers and dispensers of services who are skilled and habituated in the performance of separate and special tasks without any comprehension of the industrial process as a whole or their role in the society within which the industrial process is rooted. The principle of the division of labor is as old as the *Republic* of Plato. No society can exist without it. But underlying this principle is also Plato's conception of the social organism as a harmonious integration. Always within the social structure must exist the sense of totality and the sense of unalienated participation. Plato provided for this by the myth of the three metals which rationalized his class structure. If there is something distasteful about this to a free society—something that smacks of the less than candid manipulation of a political elite—that is wholly understandable. But the Platonic moral still remains. Every stable society needs the sense of totality, of unified effort, and this common effort can be authentically maintained only by a form of social knowledge which is dispersed into every corner of the social space. The rationale of social coexistence is the picture (myth or science) which dignifies each social place and gives to each specialized activity an indispensability inseparable from authentic human existence. Because the contemporary individual has no comprehensive picture of the social universe within which he lives and of the structure of modern society, he pays the price of meaninglessness and insignificance in his daily work and even a spiritual isolation from his fellows.

Something of the same tendency has characterized modern empirical science. The division of labor and specialization of function which has atomized the industrial and social life of our time also finds its expression in the laboratory and in the productions of scholarly research. Modern science also tends to be atomistic, to deal with smaller and smaller isolates, to become progressively specialized. This compartmentalization of the sciences, entailing as it does recourse to more specialized tools and methods, and, most significant of all, more specialized terminologies and vocabularies, means that in the one area which has always resisted the divisions of religion and the provincialisms of nationalistic feeling, colleagues can often no longer meaningfully speak to one another. Archimedes would have been able to talk with Galileo, Galileo and Newton would have no difficulty in understanding one another, Newton and Clerk Maxwell would find much in common, and Clerk Maxwell and Albert Einstein would probably share a common universe of discourse. But put together in the same room a professor of mathematical bio-physics and a historical geologist learned in the brachiopods of the Devonian age, and you have doubtless condemned two men to complete silence.

The industrialization of modern life and the growth of modern science have come together to produce a civilization divided within itself, and this division has its source in the very spirit of technology. The intrinsic meaning of technology is the application of the method of science to the productive problems of the industrial arts. Technology by definition means the intervention of man in nature, or (to use an Aristotelian phrase), the rational control of the processes of natural change for human ends. But there is a paradox here; it lies in the fundamental contrast presented by the phrase "natural change" and the phrase "for human ends." Implicit in this contrast lie all the ancient antagonisms between the regularity in the order of nature and the creative spontaneity of human life.

There is, perhaps, another and more philosophical way in which this contrast can be stated. This is by distinguishing between two very different kinds of "time," between the impersonal, constant, abstract time of nature on the one hand and the very personal, subjective, variable time of human life on the other. The first kind is natural time or Astronomer Royal's time or time by the clock. It is the time of physical science, sidereal time measured by the rotation of the earth relative to the stars. A sidereal day is the interval between the passage of a meridian eastward across a vernal equinox and its next passage across the vernal equinox. Every day is the same length. An hour is one twenty-fourth of this interval. Every hour is the same in endless repetition; every hour is substitutable for every other. This is the time of insensible matter in motion and it knows nothing of human life.

Psychological or personal time (the time of human life) is very different. It is the time which is qualitative rather than quantitative, which is given its spice and color by human feeling, and it may compass within a single moment the personal decision which will determine an entire future or the experience which gives meaning and significance to a lifetime. This is the time which Bergson speaks of as *duration*, whose recovery through the process of recollection is the entire subject of Proust's great novel *The Remembrance of Things Past*. It is, in the fine phrase of Eddington, "time lived."[11] The hours of clock time pass in eternal recurrence, but the hours of time lived cannot be substituted for one another. They are unique, variable, irreplaceable.

Here we have the clue to one of the great spiritual sicknesses of the contemporary industrial order. Modern technology has applied the method of science to the problems of industrial production. But in so doing it has not stopped with the designing of machines and factories. It has ventured into the area of the men who operate those machines and who work in those factories and in so doing has been forced by its inherent logic to impose the abstract time of physical nature upon men whose dignity and importance lies wholy in the domain of time lived. This is the philosophical explanation of the crisis in the modern industrial world.

The heart of the industrial problem in the modern world is the refusal of a technology dominated by the theoretical framework of physical science and its conception of time to submit to the demands of the time of the human person. In fifth century Athens a leisure making possible real political responsibility was the norm of the city state, while business was scorned as the occupation of the slave.[12] In the modern world it is often with the deepest misgivings that an employee requests of his employer a free afternoon to vote. In the world of the mediaeval artisan when an elderly inhabitant of a village died, everyone closed up shop and the village as a whole attended the funeral; today the birth of children or the death of friends and relatives is merely an interruption of the process of production and of distribution. Birth and death and marriage, the crucial points of reference for time lived, are only a nuisance for a productive process based upon the abstract time of physical science.

The triumph of the mechanical time of industrial production over the specific individuality of time lived is tragically illustrated by the modern practice of paying wages "by the hour" rather than by the quarter or by the year or even by longer periods. Hours of labor, like hours by the clock, are recurrent, replaceable, and without real reference to the past or to the future of persons. The modern industrial system does not employ persons, it contracts to buy hours of labor. When the industrial engineer estimates that the construction of a bombing plane will require 300,000 man-hours of labor the context of his calculation makes him indifferent as to whether this shall be accomplished by 300 men working 1,000 hours each or by 30,000 men each contributing but 10. Indeed, if speed is a consideration, he will prefer the latter alternative. But in either case the choice will be dictated not by the requirements of the life-span of the men working but by the requirements of the thing to be made.

When in 1788 Mozart composed his three last great symphonies within the space of eight weeks, this was not a case of mass production. Those eight weeks were unique segments of time lived, organically related to his total past, which was simply their prelude, and to his pitifully short future. And when in that same year Edward Gibbon brought to completion his famous *The Decline and Fall of the Roman Empire* after twenty-four years of work and meditation, this too was not something apart from Gibbon's life but its very inmost expression. In either case, labor of eight weeks or labor of twenty-four years, what was produced was intelligible only in terms of a long-time point of view. The symphonies of Mozart and the history of Gibbon are the symbols of life continuity—they certify not time by the clock but time lived.

Contrast this situation with that of the modern factory worker. He is paid by the hour. He works 2,000 hours a year. His working time is broken up into units. These units are anonymous and replaceable. The great problem is how to maintain the unity of such a life. As the partner in a marriage, as the father of children, a man must make long-time plans. But how can a man who is paid by the hour, whose life is dominated by the short-time perspective of modern industrial employment, be expected at the same moment to adapt himself to the long-time requirements of time lived?

The answer is, of course, that he cannot. And the price which he pays in consequence is again a fragmentation of life. "What a man can do nowadays," says Karl Jaspers,[13] "can only be done by one who takes short views. He has occupation indeed but his life has no continuity." What is characteristically human about labor is the possibility of real creation; it is this possibility fulfilled which gives the sense of achievement and pleasure in work. But this is exactly what the application of the time of natural science to the process of industrial production has denied: "Joy in work is ruined whenever the working of the universal order is such as to split up the whole into partial functions, those who perform them being indifferently replaceable."[14] By the dehumanization of work as well as by the loss of religious faith the organic unity of the mediaeval synthesis has been destroyed.

The attempt to contrast the deeper stratum of the self with the self which is appealed to or exploited by the system of industrial production is hardly new. Marx himself pointed to the *Verdinglichung* of modern man, to the tendency for man to become an object or a commodity. But this criticism, which Marx first suggested within a context of economic history, has been developed as general social criticism by contemporary Existentialism. Karl Jaspers has applied the point of view to the analysis of family life and of occupation. And it has led Gabriel Marcel to view our tragic loss of the sense of "being" as a direct consequence of the current misplacement of the idea of "function."[15]

Travelling on the Underground, I often wonder with a kind of dread what can be the inward reality of the life of this or that man employed on the railway—the man who opens the doors, for instance, or the one who punches the tickets. Surely everything both within him and outside him conspires to identify this man with his functions—meaning not only with his functions as worker, as trade union member or as voter, but with his vital functions as well. The rather horrible expression 'time table' perfectly describes his life. So many hours for each function. Sleep too is a function which must be discharged so that the other functions may be exercised in their turn. The same with pleasure, with relaxation; it is logical that the weekly allowance of recreation should be determined by an expert on hygiene; recreation is a psycho-organic function which must not be neglected any more than, for instance, the function of sex. We need go no further; this sketch is sufficient to suggest the emergence of a kind of vital schedule; the details will vary with the country, the climate, the profession, etc., but what matters is that there is a schedule. . . .

I need hardly insist on the stifling impression of sadness produced by this functionalised world. It is sufficient to recall the dreary image of the retired official, or those urban Sundays when the passers-by look like people who have retired from life. In such a world, there is something mocking and sinister even in the tolerance awarded to the man who has retired from his work.

The time-table, the schedule, and the clock are here the symbols of man's alienation from an intrinsically human world. And the submergence of the human in the requirements of the mechanical makes itself felt both in the conditions of life and in the philosophies which have been developed to validate this point of view.

3. THE BREAK-UP OF THE MIND

The contrast between "time lived" and "time by the clock" as this expresses itself in the impact of industrial technology upon the life of modern man has not been explored primarily for the purpose of constructing a critique of modern society, but rather because there are concepts here which find their parallel in the confusions of modern intellectual life. The impersonal time of science opposed to the personal time of human biography, the working side of life opposed to the side of leisure, the short time perspective of wages by the hour opposed to the lifetime perspective of marriage partnership and responsible parenthood suggest divisions and antagonistic perspectives in social life which have their analogue in the divisions and antagonistic perspectives of our mental life. It is unavoidable that this should be so. One does not need to be a Hegelian metaphysician to see the sense in which the most diverse aspects of a culture express its underlying spirit, whether this be a political ideal, a religious integration, or an economic conflict. The intellectual life of an age and its social structure express a recognizable congruence.

It has been suggested by Spengler, by Ortega y Gasset, and by Whitehead that in many ways our age is culturally analogous to the period between the breakdown of the classical world and the birth of Christian culture. The Hellenistic age, like our own, was a period of great cities, great commercial development and international exchange, pretentious architecture, bizarre and frequently vulgar forms of literature, and tremendous devotion to the development of science and the most meticulous and specialized forms of research.[16] But the comparison is particularly apt as regards the openness and competitiveness of the intellectual climate of opinion. The breakdown of the unity of classical culture meant not only a new materialism of outlook, but an increasing "professionalization" of philosophy into academic sects and a live competition between Greek and Asiatic religious cults for the last remnants of a decaying faith. Stoicism, Epicureanism, Agnosticism, Orphism, Cynicism, Skepticism, Tychism, and the worship of the New Dionysius existed side by side in a fine imbalance.

As the Hellenistic world stood to the Athenian synthesis, so the twentieth century stands to the unity of mediaeval culture. If one wanders into the late mediaeval room of any large metropolitan art museum and examines the Italian primitives of the Florentine or the Sienese school, unless he is experienced he will be unable to distinguish one painter from another. Not only the unity of thematic material—illustrations of the Bible, the legends of the Saints, the ritual of the Church, and the Apocrypha—but even a similarity of style and chromatic choice stand as striking testimonials to the unified cultural matrix within which this painting originated. But should the museum also be so fortunate as to possess a room devoted to the work of Picasso in all its stages, the visitor will stand in amazement and frank unbelief that the totally incongruous subjects and incompatible styles should be attributed to the life development of a single man. The sombreness of the "blue period," the "analytical cubism" of the pre-war days, and the "classicism" of the early twenties will hang together in mute incongruity. For the painting of Picasso is a perfect symbol of the intellectual and aesthetic pluralism of our age.

If, in concern over today's loss of a common mode of intellectual discourse, we turn to an examination of the mediaeval world, it becomes eminently clear that here the unity of the intellectual life is based upon a unity of social structure. It has been said with perhaps some slight oversimplification that the society of the Middle Ages is divided into three classes: the *laboratores*, those who work; the *bellatores*, those who fight; and the *oratores*, those who pray. The last class of those who pray includes "the class of those who think." It is not particularly congenial to modern democratic thought to entertain the Platonic notion that specialization of function within society extends even to the processes of the intellectual life. And yet what the democratic theorist is reluctant to adopt as a norm, the modern sociologist actually posits as a fact. "In every society," says Karl Mannheim,[17]

there are social groups whose special task it is to provide an interpretation of the world for that society. We call these "the intelligentsia." The more static a society is, the more likely is it that this stratum will acquire a well-defined status or the position of a caste in that society. Thus the magicians, the Brahmins, the mediaeval clergy are to be regarded as intellectual strata, each of which in its society *enjoyed a monopolistic control* over the moulding of that society's world-view, and over the reconstruction or the reconciliation of the differences in the naively formed world-views of the other strata. The sermon, the confession, the lesson, are, in this sense, means by which reconciliation of the different conceptions of the world takes place at less sophisticated levels of social development.

Nor do the great intellectual debates of the twelfth and thirteenth centuries weaken the general acknowledgment of ecclesiastical authority. If Roscellinus holds one extreme position on the problem of universals, and William of Champeaux holds another, and Peter Abelard reduces both to an absurdity, yet the debate is isolated within the academic circle of the intelligentsia—even though all three maintain that they are not merely debating a philosophical proposition of purely academic interest but are wagering on this debate the destiny of the Apostolic Church and the salvation of the individual. And if a century later Franciscans and Dominicans dispute the interpretation of sacred doctrine and Aquinas saves the Christian world from Averroism and Siger de Brabant, these disputations too are segregated within the confines of the cloisters and the universities. For lay society, the clergy remains unified and authoritative.

The uneasy tensions of the modern world, generated out of the multiplicity of perspectives and philosophies of human life, and the loss of the sense of intellectual security, are intimately bound up with the breakdown of ecclesiastical authority and the substitution of free competition for monopoly in the intellectual life.[18]

From a sociological point of view the decisive fact of modern times, in contrast with the situation during the Middle Ages, is that this monopoly of the ecclesiastical interpretation of the world which was held by the priestly caste is broken, and in the place of a closed and thoroughly organized stratum of intellectuals, a free intelligentsia has arisen.

The rise of the towns out of the commercial revival of the eleventh century, the slow growth of an urban middle class, the emergence of middle-class literature and art in the fourteenth century,[19] the use of vernacular languages, the spread of literacy, and finally the introduction of printing in the middle of the fifteenth century completed the breakdown of the ecclesiastical monopoly of the intellectual life. Humanists like Petrarch, Boccaccio, and later Erasmus on the one hand undermine the clergy with their social criticism, and on the other demonstrate the effectiveness of secular scholarship through their mastery of the literature and philosophy of the classical world. What had been implicit for over a hundred years was made explicit by the Reformation and Luther's insistence upon the freedom and equality of all individuals in the interpretation of the Bible. Henceforth there is no intermediary between the human person and the word of God, and the individual becomes responsible through his own free choice for his salvation and his destiny.

The last four hundred years have witnessed a series of progressive variations upon the theme of freedom of choice. The freedom to choose and practice a religion without persecution, the freedom to criticize political authority without penalty, the freedom to choose a life-partner and to rectify this choice, the freedom to choose a business or profession, the freedom to choose one's governmental representatives have slowly emerged from the wars, revolutions, and insurrections since the Protestant Reformation. And most important of all is the freedom to choose one's own picture of the human person and a philosophy of human life.

But behind the emergence of this freedom there lies a deadly paradox —a paradox rooted in the nature of human ambivalence. Man fights to the death to maintain his freedom, but once it is attained he does everything in his power to escape its consequences. In the nineteenth century there were a handful of thinkers slowly groping their way toward this insight, but none of them has expressed it with the brilliance and clarity of Dostoyevski. Its explicit statement comes, of course, in *The Brothers Karamazov* in the famous chapter "The Grand Inquisitor." Jesus has come for the second time during the inquisition and the aged Cardinal has had him placed by the guards in a prison cell. At nightfall he comes to confront him and speaking to Jesus he says:[20]

Thou wouldst go into the world and art going with empty hands, with some promise of freedom which men in their simplicity and their natural unruliness cannot even understand, which they fear and dread—for nothing has ever been more insupportable for a man and a human society than freedom . . . . So long as man remains free he strives for nothing so incessantly and so painfully as to find someone to worship. But man seeks to worship what is established beyond dispute, so that all men would agree at once to worship it. For these pitiful creatures are concerned not only to find what one or the other can worship, but to find something that all would believe in and worship; what is essential is that all may be *together* in it. This craving for *community* of worship is the chief misery of every man individually and of all humanity from the beginning of time . . . . For the secret of man's being is not only to live but to have something to live for. Without a stable conception of the object of life, man would not consent to go on living, and would rather destroy himself than remain on earth though he had bread in abundance. That is true. But what happened? Instead of taking men's freedom from them, Thou didst make it greater than ever! Didst Thou forget that man prefers peace, and even death to freedom of choice in the knowledge of good and evil? Nothing is more seductive for man than his freedom of conscience, but nothing is a greater cause of suffering . . . .

I have quoted this passage from Dostoyevski at length not because of its implications for religion, but because in a way it is symbolic of the intellectual dilemma of the modern world. For at precisely that moment when the social possibilities of freedom of intellectual choice are greatest, the very multitude of intellectual alternatives creates a painful suspension of judgment and a paralysis of the faculty of intellectual choice. Nothing is more seductive for man than his intellectual freedom, but nothing is a greater cause of perplexity. The dissolution of the closed universe of the mediaeval synthesis has brought division into the community of worship and has presented the modern world with the dilemmas of intellectual multiplicity.

For the last two centuries we have been living in what Graham Wallas has called "The Great Society," but this great society is at the same time an "open" society.[21] It is "open" in the sense that there is no longer any general consensus of belief guaranteed by a single authoritative intellectual elite. Instead there is a plurality of intellectual elites no one of which can deeply and conclusively influence the whole of society.[22] Freudians, Marxists, Existentialists, Bergsonians, Positivists, Deweyites, neo-Scholastics, followers of Whitehead and of Toynbee, and many others compete with one another for the intellectual allegiance of modern man and in the process of this competition illustrate the heterogeneity of our society and the conflict of values which confronts the modern world.

4. SALVATION AND AMBIGUITY

It has always been the problem of the scholar and the serious thinker to face the stream of intellectual history and to make his peace with the tradition into which he is born. It is for this reason that the greatest of the philosophers have themselves been learned in the history of philosophy. The works of Aristotle utilize the doctrines of his predecessors to arrive at the traditional or customary meaning of concepts and to clarify his own position whether in agreement or opposed. The *Critique of Pure Reason* indicates that Kant has assimilated the philosophic tradition from Descartes to Hume. Comte and Hegel use the entire history of philosophy and science before their time to demonstrate that their own theories are the culmination of an ongoing process of intellectual development. And in our own time thinkers as different as Dewey and Whitehead make crucial appeal to the philosophic tradition. Dewey examines the foundations of the philosophies of Plato and Aristotle in the same spirit in which Aristotle examines the doctrines of Plato: to indicate where the forerunner has gone astray and where he must be corrected in the service of truth. Whitehead re-examines the doctrines of Plato, Spinoza, and Locke to note the respects in which they have anticipated his Philosophy of Organism in the same spirit in which Plato found certain confirmations in the prior doctrines of Parmenides. In both cases what is important is a sense of the contemporaneity of the historical materials. It is precisely this sense which

T. S. Eliot has evoked for the poet in his famous essay on "Tradition and the Individual Talent":

Tradition is a matter of much wider significance. It cannot be inherited, and if you want it you must obtain it by great labour. It involves in the first place, the historical sense . . . and the historical sense involves a perception not only of the pastness of the past, but of its presence . . . .

Tradition, as Eliot says, cannot be merely appropriated; it must be won, and the historical sense which involves the "presence" of the past works in the service of a new synthesis and a higher originality. So it was with Aristotle and Kant. So it is with Dewey and Whitehead. But it is crucial to remember that these thinkers were not masters of the past in order to be its slaves, but in order to pass beyond it. It is a great temptation for the contemporary thinker and scholar to forget this.

I have spoken before of the likeness between the cultural anarchy of the Hellenistic world and of our own. One of the areas in which the similarity is most striking is in the relationship between philosophy and religion. Whitehead has brilliantly distinguished between two moments in the development of thought:[23] the moment of *speculation* and the moment of *scholarship*.

The progress of mankind proceeds by devious paths. The shift from the bright Hellenic age, whose final period was centered in Athens, to the Hellenistic age, with Alexandria as its intellectual capital, corresponds to a new direction of constructive genius. The special sciences were founded. Their principles were defined, their methods were determined, appropriate deductions were elicited. Learning was stabilized. It was furnished with methodologies, and was handed over to University professors of the modern type. Doctors of Medicine, Mathematicians, Astronomers, Grammarians, Theologians, for more than six hundred years dominated the schools of Alexandria, issuing text-books, treatises, controversies, and dogmatic definitions. Literature was replaced by Grammar, and Speculation by the Learned Tradition. These men conventionalized learning.

Athens in the fifth and fourth centuries before Christ, from the time of Protagoras to the time of Aristotle, was a period of miraculous speculation. Philosophy was in the ascendancy, whereas religious belief was a matter of civic custom and convention, altogether secondary in speculative importance. The Hellenistic age, on the contrary, was a scholarly period with speculative philosophy in the tradition of Plato and Aristotle in full decay. Both the Platonic Academy and the Aristotelian Lyceum had lost their original genius for speculative boldness and contented themselves with the more conservative task of preserving the works of their founders, reproducing them and elaborating them in endless interpretation and commentary. The consequence was that philosophy, in its new preoccupation with elaborating the minute, had lost its former capacity to be dangerous. But this was exactly the characteristic possessed by the competing Hellenistic religions. They were inconsistent, they were irrational, and they were bizarre, but for all that they had a vitality growing out of their relation to human purpose. For they were concerned with the problem of human salvation. Hellenistic religions were potentially dangerous, and when finally in the early days of the Roman empire they merged into the broadening stream of Christianity, they became so actually. They attracted to themselves political power and they asserted a way of life.

In our own day technical philosophy, the philosophy of the universities, has, like that of its Hellenistic analogue, become minute and academic. In its constant preoccupation with its own history, in its willingness to content itself with the comparison and classification of its own schools, and through a preference for the more technical and abstract problems of logic and epistemology, it has seemed to have lost touch with the more vital problems of human decision; it has almost lost the capacity for being dangerous. And perhaps when it is possible for philosophers to philosophize in comfort, when it is possible to engage in speculation without serious risk, then over philosophy has fallen the shadow of its own extinction.

In such a situation the more vital and functional role of philosophy passes out of the hands of philosophers. In contemporary culture to a very large extent this is exactly what has happened. If one wishes to find the real battleground of modern thought it is necessary to turn not to professional philosophers, but rather to psychologists, physical scientists, and social theorists. The germs of crucial controversy are not to be found in the writings of "the new Analysts," "the epistemological dualists," or "the objective relativists," but rather in the writings of Freud and Jung, Lenin and Veblen, Sartre and Toynbee. Here again the parallel with the Hellenistic world is apt. For in the modern world these writings perform the same function as the Hellenistic religions, that is, they fall more or less within the category of salvation literature. Marxism, psychoanalysis, the pessimistic philosophy of history—these are intellectual commitments which involve risks and moral consequences. And this is precisely why they have become the primary determinants of the spirit of modern art and modern literature.[24]

The parallel is apt in another respect also. For if these creeds are carefully examined, it will be found that not only their doctrinal function but also their sociological structure lends color to the religious analogy. The sociological essence of religion is the idea of the *cult*. This involves first a revelation, second a prophet, third a priesthood, and finally a discipleship or fellowship of the elect. The elect, through various purifications and demonstrations of faith, have become initiated into, if not the central mysteries, at least their peripheral symbols. And between the initiated and those outside the charmed circle lies an infinity of social distance defined by the common acknowledgment of caste and status of those within the group. In the modern world we have the Eleusinian mysteries of orthodox Marxism, the Dionysian rites of the Freudian fellowship, and the Orphic revelation of the Aristotelian canon. The important element is, of course, the divine revelation, and in the highly literate religious atmosphere of the modern world it is inevitable that this revelation should take the form of the written word. It is further inevitable in the society of contemporary Western culture, which has been so profoundly influenced by the Christian Reformation's conception of *The Book*, that each of these competing cults should have its Bible. It is in this sense that we are to understand the intellectual elites which have grown up around *Das Kapital*, *The Decline of the West*, *The Basic Writings of Sigmund Freud*, and *The Summa Theologica*.

But the crucial point is that in the deadly antagonism between these revelations and the cults which have grown up about them, in their mutual hostility and in their fierce competition for the souls of those yet unsaved, is mirrored the atomizing of the intellectual life and the philosophical chaos of the modern world. This is the sense in which those words of Settembrini from *The Magic Mountain* quoted at the head of this chapter are to be understood: the abstract, the refined upon, the ideal *is* in these cults the absolute. Each in its own way does contain the possibilities of deep and radical hatred—of unconditional and irreconcilable hostility.

There are, it seems to me, two respects in which the literature of the twentieth century also expresses the intellectual dilemmas of multiplicity and division. The first is in its technique. The second is in its subjects and in its general mood. If one considers the literary masterpieces of our age, the writings of Gertrude Stein for example, or Joyce's *Ulysses*, or *The Cantos* of Ezra Pound, one is forced to concede that much of their significance lies in the brilliance with which they have originated new techniques of expression and new patterns of craftsmanship. What is less frequently considered, however, is the possibility that their preoccupation with problems of technique is the direct outgrowth of a cultural situation in which the author no longer can be the mirror of the unified value pattern of his age.[25]

Joyce, Pound, and Stein were all (in those uncertain moments before they became recognized classics) "avant-garde" writers, and it is the peculiar function of avant-garde writers to exist in a relation to their society which causes their work to arouse resentment and to give offense. This is partly because their work seems an immoderate criticism of the conservative tradition, but even more because it shows all too clearly that there is no longer really a conservative tradition to which a creative artist can respectably belong. Extreme naturalism is one form which this protesting and "ill-natured" literature may take. The incitement to social violence—so-called proletarian literature—is another. The third possibility—that of Joyce, Stein, and Pound—which flourished and glistened after the First World War was an avant-garde of style and technique. Its attack was upon the formal structure of literature—the habits of ordinary syntax, the serial method of narration, the usual conventions of punctuation—in short, everything in literature which goes by the name of order. This "attack," creative and life-giving as it was to literature itself, did not signify a wilful destructiveness against an ordered society, but rather a reaction against a society in which norms had broken down and which was deficient in the sense of cultural integration. It is not insignificant that the major practitioners (Joyce, Stein, Pound) were expatriates from their native lands, living on foreign soil, bohemian not only in that they were unconventional but also in that they occupied no secure place within a society of well-defined classes. Rootless, they mirrored the rootlessness of an age, and where they expressed hope, it was for their craft and not for an integrated society.

It is possible that in a world in which there is real community of belief communication can itself be straightforward and unambiguous. Style and content achieve a classic unity of integration. But when the traditional sources of value within a society are called into question, when uniformity of faith disintegrates, then it may be that the artist must seek the surrogate for a diminished unity of content in an augmented sensitivity to the problems of technical construction. The expansion of technique is the major compensation which art receives when its mandate to give expression to the community of faith has been revoked by an indecisive age. It is perhaps precisely this compensatory and obsessive urge to experiment which has produced in painting Picasso, Kandinsky, Miro, and Klee and in literature the problematic constructions of surrealist poetry, *Tender Buttons, Ulysses,* and *Fin-*

negans Wake. It may be this which underlies the so-called "unintelligibility" of modern art.

Wallace Stevens, one of the greatest of contemporary American poets, has put the matter this way:[26]

The paramount relation between poetry and painting today, between modern man and modern art is simply this: that in an age in which disbelief is so profoundly prevalent or, if not disbelief, indifference to questions of belief, poetry and painting, and the arts in general, are, in their measure a compensation for what has been lost.

But it is a serious question whether this can really be true. Only if the aesthetic way of life can be taken as a substitute for ethical assertion and religious faith are the arts a compensation for what has been lost. While it is surely possible for poetry and painting to assert an ethical or a religious mode of perception—as for example the painting of Rouault and the later poetry of T. S. Eliot—yet this is not the mainstream of the contemporary arts. Their typical form is an abstract experimentalism which in the technical language of their respective media mirrors rather than overcomes "disbelief or indifference to questions of belief."

The mood of ambiguity and discontent may also be expressed as an integral part of the content of literature. We have seen how Hume's answer to Descartes's question (which has meant the fragmentation of the human ego) finds characteristic artistic expression in the central problem which has been the constant obsession of the dramatist Pirandello. In his novel *One, None, or One Hundred Thousand* the hero Moscarda, driven toward madness by his inability to fathom the structure of his own selfhood, cannot discover definitely whether he is one, nothing at all, or the multiplicity of the hundred thousand roles which life and society thrust upon him.

The same mood of ambiguity is stated in such works as Franz Kafka's *The Trial* and more systematically by Thomas Mann in *The Magic Mountain*.[27] *The Magic Mountain* is at once a documented demonstration of the degeneration of modern European middle-class society and a testimonial by one of the most gifted writers of our generation to the chaos of modern intellectual life. In Mann's work ambiguity is adopted in full consciousness as a symbol of the fragmentation of the philosophical universe of discourse (and perhaps also as a lapse into intellectual autobiography). In the protagonist, Hans Castorp, is manifested a brooding indecisiveness; the verbose liberal Settembrini is incapable of action, even (as in his duel with Naphta) when his very life is at stake. Even the commonplaces of the life at the sanatorium where the story takes place are in doubt. Does Hans really have tuberculosis or not? Are the doctors actually attempting to cure their patients quickly or are their medical decisions guided simply by the desire to retain profitable clients as long as possible? Is psychoanalysis a form of medical quackery or of real therapeutic value? Is love a deep spiritual commitment or merely the quaint uneasiness of the body?[28]

These questions are never conclusively answered, and what is more, the evidence which Mann presents might favor either interpretation. Most striking of all, however, are the long, pedantic, but somehow deeply exciting debates between Naphta and Settembrini in which most of the intellectual dilemmas of the modern world are cast upon the surging tide of controversy. Nationalism or universalism, humanism or religion, individual freedom or institutional discipline, faith or reason, Communism or economic liberalism—these are the questions. But to these questions there are no conclusive answers. Naphta, the mediaeval scholastic with a logical and anti-pecuniary bias, and Settembrini, the nineteenth-century liberal humanitarian, engage in ferocious dialectical encounters in which the stake is presumably the intellectual allegiance of Hans Castorp. But in the end it is impossible for Hans Castorp to accept any of the alternatives offered. Spectator throughout, with now and again just a momentary response to the prevailing doctrinal wind, he is left finally with all of the uncertainty with which he began. Here again *The Magic Mountain* makes its allegorical point. Caught between the cross-fire of the warring intellectual elites, the contemporary individual is caught and held in uneasy intellectual suspension. But the tension is never resolved and the atmosphere of Mann's conclusion remains that of ambiguity.

We return then to that point at which in this chapter we began. All of Western culture is haunted by the recollection of a previous golden age, an age in which there was a common language and a community of faith. The last golden age for Western man was the period of the mediaeval synthesis, with a stratified but secure organization of society, the monopoly of world interpretation by a single intellectual elite, and consequently a unified picture of human life and of the human person. But with the breakdown of mediaeval society under the impact of science and the commercial point of view, a rigidly organized and essentially closed society becomes a loosely integrated and an open society. Corresponding to the new social pluralism there develops an intellectual pluralism. The one elite is displaced by a plurality of warring elites with a plurality of intellectual points of view. The inescapable fact about the intellectual life of the modern world is the fact of multiplicity and division.

II

Rationality and Irrationality

Hast du Verstand und ein Herz, so zeige nur eines von beiden;
Beides verdammen sie dir, zeigst du beides zugleich.

HÖLDERLIN

And the most tragic problem of philosophy is to reconcile intellectual necessities
with the necessities of the heart and the will. For it is on this rock that every
philosophy that pretends to resolve the eternal and tragic contradiction, the basis
of our existence, breaks to pieces.

UNAMUNO

L'homo sapiens, seul être doué de raison, est le seul aussi qui puisse suspendre son
existence à des choses déraisonnables.

BERGSON

1. EIGHTEENTH-CENTURY RATIONALISM

The twentieth century (like any complicated historical period) is an age of contrasts, of uneasy paradoxes and striking contradictions. On the one hand is the massive beauty of our technical accomplishment—on the other, recurrent outbreaks of racial hatred and Fascist terror. Planck, Heisenberg, and Einstein produce the most magnificent formulations of the ordered system of physical nature; the devastation of Hiroshima exemplifies the madness which has been their consequence. Scarcely twenty years ago a mélange of voices filled our ears: on the one hand the hysterical and vituperative outpourings of Hitler and Mussolini, on the other the calm and gentlemanly accents of the logical Bertrand Russell and the ivory-tower serenity of the aesthete Santayana. Thomas Mann and Virginia Woolf were producing an orderly and cultivated prose. Gertrude Stein and James Joyce were producing a literature more playful and closer to the rhythms of the heart. The cold and masterly precision of Russell and Whitehead's *Principia Mathematica* was given to Western culture at almost the same moment as the tortured flow of fantasy which is surrealist painting. In politics, in society, in philosophy, in literature, and in the arts, on the one side we find logic, rationality, and structure, and on the other formlessness, passion, perhaps even the materials of neurosis. How has it been possible for these things to live together in the modern world? Where did they come from? What is the meaning of their coexistence?

If one probes more deeply into these contrasts and into the paradox which they present, it will be found, I believe, that these manifestations in economic and political life, in philosophy and science, in literature and the arts are unified and interdependent. For underlying them is an absorbing problem of our epoch—the problem of rationality and the irrational. It is the second great intellectual problem of the twentieth century and it represents the heritage of the last three hundred years of Western thought.

I do not mean that the contrast between rationality and the irrational is the peculiar property of our age. It has also haunted the past, but its claims then seemed less insistent. This is perhaps clearest in the case of the Greeks. Because of Plato's emphasis upon reason and mind, because of Aristotle's portrayal of the power of the active intellect and the primacy of the life of contemplation, there is a tendency to forget that Greek philosophy began in religious ecstasy and that the wilder emotions haunted the Greek theatre before they were banished from the Academy and the Lyceum. The wilder emotions are absent from the philosophers (except perhaps in Plato's picture of the Tyrant), but they survive in the burning drama of Euripides. In the insane jealousy of Medea, in the violent, almost uncontrollable, sexual passion of Phaedra, in the wild religious frenzy of *The Bacchae* is proof of the Dionysian and demonic elements which lurk uneasily in the background of the Greek consciousness.

Of course the philosophers do everything in their power to ignore the scandal, and to present to the world a united front for the life of reason. Plato presents a threefold picture of the human soul in which desire and emotion play their part, but he sees in the rationality of the ego a powerful principle of administration which can harmonize discord through the potency of its natural claim. Aristotle, too, cognizant of the irrational elements which may enter into moral choice, finds the realization of the Good in a purposive choice guided by the conclusions of rational deliberation. Even where the claims of passion seem most intense, as in the case of that *eros* which is the source of generation, Plato must in the *Symposium* dwarf the ideas of Phaedrus and Pausanias and Aristophanes and exalt those of Socrates, who sublimates the erotic impulse into the knowledge of beauty and the yearning for immortal life.

Yet in the *Timaeus* Plato, in order to account for the creation of the world by the operations of Reason, has to introduce another element called Necessity—the element of force or fate that lies at the heart of things, persuaded by Reason into orderly channels but never completely subdued. The myth of the persuasiveness of Reason enabled the Greeks to preserve the fiction of the rational life. This myth is asserted not only by the Greek philosophers, but by Aeschylus, the profoundest of the Greek tragedians.[1] In the *Eumenides* Orestes is hounded to the very foot of the Areopagus of Athens by the Furies demanding the price of his blood. A trial is held under the auspices of Athena wielding the authority of Zeus. Apollo confronts the Furies and defends Orestes. But the Furies will not yield. Finally Athena, representative of the divine Reason, turns herself to the task of persuasion, and eventually the forces of unreason yield to her arguments. So the ultimate moral of the *Timaeus* and the *Eumenides* turns out to be the same. Plato and Aeschylus cooperate in the preservation of the myth. Greek rationalism wins a precarious victory. For as Whitehead has said, it lives in the faith that a world of civilized order is a victory of persuasion over force.

The dominant critical problem of the twentieth century is to reconcile the role of the irrational in human conduct with the demand for reason in the ordering of society. The central position of this problem in our age derives from the intellectual history of the last three centuries in the West. It is, I think, the inevitable consequence of the conflict of two ideas, one the culmination of the intellectual climate of opinion of the seventeenth and eighteenth centuries, the other the outgrowth of the science of the nineteenth. It represents the confusion which inevitably results when the picture of the human individual implied in the philosophy of René Descartes is confronted with the picture of the human individual sketched in the biological science of Charles Darwin —when the picture of man the universal mathematician is set side by side with the picture of man the well-trained animal. If an age takes both pictures seriously, as the twentieth century has, it can hardly escape schizophrenia.

Descartes states his case clearly in the fourth part of *The Discourse on Method*, which appeared in 1637:[2]

.... I thence concluded that I was a substance whose whole essence or nature consists only in thinking, and which, that it may exist, has need of no place, nor is dependent on any material thing; so that "I," that is to say, the mind by which I am what I am, is wholly distinct from the body, and is even more easily known than the latter, and is such, that although the latter were not, it would still continue to be all that it is.

Darwin is equally explicit in the third chapter of *The Descent of Man*, which appeared in 1871:[3]

If no organic being excepting man had possessed any mental power, or if his powers had been of a wholly different nature from those of the lower animals, then we should never have been able to convince ourselves that our high faculties had been gradually developed. But it can be shown that there is no fundamental difference of this kind. We must also admit that there is a much wider interval in mental power between one of the lowest fishes . . . and one of the higher apes, than between an ape and man. . . . As man possesses the same senses as the lower animals, his fundamental intuitions must be the same. Man has also some few instincts in common, as that of self-preservation, sexual love, the love of the mother for her newborn offspring, the desire possessed by the latter to suck and so forth. . . .

Neither Descartes nor Darwin is in these passages explicitly presenting a philosophy of human nature. Descartes was simply concerned with establishing a method of inquiry which, while passing the most rigid requirements of the human faculty of doubt, should at the same time provide for man clear and distinct knowledge of God and of the physical world. Darwin was merely reporting the consequences of an investigation in the field of biological science the subject of which happened to be man in his animal role. And yet, quite unconsciously, both Descartes and Darwin were painting with bold brushwork and a sure touch the cultural self-portrait of an age. For in Descartes's famous *Cogito ergo sum*—I think, therefore I am—is implicit all of the pervasive rationalism of the eighteenth century. And in Darwin with his notable dictum "with all these exalted powers—Man still bears in his bodily frame the indelible stamp of his lowly origin" is implicit all of the romantic irrationalism of the nineteenth century.

The intellectual crisis of the modern world is the heritage of the unresolved conflicts of the eighteenth and the nineteenth centuries. And I think that it is important to present the contrast between the Cartesian and the Darwinian pictures of the human person because our contemporary failure to reconcile these two antagonistic accounts is a double-edged sword which strikes deep on the one hand at the roots of our literature and our art, and on the other at our philosophical formulations and political theories.

Descartes's picture of the human person separates the mind from the body primarily in order to exalt the mind. Man becomes *"res cogitans"* —pure thinking substance—and the passions therefore are secondary to the operations of the sovereign intellect.[4] Darwin's picture of the human person identifies the mind and the body in such a way that the former becomes simply a function of the latter. Man, instead of being qualitatively distinct from the lower animals by virtue of his intellect, is related to them on a quantitative scale. Darwin's emphasis highlights human and animal similarity with respect to sensation, instinct, and passion.

Despite the fact that he represents a certain break with the ancient and mediaeval worlds, Descartes is still very much in the Greek tradition, which has confidence in analysis and in the possibility of rational choice. He, too, would assert with Boethius, *"persona est rationalis naturae individua substantia"* (the person is an individual being with a rational nature). But Darwin in spirit, if not by explicit statement, falls within another tradition entirely. He is the symbolic midpoint in a movement which from Rousseau to Bergson has sought to minimize the intellect and to discredit the processes of rational analysis. Against the assertion of Boethius, this tradition would assert a counterclaim, *"Voluntas superior intellectu"*—the will is greater than the intellect.

The dominance of rationalism is bound up with the successful development of the science of mathematics. The generalizations and abstractions of mathematics lead to certainty, to the conviction that the independent operations of the mind can provide formulae which, however mysteriously, describe and predict the operations of the natural world. In the end Reason's self-confidence is a product of Pythagorean faith. The rationalism of the eighteenth century, whether expressed in the Deistic religion of Reason or in the budding political economy and social theory, was founded upon the scientific successes of the seventeenth. And the great achievements of astronomy and physics in the seventeenth century were due less to the increasing prestige of the method of observation and direct appeal to the immediate data of nature than to the development of the mathematical sciences.

The beauty and simplicity of mathematics elicit the wonder and admiration of Galileo and Descartes alike. Says Galileo's Sagredo in his *Dialogue Concerning Two New Sciences*,[5] almost in the emotion of religious awe: "The force of rigid demonstrations such as occur only in mathematics fills me with wonder and delight." Descartes not only echoes his sentiments but meditates upon the invidious contrast between this subject on the one hand and ethics and philosophy on the other. He says in the *Discourse on Method*:[6] "I was especially delighted with the Mathematics, on account of the certitude and evidence of their reasonings; but I had not as yet a precise knowledge of their true use; and thinking that they but contributed to the advancement of the mechanical arts, I was astonished that foundations so strong and solid should have had no loftier superstructure reared upon them." The guiding spirit of Descartes's whole work was to erect a philosophy of nature and a picture of the human person upon these mathematical foundations.

In this enterprise the seventeenth century was remarkably successful. Rational thought as a mathematical system was applied with exquisite precision to describe the operation of the forces of physical nature, and the completely articulated system of Newton became henceforth a structural model for both science and philosophy. This mathematical interpretation provided the picture of an ordered universe, a cosmos the like of which had not been seen since the Greeks, a cosmos which mirrored in its mathematical and quantitative character the explicitly rational character of human thought. It presented a structure of mechanical forces, mutually integrated, ordered throughout, and informed by the reign of causal law.

It is a matter for astonishment to note how the entire eighteenth century fell under the spell of Cartesian rationalism. As if hypnotized by mathematical magic, it attempted in its approach to religion, to politics, and to economic life to apply the methods and the critical instruments of the rational faculty. Locke, in his *Essay Concerning Human Understanding*, investigated the origin of ideas and the source of rational knowledge, and in *The Reasonableness of Christianity* he attempted to justify religion on grounds other than those of revelation. But the real essence of the eighteenth century is demonstrated in its approach to human nature, where it is dominated by a picture of the human person whose basic function is the exercise of rational choice.

The intellectual historian will find here a simple, perhaps even inevitable, carry-over of the mathematical and mechanical impetus of Newtonian and Cartesian science into the study of human nature. The sociologist may trace it to the form of intellectuality which always accompanies industrialism, the growth of the middle classes, the increasing importance of a money economy, and the movement of peoples to the towns.[7] In either case, at the heart of the eighteenth-century conception of man's rational choice lies the idea of the possibility of fixed, quantitative judgment, in short, of *calculation*. This conception of calculation is the eighteenth century's chief contribution to the intellectual dilemma of the modern age.

In the eighteenth century the ideal of rational calculation expressed itself primarily in three fields: political economy, the theory of government, and social ethics. Its classic formulations are found in three basic texts: *An Introduction to the Principles of Morals and Legislation* by Jeremy Bentham, *The Second Treatise of Civil Government* by John Locke, and *An Inquiry into the Nature and Causes of the Wealth of Nations* by Adam Smith. In the first, rational calculation became the foundation of the theory of utilitarian ethics, in the second it became the foundation of the theory of constitutional government, and in the third it became the foundation of the theory of economic society.

But the most perfect expression of the rationalism of the age is to be found in the moral philosophy of Immanuel Kant. For it is Kant who explicitly grounds the essential dignity and worth of man in the exercise of his rational faculty. He does so in the famous third formulation of the categorical imperative. "So act," he says, "as to treat humanity, whether in thine own person or in that of any other in every case as an end, never as means only." What is significant is not the content of this moral maxim but the reasoning by which Kant derives it.[8]

Beings whose existence depends not in our will but in nature's have, nevertheless, if they are irrational beings only a relative value as means, and are therefore called things; rational beings, on the contrary are called persons because their very nature points them out as ends in themselves. . . . If then there is a supreme practical, or, in respect of the human will a categorical imperative, it must be one which . . . constitutes an objective principle of will, and can therefore serve as a universal practical law. The foundation of this principle is: *rational nature exists as an end in itself.*

The last sentence might well serve as the motto for the entire eighteenth century.

2 . NINETEENTH-CENTURY IRRATIONALISM

The spirit of the nineteenth century is very different. Its social atmosphere is restless, and although much of it passes without major warfare or social revolution, there is an uneasiness of spirit which makes it hostile to the settled convictions of a previous age of social formality and rational principles. Goethe's *Faust* is a reflection of this restlessness, of the feeling that all experience is interesting, even the irrational moments (perhaps most of all the irrational moments), and that life's prizes are not won by placid contemplation but by struggle and infinite adventure. Thus the nineteenth century is a protest against the Age of Reason.

This protest sprang, I think, from two sources. Only one of them was literary. The other was scientific and philosophical; it emphasized the concepts of growth and dialectical development rather than those of mechanism and structure. In large part these concepts were the product of an emerging biological science, which came of age in the nineteenth century as physical science had come of age in the seventeenth and the social sciences had come into their adolescence in the eighteenth. The great names here are Humboldt, Lamarck, Cuvier, Claude Bernard, and Darwin.

The literary sources of the reaction against the eighteenth century represented all of those characteristics which have come to be associated with "Romanticism": the emphasis upon feeling rather than reason as the source of morality and critical standards, the supreme importance of spontaneity and imagination rather than logic and the structuring of thought—and perhaps most crucial of all, a will to succumb to illusion where that illusion guaranteed the values closest to the heart. The great figures here are Rousseau, Chateaubriand, Coleridge, Lamartine, Byron, and Wordsworth.

Cogito ergo sum was the dictum of Descartes. *Sentio ergo sum* might well have been the motto of Rousseau, the spiritual godfather of the romantic movement. "It was my conviction," said Descartes,[9] "that I could not do better than continue in that in which I was engaged, viz., in devoting my whole life to the culture of my Reason." "I have," said Rousseau in his *Confessions*,[10] "but one faithful guide on which I can depend: this is the chain of the sentiments by which the succession of my existence has been marked." Yet in Rousseau there appeared in violent form, almost as a caricature, that fatal split between intellect and sensibility which has become the hallmark of the modern age. This too he has scrupulously put down in his *Confessions*:[11]

Two things, very opposite, unite in me, and in a manner which I cannot myself conceive. My disposition is extremely ardent, my passions lively and impetuous, yet my ideas are produced slowly, with great embarrassment and after much afterthought. It might be said my heart and understanding do not belong to the same individual. A sentiment takes possession of my soul with the rapidity of lightning, but instead of illuminating, it dazzles and confounds me; I feel all, but see nothing; I am warm, but stupid; to think I must be cool.

For Rousseau the test of satisfactory conduct, even of moral rectitude, is sentiment. In him the man of rational thought has been succeeded by the man of invincible feeling, and this emphasis is prophetic not only of the poetry but of the thought of the nineteenth century.

The developing biological sciences and particularly the work of Darwin reinforced the philosophical perspective set by the romantic movement. Darwin emphasized the animal character of human behavior and the dramatic struggle in which the human species is engaged within its natural environment. In so doing he was not so much adding to the insights of romanticism as re-expressing basic ideas which were already, emotionally and impressionistically stated, a part of its philosophical outlook. Probably Darwinism is less responsible for the resurgence of the concept of human irrationality than is romanticism. This can be demonstrated indirectly by turning for a moment to the great protagonist of nineteenth-century irrationalism—the romantic pessimist Schopenhauer. Darwin published *The Origin of Species* in 1859. Schopenhauer published his great work, *The World as Will and Idea,* in 1819, forty years earlier. Yet in Schopenhauer we find a philosophical position which logically would seem to have evolved out of Darwinism rather than to have preceded it by almost half a century.[12]

The philosophy of Schopenhauer originates in Kant's metaphysical distinction between the phenomenal world of mere appearances and the unknown world lying back of these appearances. Schopenhauer uses this distinction to fix the respective places of the intellect and the will. The intellect (primarily an instrument of science) is man's guide in the phenomenal world. The furniture of the intellect, the concepts of time, space, and causation, are merely the tools of the mind which permit our animal bodies to orient themselves within a larger world of nature. But in fact the world is simply each man's "idea" of it. What we innocently call "the external world" is not simply the *discovery* but the actual *creation* of an intellect whose entire functioning is utilized in the service of the basic reality—the animal body, its uneasy strivings and unconscious impulses.[13] What lies back of these impulses and these strivings? Schopenhauer answers in no uncertain terms:[14]

. . . the answer is *will*. This and this alone gives man the key to his own existence, reveals to him the significance, shows him the inner mechanism of his being, of his action, of his movements. . . . Upon this rests the perfect suitableness of the human and animal body to the human and animal will in general, resembling, though far surpassing, the correspondence between an instrument made for a purpose and the will of the maker. . . . The parts of the body must, therefore, completely correspond to the principal desires through which the will manifests itself; they must be the visible expression of these desires. Teeth, throat and bowels are objectified hunger; the organs of generation are objectified sexual desire; the grasping hand, the hurrying feet, correspond to the more indirect desires of the will which they express. . . .

Schopenhauer's picture of the human individual dominated by instinctual forces which he can express, but hardly overcome, rests upon a cosmology: an image of the universe as itself constituting a blind, striving totality, in which the voluntary movements of our own body, the growth and reproduction of plants, the formation of crystals, the gravitational pull of the planets, and the electromagnetic fields at the surface of the earth are all expressions of the cosmic restlessness. We experience this restlessness directly in the intuitive knowledge which we have of the operations of our own bodies and in its expression in music; we experience it indirectly ("in idea") in the phenomena of nature, in the products of the arts, and in philosophy. But Schopenhauer's epistemology is less important than the descriptive terms which he uses of the cosmos: "blind striving," "inarticulate impulse," "boundless motion," "strife," "conflict." The illusion of science is an illusion of order provided by the intellect. The real consensus of nature is collusion in dynamic meaninglessness, with which the emotions of the human individual correspond. The primary fact about the human person is no longer the operation of the active intellect culminating in rational choice, but blind impulse and animal striving, due to the influence of a cosmic will working through man as simply one of the high-grade animals. Irrationalism has dethroned the sovereign intellect.

The two hundred years between Descartes and Darwin saw the germination and flowering of the great problem of rationality and irrationality. The eighteenth century took its stand upon the primacy of human reason, the nineteenth upon the primacy of feeling, instinct, and animal impulse. But already in the nineteenth century the contrast between these two currents in the stream of intellectual history had become something of a problem. The two great critical minds of the nineteenth century, those of Nietzsche and Kierkegaard, were aware of the dilemma —indeed, their thought was founded upon it—but their solutions, like that of Schopenhauer, were a further codification of the irrational.

To the youthful Nietzsche, the antagonism between the rational and the irrational appeared first as a problem of aesthetics: as the clue to our understanding of Greek tragedy and as the tension out of which the spirit of music was to be reborn in the genius of Richard Wagner. *The Birth of Tragedy*, published in the same year as Darwin's *The Descent of Man*, sets forth the dualism between the Apollonian and the Dionysian sources of art. By the "Apollonian" Nietzsche meant the quality of measured restraint, of intellectual calm, of dreamlike clarity, and of structured pictorial fantasy—almost formal properties upon which the work of plastic art depends, and which have remained throughout the course of Western civilization as the eternal source of the classic spirit. By the "Dionysian" Nietzsche meant the quality of the wilder emotions: the drunken ecstasy of the Bacchic chorus, the passionate unrestraint of peoples under the spell of the primitive fertility rites of Spring, of those demonic, dark, and hidden earth-energies upon which the worshipper calls in moments of cosmic identification, and upon which (as Plato saw) the poet and the imitative artist must ultimately depend.

It seems apparent, as one reads those earlier pages of *The Birth of Tragedy*, that Nietzsche's intention was not only to account for the origins of Greek tragedy, but somehow at the same time to harmonize as principles of life the wild Dionysius and the austere Apollo. As one reads further, it is clear that a reconciliation of rationality and the irrational is not to be the outcome after all. For imperceptibly Apollo is transformed from an aesthetic deity into an intellectual god. The patron of artistic form becomes the voice of the Delphic Oracle, and music-making is lost in the demand for rational self-knowledge. And of course it is Socrates who is the symbolic figure in this transformation. Nietzsche's original sympathy for an Apollo who arises out of dream and fantasy is changed into sharp hostility when in Socrates he has become the personification of the intellectual and critical spirit.

It is interesting that Nietzsche's denial of the Socratic spirit is at least in part the assertion of a will to illusion which he exalts almost into a metaphysical instinct. Tragedy and art, strong living, and assertive activity derive from the mystery of existence as from an underground spring, and the intellectuality which bases everything upon understanding, which insists upon tearing the veil from the facts of life, can only cripple art and impair the impulse to powerful action.

Nietzsche thus ends as a passionate devotee of Dionysius. His exaltation in *Thus Spake Zarathustra* of the intuitive man, the conscious artist as prophet in the domain of feeling and preacher of the affirmative values of life, is only equaled by *The Will to Power* with its assertion of instinct and its glorification of the will to power. It is characteristic that in *The Will to Power*, in some of the last pages which he wrote before his madness, he returned again to the subject of Dionysius, the god of passion and of the religious affirmation of Life. And in a revealing passage he summed up the ultimate effect of his own philosophy and of the age to which he belonged.[15]

Concerning the strength of the nineteenth century.—We are more mediaeval than the eighteenth century; not only more inquisitive or more susceptible to the strange and to the rare. We have revolted against *the Revolution*. . . . We have freed ourselves from the fear of reason, which was the spectre of the eighteenth century: we once more dare to be childish, lyrical, absurd, —in a word, "we are musicians."

Men of the eighteenth century prided themselves upon being as reasonable as mathematicians. Men of the nineteenth century prided themselves upon being as lyrical and childlike as artists. It was Nietzsche's peculiar genius and his fate that he should sense the conflict between the intellect and the power of irrationality without being able in the end to do more than succumb to the partisanship of his age. Erich Heller has written a suggestive essay comparing Rilke and Nietzsche. And he ends it justly:[16]

It is the redeeming achievement of Nietzsche and Rilke that they have raised, the one in the intensely felt plight of his thought, the other in his intensely meditated poetry, the abysmal contradictions of their age to a plane where doubt and confusion once more dissolve into the certainty of mystery.

While Nietzsche opposed Socratic, Kierkegaard opposed Hegelian rationalism, but in the service of different ultimate values. Nietzsche's critique of the authority of science was aimed at the re-establishment of the arts and the production of a new morality. He therefore condemned that form of intellectualism which attempted to rationalize art and to ground morality in the repression of natural feeling. Kierkegaard, on the other hand, distinguished both the aesthetic and the ethical as stages upon life's way, but found them inferior to the ultimate stage of the religious. Nietzsche denied the intellect to make way for instinct: Kierkegaard denied the intellect to make way for faith.

Kierkegaard deals with the traditional metaphysical problem of essence and existence. To him, existence means the personal existence of the subjective thinker, who is distinguished by the inwardness of his conscious direction, and by his involvement in the situation of human choice. This involvement is always intensely emotional, for it is emotion (not deliberation) which converts the mere possibility of a chosen action into the action itself. Man's emotion, therefore, is an expression of his existence. But the ontological primacy of existence over essence must express itself in the possibilities which are inherent in various modes of existence. These modes are the aesthetic, the ethical, and the religious. The aesthetic is the stage of diversified feeling. The ethical is the stage of personal commitment through earnest choice. The religious is a state of grace, where by faith one has passed beyond the postulates of morality into a direct relationship with God.

The essence of the aesthetic for Kierkegaard is its immediacy, but above all its lack of anchor and stability. It is the roving habit of perception, seeking the enlargement of feeling and the thrill of enjoyment wherever these are to be found. It is mobile and free-floating, it is enraptured by beauty and the arts, and can therefore find its expression in the Don Juan or the epicure, the confirmed play-goer or the patron of the arts. But although the aesthetic is rooted in feeling, it is lacking in personal emotion. The aesthete is always the spectator, never deeply a participant, and is paradoxically enough, therefore, a kind of intellectual. Kierkegaard's first real bow to the irrational occurs in the passage from the aesthetic to the ethical.[17]

The essence of the ethical is that it is expressed in the moment of responsible choice. The ethical man is no longer the dilettante of love or pastime. He has chosen to found his family and to follow his profession as its duties dictate. This has necessitated a choice, and the choice has been possible only by virtue of the irrational. Ethical moments are when one stands at the crossroads, and when, in Kierkegaard's words, the soul is "matured in the hour of decision." But no choice is ever made through deliberation. Deliberation is an aesthetic examination of possibilities which precedes, perhaps, but does not determine action. It is only when the endless possibilities are brushed aside by the intervention of the strong deciding will that commitment may occur. There is always a basic irrationality in the act of decision, an arbitrariness provided by the strong undercurrent of emotion upon which our life is founded.

In the passage from the ethical to the religious Kierkegaard again invokes the irrational.[18] For him the essence of the religious is that the religious individual possess God by virtue of a faith which is not based upon deliberation or reflection, but exists in the face of an objective uncertainty. The movements of faith not only lack scientific justification, they are made by virtue of an impossibility. Faith persists even in the light of its own absurdity, and the love of God pervades the consciousness as an inexplicable gift, not as a rational belief or as an ethical consequence. Faith is an immediate instinct of the heart and it is the paradox of all life and all existence.

As Nietzsche fought against the pretentions of scientific method, so Kierkegaard fights against the claims of objectivity. The objective and logical thinker can construct a system, but in this process he forgets that he himself is an existing individual. For all decisiveness, all feeling, all authentic existence inhere in subjectivity. Love is a determination of subjectivity. Passion is subjectivity. And faith is "the highest passion in the sphere of human subjectivity." An objective tendency which demands self-forgetfulness and the assumption of the posture of the impartial observer makes the individual into a function, and removes him from the stream of life. But in the moment of decision the road swings away from objective knowledge.[19]

When subjectivity is the truth, the conceptual determination of the truth must include an expression for the antithesis to objectivity, a memento of the fork in the road where the way swings off; this expression will also indicate the tension of the subjective inwardness. Here is such a definition of truth: *An objective uncertainty held fast in an appropriation-process of the most passionate inwardness is the truth*, the highest truth attainable for an *existing individual*. At the point where the way swings off (and where this is cannot be specified objectively, since it is a matter of subjectivity), there objective knowledge is placed in abeyance. Thus the subject merely has, objectively, the uncertainty; but it is this which precisely increases the tension of that infinite passion which constitutes his inwardness. The truth is precisely the venture which chooses an objective uncertainty with the passion of the infinite.

This definition of truth is, of course, simply an equivalent for faith, and in it we can see how far Kierkegaard has advanced the claims of the irrational against the whole eighteenth century and particularly against the kind of religious reasonableness advocated by Locke. Indeed, for the nineteenth century, to be reasonable was something of an affront, almost an impertinence. It is not by accident that the great Russian novelists exalt the idiot and the fool into a man of unconscious wisdom. So Dostoyevski can make Prince Myshkin an idiot, even a poor fool wise in his instinctive faith, and can make Alyosha with his simplicity and his intuitive sense of the human heart the most sympathetic of the Karamazov brothers. So after the completion of *Anna Karenina* in 1877, Tolstoi turns from literature to philosophical and religious reflection, and in the most famous of his autobiographical writings, *A Confession*, presents the same essential insights which appeared earlier in the thought of Kierkegaard. Whether one turns to the philosophers or the poets, the strategy is the same: protest against the eighteenth century and its glorification of the sovereign intellect, substitution of modes of knowledge closer to the heart.

3. EXAMPLES FROM POLITICS AND ART

The nineteenth century began to sense the dramatic conflict between faith and reason, between Descartes and Darwin, between the human individual as the agent of rational choice and the human individual as an impulsive animal mirroring the chaotic irrationality of the universe. It sensed the difficulty but did not resolve it. And so it has remained to haunt the intellectual prophets of the twentieth century, giving them their subject matter, in some cases dictating their results, and always looming large behind the tensions and the dilemmas of the modern age.[20]

The problem of rationality and the irrational has penetrated into every area of modern culture—into our system of industrial production, into the competition between rival theories of justice and political power, into our literature, painting, and music. It occurs in systems of aesthetics and metaphysics, in epistemology, and in the philosophy of history. In each of these fields the contrast between the temper of the nineteenth century and the eighteenth, the tension between the Cartesian and the

Darwinian pictures of the human person, is of crucial and unmistakable importance.

It is not possible within the compass of this chapter to document this thesis completely (indeed, to the extent that it applies to the major prophets of our intellectual life this will be the task of the remainder of this book), but some indication of what I mean can be given by two examples, one from modern political theory, the other from modern painting.

Recent discussions about the meaning of "democracy" are not always agreed on what exactly constitute the ethical presuppositions of a democratic society. But most of them fall back upon a certain assumption about the human person, an assumption expressed in the phrase "the essential dignity and worth of man." It is a phrase worthy of analysis. In precisely what respect is man an object of dignity and worth? The historic and by now traditional answer is that man's dignity lies in his ability to exercise free choice and his worth lies in the promise of his rational nature. This was the reply of Kant and the entire eighteenth century and it remains the fountainhead of contemporary democratic theory.

The entire theory of representative government depends upon faith in human rationality. According to this theory, the average citizen, on the basis of a rational consideration of alternatives, casts his ballot for a representative who, in turn, meets with others in the legislative assemblies, where after further rational discussion public policy is enacted into law. The underlying assumptions are that knowledge about society is available, that universal discussion will be the rule, and that rational persuasion will be its consequence both in the market place and in governmental assemblies.

To the theory which has just been sketched, there is one corollary which is crucial. This is a high evaluation of the language of ordinary discourse. The political enterprise is constituted by men living together in society, and the ultimate formulation of public policy by the aggregate of these persons depends upon the language through which they communicate with one another. Rational discussion takes place through the medium of language; and in order that discussion may be rational, the language it uses must be rational. This requires that language shall not be merely ceremonial in character, that it shall not consist of merely emotional appeals, and that it shall not conceal prejudices and resentments and ulterior purposes beneath the respectability of words which, on the surface, purport to be intelligible.

The acknowledged theory of political democracy is the creation of the eighteenth century and a product of the Cartesian picture of the human person. But the Darwinian picture of the nineteenth century is very different, and has equally explicit implications for political thought. Perhaps the greatest paradox of social theory in the modern world can be stated in this question: Can a political science and a sociology which are the direct outgrowths of the Darwinian assumptions of the nineteenth century be reconciled with a democratic political philosophy which stems from the Cartesianism of the eighteenth?[21]

This paradox can be examined on three different levels: the psychological, the semantic, and the political. Psychologically, the problem may be defined as that of the way in which the intellectual and the emotional elements of personality interact, the way in which they affect choice, and thus ultimately the respective roles which they play in the determination of conduct. This question has been of importance from Aristotle to Freud. Semantically, the problem involves an analysis of the various functions of language; the necessity of distinguishing between language used logically, practically, expressively, and ceremonially; and, ultimately, an investigation of the conditions under which language may be logical (informative) rather than merely manipulative or ceremonial. Politically, the problem may be defined as that of the relationship of intelligence to politics—whether, in fact, the act of deliberation is important in the process of formulating public policy; whether knowledge (and particularly the knowledge provided by the social sciences) can be used decisively in the formation of political decisions; finally (and most important), whether the democratic postulate of human beings as self-determining agents whose minds may be enlightened, rather than as passive animals whose activities may be externally manipulated, is compatible with some prevailing theories of psychology and with the actual facts of political behavior. Thus, in the tension between Cartesianism and Darwinism in the modern world is implied the contrast between rationalism and irrationalism in psychology, between logic and propaganda in the theory of communication, and between "democracy" and "totalitarianism" in political theory.

Just as the rationalistic theory makes certain assertions about human personality, social communication, the function of language, and the place of social science in the determination of social policy, so the anti-rationalist theory is based on conflicting assumptions.

The Darwinian evaluation of language is low. Passages might be quoted at length from a number of social scientists which are full of skepticism as to the ability of language to function logically in political debate. An illustration of the pattern of non-Cartesian thought in the social sciences is found in these citations from the work of Thurman Arnold.[22]

On the psychology of political action:

One of the most difficult adjustments for modern intellectuals is the realization that different points of view have equal validity provided that they are used in different settings. When one appears on the public stage to take part in some important ceremony, he should not question the assumptions on which that ceremony is based. Public debate of all kinds today, whether before a court or in a campaign, assumes the existence of group free will and a thinking man who will be persuaded. If that assumption is questioned on the stage, the advocate will be a failure. The reformer who questions it will spend the rest of his life condemning the human race because its institutions are not what they pretend to be. Public management on the other hand is based on the assumption that men in groups are not rational. That assumption has given impetus to the varied political techniques of industrial organization in which we excel. If public management is carried on under the assumptions of public debate only failure will follow.

On the relation of discussion to legislative improvement:

The notion that legislation becomes more expert because of prolonged public discussion of proposed measures is an illusion which follows the notion that public debate is addressed to a thinking man through whose decisions organizations have group free will. All prolonged public discussions of any measure can do is to reconcile conflicts and get people used to the general ideal which the measure represents.

Of the character of social science:

An institution has something which may be called a subconscious mind. This means only that its verbal conduct must be calculated to inspire morale and not to describe what it does. Law and economics are the formal language of institutions on parade.

According to these citations, the function of political language is either ceremonial or frankly manipulative. Such an assumption grows easily out of the Darwinian picture of the human person. If man is best understood in terms of his animal nature, then adaptation to environment by means of the conditioned reflex explains not only the character of human living but the pattern of human knowing as well. To speak and to listen means only to stimulate and to respond. Human conviction is then determined not by the weight of evidence which is available as scientific validation for a proposition, but by the mechanical conditions under which the proposition is suggested. Verification is inconsequential, repetition is all; and the once-told truth is impotent before the thrice-told lie. The social scientists and political theorists in question (and surely Thurman Arnold) might be reluctant to acquiesce in a theory which, when stated baldly, is so reminiscent of the techniques of totalitarian propaganda, and yet, from their Darwinian assumptions about the nature of the human person, such a theory follows inevitably.

These social scientists have indeed laid the foundation for a severe and realistic critique of the theory of a democratic society. Our common experience demonstrates that there is a wide divergence between the theory and the practice of politics. Whether in the legislature, in the market place, or on the bench, men have shown themselves to be as much the Darwinian creatures of irrational impulse as the Cartesian men of reason. Equally tempting is a cynical attitude with respect to the function of reason in bringing about a meeting of minds in matters of public policy. We need no reminder that, too often, decision comes not from the logic of evidence but from the "logic of fatigue" and that all too frequently the function of protracted debate is simply so thoroughly to exhaust all concerned as to paralyze the will to further resistance. But because the Cartesian picture proves unsatisfactory, it does not follow that the Darwinian is any less so. Social scientists with this approach cannot, I think, maintain their position without consequences disastrous to a real belief in the democratic way of life.

The idealistic picture of the Cartesian democratic myth, with its assumptions of perfect human rationality, deliberative political processes, and the use of logical language, is shattered against the rock of actuality. On the other hand, the Darwinian social science myth, with its denial of human self-determination, its assertion of political ceremonialism and the central importance of techniques of non-rational manipulation, does not hold up, either, against stubborn human facts: in particular the behavior of small, face-to-face groups and of persons out of range of the mass media. Here, in the uneasiness of our social thought and the striking ambivalence of our contemporary political theory, lie the contemporary consequences of the problem of rationality and irrationality.

The contrast between the rationalism of the eighteenth century and the irrationalism of the nineteenth haunts not only the social scientist and the political philosopher but the writer and the creative artist as well. For the domain of modern painting it sets problems which are at once peculiar and important.

The work of art, whatever else it may be, is clearly a cultural symbol. In it are reflected as at a central intersection the perplexities, the dominant attitudes, and the spiritual problems of an age. It is one of the commonplaces of modern criticism that between the creative artist of the twentieth century and the masses of people who should constitute his public there exists a curious antagonism. This antagonism is more than the aristocratic scorn which since the Renaissance has characterized the attitude of the artist toward a Philistine public, and the impatience of that public, devoted to the ideals and aspirations of a commercial and acquisitive society, with creative expression devoted to pure beauty independent of utilitarian considerations. The antagonism runs deeper than this. It arises not only from two conflicting systems of value but also from a real failure of primary communication.

On the whole, responsibility for this failure of communication probably lies less with the artist than with his public. Who can deny that the style, the quality, and the expressiveness of modern painting (particularly that of the advance guard) often produces doubt, bewilderment, anxiety, and ultimately resentment among those to whom it seems to be addressed? To many the idiom of modern art is unintelligible. But if this fact is examined without prejudice as simply one of the data of modern cultural history, one is forced to conclude that the so-called "unintelligibility" of the arts is due less to the rancor, caprice, and irresponsibility of the artist[23] than to the seriousness with which he views his mission, the integrity of his insights, and the fidelity with which he reflects the temper of his age.

If the work of art is a cultural symbol of an age, then "unintelligibility" must be one of the cultural indices of the twentieth century. I have suggested in the preceding chapter how this "unintelligibility" is the natural result of an ambiguity of content and a new experimentalism as to technique which are the direct product of the fragmentation of a unitary system of values and the resultant competition between rival claims of authoritativeness in diverse and conflicting philosophies. Unintelligibility in the arts is a function of multiplicity and division in the intellectual life.

But when it is suggested that unintelligibility is a quality of modern painting, this does not imply that modern art is without meaning. Meaning is never something established absolutely and in isolation. The "meaning" of a symbol, an idea, or a work of art is relative to the context in which it appears. The unintelligibility of modern painting to its usual audience implies neither that it is really without meaning nor that it cannot be understood. It seems unintelligible to many only because, being non-representational in spirit, it is a radical departure from that meticulous mirroring of the natural world which was the ideal of the realist and naturalist schools of the last century, profoundly influenced as they were by the successes and the prestige of nineteenth-century descriptive science.

In 1936 the United States customs officials refused to permit the Museum of Modern Art to enter as works of art nineteen pieces of abstract sculpture, among them being works by Boccioni, Laurens, Miro, and Arp, under a ruling that sculpture must represent an animal or human form, and that since these pieces did not, they were therefore dutiable as plaster, wood, stone, or bronze.[24] This illustrates the simple standards of literalism in terms of which modern art is so often judged to be unintelligible. But if such standards are abandoned, and a serious attempt is made to understand the sources and the objectives of modern painting, it will be discovered, I think, not only that it is highly meaningful, but that in the impulses and the insights of its two major branches is expressed the conflict between the rationalism of the eighteenth century and the irrationalism of the nineteenth.

There are perhaps two main traditions in twentieth-century painting. The first is abstract, highly intellectual, interested in structure and the concepts of geometry. The second is more obviously expressive of feeling; it is intuitive, and emphasizes the biomorphic, the spontaneous, and the irrational. The first originates in the aesthetic theory of Cézanne, the second in the aesthetic practice of Van Gogh, Soutine, and Matisse. The first finds its keenest expression in the painting of the Cubists (which dominated the early decades of the century) and perhaps its culmination in the Platonism of Piet Mondrian. The second finds its classic form in the earlier painting of the Surrealists, and its culmination in the "abstract expressionism" of DeKooning, Motherwell, and Franz Kline. The distance between the two traditions can be illustrated by the contrast between a suprematist composition of Malevich and one of the works of Max Ernst around 1930, or more recently in the contrast between the works of Mondrian and those of Miro. The first tradition is anti-literal and therefore "unintelligible" because of the formalism and abstractness of its method; the second is equally anti-literal and therefore equally "unintelligible" because of the fantastic inventiveness of its content.

Cubism and geometric abstraction find justification for their technique in Cézanne's recognition that underneath the seeming disorder of nature lies the regularity of geometrical forms. His letter to Emile Bernard in which he said: "You must see in nature the cylinder, the sphere, the cone," was widely known and had great influence upon the earlier Cubists, notably Picasso and Braque. But the fundamental assumption of abstract art, namely, that painting is simply a construct of neutral elements (line, color, and placement) in which the artist effects a

synthesis of geometrical forms within the picture space also finds justification at least as far back as the mathematical rationalism of Plato.
Cézanne's insight can be supplemented by an appeal to the *Philebus*:[25]

Socrates: My meaning is certainly not clear at the first glance, and I must
try to make it so. For, when I say beauty of form, I am trying to express,
not what most people would understand by the words, such as the beauty
of animals or of paintings, but I mean . . . the straight line and the circle
and the plane and solid figures formed from these by turning-lathes and
rulers and patterns of angles; perhaps you understand. For I assert that the
beauty of these is not relative, like that of other things, but they are always
absolutely beautiful by nature. . . .

Cubism and abstract art are the expression of the intellectualist point
of view in the aesthetics of the twentieth century. They derive from a
philosophy of rationalism insofar as they are dependent upon the
formalizing and mathematical activities of the human mind. Abstract
art glorifies an aesthetics of structure just as logic constitutes a science
of structure. They are both interested in formalizing and ordering (the
one the images of the natural world, the other the modalities of thought
and discourse) and they have much in common. Perhaps it is not mere
coincidence that the first decades of the twentieth century witnessed the
simultaneous growth of abstract art and of symbolic logic. The five
years preceding the first World War, when Picasso and Braque made
their greatest contributions to the field of abstract art, also produced the
epoch-making *Principia Mathematica* of Russell and Whitehead.

In contrast to this abstract and geometrical school of modern painting
is another very different one, dominated by a preoccupation with the
enigmatic, the bizarre, and the irrational—the school of Surrealism.
Springing up in Paris in 1923 under the leadership and spokesmanship
of the poet André Breton, Surrealism in painting exploited the irrational
to the fullest and took with complete seriousness the Freudian principle
that the basic source of artistic creation must always lie in the human
subconscious. Between abstract art and Surrealist art there is a crucial
difference of spirit and of aesthetic principle. Cubism places great emphasis on the structuring of materials, by the conscious imposition of
form upon matter; Surrealism demands absolute spontaneity of artistic
expression. Cubism is indifferent to the sources of inspiration and to
content; Surrealism exploits the dream and other unconscious or automatic materials, and therefore produces works rich in terror and in
fantasy. Cubism emphasizes the rational and purposive activity of the
creative artist, Surrealism exalts chance factors in aesthetic creation.

The rise of the Surrealist movement derives its real inspiration from the impact and the detailed interpretations of psychoanalysis. Sigmund Freud is its spiritual godfather. André Breton, writing on "Surrealism and Painting" in 1928,[26] at once acknowledges the debt to Freud and indicates a certain antagonism to abstract art:

We still live under the reign of logic but the methods of logic are applied nowadays only to the resolution of problems of secondary interest. . . . Under color of civilization, under pretext of progress all that rightly or wrongly may be regarded as fantasy or superstition has been banished from the mind, all uncustomary searching after truth has been proscribed. It is only by what must seem sheer luck that there has recently been brought to light an aspect of mental life—to my belief by far the most important— with which it was supposed that we no longer had any concern. All credit for these discoveries must go to Freud. . . . The imagination is perhaps on the point of reclaiming its rights. . . .

Surrealist painting not only permits the imagination "to reclaim its rights," but it conceives imagination as a source of strange and disturbing truths. In its effort to free the act of painting from the dictation of preparatory thought and the exercise of rational control, it encouraged psychic automatism, the free and constant use of sexual symbols, and a chaotic imagery which is expressed through the devices of systematically distorted perspective, composite images, and the startling isolation or recombination of human anatomical fragments.

Surrealism dominated the twenties and thirties—just those years when Freudian influence generally made its greatest public impact. Now, twenty years later, the Surrealist heresy has faded and a new heresy has taken its place in the domain of avant-garde painting, the heresy of "abstract expressionism." On the surface it might seem as if this was the very movement to resolve the conflict between rationality and irrationality in painting, for it owes something to both Picasso and Miro. But to describe it as expressionism breaking away from Cubism is accurate only as a formulation of intention. In its methods (although not in its results) it is a cousin of Surrealism, for it is hospitable to accidents upon the painting surface even when (especially when?) these are haphazard, and it asks as test of the artist's sincerity chiefly his ungoverned spontaneity.

The rationalist tradition of Mondrian devoted itself to a Platonism of mathematical experiment in painting. And it presupposed as method a course of rational and calculated preparation. Josef Albers (Mondrian's heir) speaks the matter plainly.[27]

In my paintings I adhere to what in other arts is considered a matter of course. Namely, that performance is prepared by rehearsal, that exercises precede recital, or plans, execution. It is still a good habit in music and dance and the theater, in architecture or typography. It remains a good procedure also in poetry and sculpture. And it was a rule with the old masters of painting.

This may be the essence of painterly good sense, but it is precisely what the method of abstract expressionism seems to deny. Harold Rosenberg calls this school "the American action painters" and describes them thus:[28]

At a certain moment the canvas began to appear to one American painter after another as an arena in which to act—rather than as a space in which to reproduce, redesign, analyze or "express" an object, actual or imagined. What was to go on the canvas was not a picture but an event. The painter no longer approached his easel with an image in mind; he went up to it with material in his hand to do something to that other piece of material in front of him. The image would be the result of this encounter.

Not only is the act of painting an event, but the result of the encounter must be a surprise, some new revelation which is the unforeseen product of gesturing with materials rather than the realization of a sketch prepared as a rehearsal. One after another of the paintings of De Kooning and Twarkov, of Hofmann or Franz Kline or Motherwell seem to have resisted planning almost successfully. There is no reference here to the Freudian sources of spontaneity, no Surrealist dependence upon the articulated images of the unconscious. But the consequence is the same. Creation is the game which the self plays with itself, and the more relaxed the gesticulation upon the canvas, the more surprise in store for the artist himself and for the resentful and alienated spectators.

To the usual spectator, repelled, perhaps even shocked, by any broad departure from the tradition of literal imitation in painting, Cubism and Surrealism are equally "unintelligible." But in fact they are profoundly different. Cubism and abstract art, depending upon the abstractive power of the human intellect, and upon the same love of order which informs the labors of the geometer, attempt to lay bare the formal properties implicit in objects within the natural world. Surrealism, depending upon the subconscious and irrational wells of inspiration, enthrones fantasy and superstition and looks within the self for the symbolic significance of twisted and distorted remnants of natural objects. In the contrast between these two movements—probably the most important and significant in twentieth-century painting—is to be found once again the outstanding characteristic and the most vivid quality of our age—the conflicting claims of rationality and the irrational.

4. SCIENCE AND ILLUSION

In his book *Civilization and Its Discontents* Sigmund Freud pauses a moment to review a theory about religion which he had developed in a previous work.[29]

In my *Future of an Illusion* I was concerned much less with the deepest sources of religious feeling than with what the ordinary man understands by his religion, that system of doctrines and pledges that on the one hand explains the riddle of this world to him with an enviable completeness, and on the other assures him that a solicitous Providence is watching over him and will make up to him in a future existence for any shortcomings in this life. The ordinary man cannot imagine this Providence in any other form but that of a greatly exalted father, for only such a one could understand the needs of the sons of men, or be softened by their prayers and placated by the signs of their remorse. The whole thing is so patently infantile, so incongruous with reality, that to one whose attitude to humanity is friendly it is painful to think that the great majority of mortals will never be able to rise above this view of life. It is even more humiliating to discover what a large number of those alive today, who must see that this religion is not tenable, yet try to defend it inch by inch, as if with a series of pitiable rearguard actions.

To me the passage is interesting not so much for the statement about religion as for what it shows about Freud's attitude toward the problem of knowledge and belief. To find the derivation of the need for religion in the child's feeling of helplessness and the need for a dependable father is not really startling. But what is revealing is the use of terms charged with emotion to indicate Freud's attitude. The metaphor out of which religion springs occasions Freud's condescension and pity. The whole thing is so "patently infantile," it is so "incongruous with reality" that it is painful to him; it is a source of real humiliation to the man to discover such childishness and will-to-illusion in the human race.

Back of this view of religion, if I am not mistaken, is something more than a momentary impatience, more than the temporary irascibility of the temperamental physician (this is a side of Freud that we know all too well despite the wonderful control of his literary style). There is also the emotion which underlies the methodology of the scientist: a certain tough-mindedness, an inner pride, perhaps, a stubbornness which will submit to nothing but "the facts." (Of course the man is sensitive: how else would he have accounted for the invisibility of the Analyst by exclaiming, "*Ich kann mich nicht acht Stunden taglich anstarren lassen*" [I cannot let myself be stared at for eight hours every day]). Now this stubbornness is itself a form of cognitive independence, a determination not to be fooled at any price—not by others and certainly not by oneself. This is why in the game that one plays with one's unconscious, there is so much at stake. Freud's attitude toward the religious man is something like that of the shrewd and knowing business man toward the fool who has been cheated. The pity is that his faith is so childish and his perceptions so incongruous with the world as it really is.

One of his friends writes him that he has found the ultimate source of the religious sentiment in a feeling of eternity, a sensation of something "oceanic." Another from his study of the East writes that Yogi by their practices can produce sensations which lead to the wisdom of the mystic. But Freud comments drily: I cannot discern this "oceanic" feeling in myself. This is not for me. Etc. Etc. Of course, Freud does not deny that satisfaction is to be obtained through illusions, nor does he assert that the discrepancy between them and reality always interferes with the pleasure they may bring. But if these illusions are derived from the life of fantasy they are expressly exempted from the demands of reality. Their function of mere wish-fulfilment can never blind us to the fact of their falsity, just as narcosis is not a denial of the fact of pain but only a massive retreat before reality.[30]

Religion circumscribes these measures of choice and adaptation by urging upon everyone alike its single way of achieving happiness and guarding against pain. Its method consists in decrying the value of life and promulgating a view of the real world that is distorted like a delusion, and both of these imply a preliminary intimidating influence upon intelligence. At such cost—by the forcible imposition of mental infantilism and inducing a mass-delusion—religion succeeds in saving many people from individual neuroses. But little more.

Here speaks the rationalism of the scientific spirit. The mechanisms of illusion return us to that childhood of humanity which we thought ourselves to have outgrown:

> The backward look behind the assurance
> Of recorded history, the backward half-look
> Over the shoulder, towards the primitive terror.[31]

Freud's emotional attitude toward illusion is shared by the patrons and disciples of the methods of empirical science. With respect to the scientific mood—the passion for facts, the alertness to make connections between ideas, the chastity of mind which refuses to let belief go beyond the limits of strict evidence, psychoanalysis and positivism seem to be in substantial agreement. Herbert Feigl, one of the most humanistic representatives of Positivism in the modern world, says:[32]

The main contribution that philosophical reconstruction can make in this regard lies in the direction of an education toward maturer ways of thinking, thinking which possesses the virtues characteristic of science: clarity and consistency, testability and adequacy, precision and objectivity. Immature attitudes are associated with attempts to explain experience in ways which lack the distinguishing marks of science. Certain of these pre-scientific modes of explanation, like the magical, the animistic, and the mythological are nearly defunct; others, like the theological and the metaphysical, still prevail.

The language of Freud and of Feigl is much the same. "Maturer ways of thinking," clarity, objectivity—these are the goals of thought. "Immature attitudes," magic, animism, myth, theology—these are the perils toward which humanity faces relapse. Nor is it unnatural that this should be the case. Behind both Freud and Feigl lies the optimism of an unstated doctrine of intellectual progress—a heritage from Auguste Comte. Both psychoanalysis and positivism attempt to reinstate the reign of rationality not through the assertion of an arid metaphysical rationalism, but through the development of a sense of reality and the ability to tolerate the anxieties of uncertainty in those areas in which the empirical evidence can warrant no more.

But from what ultimate sources do confidence in empirical evidence and distrust of illusion spring? On this point Freud and Feigl are not agreed and neither of them is completely satisfactory. Feigl seems to say that the difference between the worldly and the otherworldly types of thought represents an irreconcilable divergence between two types of personality and temperament. He therefore seems to despair of the possibility of decisively eliminating their perennial antagonism. Freud finds the difference to lie in an opposition between the pleasure principle and the reality principle, but asserts without further proof the superiority of the sense of reality in the struggle for existence. Ultimate values are not touched upon here either.

A somewhat different approach to this problem, which asserts the greatest sympathy with the non-rational aspects of human belief—with religion, with literature, and with the imagination—is that of Bergson. It is not merely an assertion of confidence in those sources of illusion which Freud and Feigl deplore. Its scope is cosmic. It attempts to place the will-to-illusion within the setting of evolutionary necessity, not as a primitive moment to be displaced by rational afterthought, but as an enduring answer to a question inevitably posed by the existence of human intelligence. Bergson, therefore, treats the issue less moralistically than either Freud or Feigl, but more pragmatically, with a more explicit conception of the inclusive and inevitable role which illusion plays and must play in human life.[33]

The spectacle of what religions have been in the past, of what certain religions still are today, is indeed humiliating for human intelligence. What a farrago of error and folly! Experience may indeed say "that is false," and reasoning "that is absurd." Humanity only clings all the more to that absurdity and that error. And if this were all! But religion has been known to enjoin immorality, to prescribe crime. The cruder it is, the more actual space it occupies in the life of a people. What it will have to share later with science, art, philosophy, it demands and obtains at first for itself alone. And that is indeed a matter for surprise, seeing that we began by defining man as an intelligent being.

The existence of religious belief beyond the evidence of the senses, indeed, the hold which absurd superstitions have been able to maintain over the lives of reasonable beings, remains a problem to be explained. Religious phenomena belong to the domain of imagination, to the myth-making faculty, and around this faculty cluster not only religious beliefs but poetry, mythology, and the other brilliant mechanisms of human fantasy. Is it possible to believe that these mechanisms are primitive remnants which have outlived their usefulness and now, vestigial organs, remain only as sources of infection for human rationality?

Not if we believe that our psychical structure originated in the practical necessity of preserving individual and social life. For in that case it is more reasonable to assume that the persistence of myth-making is due to its utility, and that there are certain dangers for life to be discovered where they might be least expected, in the very exercise of rationality.

Human life always presents two essential characteristics: (1) it uses intelligence and (2) its form is social. But there is reason to believe that these characteristics are not at all points mutually compatible. Intelligence can exist in a radically individualistic form, and it then constitutes a threat to the very society which harbors it. "Looked at from this point of view, religion is then a defensive reaction of nature against the dissolvent power of intelligence."[34] Intelligence is dissolvent in two senses. It presents to the living creature the image of its own death as determined and inevitable—an idea infinitely disturbing and disruptive of the flow of life. Intelligence also presents to the mind the depressingly frequent occurrences of the unforeseen and the unintended, suggesting a universe unfriendly to human purpose. Intelligence is lucid and cruel. Religion and myth provide the reassurance which is a safeguard against man's natural panic when confronted by knowledge of death and by a hostile universe; they are only the projection of a desire which fills the heart because it is the heart's need.

The myth-making faculty is not perhaps an instinct, but the role which it plays in human life is virtually instinctive. Man seems to be the only animal whose actions are subject to the hesitations of self-mistrust and the fear of failure. He alone knows that life is uncertain, that suffering is implicit in living, that he must die. This is the priceless gift of his intelligence. But if anxiety and disquiet are the gifts of intelligence, the myth-making faculty and the religions which are its outcome offer the promise of a compensating strength and an ultimate peace.

On the surface Bergson's argument is merely a naturalistic explanation of the persistence of the anti-intellectual in experience. It is nevertheless an argument for religion and myth; for with anxiety and fear pitted against strength and peace, who would choose the former? But the argument is never more than pragmatic. Bergson does not try to claim the virtues of the intellect for the anti-intellectual domain. He does not argue that religious beliefs can be proved by evidence, nor does he distort the meaning of knowledge so as to make them by epistemic trickery a form of knowledge.

In this respect Bergson approaches the Fictionalism of Hans Vaihinger, who holds that:[35] "An idea whose theoretical untruth or incorrectness and therewith its falsity is admitted, is not for that reason practically valueless and useless; for such an idea, in spite of its theoretical nullity may have great practical importance." This position has much in common with pragmatism, but does not go so far as to claim that the true and the useful are the same. Vaihinger's position had its origin in the British empirical temper but did not, like later empiricism, merge into the positivistic stream. While it denies verifiability to metaphysical and religious ideas, it acknowledges their value for human life. In this it is not far removed from Bergson's philosophy.

Fictionalism is a dualistic philosophy. It proposes a split through the center of the epistemic world. Sense data are the ultimate sources of validation for the scientific account of nature, but since the fictions of the mind serve emotional needs, many of them either are not congruent with "reality" (the sequence of our sensations) or are self-contradictory. But the "As If" world of our aesthetic, ethical, and religious fictions becomes finally for us a world of values which governs our lives at the very moment when we have least warranted certitude of their validity. This is dualism with a vengeance, for it enthrones the distinction between the rational and the irrational at the very center of our knowledge.

Vaihinger's fictionalism and Bergson's evolutionary theory of religion have roots in the nineteenth century, not only in Darwin and Schopenhauer, but especially in Nietzsche. It was he who found a "will to appearance or illusion" as a deeper and more "metaphysical" instinct than the will to truth, and his interpretation of art led him to see that the chief concepts of the understanding are simply cognitive metaphors. It is perhaps more from Nietzsche than from any other man except Plato that we have learned that the construction of metaphors is the fundamental instinct of man, his "metaphysical need."

It is natural for an artist to insist that the less merely factual accuracy an aesthetic object possesses, the greater its worth. But Nietzsche saw the aim of the philosopher as akin to that of the artist rather than the scientist:[36]

> The ascertaining of "truth" and "untruth," the ascertaining of facts in general, is fundamentally different from the creative *placing*, forming, moulding, subduing and *willing* which lies at the root of *philosophy*. *To give a sense to things*—this duty always remains over, provided no sense already lies in them.

The function of philosophy and religion is to make sense out of experience, and if the content of our knowledge consists of propositions discouraging to our present or neutral as to our destiny, perhaps Bergson and Nietzsche and Vaihinger are right that the irrational in the form of poetic myth and religious illusion must step in for the guidance of the spirit. The religious need is deeply rooted. Must it, though, always spring from a retreat into immaturity or a despair of intelligence?

In a sense the answer is yes. If maturity is defined as the employment of the methodology of science (as with Freud and Feigl), and if intelligence is conceived (as with Bergson) as the faculty which secures the adaptation of the organism in an environment presented as time, space, and matter, then belief beyond evidence must be immature and statements about the destiny of man must reflect unconcern with an intelligence unfitted by nature to originate such statements. This is why in the last two centuries Positivism and Idealism have fought such unyielding engagements. These encounters, as well as those between science and religion, surrealism and abstract art, the Darwinian theory of the social sciences and the theory of political democracy, dramatize the conflict between rationality and the irrational.

The breakdown of the pictures of the human person which sufficed for classical Greece and the mediaeval world not only resulted in fragmentation of the intellectual life and a consequent multiplicity and division, but also served to raise with renewed urgency within the chaos of that fragmentation the issue of human rationality and human irrationality. The Cartesian picture of man, with its emphasis upon the potency of the isolated intellect, dominated the eighteenth century and was essentially responsible for its mathematical bias and faith in reason. The Darwinian picture of man, preshadowed in the romanticism of Rousseau and in the voluntarism of Schopenhauer, and placing primary emphasis upon the human faculties of will and desire, dominated the literary and philosophical expression of the nineteenth century. To confront the eighteenth century with the nineteenth, and to take a stand upon the issue which is presented by their dialectic, is the second great intellectual problem of the twentieth century. It is in the light of this setting, of the past three hundred years of intellectual history, that the efforts and the insights of the philosophers and the intellectual prophets of our age are to be understood.

PART II

THE PROPHETS

III

The Creativity of Man: Henri Bergson

For the truths that the intellect grasps directly and openly in the full-lighted world are somehow less profound, less indispensable than those which life has communicated to us without our knowledge through the form of impressions, material because they come to us through our senses, but the inner meaning of which we can discern. . . . Only the subjective impression, however inferior the material may seem to be and however improbable the outline, is a criterion of truth, and for that reason it alone merits being apprehended by the mind, for it alone is able, if the mind can extract this truth, to lead the mind to a greater perfection and impart to it a pure joy. . . . It was this conception of time as incarnate, of past years as still close held within us, which I was now determined to bring out into such bold relief in my book.

MARCEL PROUST, *Remembrance of Things Past* (*The Past Recaptured*)

1. THE PROBLEM OF TIME

The year 1859, says Oswald Spengler, was a great "year of symbolic coincidences."[1] It included the publication of both Mill's *Liberty* and Marx's *Critique of Political Economy* and the creation of Wagner's *Tristan and Isolde*. It also contained two other events which Spengler did not remark—the publication of Darwin's *Origin of Species* and the birth of Henri Bergson. This, too, is a symbolic coincidence. For out of the Darwinian revolution and the new biological science grew a whole series of philosophical perplexities and intricate problems not unrelated to human destiny which were to seize upon the young Bergson and create the necessity for his philosophical life's work.

For assuredly we may say that Darwinism is one of the great starting-points from which originate the novelties of contemporary philosophy. In its shocking assertion of the physical continuity which exists between man and the rest of the animal world, it dramatizes the claims of human irrationality, and thus in effect seriously questions the major insight of a philosophic tradition which has dominated Western thought for two thousand years. Aristotle had found in "contemplation" the ultimate crown of the moral virtues, and Descartes had seen the highest expression of the intrinsic nature of the human self in the operation of the sovereign intellect. But if Darwin is right, and man is chiefly an animal evolving and developing according to the adaptation demanded by his natural environment and in response to the *ad hoc* requirements of the struggle for survival, what can one say with assurance of the place of mind, imagination, and creativity in the universe? What is the ultimate meaning of man's science, his philosophy, his religion, and his art? Stripped of all non-essentials, this, I think, is the root-problem of the Bergsonian philosophy. It is less a metaphysics than a philosophy of culture.

The theoretical formulations of a Newton or a Planck, the metaphysical passion of a Spinoza or a Plato, the value-intoxication of a Buddha or a St. John of the Cross, the paintings of a Vermeer celebrating surface quality, or the operas of a Mozart painting character like some musical Molière are all products of human life, but their humanity is diversified, and they are distinguished by the analogous, yet undoubtedly different types of insight or ways of knowing which they express. To ask the meaning of each of these various human productions would be to risk some evaluation of the different "ways of knowing" upon which they depend.

Each of them utilizes a different mode of perception, and applies a different interpretation to the world. Each of them ends by presenting its own unique "truth," and a thoughtful comparison of these truths is at once epistemological—that is, deeply concerned with ways of knowing —and metaphysical—that is, deeply concerned with each way of knowing's objective correlative. It was Kant, speaking for all philosophy since Descartes, who in the preface to *The Critique of Pure Reason* stated that the adequacy of any system of metaphysical truth must be substantiated by the validation of its principles of knowing, and that such a critique of the principles of knowing was the first task. In this belief Kant and Bergson are alike. "Theory of knowledge and theory of life seem to us inseparable,"[2] Bergson remarks.

But where does the philosopher begin? Descartes's answer had been —at the very beginning; with the knowing self. Bergson's answer is— in the middle; with the knowing self. Paradoxically, Descartes's beginning and Bergson's middle are one. For this is the narcissistic subjectivity of all philosophy since the Renaissance: that whether it begins at the beginning, the middle, or the end, it always takes as its point of departure the epistemic properties of the human self.

As early as 1889, in his *Essai sur les données immédiates de la conscience* (translated as *Time and Free Will*), Bergson had attempted to analyze the self as an entity existing through time and endowed with free will. In his *Matière et mémoire* (Paris, 1896) he continued his studies in perception with particular reference to the relation between the instrumentalities of thought and the supposed organization of phenomena in the external world. Both of these books had been directly inspired by Bergson's interest in biology and what he believed to be the psychological inferences which could be legitimately derived from biological knowledge. But it was not until the writing of his masterpiece, *L'Evolution créatrice* (Paris, 1907), that he brought together the insights of these two previous volumes and fitted them snugly within the context of a general theory of man's evolutionary development. The heart of Bergson's philosophy may be found in *Creative Evolution.*

In the years immediately preceding *Creative Evolution* Bergson produced a long and important article entitled "Introduction à la métaphysique," which appeared in January 1903 in the *Revue de Metaphysique et de Morale.* This probably provides the best introduction to his philosophy as a whole, and I shall examine its content in a moment. It is interesting for the way in which its ideas are developed, which, paradoxically enough, suggests the classic method of that other Frenchman, Descartes.

In the preceding chapter I spoke of the twentieth century as haunted by the problem of rationality and the irrational. This dualism haunts equally the whole course of French thought. The more analytic strand in French intellectual history is illustrated by the progression Descartes, Voltaire, Comte. The more intuitive strand is illustrated by the progression Pascal, Rousseau, Bergson. But whereas Descartes's original *Discourse on Method* charted a methodology for rationalism by showing that the activity of "knowing" is the point of departure which yields insight into the nature of "being," Bergson's "An Introduction to Metaphysics" proposes a methodology for mystical insight by exactly the same speculative procedure. Descartes, beginning with doubt and a doctrine of self-evidence dependent upon the notion of "clear and distinct ideas," passes from the certainty of the self to the certainty of a perfect being and hence to the existence of matter and substance. Bergson, denying the clear and distinct ideas produced by analysis in favor of the method of intuition, passes next to a consideration of the human self and from this point to a treatment of the reality behind the external world which the self may know. The Cartesian series—doubt, thinking substance, extended substance—finds its parallel in the Bergsonian series—intuitive knowing, the self, reality. "An Introduction to Metaphysics" is, therefore, the *Discourse on Method* for modern anti-rationalism.

This famous essay begins by distinguishing two different sources of knowledge. "There are," says Bergson,[3] "two profoundly different ways of knowing a thing. The first one implies that we move round the object; the second that we enter into it." The first is the way of analysis; the second is the way of intuition.

By analysis we reduce an object to elements already known, that is, we describe it and represent it in terms of our conventional system of symbols. Analysis multiplies indefinitely the perspectives from which an object may be viewed yet never exhausts the infinite possibilities of perception. But intuition is the mode of knowing through which this multiplicity can be overcome. It is "the kind of *intellectual sympathy* by which one places oneself within an object in order to coincide with what is unique in it and consequently inexpressible."[4]

It is probable that a visitor to Paris or Dublin could by the judicious use of a pocket camera provide for himself a series of photographs of the city which, taken together, would preserve something of its flavor and perhaps even a structural outline for his later contemplation. But no series of snapshots made by any particular traveler, however imaginative, could exhaust the nuances of the entity which we call Paris or distill in blacks, whites, and greys the essence of its unique character. Any set of such photographs would be relative to the interests and organizing purpose, to the delicacy and sensitivity of the photographer. They could suggest and partially describe, but they would not exhaust their object, and the knowledge which they offered to the senses of one innocent of the originals would be mysterious, approximate, and fragmentary. But one who has visited Paris and who has surrendered unconditionally to its lively indifference and sprawling beauty would have acquired an intuition, a kind of intellectual sympathy with Paris in which love and knowledge would be blended and which might continue to warm the heart even when the visitor was far away.

Although Bergson does not explicitly say so, the distinction between intuition and analysis suggests broadly the difference between the procedure of the arts and the method of science. A psychological treatise on the nature of personality or a case history of an introspective and maladjusted man could only present abstractly the unity of human personality by accumulating a series of incidents and generalizing from their effects. But a dramatist like Shakespeare in his portrayal of Hamlet can present analogous data in such a way that the reader or spectator of the drama feels for the character an intellectual sympathy which permits him to identify himself from within, as it were, with the thoughts, feelings, and actions of Hamlet. For science the understanding of the *unitary* character of the sequence of events constituting the biography or career line of the individual presents a problem. But for the intuitive reader there is no "problem of Hamlet." His hatred for Claudius, his ambivalence toward Gertrude, his strangeness toward Ophelia, his slaying of Polonius, his sending of Rosencrantz and Guildenstern off to their deaths, and his final killing of Claudius are but the realized emotions of the reader himself. Granted the reality of emotional involvement, the revelation of Hamlet's personality and the meaning of his actions flow with a kind of unquestioned inward necessity.

This is because the object of art is to provide unmediated contact with consciousness and with sense, to permit the individual to enter directly into an accord with nature and with life. The media of the arts are materials which in ordinary existence perform utilitarian functions but which are here magically transformed so as to suggest the rhythms of nature and the music which underlies reality. This is what artists do: "By setting free and emphasizing this music, they force it upon our attention; they compel us, willy-nilly, to fall in with it, like passers-by who join in a dance. And thus they impel us to set in motion, in the depths of our being, some secret chord which was only waiting to thrill. So art, whether it be painting or sculpture, poetry or music, has no other object than to brush aside the utilitarian symbols, the conventional and socially accepted generalities, in short, everything that veils reality from us in order to bring us face to face with reality itself."[5]

In this confrontation there is no form more potent than the tragic drama. Poetry always expresses inward states. It recalls us to a self with which we have partially lost contact, coated over as it is by the film of habit and the cake of custom.

Such is just the kind of pleasure that is provided for us by drama. Beneath the quiet humdrum life that reason and society have fashioned for us, it stirs something within us which luckily does not explode, but which it makes us feel in its inner tension. It offers nature her revenge upon society. . . . But . . . whether it weakens society or strengthens nature, it has the same end in view: that of laying bare a secret portion of ourselves, what might be called the tragic element in our character. This is indeed the impression we get after seeing a stirring drama. What has just interested us is not so much that we have been told about others as the glimpse we have caught of ourselves . . .[6]

Art extends an intuitive invitation to knowledge which science can only stumble upon by accident, and the laboratory report or the case history can produce no conviction within the deepest self as Hamlet or Oedipus can. But why is this the case? Why will the picture of Shakespeare or Sophocles compel responsiveness while the case history of Freud, rich in description and diagnosis, will seem like a series of disjointed fragments? The genuineness of Hamlet is guaranteed by nothing so much as the poet's sincerity. The candor of great drama provides the power

whereby the intuitive process may operate. The intuitive grasp of a
fictional character is possible, therefore, because it is simply an extension
of the more primitive and original experience of intuitive knowing—
that of one's own self. "There is one reality, at least [says Bergson], which
we all seize from within by intuition and not by simple analysis. It is
our own personality in its flowing through time—our self which endures."[7]

It is well to remember that the rather terse summary of the nature
of the self which Bergson gives in "An Introduction to Metaphysics" has
been prepared by his two earlier works. In *Time and Free Will* he began
what was intended to be a quasi-psychological investigation of the nature
of the self by means of a painstaking analysis of the diverse states of
consciousness to which Hume had called attention. But quite unlike
Hume, the burden of his argument was that though admittedly when
analyzed the states of consciousness of the individual are multiple, they
are in their inmost nature a single whole, and he concluded that in the
idea of *duration* is to be found the organizing principle of personality.

I am of the opinion that there are two equally good ways to gain
insight into Bergson's notion of the self. One is to read the doctrines
directly in *Time and Free Will* and in *Matter and Memory*. The other
is to read carefully Marcel Proust's great novel *The Remembrance of
Things Past*. For it occasionally happens that by a miracle of the creative
will (which governs both philosophers and artists) there is between a
thinker and a writer a kind of pre-established harmony of intention
which makes the creative imagination of the one a counterpart of the
creative thought of the other, so that their works are as twin branches
of a single tree—differing in their foliage and colors, but of the same
form and sprung from the same roots. It is so with Bergson and Proust.
Proust had not only fallen under the conscious spell of Bergson's
philosophy, but had in his independent creative life come to conclusions
which exactly parallel those of the philosopher.[8] Bergson says:

Certain states of the soul seem to us rightly or wrongly to be self-sufficient,
such as deep joy or sorrow, a reflective passion or an aesthetic emotion. . . .
for example, an obscure desire gradually becomes a deep passion. Now you
will see that the feeble intensity of this desire consisted at first in its appearing to be isolated and as it were foreign to the remainder of your inner life.
But little by little it permeates a larger number of psychic elements, tingeing
them so to speak with its own color: and lo! your outlook on the whole of
your surroundings seems now to have changed radically. How do you become
aware of a deep passion, once it has taken hold of you, if not by perceiving
that the same objects no longer impress you in the same manner? All your

sensations and all your ideas seem to brighten up: it is like childhood back again.[9]

And yet it is important to remember that this intermingling of surface impressions and deep passions through the mysterious operations of memory is not the most usual way in which consciousness reveals itself. If, as more commonly happens, we simply give ourselves up to the enjoyment of our immediate sensations without reflecting that they have a more profound anchorage in the deep waters of our personal life, then these sensations do reveal themselves as the disordered multiplicity of which Hume spoke, and at this level they appear to have a superficial existence more or less cut off from the concrete duration of the self which underlies them. Thus we are presented at the very threshold of Bergson's philosophy with a duality of consciousness. Consciousness can be said to be at once the inhabitant of two universes, one inner and one outer, one the universe of depth, the other the universe of surface.

The self which is most clearly displayed by analysis is the self of the surface world. Its images and impressions are in constant flux and its perceptions are distinguishable as seemingly separate and independent entities. This is the self of the ordinary stream of consciousness which gives us the fluent cascade of impressions—impressions of trees and streams, houses and streets, persons greeting one another and quarreling —in short, the everyday self which is the condition of the interaction of our being with nature and objects, with mankind and its manners.

The self of depth, on the other hand, is constituted by the form which our conscious states assume under the unity of memory. Here, below the surface of the other, is a self in which experiences do not merely follow upon one another but actually melt into one another and so (never being lost) form an organic and ever-expanding whole. It is but rarely that we are engaged with this deeper self.

The reason [says Bergson] is that our outer and, so to speak, social life is more practically important to us than our inner and individual existence. We instinctively tend to solidify our impressions in order to express them in language. Hence we confuse the feeling itself which is in a perpetual state of becoming, with its permanent external object, and especially with the word which expresses this object. In the same way as the fleeting duration of our ego is fixed by its projection in homogeneous space, our constantly changing impressions, wrapping themselves round the external object which is their cause, take on its definite outlines and its immobility.[10]

By means of the surface self we establish contact with the world of everyday existence, moulding our impressions into objects and giving to them (and to persons as well) a fixity in time and space which permits us to deal with them as solid fragments of a solid world. All honor to the surface self if it secures our place within the continuum of nature. But let us not claim for it responsibilities which it cannot fulfill. It can neither bring to the individual a personal experience of his own existence, nor can it control that primal stratum of the self which originates our decisive acts and our moral will. Interpreter of our environment to ourselves, go-between for our periphery and our center it may be, but through it we cannot act. It knows nothing of anxiety, fear, guilt, desire, or love, and so only delusion would cause us to entrust it with our freedom.

We are left, then, with this difficulty: that whereas the discontinuous flow of states of consciousness provides our basic contact with the external world, these discontinuous states are incapable of accounting for human decision and moral action. Such action in order to make sense— that is, in order to sum up our past and hold relevance for our future— cannot spring from a self which is discontinuous. It must be the whole self which is responsible for the decisive act. "In short," says Bergson, "we are free when our acts spring from our whole personality, when they express it, when they have that indefinable resemblance to it which one sometimes finds between the artist and his work."[11]

If this is so, then we have an explanation for much that is incoherent, wavering, and perhaps unconsciously dishonest in human action. The wavering and the incoherence mean really that one acts only with the surface self and without the involvement of one's deepest nature, and this abandonment of depth in favor of surface means for our life the passive abrogation of personal freedom. Here is a long passage from Bergson which casts considerable light upon the nature of free choice:[12]

. . . we will grant to determinism that we often resign our freedom in more serious circumstances, and that, by sluggishness or indolence, we allow this same local process to run its course when our whole personality ought, so to speak, to vibrate. When our most trustworthy friends agree in advising us to take some important step, the sentiments which they utter with so much insistence lodge on the surface of our ego and there get solidified. . . . Little by little they will form a thick crust which will cover up our own sentiments; we shall believe that we are acting freely, and it is only by looking back to the past, later on, that we shall see how much we were mistaken. But then, at the very moment when the act is going to be performed, *something* may revolt against it. It is the deepseated self rushing up to the surface. It is the outer crust bursting, suddenly giving way to an irresistible thrust. Hence in the depths of the self, below this most reasonable pondering over most reasonable pieces of advice, something else was going on—a gradual heating and a sudden boiling over of feelings and ideas, not unperceived, but rather unnoticed. If we turn back to them and carefully scrutinize our memory, we shall see that we had ourselves shaped these ideas, ourselves lived these feelings, but that, through some strange reluctance to exercise our will, we had thrust them back into the darkest depths of our soul whenever they came up to the surface. And this is why we seek in vain to explain our sudden change of mind by the visible circumstances which preceded it. We wish to know the reason why we have made up our mind, and we find that we have decided without any reason, and perhaps even against every reason. But, in certain cases, that is the best of reasons. For the action which has been performed does not express then some superficial idea, almost external to ourselves, distinct and easy to account for: it agrees with the whole of our most intimate feelings, thoughts and aspirations, with that particular conception of life which is the equivalent of all our past experience, in a word, with our personal idea of happiness and of honor. Hence it has been a mistake to look for examples in the ordinary and even indifferent circumstances of life in order to prove that man is capable of choosing without a motive. It might easily be shown that these insignificant actions are bound up with some determining reason. It is at the great and solemn crisis, decisive of our reputation with others, and yet more with ourselves, that we choose in defiance of what is conventionally called a motive, and this absence of any tangible reason is the more striking the deeper our freedom goes.

If Bergson is correct, human freedom is not the constant possession of personality as classic philosophy has sometimes maintained. Rather it is a quality which is not ordinarily called upon or actually possessed, but which we regain at such moments as demand the pulling together of the strands of the self in the face of dramatic decision. It is an act of self-integration. It is somewhat startling to find clearly stated in a book written at the turn of the century the same romantic notion of "the moment of decisive choice" which in Jaspers and Heidegger has become the clue to our experience of personal identity. Indeed, this doctrine has been the cornerstone of Existentialism from Kierkegaard to Sartre. Such a conception explains much about the paradoxes of human action, but the price of this explanation is the abandonment of our real individuality in all but the crisis situations in human life.[13] About this Bergson too is explicit.[14]

Hence there are finally two different selves, one of which is, as it were, the external projection of the other, its spatial and so to speak social representation. We reach the former by deep introspection, which leads us to grasp our inner states as living things, constantly becoming, as states not amenable to measure, which permeate one another and of which the succession in duration has nothing in common with juxtaposition in homogeneous space. But the moments at which we thus grasp ourselves are rare, and that is just why we are rarely free. The greater part of the time we live outside ourselves, hardly perceiving anything of ourselves but our own ghost, a colorless shadow which pure duration projects into homogeneous space. Hence our life unfolds in space rather than in time; we live for the external world rather than for ourselves; we speak rather than think; we "are acted" rather than act ourselves. To act freely is to recover possession of oneself, and to get back into pure duration.

At this point the work of Proust comes close in its intention and its method to the spirit of Bergson's philosophy. Proust's work is entitled A la recherche du temps perdu—the search for lost time. We ought to consider carefully the literal sense which this title conveys. For in Proust the attempt of the narrator Marcel to recover the past is in essence an attempt to regain contact with his deepest self, and thus recreate the possibility of freedom. It is no accident that the last volume of Proust's great work should have been entitled Le Temps retrouvé— the past regained—, for this final volume documents the culmination and the ultimate success of the long process of remembering. Proust, like Bergson, understood that the recapture of past time can be achieved only through "the process of deep introspection" and he also understood with the clarity of the intuitive artist that "the moments at which we thus grasp ourselves are rare." If to recover the possession of the self and to re-enter the stream of pure duration is a manifestation of freedom, then the work of Proust is one of the great creative acts of free will of the twentieth century.

What Proust says in Le Temps retrouvé[15] is here much to the point.

Those who have created for themselves an enveloping inner life pay little heed to the importance of current events. What alters profoundly the course of their thinking is much more something which seems to be of no importance in itself and yet which reverses the order of time for them making them live over again an earlier period of their life.

Proust also suggests how it happens that the particular past experience which is recovered is not simply one indiscriminate and inconsequential form from among the variable flow of sensations, but through the very act of its difficult recreation, it assumes an almost Platonic quality of essence, never to be expected in the more trivial context of its original occurrence.

But let a sound already heard or an odor caught in bygone years be sensed anew, simultaneously in the present and the past, real without being of the present moment, ideal but not abstract, and immediately the permanent essence of things, usually concealed, is set free and our true self, which had long seemed dead but was not dead in other ways, awakes, takes on fresh life as it receives the celestial nourishment brought to it. A single minute released from the chronological order of time has recreated in us the human being similarly released in order that he may sense that minute.[16]

These reflections of Proust originate in the accidental starting in motion of a train of ideas stimulated by a particular sense impression which has unaccountably and quite accidentally repeated itself. Thus near the beginning of his book, a crumb of cake (*petite madeleine*) dipped in tea eaten by chance in his Paris apartment recalls to Marcel, through the sense of taste, a similar cake dipped in tea which his aunt gave him when a boy and thus all of his early life at Combray. From this accident of sensation, arbitrary and fortuitous as it appears to be, the whole of *A la recherche du temps perdu* springs.[17]

And so it is with our own past. It is a labor in vain to attempt to recapture it: all the efforts of our intellect must prove futile. The past is hidden somewhere outside the realm, beyond the reach of intellect, in some material object (in the sensation which that material object will give us) which we do not suspect. And as for that object it depends on chance whether we come upon it or not before we ourselves must die.

The entire enterprise of Proust is built upon the mechanism of involuntary memory, upon those occasions where, through the medium of analogous sensations, the miracle of the recovery of past reality occurs. On the way to a reception at the Princess de Guermantes', Marcel chances to touch with his foot an uneven paving stone in her courtyard, giving him immediately an overpowering sense of joy and reminding him of the paving stones of the Baptistry of St. Mark's in Venice. A footman at a reception accidentally clanks a spoon against a plate and Marcel is transported back to a fresh summer's day in the country in a railway carriage of a train which had stopped momentarily while the brakeman clanked his little hammer against the wheels. A servant brings him a glass of orangeade and a napkin which, when it touches his lips, reminds him of the blue of the sea at Balbec, for it is starched to the same consistency as the towel with which he used to dry himself at that seaside resort. Everything by chance. Everything mysteriously pointing to the experiences of a self lost somewhere in the labyrinth of Time.

To read the subjective book of these strange signs (signs standing out boldly it seemed which my conscious mind as it explored my unconscious self went searching for, tumbled against, and passed around like a driver groping his way), no one could help me with any rule, for the reading of that book is a creative act in which no one can stand in our stead or even collaborate with us.[18]

Proust's work is devoted to the resurrection of past fragments of life. But underneath these occasions of remembering there lies a whole series of Bergsonian assumptions. (1) The important memories are not those which stem from the will, but from the deep strata of the unconscious self. (2) The character which we attribute to others is merely a representation of our fragmentary experiences of them and therefore not only has merely partial validity, but is in a state of continual change. (3) We go through life with our vision not aided but limited by our intelligence, for the innate tragedy of all psychological experience is the lack of synchronization between the calendar of facts and that of our feelings. (4) There is an affinity between art and philosophic intuition, for the mode of knowing appropriate to the artist is to experience life at the extreme limit of sensibility. (5) We grasp the truth of things not by an intellectual reduction, but by an intuition to which the intellect not only points, but to which it must finally succumb.

In Proust's conception of "time as incarnate," of the past as held close within us, and of the dignity of the human self in time—a dignity not correspondingly held in space—lies the literary and imaginative reflection of Bergson's theory of duration and of the unity of the self achieved through the act of memory. This conception is classically outlined in Bergson's second important book, *Matter and Memory*.

2. MATTER AND MEMORY

I think it is fair to say that the heart of *Time and Free Will* is Bergson's attempt to find, underlying the multiplicity of conscious states, some deeper and more integrated self. We saw how he maintained that the mind could be conceived as a series of separate mental states only if one used a method of analysis whose intrinsic character committed it to a Cartesian division of any experience into its elements. But once we clearly understand that these elements are not actually "parts" of the self, but merely the end product of a process of high abstraction, we can see that to extract a single mental state from its ground in the growing personality is unreal, and the converse fallacy of trying to synthesize personality from a series of psychic states will also become apparent.

Traditional empiricism has erred[19] in trying to discover the self through analysis. Traditional rationalism has erred equally in trying to bind together states of consciousness by employing the highly questionable mechanism of a transcendental unity of apperception. Both empiricism and rationalism fail because they make no sustained effort to deal with the self intuitively. But as *Time and Free Will* makes clear, once the method of intuition is employed, once one abandons a method of analysis which is appropriate for the merely practical understanding of the external world for a method which is uniquely appropriate for an understanding of the self, this same self will then be identified as "pure inner duration," and beneath the surface of well defined conscious states there will be discovered a deeper core whose parts interpenetrate and form a living and organic whole.

It is precisely the organic unity of this underlying self which provides the clue to man's freedom. Free will cannot be established for a self in that Newtonian space and time in which "events in the external world" are localized, but only for a self which "endures." This means that prediction from the point of view of a depth psychology is of a different order from the prediction customarily employed through the methods of an older mathematical physics. The freedom of the self is real, but this freedom is strictly indefinable, and the acts of the total self are indeterminate according to the canons of mathematical reasoning.

The paradox of *Time and Free Will* is that it leaves Bergson with a deep split between the external world of nature and the deepest personal self, and the only clues which he suggests for their relationship are reminiscent of a kind of inverted Kantianism.[20] Kant's problem—how is our knowledge of nature possible?—was resolved by explaining that our knowledge of the external world (and particularly those elements of it which are not contingent and variable but universal and necessary) is the conclusion of a process in which spontaneous impressions from "outside" filter through forms of perception which are a part of the furniture of the mind. The "external world" is partially a construct impressed by the mold of the knowing mind and is, consequently, always relative to the form which our inner sense imposes.

Bergson's initial problem is very different. His perplexity is not over how knowledge of the external world is possible, but over how knowledge of the inner self is possible. I speak of his inverted Kantianism because he shows that our faltering and mistaken attempts at self-knowledge arise when states of the self are observed through forms borrowed from the necessities of our perception of the external world. External nature is dominated by the concept of a homogeneous space. According to Bergson, Kant's mistake (which occurred because he was

under the influence of Newtonian cosmology), and that of most philosophers after him, was to accept a homogeneous time coordinate with and
analogous to a homogeneous space. Kant recognized that within the
dimensions of such a time and space any self must be a natural object
among other natural objects and hence subject to the uniformities which
we formulate as laws of nature. Consequently, he placed the self which
is free completely outside of both space and time. Kant's failure was not
in separating the realm of the free self from the space and time of the
external world, but in not seeing that the concept of time is completely
different when applied internally to the self and externally to the world.

For Bergson, the external world is primarily a spatial world, and the
conception of time which is utilized by the physical sciences (the abstract time which in Chapter I, following Eddington, I have called
"time by the clock") is modeled upon the concept of space. But that
time which is the matrix of the inner life (which Eddington has called
"time lived") has nothing to do with space and is, in fact, its absolute
opposite. External time, like external space, is homogeneous. Internal
time, which is nothing but pure duration, is heterogeneous and qualitatively unique. As this book continues, I shall try to show that the
distinction between "time by the clock" and "time lived" is one of the
focal issues of philosophy in the modern world and that it constantly
recurs in such men as Russell, Eddington, Whitehead, and the Existentialists. In Bergson, as the distinction between a time patterned upon
space and upon pure duration, it is the climactic insight of *Time and
Free Will*.

We have seen that the problem of *Time and Free Will* was to investigate the sources of personal identity and that this inquiry turned
upon a distinction between that form of perception appropriate to the
external world and the form appropriate to deep self-knowledge. In
attempting to find what constitutes the unity of the self in time, Bergson was led to suggest that the clue might perhaps be found in the
phenomenon of memory. Bergson's second important book, *Matter and
Memory*, takes up this clue and develops it further.

I think it is true that Bergson's interest in memory is twofold. He is
interested both in discovering the essence which provides the unity
of the self and at the same time in relating human consciousness to
the existence of a world of material objects. In *Matter and Memory* the
concept of memory becomes both the focus of the self's unity and the
point of intersection of mind and matter. *Matter and Memory* takes for
granted that there are different levels of mental life. We may perceive
a landscape full of objects noting the shape of its clouds, the color of its

flowing water, the freshness of its spring odor, the solidity of its trees, the massiveness of its hills and forests. We may remember a city street full of intricate detail and the meaning which its shapes and shadows possessed for us in days gone by. We may have formerly acquired a distaste for crowded places so that we habitually avoid those thoroughfares where noises abound and people congregate. It is easy to distinguish in the welter of experience (1) our perception of objects, (2) our store of memories, (3) our accumulation of motor habits. But *Matter and Memory*, in addition, suggests that these details of consciousness may be classified according to their closeness to the sphere of practical activity. Our mental life has its moods and its delicate modulations, and we live now more remote from, now closer to, the interests of the life of action.

At this point Bergson shows for the first time the real impact which Darwin and the biological science of the nineteenth century have had upon his thinking. Perception and motor habit are functions of the brain; the brain is in man the highest neural organization of a body endowed with animal life. And what is this organization if not an instrument of adaptation which ensures an appropriate response to the conditions of our natural environment? The body with its quaint apparatus of perception and motor habit becomes now not the cradle of man's reason, nor the fretful bearer of his immortality, but simply "an instrument of action, and of action only."

How the lofty role of our perceptions as given by two thousand years of philosophic tradition has been suborned! How the mighty have fallen! "We believe," says Bergson, "that the reader will find his way if he keeps a fast hold on the two principles which we have used as a clue throughout our own researches. The first is that in psychological analysis we must never forget the utilitarian character of our mental functions, which are essentially turned towards action. The second is that the habits formed in action find their way up to the sphere of speculation, where they create fictitious problems, and that metaphysics must begin by dispersing this artificial obscurity."[21] How much of historic philosophic passion is here laid waste! For if perception is not the graded slope to the bridge of contemplation, if it is not the preparation for the achievement of a purely speculative and disinterested knowledge, Plato's *Theaetetus* is a monstrous joke, Aristotle's *Metaphysics* is a delusion of our childhood, and *The Critique of Pure Reason* is but a ponderous Germanic travesty.

In the idealistic, and even mystical, twist which Bergson gives to his metaphysics there is a strong tinge of pragmatism and, although in its tang and flavor the work of Bergson is completely different from that of

John Dewey,[22] their starting-points and their insights are not unlike. That two such different philosophic temperaments include a similar strain of "instrumentalism" within their speculative systems is understandable only when it is recognized that their problems have been set by the biological science of the nineteenth century.

I have said that Bergson uses the concept of memory to serve as a point of intersection between matter and mind. But how is this possible? How could the impalpable mental stuff of memory ever reach out to embrace a world of solid bodies, of rough edges, of impenetrable surfaces? Clearly, this is possible only if we can assimilate matter to the texture of our minds—if, indeed, there is less real solidity in the external world than an older physics and a doctrine of primary qualities would have us believe. Bergson does not deny the reality of matter, but he conceives it less in terms of its independent subsistence than of its perceptual immediacy. For John Stuart Mill matter was "a permanent possibility of sensations." For Bergson matter is "the aggregate of images" and the perception of matter is "these same images referred to the eventual action of one particular image, my body."[23] But to call matter an aggregate of images (which is almost the equivalent of saying that it is a collection of sense data) suggests that it has no function except to provide a structure for the world in which we must move and act practically. The so-called material world is then discovered to be, if perhaps not quite a mere construction, at any rate a sculptured segment which our practical needs carve out of the totality of our possible experience. And the tool that creates this seeming world of solidity is our faculty of perception—a faculty which finds its ultimate rationale in the tendency which our animal body has toward movement. Bergson says:[24] "Our representation of matter is the measure of our possible action upon bodies: it results from the discarding of what has no interest for our needs, or more generally, for our functions."

But the more carefully we examine perception, the more we realize that it is not an independent act isolated or quarantined within the specific moment of its occurrence. Perceptual choice falls within a rich field of experience nourished and fed by our past. Thus it is possible for us to say: perception is the stepchild of memory. But just here occurs one of those curious inversions of our mental life so like the strong infusion of yellow light upon our retina which causes the inevitable after-image of ultramarine. Not only are the details of present perception partially selected through the agency of memory, but almost by a contrary and reverse movement, perception itself "ends by being merely an occasion for remembering."[25] And when this recollection is permitted to wander freely, unencumbered by the dictates of necessity, what was once a perception engendered by practical considerations has turned into a spiritual activity which is of absolute and intrinsic value. This is the use of memory which Proust celebrates, and which he ends by identifying with the creativity of art.

We have now come to the point where we can perceive more clearly that the "memory" of which Bergson speaks is not really a single function, but two different functions. For there are two forms under which the past survives in the experience of the self. The first is in the motor habits which our bodies have acquired, the second is in the reservoir of our independent recollections. It is almost as if here the old dualism between body and spirit reappeared again, each claiming memory for its own.

Of the two kinds of memory, one is mechanical—the repetitive mechanism which registers the body's past and permits it successful access to the world of matter. But the other—independent recollection—disdains the useful; it constitutes the free exercise of memory as a creative act.

To call up the past in the form of an image we must be able to withdraw ourselves from the action of the moment, we must have the power to value the useless, we must have the will to dream. Man alone is capable of such an effort. But even in him the past to which he returns is fugitive, ever on the point of escaping him, as though his backward turning memory were thwarted by the other, more natural memory of which the forward movement bears him on to action and to life.[26]

But what can one say of the free exercise of memory as a creative act? What a puzzle this would have been for the theories of Darwin and his disciples! The first type of memory, our conditioned reflexes embedded in our motor habits, is practical in the most obvious sense— it is a finely wrought instrument by which the animal body adapts itself to its natural environment. But these memory-images of the deeper self, these recollections which turn us moodily away from the practical situations of life, which substitute revery for action, which mingle dream with reality in such a way as to render problematic their very boundaries, far from satisfying a practical end, do they not completely distort, even deny, the practical character of our life? There can be no doubt that they do. In the first kind of memory the animal organism reveals its dependence upon the order of external nature; in the second the self states its declaration of independence from the natural world, its spontaneity, even its caprice. For Bergson this spontaneity and caprice, no less than the decisive act of the deepest self, is the meaning of human freedom.

3. CREATIVE EVOLUTION

The history of the evolution of life [says Bergson[27]] incomplete as it yet is, already reveals to us how the intellect has been formed by an uninterrupted progress on a line which ascends through the vertebrate series up to man. It shows us in the faculty of understanding an appendage of the faculty of acting, a more and more precise, more and more complex and supple adaptation of the consciousness of living beings to the conditions of existence that are made for them. Hence should result this consequence that our intellect in the narrow sense of the word, is intended to secure the perfect fitting of our body to its environment, to represent the relations of external things among themselves—in short, to think matter.

Thus at the very beginning of *Creative Evolution* Bergson states both the frame of reference within which his thought originated and a major conclusion of his philosophy as a whole.

This means that the inherent logic of all intellectual processes is that they have as their purpose the strict control of a solid environment. If Bergson is correct, the most theoretical equipment of the human mind —the total apparatus of symbolic logic and of mathematics—is but an instrumentality for the control of material objects. There is, then, no serious epistemological problem as the seventeenth century saw it—no perplexity as to how interaction is possible between mind and the external world. For between the logical structure of the mind and the perceived structure of the world of matter in motion there exists a preestablished harmony, proceeding not from the imposition of divine authority but from the automatic working of the evolutionary process.

But if to explain logic and mathematics in this fashion solves one important problem of epistemology, it poses another of even greater difficulty. If our concepts have been created in conformity with our necessity to think matter, how can we have any confidence that this natural geometry of solids can be used to explain the nature of life, or to comprehend the total meaning of that very evolutionary process through which this natural geometry has itself developed? Strangely enough, this has rarely been a stumbling-block to those philosophers or scientists who have been most preoccupied with the doctrines of biological evolution, with the result that most explanations of living processes have been given in a language and within a conceptual framework which is peculiarly appropriate to the domain of the inorganic. In his recognition of this fact Bergson again makes use of a type of philosophical apparatus which we are accustomed to associate with Kant.

In the famous section of *The Critique of Pure Reason* where Kant is dealing with the antinomies of reason, he shows the difficulties, and indeed the contradictions, into which human thought falls when we attempt to apply to the realm of nature concepts which have their origin and sole validity in the domain of pure reason. Bergson, similarly, insists that when we try to apply to the realm of the living, concepts which are derived from our experience of inert matter, similar contradictions result. For an understanding of living things, intellectual apprehension is not enough; we must add intuition.

Creative Evolution begins where *Matter and Memory* had left off— with the creativity of the self and the crucial contrast between the self and natural objects.[28]

The finished portrait is explained by the features of the model, by the nature of the artist, by the colors spread out on the palette; but even with the knowledge of what explains it, no one, not even the artist, could have foreseen exactly what the portrait would be, for to predict it would have been to produce it before it was produced—an absurd hypothesis which is its own refutation. Even so with regard to the moments of our life, of which we are the artisans. Each of them is a kind of creation. And just as the talent of the painter is formed or deformed—in any case, is modified—under the very influence of the work he produces, so each of our states, at the moment of its issue, modifies our personality, being indeed the new form that we are just assuming. It is then right to say that what we do depends on what we are; but it is necessary to add also that we are, to a certain extent, what we do, and that we are creating ourselves continually.

With non-living, unorganized bodies it is very different. Here there is no principle of inner duration, no constant process of self-creation. The world of an older physics consists of physical elements and their relationships, and these relationships generalized provide a system of rigid principles of explanation. Bits of matter may be said to be "simply located"[29] within an all-embracing absolute space and their motions are predictable as the operations of a machine are predictable. Granted such a Newtonian world, the fiction of Laplace is inevitable. An omniscient being or a superhuman intellect could at any time calculate from the past the present position of any particle in the system of universal space. Upon such a mechanistic presupposition the isolation of particular regions of the world for detailed study and a general doctrine of scientific predictability depend. As Bergson says:[30] "All our belief in objects, all our operations on the systems that science isolates rest, in fact, on the idea that time does not bite into them."

The inner self bathes in duration. The world of external nature is steeped in spatiality. In which universe are we to find the place of other living things? For Bergson the answer is clear. The home of matter is space. The home of life is time.

Bergson is not unaware that the concept of time plays its role in the physical sciences. But he distinguishes "duration," or time lived, from the abstract "time by the clock" which is used in physics; a time which knows nothing of qualitative uniqueness, but is characterized by the uniformity of our experience of space. Unorganized bodies have a future which is but the repetition of their past. Living bodies, on the other hand, *endure*. They mature and grow old and the moving path of their life is a constant recording of their time. "Whenever anything lives, there is open somewhere a register in which time is being inscribed."[31]

Mechanistic explanation pervades the mentality of biological science, but any radically mechanistic approach to the phenomena of life is at once rendered inadequate by an appeal to our experience of "real time."[32]

We perceive duration as a stream against which we cannot go. It is the foundation of our being, and, as we feel, the very substance of the world in which we live. It is of no use to hold up before our eyes the dazzling prospect of a universal mathematic; we cannot sacrifice experience to the requirements of a system. That is why we reject radical mechanism.

Explanations of the development of the series of living forms are generally divided into two primary types: mechanistic and teleological. The first views biological change as the inevitable operation of a rigid system of cause and effect, predictable as the outcome of the mutual interaction of organisms and natural environment. The second views biological change as the unfolding of an original purpose, the progressive realization of a program previously arranged. But in this view finalism is as unsatisfactory as mechanism. For if we merely substitute the attraction of the future for the push of the past, there is still no escape from the predictable outcome. No room is left for the mysterious agency of novelty and creation. Finalism, like mechanism, is an outgrowth of the practical orientation of the intellect—of its vast disinclination to submit to the unforeseeable.

Insofar as we are geometricians, then, we reject the unforeseeable. We might accept it assuredly, insofar as we are artists, for art lives on creation and implies a latent belief in the spontaneity of nature. But disinterested art is a luxury like pure speculation. Long before being artists we are artisans;

and all fabrication, however rudimentary, lives on likeness and repetition, like the natural geometry which serves as its fulcrum.[33]

For Bergson, neither mechanism nor finalism presents the real clue to the nature of the evolutionary process. This clue is to be found only in the *élan vital*—the spirit of life itself—a mysterious, creative agency which is at once the original impetus from which life springs, and the force which, passing through the individuated forms of life like an electric current through a series of conductors, serves to bridge the gap between the generations of living organisms and at the same time to cause those variations and mutations which create new forms of life in an ever broadening stream of productivity. All life, from the simplest protozoa to the most complicated forms, is the proliferation of the same vital impetus emerging in the most varied species and passing into divergent lines of evolution. The vital impetus is the creative well out of which all living things emerge, and its creativity produces types which can be neither calculated nor foreseen. Here then is the crucial cosmological divide which bifurcates the universe—that between the deadness of inert matter and the vitality of organic forms. And this divide has also profound significance for human life. For if man's deepest despair is his sense of homelessness in a universe of alien matter, his profoundest comfort lies in the sense of solidarity with the world of living things and his participation in its source—the vital impetus.[34]

The vital impetus is the prime power for the course of life. But that initial unity diversifies itself endlessly in the various lines of development of living forms. In what fashion are we to understand this movement? A metaphor provides the answer:

The evolutionary movement would be a simple one, and we should soon have been able to determine its direction, if life had described a single course, like that of a solid ball shot from a cannon. But it proceeds rather like a shell, which suddenly bursts into fragments, which fragments, being themselves shells, burst in their turn into fragments destined to burst again, and so on for a time incommensurably long. We perceive only what is nearest to us, namely, the scattered movements of the pulverized explosions. From them we have to go back, stage by stage, to the original movement.

When a shell bursts, the particular way it breaks is explained both by the explosive force of the powder it contains and by the resistance of the metal. So of the way life breaks into individuals and species. It depends, we think, on two series of causes: the resistance life meets from inert matter, and the explosive force—due to an unstable balance of tendencies—which life bears within itself.[35]

If this metaphor has substance, it would suggest that such harmony as exists in the evolutionary process is a harmony which is greatest in the beginning and becomes progressively less as the evolutionary process proceeds. And it would also suggest that in the many bifurcations which have occurred throughout the development of living beings, many forms have been generated which in the end turned out to be blind alleys. Indeed, only that one grand thoroughfare which leads through the vertebrate series up to man is really significant in the revelation of nature's intrinsic intent.

The first fork in the evolutionary highway is that which marks the divergence between the plant and the animal. The difference between them cannot be defined by clear and definite characteristics but only by their respective emphases and tendencies. The animal has mobility in space, the plant has torpor. The animal is conscious, and this consciousness is related to its power to move freely. The plant, being fixed in the earth, has no need of movement to gain its sustenance and thus no need for consciousness. The vegetable manufactures organic substance directly from its mineral environment, and this frees it from the necessity of movement and sensation. Animals, obliged to search for their food, must move, and in consequence must develop an ever-expanding and ever more supple consciousness. The basic function of plant life is to store up energy. The basic function of animal life is to expend energy. Deeply considered, animality means the constant release of stored energy into explosive action. The agent of this release is the central nervous system, which becomes the transformer of potential into kinetic energy.

Yet the maintenance of the energetic character of animal life is precarious. It is almost as if the inertness of matter were a constant peril awaiting its opportunity to overcome the forces of life. The pitfalls of the plant, torpor and unconsciousness, perpetually lie in wait for the animal, and eventually overcome it in death. It is exactly what we might expect if we were to analogize for nature the precariousness of our own human freedom.

Out of an original vital impetus two branches of living things spring, the animal with motion, the plant with torpor. Of these two the plant is the terminus, the animal is the thoroughfare. The animal is in turn divided into two main streams. In one direction goes the vertebrate series culminating in man, in another the line culminating in the arthropods (crustaceans and insects). What is the inner meaning of this divergence? In the separation of these two streams can be discerned two powers, both contained in the original vital impulse, and destined to increasingly part company as the evolutionary process matures—in the insects the power of instinct, in man the power of intelligence.

Yet, opposite as they are, instinct and intelligence are also complementary in their functioning. Also, having sprung from the same vital impetus, neither has been absolutely refined and purified through the evolutionary process. Thus there is no intelligence without some trace of instinct, no instinct apart from its vague fringe of intelligence. Neither lends itself to rigid definition. They are not absolutes but tendencies.

The function of intelligence is to produce mechanical inventions. The function of instinct is to operate immediately upon the world. Instinct is the natural ability to use an inborn mechanism. Intelligence is the perfected faculty of contriving external tools for the manipulation of the environment. Instinct is magnificently specialized, but narrow. Intellect gives man infinite potentialities of discovery and of use. Instinct is confined and limited, but safe. Intelligence is free, full of possibility, but risky.

Once intellect is seen for what it really is—neither a speculative luxury nor the blinding light to pierce the curtain of reality, but the functional machinery of animal adaptation—its nature and its limitations become clear. It manipulates, it aims at the practically useful, it constructs tools, it works with matter and with solids, it favors atomicity over continuity, it feels at home with the static rather than the mobile. And of all its contrivances the most potent is language.

Through language the human community of action is made possible. And through the abstract generality of language man is freed from the bondage of matter. Were sensation alone the condition of human experience we should live out our lives bounded by the limits of an everlasting present. But by extending perception to include the recollection of like percepts, and by crystalizing this comparison in an idea, we round out our past and construct for ourselves a partially predictable future. Language fixes our ideas in the form of concepts and combines them according to a systematic grammatical structure. And the set of relations imbedded in this universal grammar is the content of our logic.[36]

Our logic is the complete set of rules that must be followed in using symbols. As these symbols are derived from the consideration of solids, as the rules for combining these symbols hardly do more than express the most general relations among solids, our logic triumphs in that science which takes the solidity of bodies for its object, that is, in geometry. It is from the extension of a certain natural geometry, suggested by the most general and immediately perceived properties of solids, that natural logic has arisen; then from this natural logic, in its turn, has sprung scientific geometry, which extends further and further the knowledge of the external properties of solids. Geometry and logic are strictly applicable to matter; in it they are at home, and in it they can proceed quite alone.

But precisely because "symbols are derived from the consideration of solids" we may raise serious questions about the metaphysical adequacy of language. The measure of its success in understanding matter is the measure of its failure in expressing the nature of life or of penetrating into dynamic reality. Language, since it is the creature of intellect, is bound by the demand for clarity, simplicity, and economy. This was Descartes's meaning in his demand for clear and distinct ideas. But life and creative evolution cannot be approached through the channels of clarity and distinctness.[37] And herein lies the superiority of instinct.

Instinct is modeled on the very form of life. We know it as fullness of feeling, as organic sympathy. And it is in the direction of sympathy rather than of intelligence that metaphysical truth must be sought. This does not mean that intelligence cannot play an indispensable role in the drama of knowledge, for indeed it is the catalyst which transforms brute instinct into human intuition.[38] Intuition is instinct which has been freed from its practical uses, which has become disinterested, reflective, and self-conscious. And this liberation from the necessities of practice has been gained from the push of intelligence. Intuition is the culminating form of consciousness which has developed in the evolutionary process. The long series of biological changes which began with the most primitive expressions of the vital impetus ends now with the production of nature's supreme creative gift.

And yet, says Bergson, philosophy itself has not accepted this gift with unbiased graciousness. How could it, since philosophy itself has traditionally served as willing victim of the intellectualization of consciousness? Philosophers since Plato and Aristotle have taken for granted the centrality of the intellect, and from this belief has grown a faith that the unity of nature can be best expressed in the abstract and geometrical form imposed by the intellect. For the Greeks the philosophy of nature is an inferior, because more contingent, "logic," but it is a logic nevertheless. Once this is granted, "intelligence" and "reality" are seen to mutually imply one another. Through an inherent correspondence between the realm of events and the realm of mind mathematics inevitably becomes the clue to the pattern of the natural world. For Plato, for Hegelian metaphysics, and for modern philosophy of science, "what is rational is what is real."

Once it sees, however, that reason is pragmatic through and through, that intelligence is primarily the servant of action, then philosophy can no longer accept the intellectualist account of the relation of science and metaphysics. Intelligence would have to be thrust aside by an act of pure will before philosophy could proceed by a method truly appropriate to the dignity of its search. For then it would be the business of philosophy to examine into the ultimate meaning of life not by the method of intelligence but by the method of intuition.

But the abandonment of the method of intellect would have one peculiar consequence—it would severely injure the reputability of the assumption of the mathematical order of nature. If one were to inquire why the mind is so intent upon finding a mechanical uniformity in the natural world, one would see that there is at the source of our intellectual operations a need, and consequently a passion, for order. The mind clings tenaciously to the application of mathematics to the realm of natural events because of a certain restless anxiety which it normally feels in the presence of chaos and disorder. But suppose that the world in its inmost nature is not mathematically ordered. It does not therefore follow that it exhibits no order at all. In place of the fiction of a cosmic mathematics we might have confidence in the existence of an order of quite another sort—a willed and vital, indeed, a creative order, an order for the world of living things analogous to that implicit in a work of art.

Of course, the invitation to adopt the method of intuition is qualified by its own irony, for man's limitation is that his consciousness is permanently intellectual. It might have been given a greater admixture of intuition. In a perfect humanity, produced by a completely creative evolution, intuition and intellect would have been perfectly blended, but in the humanity of which we are a part, intuition haunts the operations of intellect, although it is submerged by it. In this lies human imperfection, and in the recognition of this imperfection lies the task of philosophy.

Intuition is there, however, but vague, and above all discontinuous. It is a lamp almost extinguished, which only glimmers now and then, for a few moments at most. But it glimmers wherever a vital interest is at stake. On our personality, on our liberty, on the place we occupy in the whole of nature, on our origin and perhaps also on our destiny, it throws a light, feeble and vacillating, but which nonetheless pierces the darkness of the night in which the intellect leaves us. These fleeting intuitions, which light up their object only at distant intervals, philosophy ought to seize, first to sustain them, then to expand them and so unite them together.[89]

But suppose that by an act of will the philosopher were to throw back the heavy draperies of the intellect so that the bright power of intuition should have a freer entree. What dark corners would it illumi-

nate? What light would it throw upon the nature of the real? To ask
this question is to pass to Bergson's own intimations of the nature
of ultimate reality—to explore his own characteristic "metaphysics of
process."

Already in "An Introduction to Metaphysics" Bergson had said:[40]

There is a reality that is external and yet given immediately to the mind. . . .
This reality is mobility. Not *things* made, but things in the making, not
self-maintaining *states*, but only changing states, exist. Rest is never more
than apparent, or, rather, relative. The consciousness we have of our own
self in its continual flux introduces us to the interior of a reality on the model
of which we must represent other realities. *All reality, therefore is tendency.*
. . . Our mind, which seeks for solid points of support, has for its main
function in the ordinary course of life that of representing *states* and *things*.
It takes, at long intervals, almost instantaneous views of the undivided
mobility of the real. It thus obtains *sensations* and *ideas*. In this way it
substitutes for the continuous the discontinuous, for motion stability, for
tendency in process of change, fixed points marking a direction of change and
tendency. This substitution is necessary to common-sense, to language, to
practical life and even in a certain degree to positive science.

If, then, we force ourselves to "think" being directly, we shall find
it patterned upon the model of our own duration, akin to the data of
our deepest introspection: a process of perpetual becoming, an endless
creative flow. That we are not constantly aware of this reality is due to
the urgency with which appearance dominates our practical life, and to
the grossness of our organs of sense perception. If, looking at an impres-
sionist painting while standing a little way off (a Sunday promenade of
Seurat or one of Monet's studies of Amiens), one fixes one's attention
upon a patch of dull blue or greyish-purple, it seems as though this
segment of the canvas is homogeneous and uniform in color. But
coming closer to the picture one sees that this is not the case. What
seemed a patch of uniform grey is in reality a nosegay of red, blue,
black, and white points of brilliant color dotted by the artist in order
that the eye of the beholder might mix them into grey at a distance.
The semblance of an atmospheric mist is revealed technically as the
reality of many brilliant centers of violent color. Or again, who has not
seen a round ball sustained in the air over a jet of water? From a distance it seems as though the ball were held steady like the capital upon
a column of stone, but close up one sees that it is the ever-moving
stream of water which by a series of constant and ever-changing thrusts
maintains the ball upon its sparkling surface. Just so, the world of
material objects carved out by perception, when seen intuitively, can

be recognized as the momentary solid form which intellect imposes upon a substratum whose movement is constant and iridescent as a flowing stream in sunlight.

The very perceptions which permit us to discriminate the massive qualitative differences of our world, upon close inspection turn out to be grounded in an infinite number of vibrations within the structure of the real.

In the smallest discernible fraction of a second, in the almost instantaneous perception of a sensible quality, there may be trillions of oscillations which repeat themselves. The permanence of a sensible quality consists in this repetition of movements, as the persistence of life consists in a series of palpitations. The primal function of perception is precisely to grasp a series of elementary changes under the form of a quality or of a simple state, by a work of condensation.[41]

The more imperative the demand for practical activity, the more our mind with a kind of conceptual shorthand concentrates these vibrations into a thick focus of attention. This is the measure of our mastery over our environment. A man is gifted practically in proportion as he can encompass at a glance a series of events; lingering over them as successive movements, or brooding over their significance as simple appearances, he is lost in an aesthetic moodiness which blunts the edge of his determination to act. Only those circumstances which we grasp instantaneously as a whole are ours to dominate.

But it would be the crassest metaphysical deception to believe that this telescoping of the continuous movement of the real brings us any closer to the nature of things.

What is real is the continual *change of* form: *form is only a snapshot view of a transition.* Therefore, here again, our perception manages to solidify into discontinuous images the fluid continuity of the real. When the successive images do not differ from each other too much, we consider them all as the waxing and waning of a single *mean* image or as the deformation of this image in different directions. And to this mean we really allude when we speak of the *essence* of a thing, or of the thing itself.[42]

The transition from the reality of underlying movement to the perceptual presentation of objects takes place through the condensation of many images into a single image, and the single image which perception chooses is, as it were, generally the most typical. It is as though the practical requirements of our life dictated that we take an average or *statistical view of reality* in order to dominate that real multiplicity which, although metaphysically authoritative, would in practice be a source of endless clumsiness and embarrassment. And the stable images which the mind distills from the flux of reality are those of the *qualities* of bodies, the *essences* of things, and the *acts* of individuals. These three are the chief denominations of our intellectual monetary system and they find their natural expression in the currency of language. Adjectives, substantives, and verbs are the primordial elements of language: they are the linguistic correlatives of qualities, essences, and acts.

Although the intellect does not penetrate to the inmost activity of the real, through the aid of our sensory apparatus it does nevertheless provide us with an image of Becoming. The fact of change is rudimentary in experience. We are convinced that we inhabit a world of process, and although for practical purposes we are guided by "the illusion of permanent solids," the mechanism through which knowledge takes place imparts a qualitatively neutral movement to the objects of our perception. This is because the mind operates according to the model of a moving-picture projector.

Suppose we wish to portray on a screen a living picture, such as the marching past of a regiment. There is one way in which it might first occur to us to do it. That would be to cut out jointed figures representing the soldiers, to give to each of them the movement of marching, a movement varying from individual to individual although common to the human species, and to throw the whole on the screen. We should need to spend on this little game an enormous amount of work, and even then we should obtain but a very poor result: how could it, at its best, reproduce the suppleness and variety of life? Now, there is another way of proceeding, more easy and at the same time more effective. It is to take a series of snapshots of the passing regiment and to throw these instantaneous views on the screen, so that they replace each other very rapidly. This is what the cinematograph does. With photographs, each of which represents the regiment in a fixed attitude, it reconstitutes the mobility of the regiment marching. It is true that if we had to do with photographs alone, however much we might look at them, we should never see them animated: with immobility set beside immobility, even endlessly, we could never make movement. In order that the pictures may be animated, there must be movement somewhere. The movement does indeed exist here; it is in the apparatus. It is because the film of the cinematograph unrolls, bringing in turn the different photographs of the scene to continue each other, that each actor of the scene recovers his mobility; he strings all his successive attitudes on the invisible movement of the film. The process then consists in extracting from all the movements peculiar to all the figures an impersonal movement abstract and simple, *movement in general*, so to speak: we put this into the apparatus, and we reconstitute the individuality of each particular movement by combining this nameless movement with the personal attitudes. Such is the contrivance of the cinemato-

graph. And such is also that of our knowledge. Instead of attaching ourselves to the inner becoming of things, we place ourselves outside them in
order to recompose their becoming artificially. We take snapshots, as it
were, of the passing reality, and, as these are characteristic of the reality, we
have only to string them on a becoming, abstract, uniform and invisible,
situated at the back of the apparatus of knowledge, in order to imitate what
there is that is characteristic in this becoming itself. Perception, intellection,
language so proceed in general. Whether we would think becoming, or express it, or even perceive it, we hardly do anything else than set going a kind
of cinematograph inside us. We may therefore sum up what we have been
saying in the conclusion that the *mechanism of our ordinary knowledge is
of a cinematographical kind.*[43]

The difficulty is that this mechanism provides an image of Becoming
which, since it is constructed of immobile parts, is but a semblance of
the continuous movement of the real. But no insight into continuity
can be achieved by the juxtaposition of discontinuous images. Action
is discontinuous, and knowledge serving as expeditor of action shares
in this discontinuity. A speculative attempt to uncover the metaphysically real which relies upon this intellectual equipment is doomed
to failure. But philosophy is the very antithesis of action, and its method,
transcending practical requirements, only demands of the philosopher
that he shall advance with the moving reality, install himself by an act
of intuition within change itself and thus become immersed in a mystical
reality which the classifying intellect and a solidified language cannot
hope to illumine.

Philosophical ideas are often the consequence of theoretical advances
in the sciences. An age in which physics is the dominant scientific
concern might naturally be preoccupied with primary qualities and with
the evidences of materiality. But since Darwin and Wundt it is the
sciences of life and of consciousness which occupy men's minds and in
which they might rightfully seek the clue to an adequate metaphysics.
It is Bergson's great discovery that in the evolutionary series are to be
found the secrets of mentality, that the nature of the real was less
adequately grasped by Parmenides than by Heracleitus, and that the
task of philosophy is an intuitive recovery of relationship with the creative effort of the universe of which it is the profoundest expression.

The philosopher must go further than the scientist. Making a clean sweep
of everything that is only an imaginative symbol, he will see the material
world melt back into a simple flux, a continuity of flowing, a becoming. And
he will thus be prepared to discover real duration there where it is still more
useful to find it, in the realm of life and of consciousness. For, so far as inert

matter is concerned, we may neglect the flowing without committing a
serious error: matter, we have said, is weighted with geometry; and matter,
the reality which *descends*, endures only by its connection with that which
ascends. But life and consciousness are this very ascension. When once we
have grasped them in their essence by adopting their movement, we understand how the rest of reality is derived from them. Evolution appears and,
within this evolution, the progressive determination of materiality and intellectuality by the gradual consolidation of the one and of the other. But,
then, it is within the evolutionary movement that we place ourselves, in
order to follow it to its present results, instead of recomposing these results
artificially with fragments of themselves. Such seems to us to be the true
function of philosophy. So understood, philosophy is not only the turning
of the mind homeward, the coincidence of human consciousness with the
living principle whence it emanates, a contact with the creative effort: it is
the study of becoming in general, it is true evolutionism and consequently the
true continuation of science.[44]

4. SOCIETY AND RELIGION

Creative Evolution appeared in 1907. Twenty-five years later, in 1932,
Bergson published *The Two Sources of Morality and Religion*. The
intervening period was a time of patient reflection in which Bergson
steeped himself not only in the studies of Durkheim and Lévy-Bruhl,
the famous French sociologists of religion, but also in the documents
of the great religious mystics—St. Bernard of Clairvaux, St. Theresa of
Avila, St. John of the Cross. The book thus, characteristically, bears the
impress both of the most mundane facts of social life and of the most
exalted religious aspirations of the human spirit.

This dualism of outlook is not accidental. It is not that the preparation determined the thesis, but rather that the thesis determined the
preparation. *Creative Evolution* expressed the same range of comprehension, the same vivid interest in the factual details and the ultimate
outcome of biological phenomena that *The Two Sources* shows for the
moral and the religious life. And as for the dualism, that seems to me
to be almost the ruling form of Bergson's perception.[45] *Creative Evolution* had explored the major dichotomies of matter and life, instinct
and intelligence, intuition and practical action. *The Two Sources* explores the comparable dichotomies which pertain to morality and to
religion.

Of these, the most important is that of the open versus the closed
society. In a closed or finite society, the moral laws by which we guide
our conduct are often interpreted as fixed and inevitable laws of nature
(just as the laws of nature are sometimes interpreted as divine impera-

tives). This is both because the role of religion is to reinforce the claims of society and because the sense of obligation represents the pressure of society felt both as external restraint and as internal compulsion. The verdict of conscience is always the verdict of our social self, and we feel the pull of duty not primarily as the result of an act of deliberation but as a kind of automatic response to the fixity of our social obligations.[46] Kant was wrong. Obligation is not a requirement of reason. It is a pressure of social necessity upon the will, and it always has in view the preservation of some finite community, some "closed" society.

In contrast to the closed is the "open" society, the society which includes all mankind. We are led to the ideal of this society through those universalizing agents: God and Reason. But they operate in very different ways. It is the rationalist dream that all men live outward from the center of a circle and that although what is nearest the center is most real to them, yet by a process of progressively enlarging identification they may pass from ethnocentrism to the love of humanity. But this is a delusion. There is no continuity between the closed and the open society. Theirs is a difference not of degree but of kind. And so God is more relevant here than Reason, not because the idea is more universal (Stoic morality disproves that), but because it adds a new dimension of emotion, a new dynamic of feeling. The absolute morality of the "open" society is always exemplified by the extraordinary man; it is incarnate in a privileged person.

Founders and reformers of religions, mystics and saints, obscure heroes of moral life whom we have met on our way and who are in our eyes the equals of the greatest, they are all there: inspired by their example, we follow them, as if we were joining an army of conquerors. They are indeed conquerors: they have broken down natural resistance and raised humanity to a new destiny. . . . Look at it as you will, you must always come back to the conception of moral creators who see in their mind's eye a new social atmosphere, an environment in which life would be more worth living, I mean a society such that, if men once tried it, they would refuse to go back to the old state of things. Thus only is moral progress to be defined; but it is only in retrospect that it can be defined, when some exceptional moral nature has created a new feeling, like a new kind of music, and passed it on to mankind, stamping it with his own vitality.[47]

There are, then, two sources of morality, which are exemplified respectively in the universal acceptance of a law and the common imitation of an ethical model. The first source of morality lies in the necessity for social solidarity felt by all closed societies and expressed in the distinct pressures exerted by society through the agency of obligation.

The second source of morality is the emotional appeal of great men—
the morality of aspiration and contagion through which the limitations
of a closed society are broken. Articulated moral structures are stamped
with the forms of reason, but they express the same natural requirement
for communal social living as are expressed in the instinctive behavior
of insect societies. The morality which flowers in the lives of great
spiritual leaders breaks through the mere requirements of nature toward
some higher potential of the human person for the brotherhood of all
mankind. It is this which St. Paul preached of a kingdom not of this
world and which Plato suggested might be the Republic of dedicated
spirits even though that Republic were never to come into actual being.

But the great moral figures that have made their mark on history join
hands across the centuries, above our human cities; they unite into a divine
city which they bid us enter. We may not hear their voices distinctly, the
call has none the less gone forth, and something answers from the depth of
our soul; from the real society in which we live we betake ourselves in thought
to this ideal society; to this ideal society we bow down when we reverence
the dignity of man within us, when we declare that we act from self-
respect.[48]

The two sources of morality (pressure and aspiration) are embedded
in the formulae of moral activity which drive all civilized societies,
the imperatives dictated by impersonal social requirements and the
series of appeals to the conscience made by persons who are in advance
of humanity. And both of these forces, working upon different aspects
of our moral nature, are moulded and formalized by our intelligence.
Reason coordinates legal codes and it also systematizes the prophecies
of the sage. It does not, however, originate either. Back of Reason's
manipulations are the true origins: social necessity, moral passion. The
dualism seems absolute but in truth it is not, for it merges into a higher
unity. Just as instinct and intelligence are two complementary manifestations of the *élan vital,* so also are social pressure and the impulse
toward love.

The distinction between the open and the closed society is the first
dichotomy which Bergson's *Two Sources* explores. A second, equally
important one is the distinction between static and dynamic religion.

For the rationalistic mind, the very existence of religion presents a
problem. How is it that obviously absurd superstitions are able to exert
such coercive force upon the lives of reasonable beings? The facts are
indubitable and impressive. Religion is a pervasive feature of social life
at every level. There has never been a society without religion. From

Bergson's point of view (that of a biologist who translates human phenomena into biological categories of explanation), this fact is decisive. Religion being as wide as the human species, its existence must be attributed not to chance or to accident, but to some inherent property of our structure. Men dream and they philosophize, but first of all they must live. And since our psychic structure is fitted to the necessities of preserving individual and social life, that which is pervasive in our makeup must have some social and biological utility. And so it is with religion.

Religion is created through the myth-making faculty, which is the answer to a basic demand of life. It is true that the art of creating "fictions" is wider than the sphere of religion, that it comprehends poetry, art, dreams and fantasies of every description, but these are extras—a super-abundance of creativity coming into existence because the mind knew how to make myths; but religion is really what explains the myth-making function. We see this more clearly if we remember that the essence of human life is always close to animal instinct, that in man instinct has to some extent made room for intelligence, but that from intelligence spring possible dangers for life which must be guarded against by other psychic mechanisms. This is the utility of the myth and of religion.

The destructive potentialities of intelligence are of two kinds: (1) it can generalize the experience of death and apply it to the individual case, and (2) it knows its own limitations in predicting the outcome of events and activities. Human beings are thus confronted both with the knowledge that their own death is inevitable and that there is a critical disparity between human desire and the way of the world. Each of these modes of knowledge is destructive, for they mobilize our fears and give rational justification for our insecurity. But such fears are overcome by religion. Religious belief means a relating of the self to the mysteries of the universe in such a way that death is seen to be an illusion, and that forces sympathetic to human purposes can be read even into the suffering and frustrations of human life. Religious belief means confidence and reassurance against fear. It is therefore a defensive reaction of nature against the socially destructive influence of intelligence.

It is this kind of religion which Bergson terms "static." It is religion which supplies strength and discipline, which therefore needs rites and ceremonies, and which is embedded in the texture of society. Static religion is analogous to moral obligation; it is institutionalized. It binds together the members of a society through the creation and preservation of a tradition; it therefore tightens the social bond. In the operations of intelligence there is not only fear, but a certain tendency toward individualism. But static religion stamps out those impulses which are merely individual, and turns man toward his society.

Just as there are two types of morality, one of pressure and one of aspiration, so there are two types of religion: one the natural religion of social conformity, the other the "dynamic" religion which leans toward a unification of all cosmic experience. The soul strong enough (and noble enough) to seize upon intuition, intensify it, and then feel itself pervaded by a kind of being infinitely superior to itself would experience this unification. Dynamic religion, intuition, mysticism (they are all one) is thus a striking out of the self beyond the limits of intelligence in search of vision and of contact.

> We must be still and still moving
> Into another intensity
> For a further union, a deeper communion
> Through the dark cold and the empty desolation. . . .[49]

Or, as Bergson himself puts it:[50] "In our eyes, the ultimate end of mysticism is the establishment of a contact, consequently of a partial coincidence, with the creative effort which life itself manifests. This effort is of God, if it is not God himself. The great mystic is to be conceived as an individual being, capable of transcending the limitations imposed on the species by its material nature, thus continuing and extending the divine action."

> Man's curiosity searches past and future
> And clings to that dimension. But to apprehend
> The point of intersection of the timeless
> With time, is an occupation for the saint. . . .[51]

The great mystic, like the great moral creator, has as his task the radical transformation of humanity, not through precept, but through example. And so, between the institutionalized natural religion of tradition and the dynamic religion of mystic inspiration lies an interval as great as that between life and death. Yet there is a relationship between them. "We represent [static] religion, then, as the crystalization, brought about by a scientific process of cooling, of what mysticism had poured, white hot, into the soul of man."

5. CONCLUSION

The permanent merit of Bergson's philosophy is that, taking the theory of biological evolution with the utmost seriousness, it shows the place of human creativity in the cosmic scheme. Its subsidiary merits are great. In distinguishing between the mechanical time by which physical events are measured and the "duration" in which the self exists, Bergson has made possible the separation of an artificial world of scientific description from an emotional world of human experience. And in distinguishing between the surface self which adjusts itself to the natural and social worlds simply as an episode in its survival, and the deeper self which can act with all the resources of its nature in moments of decisive importance, and which in memory recovers every shade and every nuance of its past, Bergson has provided a clue to much that is mysterious and obscure in mental operations and social behavior. To these merits must be added a third: that of accounting for the process of biological evolution in such a way that intellect and instinct are each given their reasonable and proper function, so that the former is not viewable as a divine intervention in a wholly animal series, and the latter is not a fact of human embarrassment. These subsidiary merits all take their place as parts of the ultimate demonstration, which is that human art, religion, and philosophy are not simply the accidental by-products of a course of mechanistic change, but are the expressions of the very *raison d'être* of the evolutionary process itself.

The theory of instrumentalism is a natural inference from Darwinism. That our mental faculties are instruments for our adaptation, our growth, and our survival agrees with much that we know concerning the course of life and the operations of our minds. But it has a certain distressingly practical ring which, although it fits in well with the practical and mechanistic presuppositions of modern life, is at the same time discouraging to the spiritual values implicit in philosophy, religion, and the arts. It is the paradoxical originality of Bergson that admitting (in fact, insisting upon) the instrumental theory of mind, he at the same time subordinates that instrument to values which have little to do with practicality.

All of this is accomplished through a dualistic epistemology. Granted that instinct and intelligence are complementary in their functioning and interpenetrate each other, that they are tendencies rather than absolutes, nevertheless the function of intelligence is to contrive tools (symbolic or otherwise) for the manipulation of the environment. And instinct, fringed about by intelligence, grown almost self-conscious as it were, turns into that higher form of awareness which is intuition. Intuition as knowledge can be defined only poetically, that is, by suggestion. In *An Introduction to Metaphysics* Bergson has called it "the kind of intellectual sympathy by which one places oneself within an object in order to coincide with what is unique in it and consequently inexpressible." He has also said that intuition provides an absolute and not a relative awareness, and the conclusion of *Creative Evolution* is that it is the culminating form of consciousness which has developed in the evolutionary process. But if we ask how concretely does it operate, it is necessary to turn from a generalized form of perception to specific areas and to examine respectively art, philosophy, and religion.

What is the purpose of art? It is to provide a vision of reality which is direct, vivid, feelingful.

Between nature and ourselves, nay, between ourselves and our own consciousness a veil is interposed: a veil that is dense and opaque for the common herd,—thin, almost transparent for the artist and the poet. What fairy wove that veil? Was it done in malice or in friendliness? We had to live, and life demands that we grasp things in their relations to our own needs. . . . We move amidst generalities and symbols, as within a tilt-yard in which our force is effectively pitted against other forces; and fascinated by action, tempted by it, for our own good, on to the field it has selected, we live in a zone midway between things and ourselves, externally to things, externally also to ourselves. From time to time, however, in a fit of absentmindedness nature raises up souls that are more detached from life. Not with that intentional, logical systematic detachment—the result of reflection and philosophy —but rather with a natural detachment, one innate in the structure of sense or consciousness, which at once reveals itself by a virginal manner, so to speak, of seeing, hearing or thinking. Were this detachment complete, did the soul no longer cleave to action by any of its perceptions, it would be the soul of an artist such as the world has never yet seen. It would excel alike in every art at the same time; or rather, it would fuse them all into one. It would perceive all things in their native purity: the forms, colors, sounds of the physical world as well as the subtlest movements of the inner life. But this is asking too much of nature. Even for such of us as she has made artists, it is by accident, and on one side only that she has lifted the veil. In one direction only has she forgotten to rivet the perception to the need.[52]

The intuitive vision of the real which the artist presents is possible because of his detachment from the demands of every-day living. Sometimes, by a lucky accident, men arise whose consciousness is less oriented to action than that of the ordinary man. When such men perceive an object, they are less concerned with deliberation and action than with the significance of the object itself. Here perception is not an instrument; it is intrinsically valuable, and the less the artist is habituated to the utilization of perception, the more he perceives and the deeper his vision of the object. The communication of this deeper vision of the real (which enlarges the vision even of those who are not artists) is the function of art.

I have dwelt upon Bergson's theory of art (fragmentarily as it is put forth in *Laughter* and "The Perception of Change") partly because it shows one of the areas where practicality is thrown aside and intrinsically valuable experience can be garnered, but mainly because it is through the example of art that Bergson suggests what philosophical intuition might be.

The vision of pure Becoming which a philosophical intuition might yield would perhaps penetrate all our activities, and through it we might obtain satisfactions similar to those of art, but more continuously and with even greater accessibility. For, although art enlarges our perception and enriches our present, its appeal is to surface quality rather than to depth, and its appeal to our present makes no demands upon the deepest self and its accumulated past. Philosophy is different.

Through philosophy we can accustom ourselves never to isolate the present from the past which it pulls along with it. Thanks to philosophy, all things acquire depth,—more than depth, something like a fourth dimension which permits anterior perceptions to remain bound up with present perceptions, and the immediate future itself to become partly outlined in the present. Reality no longer appears then in the static state, in its manner of being; it affirms itself dynamically, in the continuity and variability of its tendency. What was immobile and frozen in our perception is warmed and set in motion. Everything comes to life around us, everything is revivified in us. A great impulse carries beings and things along. We feel ourselves uplifted, carried away, borne along by it. We are more fully alive.[53]

Philosophical intuition permits us to plunge into pure duration, and the consequence of this leap is that we feel ourselves somehow close to the moving center of the universe. We are possessed of a new spirit, and all experience achieves a new quality of vividness. But this intuition is not easily come by. Already in *Creative Evolution* Bergson has indicated how consciousness is pre-eminently intellectual, and how intuition, like a lamp almost extinguished, glimmers fitfully. An act of will is needed to thrust intelligence aside so that the light of intuition may flare up and introduce us further into the spiritual life.

For philosophy this poses a particular problem. Philosophical systems (even Bergson's own) are edifices constructed with symbols, and symbols are tools of the intellect with which Bergson's metaphysics claims to dispense. The paradox is resolved, I think, if we distinguish between the intuitive experience, which is pure, immediate, and non-symbolic, and the attempt to express it, which is always symbolic, but for that very reason inadequate, frustrating, never more than suggestive and approximate. After all, the same holds true for the artist and the religious mystic. The artistic vision is pure and ineffable; only the attempt at communication which involves the construction of the art object brings with it the struggle to impose the quality of spiritual vision upon recalcitrant materials. The difficulties in the case of religious mysticism are classic and Bergson himself has referred to them:[54]

The enterprise was indeed discouraging: how could the conviction derived from an experience be handed down by speech? And above all, how could the inexpressible be expressed? But these questions do not even present themselves to the great mystic. He has felt truth flowing into his soul from its fountainhead like an active force. He can no more help spreading it abroad than the sun can help diffusing its light. Only, it is not by mere words that he will spread it.

Eliot, too, speaking at once for poetry and for the poet trying to assimilate the religious impulse to his craft, says:[55]

> That was a way of putting it—not very satisfactory:
> A periphrastic study in a worn-out poetical fashion,
> Leaving one still with the intolerable wrestle
> With words and meanings. . . .

The wrestle with words and meanings is the fate of any symbolism which attempts the communication of truths intuitively revealed, whether poetic, mystical, or philosophical. We must not forget, therefore, that every philosophy is founded upon something extremely simple —so simple, in fact, that the philosopher has never succeeded in saying it and therefore he had to keep talking: expanding, correcting, introducing one complication after another to approximate the original intuition. This mass of complexity and doctrinal refinement is therefore only the measure of the incongruity between his simple original intuition and the means at his disposal for expressing it. The nature of philosophical interpretation is, then, much like the activity whereby we explore our deepest selves. It demands an act of penetration which pierces the verbiage and the paraphernalia, and seeks to grasp the simple intuition upon which all is founded.

A philosopher worthy of the name has never said more than a single thing: and even then it is something he has tried to say, rather than actually said. And he has said only one thing because he has seen only one point: and at that it was not so much a vision as a contact: this contact has furnished an impulse, this impulse a movement, and if this movement, which is as it were a kind of swirling of dust taking a particular form, becomes visible to our eyes only through what it has collected along its way, it is no less true that other bits of dust might as well have been raised and that it would still have been the same whirlwind. Thus a thought which brings something new into the world is of course obliged to manifest itself through the ready-made ideas it comes across and draws into its movement.[56]

Art, philosophy, and religion are the three areas in which intuition may operate, or better, they are the three channels through which the stream of intuition may flow, for Bergson is never exact in distinguishing philosophic, artistic, and religious intuitions as separate species of a single genus. But all these intuitive expressions represent the overcoming of an obstacle, the exercise of an effort against the usual and the customary, a kind of creative *break-through*. The artist must overcome the one thing that is death to his art—practicality—so that in his detachment from life ("absentmindedness") he may enjoy perception for itself. The philosopher must overcome the one thing that is death for his philosophy—the tendency to intellectualize—so that by avoiding the pitfalls of static conceptualization, he may immerse himself in the process of the world. The great spiritual leader, the mystic, must overcome what is fatal to dynamic religion—the dead hand of custom and the drag of social institutions—so that he may gain connection with the mystery which lies behind it all. As torpor perpetually lies in wait for the animal to overcome it and degrade it to the level of vegetative existence, so routine, practicality, and conceptualization lie in wait for mankind to imprison it and cut it off from the possibilities of vision, of contact, and of feeling.

The sense of exertion which the ultimate values demand for their realization is never absent from Bergson's philosophy. Principally it lives in his metaphors. The *élan vital* bursts into life as a shell explodes, and as the powder bursts through the cartridge, so life bursts through the restraints of matter. Intuition is a light flickering in the wind, and only nurture and protection enable it to flare up and overpower its hostile environment. The real self is like a dormant volcano over which a thick crust of habit has formed, and only the decisive moment activates it to break through the crust and express its true nature. But the exercise of intuition is the ultimate break-through and in its possibility lies the creativity of man.

IV

History and Destiny: Oswald Spengler and Arnold Toynbee

"History," Stephen said, "is a nightmare from which I am trying to awake."

JAMES JOYCE, Ulysses

> I pace upon the battlements and stare
> On the foundations of a house, or where
> Tree, like a sooty finger, starts from the earth;
> And sends imagination forth
> Under the day's declining beam, and call
> Images and memories
> From ruin or from ancient trees,
> For I would ask a question of them all.

W. B. YEATS, The Tower

History, it appeared, could be like the delirium of a madman, at once meaningless and yet charged with a dreadful meaning; and there existed a new agent to face this character of our age and intensify it.

REBECCA WEST, Black Lamb, Grey Falcon

1. THE PHILOSOPHY OF HISTORY

When Nietzsche's brilliant early book, *The Birth of Tragedy*, first appeared, Ulrich von Wilamowitz-Moellendorff, later to become the ruling prince of German classical philology, said of it: "This work does not exist for science." The boycott so pontifically pronounced by Wilamowitz has not, however, prevented the book from being read and admired, and classical scholarship itself has learned from it and even learned to praise it. A similar destiny may be in store for another brilliant first book: Oswald Spengler's *The Decline of the West*.

Upon its appearance and for a decade afterward, the recognized custodians of historical scholarship echoed the judgment of Wilamowitz. "This work," they said, "does not exist for science." But the criticisms of Spengler and of Nietzsche spring from a common positivistic assumption. In *The Birth of Tragedy* Nietzsche was not primarily interested in tracing the drama from Homer and Archilochus to Euripides, but in determining its spiritual components and the meaning of its ultimate decay. He was interested therefore not in drama as a mode of stagecraft or literature but as cultural symbolism. And Spengler in *The Decline of the West* is less concerned with the detailed narrative account of universal history than with its ultimate significance. Of course, in the strict sense neither *The Birth of Tragedy* nor *The Decline of the West* exists for science; that does not however prevent them from existing for philosophy.

The difference between history and the philosophy of history is obvious. The first, since it deals with the continuity of particular events, cannot be scientific in the Greek sense of demonstrating forms of generality, but it can be scientific in utilizing strictly the methods of observation, inference, formation of hypotheses, and criteria of evidence according to a logic of probability. Its aim is the approximation of actual fact. It seeks a narrative reconstruction of the past as von Ranke said: *"wie es eigentlich gewesen ist"*—as it actually happened.

Philosophy of history, on the contrary, is oriented not toward description but interpretation. Philosophy in general is a reflection upon experience, and the philosopher of history brings to his experience of history a contemplative and an interrogative mind. It is as Yeats said: to call images and memories from ruins and from ancient monuments—"For I would ask a question of them all." And to this question the philosophy of history should provide an answer.

The minimum requirements of a contemplative approach to history are (1) that it should be systematic, (2) that it should provide an interpretation of the totality of historical experience, and (3) that it should utilize some principle according to which the multiplicity of historical events are unified through their exhibition of an ultimate meaning. But one of the most disputed questions especially among those who, like Burckhardt, "seek to safeguard our impartiality against the invasion of history by wishful thinking," is, indeed, whether any such ultimate meaning is to be discerned. Many historians would agree with H.A.L. Fisher in the preface to his three-volume A *History of Europe*:[1]

One intellectual excitement has, however, been denied me. Men wiser and more learned than I have discerned in history a plot, a rhythm, a predetermined pattern. These harmonies are concealed from me. I can see only one emergency following upon another, as wave follows wave, only one great fact with respect to which, since it is unique, there can be no generalizations, only one safe rule for the historian; that he should recognize in the development of human destinies the play of the contingent and the unforeseen.

It has become fashionable among philosophers as among historians to deny that history has "a plot, a rhythm, a pre-determined pattern," to reject previous philosophies of history in the grand manner, whether those of Plato, St. Augustine, Comte, or Hegel. It is significant that this denial comes not only from the side of positivism, where it might be expected, but also from the side of theological commitment, which has historically asserted some version of the Augustinian eschatology. When Karl Popper, speaking from the standpoint of science, denies in the name of objectivity that there can be any universal historical laws, and asserts that all interpretations in history are subjective, that is, express an individual point of view or a cultural preference, it makes good sense.[2] For this permits him a certain generosity toward the philosophy of history considered outside the bounds of science. Pragmatically he can then say: "Each generation has its own troubles and problems and therefore its own interests and its own point of view; it follows that each generation has a right to look upon and re-interpret history in its own way." And he can countenance an act of valuation which, although it is not a valid generalization from the facts, is an understandable imposition upon the facts. "Although history has no ends, we can impose these ends of ours upon it; and *although history has no meaning, we can give it a meaning.*"

But Karl Löwith, writing as philosopher and theologian, on the basis of an inquiry into meaning in history states:[3] "The problem of history as a whole is unanswerable within its own perspective. Historical processes as such do not bear the least evidence of a comprehensive and ultimate meaning. History as such has no outcome." This is as refreshing as it is unexpected. It indicates a certain meeting of extremes on the problem of history where skeptic and believer argue a common case against uncritical generalization and the susceptibility to illusion.

It may be that both Popper and Löwith are more severe toward the search for meaning in history than even traditional historians. Jacob Burckhardt, the colleague of the young Nietzsche at Basle, and one of the great historians of the nineteenth century, found his greatest task not in the prosaic construction of narrative history but in the analysis of the composition of the life-interests of historical periods, in the hierarchy of values exemplified in such ideal types as the man of the Italian Renaissance or the Greek of the heroic age. The characterization of vast epochs and preoccupation with the historical emergence of value patterns are quasi-philosophical and perhaps intuitive. Burckhardt had small sympathy for the linear philosophies of history which dominated the nineteenth century. He held that Hegel's views were little more than an over-obvious theodicy, and he viewed the theory of historical progress as the vulgar consequence of the complacency of a crude and arrogant bourgeoisie. He tried conscientiously to distinguish between philosophy and history:[4] "The philosophy of history is a centaur, a contradiction in terms, for history co-ordinates and hence is unphilosophical while philosophy subordinates and hence is unhistorical. . . . Philosophy grapples direct with the great riddle of life, it stands high above history, which at best pursues that goal imperfectly and indirectly." But he was not without sympathy for their combination. "All the same we are deeply indebted to the centaur, and it is a pleasure to come across him now and then on the fringe of the forest of historical study. Whatever his principles may have been, he has hewn some vast vistas through the forest and lent spice to history."

The justification for the philosophy of history is, I think, just this. It is an attempt to grapple with one of the great riddles of our existence, that of the broad meaning of historical experience, and if it has "hewn some vast vistas through the forest," it is always in some sense as an answer to a vivid need for order. Staring into chaos is hardly productive of energy or contentment, and the philosopher of history has always in some measure been the agent of a recall to order.

Of course I do not mean that the philosophy of history is always the servant of moral considerations. Rather I have in mind that kind of reflective history which Hegel called "pragmatic":[5]

When we have to deal with the Past, and occupy ourselves with a remote world, a Present rises into being for the mind—produced by its own activity, as the reward of its labor. The occurrences are, indeed, various; but the idea which pervades them—their deeper import and connection—is one. This takes the occurrence out of the Past, and makes it virtually Present. Pragmatic reflections, though in their nature quite abstract, are yet truly of the Present, and quicken the annals of the dead Past into the life of today.

The "quickening" of history into the contemporary is little more than the demonstration that the past is relevant to modern concerns, relevant for understanding as well as for action. Indeed, underlying the issue of relevance and of order is an ancient epistemological issue of some consequence. It is expressed in Hegel in the implied contrast between an actuality which arises out of the mind's own activity, and the universal idea and the inner connection of events. In Aristotelian language it is the question whether historical work is to be assimilated to the activity of the scientist or the artist, that is, whether it is the eliciting of form from the empirical particulars or the imposition of form upon the matter of history. Hegel argued for a monistic view of the cosmos in which (by a pre-established harmony of mind and reality) these two activities are identical. Modern epistemology lacks this conviction.

Whitehead, for example, treats the analogue of the question of law in history, the status of law in science.[6]

The notion of Law, that is to say, of some measure of regularity or of persistence or of recurrence, is an essential element in the urge towards technology, methodology, scholarship, and speculation. Apart from a certain smoothness in the nature of things, there can be no knowledge, no useful method, no intelligent purpose. Lacking an element of Law, there remains a mere welter of details with no foothold for comparison with any other such welter, in the past, in the future, or circumambient in the present. But the expression of this notion of Law with due accuracy and with due regard to what in fact is presupposed in human purposes, is a matter of extreme difficulty.

If history, like the particular occasions of nature, is not to be a mere welter of detail, it too must contain an element of regularity or of law. But Whitehead goes on to add that there are at least four interpretations of the nature of law: law as immanent, law as imposed, law as observed order of succession, and law as conventional interpretation. It is the first two which are relevant for the philosophy of history. A doctrine of law as immanent means that there is indeed a historical order and that events have a real and intrinsic character. In understanding this quality of events we discern mutual relations between them which constitute an actual pattern. The philosophy of history is the discernment of this pattern. The doctrine of law as imposed means that cognitive patterns are projected onto the perceptions and inferences which are the ultimate elements of history, with the consequence that such order as the facts exhibit is due to a power lying outside the facts themselves. In the realm of cosmology both doctrines are implicit in Plato's *Timaeus*, where the elements contribute to the universe the qualities of their own natures, but where the pattern is imposed by the divine creator. In terms of epistemology the distinction is illustrated by the *tabula rasa* theory of Locke as against Kant's derivation of the categories.

Any justification of the conclusions of a philosophy of history must hinge upon the issue of whether such conclusions represent a process of imposition or a process of extraction, and how in either case the generalizing activity can be protected against charges of wilfulness and irresponsibility. This issue arises in dealing with both of the great contemporary philosophers of history, Oswald Spengler and Arnold Toynbee. Before turning to the former, I should like to consider one other aspect of the philosophy of history: the limitation of its available patterns.

In 1750 Turgot, delivering his famous Sorbonne lecture, "On the Progress of the Human Mind," began it thus:

The phenomena of nature, subject as they are to unvarying laws are enclosed within a circle whose revolutions are ever the same; everything is born and born again, everything perishes and in the successive generations that reproduce the vegetal and the animal forms, time does but restore at every moment the image of what it has already made to disappear. The succession of men on the contrary offers from century to century an ever varied spectacle. Reason, passions, liberty give rise unceasingly to new events. All the ages of mankind are enchained one with another by a sequence of causes and effects that binds the present to the whole preceding past.

Turgot's entire thesis rests upon the contrast between the cyclical phases of nature and the linear continuity of human history. Obviously the doctrine of progress presupposes cultural continuity. But the chief interest of his remarks lies in the fact that the cyclical phases of nature are, by analogy, themselves the source of another philosophy of history which is as old as the speculations of Heracleitus, and which constitutes the chief alternative to the linear interpretations which dominated the nineteenth century.

Turgot is right that the idea of phenomena enclosed within a circle whose revolutions are ever the same is a part of the concept of nature, and this concept of nature is an inheritance from the Greeks. It originates in the cosmological speculations of Heracleitus and Empedocles, where the flux of events is rationalized by a logic of passage, and where the orderliness of the cosmos consists in a perpetual process of ebb and flow, generation and corruption, life and death. Pythagoreanism adds to this latent conception a broader and more detailed inclusiveness, so that the movements of the heavenly bodies, the beat of the human heart, and the twang of the lyre all express a periodic regularity reducible to numerical expression. By means of the cycle of eternal recurrence, the constancy of life and motion for which the Greeks yearn with a metaphysical passion is guaranteed even against the mutations registered by sense.

In such an atmosphere, dominated by the cosmological sense, there is little need for the later Sophistic distinction (which Turgot would have eminently understood) between cosmic nature and man-made convention; human history is dwarfed by the spectacle of nature. And even after the Sophists have made the dichotomy of "nature vs. law" a commonplace, Herodotus and Thucydides view history within its proper local perspective, as an inquiry into causes within a limited area of human concern. The concept of the "epoch-making event" is unGreek.[7]

With the Judeo-Christian outlook, the Greek is reversed. Moral experience is central and the ultimate "meaning" of existence—the drama of sin and redemption—works itself out in the process of history. The Greek view of life subordinates the uniqueness of history to the periodicity in nature. The Judeo-Christian view sees nature as the mere backdrop against which the real story unfolds, a property for the expression of God's purposes in human actions. Also the Judeo-Christian point of view is based upon the moment of the transcendent event—"the point of intersection of the timeless with time" in which God and man are one—and the consequences which flow from this fact for man. Upon it salvation hinges, and salvation lies in a distant and indeterminate future. Therefore, as Collingwood says,[8] "Any history written on Christian principles will be of necessity universal, providential, apocalyptic and periodized."

For the Greeks "meaning" in history would be the sense which emerged from a rational understanding of the past and the present. For the Christians "meaning" in history would relate to a direction or purpose in the course of events realizable in the future. All cyclic theories, whether Vico's doctrine of *ricorsi* (recurrences), Nietzsche's theory of *die ewige Wiederkunft* (the eternal recurrence), or Pareto's theory of the upward and downward paths of the ruling elites, are Greek in inspiration. All directional theories, whether those of Marx, Comte, or Hegel, are the consequence of a secularization of theological principles and the latent employment of an eschatological motivation whether recognized or concealed. It almost seems, as Löwith says,[9] "as if the two great conceptions of antiquity and Christianity, cyclic motion and eschatological direction have exhausted the basic approaches to the understanding of history."

The nineteenth century by and large lay under the spell of a linear conception of history, and its problem therefore consisted in interpreting historical movement either optimistically or conservatively (that is to say, following the impulse either of the science of Darwin or of Sadi Carnot). But a simple theory of progress or of degeneration was obviously inadequate, and in Nietzsche and Henry Adams the paradoxes of linear history turned imperceptibly into a theory of phases. Again it is the influence of the Greeks, whether in Toynbee's perpetual interaction of man and environment, in Spengler's waxing and waning of cultures, or in Whitehead's ingression of eternal objects into the stream of events, which dominates the philosophy of history in the modern world.

Despite the renewed influence of modes of pre-Socratic thought toward the end of the nineteenth century, Western culture is a Christian culture, and the very impulse to philosophize about history has roots which are not to be denied in an apocalyptic tradition. Philosophy of history as a contemporary phenomenon is a plant which has grown up as the result of a graft combining the Greek concept of nature with the Christian concept of man's meaningful destiny. This dual origin has wrought in the product some of the dilemmas and the internal contradictions from which both the theories of Spengler and of Toynbee suffer.

Perhaps the most interesting of these emerges in the problem of destiny—the dialectic of fate and freedom. For the Greeks, as Bergson has noted, time lacks the vividness accorded to space, and a future which is doomed to be but the revolution of the cycle of the past cannot draw intensity from the suspense of an unknown outcome. The spectators of the Greek tragic drama sit spellbound before the preparation of a denouement which they know in advance, and free will in the sense of radical self-determination seems irrelevant to the future which an over-arching fate has prepared for Oedipus or to the consequences for Phaedra and Hippolytus which follow from the hostility between Artemis and Aphrodite at a level above their powers and their comprehension. Not so with the protagonists of Shakespeare, Milton, Goethe, or Racine. Atheist or believer, they have been infected with the Christian ideology, and their free will sends them toward a future upon which everything of significance hinges. The philosophy of history of Spengler and Toynbee purports to be a serious treatment of the organic structure of different societies—a morphology of culture; but a comparative "science" of historic cultures in itself promises little and, indeed, asks little concerning questions of political or spiritual guidance. But neither Spengler nor Toynbee can restrain a desire to prophesy in advance and to commit themselves to an outcome. Under the spell of the Greeks as they undoubtedly are, they cannot at the same time resist the Christian lure of the significant future.

It may be that Burckhardt, conservative as he surely was, was more perceptive in these matters, more Greek, for he turned his back upon the future not only out of methodological reserve, but out of prudence. "To know the future," he said,[10] "is no more desirable in the life of mankind than in the life of the individual. And our astrological impatience for such knowledge is sheer folly." He continues in a fashion reminiscent of Bergson: "Whether we imagine a man, for instance, knowing in advance the day of his death and the situation it would find him in, or a people knowing in advance the century of its downfall, both pictures would bear within themselves the inevitable consequence —a confusion of all desire and endeavor. For desire and endeavor can only unfold freely when they live and act 'blindly,' i.e., for their own sakes and in obedience to inward impulses."

The contemporary crisis in the philosophy of history lies in the difficulty of assimilating the Christian concern with a prophetic future to an impassive Greek concept of destiny; in the profound ambiguity which results when natural fate is combined with the operations of the decisive will. This ambiguity is revealed in all its complexity in the brilliant theories of Oswald Spengler.

2. SPENGLER'S PHILOSOPHIC SOURCES

The Decline of the West: Outlines of a Morphology of World History (*Der Untergang des Abendlandes: Umrisse einer Morphologie der Weltgeschichte*)[11] was composed between 1911 and 1914, worked over and published in the beginning of 1918, and in response to numerous attacks and critical notices republished in 1922-1923 in the revised edition as it now stands. Volume I, "Form and Actuality," contains the heart of Spengler's theory; Volume II, "Perspectives of World History," is a more detailed elaboration of the theories of Volume I and a further exploration of the chief concepts necessary for a theory of civilization. The two volumes taken together constitute a brilliant, dogmatic, intuitive, provoking, arrogant, wide-ranging, insightful, wrong-headed, repetitious, pessimistic, diffuse, unscientific, original, pseudo-systematic, aphoristic, passionate, long-winded, metaphysical attempt at a complete philosophy of history. In short, it is a fascinating, equivocal performance, and can be neglected only at their peril by those who are interested in the intellectual life of the modern world.

The title and subtitle of the work state its basic themes: on the one hand a general morphology of history which meets the three demands of a philosophy of history as to system, universality, and unity of explanatory principle, and on the other a theory of the present crisis of Western culture which, although it depends logically upon the general morphological principle (as any exemplification of fact depends upon an ordering of perception), is dramatically the central theme of the work rather than a secondary one. Uniting those two is a comparison between the course of classical civilization after Knossos and the course of Western civilization since the tenth century in which both culminate in the inevitable destiny of "an Alexandrian age."

Behind both the morphological principle and the theory of cultural crisis lies a series of metaphysical presuppositions, and it is only by careful attention to them that the methodology of *The Decline of the West* can be understood and its contemporary relevance established. I believe that the axioms which underlie Spengler's work are closely related to those of Bergson, and that quite apart from any question of influence or borrowing,[12] Spengler's work must be recognized as flowing from the same inherent mode of perception which flowers in *Creative Evolution* and *The Two Sources of Morality and Religion*.

Both Bergson and Spengler utilize an angle of vision which is radically dualistic, which sees a metaphysical split running clear through the universe of experience. As the world falls into two pieces, it develops that for each realm there is a pre-ordained method of knowing and a methodological principle which is its consequence. For Bergson the great divide through the center of the universe is that which sets off life from matter; the two cognate methods of knowing are intuition and analysis; and the methodological principle which follows is to forever distrust the lure of mechanistic repetitiveness and to lay oneself open to all those influences which represent the forces of "real time." For Spengler the great divide through the center of the universe is that which sets off "the world as history" from "the world as nature;" the two methods of knowing are those which identify mathematical laws and those which utilize a technique of analogies to discover the morphology of world history; and the methodological principle which follows is to voluntarily relinquish the principle of causality and substitute a more appropriate mistress—the Idea of Destiny.

Spengler, whose first love was Latin and Greek and the ancient world, studied mathematics and natural science at the Universities of Munich, Berlin, and Halle, and received his doctorate for a thesis on Heracleitus (1904) which already at this early date shows the philosophical trend of his ideas.[13] A scientific training which would concede scientific relevance to a mystical cosmic philosopher like Heracleitus shows the extent to which the humanism of Goethe and Nietzsche had influenced the German scientific world. But a narrower laboratory empiricism still existed as a covert threat, and it had profoundly affected the writing of history in the late nineteenth century. Spengler was struck by the fact that the cultural sciences were pursuing a methodology more narrow and unfruitful even than that of physics and chemistry.[14] He was led to the conclusion that there is not one but two series of reality, and that nature experience and historical experience are not continuous, but absolutely dichotomous and unique.

It may be that Bergson's view is more metaphysical than Spengler's, more deeply committed to a real division in the cosmos between what is living and what is not, whereas Spengler's approach is subjective and celebrates an unbridgeable gap between different perspectives or modes of apprehension. But at any rate, for both there arise the same epistemic consequences. Spengler says:[15]

The *world-as-history*, conceived, viewed and given form from out of its opposite the *world-as-nature*—here is a new aspect of human existence on this earth. And yet, in spite of its immense significance, both practical and theoretical, this aspect has not been realized, still less presented. . . . We have before us two possible ways in which man may inwardly possess and experience the world around him. With all rigour I distinguish (as to form, not substance) the organic from the mechanical world-impression, the content of images from that of laws, the picture and symbol from the formula and the system, the instantly actual from the constantly possible, the intents and purposes of imagination ordering according to plan from the intents and purposes of experience dissecting according to scheme; and . . . the domain of *chronological* from that of *mathematical number*.

Organic vs. mechanical, picture vs. formula, imagination vs. system—these are the distinctions which we have already found in Bergson, and which indeed are current wherever a romanticism of feeling has supervened upon a period of successful scientific formulation. Spengler is perhaps even more candid than Bergson in expressing his debt to the "romanticism" of his predecessors.

The philosophy of this book I owe to the philosophy of Goethe, which is practically unknown today, and also (but in a far less degree) to that of Nietzsche. The position of Goethe in West-European metaphysics is still not understood in the least; when philosophy is being discussed he is not even named. For unfortunately he did not set down his doctrines in a rigid system, and so the systematic philosophy has overlooked him. Nevertheless he was a philosopher. His place *vis-à-vis* Kant is the same as that of Plato—who similarly eludes the would-be systematizer—*vis-à-vis* Aristotle. Plato and Goethe stand for the philosophy of Becoming, Aristotle and Kant the philosophy of Being. Here we have intuition opposed to analysis.[16]

The anti-rationalist bias of both Bergson and Spengler is obvious. The emphasis upon the fatal character of reason and system, upon the frozen rigidity of that which is known through the intellect against the suppleness of that which is felt through the emotions is common to both. If we have learned from Bergson that calculation and cognition are inseparable, we are to learn from Spengler that poetry and historical study are akin. If Bergson has reserved intuition for religion, philosophy, and the arts, Spengler has added history to the list.

The kinship between poetry and history is not that they are both imaginative, relatively undisciplined, and unanchored in fact, but that their utilization of language is primarily metaphorical and that they are concerned less with strict description of natural processes (and the repeatable forms implicit within such processes) than in the suggestive likenesses which are discernible in hitherto separately perceived entities. Both history and poetry service the sense of connectedness. Kant has drawn attention to the analogies of experience whereby all phenomena are capable of mutual relatedness. Wallace Stevens has said that poetry "is a satisfying of the desire for resemblance." If, indeed, poetry makes brilliant the resemblances between things and gives to the fact of similarity its own dramatic grandeur, a like (but more purposive) interest in analogy governs Spengler's approach to history.

The role of analogy in poetry is casual, based perhaps upon an unconscious Platonism where anything may become everything. The analogy in Spenglerian history is a *technique* controlled by two basic principles of organicity: (1) that there is a morphological relationship which unifies every aspect of a culture and (2) that there is an analogy between the developmental stages of each individual culture and every other. Naturally, Spengler believes that this commonplace of Platonic sociology is original with him.[17]

I have not hitherto found one who has carefully considered the *morphological relationship* that inwardly binds together the expression-form of *all* branches of a Culture, who has gone beyond politics to grasp the ultimate and fundamental ideas of Greeks, Arabians, Indians, and Westerners in mathematics, the meaning of their early ornamentation, the basic forms of their architecture, philosophies, dramas and lyrics, their choice and development of great arts, the detail of their craftsmanship and choice of materials. . . . Who amongst them realizes that between the Differential Calculus and the dynastic principle of politics in the age of Louis XIV, between the space-perspective of Western oil-painting and the conquest of space by railroad, telephone and long-range weapon, between contrapuntal music and credit economics, there are deep uniformities? Yet viewed from this morphological standpoint, even the humdrum facts of politics assume a symbolic and even a metaphysical character, and . . . things such as the Egyptian administrative system, the Classical coinage, analytical geometry, the cheque, the Suez Canal, the book-printing of the Chinese, the Prussian army, and the Roman road-engineering can, as symbols, be made *uniformly* understandable and appreciable.

The possibility of building up the principle of analogy into a technique of historical understanding rests upon the fact that the events of history and the facts of culture constitute an all-embracing symbolism.

Each culture has its own unique *"gestalt"* or "soul" and its politics, economics, philosophy, art, and religion are only media through which this form reveals itself. Each of the great cultures has finally produced what Spengler calls "a secret language of world-feeling," which is fully comprehensible only by one who belongs to that culture, but which through sympathy and intuition can be appreciated and partly understood by others. Certain aspects of thought and feeling are particularly revealing of the soul of a culture: its sense of depth, the way it looks at space (in terms of flat dimensionality or deep perspective); its attitude toward death (whether it has a cult of the dead like the Egyptians, where the disposal of the dead and the forms of adornment of the graves of the dead are of the greatest importance, or whether, as with the Greeks, the body is burned or quickly disposed of and forgotten); its attitude toward history (whether like the Chinese it attempts to preserve its total past in the form of elaborate calendars and dynastic chronicles, or whether like Hindus and Greeks it lives in a world where the present or future is everything and the past hardly worth preserving). Space, time, and death are the crucial categories of significance, and they provide a continuum of possible attitudes in which every great culture expresses its own frozen cross-section. The analogies to which Spengler has referred between the differential calculus, long-range communication, the infinite perspective of Raphael, and the contrapuntal music of Bach are based upon a single image of infinite depth, in contrast with the finite extension which dominates the classical world and informs the bodily sculpture, plane geometry, flat vase painting, city-state organization, thick earth-bound architecture, and political rhetoric of the Greeks.

The first anchorage of the technique of analogy is the universal participation of cultural entities in a common "feeling" or Platonic form which they exemplify. The second is the similarity of the cycles of development through which every great culture passes. Here Spengler denies the linear assumption upon which the famous philosophy of the Enlightenment was based. Kant saw history as the contemplation of the operations of human will on a vast scale which would "aim at unfolding to our view a regular stream of tendency in the great succession of events," and he even thought (with typical rationalistic optimism) that "the history of the human species as a whole may be regarded as the unravelling of a hidden plan of nature for accomplishing a perfect state of civil constitution for society. . . ."[18] Our own perspective has perhaps dispensed with the optimism but it characteristically sees everything from the provincial angle of the centrality of Western culture, from which all else is tangential, even historically dispensable. It is this provincialism which Spengler decries.[19]

The most appropriate designation for this current West-European scheme of history, in which the great Cultures are made to follow orbits round *us* as the presumed centre of all world-happenings, is the *Ptolemaic system* of history. The system that is put forward in this work in place of it I regard as the *Copernican discovery* in the historical sphere, in that it admits no sort of privileged position to the Classical or the Western Culture as against the Cultures of India, Babylon, China, Egypt, the Arabs, Mexico—separate worlds of dynamic being which in point of mass count for just as much as the Classical, while frequently surpassing it in point of spiritual greatness and soaring power.

If no privileged position is to be given to Western culture as a unique and supremely valuable node of historical experience, it is because the logic which is discoverable in history is derived from the classical conception of nature and from the biological analogy which dominated the nineteenth century. If history expresses not mechanism but organicity, then cultures are like individuals. Life is a series of stages which mankind traverses in orderly and inescapable sequence: birth, youth, middle age, maturity, old age. The essence of man is implicit in the concept of his lifetime; may not the same be true of history? Its logic is founded upon a general biographic archetype.

But only bring analogy to bear on this aspect as on the rest, letting the world of human Cultures intimately and unreservedly work upon the imagination instead of forcing it into a ready-made scheme. Let the words youth, growth, maturity, decay . . . be taken at last as objective descriptions of organic states. Set forth the Classical culture as a self-contained phenomenon embodying and expressing the Classical soul, put it beside the Egyptian, the Indian, the Babylonian, the Chinese and the Western, and determine for each of these higher individuals what is typical in their surgings and what is necessary in the riot of incident. And then at last will unfold itself the picture of world-history that is natural to us, men of the West, and to us alone.[20]

General biology demonstrates the cycle of birth, growth, and death. Comparative anatomy speaks of the homology of organs to signify a morphological equivalence. The concept is equally fruitful for Spengler's comparative study of cultures. In terms of relative rather than absolute time this notion of homology provides a redefinition of the "contemporary." Historical facts are contemporary in the Spenglerian scheme when they occur in exactly the same relative position in their respective cultures and so possess exactly equivalent importance. From this point of view classical sculpture and the orchestration of Haydn, the pyramids of the Egyptian fourth dynasty and the Gothic cathedrals, Buddhism and Roman Stoicism are homologous (equivalent in cultural significance) and Pythagoras and Descartes, Archimedes and Gauss, the Ionic and the Baroque, Polygnotus and Rembrandt, Aristotle and Kant are "contemporaries." This notion of growth and of homology is the foundation for Spengler's extremely ambitious program for the outline of a comparative anatomy of the great historic cultures.

I hope to show that without exception all great creations and forms in religion, art, politics, social life, economy and science appear, fulfil themselves and die down *contemporaneously* in all the Cultures; that the inner structure of one corresponds strictly with that of all the others; that there is not a single phenomenon of deep physiognomic importance in the record of one for which we could not find a counterpart in the record of every other; and that this counterpart is to be found under a characteristic form and in a perfectly definite chronological position.[21]

The dichotomy of "factuality" and "significance" lies back of Spengler's work. He develops it as the antithesis between the principle of causality and the idea of destiny. The concept of destiny performs the same role in Spengler's philosophy as intuition does in Bergson's. It is central in its import, mystical in its nature, and inexplicable in a language designed for purposes of connotative clarity. It provides one of the most elusive points in Spengler's philosophy of history, because it is the point of meeting between a Greek theory of natural cycles uninterested in futurity and the Christian eschatology. Something like it, of course, occurs as backdrop for the tragic spirit of the Greeks. The king and hero is not free and independent in the face of the universe, he is (as Heracleitus' position assumes) part and parcel of the cosmic ebb and flow. In such an electric universe man is intimately connected with the macrocosm; Oedipus, struggling, meets his fate; Hector more stoically goes down to his doom. But neither fate nor doom is quite the same as destiny. They smack too much of Kant's third Critique—the form of purposiveness without a glimmer of actual purpose. A destiny instinct with real purposiveness is the gift of Christian belief.

Destiny is somehow connected with the knowledge that life is "directed, irrevocable in every line, fate-laden." The primitive feels it dimly and anxiously, the man of a historic culture feels it mediately, in the vision of the world communicated through the form-languages of art and religion. Words such as "fortune," "providence," "doom," "vocation" indicate its presence. Words like "hope," "repentance," "devotion," "consolation" reveal its religious source. It is the metaphysical and emotive counterpart of the rational causation of science, but it is as opposed to science as light is to dark.

He who expects here, in the domain of the living, to find reasons and consequences, or imagines that an inward certainty as to the meaning of life is the same thing as 'Fatalism' or 'Predestination,' simply knows nothing of the matters in question, confusing experience lived with experience acquired. Causality is the reasonable, the law-bound, the describable, the badge of our whole waking and reasoning existence. But destiny is the word for an inner certainty that is *not* describable. We bring out that which is in the causal by means of a physical or an epistemological system, through numbers, by reasoned classification; but the idea of destiny can be imparted only by the artist working through media like portraiture, tragedy and music.[22]

Spengler's conception of destiny owes much to the Greeks, but it also re-echoes Schopenhauer. The latter's notion of "will" as a cosmic principle working inexorably everywhere (and especially in the life of man) with an outcome which is at once fated and tragic led to a general pessimism which was as characteristic of German romanticism as it was *fin de siècle*. A hundred years later, by the transference of fate from nature to history, Spengler produces a doctrine no less romantic, no less pessimistic, no less *fin de siècle*.

3. CULTURE AND CIVILIZATION

In history it is not individuals who are important, according to Spengler, but those mighty beings which we know as the higher Cultures. They are "inspired mass-units," beings of a higher order, for, historical as they are, they mark the point at which history intersects with the cosmic pulse. Membership in them is involuntary but desperately real. The majority of social institutions which have grown up in the West since the French Revolution are products of the intellectual consciousness; they are schools, clubs, associations, parties which one may join upon impulse and from which one may withdraw at will. But to a Culture one is *committed* with one's entire being and without possibility of withdrawal. All of the great events of history are produced by the larger units—peoples, parties, armies, social classes—but these aggregates of lower degree are welded together in the Culture. This Culture is pervaded by its own unique spirit, it unifies all parts by its own peculiar vision of the world. It is born of spiritual upheaval, enjoys a thousand years of existence, and then falls upon evil days. For every Culture, every inspired aggregate is born and dies.

It is, of course, only the unique standpoint of our own Western Culture which permits us to see it so. History is not a natural fact objectively standing in the world and making a claim upon perception. It is itself a form of perception, a mode of experiencing which we impose upon an indeterminate flux. For the first time perhaps Spengler has shifted the methodological question from "Through what evidences may the past be known?" to "For whom is there History?" There are those Cultures like the Greek and the Hindu which conceive of their own existence as timeless and rounded-off, hermetically sealed and self-sufficient in time and space. There are people like the Chinese and Egyptians who live under the impression that their lives are part of a determinate chronology which goes back to dimmest memory. And there are those of us, members of the Faustian world, who are unwilling to forget anything, for whom historical research yields for Cultures precisely what diaries and autobiographies yield for individuals—an all-inclusive reconstruction of a series of thick cultural worlds. The perspective of the Greeks is always insular and provincial; it is the vision of "the narrow horizon," but today in the West not only do our "time horizons melt in the double endlessness of the calendar before and after Christ," but we are approaching the ultimate achievement of which our historical understanding is capable—"the organic linking and disposition of these historical planes in a single vast world-history of uniform physiognomic that shall enable our glance to range from the life of the individual man without a break to the first and last destinies of the universe."[23]

The higher Cultures spring up suddenly out of the dim uniformities of primitive life. About 3000 B.C. on the lower Nile and the lower Euphrates arise the earliest Cultures, the Egyptian and the Babylonian. Fifteen hundred years later, when these are already far along the path to old age, three new Cultures begin: the Indian in the upper Punjab, the Chinese on the middle Hwang-Ho, and shortly afterward (about 1100 B.C.) the Classical Graeco-Roman on the shores of the Aegean Sea. About the time when the Classical is reaching its final phase, the Arabian Culture comes into being: a polyglot mixture containing late Hellenistic Jewry, early Christianity (and the whole area from Alexandria to Byzantium), unified in its later stages by Islam, and slowly spreading over the remnants of the Classical world in the western Mediterranean: southern Spain, Sicily, Provence. Almost simultaneous with the Arabian Culture in the Old World is the Aztec Culture in the New, reaching its height around 600 A.D., and already with the Mayas entering upon its old age. The eighth Culture which Spengler fully distinguishes is the Western, beginning around the time of the Crusades, ripening into consciousness with Calvin and Galileo, reaching its zenith of intellectual creativeness with Goethe and Kant, and with the nineteenth century entering upon its inevitable winter. These eight Cultures (Egyptian, Babylonian, Indian, Chinese, Classical, Arabian, Aztec, Western) are the basic materials for Spengler's history.

This type of historical inquiry is not an investigation of causal sequences, but an attempt at the characterization of epochs. There is a relationship between causality and the smooth sequence of events, but the changes which occur in the Spenglerian cultural cycle are abrupt— even mutational. No reason can be assigned why a Chinese Culture should arise in the second millennium or why an Aztec Culture should spring up in central America about the time of the birth of Christ. Likewise no reasons can be assigned for the swift changes which occur within a Culture; for example, the sudden flowering of the Pyramid style in Egypt or that of Gothic in the West, the quick emergence of imperialism in the China of Shi Hwang-ti or in the Rome of Augustus. Origins and turning-points in history are like origins and turning-points in nature—mysteries which we must only accept.

If there is a cultural logic, it is a logic of immanence. What develops grows out of an inherent tendency within, and although disturbances from outside may arise, the presence of external forces never really alters historical occurrence. All great Cultures are in full march toward self-fulfillment but there is no real impingement of one Culture upon another. It is at this point that Spengler's doctrine most clearly offends not only the traditional view of the continuity of Greek, mediaeval, and modern history, but also the sociological axiom of the cross-fertilization of cultures, for this is precisely what Spengler's theory denies. Every great Culture is a water-tight, hermetically sealed organism. To be sure, two cultures may touch and a living man in one may be confronted with the relics or crystalized expression-forms of the other. It is even possible that what looks like borrowing may take place, but it is always merely superficial: the forms are transferrable, the spirit never.

There was no movement of "Buddhism" from India to China, but an acceptance of part of the Indian Buddhists' store of images by Chinese of a certain spiritual tendency, who fashioned out a *new* mode of religious expression having meaning for Chinese and only Chinese Buddhists. What matters in all such cases is not the original meanings of the forms, but the forms themselves, as disclosing to the active sensibility and understanding of the observer potential modes of his own creativeness. Connotations are not transferrable. Men of two different kinds are parted, each in his own spiritual loneliness, by an impassable gulf. Even though Indians and Chinese in those days both felt as Buddhists, they were spiritually as far apart as ever. The same words, the same rites, the same symbol—but two different souls, each going its own way.[24]

The crucial case is the Western Renaissance. It is supposed to have been completely under the spell of Classical art. But a moment's glance will show that its borrowings were selective and histrionic; no Doric temples, no Ionic columns, no flat vase painting, no painted statuary—only what an expansionist tendency (wholly un-Greek) could use. Not the full Greek legacy, merely what the "accidents" of survival and the pedantic censorship of the Augustan scholars permitted to "survive" has produced the imaginary portrait of "Classical Civilization" both for Medician Florence and for Winkelmann, Hölderlin, and Pater. In Spengler's perspective it must be so. Cultures are self-determining and impenetrable. When one looks at another it is through its own eyes, and when it appropriates, it is through the "art of deliberate misunderstanding." For there is no stream of civilization, only the periodic growth and decay of unique Cultures determined from within by their own peculiar properties.

I see, in place of that empty figment of *one* linear history which can only be kept up by shutting one's eyes to the overwhelming multitude of the facts, the drama of a *number* of mighty Cultures, each springing with primitive strength from the soil of a mother-region to which it remains firmly bound throughout its whole life-cycle; each stamping its material, its mankind, in *its own* image; each having *its own* idea, *its own* passions, *its own* life, will and feeling, *its own* death.[25]

The eight Cultures which Spengler distinguishes are the materials of his morphology, but *The Decline of the West* does not treat them all with the same detail and completeness. It is like a stage setting where the portraits and the books of the library are only painted in; the windows, fireplaces, and doors must be more functional though created of lath and canvas; and only the table and chairs down-stage are real tables and chairs upon which the actors sit and about which the action revolves. The Babylonian and the Aztec are like the painted books, the Egyptian, Indian, and Chinese are like the windows of lath and canvas, only the Classical, the Arabian, and the Western are the real tables and chairs in the foreground. Thus the discarded scheme of Ancient, Mediaeval, and Modern History takes its revenge upon Spengler after all.

Each of the great Cultures (in particular the Classical, the Arabian or Magian, and the Western or Faustian) has its own language of world-feeling, its intuition of the nature of experience which is fully comprehensible to it and to it alone. In consequence, each of the great Cultures has its prime symbol which stands as the embodiment of its unconscious intuition.

The Classical Culture is primarily Euclidean. Its apprehension is finite, anchored in perception and above all in the perception of magnitude. Greek mathematics culminates in a geometry which is a science of perceivable quantities. Analogously Greek politics is a politics of limited geographical scope, operating within the determinate confines of the city-state. And Greek art is either two-dimensional and lacking in perspective and depth, or rooted in the solid earth as the squatting Doric temple. In no other Culture is "the firm footing," the earth-bound, so emphasized, whether in the Parthenon, the temple at Paestum, or the solidly footed, always heavily corporeal Greek statuary.

The drama of the Greeks is a drama of situation where action has become ritual and is formalized in mask and gesture. The drama of the West is a drama of character where the inward nature of an Othello or an Andromache develops and is slowly expressed. This difference is not incidental but crucial for an understanding of the difference between the Classical and the Faustian spirit. Whereas the symbol of Classical world-feeling is the finite body, the symbol of Western man is the stretching perspective of infinite space. Analogously, Western mathematics is oriented toward the infinite: it views numbers as pure relations and its characteristic form is not geometry but the calculus. In architecture the West loses itself in an upward thrust whether in the Gothic pinnacle or the modern skyscraper, and its discovery of perspective made out of every Renaissance picture frame a window for the long look into the infinite space of the horizon. But perhaps the two most significant features of Western man are his autobiographical tendency and his bondage to the concept of time. There is no autobiography among the Greeks. Not until literary forms grew out of the formulae of Christian penitence was it possible to produce Augustine's *Confessions* and the modern novel. And in the same way, only a Culture interested in a chronology of becoming would generalize this interest in both the communal and the private spheres—in the bells of cathedral and town hall chanting the hours, and in the pocket watch, constant companion of the individual and symbol of the constraint which an exact chronology imposes upon him.

Out of the autobiographical tendency of Western man and out of the time sense which produces his infinite memory grows his approach to history, which is expressed by Spengler himself in *The Decline of the West*. It is a heroic effort to construct a vast historical museum of a thousand pages, in which the cultural development of every civilization lies embalmed under glass ready for our inspection as we walk pensively from case to case. The Greeks knew no such enterprise. Athens and Corinth possessed no museums of any kind, and the Greeks were even hazy about the dates of their own scientists and philosophers who had lived but a hundred years before. But the West knows the birthdays and deathdays of almost every great man since the twelfth century.

The Faustian symbol is pure and limitless space; the Apollonian is the sensuously perceived individual body; the Magian is the earth-bound cave. Classical Culture has geometry and statics; Arabian Culture has algebra, astrology, and alchemy; Western Culture has the calculus and Galilean dynamics. The Greeks have the nude statues of Polygnotus and Myron, the Arabs have mosaics, arabesques, and mosques; the West has Chartres, the chiaroscuro of Rembrandt, and the fugues of Bach. It is the merit of Spenglerian history, not that it should recall these commonplaces to our attention, but that it may instruct us "why" it is so. For it presents an entirely new symbolism of connectedness which is suggestive for an understanding of the types of science and the forms of art. There are sculptured figures on the porches of Chartres and on the porch of the Erechtheum, and both are covered with drapery, but it is significant of the difference between Faustian and Apollonian Culture that in the one case the drapery is used only to emphasize the body beneath and in the other to conceal it and point to the spirituality of the face. Santa Sophia, the Patriarchate at Peć, Amiens, and Maria am Gestade are all Christian churches, but anyone who has experienced them knows that the former two are Magian caverns in which magic was performed, while the latter are Faustian fingers of light reaching up to heaven. Classical vase painting and the portraiture of the great sixteenth-century Venetian painters both utilize color, but the Greeks limit their palette to clay yellow, black, and brick red—popular colors and colors drawn from the earth—while the Venetians delight in backgrounds of green and blue suggesting the loneliness and depth of infinite sea or sky. If Spengler is correct, these facts are not merely data of art history, they are bridges to Cultural understanding.

Each of the eight Cultures distinguished by Spengler passes through the age-phases of the individual man. For each one there is a childhood, youth, manhood, and old age. But the Heracleitean bias is apparent when the seasons of the year are substituted for the ages of man and each cultural entity is spoken of in terms of its springtime, summer, autumn, and winter. Even a philosophy which sets great store by the distinctions between the-world-as-history and the-world-as-nature finds the focus of Culture in a cycle of blooming, flowering, and withering. But at this point the dichotomy collapses into a single concept of history-as-nature.

Each cultural springtime marks the birth of a myth, a new religious feeling. Such was the Vedic religion in India, the Gods of Homer, the piety of Bernard and Francis of Assisi. Each cultural summer is an era of religious reformation and the beginning of philosophical thought. Such were the Brahmanas, Orphism, the ideas of Savonarola, Luther, and Calvin. Philosophy began in the Upanishads, the great pre-Socratics of the sixth century B.C., and with Bacon, Descartes, and Galileo. Each cultural autumn has its rationalistic enlightenment and its great conclusive philosophical systems: Yoga and Vedanta in India, Plato and Aristotle in the Classical world, Averroes and Avicenna in Islam, Kant and Hegel in the West. And, finally, each cultural winter has its materialistic world outlook, its cult of science and utility, its emphasis upon ethics and society: Stoics, Epicureans, Cynics among the Greeks; Bentham, Comte, Marx in the West.

From primitive religious feeling to reformation and early philosophy, from early philosophy to enlightenment and great philosophical systems, from philosophical systems to materialism and the cult of science—this is the spiritual history of each of the great Cultures. But Spengler's elaborate (and not always successful) attempt to fill in the details of cultural development is less convincing than his brilliant adaptation of a distinction borrowed from Nietzsche—that between "culture" and "civilization."* For every great historical society there is a crucial turning-point, a moment of maximum tension and fruition, beyond which the forces of death are in the ascendancy. If one can assimilate the history of Cultures to a dramatic schema forever established in the *Poetics* of Aristotle, one would say that the complication of the plot which is "culture" gives way after a climax of maximum fruition to the denouement which is "civilization."

Every Culture awakens in the actualization of a particular intuition

* There is an unavoidable ambiguity here in the term "culture," which is eased by systematically distinguishing between "culture" and "Culture." A "Culture" for Spengler is the total socio-historical complex from birth to death, and he distinguishes eight of them. But "culture" is the period of flowering which is always used in opposition to "civilization," or a period of decay. Every Culture therefore has its phase of culture and of civilization.

of existence. It blooms within the set of natural conditions which are at once its sustenance and its boundaries. It dies when it has realized the full possibilities of its languages, arts, sciences, peoples, and politics. But its sequence of epochs is always a struggle to maintain its living force against the powers of disorder without and the implicit death within, that is to say, to attain its aim. But "the aim once attained—the idea, the entire content of inner possibilities, fulfilled and made externally actual—the Culture suddenly hardens, it mortifies, its blood congeals, its force breaks down, and it becomes *Civilization*, the thing which we feel and understand in the words Egypticism, Byzantinism, Mandarinism."[26]

This is the finality which awaits every living Culture. It is the meaning of those "declines" and "falls" which since Gibbon we have associated with the end of the classical world and which Spengler believes are already perceptible in the world today. The idea of cultural death is therefore intimately bound up with the concept of "civilization."

"Civilization" follows "culture" by a strict and necessary organic succession. Civilization is the most external, the most crystalized, the most artificial state of which a Culture is capable. It is the destiny of every cultural springtime, and in the total perspective of the great Cultures it is reached again and again. That peculiar moment of transition which Nietzsche noted in classical Culture between the primitive vitality and metaphysical flair of Homer and Heracleitus and the tired, formal intellectuality of Euripides and Aristotle is accomplished in every Culture, and was, if Spengler is correct, accomplished for Western man in the nineteenth century.

All "cultures" and all "civilizations" are alike whether Chinese, Western, or Greek, and they are distinguishable by a series of indices: culture vs. civilization means province vs. world-city, folk vs. mass proletariat, intuitive feeling vs. intellect, productivity vs. money, gymnastics vs. sport, localism vs. imperialism. Of these, the most sociologically important is that between the quiet country world of the peasant or farmer dwelling and the civilized, mobile, restless, and essentially homeless existence of the great urban proletariat.

World-city and province—the two basic ideas of every civilization—bring up a wholly new form-problem of History, the very problem that we are living through today with hardly the remotest conception of its immensity. In place of a world, there is a *city, a point* in which the whole life of broad regions is collecting while the rest dries up. In place of a type-true people, born of and grown on the soil, there is a new sort of nomad, cohering unstably in fluid masses, the parasitical city dweller, traditionless, utterly matter-of-fact, religionless, clever, unfruitful, deeply contemptuous of the countryman and especially that highest form of countryman, the country gentleman. This is a very great stride towards the inorganic, towards the end—what does it signify? France and England have already taken the step and Germany is beginning to do so. After Syracuse, Athens, and Alexandria comes Rome. After Madrid, Paris, London comes Berlin and New York. It is the destiny of whole regions that lie outside the radiation-circle of one of these cities . . . to become "provinces."[27]

The consequences which follow are at once spiritual and institutional. The man of the land and the man of the city are different essences, and they live as differently and understand each other as little as a peasant of Sicily or Santorini understands a dweller on Telegraph Hill or Madison Avenue. The country lives close to the necessities of life; its productivity is related to the simplest and most explicit needs, while the commerce which flourishes in the city turns in the phase of "civilization" to high finance, paper credits, and the manipulation not of economic entities but of their symbolic tokens. The money markets are but dimly related to the real facts of productivity; money has become a power in its own right, and the monetary consciousness is calculating and, in this sense, intellectual. The metropolitan center of "civilization" is wholly intellect, and this intellectuality, this lure of abstraction finds expression in two obvious areas. The first is the artificial, geometric chessboard of buildings and thoroughfares, constructed by those city planners who are the architects of "civilization." The second is the transformation of the home into "a machine for living" (Le Corbusier) or "a housing project."

Their houses are no longer, as those of the Ionic and the Baroque were, derivatives of the old peasant's house, whence the Culture took its spring into history. They are, generally speaking, no longer houses in which Vesta and Juno, Lares and Penates, have any sort of footing, but mere premises which have been fashioned, not by blood but by requirements, not by feeling, but by the spirit of commercial enterprise. So long as the hearth has a pious meaning as the actual and genuine center of a family, the old relation to the land is not wholly extinct. But when *that*, too, follows the rest into oblivion, and the mass of tenants and bed-occupiers in the sea of houses leads a vagrant existence from shelter to shelter like the hunters and shepherds of primitive times, then the intellectual nomad is completely developed. This city is a world, is *the* world. Only as a whole, as a human dwelling-place, has it meaning, the houses being merely the stones of which it is assembled.[28]

The inhabitants of such a city world are faced daily with a thousand noises, meetings, explosions, crises. The need for watchfulness, for ever being on the alert is constant and the state which this need produces is tension. Civilization is nothing but tension, and since "intelligence is only the capacity for understanding at high tension," the city-dweller is a creature of thought with a need for "elucidation" and a mounting dependence upon causal rather than intuitive modes of knowledge. The tension of the city worker grows unbearably and is relieved only by that form of relaxation which is specific to the world-city: relaxation through a further series of excitements—athletics in which the city man is spectator, not participant, betting, racing, burlesque or its equivalent, gambling. The Hellenic *palaestra* was an institution of "culture," the Roman *circus* of "civilization," and all of the contests and fleshpots of the modern empire city could have been found in the alleys of Alexandria and the thoroughfares of Rome. For the "late city man" is the representative of a cosmopolitanism, of a mannerism which is indigenous to no specific Culture but appears in each when the winter of "civilization" has come upon it.

As to the living representatives of these new and purely intellectual creations, the men of the "New Order" upon whom every decline-time founds such hopes, we cannot be in any doubt. They are the fluid megalopolitan Populace, the rootless city-mass (oi polloi as Athens called it) that has replaced the People, the Culture-folk that was sprung from the soil and peasantlike even when it lived in towns. They are the market-place loungers of Alexandria and Rome, the newspaper-readers of our own corresponding time, the "educated" man who then and now makes a cult of intellectual mediocrity and a church of advertisement; the man of the theatres and places of amusement, of sport and "best-sellers." It is this late-appearing mass and *not* "mankind" that is the object of Stoic and Socialist propaganda, and one could match it with equivalent phenomena in the Egyptian New Empire, Buddhist India and Confucian China.[29]

Spengler's proposal of the syndrome of "civilization" is perhaps one of his least original ideas. But it is no less persuasive for that. Into it has gone Nietzsche's distinction between cultural vigor and dead intellect, Max Weber's prophetic analysis of modern materialism and bureaucracy, Ernst Simmel's brilliant bringing together of money, mathematics, and intellectuality as functions of urban existence. All this of course is seasoned with a mixture of post-Hegelian romanticism which glorified the people and the soil, and a Prussian conservatism (also to be found in the Tolstoi of *Anna Karenina* and *War and Peace*) which sees the landed proprietor the natural center of all the virtues. But unconscious motivation and borrowed glories aside, it has the impact of inescapable truth.

4. DESTINY AND DECLINE

Spengler is right that the assertion of "the decline of the West" is simply an inference from the general theory of "civilization." Such a decline is the destiny of every Culture, and the only empirical problem is to chart the phases through which a Culture passes and principally to identify the epoch-making moment which signifies that its "culture" is over and that it has entered upon the period of its "civilization." If, as Spengler hints, the life span of any Culture seems to be about a thousand years, and if, as he clearly asserts, the origins of Western Culture are to be found at the end of the Carolingian era and the beginning of the Crusades, the conclusion is obvious.

The springtime of the Faustian "culture" lasts through the Middle Ages. Feudalism and chivalry are of its essence; Christian mysticism and scholastic philosophy are its ripest cultural fruits. The summer of the Western world begins with the Renaissance, the rise of the national states, and the growth of capitalism and town economy; its "culture" is expressible in the great mathematics and philosophy of the sixteenth and seventeenth centuries, in the flowering of Italian painting and in the origin of contrapuntal music. The Faustian autumn is the late Baroque, the eighteenth century, and with Mozart, Goethe, and Kant the Faustian spirit reached the ultimate creativity of which it was capable. The beginning of the nineteenth century is, therefore, the symbolically crucial date for the Western world.

Culture and Civilization—the living body of a soul and the mummy of it. For Western existence the distinction lies at about the year 1800—on the one side of that frontier life in fullness and sureness of itself, formed by growth from within, in one great uninterrupted evolution from Gothic childhood to Goethe and Napoleon, and on the other the autumnal, artificial, rootless life of our great cities under forms fashioned by the intellect.[30]

The nineteenth century ushered in the winter of the Western world. A materialistic world-outlook centered in Comte, Darwin, and Marx; the spread of anarchistic and socialistic ideas; the degradation of abstract thought into professional lecture-room philosophy and the new popularity of "logicians," "positivists," and "psychologists;" the beginnings of "modern" art with its attempts to excite the metropolitan consciousness; the development of pretentious, artificial architecture—all signify the beginning of the end—that is, the period in which we now live. And to these cultural indices must be added the political and sociological facts: an age of massive imperialisms, of dictators, of periodic world wars; the domination of a machine culture where the Faustian passion of discovery and invention has turned into the ultimate dominance of the industrial administrator and the engineer. It is not an appetizing picture which Spengler has painted in the last chapters of *The Decline of the West*, but infinitely more disturbing than the "facts" which he details is the "attitude" which he proposes in his final words.[31]

For us, however, whom a Destiny has placed in this Culture and at this moment of its development—the moment when money is celebrating its last victories, and the Caesarism that is to succeed approaches with quiet, firm step—our direction, willed and obligatory at once, is set for us within narrow limits, and on any other terms life is not worth the living. We have not the freedom to reach to this or to that, but the freedom to do the necessary or to do nothing. And a task that historic necessity has set *will* be accomplished with the individual or against him.

This is the challenge of historical determinism.

But it is a perverse and by no means consistent form of determinism. It is clear from biological analogy that increasing age means approaching death, and that this is indeed the "destiny" of all life, but why assume that death is both "obligatory" and "willed;" that if increasing age does set certain narrower limits, "on any other terms life is not worth the living;" and finally why assume that we no longer have freedom to reach out to new possibilities, but only "freedom to do the necessary or to do nothing"?

It is, I think, because Spengler's concept of destiny includes something sinister and meaningless, some almost malignant natural force which operates like the Greek "*moira*" behind the curtain of intelligible causality. It is so in the case of the inevitable imperialism of our age.

Imperialism is Civilization unadulterated. In this phenomenal form the destiny of the West is now irrevocably set. . . . It is not a matter of choice —it is not the conscious will of individuals, or even that of whole classes or peoples that decides. The expansive tendency is a doom, something demonic and immense, which grips, forces into service, and uses up the late mankind of the world-city stage, willy-nilly, aware or unaware. Life is the process of effecting possibilities, and for the brain-man there are *only extensive* possibilities. . . . He who does not understand that this outcome is obligatory and insusceptible of modification, that our choice is between willing *this* and willing nothing at all, between cleaving to *this* destiny or despairing of the future and of life itself; he who cannot feel that there is a grandeur also in the realizations of powerful intelligences, in the energy and discipline of metal-hard natures, in battles fought with the coldest and most abstract means; he who is obsessed with the idealism of a provincial and would pursue the ways of life of past ages—must forgo all desire to comprehend history, to live through history or to make history.[32]

But if it is not the conscious will of individuals that decides, wherein lies the obligation to acquiesce? Above all, wherein lies the "grandeur" of furthering tendencies which are either definitely malevolent or at the very least devoid of intrinsic value? Sensitive as he undoubtedly is to the impact of literature, philosophy, and the arts, there is something in Spengler's nature which is naturally attracted to ruthlessness, to power politics, and to the unlimited expansiveness of technology. It is as if he is the conscious heir to the Nietzschean legacy of power and moral strength without having remembered Nietzsche's central conviction "that art is the highest task and the proper metaphysical activity of this life."[33] Only such forgetfulness could produce Spengler's indifference to the future of philosophy and the arts, which shows itself not in his brilliant diagnosis of our age, but in his recommended acquiescence to its painful direction.

We are civilized, not Gothic or Rococo people; we have to reckon with the hard cold facts of a *late* life, to which the parallel is to be found not in Pericles's Athens but in Caesar's Rome. Of great painting or great music there can no longer be, for Western people, any question. Their architectural possibilities have been exhausted these hundred years. Only *extensive* possibilities are left to them. Yet, for a sound and vigorous generation that is filled with unlimited hopes, I fail to see that it is any disadvantage to discover betimes that some of these hopes must come to nothing. And if the hopes thus doomed should be those most dear, well, a man who is worth anything will not be dismayed. It is true that the issue may be tragic for some individuals who in their decisive years are overpowered by the conviction that in the spheres of architecture, drama, painting there is nothing left for them to conquer. What matter if they do go under! . . . The lesson, I think, would be of benefit to the coming generations, as showing them what is possible— and therefore necessary—and what is excluded from the inward potentialities of their time. . . . And I can only hope that men of the new generation may be moved by this book to devote themselves to technics instead of lyrics, the sea instead of the paint-brush, and politics instead of epistemology. Better they could not do.[34]

But again, why should the new generation abandon painting, philosophy, and poetry to devote itself to technics and politics if this means (as Spengler surely understands that it does) to the technics of destruction and the politics of conquest? Erich Heller among many others has been distressed by this perversity, and has said:[35]

Spengler must be rejected on different grounds: not because his history is incorrect, but because it is untrue. And between the two reasons lies a world of difference. Spengler's history is untrue because the mind which has conceived it is, despite its learning and seeming subtlety, a crude and wicked mind. The image of man which lurks behind Spengler's vast historical canvas is perverted, and could only be accepted by a hopelessly perverted age. For Spengler has no idea of the true stature of the problem of human freedom. Therefore his historical vision is lacking in depth as well as in love, pity and pathos. It is a worthless and deeply untruthful sort of history which lacks these qualities for they are the proper tools of human understanding.

I believe that Heller's statement is inaccurate but that its implication is true. No history could be untrue simply because the mind which had created it was wicked. The criteria belong to different levels of value. Spengler's pessimistic account of the decline of the West may well be true and, distressing as his portrait of the contemporary Alexandrian age may be, it has the colors of authenticity. But no mere "description" of an age of degraded values entails a "conscious decision" for those degraded values. It is not because Spengler has charted the decline of our Culture that he is to be decried, but we must cease to follow him because, departing from the brilliant role of analyst, he has demanded that we put ourselves on the side of those false values. That man should be forced against his will to suffer death or endure evil would be an apt theme for the tragedy of the Greeks. But that he should lend a helping hand to an evil destiny would be beyond the comprehension of Sophocles or even Seneca.

The deliberate choice of decline, the deliberate desire to embrace those elements of technology and conquest which characterize Western Culture in the phase of its Civilization is, I think, bound up with another presupposition of Spenglerian history: the relativity of all values. If there are eight (or any number for that matter) separate, individually sealed Cultures, each with its own soul, each with its own thought-forms and modes of perception, there must also be eight moral systems. "Each Culture possesses its own standards, the validity of which begins and ends with it. There is no general ethics of humanity."[36] Not only our world-feeling, but the ethical basis of our entire daily existence is culturally *a priori*. When Plato speaks of humanity, he means the Greeks in contrast to the barbarians, the free man in contrast to the slave. Whatever universality we are tempted to import into the doctrines, no Greek would ever construe the ethics of Plato and Aristotle as holding beyond the provincialism of the Classical world. With Kant, however, it is otherwise. His categorical imperative he tries to validate universally, for all times and for all places. But this is the characteristic myopia of Faustian man.

It is *this* that is lacking to the Western thinker, the very thinker in whom we might have expected to find it—insight into the *historically relative* character of his data, which are expressions of one *specific existence and one only*; knowledge of the necessary limits of their validity; the conviction that his "unshakable" truths and "eternal" views are simply true for him and eternal for his world-view; the duty of looking beyond them to find out what the men of other Cultures have with equal certainty evolved out of themselves. That and nothing else will impart completeness to the philosophy of the future, and only through an understanding of the living world shall we understand the symbolism of history. Here there is nothing constant, nothing universal. We must cease to speak of the forms of "Thought," the principles of "Tragedy," the mission of "The State." Universal validity involves always the fallacy of arguing from particular to particular.[87]

From Spengler's history no absolute values can ever emerge, and if absolute values are a delusion, what difference does it make whether we follow the *Zeitgeist* or resist it, whether we are frustrated as artists or brilliantly successful as engineers? No reason intrinsic to history can be given, and since Spengler does give a dogmatic and unhesitating answer, it must spring from some source outside the historical process. Spengler's role as counselor to Western civilization has no logical connection with his vocation as a morphologist of culture. Therefore his admonition to bow before the inevitable and will our tragic destiny lies either with some deep but unacknowledged sympathy for the content of that destiny, or a pathetic longing for the splendors of success however empty. Unless, of course, Spengler's history is the dramatic exemplification in the modern world of that bankruptcy of traditional values which ends by making what is the test of what ought to be, and which manages to produce out of absolute historical relativism absolute axiological meaninglessness. In that case "history" would indeed be the nightmare from which Stephen Dedalus was trying to awake and the delirium of a madman of which Rebecca West has spoken.

5. THE WORK OF TOYNBEE

If the upshot of Spengler's philosophy of history is a denial of absolute values, and if the laborious outcome of *The Decline of the West* is a pervasive historical skepticism, precisely the opposite emerges from the massive ten-volume *A Study of History* by Arnold Toynbee, a work upon which he spent thirty years of his life and which appeared part by part between 1934 and 1954.[38]

Edward Gibbon, writing from Lausanne in 1787, ended his monumental *The Decline and Fall of the Roman Empire* with a modest note: "The historian may applaud the importance and variety of his subject; but, while he is conscious of his own imperfections, he must often accuse the deficiency of his materials. It was among the ruins of the Capitol that I first conceived the idea of a work which has amused and exercised near twenty years of my life, and which, however inadequate to my own wishes, I finally deliver to the curiosity and candour of the public." Toynbee, before completing his work in London in 1951 ("June 15, 6:25 p.m., after looking once more this afternoon at Fra Angelico's picture of the Beatific Vision"), had much more to say (almost all of Volume X) about his own biography, the feeling for poetry in the facts of history, and the sources of the inspiration of historians. And, dealing quite frankly with his own "angle of vision," he summed it up thus:[39]

Why do people study History? Why, to put the question *ad hominem*, had the writer of the present work been studying History since he was a child and been spending thirty years on this book which he was now finishing? . . . The present writer's personal answer was that an historian, like anyone else who has had the happiness of having an aim in life, has found his vocation in a call from God to 'feel after Him and find Him.'

If this personal answer finds any favour with the reader, it may help us also to answer a second question that is implicit in the one from which we have started. In beginning by asking ourselves why we study History we have begged the question: What do we mean by History? And the writer, continuing to speak simply for himself from his personal experience, would reply that he meant by History a vision . . . of God revealing Himself in action to souls that were sincerely seeking Him. . . . History's contribution is to give us a vision of God's creative activity on the move in a frame which, in our human experience of it, displays six dimensions. The historical angle of vision shows us the physical cosmos moving centrifugally in a four-dimensional frame of Space-Time; it shows us Life on our own planet moving evolutionarily in a five-dimensional frame of Life-Time-Space; and it shows us human souls, raised to a sixth dimension by the gift of the Spirit, moving, through a fateful exercise of their spiritual freedom, either towards their Creator or away from Him.

Spengler's work is a little like that of Gibbon: both take as their subject-matter the area of "decline and fall," both treat this area with seriousness, but with an irony that sometimes suggests sympathy with the mechanisms of decay rather than the institutions which conventional piety considers the chief bulwarks against it. But if Spengler belongs to the tradition of Gibbon, then obviously Toynbee is a modern Augustine, writing his study of history like the Bishop of Hippo in "a time of troubles," and bringing all of the resources of a positivistic historiography (as Augustine did of pagan wisdom) to the service of a Christian view of the world.

Nevertheless there are important similarities between A *Study of History* and *The Decline of the West*, similarities due less to any basic sympathy of *Weltanschauung* than to the climate of opinion of histori- cal studies since 1900 and the peculiar problems with which the philosophy of history finds itself confronted in the modern world. *The Decline of the West* first reached Toynbee in 1920.

As I read those pages teeming with firefly flashes of historical insight, I wondered at first whether my whole inquiry had been disposed of by Spengler before even the questions, not to speak of the answers, had fully taken shape in my own mind. . . . But when I looked in Spengler's book for an answer to my question about the geneses of civilizations, I saw that there was still work for me to do, for on this point Spengler was, it seemed to me, most unilluminatingly dogmatic and deterministic. According to him, civilizations arose, developed, declined, and foundered in unvarying conformity with a fixed time-table, and no explanation was offered for any of this. It was just a law of nature which Spengler had detected, and you must take it on trust from the Master: *ipse dixit*. This arbitrary fiat seemed disappointingly unworthy of Spengler's brilliant genius; and here I became aware of a difference in national traditions. Where the German *a priori* method drew blank let us see what could be done by English empiricism. Let us test alternative explanations in the light of the facts and see how they stood the ordeal.[40]

It is perhaps not quite appropriate for a modern St. Augustine to complain about the arbitrary fiats of another, for it is difficult to see how even English empiricism could be invoked to furnish evidence that history demonstrates "God's creative activity on the move." The fact is that every philosophy of history has its own type of *a priori*.

Toynbee, like Spengler, considers the Society or the Civilization as "the intelligible field of historical study,"[41] but instead of Spengler's eight Cultures, he distinguishes twenty-one,[42] of which five (Western, Orthodox Christian, Islamic, Hindu, and Far Eastern) are extant today. But perhaps the most significant difference is that whereas for Spengler each Culture is sealed within the confines of its own mode of perception, for Toynbee there is a range of relatedness differentially illustrated by the various Civilizations. Some (like the Egyptian and the Andean) are wholly unrelated to any others; others (like the Minoan) are wholly unrelated to earlier Civilizations but are affiliated to a later (Hellenic) culture. And some are the very sources of later ones, are in short their parents (as the Indic is to the Hindu, or the Hellenic to the Western).

Toynbee is indeed an empiricist, but it is a paradoxical empiricism, because the hypotheses which the empiricism is used to substantiate are derived not from the data of cultural morphology, but from the content and the theory of literature. This has its own irony, because it is upon somewhat similar grounds that Toynbee is especially critical of Spengler. It is obvious that Spengler's philosophy of history rests upon a biological analogy. After quoting one of the famous passages from *The Decline of the West* in which this analogy is asserted, Toynbee says:[43]

In this passage we may acknowledge a fine appreciation of the successive changes in ethos that can be observed in the course of the histories of certain civilizations which, at some point in their growth, have in fact had the misfortune to break down and to lapse into a decline. But Herr Spengler is here demanding from us much more than a recognition of empirically verifiable facts. He is asking us to induce from this handful of facts a universal and inexorable law; and with (no doubt, unconscious) jugglery, he is attempting to mask the inadequacy of the evidential basis on which his tremendous induction has to stand, behind the simile in which he likens the career of a civilization to the life-history of a human being or other living organism. As an effective artifice of literary expression, this simile might have been allowed to pass; but, when we detect its author in the act of misusing it for the purpose of glazing over a weakness in his chain of argument, we are bound to point out that this simile has no basis in fact.

Now it is not really so easy in the philosophy of history to distinguish between "a chain of argument" and an "effective artifice of literary expression," and in the case of Toynbee himself it is difficult to separate his cultural hypotheses from the forms of his literary expression. All Platonic history is innately metaphorical, and this is as true of A *Study of History* as it is of *The Decline of the West*. The only difference is that Toynbee's metaphors are derived from art rather than from nature, from Goethe, Aeschylus, and Aristotle rather than from the ages of men and the seasons of the year.[44]

The principal subject of A *Study of History* is an inquiry into the geneses of civilizations, the growth of civilizations, and the breakdown of civilizations. But genesis, growth, and breakdown are only substantives which represent a dynamics of process, and the clue to that dynamics has in every case been suggested to Toynbee's cultivated intelligence by an episode from the literary or philosophic tradition. For him the mechanism of genesis is the central insight of the Prologue to Goethe's *Faust*; the mechanism of growth is exemplified in Aeschylus' *Prometheus Bound*; the mechanism of breakdown is nothing but the "peripeteia" of Aristotelian tragedy.

In seeking the rationale for the genesis of civilizations, Toynbee examines the customarily proposed factors of environment and race and rejects them both. "If our unknown quantity is neither Race nor Environment, neither God nor the Devil, it cannot be a simple quantity but must be a product of two: some interaction between Environment and Race, some encounter between the Devil and God. That is the plot of the Book of Job and the plot of Goethe's *Faust*. Is it, perhaps, the plot of Life and the plot of History?"[45] But to talk about "the plot" of life or "the plot" of history is to resort to a metaphorical mode of discourse no less imaginative than Spengler's. It is almost to abandon historical positivism, and about this Toynbee himself seems to have had certain initial doubts.

Race and environment were the two main rival keys that were offered by would-be scientific nineteenth-century Western historians for solving the problem of the cultural inequality of various extant human societies, and neither key proved, on trial, to unlock the fast-closed door. . . . The breakdown of these would-be scientific impersonal explanations drove me to turn to mythology. I took this turning rather self-consciously and shamefacedly, as though it were a provocatively retrograde step. . . . If I had been acquainted at the time with the works of C. G. Jung, they would have given me the clue. I actually found it in Goethe's Faust. . . .

Goethe's 'Prologue in Heaven' opens with the archangels hymning the perfection of God's creation. But, just because His works are perfect, the Creator has left Himself no scope for any further exercise of His creative powers, and there might have been no way out of this *impasse* if Mephistopheles—created for this purpose—had not presented himself before the throne and challenged God to give him a free hand to spoil, if he can, one of the Creator's choicest works. God accepts the challenge and thereby wins an opportunity to carry His work of creation forward. An encounter between two personalities in the form of challenge and response: have we not here the flint and steel by whose mutual impact the creative spark is kindled?[46]

"Challenge and response" thereupon becomes the lever whereby to understand the genesis of civilizations, and this may now be construed as the interactive function either of environmental factors or of peoples.

The genesis of Egyptian civilization is the response to the challenge of the Nile as that of Sumerian civilization is the response to the Tigris and Euphrates. The challenge of the tropical forest brought the Mayan civilization into existence, and the Minoan civilization arose as a response to the challenge of the Aegean Sea. With this theoretical model, it becomes possible for Toynbee to carry forward the empirical examination into causes as an inquiry into "the range of challenge and response;" the stimulus of hard countries, of new lands, of blows from outside, of interior pressures and penalizations. This is the burden of all of Volume II.

From that of genesis Toynbee turns to the problem of the growth of civilizations. Here he derives his guiding principle from Aeschylus' Promethean trilogy.[47] He sees the universal imagery of Aeschylus' drama as a generalization of the plight of an infant Hellenic Civilization: Is it to grow? And the Promethean legend tells us that growth occurs when there is a triumph of thought against force, of progress against arrest of movement, in short, of energy against the death-dealing powers of lethargy.

Now all this sounds suspiciously like something we have encountered before—like the torpor which Bergson in *Creative Evolution* has seen as perpetually lying in wait for the animal, and like the lethargy of habit and institutionalized routine which in *The Two Sources of Morality and Religion* he has seen as the eternal enemy of human creativity. So we are not surprised when a few pages further, Toynbee quotes Bergson at length[48] and asserts that "In Bergson's philosophy as in the poetry of Aeschylus the personality of Prometheus . . . is drawn for us with a masterly touch." From Bergson Toynbee derives the language and the ideology of "the creative effort," and, indeed, it can be said that Bergson's ideas dominate Volumes III and IV of A *Study of History*. We have already seen that the same Bergsonian mode of perception dominates the thinking of Spengler. Whitehead has said that all of Western philosophy is simply a series of footnotes to Plato. It would be equally appropriate to say that the philosophy of history of the contemporary Western world—illustrated by *The Decline of the West* and A *Study of History*—is simply a series of footnotes to Bergson.

For Toynbee the criterion of growth applied to civilizations is a progressive movement toward self-determination. Self-determination means self-expression, and the agencies of self-expression within a society are either individuals or small groups. It follows that growth within a civilization is always the work of either "creative individuals" or "creative minorities." The former are those superior personalities or artistic geniuses or great mystics to whose achievement the work of Bergson has called attention.[49] Toynbee studies at length the course which is followed by creative personalities at their highest spiritual level. This turns out to be a "movement of withdrawal and return," symbolized not only in the ancient vegetation and fertility rites which have left their traces on such diverse cultural products as Attic tragedy and T. S. Eliot's *The Waste Land*, but also in "the dark night of the soul" of the Christian mystics, the aloneness of Moses on Mt. Sinai, and the Platonic philosopher who, having ventured forth alone to apprehend the supreme form of the good, returns again to his companions within the Cave. Toynbee's study of growth ends with a long series of case studies of withdrawal and return in the creative personalities of civilization. They include the Buddha, Lenin, Solon, Mohammed, Loyola, Thucydides, Caesar, and Confucius.

For Toynbee the growth of civilization is a Promethean experience, in which the *élan vital* of peoples is freed for the creative effort; it follows that the breakdown of civilizations is a losing of Promethean *élan*, a loss of creative power. Because Toynbee is dominated here too by the philosophy of Bergson and by the peculiar Bergsonian form of the doctrine of emergent evolution, the mechanism of breakdown must be essentially an internal alteration. "In demonstrating that the broken down civilizations have not met their death from an assassin's hand, we have found no reason to dispute the allegation that they have been the victims of violence, and in almost every instance we have been led, by the logical process of exhaustion, to return a verdict of suicide."[50] Now, this is neither exclusively Bergsonian nor modern. Jacob Burckhardt, in proposing the difference between the operation of causal agency in nature and society in the nineteenth century, was led to a doctrine very like it. "In nature, annihilation only comes about by the action of external causes, catastrophes of nature or climate, the overrunning of weaker species by bolder, of nobler by baser. In history the way of annihilation is invariably prepared by inward degeneration, by decrease of life. Only then can a shock from outside put an end to the whole."[51] Toynbee, however, spells out the consequences of a "decrease of life" in terms of the loss of self-determination, the transformation of "creative" minorities into merely "dominant" minorities, and the various forms of mechanization of impulse which follow.

Despite the profound differences in their approach to history, Toynbee's work is strikingly like that of Spengler. For he also attempts to establish a cyclical rhythm which applies to every civilization—a recurrent pattern of genesis, growth, breakdown, and disintegration. And if Spengler describes with loving attention the complicated mechanisms of decline and fall and the fateful re-occurrence of an Alexandrian age for Western Culture, Toynbee is not less assiduous in the examination of the mechanics of disintegration. He exhibits the disintegration of civilizations partly as "a schism in the body social"[52] (in which there is an alienation between dominant minorities and internal proletariats or a threat from an external proletariat or large body of the disinherited in the vicinity of the civilization), but more prominently as "a schism in the soul."[53] The schism in the soul of a civilization is that loss of organic unity which Spengler had noted in every Alexandrian age; the perplexing pluralism in modes of behavior and feeling for life, the antithetical roles of truancy and martyrdom, the sense of drift and the sense of cultural promiscuity which comes with the weakening of the cultural tradition. Here disintegration is symbolized by vulgarity and barbarism in art, by a general debasing of the linguistic coinage and a confusion of tongues, and a weak syncretism in religion.

These are the details, the burdensome accidents of disintegration, but its essence can be stated in a simple phrase; "the Nemesis of Creativity."[54] Again Toynbee has recourse to a literary analogy. The failure of a creativity once brilliantly asserted by a civilization and now conspicuously absent is like the fortune of the unhappy Oedipus. King of Thebes when the play begins, haughty saviour of his people, he is reduced to blind and pitiful weakness, crushed in spirit as the drama ends. This ironical twist of human fortune is a persistent theme of Greek tragedy, and under the name of "peripeteia" is taken by Aristotle as one of the hallmarks of the tragic play. A similar "reversal of roles" is also the paradigm of the disintegration of civilizations, and it becomes therefore a suggestive analogy of "the plot of civilization."

This second version of the plot is a tragedy in three acts which are familiar in Greek literature under the titles *koros, hubris, ate;* and in this context these three Greek words all have a subjective as well as an objective connotation. Objectively *koros* means 'surfeit,' *hubris* 'outrageous behavior,' and *ate* 'disaster.' Subjectively *koros* means the psychological condition of being 'spoilt' by success; *hubris* means the consequent loss of mental and moral balance; and *ate* means the blind headstrong ungovernable impulse that sweeps an unbalanced soul into attempting the impossible. This active psychological catastrophe in three acts was the commonest theme—if we may judge by the handful of extant masterpieces—in the fifth-century Athenian tragic drama.[55]

But whole civilizations too can have the experience of being spoilt by success, engaging in outrageous acts, and meeting disaster. One could develop the Aristotelian poetics even further (although here Toynbee is not quite so literal) to find in every civilization its *hamartia* or tragic flaw and the moment of its *anagnorisis* or dread consciousness of final inescapable destiny. Spengler's philosophy of history lies under the spell of Heracleitus and the eternal rhythms of birth and death. Toynbee's philosophy of history lies under the spell of Aristotle's *Poetics* and the tragic drama which it unfolds. Both are Hellenists, and their contributions to our knowledge of the rise and fall of civilizations bear the indelible stamp of this cultural influence.

Yet it is a Hellenism which eventuates in two profoundly different versions of fate, for Toynbee's is a Christian Hellenism which is unwilling to accept the ultimacy of cultural finitude. The Cultures in Spengler's sequence move toward death with an inevitability which admits of no reprieve, and when they have suffered the last agonies and lie cold, there is nothing which can be done. The Civilizations in Toynbee's sequence also blaze up and die away, but if you poke long enough among the ashes you may find a phoenix. Volume VI of *A Study of History* is Toynbee's poking and sifting among the ashes, and here he comes up with the phoenix which is not only to prolong his work, but to give it the characteristic twist of his later philosophy of history.[56] It is the phoenix of "*palingenesia*."

Civilizations which are in the throes of disintegration and souls who are born into a socially disintegrating world are faced with certain options, certain ways of life and feeling which still lie open.[57] One of these is "Archaism," the conservative effort to return to an old established order in conduct, art, religion, and language. Its contrary is "Futurism," the denial of tradition and the pursuit of relentless experimentation in economics and the arts. A third is "Detachment," the Stoic resignation to death and catastrophe, or the sense of an over-arching nature (as in Lucretius and Ecclesiastes) which offers a vantage-point "for levering the Soul away from its attachment to life." Finally, there is "Transfiguration," a spiritual entrance into "the Kingdom of God in This World," the path of messianic Christianity into Augustine's *Civitas Dei*. At this point it becomes crystal-clear beyond all doubt that Toynbee's parochialism has really overcome him, that he has given up the empirical description and analysis of the options of disintegration to announce himself, no longer a mere spectator, as a partisan for the path of "Transfiguration." It is an enormous price to pay, and it means that all prior claims to the purity of his empiricism must be abandoned. But the stakes too are high, and only in this way can he win through to his beloved phoenix.

The rebirth, regeneration, or resurrection to which Toynbee gives his unqualified commitment is not the birth of a new mundane society from the ashes of the old; it is the attainment of the soul to "a higher spiritual dimension than the life of This World." It is "the palingenesia of which Jesus speaks to Nicodemus."[58] The *palingenesia* announced in Volume VI becomes the essential principle upon which the remainder of A *Study of History* is founded, with the consequence that Toynbee's entire focus of attention shifts from a concern with civilizations to a concern with universal churches. What was to have been a scientific inquiry into the nature of universal states, universal churches, and heroic ages[59] turns into an undisguised assertion of religious values. Toynbee has found that a universal church (like the Christian) is likely to arise during the time of troubles following the breakdown of a civilization (like the Hellenic) and to flourish under the universal state (like the Roman Empire), which is the mark of a merely temporary recovery of the disintegrating civilization. The consequence is that universal churches are like "chrysalises" which preserve the culture of the dying civilization until a new civilization can come to birth (as the early Christian Church bridged the gap between the Classical and the Western worlds.)[60]

But Toynbee is determined to deny this analogy, because such a schema would make the universal church merely an instrument in the service of the continuity of the civilizations, and the new idea which has suddenly reoriented the perspective of his historiography suggests just the reverse.

On this view, we shall have first of all to revise our previous tacit and uncritical assumptions about the *raison d'être* of civilizations. We shall have to think of the civilizations of the second generation as having come into existence, not in order to perform achievements of their own, and not in order to reproduce their kind in a third generation, but in order to provide an opportunity for fully fledged higher religions to come to birth; and, since the genesis of these higher religions was a consequence of the breakdowns and disintegrations of the secondary civilizations, we must regard the closing chapters in the secondary civilizations' histories—chapters which, from their standpoint, spell failure—as being their justification for existence and their title to significance.[61]

This is a "*peripeteia*" in Toynbee's own philosophy of history, and its consequence is that the former clarity in the cycle of rise and fall is now clouded with ambiguity. A declining civilization may mean a rising religion; a successful secular life may be the nemesis of spirituality.

Birth and death are here confused as in the central episodes of the Christian mystery. As Eliot has said it in "Journey of the Magi":[62]

> . . . were we led all that way for
> Birth or Death? There was a Birth, certainly,
> We had evidence and no doubt. I had seen birth
>   and death,
> But had thought they were different; this Birth was
> Hard and bitter agony for us, like Death, our death.

From the new perspective which Toynbee has adopted, it might seem as if the Greek cyclical idea had been abandoned and the Christian eschatology had been espoused. It might appear, therefore, as if Christianity were the apex of a continuous movement of spiritual progress which had not merely survived secular catastrophes, but had fed upon them for its own sustenance. Indeed, this is largely Toynbee's belief. He has insisted that "spiritual and secular ideals are at variance; they are perpetually striving with one another for mastery over human souls." And he has said:[63]

When the house that Man has built for himself falls in ruin about his ears and he finds himself standing again in the open at the mercy of the elements, he also finds himself standing again face to face with a God whose perpetual presence is now no longer hidden from Man's eyes by prison walls of Man's own making.

But at the same time Toynbee's Christianity is not particularist. He is willing to acknowledge the spiritual insight in all the existing higher religions: Christianity, Mahayana Buddhism, Islam, Hinduism. In a famous passage in which he denies that Christianity or any other higher religion has a monopoly of spiritual truth, and calls himself less a Christian than a "Symmachan" ("The heart of so great a mystery can never be reached by following one road only."), he has said:[64]

The personal *tour de force* which an historian has to attempt if he is to perform his professional service for his fellow human beings is to correct, by imagination, the bias inherent in the standpoint at which he has been placed by the historical accidents of his birth and upbringing, in order to see and present the flux of human life *sub specie aeternitatis*. But human attempts to see human affairs through God's eyes must always fall infinitely short of success; and, while it is difficult enough for the historian to correct his political bias as a citizen of a state and his cultural bias as a member of a society, the hardest of all the feats of imagination that are required of him is to see beyond the *Weltanschauung* of an ancestral higher religion. If he turns savage against it and tries to break out of its confines by force, the faith of his fathers revenges itself upon him by becoming a veritable prison-house whose magic walls pen the ex-Christian atheist and the still Christian believer together in a common mental captivity which is palpable to a non-Christian looker-on. With this warning to himself and his readers, the writer of this Study will venture to express his personal belief that the four higher religions that were alive in the age in which he was living were four variations on a single theme, and that, if all the four components of this heavenly music of the spheres could be audible on Earth simultaneously and with equal clarity, to one pair of human ears, the happy hearer would find himself listening not to a discord, but to a harmony.

Toynbee's personal stand upon the issue of Christian revelation would hardly matter, and his belief that civilizations are the handmaiden of the higher religions and that these higher religions are but diverse approximations of the *Civitas Dei* would be the important thing, if it were not also true that by this time all of Toynbee's judgments as historian or as spectator of the historiography of others are so deeply entangled in his compulsive religiosity. When in Volume VIII he turns to "The Drama of the Encounters between Civilizations," where much that is original and exciting was to be expected of him, he can only deal with the diffusion and diffraction of culture in terms which have been the commonplaces of Western sociology for the last forty years. When, finally, we turn to Volume IX for the crucial treatment of the problem which underlies the philosophy of history as the sea underlies the ships upon it—the problem of "Law and Freedom in History,"[65] we find Toynbee again hopelessly enmeshed in the toils of theology.

Once again Toynbee criticizes Spengler for having laid down not a law of inevitable progress, but a law of inevitable dissolution, and he claims to have disposed once and for all of "the fallacy of Spengler's confusion of societies with organisms, and the groundlessness of his belief in the omnipotence of the savage goddess Necessity."[66] But a scant hundred pages later he is himself laying it down as an observation about the drama of social disintegration that it has a plot more regular and more precise, more empirically generalizable in fact and in time-span than any *inevitability* which is asserted in *The Decline of the West*.[67] The fact is that on the issue of the disintegration of civilizations, for all that Toynbee refuses "to cast the horoscope of our own civilization or of any other that is still alive,"[68] and for all that he substitutes the language of empirical generalization for the metaphysical language of destiny, the results of Spengler and of Toynbee are the same.

But on the theoretical issue of law and freedom, there is real divergence. The recurrent Greek naturalism, not completely articulated and not consistently expressed, which nonetheless lies at the heart of Spengler's view of the world, is denied by Toynbee, as it must be by one whose concept has been forged, however imperfectly, in the crucible of Christian supernaturalism. I say imperfectly because for all of his piety, Toynbee is not a good or a persuasive theologian. He does not take the Augustinian path of a strict separation between the City of God and the earthly city, but tries naively (that is, without really wrestling with the problem of evil or of design) to establish a correspondence between the "Law of God" and the "laws of Nature."

We can, indeed, conceive of them as being co-regnant, not only without conflict, but in positive cooperation with one another, in virtue of the very diversity between the two notions of regularity which they respectively embody. 'The Law of God' reveals the regularity of a single constant aim pursued unwaveringly, in the face of all obstacles and in response to all challenges, by the intelligence and will of a personality. 'Laws of Nature' display the regularity of a recurrent movement—for instance the motion of a wheel revolving any number of times round its axis. . . . In real life, of course, we find no wheels without wheelwrights, and no wheelwrights without drivers who commission these artificers to build wheels and fit them to carts in order that the wheels' repetitive revolutions may recur, not in vain, but for the practical and practicable purpose of conveying a cart towards the driver's intended goal. . . . In fact, the apparent incompatibility between the two kinds of regularity is merely a mirage in the shadow-world of abstract logic; in real life they are not only compatible with one another but are inseparably complementary in a divinely inspired interplay. . . .[69]

I am afraid that the incompatibility (incommensurability would be more exact) between observed sequences of natural events and the demonstrable proof of divine teleology depends on more than what Toynbee calls a faulty logic, and the point is hardly carried by his tired and careworn metaphor of the chariot of history with God in the driver's seat moving forward toward the divine purposes by means of the wheels of cyclical social movement. Too many helpless victims have been mutilated beneath the heavy wheels to make the picture of "Eternal Love behind the reins" either comfortable or persuasive.

On the issue of the laws of nature Toynbee is as naturalistic as Spengler, but his attitude is more moderate. Human affairs are amenable to laws of nature and at least to some extent are knowable and subject to scientific formulation, but the laws of nature current in history are not "inexorable," they are "controllable."[70] Man cannot suspend their operation but he can affect their incidence. This is no more than the historicism of the nineteenth century imported into a contemporary setting; Comte and Marx would have said no less. The difference is that the prospects of man as seen by Comte and Marx are solely dependent upon the control of laws of nature, whereas for Toynbee the reality of the spiritual world imports an incalculable dimension into the problem of progress.

If the prospects of Man in Process of Civilization, on his arduous climb up a precipitous cliff-face towards an unattained and invisible ledge above, evidently depended above all on his ability to recover a lost control of the pitch, it was no less evident that this issue was going to be decided by the course of Man's relations not just with his fellow men and with himself, but above all, with God his Saviour.[71]

The reality of the spiritual world has this effect: that because of the freedom of choice which God has granted to human souls, they may in various civilizations respond differentially to the ordeal of challenge and response. We see this effect in the diversity in duration of the growth-phases of the civilizations, and the diversity in the relations of the higher religions to the civilizations which they have touched. Toynbee's inquiry into law and freedom in history is philosophically superficial and adds nothing toward a new or original solution of the problem. It can only conclude with the immemorial wisdom of Dante—*La sua voluntade e nostra pace* (In Thy will lies our peace)—and the reiteration of the Christian theme: the freedom of human souls in history is their submission to the law of God.[72]

Finally Toynbee comes to the end, to the coping-stone which is to crown this edifice of different architectural orders, top-heavy cornices, jewel-studded entry-ways, and ponderous Roman facades which is A *Study of History*; he comes to "The Prospects of the Western Civilization." He comes to it reluctantly: "As he took up his pen to write the present Part of this book, the writer was conscious of a sense of distaste for this self-imposed task which was due to something more than a natural shrinking from the obvious hazards of a speculative subject."[73] The reluctance was due to the sense of abandonment of the universal standpoint from which he hoped A *Study in History* had been written, and the special concern for one particular civilization. But Toynbee need not have worried. The parochialism which he acknowledges at this point has been implicit in the work from its sixth volume. Morphologists of culture as he and Spengler both pretend to be, their ultimate subject has always been "the decline of the West." Toynbee's analysis is almost three decades later than Spengler's, but his treatment only spells out in specific political and social detail what Spengler had brilliantly sketched in: the infinite growth of technology, imperialism on the move, the rise of the Asian peoples, class conflict within the body social, and the threat of war without.[74]

But whereas Spengler saw no escape from the impasse, Toynbee is at least willing to hope that "Under the aegis of Religion, Western Man might find himself able to handle with spiritual impunity the material power thrust into his hands by the mechanization of Western technology." He sees a difficult voyage through "The Straits Ahead": "Midway through the twentieth century of the Christian Era the Western Society was in imminent danger of destroying itself by failing to stop making War now that a demonic drive had been put into War by the progress of a Western physical science; and it was in hardly less imminent danger of stultifying itself by seeking asylum from War and Class-Conflict in Circe's pig-sty."[75] Between War and Circe's pigsty, between the Christian heresy of Communism and the stultification of a backward-looking ecclesiastical tradition, Toynbee glimpses a narrow passage. But the curious thing that strikes us as we conclude Toynbee's work is that Spengler's "pessimism" and Toynbee's "hope" inhabit a psychological and emotional climate which are very similar. *The Decline of the West* and *A Study of History* end very much on the same note. Between the lesson of Stoic endurance and the lesson of early Christian humility there is really not much to choose; no more perhaps than we find between Toynbee's gloomy radiance and Spengler's radiant gloom.

6. SPENGLER AND TOYNBEE

The Decline of the West and *A Study of History* are the most penetrating and the most sustained meditations upon the content and the meaning of history which the twentieth century has produced. Spengler believes that by attending to the content of the past through that form of perception which is characteristic of the Western Culture, we may in some sense discover the secret and unveil the essence of human destiny. Toynbee believes that the employment of a patient empiricism will permit us to approach the designs of the Creator, for, however reluctant he might be to affiliate himself with the idealist tradition, he is in spirit a vestigial Hegelian, and his work is a remnant of the view which holds that God reveals Himself in history. History of this sort is not for the scientifically minded gatherer of facts. It belongs in another domain entirely. It belongs with Plato's *Timaeus* rather than Aristotle's *Constitution of Athens*, and with those other poets of the historical imagination who, while not above appealing to the literal histories of other men, take advantage of them by adapting them to uses for which they were never intended—that is, uses connected with the characterization of great epochs and the discovery of types of order throughout vast expanses of historical time.[76] But our age has a fondness for this type of historical philosophy.

Still, the nature of the epochs and the types of order is of a very particular kind. For all their differences, Spengler and Toynbee agree upon one crucial axiom of methodology: that the "Civilization" or the "Culture" is the intelligible unit of historical study. Both abandon the eighteenth and nineteenth-century preoccupation with historical continuity in favor of a theory of periodicity—what might almost be called a quantum theory of historical experience. To Turgot or Hegel, Condorcet or Marx, history might be a progressive crescendo or a fatal lapse, but it was continuous, and its focus was the moving center of the Western world. In one sense this is very cosmopolitan, for it has at its base a Christian generalization concerning the solidarity of all mankind. But in fact it is very provincial, for it is blind to all cultural events which lie outside the narrow compass of Western civilization. When Turgot talks about "humanity," no image of Hittite, Iranian, or Andean enters his head, and when Marx speaks of "man" it is without any interest in the Sinic, Syriac, or Minoan pre-capitalisms. This meant a narrowing of vision, but at the same time a corresponding intimacy of attitude. It meant that eighteenth and nineteenth-century philosophy of history could be written *from the inside.* For the modern philosopher of history with the "world-historical perspective" this is impossible.

We can see this difference very clearly, I think, if we notice for a moment R. G. Collingwood's criticism of Toynbee. It is directed specifically at Toynbee, but it might just as well have been aimed at Spengler—that is, at any contemporary philosopher of history with an interest in "Cultures" and an urge to examine them on their own terms.

The criticism which must be passed on Toynbee's principles is thus twofold. First, he regards history itself, the historical process, as cut up by sharp lines into mutually exclusive parts, and denies the continuity of the process in virtue of which every part overlaps and interpenetrates others. His distinction between societies or civilizations is really a distinction between focal points in the process: he has misunderstood it as a distinction between chunks or lumps of fact into which the process is divided. Secondly, he misconceives the relation between the historical process and the historian who knows it. He regards the historian as the intelligent spectator of history, in the same way in which the scientist is the intelligent spectator of nature: he fails to see that the historian is an integral element in the process of history itself, reviving in himself the experiences of which he achieves historical knowledge. Just as the various parts of the process are misconceived as placed outside one another, so the process as a whole and the historian are placed outside one another. And these two criticisms come in the last resort to the same thing: namely that history is converted into nature, and the past, instead of living in the present as it does in history, is conceived as a dead past, as it is in nature.[77]

Collingwood is right, I think, that for both Toynbee and Spengler "history is converted into nature." This is paradoxical, because both are dominated by a Bergsonian methodology which looks askance at the crude instruments of science, but it fits in perfectly with a pluralistic history which envisages "Civilizations" as case histories and the intuitive historian as the coordinator of their results.

Collingwood's criticism probably does Toynbee's work a graver injustice than it would Spengler's. Even if he has succumbed to the current trend toward comparative morphology, Toynbee is still sufficiently the heir of the eighteenth-century rationalists to look forward to a great task of cultural unification in which the historian performs an important role. An Alexandrian age is profoundly cosmopolitan and intellectualistic, and therefore committed to moral relativism. Spengler expresses this moral relativism but Toynbee does not; instead he has a strong impulse to see the world through the perspective of a Christian unity.

History, seen in this perspective, makes, I feel, the following call upon historians of our generation and of the generations that will come after ours. If we are to perform the full service that we have the power to perform for our fellow human beings—the important service of helping them to find their bearings in a unified world—we must make the necessary effort of imagination and effort of will to break our way out of the prison walls of the local and short-lived histories of our own countries and our own cultures, and we must accustom ourselves to taking a synoptic view of history as a whole.

Our first task is to perceive, and to present to other people, the history of all the known civilizations, surviving and extinct, as a unity. . . .[78]

It is ironic, I think, that the impulse which guides his work is so much at odds with the methodology which he employs.

The Decline of the West and *A Study of History* are vast museums of history, using similar devices of classification and division, but arranged with different ideas in mind and therefore providing somewhat different total impressions. Spengler's exhibits show that history is heavy with fate but free of laws. Those of Toynbee show that history is lawful through and through and that in these laws are to be discovered dimly but surely the Divine teleology. But for all the differences, the exhibits seem to be much alike and to spring from a common source.

When Spengler in the preface to the revised edition of *The Decline of the West* acknowledges his debts, they are above all to Goethe and Nietzsche. When Toynbee, having like Augustine produced a *City of God* in Volumes I-IX of *A Study of History*, adds to this in Volume X his *Confessions*, his acknowledgments are both orthodox and extensive.[79] They include Gibbon, Cyril Bailey, Mommsen, Rostovtzeff, Bury, Zimmern, Bergson, and Plato.

But apart from these overt statements of debt, there are similarities of influence which appear only from a comparison of the works themselves. From this point of view one could isolate four important characteristics of the contemporary philosophy of history: (1) Its root ideas are strikingly akin to those of Bergson. (2) It finds important inspiration in the works of Goethe. (3) Perhaps as a consequence of the first two, it sees poetry and historical study as akin in their reliance upon metaphor. (4) It is dominated by the looming shape of the Classical Culture (and its preoccupation with the idea of disintegration springs largely from an inability to forget what happened to the ancient world).

The influence of Bergson upon Toynbee is profound and direct, and although Spengler shows no direct influence, Nietzsche's impact upon him was bound to produce effects which are Bergsonian. Both men have learned from Goethe. Spengler said: "Goethe gave me method," and Toynbee might have said the same, for from Goethe came the root metaphor which gave substance to both *The Decline of the West* and *A Study of History*. From Goethe Spengler learned the lesson of organicity, of living nature, and on this analogy he constructed his paradigm of Cultures. From Goethe Toynbee learned the lesson of "challenge and response" and on this analogy, given in the prologue to Faust, he interpreted the life-history of his civilizations. Both men were of course profound Hellenists and classical scholars, and upon the concept of the decline and fall of Classical Culture and the analogy which this provides for the modern world the validity of their work really hinges. But in addition, both men are steeped in the very spirit of the classical Greeks. Spengler's mentality is formed upon the image of Heracleitus, and Toynbee's mode of dramatic perception is patterned on the practice of Aeschylus and Sophocles and upon the theory of Aristotle's *Poetics*.

These similarities are dramatic, and it is tempting to dwell upon them, but equally important are their differences. These are partly temperamental, partly ideological. The relationship between Spengler and

Toynbee, the two greatest contemporary philosophers of history, is much like that of Ezra Pound and T. S. Eliot, the two greatest contemporary poets. Like Pound, Spengler is brilliant, temperamental, oriented toward politics, keenly aware of architecture, music, and the arts, ill-tempered, histrionic, outrageous, drawing upon other cultures in a way which is profoundly original. And like Eliot, Toynbee is reserved, mystical, genteel, drawing upon the literatures of the world with a dry pomposity, deeply committed to the drama and to the Church. But of course the profoundest difference is that Spengler, like Pound, is theologically uncommitted, whereas Toynbee, like Eliot, has staked his fate upon the Christian faith. This serves to remind us of how deep in the modern world is the split between the secular and the religious approach to life. Existentialism has long been divided between a Christian and an atheistic branch—Sartre and Heidegger on one side, and Marcel and Jaspers on the other. In Spengler and in Toynbee the contemporary philosophy of history shares this divisive quality of the modern world. The terrible extremes of Spengler's relativistic atheism and Toynbee's obtrusive piety show how even the profound waters of historical prophecy are troubled by the schism in the modern soul.

V

The Inner Life: Sigmund Freud
and His Followers

One rational voice is dumb: over a grave
The household of Impulse mourns one dearly loved.
    Sad is Eros, builder of cities,
    And weeping anarchic Aphrodite.

    W. H. AUDEN, *"In Memory of Sigmund Freud"*

Freud's eye was the microscope of potency.
By fortune, his grey ghost may meditate
The spirits of all the impotent dead, seen clear,
And quickly understand, without their flesh,
How truly they had not been what they were.

    WALLACE STEVENS, *"Mountains Covered with Cats"*

They will get it straight one day at the Sorbonne.
We shall return at twilight from the lecture
Pleased that the irrational is rational.

    WALLACE STEVENS, *"Notes Toward a Supreme Fiction"*

1. THE METHOD OF SCIENCE

When in 1873 at the age of seventeen Sigmund Freud graduated from the Classical Gymnasium and entered the University of Vienna, he was already under the spell of Darwin and Goethe.[1] Darwin was the great iconoclast of nineteenth-century science who broke with the axioms of Cartesian rationalism, denied the dualism between a realm of reasonable human decision and a realm of animal impulse, and therefore destroyed one of those discontinuities in nature which had been elevated into a cherished doctrine by philosophy and religion. Goethe, more poet than natural scientist, but natural scientist none the less, brought to the conception of the natural world a romantic metaphysics which stressed the living questions which man addresses to his world, and the deep feelings through which this world is understood. There is one passage from Goethe's great essay *On Nature* which Freud never forgot.[2] "Nature has neither language nor speech, but she creates tongues and hearts through which she feels and speaks. . . . Her laws are unchangeable—she has few springs of action, but they never wear out; they are always operative, always manifold. . . . Even the most unnatural things are natural. . . . Whoever does not see nature everywhere, does not see her at all. . . . Her crown is love; and only through love can we understand her."

For Freud the romantic conception of nature within this passage was less impressive than the scientific. Freud was the child of the materialism of nineteenth-century science, the materialism of Mach and Helmholtz, which took for granted the assumptions of determinism and physicalism. Nature is subject to universal causal law. There are no cosmic accidents. And the phenomena of biological science are in the end reducible to the elements of physical occurrence. Any attempt to discover Freud's philosophy of culture or his view of the world, any attempt to account for his treatment of the inner life and his image of man, must begin with his life-long commitment to the methodology of natural science.

There have been those who have sensed in Freud a deep romanticism which they thought came to expression in his sense of the role of impulse in human life and his suggestion that there might be irrational ways of knowing competing with the more respectable manifestations of the cognitive process. D. H. Lawrence, always moody and violent in his intellectual reactions, begins with the deepest interest:

Long ago we watched in frightened anticipation when Freud set out on his adventure into the hinterland of human consciousness. He was seeking for the unknown sources of the mysterious stream of consciousness . . . and so who could remain unmoved when Freud seemed suddenly to plunge toward the origins? Suddenly he stepped out of the conscious into the unconscious, out of the everywhere into the nowhere, like some supreme explorer. He walked straight through the wall of sleep, and we hear him rumbling in the cavern of dreams.

But he ends with irony and mistrust:[3]

Psychoanalysts know what the end will be. They have crept in among us as healers and physicians; growing bolder, they have asserted their authority as scientists; two more minutes and they will appear as apostles. Have we not seen and heard the *ex cathedra* Jung? And does it need a prophet to discern that Freud is on the brink of a Weltanschauung?

Were Lawrence's suspicions justified? Had Freud passed from scientific to apostolic authority? And was he indeed on the brink of a *Weltanschauung?*

Ten years after Lawrence asked the question Freud himself turned specifically to its answer. "We will now take a bold step, and risk an answer to a question which has repeatedly been raised in non-analytic quarters, namely, the question whether psycho-analysis leads to any particular *Weltanschauung,* and if so, to what."[4] The word, of course, itself demands a definition. Freud means by it any intellectual construction which serves to give a unified solution to the problems of our existence. Recognizing that such a goal is one of the ideal wishes of mankind because it might provide security in life and certainty in the organization of one's emotions and purposes, he repudiates it at once.

If that is what is meant by a *Weltanschauung,* then the question is an easy one for psycho-analysis to answer. As a specialized science, a branch of psychology—depth psychology or psychology of the unconscious—it is quite unsuited to form a *Weltanschauung* of its own: it must accept that of science in general. The scientific *Weltanschauung* is, however, markedly at variance with our definition. The *unified* nature of the explanation of the universe is, it is true, accepted by science, but only as a programme whose fulfilment is postponed to the future. Otherwise it is distinguished by negative characteristics, by a limitation to what is, at any given time knowable, and a categorical rejection of certain elements which are alien to it. It asserts that there is no other source of knowledge of the universe, but the intellectual manipulation of carefully verified observations, in fact, what is called research, and that no knowledge can be obtained from revelation, intuition or inspiration.

The implications of Freud's uncompromising stand upon the primacy of the method of empirical science are unmistakable. The creations of art and the systems of religion and philosophy have fulfilled certain needs within the lives of human beings. But to grant them standing as knowledge would be to open the door to every form of human irrationality, to place neurosis on the same plane as health, and to drain off for these illusions whatever precious energy can be directed toward reality.

From the point of view of science we must necessarily make use of our critical powers in this direction, and not be afraid to reject and deny. It is inadmissible to declare that science is one field of human intellectual activity, and that religion and philosophy are others, at least as valuable, and that science has no business to interfere with the other two, that they all have an equal claim to truth, and that everyone is free to choose whence he shall draw his convictions and in what he shall place his belief. Such an attitude is considered particularly respectable, tolerant, broad-minded, and free from narrow prejudices. Unfortunately it is not tenable; it shares all the pernicious qualities of an entirely unscientific *Weltanschauung* and in practice comes to much the same thing. The bare fact is that truth cannot be tolerant and cannot admit compromise or limitations, that scientific research looks on the whole field of human activity as its own, and must adopt an uncompromisingly critical attitude towards any other power that seeks to usurp any part of its province.[5]

It seems clear, then, that Lawrence's suspicions concerning a Freudian *Weltanschauung* in the ordinary philosophical sense of that term were groundless. As a profession of faith, Freud's *Weltanschauung* is simply an adherence to the acknowledged principles of nineteenth-century scientific methodology: a more rigorous application of the logic of ordinary thought, the elimination of those interests and emotions which might compromise the most stringent objectivity, a careful examination of the trustworthiness of those immediate sense perceptions upon which experiments are grounded. And it is worthy to note that the two foundations upon which Freud's scientific faith rests are (1) a theory of representative perception and (2) a determinism so pervasive as to encompass all mental phenomena (including those previously considered universally as both "meaningless" and "irrational").

Freud never doubts the assumptions of a realistic epistemology concerning the world. Reality is objective. It is that which exists outside us and independently of us, and the adequacy of scientific knowledge is measurable by the degree to which it corresponds with reality. "This correspondence with the real external world," says Freud,[6] "we call truth. It is the aim of scientific work, even when the practical value of that work does not interest us." What else could be expected from one trained in the physiological laboratory of Ernst Brücke and in Meynert's Institute of Cerebral Anatomy?

In the beginning the theory of a universe dominated by efficient causation also served Freud well. It was derivable from the neurology in which he had been trained, and it permitted him to investigate the mind in such a way as to isolate its psychic *mechanisms*. It was characteristic that Freud should adopt a terminology which shows the residual influence of nineteenth-century physical science, and that he should accept those principles of psychological explanation congruent with a physiological model. Precisely such a view of causation was responsible for his startling views of "the unconscious."

When in the two winter terms of 1915-1916 and 1916-1917 a large mixed audience of students and professors crowded into the lecture room of the Vienna Psychiatric Clinic to hear Freud's Introductory Lectures on Psycho-Analysis, he told them at once candidly and disarmingly that the whole trend of their training and their accustomed modes of thought must inevitably have made them hostile to psychoanalysis. First of all, he said to his audience,[7] you will have been accustomed to learn science through your eyes. You *see* the anatomical specimen, the chemical solution, the muscle contraction which you have purposely stimulated. But in psychoanalysis all this is different. In this mode of treatment nothing happens but an exchange of words between patient and physician. The patient talks, tells of his past experiences, complains, expresses his wishes and his emotions. The physician listens, directs the patient's thought processes, sometimes forces his attention in certain directions, gives him certain explanations, and looks for signs of his understanding and enlightenment. It is all words and symbolic interchange. Worse, it is not publicly verifiable. The dialogue which forms the analysis can have no audience. The process cannot be demonstrated. It can only be reported secondhand.

Now this frank denial of objectivity in the usual sense and of science as the registration of sensations publicly verifiable seems to contradict the previous assumption of truth as "correspondence with the real external world," and Freud hastens to appeal to the sympathy of a physiologically minded audience by asserting that "conceptions of a purely psychological order" may play an important role in bridging the gap between the mystery of the recognizable symptoms of mental disturbance and the identification of the neurological patterns which might explain them. Thus psychoanalysis is striving to provide psychiatry with the psychological connective tissue permitting a correlation of bodily and mental disease.[8]

But Freud goes further. There are two tenets of psychoanalysis, he says, which are offensive to the whole world. The first of these displeasing propositions is that mental processes are essentially unconscious, and that those which are conscious (and which have hitherto defined the totality of psychic life) are merely isolated parts of a deeper and more pervasive total psychic entity. The second offensive proposition is that impulses which can only be described as sexual play a peculiarly large part in the causation of nervous disorders and, indeed, in the whole constellation of normal human motivations. The offensiveness of the second proposition is moral, perhaps even aesthetic, but the offense in the first is probably even greater, for it conflicts with an intellectual prejudice which consists in a pervasive human habit of finding certain human psychological phenomena to be "mysterious," "meaningless," or "inconsequential"—which is in one sense to assert by implication that there is an irreducible surd in human mental behavior, an ultimate irrationality which resists explanation or understanding.

Now, the whole of Freud's Introductory Lectures on Psycho-Analysis is a brilliantly sustained effort to deny this mystery and seeming meaninglessness in human conduct so that through the illumination of the unconsciousness, no gesture, however trivial, no compulsion, however perverse, resists classification as *understandable, motivated* behavior. The strategy which he employs is to train the attention first upon the perplexing errors of everyday life, then upon the generalized dream-life of mankind, and finally upon neurotic symptoms in such a way as to make crystal clear that they are not discontinuous parcels, but localized segments within a broad continuum of behavior having its foundation in the realm of the unconscious. Thus, dream and waking experience, the normal and the pathological in mental life form an ordered series of lawful continuity.

What of those ordinary errors that every healthy person commits, those slips of the tongue or of the pen, that temporary forgetting of names and obligations, that mislaying of objects, and all the other countless mistakes of everyday living? The average man asserts that they are inexplicable accidents. But Freud at once takes him to task as any scientist must. "Does he mean to maintain that there any occurrences so small that they fail to come within the causal sequence of things, that they might as well be other than they are? Anyone thus breaking away from the determination of natural phenomena, at any single point, has thrown over the whole scientific outlook on the world."[9] The alternative is to discover that such mistakes have meaning, that they play a role in our mental economy, and that back of their apparent aimlessness is an unconscious intention or tendency. Our slips of the tongue are compromise formations which result from the mutual interference of two different intentions. One forgets those names which are somehow unpleasant to remember. One loses or "accidentally" breaks objects when there exists some unconscious aggressiveness or resentment against their giver. The very repetitiousness of these experiences displays a persistence which denies the possibility of "chance" and fits in perfectly with the idea of design. On the one hand, we seem to have ideas which are too painful to express directly, but on the other we cannot repress them completely, and they break forth distorted and disguised. Freud's conclusions from this consideration of "the psychopathology of everyday life" are clear:[10]

You can perceive from these examples what the aim of our psychology is. Our purpose is not merely to describe and classify the phenomena, but to conceive them as brought about by the play of forces in the mind, as expressions of tendencies striving towards a goal, which work together or against one another. We are endeavoring to attain a *dynamic conception* of mental phenomena. In this conception, the trends we merely infer are more prominent than the phenomena we perceive. . . . It is important to begin early to reckon with the fact that the mind is an arena, a sort of tumbling-ground for the struggles of antagonistic impulses; or, to express it in non-dynamic terms, that the mind is made up of contradictions and pairs of opposites. Evidence of one particular tendency does not in the least preclude its opposite; there is room for both of them. The material questions are: How do these opposites stand to one another and what effects proceed from one of them and what from the other?

This dynamic conception of mental phenomena which arises out of the consideration of everyday mistakes also is strengthened by the analysis of dreams. Since psychoanalytic technique endeavors to let the person being analyzed provide the answers to his own problems, the assumption is that the dreamer himself should ultimately be able to interpret his own dream. This is accomplished by asking of the dreamer that he relax the rigid mental controls ordinarily structuring the mental life so as to utter whatever comes into his mind in connection with some given element of the dream. This "free association" turns out to be not really so "free" after all, but to engender a whole train of associations which inevitably reveal a hidden goal in whose service the dream functions, thus indicating once again that there is really no aimlessness and indeterminacy in the mental life.

Every dream is a substitute for an unconscious wish. Every dream as remembered and related is but a mask, a manifest content which covers and conceals a latent dream thought. It is characteristic of the repressive economy of the psyche that dream interpretation should encounter resistance, and that those very associations which the dreamer most wishes to keep hidden are the most important for the discovery of the unconscious thought. Every actual dream is a distorted product because the shocking nature of certain unconscious wishes (whether for sexual gratification or revenge) is countered by a dream censorship which omits, modifies, and displaces the accent of the original unconscious material. In fact the very degree of dream distortion is in proportion to the shocking character of the unconscious wish and the prudishness of the censor which controls it.

Distortion is the protective device of an inner critical standard closely allied to the demands of conscious life, and this faculty easily takes moral, aesthetic, and social offense at the radical evil of unrestrained natural desire. But to understand the reality behind the dream distortion, psychoanalysis has produced a specific technique of dream interpretation which finds in all dreams a symbolism which can be deciphered. And the curious thing about this symbolism is that it contains archaic and regressive elements, that is, those which are doubly primitive because they go back at once to the childhood of the individual and to the childhood of the race. Our dream life expresses the unconscious, and the unconscious is largely the residue of infantile mental life with its carefully repressed wishes.

There is perhaps nothing so strange and so mystifying, so expressive of the irrational in man as the infinite variety of neurotic symptoms. One patient experiences the most terrifying attacks of anxiety whenever he sees or is forced to ride in a railroad train. Another has an obsession with cleanliness, and must wash and re-wash his hands in antiseptic soap two or three times each hour. Still a third has a strange delusion that his wife is trying to poison him and will eat nothing unless someone else has tasted it first. It is useless to explain that railroad trains are relatively safe, that the hands are not dirty, that the wife is a benevolent and affectionate spouse. Ideas of this kind are inaccessible to logic and to the facts, and when a delusion does not yield to the facts of reality, then the probabilities are that it does not spring from reality. What else, then, does it spring from?

This is the question with which Freud opens the second series of his lectures on the General Theory of the Neuroses,[11] and the answer which he gives, based not upon a mere speculative system of ideas, but upon a long series of observations of neurotic patients, is that neurotic symptoms, just like errors and dreams, have their own meaning and are functionally related to the life of the person in whom they appear. When the context of past experience and mental predisposition is supplied, delusions are no longer senseless and incomprehensible but logically motivated and sensible according to the emotional experience of the patient. And furthermore it grows clearer that the delusion has arisen as a necessary reaction to another mental process which is revealed by other indications in the course of analysis. The symptom, painful as it may seem on the surface, is a kind of substitute gratification, a consolation for something denied or lost.

The patient's neurotic symptoms are, of course, conscious to him and indeed painfully obvious, but their mental antecedents, their causes, or perhaps better, their motives, are beyond his immediate understanding. This gives the inherent rationale upon which all psychoanalytic treatment is based. Since in every neurosis the meaning of his symptoms is unknown to the sufferer, analysis invariably shows that these symptoms are derived from unconscious mental processes, and under favorable circumstances in the course of psychoanalytic therapy these can be made conscious. For a symptom can only be produced by its unconscious meaning, and as this is brought to consciousness, the symptom disappears.

The difficulty is that the psychoanalytic "bringing to consciousness" of unconscious materials is not a simple intellectual act. It involves not so much the introduction of a cognitive content into the mind as the production of that kind of emotionalized and felt "insight" which comes only through a new integration of experience. The Freudian procedure is designed to break through a rhythm of life grown obsessive,[12] to effect the salvation of the self through a substitution of motive which involves a real purification of identity. The technique through which this is effected is the restoration of the individual memory.

Freud's great discovery was that "insight" or the bringing to consciousness of unconscious materials required a long and arduous process in which all gaps in the patient's memory must be filled in. His enormous experience with the transference neuroses (anxiety-hysteria, conversion-hysteria, and the obsessional neuroses) convinced him that these latter are characterized by amnesias on a grand scale, and that therapy is effective only when, against the most strenuous resistance, the patient is enabled to recall memories (freighted with the utmost painfulness) which are connected with the original production of his neurotic symptoms. The elevation of such unconscious material immediately illuminates the meaning of these symptoms: the experiences and impressions from which they sprang, and the purpose which they have served in the total mental economy of the patient.

The consideration of the mistakes of everyday life, of dreams, of neurotic symptoms leads to a common terminus: the central role of the unconscious in mental life. And, as Freud foresaw,[13] this third assault upon man's rationalistic self-esteem inevitably led to criticism and resentment.

Actually there is a deeper criticism of the theory of the unconscious, which, ironically enough, stems from the presuppositions of the very nineteenth-century scientific *Weltanschauung* which Freud himself embraces. Although the Freudian search for the principles of the inner life has been guided by a respect for empirical evidence, it has ended with a construct not directly but only inferentially established. Here again Freud is disarmingly candid. "You will understand," he says,[14] "that we cannot dispense with the unconscious part of the mind in psychoanalysis, and that we are accustomed to deal with it as with something actual and tangible." But tangible it obviously is not, and actual only in the practical sense that any scientific construct not directly a product of sense perception may account in a systematic and unified way for a series of empirical observations. Toward the end of his life Freud grew more sensitive to criticisms of psychoanalysis from the standpoint of empirical methodology. In the last work of any importance that he wrote (the *Abriss der Psychoanalyse* written in the summer of 1938) he returns somewhat uneasily to the question of empirical validity.[15]

We have adopted the hypothesis of a psychical apparatus, extended in space, appropriately constructed, developed by the exigencies of life, which gives rise to the phenomena of consciousness only at one particular point and under certain conditions. This hypothesis has put us in a position to establish psychology upon foundations similar to those of any other science, such as physics. In our science the problem is the same as in the others: behind the attributes (i.e., qualities) of the object under investigation which are directly given to our perception, we have to discover something which is more independent of the particular receptive capacities of our sense organs and which approximates more closely to what may be supposed to be the real state of things. There is no hope of our being able to reach the latter itself, since it is clear that everything new that we deduce must nevertheless be translated back into the language of our perceptions, from which it is simply impossible for us to set ourselves free. But in this lies the nature and limitation of our science. . . . So we endeavour to increase the efficiency of our sense organs as far as possible by artificial aids; but it is to be expected that such efforts will fail to affect the ultimate result. Reality will always remain "unknowable." What scientific work elicits from our primary sense perceptions will consist in an insight into connections and interdependences which are present in the external world, which can somehow or other be reliably reproduced or reflected in the internal world of our thoughts, and the knowledge of which enables us to "understand" something in the external world, to foresee it and possibly to alter it. Our procedure in psychoanalysis is exactly similar.

It is as though Freud had in the course of his lifetime imperceptibly passed from the epistemology of Locke to the epistemology of Kant without traversing the stage of Hume, which comes in between. Beginning with a representative theory of perception in which "truth" is simple correspondence with the external world (a position which is perfectly adequate to the orientation of a mechanistic biology), he is in his investigations of man's inner life led farther and farther toward the postulation of a psychical apparatus which is not accessible to direct perception. For what is the unconscious but a kind of psychological *ding-an-sich*, a thing-in-itself, metaphysically ultimate and causally efficacious, but beyond the reach of immediate perceptual knowledge? At the end of his life Freud arrives at a Kantian phenomenalism, a distinction between "appearance" and "reality" somewhat at variance with the naive realism and the easy scientific optimism of his youth. For now he cheerfully acknowledges: "Reality will always remain unknowable."

The status of psychoanalytic theory as scientific knowledge in the narrow sense of strict causal determination remains problematic. But it is doubtful whether the enthralled audience which sat in the lecture room of the Vienna Psychiatric Clinic in 1915-1917 raised to itself narrow questions of scientific methodology. "They will get it straight one day at the Sorbonne," wrote Wallace Stevens. But they *had* gotten it straight one day twenty-five years earlier, not at the Sorbonne but in a lecture room of the University of Vienna. And many of those returning at twilight from Freud's last lecture must surely have been, as Stevens puts it, "pleased that the irrational is rational."

2. FREUD'S METAPSYCHOLOGY

Freud's early disavowal of a *Weltanschauung* other than that of the methodology of empirical science was perhaps premature (if not disingenuous), and there was doubtless more to D. H. Lawrence's suspicions than he himself realized. Certainly Freud had no conscious metaphysical ambitions, no intention of constructing a *Weltbild* in the classical model of Hegel or Spinoza. But in a sense he could not avoid it. For psychoanalysis is founded upon a theory of man, *a logic of the soul* in the strictest sense of that phrase, and whenever there arises in any age a new image of man, the theory which presents it becomes a part of the philosophical tradition.

Any image of man has social, political, ethical, even religious consequences, for it affects our standards of human dignity, our beliefs about what is humanly achievable, our conceptions of what is socially to be desired. Any new image of man qualifies the laws we construct, the moral standards by which we judge the fitness of human acts, and the hopes we indulge for the reformation of social disorder. Therefore, although the picture of man may arise within the limited environment of a laboratory, the clinic, or the consulting room, it is, as Jerome Brunner has suggested,[16] *res publica*, and as such not to be changed without wide consideration and public debate. If Freud has become perhaps the chief architect of our present conception of man, then there is all the more reason to see the philosophic implications of his theories and to place them under philosophical criteria.

In all fairness to Freud, however, it must be admitted that he attempted to distinguish his science from his philosophy, his clinical reports from his speculations concerning the cosmic setting within which these might be given a unified interpretation. For him the distinction is not between philosophy and science, but between the case histories of psychoanalysis and the more general and "speculative" theory which he developed to account for them. In his own phraseology it is the difference between psychology and *metapsychology*.[17]

In the end, I do not believe that Freud's distinction between psychology and metapsychology can be sustained, or that we may conceive of him now as scientist, now as philosopher, shifting swiftly and comfortably from role to role with hardly any appreciable dislocation. The philosophy and the science are parts of a single unified enterprise, and if they exist at different levels of analysis, their co-existence yet requires a constant shift back and forth between the psychoanalytic procedure of the physician and the speculative theory of the cosmic biologist and social critic. After all, it is the compulsive repetitions of the neurotic patient which take theory "beyond the pleasure principle" and it is the bitter misery of the melancholic which shows us the death instinct deep in the heart of the superego.

Freud's metapsychology begins in the context of a Darwinian approach to the status of human life within a natural environment. Bergson's speculation about the purposiveness of our mental functions had had a similar genesis. But whereas Bergson concludes with a frankly instrumental view of the development of human intellect in its confrontation with matter, Freud arrives at this point more indirectly, through the initial postulation of a principle of psychological hedonism. "We may put the question," says Freud,[18] "whether a main purpose is discernible in the operation of the mental apparatus; and our first approach to an answer is that this purpose is directed to the attainment of pleasure. It seems that our entire psychical activity is bent upon *procuring pleasure* and *avoiding pain*, that it is automatically regulated by the PLEASURE-PRINCIPLE." But of course this raises a question as much as it provides an answer, for it makes us wonder not only what are the conditions which give rise to the phenomena of pleasure and pain, but also what purposive function they play in the general scheme of animal life. Here it is clear that Freud's acceptance of hedonism comes not from Epicurus, Hobbes, or the usual ethical sources, but from biological theory. For he accepts the view of Fechner that pleasure is connected with the discharge of energy which lessens or extinguishes the stimulating tensions of the psychical apparatus, whereas pain involves the heightening of such tensions and stimulation. The pleasure principle is thus a special case of the biological tendency toward stability. But a moment's consideration will show that although the tendency toward pleasure is strong, from the point of view of the self-preservation of the organism amidst the difficulties of the external world, it is inefficient and may even be highly dangerous.

The sexual instincts are closely allied to the pleasure principle. They are not easily molded, and in most people they retain throughout life this character of obstinacy and inaccessibility to influence which we call "unreasonableness." But the self-preservative or ego instincts comprehend with greater clarity the necessities of organic living. They are more receptive to the frustrations exacted by reality, and they adapt themselves to the mandate of the inevitable. The transition from *the pleasure principle* to *the reality principle* is the great advance in the development of the self, and it shows how closely connected "rationality" is to the demands of an external environment. The neurotic turns away from reality because it is unbearable either in whole or in part, and normalcy as a polar concept testifies to a certain intrinsic fortitude with which one endures the frustrations exacted by reality.

To the natural hedonism of the pleasure principle, the reality principle adds a new concept, that of *the useful*, and certainly the reality principle is conservative in so far as it strives for the protection of the self against damage. The products of culture and civilization are a tribute to this intrinsic conservatism. Religion with its quest for the absolute renunciation of pleasure, science with its intellectualizing of the practical apparatus, education as a patient exercise in instinctual renunciation, all serve reality. But the conquest is never complete. Not only does sexuality remain eternally "unreasonable" (a kind of restless internal proletariat ever ready to break forth in rebellion), but also it mobilizes in its service that part of the mental apparatus which remains free from the testing of reality and subordinated to the pleasure principle: the act of fantasy-making which has abandoned dependence upon real objects and hence remains a dark center of potential anarchy.

The dualistic assumption which underlies the Freudian metapsychology is typical of Freud's theoretical formulations, but its chief virtue is that it indicates the mode of socialization which transforms the human individual as an impulsive animal mirroring the chaotic irrationality of the universe into the purposive agent exercising rational choice. As such it mediates between the Cartesian and Darwinian pictures of the human person, whose conflict underlies the intellectual dilemmas of the modern world.

The transformation of the pleasure principle into the reality principle requires a profound modification of the original instinctual structure of man, a deflection of impulse from its original goal and an inhibition of its primal aim. It means that immediate satisfaction must be sacrificed to delayed, spontaneous freedom to repression, enjoyment to security, play to work, intrinsically interesting fantasy to useful productivity. For the unrestrained pleasure principle comes into conflict with the environment constituted by nature and society. That brute necessity at the heart of things which the Greeks expressed physically as matter and ethically as fate reappears in the formulation of Freud as *a cultural a priori* to whose mandates the biological individual must conform. It is the price which he pays for the realization of his humanity.

The conflict between man's original animal nature and the cultural *a priori* can be studied in the growth of the individual to maturity or in the transformations of primitive into civilized societies. But in either case the struggle expresses itself as *a limitation of satisfactions*. When the reality principle slowly begins to win its war of attrition against somatic pleasure, tensions remain, whether in the latent powers of social violence or in the individual unconscious. And behind these tensions, built into the very structure of organic life, lie those permanent somatic demands which are the ultimate cause of all activity. They are the deepest drives, the final wells of impulse. Freud calls them instincts.[19]

In his earlier formulation Freud proposed the distinction between two groups of primal instincts: the "self-preservative" or "ego" instincts, and the "sexual" instincts. But he put forward the suggestion lightly, calling it merely an auxiliary construction to be retained only so long as it proves useful rather than a necessary postulate. He admitted that while the concept of a conflict between the claims of the ego and sexuality had been derived from the transference neuroses whose origin it clarifies, it was always possible that exhaustive study of the narcissistic neuroses might oblige the formula to be altered.[20] Still, the formula was congruent with the biological distinction between the individual and the species. And of course the Freudian formula can be conceived as a psychological analogue of the metaphysical opposition which Schopenhauer had discovered between the undifferentiated "Will" and the "principle of individuation."

But Freud was not concerned with metaphysics but with psychoanalytic investigation. What first forced itself upon his attention, therefore, was not the immutability of the instincts, but their vicissitudes. An inquiry into these vicissitudes (particularly those of the sexual instincts) provides insight into the great psychic mechanisms: "reversal into the opposite," sometimes called "ambivalence," where love turns into hate; "turning upon the self," where an aggressiveness formerly directed sadistically outward turns masochistically inward; "repression," where instinctual claims are driven into the underground of the unconscious; and "sublimation," where a dangerous impulse is turned into a harmless or approved channel of expression. The existence of these mechanisms is a testimony to the involutions of instinctual expression, to that quaint necessity of civilized life which prevents instinct from pursuing its straightforward course, and to the paradox that although the instincts are the primitive material of every self, it is yet necessary for the safety of every self that it mobilize its defenses against them.

The experience of ambivalence is of particular importance, for it not only denies a logic of strict contradiction, but also leads Freudian instinct theory from an original opposition of ego and sexuality to a transitional opposition of love and hatred. Love is not conceived by Freud as a special component of sexuality. He prefers to regard it rather as the whole sexual current of feeling. But loving admits of many antitheses, and Freud (in language which strongly calls to mind the philosophical distinctions of Plato's *Lysis* and *Symposium*) suggests that we shall perhaps come to a better understanding of the manifold opposites of loving if we remember that mental life as a whole is governed by the three basic polarities of *subject and object, pleasure and pain, activity and passivity*. These three polarities within the mind are connected in various highly significant ways, but particularly in the relation of the subject to pain.

The ego hates, abhors and pursues with intent to destroy all objects which are for it a source of painful feelings, without taking into account whether they mean to it frustration of sexual satisfaction or of gratification of the needs of self-preservation. Indeed, it may be asserted that the true prototypes of the hate-relation are derived not from sexual life, but from the struggle of the ego for self-preservation and self-maintenance.[21]

Here we see that love and hate stand in no very simple relation to one another, do not originate in the cleavage of a common primal element, but rather spring from the different sources of ego and sexuality.

In 1920 Freud was forced to revise his earlier formulation of the ego and the sexual instincts. The revision came about through the necessity of a somewhat different approach to the pleasure principle. The dramatic manifestations of "a compulsion to repeat" in the events of psychoanalytic treatment seemed to exhibit in high degree an *instinctual* character, and, since this compulsion was in obvious opposition to the pleasure principle, it seemed to manifest an outside force at work. But how is "the compulsion to repeat" an expression of the instinctual? Freud's answer was both deceptively simple and at the same time revolutionary.

At this point we cannot escape a suspicion that we may have come upon the track of the universal attribute of the instincts and perhaps of organic life in general which has not hitherto been clearly recognized or at least not explicitly stressed. It seems, then that an instinct is a compulsion inherent in organic life to restore an earlier state of things which the living entity has been obliged to abandon under the pressure of external disturbing forces; that is, it is a kind of organic elasticity, or, to put it in another way, the expression of the inertia inherent in organic life.[22]

This view of instinct is profoundly disturbing because, whereas it is usual to consider the instincts as drives toward change and development, we are now asked to recognize in them exactly the opposite, that is, to see them as an expression of the underlying conservatism of living things. For a theory of evolution which hinges upon the push toward a creative future, it is paradoxical to insist that organic instincts which are historically acquired tend actually toward the restoration of an earlier state of biological existence. But it is so nevertheless. Every living thing dies for *internal* reasons and in death becomes inorganic once again. We are thus compelled to say that the goal of all life is death and that what was inanimate existed before what is living.

It is clear that Freud's biological presuppositions are precisely the same as Bergson's and, indeed, that both are the literate sons of the Darwinian revolution. For each believes that the attributes of life were at a certain moment evoked in inert matter by the action of a force of whose exact nature we can form no conception. And each believes in the developmental rise of consciousness in a particular stream of living matter. The progressive series—matter, life, mind—which summarizes the course of emergent evolution conditions at once Bergson's account of intuition and Freud's theory of the instincts. It is natural that this should be so, for both owe much to a doctrine of biological time which stresses the creative advance into the future. But such a theory of time also takes its mechanistic revenge, for, particularly in Freud, it makes psychology in the truest sense a species of *natural history*. For Freud a genetic account of origins is always a method of explanation.

If, reasons Freud, life grows out of matter, then the living thing is under a constant compulsion to return to the inanimate state, and, indeed, this must remain even for conscious human beings the first of the instincts.

The hypothesis of self-preservative instincts such as we attribute to all living beings, stands in marked opposition to the idea that instinctual life as a whole serves to bring about death. Seen in this light, the theoretical importance of the instincts of self-preservation, of self-assertion and of mastery greatly diminishes. They are component instincts whose function it is to assure that the organism shall follow its own path to death, and to ward off any possible ways of returning to inorganic existence other than those which are immanent in the organism itself. We have no longer to reckon with the organism's puzzling determination (so hard to fit into any context) to maintain its own existence in the face of every obstacle. What we are left with is the fact that the organism wishes to die only in its own fashion. Thus these guardians of life, too, were originally the myrmidons of death. Hence arises the paradoxial situation that the living organism struggles most energetically against events (dangers, in fact) which might help it to attain its life's goal rapidly—by a kind of short-circuit. Such behavior is however precisely what characterizes instinctual as contrasted with intelligent efforts.[23]

But this presents only one side of the picture. For the germ cells, distinguishable from the organism as a whole and seeking to unite with other germ cells in the production of a new organism, therefore work against the death of the living substance and succeed in winning for it at least a potential immortality. Each animal body, itself doomed to death, carries within its protecting envelope the seeds which comprise the true life instincts. These operate against the death instincts and thus yield the biological opposition which lies back of the economy of the mental life.

It is as though the life of the organism moved with a vacillating rhythm. One group of instincts rushes forward so as to reach the final goal of life as swiftly as possible; but when a particular stage in the advance is reached, the other group jerks back to a certain point to make a fresh start and so prolong the journey. And even though it is certain that sexuality and the distinction between the sexes did not exist when life began, the possibility remains that the instincts which were later to be described as sexual may have been in operation from the very first, and it may not be true that it was only at a later time that they started upon their work of opposing the activities of the 'ego instincts.'[24]

The upshot of this inquiry is not merely the drawing of a sharp distinction between the ego instincts and the sexual instincts, but the posing of a view of the world whose radical dualism possesses almost a Manichean flavor. As Ezra Pound expresses it:

> Life and death are now equal.
> Strife is between light and darkness.
> (Canto LII)

Is this view of cosmic polarity too manifestly romantic? Has Freud been led by the compulsiveness of his dualistic mode of perception into a metaphysical lapse which passes the bounds of all biological and psychological sobriety? The answer is not absolutely clear. But it is certain that Freud himself was not unconscious of the direction in which his thought was tending.

Let us pause for a moment [he says] over this preeminently dualistic view of instinctual life. According to E. Hering's theory, two kinds of processes are constantly at work in living substance, operating in contrary directions, one constructive or assimilatory and the other destructive or dissimilatory. May we venture to recognize in these two directions taken by the vital processes the activity of our two instinctual impulses, the life instincts and the death instincts? There is something else, at any rate, that we cannot remain blind to. We have unwittingly steered our course into the harbour of Schopenhauer's philosophy. For him death is the true result and to that extent the purpose of life, while the sexual instinct is the embodiment of the will to live.[25]

But if Freud has unwittingly steered his course into the harbor of Schopenhauer's philosophy, it is for momentary refuge only, and he quickly steers it out again, mistrustful of so monistic a haven. For if (as has so often been recognized) there is a similarity between the pessimism of the two men, and in both cases a somber realism which seeks to rend the veil of human illusion,[26] still, the difference between Schopenhauer's voluntaristic monism and Freud's implacable dualism sets them apart, not only in their perception of the radical evil in human life, but in their attitude toward its treatment and possible cure. Surely what has taken Freud "beyond the pleasure principle" to the instincts of Eros and destruction is neither an abundantly developed sense of drama nor a romantic metaphysics, but a serious speculative enterprise in the field of general biology.

Of course, libido theory cannot be taken too far. For if one holds that the powerful compulsion of libidinal energy informs both the sexual instincts and the self-preservative instincts, then one would have arrived at the innovation (mistaken) of Jung, whose error is that he uses the word "libido" to mean instinctual force in general. Freud specifically denies the monism of Jung as he would have denied the monism of Schopenhauer. The sharp opposition of the instincts of life and death renders such a monism untenable.

Yet it may be the case that whether stated monistically or dualistically, what is really important here is the biological orientation which finds in the crucial characteristics of living organisms a clue both to creativity and the mechanisms of the mental life. Bergson too, like Jung, was a species of monist, for he found in the *élan vital* an original impetus from which all life springs, a current of energy passing through all the individuated forms of life. But though stated in this "monistic" fashion, Bergson's theory is, with one very slight change, virtually identical with Freud's. For Bergson also inorganic nature preceded living, and the inertness of matter was a constant peril awaiting its opportunity to overcome the forces of life. The threat of the relapse into torpor is Bergson's analogue of Freud's death instinct, just as his *élan vital* is Eros personified. The difference is that whereas for Bergson the life instinct courses through the biological creature and the threat of relaxation is symbolized by the external world of matter, Freud has internalized them both.

The aim of *Eros* is to bind together, to preserve by fusion, to establish ever greater unities. The aim of *Thanatos* is to disperse, to undo connections, to destroy things. The life instinct aims at organic complexity, the death instinct at inorganic atomicity. But although they are to be analytical distinguished, all actual experience is both a conflict and a compromise between these two trends. War and artistic creation, melancholia and mania, procreation and suicide are the two sides of an eternal dialectic which rages in the cell, in the psychology, and in the society. But it is a dialectic in which the two extremes mutually imply one another. Herbert Marcuse has put it well:[27] "Freud's metapsychology is an ever-renewed attempt to uncover and to question the terrible necessity of the inner connection between civilization and barbarism, progress and suffering, freedom and unhappiness—a connection which reveals itself ultimately as that between Eros and Thanatos."

The strife of opposites is the stuff of which drama is made, and a Manichean struggle between Eros and Thanatos which reaches down into the very chemistry of the cell is bound to stimulate the dramatic appetite whether in the social or in the cosmic theater. But the Freudian drama does not merely stress the opposition of love and destruction; it also insists upon their inner connection. At this point there is a hint of the essential character of tragedy. According to the tragic attitude, good and evil, even life and death necessarily imply one another.[28] The more intensely the tragic hero appreciates the good, the more intensely will he suffer from the evil. The more drastic his fall from prosperity, the deeper becomes the self-awareness and insight into the premises of his fall. And surely it is a tragic predicament when men in society are simultaneously attracted and repelled by creativity, love, and even life itself.

But in the tragic sense of life implied by Freud's instinct theory is to be found the seed of an important psychological principle. If the work of the tragic dramatist posits the opposition between good and evil or life and death, it is only that it may establish an inevitable order between them within the work of art. This ordering or organic unification has value in its own right. The principle of harmony is not entirely absent from Freud's metapsychology. It finds its chief application in his anatomy of the self.[29]

The theory of the mental personality with which Freud's metapsychology concludes is the inevitable climax of the empirical development of psychoanalytic experience. That experience begins with the symptoms of the patient, which are intelligible only as the substitute for wishes deeply repressed in the unconscious. Consideration of the anatomy of the unconscious leads to the theory of the biological grounding of the unconscious in the two original instincts. The mediating link between the amorphous instinctual equipment and the acts of the social self is the structure of the mental personality.

This structure of the mental personality consists, according to Freud, of three parts: the *id*, the *ego*, and the *superego*. The first is the great representative of instinct. It is that which each individual experiences in himself as biological need, as imperative impulse, as the reservoir of the passions. The second is the administrative self, the regulative function engaged in the testing of reality, and it is, therefore, according to Hegel's famous equation, that part of the self in which inheres man's substantive rationality. The third is experienced as ego-ideal, as moral principle, as conscience, as those socially acquired inhibitions which limit the expressions of natural impulsiveness. Freud's anatomy of the self is thus the expression of a theory of personality which combines the archaic heritage of the biologically given, the individuality which arises through the earliest family experiences of the child, and the moral education which is the outcome of the demands of society. Passion, reasonableness, the sense of obligation are, therefore, the stuff of which every self is made.

Of the three elements, the id is the most mysterious, most foreign to the ego and to our waking consciousness. The enigma of selfhood is generally most intimately connected with its peculiar nature. Freud himself can hardly describe it except in negative terms.[30]

You must not expect me to tell you much that is new about the id, except its name. It is the obscure inaccessible part of our personality; the little we know about it we have learnt from the study of dream-work and the formation of neurotic symptoms, and most of that is of a negative character, and can only be described as being all that the ego is not. We can come nearer to the id with images, and call it a chaos, a cauldron of seething excitement. We suppose that it is somewhere in direct contact with somatic processes, and takes over from them instinctual needs and gives them mental expression, but we cannot say in what substratum this contact is made. These instincts fill it with energy, but it has no organization and no unified will, only an impulsion to obtain satisfaction for the instinctual needs, in accordance with the pleasure-principle. The laws of logic—above all, the law of contradiction—do not hold for processes in the id. Contradictory impulses exist side by side without neutralizing each other or drawing apart; at most they combine in compromise formations under the overpowering economic pressure towards discharging their energy. There is nothing in the id which can be compared to negation, and we are astonished to find in it an exception to the philosopher's assertion that space and time are necessary forms of our mental acts. In the id there is nothing corresponding to the idea of time, no recognition of the passage of time, and (a thing which is very remarkable and awaits adequate attention in philosophic thought) no alteration of mental processes by the passage of time.

There is something acutely disturbing about this conception of the id, for it suggests that there is a part of the mental personality which is forever beyond the reach of civilization and its domesticating tendencies. For, of course, the id knows no ethical values. It is beyond good and evil, wholly without morality because the pleasure-principle which dominates all its processes seeks only the discharge of instinctual tensions. Also it is blind, without any focused method of showing either love or hate. "It cannot say what it wants; it has achieved no unity of will. Eros and the death-instinct struggle within it."[31] Beyond the ordering structures of space and time, outside the rules of logic and the imperatives of the moral life, a battleground for the bloody struggle of the instincts, it is an irreducible surd of animality upon which the human superstructure is reared. To the reasonable ego and to the moralistic superego it is indeed an acutely disturbing idea, but perhaps in the end this biological primacy is a liberating idea as well. For it proposes that culture is not all-powerful, that there is a residue within personality which is beyond the control of civilization, and that this ineradicable power may be the last refuge of an individuality battered and torn in the modern world by the demands of a coercive sociality.

Sociality is coercive not only because it demands the conformity of the individual to norms which it imposes. Its most subtle form of coercion lies in its creation of the individual's superego, a process in which moral demands originating outside the self are at a certain stage of the child's development internalized in such a way that they seem to originate in the very depths of the self and to have been there always. The superego performs a judicial function, for it has taken over the power, the aims, even the methods of parental authority.[32] But its selection has been one-sided. It has chosen only the harshness and severity of the parents, their preventive and punitive functions. Naturally! For it is in the exercise of these functions that they express the trusteeship of society. The superego is at once the seat of the conscience and the compulsive authority for human ideals. It is morally restricting, but it is at the same time the advocate of whatever impulse toward perfection is to be discerned in human life. The superego retains throughout its lifetime the character of the stern and the demanding father, and it is the foundation of an ego-ideal which admits no compromise with laxness or mediocrity. In consequence all self-judgment which declares that one's ego falls short of its ideal produces, as Freud says, that sense of worthlessness which every religious believer manifests before his god. And every incongruity between the demands of conscience and the actual attainments of the ego is experienced as a sense of guilt.

But what, indeed, is the ego? And how is it related on the one hand to man's instinctual original nature and on the other to society's coercive demands? If the id is the representative of man's animal nature, and the superego is the internalized agent of society, then it can be said that the ego is the representative of inherent individuality, and that it plays a mediating role in the psychical apparatus. Whereas the id is chaotic and the superego is compulsive, the ego is capable of deliberation and to some extent of control. For it provides in every individual *the coherent organization* of the mental processes. The role of the ego is protective. It has taken over the task of representing the external world to the self, its dangers and its threats. It must therefore build an image of reality through the organs of perception and of memory and guide the activities of the self in the light of this image. The ego controls the pathway to activity, and it does so by interposing between the immediate desire and the eventual act the whole procrastinating factor of thought and deliberation. In this way it modifies the immediacy of our instinctual nature. It controls the pleasure principle, which is the driving force of the id, and regulates it by the reality principle, which is consequent upon its own external perceptions. In this way it secures the safety and adaptation of the organism.

Unlike the id, the ego exists in time, constitutes in fact those very forms of perception (space and time) which Kant attributed to the understanding. But what especially seems to characterize the ego is (as Kant also remarked) a tendency to synthesize its own contents, to unify and bring together the mental processes. There is something here that we have heard before. In fact the tripartite division of an impulsive id, a demanding superego, and an organizing ego is not unlike the tripartite psychology of Plato—a psychology from which one derives a principle of harmonious integration as constituting the health of the soul. For Plato this is possible, for he sees in the rationality of the ego a principle of administration which is powerful as well as reasonable and which can harmonize the discords of the self through the very potency of its natural claim. But, unfortunately for the unity of the self, Freud does not read the signs in this fashion.

The fact is that the ego (instead of the harmonizing authority which Plato believed it to be) is a poor creature, subservient to three masters and therefore menaced by three dangers. These are respectively the objective dangers of the external world, the perpetual threat of the residual passions, the cruel severity of the sense of guilt. Faced by these dangers, the ego lacks the confidence to be strong and single-minded. Now it compromises its ethical ideal before external pressure; a moment later it submits to some nameless passion. Caught between the id, the superego, and reality, it is opportunistic, sycophantic, and false to itself.

In this way, goaded on by the id, hemmed in by the super-ego, and rebuffed by reality, the ego struggles to cope with its economic task of reducing the forces and influences which work in it and upon it to some kind of harmony; and we may well understand how it is that we so often cannot repress the cry: "Life is not easy." When the ego is forced to acknowledge its weakness, it breaks out into anxiety: reality anxiety in face of the external world, normal anxiety in face of the superego, and neurotic anxiety in face of the strength of the passions of the id.

We have now returned to our starting-point. The wheel has come full circle. From the neurotic symptoms we have (through the unconscious, the psychic economy, and the instincts) derived the self. From the structure of the self (that weak but good-hearted ego trying vainly to establish its ordered harmony over the residual self) we have arrived once more at the neurotic symptom. But in our roundabout journey we have again proved that Plato's ancient insight was indeed correct. Sickness in the mind is the result of conflict. Harmony and integration are the health of the soul. This leads to the psychoanalytic therapy and to that unspoken social compact which sets in motion the analytic transaction.

Our plan of cure is based upon these views. The ego has been weakened by the internal conflict; we must come to its aid. The position is like a civil war which can only be decided by the help of an ally from without. The analytical physician and the weakened ego of the patient, basing themselves upon the real external world, are to combine against the enemies, the instinctual demands of the id, and the moral demands of the superego.

We form a pact with each other. The patient's sick ego promises us the most complete candor, promises that is, to put at our disposal all the material which his self-perception provides; we, on the other hand, assure him of the strictest discretion and put at his service our experience in interpreting material that has been influenced by the unconscious. Our knowledge shall compensate for his ignorance and shall give his ego once more mastery over the lost provinces of his mental life. This pact constitutes the analytic situation.[33]

The meaning of the psychoanalytic therapy is the strengthening of a weakened ego by an increase in the ego's self-knowledge. The work is difficult, for the restoration of memory is constantly resisted.[34] But the value of the Freudian therapeutic effort is that it is the perfection of a technique for being frank which lies beyond any merely conscious motivation or censorship. In the end the hope is that an ego, at first no longer able to fulfil the task imposed upon it by the external world, its activity inhibited by the strictures of the superego, its energies sapped and consumed by vain efforts to keep the demands of the id at bay, will regain its wholeness and unity of aim, no longer split by discordant impulses and hopeless conflicts.

The intervention of the analyst is not always a success. The Manichean struggle for the patient's soul is often doubtful, depending as it does upon quantitative factors—upon the amount of energy which can be mobilized within the patient to his own advantage, as against those forces working against him. "Here once again," says Freud, "God is on the side of the big battalions. It is true that we do not always succeed in winning, but at least we can usually see why it is that we have not won."

The father of the psychoanalytic movement was an impatient man. Also he was deeply moralistic. (The story goes that he rushed from the consulting room one day shouting: "*Warum soll ich solcher Schweinerei zuhören?*" [Why must I listen to such nastiness?]). His moralism predominates in his account of the aim of the therapeutic efforts.[35] "For their object is to strengthen the ego, to make it more independent of the super-ego, to widen its field of vision, and so to extend its organization that it can take over new portions of the id. Where id was, there shall ego be." But he added impatiently: "It is reclamation work, like the draining of the Zuyder Zee."

3. THE ATTACK ON CIVILIZATION

Freud, like Goethe and like Leonardo, was one of those gifted individuals lured both by the exact sciences and by the humanistic arts. As a schoolboy he confesses that his curiosity was "directed more towards human concerns than towards natural objects." His subsequent choice of a medical career, although ultimately coming to rest in the psychiatry which is the most humane of the biological arts, only resolved the tension paradoxically, for it required of him that he should treat "human concerns" as though they were indeed "natural objects." But in *An Autobiographical Study* he tells of that rebirth of the repressed humanism of his youth which returned after he was seventy, of "an alteration in myself, with what might be described as a phase of regressive development."[36]

My interest, after making a lifelong *détour* through the natural sciences, medicine and psycho-therapy, returned to the cultural problems which had fascinated me long before, when I was a youth scarcely old enough for thinking. At the very climax of my psycho-analytic work in 1912, I had already attempted in *Totem and Taboo* to make use of the newly discovered findings of analysis in order to investigate the origins of religion and morality. I now carried this work a stage further in two later essays, *The Future of an Illusion* (1927) and *Civilization and Its Discontents* (1930). I perceived ever more clearly that the events of human history, the interactions between human nature, cultural development and the precipitates of primaeval experiences (the most prominent example of which is religion) are no more than a reflection of the dynamic conflicts between the ego, the id, and the super-ego, which psycho-analysis studies in the individual—are the very same processes repeated upon a wider stage.

Again it reminds us a little of Bergson, who twenty-five years after *Creative Evolution* published *The Two Sources of Morality and Religion*. Likewise, after the crucial formulations of his metapsychology, come Freud's own reflections upon religion and culture. Throughout his scientific lifetime he has been asking question after question about symptom formation, psychological structure, therapeutic procedure. Now he wishes for more generalized answers. Perhaps he wants to grasp the meaning of community life as a whole and to make a psychoanalysis of the epoch. But at any rate the procedure which we may expect is less formal than metaphorical. We are back at the procedure of Plato's *Republic*. Culture is the projection of the self. The civilization is the individual "writ large."

We may begin, philosophically, with the question of the meaning and purpose of life, not as religion formulates it, but as it reveals itself in the behavior of men, as they express their demands and reveal their wishes. The answer is clear.[37] Men seek happiness. But if the pleasure principle gives the program of life's purpose, and if from the beginning it (as we have seen) dominates the mental apparatus, yet it is doomed to failure and frustration. For it is in conflict with the whole world. "It simply cannot be put into execution, the whole constitution of things runs counter to it; one might say the intention that man should be happy is not included in the scheme of Creation."[38] Here is the ultimate source of the Freudian pessimism: that "necessity" in the struggle for life which ordains the frustration which shall be exacted by reality.

The possibilities of happiness are limited from the very beginning by the constitution of the self and by the curious world in which it is doomed to live. Suffering comes from three quarters: from the human body, destined for death, which slowly decays with the warning signals of pain and anxiety; from the world of nature and its constant threats; and finally from the world of social living, the relations with other men, which perhaps are a more painful source than any of the others and according to Freud no less inevitable.

It is surely little wonder if under the pressure of these necessities the moral economy becomes transformed, human demands and expectations are reduced, and the pleasure principle changes into the more easy-going reality principle. But this transformation enthrones a new moral strategy. Effort is henceforth devoted not to the acquisition of pleasure, but to the avoidance of pain. Every search for moral wisdom has concluded with a recommendation for performing this task. Unbridled gratification of desire may be the most alluring guide to life but the art of life entails the preference of caution to enjoyment, and its various recommendations are therefore directed against the different sources of suffering.

Voluntary loneliness in isolation from others is a search for peace which is aimed against the unhappiness of human relations. Combining with the human community under the guidance of science is a method for subjugating the threats of nature. But the most interesting methods for averting pain are those which are aimed at the organism itself. Intoxication can so alter the conditions of perceptivity that we become insensible to the disagreeable; its virtue is that it negates pain through granting us a certain independence of the external world. Another type of escape seeks to control the internal sources of our needs; it operates by a systematic annihilation of the instincts as advocated by the wisdom of the East. A similar, though less extreme, form of the abandonment of direct instinctual gratification comes through sublimation, that is, by transferring the instinctual aims into such channels as will not be frustrated by the outer world. This latter succeeds best when there is a heightening of the ability to obtain pleasure from intellectual and creative work. The artist's joy in creation through the embodiment of erotic fantasy and the scientist's involvement in the solution of problems or the discovery of truth is so absorbing that it almost places art and science beyond the domination of Fate. Almost, but not quite.

The difficulty with this method of flight from pain is that it is not widely available; it is a gift of the few. For the many there is, of course, work. Freud sees work as culturally valuable not merely as indispensable for subsistence, but also because it provides discharge for those impulses (narcissistic, aggressive, even erotic) which otherwise might alienate the individual from reality and from the mainstream of his society.[38]

The last escapes from pain are, characteristically enough, more loosely connected with reality. In fact satisfaction is obtained through a conscious commitment to illusion. One kind comes through the enjoyment of works of art, through a contemplation of form which is obviously cut off from all contact with reality. It is the devotion to the Platonic idea of things for its own sake which Schopenhauer sensed as the essence of aesthetic appreciation. But as narcosis aesthetic appreciation is weak. It is (as both Freud and Schopenhauer saw) but a temporary refuge from the cruelties of life. Its effect is too weak to outlaw real suffering. Each of us in his own way makes some individual use of the instruments of illusion. Some substitute a mild illusion or wish-fulfilment for an aspect of the real world which is unbearable. Others band together and try to obtain the assurance and protection from suffering by that "delusional transformation of reality" which Freud calls religion. And of course a last (and by no means negligible) method of dealing with life remains. It is the flight into neurotic illness.

Isolation, intoxication, intellectuality, work, art, religion, neurosis: the Freudian catalogue of remedies against the sufferings of mankind reads like Schopenhauer's anthology of the human condition. The second chapter of Civilization and Its Discontents appears like a condensed version of the last two books of The World as Will and Idea. But Freud offers us here no ultimate metaphysical explanation like Schopenhauer's. If we ask why is it so hard for mankind to be happy, the answer is factual and clear: because of the superior forces of nature; because of the disposition of our bodies to decay; because of the pitful inadequacy of our methods of regulating human relations in the family, the community, and the state.

With respect to the first two we are willing to submit to the inevitable. But when we approach the third we come face to face with a certain irritability in human nature which baffles us. For there are some individuals who seem to hold that civilization itself is to blame for much of our misery, and who like Rousseau or Thoreau consider that we should be better off if we lived amidst more primitive conditions. Moreover, many who do not preach this creed as a philosophy hold to it in some quiet niche of their unconscious. Why is it that so many people have adopted this strange attitude of hostility to civilization?

The psychoanalytic experience in individual cases has provided the clue to an answer. For here "it was found that men become neurotic because they cannot tolerate the degree of privation that society imposes on them in virtue of its cultural ideals."[39] Civilization demands cleanliness and order in the lives of men. It sets a superior value upon the higher mental faculties and concedes a leading role to religious and ethical ideals. Above all, it sets radical limits to the sexual life of the individual, and this can so seriously cripple sexual response as to inhibit the functioning of the entire pleasure mechanism of the person. As a young man of twenty-four writing at Paris in the springtime André Gide noted in his *Journal*:[40] "That ethic of privation had so thoroughly established itself as my natural rule of conduct that the other is now very painful and difficult for me. I have to urge myself to pleasure. It is painful for me to be happy."

It is little wonder then that "every individual is virtually an enemy of culture,"[41] and that there remains a deep resentment against a civilization which has been built up on coercion and renunciation of instinct. For whether one looks at the development of the individual or at the historical genesis of society itself, this is the picture presented:

Human life in communities only becomes possible when a number of men unite together in strength superior to any single individual and remain united against all single individuals. The strength of this united body is then opposed as 'Right' against the strength of any individual, which is condemned as 'brute force.' This substitution of the power of a united number for the power of a single man is the decisive step towards civilization. The essence of it lies in the circumstance that the members of the community have restricted their possibilities of gratification, whereas the individual recognized no such restrictions.[42]

A state of lawful society to which each has contributed by making some sacrifice of his own desires leaves none at the mercy of brute force to be sure, but it can hardly avoid some residue of the desire for freedom; a vestigial desire no doubt, originating in the primitive roots of the personality, but still somehow undomesticated by civilizing influences and permanently waiting its time to break forth afresh and express its antagonism to culture. If the state of nature without[43] has been overcome by some Hobbesian expedient of a social contract, the state of nature within—the eternal presence of the instincts—remains a constant source of that irritable conflict between the individual and his society of which Freud was so continuously aware.

The study of civilization is a study of the forms of expression of the instincts, of their repression, sublimation, transformations. Since it is impossible to ignore the extent to which civilization is built up through a process of renouncing the gratification of the instincts, it follows that there is a contradiction lying deep within the structure of civilization itself. Cultural privation dominates the entire field of social relations. But this same cultural privation is the cause of the latent and eternal antagonism against which all civilization has to fight. To what influence does this conflict owe its origin?

There is no question that the similarities between Freud and Hobbes are striking. Both utilize a state of nature, both see its destructive force overcome by a species of social contract which displaces a scattered power constellation by the authority of a sovereign. But there the similarity ends. For Hobbes' account is predicated upon a rational assessment of self-interest, whereas Freud bases everything upon a primal crime.[44]

In primaeval times men lived in small primitive hordes. In each a strong male was master and *father* to the whole, unlimited in his power, which he used brutally. All females were his property, wives and daughters alike. The lot of a son was hard. If he aroused the father's fear or jealousy, he was killed, castrated, or driven out. But a decisive change takes place in this type of social organization through the hatred of the sons for the father. Banding together, they form a pact, murder the father and then eat his body. This is the same ambivalent emotional attitude which marks the eternal relations of fathers and sons. They hate his domination but they admire his strength, and after his death they seek to identify themselves with his power.

The killing of the primal father introduces a new organization of society—a union among the brothers, consolidated by the memory of the deed of liberation they had achieved together. In their compact (in which they all agree to renounce unrestrained gratification) is a recognition of mutual obligations toward peace and order, in short, is the foundation of morality and law. But there is a paradox here. For although morality and law are rational enough in themselves, their origin is a deed which its authors recognized as a crime. Regretting the deed and deciding that it should not be repeated, they invoked the sanctions of law. Thus the motivation for civilized order is remorse rooted in the sense of guilt of sons who have committed a nameless crime against a primal father.

The ultimate paradox lies in the nature of that ambivalence which characterizes the relationship of father and son. For if the pattern of political domination resides in this analogy (as Freud thought it does), then there is a fateful dialectic which must pervade the history of culture. Regretting the deed and deciding that it shall not be repeated, the primal sons have nevertheless condemned society to its eternal recurrence. For any power is like the paternal authority. It is feared and hated, but it is also sought and admired. Therefore every revolt against authority contains a hidden love for authority which in turn leads to its restoration and glorification. Authority, enslavement, rebellion, enforced domination, fresh revolt with subsequent restoration of authority form a cycle ever new in the history of civilization.

The account of the primal crime in *Totem and Taboo* is incapable of historical verification. But it is no more meant to represent an actual historical event than the establishment of the political covenant in the *Leviathan*. Both accounts are social fictions and their value lies in the potentiality of any generic, timeless explanation which underlies recurrent and mysterious social processes and gives increased meaning to widespread human institutions.[45] They are not strictly *true*, but they are also far from being nonsense.

Freud's fiction has the same logical status as that of Hobbes, but as a generic explanation it carries with it one powerful corollary which is absent in Hobbes. For it suggests that the cycle of development of each individual is inextricably bound up with the cycle of development of society. Civilization is still haunted by its archaic heritage, not merely through the survival of a legal system founded upon the sense of guilt, but because by a pre-established harmony of fate each child must deal with the Oedipus complex symbolically as the original sons in the primitive family dealt with it in actuality. Here again we are made aware how the individual's present has given hostages to the fortune of the archaic past. The contemporary individual is indissolubly bound to the experiences of the race; each self in its individual development re-lives the universal fate. "We cannot disregard the conclusion," says Freud,[46] "that man's sense of guilt has its origin in the Oedipus complex and was acquired when the father was killed by the association of the brothers." This is a conclusion of *Civilization and Its Discontents*. But it has been carefully prepared by *Totem and Taboo*. For there Freud had said:[47] "I want to state the conclusion that the beginnings of religion, ethics, society, and art meet in the Oedipus complex. This is in entire accord with the findings of psychoanalysis, namely, that the nucleus of all neuroses as far as our present knowledge of them goes is

the Oedipus complex. It comes as a great surprise to me that these problems of racial psychology can also be solved through a single concrete instance, such as the relation to the father."

It is perhaps disingenuous of Freud that it should "come as a surprise"
to him that problems of racial psychology could be solved through "the
concrete instance" of "the relation to the father." For the relation to
the father is the archetypal pattern for all Freudian explanation. It
might even be said to be the essential mode of his perception. Freud's
psychology is as much a social psychology as an individual psychology,
for it derives the nature of the individual as well as the social complex
from the situation within the family. The derivation of individuality is
through the critical handling of the identifications with the stern
authoritative father and the tender permissive mother. Society finds
its measures of status and its conventional roles from the hierarchies
of the family constellation. The ideals of political power pit the decree
of the authoritative father against the consensus of the equalitarian
brotherhood. Ethics as categorical imperative grows out of the model
of fatherly commands that brook no opposition. Artistic creation is a
fatherhood generated by the imposition of form upon matter. And
finally, religion itself is derived from the child's feeling of helplessness
and the longing for a protective and life-giving father. If it is Freud's
surprising conclusion that "the beginnings of religion, ethics, society,
and art meet in the Oedipus complex," this is only because by a simplicity of concentration which amounts to genius, the psychoanalytic
perspective is riveted to the traumas and perplexities of the child fighting
for selfhood against the unalterable necessity of parental determination.

Their accounts of the relation between society and individuality are
different, but the most striking similarity between Hobbes and Freud
exists in their image of "the natural man." In Hobbes, it is true, there
is a certain ultimate reasonableness about the desire for self-protection,
but this quickly turns into the use of force and fraud "to master the
persons of all men," and the ruthless desires for gain, safety, and deference soon erupt in the unrestrained resort to violence. In Freud the
rationality has disappeared, and what is left is the inherent destructiveness latent in the instinctual equipment.[48]

The bit of truth behind all this [says Freud]—one so eagerly denied—is
that men are not gentle, friendly creatures wishing for love, who simply
defend themselves if they are attacked, but that a powerful measure of
desire for aggression has to be reckoned as part of their instinctual endow-
ment. The result is that their neighbor is to them not only a possible helper
or sexual object, but also a temptation to them to gratify their aggressiveness

on him, to exploit his capacity for work without recompense, to use him sexually without his consent, to seize his possessions, to humiliate him, to cause him pain, to torture and to kill him. *Homo homini lupus*; who has the courage to dispute it in the face of all the evidence in his own life and in history?

This "aggressive cruelty" which lies close under the surface of the veneer of civilized man only awaits its glancing provocation: it requires only a slight relaxation of the usual inhibiting mental forces before its almost spontaneous outbreak demonstrates a savagery in the human animal incompatible with the image of benevolence and rationality. This tendency to aggression is the nightmare of culture, which infects the relations between man and man, and which calls into operation the entire controlling and inhibiting apparatus which civilization has at its disposal. When one considers the manner in which civilization has disabled the sexual life of man, denigrating it as a source of pleasurable sensation and forcing it in the direction of an inhibition of its aim, one's sympathies are with the individual, and the torment of the superego becomes (as in the case of Gide) a cause of poignant regret. But when one recognizes how society is perpetually menaced by complete disintegration through that primary hostility which men express in their relations with one another, then the evaluation shifts and we are reconciled to that necessity which, according to Freud, culture feels "to call up every possible reinforcement in order to erect barriers against the aggressive instincts of men." At the same time we also recognize that a civilization which requires sacrifices of both sexuality and aggressiveness can hardly have been tailor-made for human happiness.

Hobbes' account of man in the state of nature—*Homo homini lupus*—is pessimistic, like Freud's, but it is mitigated by his faith in the existence of natural laws, those general precepts of reason which counsel peace, the fulfilment of obligations, and justice. From these comes the motive to maintain political order on the basis of contractual commitments. The state of nature is therefore eventually and finally overcome. But for Freud the state of nature is never overcome. The tendency to aggression is an innate independent instinctual disposition in man. It is the way that the death instinct manifests itself in the life of society. Such an admission prevents any optimism concerning social reform. It saves us from utopian hopes for the progressive development of social institutions. Freud's criticism of the Marxian solution in the end reduces to this point. He has no concern with any purely economic criticisms of the Communist system. Nor does he inquire whether the abolition of private property is morally just. But he recognizes that as a program it is founded upon a psychological illusion. The abolition of private property might indeed deprive the human love of aggression of one of its channels of expression, but it leaves the instinct itself unchanged. Free-floating aggressiveness remains to attach itself to whatever issues of sexual competitiveness and prestige remain. This is the eternal destiny of human instinct.

There is an admirable consistency in Freud's doctrine. The social theory of *Civilization and Its Discontents* hinges directly upon the metapsychology established in *Beyond the Pleasure Principle*. The metapsychology is infected through and through with Darwinian presuppositions, and it therefore yields little to a merely sociological frame of reference. The dualistic opposition of the instincts here breaks out afresh. For it now becomes the clue to the evolutionary development of civilization.[49]

The natural instinct of aggressiveness in man, the hostility of each against all and of all against each one, opposes this programme of civilization. This instinct of aggression is the derivative and main representative of the death instinct we have found alongside of Eros, sharing his rule over the earth. And now, it seems to me, the meaning of the evolution of culture is no longer a riddle to us. It must present to us the struggle between Eros and Death, between the instincts of life and the instincts of destruction, as it works itself out in the human species. This struggle is what all life essentially consists of and so the evolution of civilization may be simply described as the struggle of the human species for existence.

We have come at last to the heart of the problem of the evolution of culture which is the final conclusion of the whole investigation. It is "the fatal inevitableness of the sense of guilt." The eternal price which the progress of civilization exacts is the diminution of happiness through a heightening of the sense of guilt. This guilt originates in the primal crime, in that remorse which expresses the ambivalent feelings of the sons toward the father, but since the aggressive impulses toward the father are repeated in every generation, the fateful dialectic continues. The Oedipus complex is the re-enactment of the primal crime, and the superego is the heir of the Oedipus complex. But this dialectic is not a cosmic accident. It is the expression of an ambivalence which represents the eternal struggle between Eros and Thanatos—the instinct of love and the instinct of destruction. This struggle, implicit in organic life in general and in the development of the individual, also invades the wider forms of communal life. The family (following the inner erotic impulse which seeks ever broader forms of binding and juncture) becomes the community, the community becomes the state, and that sense of guilt which began in relation to the father ends as a relation to the sovereign power of the social institutions, and increases until its magnitude is well-nigh insupportable.

The incorporation of the individual within the society subjects him to the prohibitions which it has developed. For the community, like the individual, develops a superego under whose influence social life is regulated. Freud's account of the genesis of the social superego is much like Bergson's description of the morality of aspiration in the open society. "It is based on the impression left behind them by great leading personalities, men of outstanding force of mind, or men in whom some one human tendency has developed in unusual strength and purity."[50] But in truth Freud's assessment of the efficacy of moral prescriptions of this ideal nature is rather negative. Since the constitutional tendency toward aggression is such an obstacle to civilization, those ethical systems which have demanded altruistic love have been highly valued, and men have expected them to achieve something especially important. And in fact they are directed toward the really vulnerable spot in the fabric of civilization. "Ethics must be regarded therefore as a therapeutic effort: as an endeavour to achieve something through the standards imposed by the super-ego which had not been attained by the work of civilization in other ways."[51] Unfortunately these ethical systems make demands upon the ego which it is constitutionally unable to fulfil. And as in the individual the cruel and unreal demands of the superego may motivate misery and even the flight into neurotic illness, so may the strictures of the moral code lead in the direction of a sick society.

This is the final conclusion to which the Freudian analogy of individual and social development must lead. For if psychoanalysis is applied in such a way that society becomes the patient, then perhaps the diagnosis is justified that whole epochs of civilization (perhaps even society itself) have become neurotic under the brutal impact of the pressures of civilizing trends. This is not only a matter of theoretical interest. It is also the fateful question of the future of the human species. Can the cultural process succeed in repairing the rips and tears in communal life caused by human aggression and the instinct of self-destruction? Can "eternal Eros" maintain itself alongside his immortal adversary? The powers of science have reached such a peak now that for the first time radical self-destruction is a real possibility. It is the knowledge of this fact which produces the latent unrest, the anxieties, and the apprehensions of our current mood.

4. RANK AND THE REVISIONISTS

The private history of the psychoanalytic movement is a record of misunderstandings, comedies of errors, schisms, heresies, and deviations within the interpretation of the sacred doctrines. Alfred Adler resigns from the Vienna Psychoanalytic Society in 1911. Stekel resigns from it in 1912. In 1913 Jung breaks off all relations with Freud. In 1912 the inner circle, the prime initiates of the Eleusinian mysteries (Ferenczi, Jones, Abraham, Rank, Sachs, Eitingon, Freud) form the mystic seven to consolidate the ritual. They agree to publish only upon mutual consultation. The master gives to each one the precious talisman of an identical gold ring.[52] The breaches are healed—but not for long. In 1925 Otto Rank, the gifted and many-colored Joseph of this band of brothers, is guilty of treasonable desertion and old Jacob is struck to the heart. So it continues. It is family tragedy—with Biblical overtones.

The private history of the psychoanalytic movement has its own pathos, but it is not strictly a part of the intellectual history of the modern world. But the multiple deviations from the orthodox Freudian position are intrinsically of the greatest importance. Often they seem to center about minor points of doctrine or of the technique of analytic therapy, but dwell upon them long enough, push them back further to the doctrines which they imply, and you will discover that ultimately they represent a conflict between differing images of man and even differing speculative metaphysical positions. It is both interesting and ironic that a discipline which originated in one of the more rigorous branches of empirical science and which prided itself upon the lack of a *Weltanschauung* other than that of science in general should be so irrevocably infected with philosophical implications and metaphysical importance. Each of the earlier generation (Adler, Jung, Rank) constructed a system with different presuppositions, and the second generation also (Horney, Sullivan, Fromm, Reich in his earlier writings) has created a structure based upon Freud but differing from him in significant respects.[53] Is it possible in this multiplicity to discern any generalized philosophic direction?

I think that it is. The strategic center of the Freudian position is the way in which it structuralizes and explains the irrational in man. It therefore holds in uneasy suspension the Darwinian and Cartesian images of the human person. It is paradoxical, but perhaps inevitable, that on the one hand Freud should be criticized as too Cartesian in his point of view, and on the other as too Darwinian. For I believe that the

two principal attacks upon him are (1) against his scientific intellectualism and (2) against his commitment to essentially biological
categories. The first attack, a partisanship for the spirit of Rousseau
and Bergson rather than Descartes (for the enthronement of feeling
rather than analysis) comes from Jung and Rank. It is the latter, less
cumbersome, less obscurantist than Jung, whom I shall take as representative of this position in the following necessarily brief remarks. The
second attack, which springs from a partisanship for the spirit of
Auguste Comte rather than that of Darwin (for sociological factors
rather than biological in the determination of man's nature) originated
with Alfred Adler, although it is best known in the contemporary world
through the neo-Freudian revisionists Fromm, Horney, and Sullivan.

The concluding pages of Freud's *The Future of an Illusion* are a sober,
even majestic, glorification of the spirit and method of science. The
whole book has been an attempt to show religion up for what he thinks
it is: a wish-fulfilment, a childish consolation, a narcosis for the immature mind. He agrees of course that men in general cannot do
without the consolation of the religious illusion, but this, he says, is
because the bitter-sweet poison has been instilled from childhood on.
But what of the man who has been brought up in scientific sobriety?
Of course he will be in a difficult position. He will find himself helpless in the universe—no longer the center of creation. "But after all,"
says Freud,[54] "is it not the destiny of childishness to be overcome? Man
cannot remain a child forever; he must venture at last into the hostile
world. This may be called '*education to reality*'; need I tell you that it
is the sole aim of my book to draw attention to the necessity for this
advance?"

And of course religion is doomed. For surely nothing can really with-
stand man's reason and the testimony of his senses, and that religion
contradicts both of these is only too clear. Back of Freud's strictures
against religion lies his relentless Cartesianism, the faith in reason which
makes him really a man of the eighteenth-century Enlightenment, an
extreme confidence in the power of the intellect which even mitigates
his pessimism about the future of man's destructive instincts.[55]

We may insist as much as we like that human intellect is weak in comparison with human instincts, and be right in doing so. But nevertheless
there is something peculiar about this weakness. The voice of the intellect
is a soft one, but it does not rest until it has gained a hearing. Ultimately,
after endlessly repeated rebuffs, it succeeds. This is one of the few points
in which one may be optimistic about the future of mankind, but in itself
it signifies not a little. And one can make it a starting-point for yet other

hopes. The primacy of the intellect certainly lies in the far, far, but still probably not infinite, distance.

Some of this same confidence in the primacy of the intellect underlies the Freudian analytic therapy, bringing about the re-creation of the self through an enlargement of self-knowledge. Here Rank's counter-claim strikes its first decisive blow.

For if in truth, thinks Rank,[56] there is any powerful acid which eats away the binding unity of the human self, it is the tormenting self-consciousness of the modern individual. When the intellect is expressed as self-knowledge, it leads finally to constant awareness of the subject, which disturbs if it does not block completely the flow of immediate experience. Such self-consciousness leads to the neurotic self-restriction upon living rather than to a free commitment to its fluid demands. Knowledge, because of its relentless striving for the truth, separates consciousness from experience. And truth as a cognitive claim which is affirmed or rejected can influence us only as it attaches itself to the emotional life and is "stamped with psychic reality or unreality." Thus the only "trueness" in terms of actual psychic reality is found in emotion and not in thinking (which disregards reality, when it is not rationalizing it). From this follows an alternative to the Freudian concept of human behavior, a view of life which is therapeutic in an anti-analytic sense.[57]

It is to the effect that our seeking the truth in human motives for acting and thinking is destructive. With the truth one cannot live. To be able to live one needs illusions, not only outer illusions such as art, religion, philosophy, science and love afford, but inner illusions which first condition the outer. The more a man can take reality as truth, appearance as essence, the sounder, the better adjusted, the happier will he be. At the moment when we begin to search after truth we destroy reality and our relation to it.

Suppose that we find in a lover a substitute for the mother, or in a hated business associate the image of a domineering father. The reality of contemporary life is then the displacement of the childish past. But what difference that we analytically perceive this fabric of illusion? We can never bring it to an end, and this the analytic situation teaches us best of all, for the analyst himself is only a displacement of the patient's past. "In a word, the displacements are the real. Reality unveils itself to analysis always as something displaced, psychologically untrue. This is a cognitive fact but no life principle."[58] For displacement if successful is not pathological, but normal and healing in its effects. Self-deception, pretense, role-taking and role-assigning, stumbling and blundering are the very nature of reality. And this, Rank believes, is the authentic wisdom of the Greek Oedipus myth, "whose hero would live happily in his displaced world of appearance if he were not driven by his intellectual pride, the will to truth, to expose his reality as lies, as appearance, as falsehood."[59]

From this conception follows a curious insight into the nature of neurosis. The more a man can accept the appearance as the reality, the more normal, healthy, and happy he is. The neurotic unfortunately sees through the deception of the world of sense, sees the falsities of reality, and it is this insight which robs him of the illusions important for living. Psychologically the neurotic is much nearer to actual truth than the others. That is why he suffers.

It is in relation to this theory of truth and reality that Rank explodes Freud's claim to dispense with illusion. He does this by showing the insoluble conflict in which psychoanalysis itself is caught. This is because it wants to be theory and therapy at the same time. "As psychological theory it seeks truth, that is, insight into psychic processes themselves and this works destructively, as neurotic self consciousness shows only too clearly. As therapy it must offer the patient contentual consolations and justifications which again cannot be psychologically true, or, as far as they are true, cannot work therapeutically."[60] This is the ultimate dilemma of Freud's position. It wishes to know the final truth about man and it wants to reconcile the alienated to reality. But these intentions are incompatible.

If there is a methodological error in Freud's psychology, it lies in an overestimation of the inherent power of rationality. This turns it from the problems of the positive creative affirmation of the will, where it might do useful work, toward cognitive issues which are therapeutically insignificant. The neurotic fails in life because he knows too much truth about himself, whether he experiences this truth as guilt, incapacity for love, or feelings of gross inferiority. And this "knowledge" is always at bottom an incapacity for illusion—but an incapacity for illusion with respect to the decisive power of his individual will. At this point it should be clear in which direction Rank's critique is headed: away from a psychology of cognition and directly toward a psychology of the will.

To restore the conscious will as the central point of psychology and to view the task of analytic therapy as the activation of a constructive will is to minimize the significance of the unconscious and at the same time to deny the claims of the intellect. It therefore represents philosophically the same kind of development symbolized by the passage from the philosophy of Schopenhauer to the philosophy of Nietzsche. No doubt Rank was not moved primarily by philosophical considerations, but by a root contradiction in the whole Freudian theory which could be attributed to an inability to recognize the relationship between the glorification of the will and the existence of the sense of guilt in man.

According to Rank, will and guilt are two sides of the same phenomenon, as Schopenhauer also saw. But it follows that a voluntaristic philosophy will be deeply pessimistic (like Schopenhauer's and probably like Freud's also) if it emphasizes the aspect of guilt, or extremely optimistic like Nietzsche's if it affirms the creative power of the will. But now for the problem. In Freudian psychoanalysis Rank discovered both aspects, not reconciled in theory, but rather as an open opposition between what the theory says about man and how the therapy works for his reconstruction.

As therapy, analysis is optimistic, believes as it were in the good in men and in some kind of capacity for and possibility of salvation. In theory it is pessimistic; man has no will and no creative power, is driven by the id and repressed by the super-ego authorities, is unfree and still guilty. Here lies before us so transparent a contradiction that one can only wonder how it is possible, and must again recognize therein a psychological problem so fundamental that it leads far beyond a critique of psychoanalysis.[61]

The problem is that of free will, the metaphysical issue underlying all psychological theory. Rank holds that the fact of the human consciousness of guilt is alone sufficient to prove this freedom as it is relevant psychologically. This becomes the crux of his deeper criticism of the theory of Freud. For he sees Freud as a man of the nineteenth century, holding to a determinism as rigid psychologically as Darwin's was biologically and Marx's was economically. But in psychology it is the less excusable error. For it deprives the personality of the very qualities which make it human: autonomy, responsibility, and conscience. No deterministic interpretation of behavior can serve as a therapeutic foundation. Such an interpretation may explain neurotic attitudes from without, but it leaves no room (theoretically) for a re-education of the will. "The whole question of psychological therapy," says Rank, "resolves itself in the last analysis to the philosophical problem of a deterministic versus a vitalistic point of view."

Any humanistic philosophy has always acknowledged that individual personality is a practical causative factor, that the individual will (using impulse and environment alike) creates an inner causality of its own. Such a creative exercise of the will automatically passes beyond a mechanistic causality (which makes the individual analyzable without remainder into his heredity and environment) to a dynamic causality of the will, creating personality as well as transforming the culture into which it moves.

Almost all contradictions and controversies of the psychoanalytic schools are due to this confusion between mechanistic causality on which theory has to be based and dynamic causality on which therapy rests. That means, explanatory psychology has to trace the causal links beyond the individual to its social and collective sources in the remote past, where the basic conceptions of human culture and personality originated. Therapy, on the contrary, has to be based on the individual's will as an autonomous force operating beyond and above heredity and environment.[62]

Thus it becomes clear that Rank's criticism of Freud is twofold. As theory psychoanalysis is too mechanistic. And as therapy it relies too much upon the transforming character of self-knowledge. The neurotic suffers from the fact that he cannot accept his own nature although he wishes it otherwise. His salvation therefore lies not in a "correction" of his character, but in a "reinforcement" of the latent powers of his will. He must be transformed from a negative person of suffering and guilt into a positive man of will and action. It is Neitzsche all over again but psychologically adapted and without the overtone of shrillness and hysteria.

The final culmination of Rank's critique of Freud is a typology of selfhood which sees the neurotic personality against the background of its two co-ordinates—the normal individual and the artist. This distinction between the normal, the neurotic, and the artist is not merely psychological; it is also ethical and metaphysical. It does not hang upon mere mental processes and symptoms but upon a mode of dealing with reality. In the last analysis, it is a difference between three distinct qualities of the will. The normal or adjusted individual takes the generally accepted reality of his environment as his own. He approximates it and lives by it as his own truth without disturbance or displacement. The artist or creator denies the truth of his environment, refuses to live by it, but discovers or creates his own truth and creates the reality according to which he lives out of the truth which he has discovered. The neurotic falls in between. He finds his truth, but is unable to accept it, and therefore destroys the given reality without the possibility of a creative substitute. He is too much of an artist to accept the socially given; he is not enough of an artist to construct his own.

Just here, of course, arises the dilemma of the therapist. Is he on the side of the will or the powers of submission? Shall he try to make the patient into a good citizen who accepts general ideas without contradiction, or shall he push him further in the direction of the artist—strengthening his will, permitting him to develop into what he is without guilt, helping him further along the path of strong self-affirmation? At this point clinical medicine becomes a matter of ultimate ethics.

The striking thing about Rank's typology is that it equates autonomy in the full Kantian sense of self-legislation with the activity of the artist, and thereby suggests that the development of the self is not merely an issue of sociological emergence but of fine art. The creation of individuality is like artistic activity. Whether in the experience of "rebirth" or in the organic unification of his diverse experiences, the individual creates himself, evolves his ego-ideal from himself not by merely given but by "self-chosen" factors consciously striven for. At this point the break with Freud is decisive and complete.

The neo-Freudian revisionists have learned much from Rank, but at heart their doctrines are founded not upon a preference for the will rather than the intellect, but upon a preference for social rather than biological categories of explanation. Their inspiration has grown out of the last few pages of *Civilization and Its Discontents*, where Freud has hinted that there may be such a thing as a sick society. But this point of Freud's has been warped beyond recognition by the elimination of its biological base—the theory of instincts without which Freud's position is completely unintelligible.

But if the explosive instinctual roots of the personality are neglected, then the immediate processes of social adaptation can be elevated to the role of primary causal factors. Social reality becomes the chief element in the formation of the personality, and even the criteria of mental sickness and health are seen to be social through and through. Neurosis will still be characterized by conflicts, anxieties, difficulties and suffering, and may even have a formal structure which recurs in almost all neurotic persons, but the emphasis will not be placed upon the traumas of early childhood, but upon the shaping role of specific cultural conditions. There is then no "normal psychology" which holds for all mankind. Normality becomes a standard imposed by a group according to culture and period. Such obvious criteria of neurosis as rigidity of reaction and discrepancy between potentiality and accomplishment are socially interpreted. "Rigidity" and "accomplishment" are terms given their full sense and flavor only by reference to the customary behavior within the society in question. Neurosis for Freud is a critical dislocation of the instinctual economy. For Fromm, Horney, and the revisionists it is a disturbance deviating from the pattern of a particular culture.[63]

The difficulty is, of course, that the revisionists are also extremely conscious of the factors within the society which produce neurotic conflict. Alfred Adler had long before abandoned Freud's emphasis upon sexuality and substituted the individual's striving for power as a compensation against feelings of inferiority. The revisionists revive this ancient heresy by describing the obsessive quest for power, prestige, and possessions as modes of reassurance against basic anxiety. And they see the tendency to dominate and destroy radiating out from economics into the whole field of social relations; love, play, and the family. Therefore those conflicts from which the neurotic suffers are also characteristic of the lives of normal individuals. For our society suffers from certain basic contradictions: a worldly emphasis upon competition and success versus a Christian ideal of humility and brotherly love; a constant stimulation of consumer wants without the kind of distribution of income which could reasonably satisfy them; a theory of individual free will combined with a knowledge of the individual's factual limitations in a society dominated by forces which no individual can control. There are then certain difficulties inherent in the very nature of modern machine culture, which produce the accentuation of competitive feelings, an exaggerated fear of failure, a sense of isolation in the individual, and an intensified need for affection which produces an almost hysterical demand for love and an over-valuation of sociality. The neurotic is only the one who has experienced the cultural difficulties of his civilization in an accentuated and virulent form.

The result of the revisionist critique of Freud is that all the deepest problems of a biological psychology are transformed into problems of sociology. The influence of instinctual drives upon the Oedipus complex, infantile sexuality, and the formation of character structure are eliminated, and in their place is a personality which is the exclusive product of social interaction. Anxiety remains the heart of neurosis, but it is explained not, as in Freud, as a product of instinctual repression, but as the fear of the individual against "irrational authority" first expressed in the family situation. At this point psychology becomes the tool of a program of social reform. Freud's social pessimism is the inevitable consequence of his psychological theory. For him neurosis grows out of an inability to handle the problem of instinctual deprivation, and instinctual deprivation is the inevitable price of civilization. But if, on the contrary, as the revisionists believe, neurosis is the consequence of "irrational authority" within society, the elimination of such authority eliminates the disease; the reform of institutional patterns is the hope of civilization, and an optimistic outcome is a real possibility.

If there is a certain shallowness about revisionist theory—an attempt to build up personality out of merely cultural elements, an elimination of the darker forces of the self inaccessible to rational control—this represents a view of the world which is itself conditioned by cultural factors within our society. For despite the fact that Rank criticizes Freud's position as too Cartesian, and the revisionists criticize it as too Darwinian, there is a certain similarity in the attitudes out of which the two criticisms spring. Both are moralistic, active, and inherently romantic. For they dwell upon the human powers of manipulation and re-making. Rank's psychology enthrones the concept of the improvable will; the revisionists' psychology enthrones the concept of the improvable institutional structure. What both lack is the sense of the inevitability of the instinctual struggle—that imponderable necessity which lies within the nature of the human animal. In Freud's theory civilization perpetually imposes its own necessities, and the instincts make their eternal protest. Such health and pleasure as is attainable could almost be said to be the peace of successful resignation. Rank's education of the decisive will and Fromm's proposals for the economic transformation of society are in Spengler's terms *Faustian* to the core. But in Freud the classical spirit of Sophoclean tragedy survives into the modern world.

5. FREE WILL AND FATE

Arthur Koestler's novel, *Arrival and Departure*, set in the political atmosphere of the second World War, was an interesting fictional attempt to confront the ideology of Marxism with the therapy of Freud. Peter Slavek, a middle-European refugee from the Nazis (by whom he has been tortured), young, short, strongly built, and a long-time Communist, arrives in Portugal as a stowaway, and there makes plans either to enlist in the British air force to fight the Nazis further or to leave for America. After a number of weeks of waiting he is found by Dr. Sonia Bolgar, a psychoanalyst and an old friend of his mother, and given a room in her apartment. But when his English visa finally arrives, Peter suddenly develops hysterical paralysis and Dr. Bolgar starts to treat him with psychoanalysis. The analysis reveals a number of significant facts: that his heroic behavior under torture was connected with the fact that Peter had identified the sadistic police chief Raditch with his father, and that Peter had never lost his sense of guilt over the accidental death of a younger brother who died when Peter was only five. He now sees that his brother's death was no accident. He himself had unconsciously desired it, and this is the source of that latent feeling of guilt for which his whole life in the revolutionary movement has been one long atonement.

With this realization comes catharsis. Peter's paralysis slowly disappears, and his hysteria comes to an end. The implication is clear. The motivation of the Marxist revolutionary hero is reduced to a neurotic and unconscious impulse toward self-punishment. Peter's recovery is now complete, but it seems to leave him with a philosophical problem no less disturbing than his previous physical symptoms. For it appears to suggest not only that there is always a latent morbidity behind the values we admire, but that these values themselves dissolve under the influence of causal modes of explanation.

And he also realized in his more lucid hours that under Sonia's influence the proud structure of his values had collapsed, and imperative exclamation marks had been bent into marks of interrogation. What, after all, was courage? A matter of glands, nerves, patterns of reaction conditioned by heredity and early experiences. A drop of iodine less in the thyroid, a sadistic governess or over-affectionate aunt, a slight variation in the electric resistance of the medullary ganglions, and the hero became a coward, the patriot a traitor. Touched with the magic rod of cause and effect, the actions of men were emptied of their so-called moral contents as a Leyden jar is discharged by the touch of a conductor.[64]

Fortunately Peter does not remain at this point of complete skepticism. As he reflects further, he finds that Sonia the psychoanalyst herself has values and a sense of moral discrimination and slowly, impelled by some inner urge, he moves once again to join the forces fighting against Fascism. But what then is the difference between his first crusade which had ended with his breakdown on Sonia's couch and the second on which he was about to depart? The first time he did not know his reasons. This time he knew them but understood also that reasons do not matter so much. "They are the shell around the core; and the core remains untouchable, beyond the reach of cause and effect." The conclusion is not so much a mystique of personality as a kind of quaint dualism which sees on the one hand the cool operation of scientific causality, and on the other the equal validity of intuition and ethical belief. As the book ends, Peter writes to a former friend:[65]

Today I am going to fly off at a tangent from the twisted path. I have not many illusions about the reasons why I am doing it nor about the cause which I serve. As children we used to be given a curious kind of puzzle to play with. It was a paper with a tangle of very thin blue and red lines. If you just looked at it you couldn't make out anything. But if you covered it with a piece of transparent red tissue paper, the red lines of the drawing disappeared and the blue lines formed a picture—it was a clown in a circus holding a hoop and a little dog jumping through it. And if you covered the same drawing with blue tissue paper, a roaring lion appeared chasing the clown across the ring. You can do the same thing with every mortal living or dead. You can look at him through Sonia's tissue paper and write a biography of Napoleon in terms of his pituitary gland as has been done. . . . You can explain the message of the prophets as epileptical foam and the Sistine Madonna as the projection of an incestuous dream. The method is correct and the picture in itself complete. But beware of the arrogant error of believing that it is the only one. The picture you get through the blue tissue paper will be no less true and complete. The clown and the lion are both there, interwoven in the same pattern. . . .

Koestler puts the issue in a metaphor, but the question of the equal reality of the clown and the lion haunts the Freudian formulation like some ghost from the theological past. On the question of the philosophical status of human values in psychoanalytic theory, Freud himself is curiously silent. This is not to say that as a person he is without strong moral attitudes. Quite the contrary. With perhaps a certain simplicity he has said of himself:[66] "I consider myself to be a very moral person who can subscribe to the excellent maxim of Theodore Vischer, 'What is moral is self-evident' (Das Moralische versteht sich von selbst)." Can this be meant ironically? Apparently not. And yet what a superb inconsistency to find the insistent methodologist of science committed to moral intuitionism! And at the same time how Jewish to combine the Prophets' conception of morality with the scientist's distrust of illusion! But also how close to the dangers of Peter Slavek's disillusionment upon the psychoanalytic couch!

If there is no provision in Freud for a justification of human values, there is nonetheless an implicit argument concerning the human condition. Here Freud places himself not on the side of Old Testament prophecy but in the ranks of the Greek dramatists and the Stoic philosophers. "Even I myself am struck," he said, "by the fact that the histories of the diseases which I write read like novels." He might more appropriately have said that they read like Attic tragedy.

In a famous passage in *Science and the Modern World* Whitehead has suggested that the conception of fate implicit in Greek drama was a precursor of the modern conception of scientific law. In Freud the two strands cooperate. Combined with the determinism of science, there is in Freud a constant recognition of the repetitive mechanisms in human behavior which are a kind of analogue to the periodicity of nature. The "return of the repressed" and the compulsive repetition of obsessive acts are cases in point. But the conception goes further. The primal crime which *Totem and Taboo* has discovered at the foundation of civilized life is repeated in the fantasy of every son. The Oedipus complex demonstrates that for the individual there is no escape from the destiny of the race.

The concept of destiny is, of course, a contemplative and a poetic idea. For the Greeks it was sometimes conceived of as a curse hanging over a noble house, and at others as a weakness or flaw of individual character. It is not certain that the two perspectives are logically compatible or that the Greeks ever succeeded in relating them in their theories of tragedy. But in Freudian theory they find psychological reconciliation. The instincts are a heritage prior to individuality, but individuality itself is produced within the family constellation. Thus, if the Oedipus situation be translated as the curse hanging over all humanity, then certainly the flaws of individual character are produced as the nascent individual experiences the details of this destined situation.

Spengler has distinguished between the classical drama of *situation* and the Faustian drama of *character*. This means in part that for the Greeks a man's character is his *being*, and what happens in the drama is the consequence of character already formed. For the Faustian man, a man's character is his *becoming*, and therefore what happens in the drama is a real development of character itself. One consequence of this distinction is a difference in the sense of inevitability. For Oedipus the oracle has spoken unavoidable truth. Any choice which Oedipus might have made would have led to the same result. With Macbeth the case is different. What the witches gave was not an oracle but a conditional promise, a lure to temptation. To these voices Macbeth could, and indeed should, have refused to listen. Thus Macbeth's is the tragedy of free will while Oedipus' is the tragedy of destiny.

The distinction is perhaps superficial, and cannot be defended in all its implications. But for an understanding of the spirit of Freud it is, I believe, suggestive. Freudian theory puts the critical experience of character formation in the depths of the infantile memory. Thus the climax comes too soon; it is the prelude to the play, and the play itself is all denouement and unraveling. A plot so formalized can advance only through the mechanism of countless repetitions. In two respects, therefore, the Freudian account of the human condition is typically Greek. It is a drama of universal situation, and its mood is framed by the sense of inevitability. In one section of "Esthétique du Mal" Wallace Stevens has epitomized the Freudian position:[67]

> It may be that one life is a punishment
> For another, as the son's life for the father's.
> But that concerns the secondary characters.

It is a fragmentary tragedy
Within the universal whole. The son
And the father alike and equally are spent,
Each one, by the necessity of being
Himself, the unalterable necessity
Of being this unalterable animal.
This force of nature in action is the major
Tragedy. This is destiny unperplexed,
The happiest enemy.

How better to express the pathos of the Oedipus situation? The son and the father alike are spent, each by the necessity of being himself. And it is "necessity" here in the full Greek sense of unalterability at the heart of things. In the end the tragedy comes down to this: that the Darwinian assumption cannot be brushed aside. The drama of human life is set within the unbreakable bonds of nature and nature herself in action is the major tragedy. Against this insight all protests about chance, coincidence, accident, fortune, or contingency are quaint and superficial. The moral arithmetic used to settle the issues of "accountability" as well as the retrospective anxieties about "avoidability" are also completely beside the point. If there is any lesson to be learned, it must be something like that of Oedipus himself: to take the jealousy of the gods for what it is, to learn by "wisdom through suffering" that the cosmos has a rationale of its own which is not to be set aside.

It would be a mistake to believe that in the Freudian analogue this rationale has anything to do with the promotion of human values. There is no divine providence brooding over the affairs of men, and if the cosmos has a harmony of its own, it is blind to human suffering. About this matter Freud is as explicit as he is uncompromising.[68]

It seems not to be true that there is a power in the universe, which watches over the well-being of every individual with parental care and brings all his concerns to a happy ending. On the contrary the destinies of man are incompatible with a universal principle of benevolence or with— what is to some degree contradictory—a universal principle of justice. Earthquakes, floods and fires do not differentiate between the good and the devout man, and the sinner and unbeliever. And, even if we leave inanimate nature out of account and consider the destinies of individual men in so far as they depend on their relation with others of their own kind, it is by no means the rule that virtue is rewarded and wickedness punished, but it happens often enough that the violent, the crafty and the unprincipled seize the desirable goods of the earth for themselves, while the pious go empty away. Dark, unfeeling and unloving powers determine human destiny; the system of rewards and punishments, which, according to religion, governs the world, seems to have no existence.

"Dark, unfeeling and unloving powers determine human destiny." This is the philosophical crux of the entire Freudian position. Therefore its ultimate wisdom of life suggests the solution of the Stoics and of Spinoza. The recognition and understanding of one's own nature is the way of peace. The acceptance of the laws of nature is a species of contentment. The acknowledgment of necessity is the only mode of freedom.

VI

Society in Distress:
V. I. Lenin and Thorstein Veblen

> With usury has no man a good house
> made of stone, no paradise on his church wall
> With usury the stone cutter is kept from his stone
> the weaver is kept from his loom by usura
> Wool does not come into market
> the peasant does not eat his own grain
> The girl's needle goes blunt in her hand
> The looms are hushed one after another
> ten thousand after ten thousand
> Duccio was not by usura
> Nor was 'La Calunnia' painted.
> Neither Ambrogio Praedis nor Angelico
> had their skill by usura
> Nor St Trophime its cloisters;
> Nor St Hilaire its proportion.
> Usury rusts the man and his chisel
> It destroys the craftsman, destroying craft . . .
>
> EZRA POUND (Canto LI)

For mechanization is perhaps not merely an economic and social error but also a vice of man, comparable with that of heroin or morphine, as if all that both or all three do is to betray the same nervous disturbance, a double defect of the imagination and of the will.

GEORGES BERNANOS

As far as I am concerned, I, too, am a "seeker" in philosophy.

V. I. LENIN

1. THE MARXIAN PREPARATION

In one of his famous philosophical essays, Jean-Paul Sartre says:[1]

Freedom is one and indivisible, but it manifests itself in a variety of ways, according to circumstances. The following question may be asked of all philosophers who set up as its defenders: in connection with what exceptional *situation* have you experienced your freedom? It is one thing to test your freedom in the realm of action, of social or political activity, or of artistic creation, and another thing to test it in the act of understanding and discovering.

And he continues:

A Richelieu, a Vincent de Paul or a Corneille would, had they been meta-physicians, have had certain things to tell us about freedom because they grasped it by one end, at a moment when it manifested itself by an absolute event, by the appearance of something new, whether poem or institution, in a world which neither asked for it nor rejected it. Descartes who was primar-ily a metaphysician, grasped things by the other end; his primary experience was not of creative freedom . . . but of autonomous thinking.

In some sense both of the two social philosophers with whom we are here concerned, V. I. Lenin and Thorstein Veblen, set themselves up as defenders of freedom, but in the terms of Sartre's distinction, each experienced his own freedom in quite different exceptional situations. Defender of the Marxist faith and theorist of the Russian Revolution, Lenin tested his freedom in the realm of thought always with an am-biguous reference to the realm of social and political activity. A purer intelligence, free-floating, socially unanchored, and personally strange, Veblen realized his freedom in the act of autonomous thinking, in ironic and detached understanding of the organization of modern in-dustrial society. Lenin's social theory is always geared to the absolute event of revolution. Veblen's social theory "grasps things by the other end;" it is social portraiture through a very sensitive if slightly distorted lens. Between the two of them there emerges a critical literature which displays a contemporary social milieu in considerable distress.

The problem goes back at least five hundred years, to the slow emergence of capitalist society out of the disintegration of the mediaeval social order. The two crucial events in the life of Western man are the growth of modern science and the industrialization of human society, and they have confirmed and supported one another throughout their history. It matters little, therefore, whether we say with Pound that the sin of usury (by which is meant not merely the profit motive as a mon-strous force, but all lapses from perfect integrity in economic behavior) corrupts the man and destroys his honest making, or say with Bernanos that mechanization is a vice like heroin or morphine. They are but two sides of the same coin of social criticism; they spring from the same mode of indignant perception which moralizes the defects of a society dominated by industry and the machine.

There are many ways in which this social criticism expresses itself in the modern world.[2] One can point, as R. H. Tawney does, to the dis-tinction between an acquisitive society in which the profit motive rules the social organization, and a functional society in which the acquistion of wealth should be contingent upon the discharge of social obligation. One can with John Dewey indicate that a laissez-faire attitude toward industry and finance breeds a wrong distribution of political power, and that "the only form of enduring social organization that is now possible is one in which the new forces of productivity are cooperatively controlled and used in the interest of the effective liberty and the cultural development of the individuals that constitute society."[3] One can with Georges Sorel cry out that under capitalism the proletariat is crushed, and that its salvation lies in the resort to violence symbolized in the general strike. One can point, as Karl Jaspers and Ortega y Gasset do, to the undesirable tension between a technical mass order and the requirements of genuine human life, and one can show with Gabriel Marcel how in the conception of man as a mechanical assemblage of mere functions fostered by industrialized society, modern man has lost the sense of his own unique identity.

All of these criticisms, liberal-democratic, revolutionary, or existentialist, share one characteristic. All of them are unintelligible without reference to the nineteenth-century paradigm of all contemporary social criticism—the economic doctrines of Karl Marx. Every age needs its rationale of social co-existence; needs its picture (myth or portrait) which dignifies or at least evaluates each social place. Marxism was the great revaluation of social place in the nineteenth century, and knowledge of its presuppositions is therefore necessary for an understanding of all contemporary philosophies of social distress. It is also required to put the work of V. I. Lenin and of Thorstein Veblen in their proper perspective.

In a certain sense Lenin himself has given to Marxism its most sympathetic exposition and exegesis.

The teaching of Marx [he said] evokes throughout the civilized world the greatest hostility and hatred on the part of all bourgeois science (both official and liberal) which regards Marxism as something in the nature of a pernicious sect. No other attitude is to be expected, since there can be no "impartial" social science in a society which is built up on the class struggle. *All* official and liberal science defends wage-slavery in one way or another, whereas Marxism has declared relentless war on that slavery. To expect science to be impartial in a society of wage-slavery is as silly and naive as to expect impartiality from employers on the question as to whether the worker's wages should be increased by decreasing the profits of capital.[4]

It is completely characteristic that Lenin should deny the possibility of objectivity in economic analysis and of "impartiality" in the social sciences. But his pragmatic bias partially warps his own interpretation of Marxist theory. For while Lenin and Veblen split between them the theoretical and the practical impulse of the social theorists, in the life of Marx the two strands are more intimately combined. It is true that Marx's development of the doctrine of dialectical materialism between 1844 and 1848 occurred within the context of a career of revolutionary ambition, but the development of the theory of surplus value and the other theoretical constructs of *Das Kapital* of 1867-1883 were accomplished in the scholarly quiet of the British Museum, all dreams of violence seemingly left far behind.

Marxism itself claims to be reliable "social science," yet it too originates within a society which is built upon the class struggle. If the official doctrines of defense could hardly be expected to be impartial, no more could the passionate theoretical weapons of attack. If Lenin had taken the position of Sorel, if he had interpreted Marxism not as a description of economic fact, but as the expression of a determination to act, a kind of handbook for the *revolutionary apprenticeship* of the proletariat, there would have been no difficulty. But at the same time Lenin entered a truth-claim; he wished to invest Marxism at once with the heritage of philosophic wisdom and the authority of economic fact.

The teaching of Marx [he said] is all-powerful *because it is true*. It is complete and harmonious, providing men with a consistent view of the universe, which cannot be reconciled with any superstition, any reaction, any defence of bourgeois oppression. It is the lawful successor of the best that has been created by humanity in the nineteenth century—German philosophy, English political economy and French socialism.[5]

We are confronted here with that kind of embarrassment which arises when two aspects of the same theory seem to be irreconcilable with one another. The Marxian dilemma, as illustrated by these two adjacent passages from Lenin, is that whereas it asserts the cultural determinism of ideologies in a fashion so strong as to preclude all objectivity in social theory, at the same time it produces a social theory which claims to be objectively true. Such dilemmas haunt the domain of social philosophy no less than that of metaphysics.

That Marxism is a continuation of English political economy must be clear to anyone who has looked into *Capital* and who has followed the metaphysics of "the commodity," the distinction between "value in use" and "value in exchange," and the quixotic twist which Marx gives to Ricardo's labor theory of value. That Marx has felt the influence of French socialism (of men like Sismondi, Proudhon, and Fourier) is clear even though in the third section of *The Communist Manifesto* he so emphatically characterizes it as utopian, bourgeois, or even downright reactionary. But the relation to German philosophy (meaning the system of Hegel) is problematic, because "philosophy" for Marx always has a quality half serious, half ironic, which is expressed to perfection in that ambivalence which generally marked his relation to the thought of Hegel.

In the early "Critique of the Hegelian Dialectic and Philosophy in General" of 1844 (one of the Paris Philosophic-Economic Manuscripts) Marx wrote:[6]

The Hegelian Encyclopedia . . . is nothing but the expanded essence of the philosophic spirit, its self-objectification. And the philosophic spirit is nothing but the alienated spirit of the world, thinking within its self-alienation. . . . Logic, the *money* of the spirit . . . has become completely indifferent to all actual determinateness and is therefore mere essence. It is estranged thinking, abstracted from the actualities of man and Nature. It is completely abstract. . . .

Hegel commits here a double error which appears most clearly in the Phenomenology. . . . When, for example, he considers wealth, the power of the state etc. as entities alienated from human existence, this is only in their ideal form. They are ideal entities, and thus simply the alienation of pure philosophic thought. . . . The whole movement ends therefore with absolute knowing. . . . It is precisely abstract thinking from which these objects are alienated and to which they stand opposed with their pretension of reality. The philosopher, who is himself an abstract form of alienated man, takes himself as the yardstick of the alienated world. The whole history of alienation . . . is therefore nothing but the history of the production of abstract thought, that is, thought which is absolute, speculative, logical. . . .

In this passage one finds the clue to what for Marx was negotiable and what was useless in the philosophy of Hegel, couched, symbolically enough, in the same opaque and involuted phraseology which characterized the master. The sin of Hegelianism is the pride of *abstraction*, and abstract thought is the very essence of the philosophic spirit. It is characteristic that Marx should speak of logic as the "money" of the spirit, for this suggests not merely an essence but lack of real concreteness, the merely symbolic manipulation of the token of value abstracted from all that is actually, *substantially* valuable. The somber realities of economic inequality and political coercion are subordinated by Hegel to the ultimate reality of an absolute knowing which becomes for him the truly concrete. Not since Plato's theory of ideas have the intuitions of common sense concerning the abstract and the concrete been so affronted.

But if Hegel has turned things upside down, then another simple reversal of Hegel himself (a negation of the negation, so to speak) ought to put things right. Thirty years later (in the preface to the second edition of *Capital*) this is precisely what Marx confesses he has done:[7]

My dialectic method is not only different from the Hegelian, but is its direct opposite. To Hegel, the life-process of the human brain, i.e. the process of thinking, which, under the name of "the Idea," he even transforms into an independent subject, is the demiurgos of the real world, and the real world is only the external, phenomenal form of "the Idea." With me, on the contrary, the ideal is nothing else than the material world reflected by the human mind, and translated into forms of thought.

The mystifying side of Hegelian dialectic I criticised nearly thirty years ago, at a time when it was still the fashion. . . . The mystification which dialectic suffers in Hegel's hands, by no means prevents him from being the first to present its general form of working in a comprehensive and conscious manner. With him it is standing on its head. It must be turned right side up again, if you would discover the rational kernel within the mystical shell.

Another basic concept which Marx derived from Hegel is the concept of *alienation* (*Entfremdung*) or *self-alienation* (*Selbstentfremdung*). The passage from the Paris Manuscript which I have quoted is full of it. The philosophic spirit is nothing but the *alienated* spirit of the world thinking within its *self-alienation*. Wealth and state power are entities *alienated* from human existence. The philosopher is the abstract form of *alienated* man, the yardstick of the *alienated* world. The whole history of *alienation* is the production of abstract thought. We have here a rhythm grown almost obsessive.

At the same time, the concept of alienation or estrangement has a familiar sound to modern ears. It is a commonplace of all advance-guard literature. It is the mood of Rilke's *Malte Laurids Brigge*, of Kafka's novels, of Sartre's *Nausea* and Camus' *The Stranger*. It burst upon the modern world with Dostoievsky's *Notes from Underground*, and, indeed, all of his problematic heroes—Raskolnikov, Stavrogin, Ivan Karamazov—are creatures of alienation and estrangement. Also (derivative likewise from Hegel) it is a favorite theme of contemporary existentialism. But from Marx we learn that alienation has a crucial economic dimension.

The system of capitalist production rests upon wage-slavery; it is a system of compulsion in which the power to compel rests with those in possession of the instruments of production.[8] The laborer has nothing to sell but himself, the value of his labor is fixed by impersonal conditions of exchange beyond his powers of control, and the product which he creates is then separated from his life situation in a fashion which constitutes a violation of his human nature. The worker is thus alienated from the instruments of production; from all human relations constituting the process of production; and finally, from identification with the product which he himself creates.[9] In these three ways the capitalist process promotes a situation in which man is robbed of his essential human dignity because his life's time, unique and irreplaceable, is degraded to the level of impersonal economic relations.

Any attempt to reach and develop the sources of human selfhood is doomed to defeat by the organization of capitalist production, for it brings about that V*erdinglichung* (that is, the tendency for men to become mere natural objects) which is the antithesis of his humanity. Marx's treatment of the alienation of labor is, in the end, reducible to his remarkable insight into the mystical character of *the commodity*.[10]

A commodity is therefore a mysterious thing, simply because in it the social character of men's labor appears to them as an objective character stamped upon the product of that labor; because the relation of the producers to the sum total of their own labor is presented to them as a social relation, existing not between themselves, but between the products of their labor. This is the reason why the products of labor become commodities, social things whose qualities are at the same time perceptible and imperceptible by the senses. . . . There it is a definite social relation between men, that assumes in their eyes, the fantastic form of a relation between things. . . .

The clue to the entire position lies in the last sentence, in the tendency of "definite social relations between men" to assume "the fantastic form of a relation between things." And it is but a specific economic documentation of the older uneasiness of Emerson:

> There are two laws discrete
> Not reconciled,—
> Law for man, and law for thing;
> The last builds town and fleet,
> But it runs wild,
> And doth the man unking.

The Marxian point is that in a society in which "values in use" are subordinated to "values in exchange," labor itself becomes a commodity, and the lives of men are bartered on an openly competitive and impersonal market.

It is now possible to see the peculiar relevance of Marx's metaphor—logic is "the *money* of the spirit" which suggests the contrast between an abstract mathematical calculation of value (the impersonal measurement of the natural sciences) and a warm human assessment of worth. Marx's general sociology is based upon recognition of the degradation of a society infected by the bourgeois system of value, where the ancient institution of the family has had its sentimental core reduced to a money relation, and where the dignity of the professions is fast turning into the opportunism of business enterprise. When Sir Henry Maine characterized the transformation of mediaeval into modern law as the passage "from status to contract," he was stating impersonally a fact of social change. But this same fact becomes for Marx the ground for a critique of the capitalist order. Its most heated (and in many ways its most effective) statement comes in the intemperate language of "the call to action"—*The Communist Manifesto* of 1848.[11]

The bourgeoisie, wherever it has got the upper hand, has put an end to all feudal, patriarchal, idyllic relations. It has pitilessly torn asunder the motley feudal ties that bound man to his 'natural superiors,' and has left no other nexus between man and man than naked self-interest, than callous 'cash payment.' It has drowned the most heavenly ecstasies of religious fervor, of chivalrous enthusiasm, of Philistine sentimentalism, in the icy water of egotistical calculation. It has resolved personal worth into exchange value, and in place of the numberless indefeasible chartered freedoms, has set up that single unconscionable freedom—Free Trade. In one word, for exploitation, veiled by religious and political illusions, it has substituted naked, shameless, direct, brutal exploitation.

Marx speaks here not merely of "alienation," but of "shameless, brutal, exploitation." When the quality of alienation rises from simple estrangement into active disaffection, then this new-won self-consciousness of the industrial working class transforms "alienation" into "exploitation," and a vague (however severe) discontent is transformed into an effective aim. When the proletariat comes to recognize that its labor is a mere commodity, and that the cash nexus has reduced the relationship of employer and employee to a situation without human significance or moral obligation, then a revolutionary situation is in the making. This, for Marx, is the potentially explosive fact of modern history.

It might seem from Marx's account of alienation that he was espousing some idealistic essence of human nature against the material necessities of the economic order.[12] But such an interpretation would be a complete mistake. Marx's chief antagonism is not toward matter (quite the contrary), but toward that which is inherently abstract. His real quarrel with Hegel is that his emphasis upon abstract thought (the mere "Idea") inverts the order of conceptual valuation, and that it is precisely the material order of human life in which an adequate system of living value can be ascertained. He is therefore opposed to Hegel's dialectical idealism, not because it is dialectical, but because it is abstract. And he denounces money and the cash-nexus not because they are materialistic, but because they are impersonal. His own dialectical materialism, concisely expressed in the early pages of *The German Ideology*, is epitomized in the preface of *The Critique of Political Economy*.[13]

In the social production which men carry on they enter into definite relations that are indispensable and independent of their will; these relations of production correspond to a definite stage of development of their material powers of production. The sum total of these relations of production constitutes the economic structure of society—the real foundation on which rise legal and political superstructures and to which correspond definite forms of social consciousness. The mode of production in material life determines the general character of the social, political and spiritual processes of life. It is not the consciousness of men that determines their existence, but, on the contrary, their social existence determines their consciousness.

It is here, of course, that Marx really stands Hegel on his head. The Marxian materialism is interesting, moreover, because it has unconsciously become the methodological premise of contemporary social science. Modern sociological analysis conceptualizes culture as a segmented pyramid resting squarely upon a broad base of natural and human resources. The level above this is the level of current technology. The next level is the structure of social organization, political, economic, and otherwise; and the narrow apex of the pyramid is the domain of ideology, of theoretical science, philosophical construction, religious belief, literature and the fine arts. The implicit assumption is that the "lower" or "material" factors sustain the "higher" or "non-material," and that therefore, in some sense, the higher are socially reducible. This is precisely the Marxian contention.

The Marxian assumption that social existence determines consciousness, that the higher functions of culture are reducible to the lower, and that thought is the creature of social milieu has another consequence which is crucial for an understanding of the modern world: it constitutes a staggering assault upon objectivity. When in *The Communist Manifesto* Marx is describing the conditions of the proletarian—his propertylessness, his warped family relations, his dispossession of property and tradition—he adds: "Law, morality, religion are to him so many bourgeois prejudices, behind which lurk in ambush just as many bourgeois interests." And a moment later, when he is scolding the bourgeois for his opposition to the Communist criticisms of property, he continues:[14]

But don't wrangle with us so long as you apply to our intended abolition of bourgeois property, the standard of your bourgeois notions of freedom, culture, law, etc. Your very ideas are but the outgrowth of the conditions of your bourgeois production and bourgeois property, just as your juris-prudence is but the will of your class made into a law for all, a will whose essential character and direction are determined by the economical conditions of existence of your class.

The selfish misconception that induces you to transform into eternal laws of nature and of reason the social forms springing from your present mode of production and form of property—historical relations that rise and disappear in the progress of production—this misconception you share with every ruling class that has preceded you. What you see clearly in the case of ancient property, what you admit in the case of feudal property, you are of course forbidden to admit in the case of your own bourgeois form of property.

The general conclusion is clear. Men's conceptions, philosophies, views of the world change with the transformations of their material condi-tions and social relations. The ideas which rule each age are the ideas of its ruling class. There is, no doubt, always a social or existential determination of actual thinking, and the emergence of actual thought is influenced at many points by extra-theoretical factors. But the systematization of logical principles and the content of the natural sciences have always been held to be beyond the influence of ephemeral social conditions. That there is a structure of theoretical and practical reason which transcends sociology has been presupposed from the days of Plato and Aristotle. If Marxism were only to insist that all knowledge must be dated and contextualized (that it is inherently relational and historic), this would be a sufficient assault upon a narrow conception of objectivity.[15] But it goes further. Because it takes as central the doc-trine of the class struggle, because it polarizes society into bourgeois and proletarians, the rulers and the ruled, it must polarize thought as well. This leads to the doctrine that ideas are not to be judged primarily according to their theoretical truth or falsity, but according to their social role.

That *ideas have roots* is a commonplace of any organic theory of knowledge. That *ideas have consequences* is the insight of any pragmatic approach to the world. But that *ideas are weapons* is the peculiar con-tribution of Marxism to the intellectual history of the modern world.

Here is "pragmatism" with a vengeance, for it suggests that political considerations (I mean here considerations of the seizure and enjoyment of power) are the tests of theory. "To discover the truth" becomes a problematic activity. "To forge the intellectual weapons of the proletariat" becomes the responsibility of the intelligentsia. The very conception of the intelligentsia as a free-floating, essentially classless group whose calling is *the exercise of independent thought* is alien to the Marxist mentality. When Lenin said, "The teaching of Marx is all-powerful because it is true," either he was guilty of an inconsistency which cannot be mitigated by any merely logical appeal to "the theory of types," or else by "truth" he meant "harmony with the interests of the proletariat," rather than "that which is congruent with the method of scientific inquiry and which compels the assent of all reasonable men."

The contemporary practitioners of "The Sociology of Knowledge" have founded their discipline upon the Marxian insight. "In principle," says Karl Mannheim,[16] "it was politics which first discovered the sociological method in the study of intellectual phenomena. Basically it was in political struggles that for the first time men became aware of the unconscious collective motivations which had always guided the direction of thought." But his results go much further than this awareness. They lead to the intensification of the split between two polarized modes of thought:

The concept "ideology" reflects the one discovery which emerged from political conflict, namely that ruling groups can in their thinking become so intensively interest-bound to a situation that they are simply no longer able to see certain facts which would undermine their sense of domination. . . .

The concept of *utopian* thinking reflects the opposite discovery of the political struggle, namely that certain oppressed groups are intellectually so strongly interested in the destruction and transformation of a given condition of society that they unwittingly see only those elements in the situation which tend to negate it. . . . Their thought is never a diagnosis of the situation; it can be used only as a direction for action. . . .

Here is the Marxian dogma of the social role of ideas elevated into a method of social research. From the political distinction between bourgeois and proletarians follows the psychological distinction between the conservative and radical impulse within any social order, and from the psychological distinction follows the doctrine of the ideological and utopian dimensions of all thinking whatsoever. The technique is valuable, but it is also dangerous. For it seriously limits the potentialities of reconciliation within a divided society. The adamantine nature of contrary political interests is a fact which can only be acknowledged. If science, philosophy, and art are viewed as autonomous products of a rationality and an ordering of feelings which transcends politics, then they may by their spontaneous therapies heal the wounds of division. But if they too are but compliant instruments in the struggle for power, then the breach is absolute.

It is, of course, the contention of Marx that the breach *is* absolute. In his opinion "society as a whole is more and more splitting up into two great hostile camps, into two great classes directly facing each other: Bourgeoisie and Proletariat."[17] This is not merely a modern phenomenon. The history of all previously existing society has been a history of class struggle in which manifold gradations of social rank have produced a class of victims and a class of oppressors. What is new is not so much the formal structure of oppression, but its total nature, and therefore the simplification of the opposition between classes. When Marx speaks of class struggle, he does not speak only as a neutral social historian impersonally describing the incidence of social power. He also speaks as an indignant moralist, treating "oppression" with the ethical outrage which makes its existence a call to action. George Bernanos, anything but a follower of Marx, has diagnosed the contemporary social disease in terms which restate perfectly the Marxist position.[18]

Every civilization has, unquestionably, had its injustices. But injustice itself was always done by the hands of men, that is by hand, and what hands had done, other hands could undo. What we call modern civilization, on the other hand, is technological. Injustice is no longer handiwork, but machine-made, so that the slightest of errors can have incalculable consequences. Technology at the service of injustice or violence gives both of these a character of particular gravity. Injustice now is in danger of quickly becoming total, like war.

The contemporary situation is the outcome of a long process of dialectical development. For the consolidation of political power by the bourgeoisie is only the culmination of a series of revolutions in the modes of production and exchange since the breakdown of the feudal age. But, just as society is a moving balance of antithetical forces whose constant tension operates for the production of social change, and just as economic history presents an internal evolution which is the logical expression of these antithetical forces, so the bourgeois order has called into existence the modern working class (the proletariat) which is fated to bring about its downfall. That downfall is to come about through flaws within the system of capitalist production itself, which provoke periodic crises of overproduction, unemployment, and idle capital resources.[19] Through these periodic crises come two results:

first, the slow liquidation of the lower strata of the middle class—
the small tradesmen, shopkeepers, and businessmen who "sink gradually into the proletariat," and second, the gradual embitterment of
the industrial proletariat:[20]

Modern industry has converted the little workshop of the patriarchal
master into the great factory of the industrial capitalist. Masses of laborers,
crowded into factories, are organized like soldiers. As privates of the industrial army they are placed under the command of a perfect hierarchy of
officers and sergeants. Not only are they the slaves of the bourgeois class
and of the bourgeois state, they are daily and hourly enslaved by the
machine, by the overlooker, and above all, by the individual bourgeois
manufacturer himself. The more openly this despotism proclaims gain to
be its end and aim, the more petty, the more hateful and the more em-
bittering it is.

All that is then needed is the spur of revolutionary activity. The
proletariat, originally forming an incoherent mass, gradually unites to
form compact local bodies. Naturally they are harassed by the bourgeoisie, who encourage enmity and competition among the workers.
But as the class struggle "nears the decisive hour," a small section of
the ruling class splits off and joins the proletariat. Their leadership is
precisely what is needed to organize the proletariat into a class and
ultimately into a powerful political party. And with this organization
the revolution is at hand. The internal dialectic has thus worked itself
out, and what the bourgeoisie has wrought (in true Hegelian fashion)
is its own negation.[21]

The essential condition for the existence and for the sway of the bourgeois
class, is the formation and augmentation of capital; the condition for capital
is wage labor. Wage labor rests exclusively on competition between the
laborers. The advance of industry, whose involuntary promoter is the
bourgeoisie, replaces the isolation of the laborers, due to competition, by
their involuntary combination, due to association. The development of
Modern Industry, therefore, cuts from under its feet the very foundation
on which the bourgeoisie produces and appropriates products. What the
bourgeoisie therefore produces, above all, are its own grave diggers. Its fall
and the victory of the proletariat are equally inevitable.

Believing firmly in a rigid economic determinism, Marx asserts that
the fall of the bourgeoisie and the victory of the proletariat are historically inevitable; but at the same time he calls for a program of
revolutionary action to bring about the "inevitable" event. This is
probably less inconsistent than is usually assumed. Recognizing that

capitalism is only one phase in the evolution of modern society, Marx noted that the period of its dissolution would see a series of struggles for political power. His ultimate purpose was both theoretical and practical. He wished to formulate a theory of economic development, and he wished to provide a program of action to influence the course of history. There may be nothing incompatible between the role of social observer and that of social partisan. At any rate Marx was no more inconsistent in this respect than Hegel or Auguste Comte, both of whom also adhered to a philosophy of history that described a course of inevitable progressive development, and at the same time prescribed a program of social action. Hegel promoted the rise of the Germanic nations to the spiritual leadership of Europe. Comte promoted the religion of humanity under the priesthood of a scientific fraternity. Marx promoted the proletarian revolution under the leadership of the Communist Party.

Communists, according to Marx, have no interests separate from those of the proletariat as a whole. They are merely "the most advanced and resolute section of the working-class parties of every country," having over the great mass of the proletariat the advantage of clearly understanding the aims, the possibilities, and the historic role of the proletarian movement. Their aim is to guide the revolution: to form the proletariat into a self-conscious class, overthrow the supremacy of the bourgeoisie, gain political power, and abolish all private property. Only so can the repetitive mechanism of history be brought to its desired end. If the history of society is the history of class antagonisms growing out of the exploitation of one part of society by another, a Communist revolution which eliminates traditional property relations may prepare the way for the classless society.

The Marxian social philosophy is undoubtedly an enormous simplification. It is, however, as John Dewey has pointed out,[22] a simplification which has the great merit of combining "the romantic idealism of earlier social revolutionaries with what purports to be a thoroughly objective scientific analysis, expressed in formulation of a single all-embracing law." In Marx the theoretical interest in "scientific analysis" and the practical interest in revolutionary reform coalesce. But his followers have chosen the latter path rather than the former. Years after Marx was dead, Frederick Engels found an old notebook of his, written in Brussels in 1845, containing the rudimentary "Theses on Feuerbach." Its last "thesis" has been the acknowledged program for all of his followers. "The philosophers," said Marx, "have *interpreted* the world in various ways; the point however is to *change* it." This may serve perfectly as transition to the work of Marx's heir—V. I. Lenin. It was to be his destiny less to interpret the world than to change it.

2. LENIN'S EPISTEMOLOGY

Marx was the product of the cosmopolitan culture of the nineteenth century. He was intimately acquainted not only with English political economy and French socialism, but with the history of philosophy since Aristotle (whose texts he quotes in *Capital* in the original Greek) and with the world literature which since Goethe had been the requisite possession of the European intellectual. His work is therefore, as Edmund Wilson has noticed, "heavily loaded with the old paraphernalia of culture." But with Lenin it is different; all of his writing is strictly pragmatic. It is functional and purposive, and even if it grows dull with repetitions and pedantic with endless quotation, it is nevertheless directed toward the accomplishment of an immediate purpose.

This is not to say that Lenin was without culture or aesthetic sensibilities. Quite the contrary. It is said in Russia that his early love of Latin left a permanent mark on his literary style, and Maxim Gorky relates his enthusiasm for Tolstoi: "What a colossus, eh? What a marvelously developed brain! Here's an artist for you, sir. And do you know something still more amazing? You couldn't find a real muzhik in literature till this count appeared on the scene." He also quotes Lenin upon listening to Beethoven's *Appassionata*: "I know nothing that is greater than the *Appassionata*; I'd like to listen to it every day. It is marvelous superhuman music. I always think with pride—perhaps it is naive of me—what marvelous things human beings can do! . . . But I can't listen to music too often. It affects your nerves, makes you want to say stupid nice things and stroke the heads of people who could create such beauty while living in this vile hell. And now you mustn't stroke anyone's head—you might get your hand bitten off. You have to hit them on the head without any mercy, although our ideal is not to use force against anyone. Hm, hm, our duty is infernally hard."[23] The emotional sense of this passage is clear, and it is as characteristic of Lenin's approach to philosophy as to music. His philosophy (however reluctantly) is without curiosity, intellectual imagination, or *metaphysical* need.

When Lenin in the 1908 preface to his chief philosophical venture, *Materialism and Empirio-Criticism*, says (as I have quoted at the head of this chapter), "As far as I am concerned, I, too, am a 'seeker' in philosophy," he is speaking ironically. In the first place he is referring directly and sarcastically to a sentence of Lunacharsky's: "Perhaps we stray, but we are seekers." Lenin continues: "The task which I have set for myself in this book is simply to find out what is the trouble with those who under the guise of Marxism are offering something baffling, confusing and reactionary."[24] His seeking is, therefore, an expedition in search of heresy.

Marxism as social philosophy functions both as a semi-religious symbol to call out and maintain the most absolute loyalty to a cause and at the same time as a body of doctrine whose application yields directives for social policy. Lenin's own philosophic contributions are most often presented by him as mere "restatements" of the principles of Marx and Engels, and he pretends (perhaps even deceiving himself) to the most rigorous orthodoxy, which he supports by a rigid exegesis of the original writings. It is perhaps not surprising therefore that he should charge his opponents with "revisionism" and "deviations," and that he should set himself up as the protector of "the truth" against all "bourgeois and reactionary views."

The necessity of protecting the truth against the deviations and the revisions of the misguided and the evil-minded does not entail the absolute suppression of philosophical discussion; it merely confines it within the kind of limits which the medieval Christian tradition always imposed. As late as the end of the nineteenth century Cardinal Newman in A Grammar of Assent was distinguishing between inquiry, in which one entertains a hypothesis and inquires into it to discover whether it is true or false, and investigation, in which one looks into the grounds and the reasons of a truth to which one initially assents. Since the outcome of inquiry is always problematic, and since it is based upon an initial uncertainty, it is not permitted to the faithful. Investigation, on the other hand, is a legitimate enterprise. A similar situation holds within the Marxist community. Lenin is a "seeker" in philosophy in the sense that although he never engages in what the West knows as free philosophical discussion (that is, inquiry), he does frequently and interestingly "investigate."

Naturally Lenin cannot assert that Marxist doctrine is accepted upon the grounds of faith, for fideism is the great enemy. His argument is at the same time more pedestrian and more subtle, for it is an appeal to "practice." "From the standpoint of life," says Lenin, "practice ought to be the first and fundamental criterion of the theory of knowledge. It inevitably leads to materialism, brushing aside the infinite inventions of professional scholasticism." But practice is notoriously inconclusive, and also there is the prestige of the method of science, for which Lenin claims to have the greatest respect, and which, therefore, he must somehow appropriate. He thus continues:

Of course, we must not forget that the criterion of practice, in the nature of things, neither confirms nor refutes completely any human presentation. This criterion is sufficiently indefinite not to allow human knowledge to become "absolute," and at the same time sufficiently definite to wage a bitter struggle with all varieties of idealism and agnosticism. If that which our practice confirms, is the sole, ultimate and objective truth, then it follows that the sole path to this truth is the road of science which stands by the materialist creed. For instance, Bogdanov agrees to recognize Marx's theory of the circulation of capital as an objective truth only "for our time," regarding as "dogmatism" the designation of this theory as an "historically objective" truth. This again is a blunder. No further circumstances can change the correspondence of this theory with the fact, for the simple reason that such a truth is as eternal as that Napoleon died on May 5, 1821. But inasmuch as practice, i.e., the development of capitalist countries in the last few decades, actually proves the objective truth of the whole social and economic theory of Marx in general, and not only some of its specific formulations, it is obvious that to speak here of the "dogmatism" of the Marxists, is to make an inexcusable concession to bourgeois economy. The sole inference from the proposition upheld by Marxists, that the theory of Marx is the objective truth, is this: Following in the direction of the Marxian theory, we shall draw nearer and nearer to the objective truth (without exhausting it); following another path, we shall arrive at confusion and falsehood.[25]

The conclusion is thus: (1) a denial of the "absoluteness" of Marxian theory, while at the same time (2) an insistence on its "objective truth;" (3) the assertion that a *theory* is just as eternally true as an *elementary proposition of fact*; and (4) the statement that Marxism is objective truth in the sense that to follow its guidance *leads* nearer and nearer to objective truth. The logical incompatibility of these four propositions is not difficult to demonstrate. But as Lenin states them, they are a plausible attempt to sustain a dogmatic Marxism without removing the scientific insistence upon the successive approximateness of all theory.

Materialism and Empirio-Criticism is without doubt a work of philosophical partisanship which can be more clearly understood in terms of the context out of which it was produced. The hundredth anniversary of the death of Kant occurred in 1904, and the years immediately following were given over to discussions both of Kant's ethics and of the neo-Kantian epistemology which had so much influenced Ernst Mach and through him the early philosophers of modern science. Moreover, the works of Mach and Avenarius had penetrated into Russia, where they had influenced even those who were professed followers of the dialectical materialism of Marx and Engels. Lenin's first impulse is thus the criticism of the neo-Kantian tendencies (he terms them Empirio-Criticism) as a reinforcement of the position of orthodox materialism. But there were other motivations at work also. Bogdanov, the chief target of Lenin's attack, was a rival of his for the ideological leadership of the Bolshevist Party, and therefore *Materialism and Empirio-Criticism* was also originally conceived as a weapon in an intra-Party struggle for power.[26] This is of interest in the historiography of the Russian Revolution, but it is not to our purpose. For what we are more particularly concerned with is Lenin as social philosopher, and what the argument of *Materialism and Empirio-Criticism* demonstrates to perfection is an asserted relationship between a general theory of social criticism and the epistemological foundation upon which it is presumed to rest.

This assertion originates not primarily with Marx but with Engels. The latter had in his *Ludwig Feuerbach and the Outcome of Classical German Philosophy* noted that "the great basic question of all philosophy, especially of modern philosophy, is that concerning the relation of thinking and being," and (with that power of simplification of difficult and complex issues in which any impatient social theorist excels) he had succeeded in reducing all possibilities to two. For he continues:[27] "The answers which the philosophers gave to this question split them into two great camps. Those who asserted the primacy of spirit to nature . . . comprised the camp of idealism. The others, who regarded nature as primary, belong to the various schools of materialism." Here is again that strategy of dualistic reduction which we have experienced in the metapsychology of Freud, and which also characterizes the Marxist mode of perception. To the class distinctions of proletarian and bourgeois, and the distinction within general theory of "utopian" and "ideological," we must now add the philosophical distinction between idealism and materialism. And just as Marx sharpens the social dialectic until the mean between the extremes—in this case the middle class —disappears through radical absorption by the extremes, so the philosophical strategy of Engels and of Lenin is to reduce any compromise position—whether the agnosticism of Hume, the subjectivism of Kant, or the empirio-criticism of Mach and Karl Pearson—to Berkeley's idealism, which, with its solopsistic implications, constitutes for them the final philosophical *reductio ad absurdum*.

Lenin's theory of perception begins with the affirmation of the epistemic application of the materialism-idealism dichotomy. One is a materialist if he recognizes that there are "objects in themselves," that they exist outside the mind, and that our ideas and sensations are "copies" or "images" of these objects. One is an idealist if he asserts that objects do not exist outside the mind, and if he believes that objects are nothing but simple "combinations of sensations."[28] There are two parts to the materialist theory: (1) the naive realistic assumption of the common-sense givenness of the external world, and (2) a simple representative or causal theory of perception. The clue to the entire position lies in the mediating role of sensation.[29]

For every scientist who is not led astray by professorial philosophy, as well as for every materialist, sensation is nothing but a direct connection of the mind with the external world; it is the transformation of energy of external excitation into a mental state. . . . The sophistry of idealist philosophy consists in that it takes sensation not as a connection of the mind with the outer world, but as a screen, a wall which separates the mind from the outer world. . . .

Independent of the knowing mind and its states of consciousness there exist the vibrations of matter and ether waves of a certain length and velocity, and when these act upon the retina, color sensations are produced. This is the simple consequence of Lenin's epistemology: that matter acting upon the sense-organs produces sensation. Naive realism, as Lenin says, is the "instinctive materialist viewpoint," but he hastens to remove from the term "naive" all tinge of innocence or simple-mindedness. It is, in fact, the realism of a healthy common sense.[30]

The "naive realism" of any healthy person, who is not an inmate of an insane asylum or in the school of the idealist philosophers consists in this, that he believes reality, the environment and the things in it, to exist independently of his perception—independently of his conception of himself in particular, and of his fellow men in general. . . . Our sensation, our consciousness is only a representation of the outer world. But it is obvious that although a representation cannot exist without someone for whom it is a representation, the represented thing exists independently of the one for whom it is a representation. The "naive" belief of mankind is consciously taken by materialism as the basis of its theory of knowledge.

It is clear that the entire dynamic of Lenin's position is against any form of sensationalism which asserts that bodies or things are *complexes of our sensations* and toward a position which views sensations as themselves *images or copies* of bodies and things. But this only suggests the recurrent problem of a representative theory of perception. Any theory which asserts (as Lenin does) "a reality which is copied, photographed, and reflected by our sensations, but which exists independently of them" must account for the existence of truth and error; must show by what procedures a "copy, photograph, or reflection" may be compared with its original in order to ensure its accuracy. Since this seems to involve either an immediate intuition of reality (things-in-themselves) or an infinite series of congruent comparisons, the position seems untenable.[31] Lenin obviously would find neither alternative acceptable, nor indeed does he really deal with the difficulty. The closest he comes is to appeal to the pragmatism of Engels, who, he says, "in 1888 and 1891 introduced the criterion of practice into the theory of knowledge of materialism." If we ask what proves the correspondence of our perception with the independent object perceived, the answer is "the success of our actions." But this notion of successful action remains unanalyzed in detail as to its bearing upon epistemological theory.

Lenin's theory of the independent existence of material things leads to the further doctrine of the independence of the system of relations which contains them. From the reality of the outer world of objects follows the objectivity of the laws of nature. A recognition "of the fact of natural order and the approximate reflection of that order in the mind" is also a tenet of materialism. Neither Engels nor Lenin ever doubts the objective existence of law, order, causality, and necessity in nature. Just as this constitutes a denial of Kant's doctrines in the "Transcendental Analytic" that those things which are universal and necessary in experience are the product of forms of understanding imposed by the mind, so it denies the doctrine of Kant's "Transcendental Aesthetic" of the objective ideality of space and time. Space, time, causality, matter, and law form a simple set or complex of external nature, and the progress of science (to which assumption, again, both Engels and Lenin adhere) is simply the way in which "our experience and our cognitions adapt themselves more and more to objective space and time, continually reflecting them with greater and greater accuracy."[32]

Materialism and Empirio-Criticism concludes with a chapter (Chapter V, "The Latest Revolution in Natural Science and Philosophic Idealism") which is of the greatest interest, not only because it illustrates the type of philosophy of science to which dialectical materialism leads, but also because it represents a particular response to the problem of the philosophical implications of the revolution in physical science which has been in operation since the turn of the century. The period 1900-1908 not only included the failure of the Revolution of 1905 and the new influence of Mach and Avenarius upon the Russian Marxists, but also the new discoveries concerning cathode rays, radioactivity, and electrons (the electrical theory of matter) associated with the work of

Röntgen, J. J. Thomson, Lorentz, and Rutherford. Lenin is therefore interested in exploring the epistemological consequences of "recent physics," particularly since its conclusions had stimulated a revival of idealistic interpretations of the nature of the world of science. The discovery of radium was thought to have undermined the principle of the conservation of energy. The electron theory of matter was thought to have undermined the conservation of matter. Mass disappears. The foundations of mechanics are destroyed. And Henri Poincaré, the famous mathematical physicist, was saying precisely what Sir Arthur Eddington was to repeat just twenty years later:[33] We have before us the ruin of old principles. Materiality has vanished. In dissecting matter into electric charges, we have lost the conception of substance. The world of physics has become a world of shadows. All we have left is pointer readings, symbols, signs, and prescriptions for practice.

Engels had said explicitly that "with each epoch-making discovery in natural science, materialism has been obliged to change its form," and Lenin sees that this in no way affects the basic issue, which is after all not a matter of metaphysics but of epistemology. To say that the dematerialization of the atom has devaluated Marx and Engels is to miss the point. The insistence upon the solidity of body, or the theory of immutable substance, is metaphysical materialism, but it is not dialectical materialism. For what is really at stake is not the metaphysical problem of *substance*, but the epistemological problem of *objectivity*.

To put the question from the only correct, that is, the dialectico-materialistic standpoint, we must ask: do electrons, ether, etc. exist as objective realities outside of the human mind? The scientists must answer this question without hesitation and the answer must be an affirmative one, for they recognize without hesitation the existence of nature prior to man and organic matter. Thus is the question decided on the side of materialism, for the idea of matter as we already stated, epistemologically means nothing new, besides some objective reality existing independently of the human mind and reflected by it.[34]

The alternative is, of course, idealism, and this "deviation toward reactionary philosophy" manifested by some schools of physicists is but "a temporary relapse in a sickly period in the history of science—is the effect of growing pains brought on by a sharp crisis in old established ideas." The result of the inquiry into the revolution in natural science is, in the end, the same as that into the effects of the philosophy of Mach. The interpretation of physical phenomena is as fraught with significance as the interpretation of the status of our sensations. Science is no more neutral and autonomous than philosophy, for in the end, its uses and interpretations are indeed a species of philosophy. Poincaré is as dangerous as Avenarius for in both "it is impossible not to discern clearly the partisan struggle in philosophy, a struggle which ultimately expresses the tendencies and ideology of classes hostile to one another in modern society."[35]

3. THE THEORY OF VIOLENCE

Materialism and Empirio-Criticism is an impressive link in the chain of Marxist ideology. It expands the theoretical philosophy first worked out by Engels and adapts it to the challenge of modern empirical science. It therefore solidifies the philosophical substructure upon which all subsequent Marxist interpretation may rest. And yet, one lays it down with a certain disappointment. A critique of philosophical idealism, an attempt to prove that materialism is the philosophy of science, the assertion of an almost naively realistic theory of knowledge, it seems far removed from the conspiratorial mood and revolutionary acts. One cannot even say that it is a contribution to the epistemology of violence.

But the Marxism of the second generation did produce its theoretical incitements to violence. As the over-all criticism of a society in distress, of a social order in which "injustice had become total," this was no less than its assertion of responsibility. The chief theoretician of violence is again Lenin, but this time he has been partially anticipated by the paradoxical advocate of revolutionary syndicalism, the Frenchman Georges Sorel, whose famous *Reflections on Violence* was published in 1907 (the year of Bergson's *Creative Evolution*). Lenin's own theory of revolution was not published until ten years later, in 1917, on the eve of the Russian Revolution.

Reflections on Violence seems curiously outside the spirit of the Marxist tradition, although it utilizes the Marxist vocabulary, and although Sorel himself considered that he had been inspired by the principles of Marx rather than by "the formulas taught by the official proprietors of Marxism." It is the abandonment of formula and the recourse to revolutionary passions which gives his work its freshness. Fascism, for all of its crude disorderliness in Germany, was dominated by a paradoxical obsession with "legality." And Marxism, however opportunistic in practice, in theory is infected with the normal obsession of the Hegelian mentality: commitment to a "logic" of historical action and a theory of dialectical inevitability which easily yields to formula and simplification. But if there is any logic in Sorel, it is a logic of passion, guided by the same sympathies for the irrational in man which appear in Bergson, at whose lectures at the Collège de France Sorel was not infrequently to be found.

The logic of Sorel is the logic of the *myth*. All men who participate in a great social movement guide their action by the picture which they hold of the triumph of their cause. These pictures are symbolic constructions incapable of logical dissection into smaller elements, but dynamic as historical forces within the great social movements where they appear. To borrow a phrase from Whitehead, they are "lures for feeling" and for action.

Sorel's criticism of the "degenerate" Marxism of his time (Bernstein's evolutionary socialism, for example) was precisely at the point of its analytic rationalism. "As long as there are no myths accepted by the masses, one may go on talking of revolts indefinitely, without ever provoking any revolutionary movement; this is what gives such importance to the general strike and renders it so odious to socialists who are afraid of a revolution."[36] A myth is not an intellectual construction, but an organization of feelings of those preparing themselves to enter into a decisive struggle; myths are not descriptions of things but expressions of a determination to act. In this the myth is to be distinguished from a utopia, which is an intellectual product, the work of theorists who seek to establish a model for the critical evaluation of the evils of the contemporary society, and which is, therefore, itself a model for possible legislation and open to critical attack. A utopia can be discussed like any other proposed constitution for society, and it can even be "refuted" by showing, for example, that it violates all reasonable requirements of economic productivity, or is incompatible with the assumed nature of man. But a myth cannot be refuted; being, at bottom "identical with the convictions of a group; being the expression of these convictions in the language of movement."

To speak of social "myths" is in no sense an indication that one does not take them with the utmost seriousness. The class struggle is drama perhaps, but it is drama in which the actors must be committed beyond withdrawal. This implies that the souls of the revolutionary *dramatis personae* must receive a deep and lasting impression.[37]

These results could not be produced in any very certain manner by the use of ordinary language; use must be made of a body of images which, by *intuition alone*, and before any considered analyses are made, is capable of evoking as an undivided whole the mass of sentiments which corresponds to the different manifestations of the war undertaken by Socialism against modern society. The Syndicalists solve this problem perfectly, by concentrating the whole of Socialism in the drama of the general strike; there is

thus no longer any place for the reconciliation of contraries in the equivoca-
tions of the professors; everything is clearly mapped out, so that only one
interpretation of Socialism is possible. This method has all the advantages
which "integral" knowledge has over analysis, according to the doctrine of
Bergson; and perhaps it would not be possible to cite another example
which would so perfectly demonstrate the value of the famous professor's
doctrines.

The myth of the general strike is Sorel's contribution to Marxist
revolutionary strategy, for it is a concept which, he thinks, invokes all
the sentiments of class war and brings them to a pitch of maximum
intensity, reinforcing the painful memories of particular conflicts and
coloring Socialism with the most intense class loyalty. The chief weakness of Marxism has always resided in the tendency of the middle class
to grow rather than to collapse, and for the sharply etched outlines of
rigid social classes to grow dim as social mobility increases under the
aegis of economic prosperity. But Sorel saw the general strike as really
polarizing society in a crisis of class loyalty which could effect infinitely
more than the placid circumstances of daily life. All oppositions become
extraordinarily clear when enlarged to the proportions of a general strike;
society would then be plainly divided into two camps as on a field of
battle. The image of the field of battle is no thoughtless metaphor; it is
essential to the myth.

The social revolution [says Sorel] is an extension of that war in which each
great strike is an episode; this is the reason why Syndicalists speak of that
revolution in the language of strikes; for them Socialism is reduced to the
conception, the expectation of, and the preparation for the general strike,
which, like the Napoleonic battle, is to completely annihilate a condemned
régime.[38]

The whole point is the drama of annihilation, which must be as brutal
as lightning—and as instantaneous. No quantum theory of revolution
is proposed here, no sum of historical details. "*The general strike must
be taken as a whole and undivided, and the passage from capitalism to
Socialism conceived as a catastrophe, the development of which baffles
description.*"[39]

Clearly the psychology which is here implicitly presupposed is that
of "all or nothing." Social conditions form a system bound together by
an iron law of necessity, "so that the system is given as it were in one
block." Therefore it cannot disappear except in a catastrophe which
involves the whole. This histrionic view of social change is closely
bound up with a faith in the efficacy of violence. Violence and catas-

trophe alike appeal to some deep, almost mystic anarchism hidden deep in Sorel's romantic soul, even if it is expressed in a calculated Marxian terminology. It is, of course, difficult whether for bourgeois or proletarian to "feel" the necessity of tumultuous rioting. To step out of the region of legality requires an extraordinary push of circumstance. Hence the incitement to proletarian violence depends upon a virtually Nietzschean transvaluation of the ordinary values, whereby criminal acts are by a single stroke converted into heroic and meritorious deeds. Sorel understood this perfectly well. "If Socialism comes to grief," he said, "it will evidently be . . . because it will have been alarmed at its own barbarity."

Sorel's attempt to assimilate the heroic virtues to a violent proletariat carries with it a corresponding contempt for the ideology of a timorous humanitarianism, and for middle-class cowardice which always sur- renders before the threat of violence, thus showing that it is incapable of self-preservation. In this it joins hands with a more orthodox Marxism, which only asks that the proletariat cling with perfect obstinacy to its revolutionary aim. But the difference is that whereas for Marx violence is always a means to a revolutionary end, and loses its usefulness when that end has been accomplished, for Sorel there is something excellent in violence itself.[40]

In the total ruin of institutions and of morals there remains something which is powerful, new and intact, and it is that which constitutes, properly speaking, the soul of the revolutionary proletariat. Nor will this be swept away in the general decadence of moral values, if the workers have enough energy to bar the road to the middle-class corrupters, answering their advances with the plainest brutality.

I believe that I have brought an important contribution to discussions on Socialism. . . . The bond which I pointed out at the beginning of this inquiry between Socialism and proletarian violence appears to us now in all its strength. It is to violence that Socialism owes those high ethical values by means of which it brings *salvation* to the modern world.

Sorel's doctrine of violence has not found general favor in the modern world. Perhaps its saving quality was not apparent to the French bourgeois spirit, which has never recovered from the intense shock of the French Revolution. Perhaps also Freud has made us too aware of the relation between aggression and the death instinct to permit us to be persuaded of its therapy. Only in the early days of the Russian Revolution was there a direct translation of Sorel's theory into action. It is doubtful if there was direct influence between the two. It is true that sometime in 1907 or 1908 Lenin was in Paris writing endless political tracts at *La Rotonde* in Montparnasse, and that this was the very time that Sorel was expounding Bergson and his own theories in the tiny front office of Péguy's *Cahiers de la Quinzaine* in the Rue de la Sorbonne, but there is no evidence that the two ever met. Ten years later (September, 1919) after Lenin had come to power in Russia, Sorel wrote for the fourth edition of *Reflections on Violence* an appendix "For Lenin" in admiration and respect. Here he said:[41] "I have no reason to suppose that Lenin may have accepted any ideas in my books; but if it were so, I should be in no small degree proud of having contributed to the intellectual formation of a man who seems to me at once the greatest theorist that socialism has had since Marx and a head of the State whose genius recalls that of Peter the Great." The rise of the Soviet Union was in some sense a vindication of Sorel's contention that the principles which he had defended in *Reflections on Violence* were not mere romantic nonsense. But on the other hand it was not his theories which the Russian Revolution adopted, but those of Lenin.

Lenin's own treatment of violence comes in the second most important of his philosophical works, *State and Revolution*, written in August and September 1917, just before the October Revolution. In a sense it too is an attempt to vindicate the technique of revolutionary violence, not like Sorel by showing its intrinsically moral properties, but by attempting to undermine the claims to justice and legality of the whole state apparatus against which the Communist revolution is directed. This is, in effect, a major revolution in the domain of political theory, for it projects the violence of illegal action into the very stronghold of legality—the political commonwealth.

The liberal-democratic conception of the political state is that it is the machinery of representation and compromise whereby interests which conflict (whether economic, religious, social, or personal) may be adjudicated somehow short of the appeal to force. It does not deny the fact of conflict of interest among men; it merely assumes that such conflicts can be regulated without the explosion of the community. It therefore emphasizes just those political expedients which exist below the threshold of violence: discussion, compromise, consent, resignation, good sportsmanship, and the achievement of generosity wherever these are possible. All this, of course, within the framework of a quasi-Aristotelian view of politics which sees the state as the community of those who in some sense share a common system of values, and whose purpose in coexisting is not merely to live, but to live well.

All of this Lenin denies. He agrees with Engels that the state is merely a product of society at a certain stage of its development; at that stage, in fact, where class antagonisms, if taken at the level of their real meaning, would contradict the public assumptions of shared values which the state pretends to represent. The power of the state apparently stands above society, regulating it, moderating it, keeping it within the bounds of order—an impersonal and higher authority of justice. But this conception is the measure of bourgeois fraud. In reality, "the state is the product and the manifestation of the *irreconcilability* of class antagonisms. The state arises when, where, and to the extent that the class antagonisms *cannot* be objectively reconciled. And, conversely, the existence of the state proves that the class antagonisms *are* irreconcilable."[42] Once it is recognized that the state is the organ for the oppression of the proletariat, and that the "order" which it claims to create is but the legalization and continuation of this oppression, there can be no conclusion to the class struggle short of a violent revolution which brings about the destruction of the apparatus of state power.

The liberal-democratic version of the state fits best with its everyday operations, when economic life is "normal" and when there are no convulsions of labor unrest or threats of foreign domination. But the intent of Marxist theory is to force us to consider the state at that moment when its back is to the wall. What in effect, Lenin asks, is the state in time of domestic or foreign crisis? What is the state when the chips are down? The answer is obvious and clear. A local strike occurs and the police are called in. If it persists and spreads, the National Guard is called out. If the boundaries of the nation are threatened, the army is mobilized. The public force exists in every state: not merely army and police, but prisons, judges, tax-collectors, repressive institutions of all kinds. But the army and the police power are at the core, and in them is illustrated the real nature of the state as an organization of violence. It is completely within the Marxist tradition to define the state not as an agency of public welfare, but as that institution which enjoys a monopoly of what it is pleased to call *legitimate* violence. Revolution is thus not the substitution of immoral for moral, or of illegitimate for legitimate violence; it is the pitting of power against power where the real issue is freedom or exploitation.

Lenin is very anxious to combat the current misconception that according to Marx and Engels, the state will naturally "wither away," for this means a slurring over of revolutionary fervor and a blunting of the weapons of action. Such an interpretation is, as he says, the crudest distortion of Marxism. The bourgeois state does not "wither away." It is only annihilated by the proletariat in the course of the revolution.[43]

. . . the 'special repressive force' of the bourgeoisie for the suppression of the proletariat, of the millions of workers by a handful of the rich, must be replaced by a "special repressive force" of the proletariat for the suppression of the bourgeoisie (the dictatorship of the proletariat). It is just this that constitutes the destruction of the state as the state. It is just this that constitutes the act of the seizure of the means of production in the name of society.

It is clear that the successful revolution, having established the dictatorship of the proletariat, still operates as a political power; it still needs to exercise a repressive force in order to consolidate the revolutionary idea and to spread its doctrine into every joint of the social structure.[44]

The proletariat needs state power, the centralized organization of force, the organization of violence, both for the purpose of crushing the resistance of the exploiters and for the purpose of *guiding* the great mass of the population—the peasantry, the petty-bourgeoisie, the semi-proletarians—in the work of organizing Socialist economy. By educating a worker's party, Marxism educates the vanguard of the proletariat, capable of assuming power and of *leading the whole people* to Socialism, of directing and organizing the new order, of being the teacher, guide, and leader of all the toiling and exploited in the task of building up their social life without the bourgeoisie and against the bourgeoisie.

At this point Lenin suggests one of his most original ideas (and one which goes considerably beyond the theories of Marx and Engels): the centrality of the Communist Party. Although Marx had advocated the strategy of proletarian revolution, his grounding of social process in the material conditions of productivity had caused him to recognize that social revolution cannot (either by force or by persuasion) be made to run in advance of the underlying industrial situation upon which the making of a proletarian mentality depends. Lenin's peculiar insight was this: that the proletarian mentality is not really socialistic, but only trade-union, and that it requires bourgeois intellectuals (of whom, naturally, Marx and Engels are themselves prime examples) to educate the proletariat to socialism. This has two consequences. First, it gives a dominating role to intellectuals in the revolutionary enterprise. Second, in building a small, compact, fanatically devoted Communist Party from their nucleus, it conceives of the Party as an intellectual and moral elite whose jealous monopoly of Marxian scholarship makes them the watchdogs of the purity of Communist doctrine, and the wielders of total power for the ultimate good of the proletariat.

Perhaps no single feature of Lenin's political theory has seemed so obvious and yet so paradoxical. In Dostoievski's great novel *The Possessed* there is an intense and sometimes comic conspiratorial scene where the plotters meet at the home of Virginsky and listen to the plan which Shigalov has drawn up for the revolutionary reorganization of society. The plan is dogmatic, ruthless, and confused, and in it Dostoievski quietly expresses some of his most deadly irony. The whole point is made by Shigalov as he sums up the logic of his plan. "Starting from unlimited freedom," he says seriously, "I arrive at unlimited despotism. . . ." There have been many who have seen in Communism a kind of Shigalovism where the aspirations for freedom of the proletarian revolution have been transformed into the unlimited despotism of the leaders of the Communist Party. If they are correct, it is the political theory of Lenin which has prepared the way.

Certainly in Shigalov's plan is expressed some of the latent Hegelianism which from time to time takes its revenge upon those Marxists who have "stood it on its head," for in Hegel everything passes over into its opposite. Lenin's theory of the Party doubtless had no such ultimate intention, but its emphasis upon an elite absolute in power and intelligence gives to this corporate entity an importance which submerges all individualism in the service of its goal, and which, like the national state for Hegel, becomes the representative and the bearer of historic destiny. Arthur Koestler's novel of Stalinist Russia, *Darkness at Noon,* faces unflinchingly many of the dilemmas which follow from Lenin's theory of the Party, and no scene is more poignant than that between the old Party stalwart Rubashov and the youthful rebel Richard:

> Rubashov waited to see whether he still had anything to say, but Richard said nothing. Dusk was falling rapidly now. Rubashov took his pince-nez off and rubbed it on his sleeve.
>
> "The Party can never be mistaken," said Rubashov. "You and I can make a mistake. Not the Party. The Party, comrade, is more than you and I and a thousand others like you and I. The Party is the embodiment of the revolutionary idea in history. History knows no scruples and no hesitation. Inert and unerring, she flows toward her goal. At every bend in her course she leaves the mud which she carries and the corpses of the drowned. History knows her way. She makes no mistakes. He who has not absolute faith in History does not belong in the Party's ranks."
>
> Richard said nothing. . . .[45]

Because the party is infallible, because it is "the embodiment of the revolutionary idea in history," it must exercise power subsequent to the revolution, but it is not to simply take over the existing state machinery ("the rotten parliamentarianism" Lenin calls it) and administer it.

Marx's idea, which Lenin approves, is that the working class must shatter and completely destroy the ready-made state machinery which it finds. Marx was too pragmatic to produce a utopian answer to the question: What is to replace the shattered state machinery? (waiting rather for experience to dictate the exact form of the organization of the proletariat as ruling class), but he hinted at certain necessary developments: for the bourgeois standing army, the substitution of the armed proletariat as a whole; for the minority of privileged officialdom, a series of proletarian managers to be elected and subject to recall at any time with salaries reduced to "workingmen's wages."

Lenin was too practical to indulge in anarchist or utopian dreams of how best to immediately do away with all administration, all officialdom, all subordination, for that would put off the Socialist revolution until human nature had itself been revolutionized. "No," he said realistically, "we want the Socialist revolution with human nature as it is now, with human nature that cannot do without subordination, control, and managers." But if there is to be subordination, let it be to the proletariat—the armed vanguard of the laboring and exploited—and to the simple functionaries who do its bidding.[46]

We will organize large-scale production, starting from what capitalism has already created; we workers *ourselves*, relying on our own experience as workers, establishing a strict, an iron discipline, supported by the state power of the armed workers, shall reduce the role of the state officials to that of simply carrying out our instructions as responsible moderately paid 'managers' (of course with technical knowledge of all sorts, types and degrees). This is *our* proletarian task, with this we can and must *begin* when carrying through a proletarian revolution. Such a beginning, on the basis of large-scale production, of itself leads to the gradual 'withering away' of all bureaucracy, to the gradual creation of a new order, an order without quotation marks, an order which has nothing to do with wage slavery, an order in which the more and more simplified functions of control and accounting will be performed by each in turn, will then become a habit, and will finally die out as *special* functions of a special stratum of the population.

There is a certain historical irony in Lenin's conception that the task of the proletariat is to reduce the role of officials to that of paid managers, which "of itself leads to the gradual withering away of all bureaucracy," and his hope that public functions will cease to be "political" and become simply "administrative." This is the most dreamy-eyed utopianism, involving the complete undoing of the economic requirement of a division of labor within society. It would require, as he says, the reduction of the functions of public service "into such simple operations of control and accounting as are within the reach of the vast majority of the population, and ultimately, of every single individual."

It is true, of course, that Lenin made no attempt to define the exact moment of the future withering away of the state, particularly since he thought it must obviously be a rather lengthy process. The Marxist theory of the inevitable annihilation of capitalism and the bourgeois state suggests that the epoch of transition between capitalism and communism must face certain typical socialist problems. It must substitute a democracy of the poor for a democracy of the rich. It must use force for the crushing of the bourgeois remnants, so that no class differences remain. It must maintain peace without exploitation so that, freed from "capitalist slavery," men will "gradually *become accustomed* to the observance of the elementary rules of social life that have been known for centuries and repeated for thousands of years in all school books; they will become accustomed to observing them without force, without compulsion, without subordination, without the *special apparatus* for compulsion which is called the state."[47]

In May, 1931, André Gide wrote in his Journal:

But above all I should like to live long enough to see Russia's plan succeed and the states of Europe obliged to accept what they insist on ignoring. How could so novel a reorganization have been achieved without, first, a period of profound disorganization? Never have I bent over the future with a more passionate curiosity. My whole heart applauds that gigantic and yet entirely human undertaking.

And a year later (February, 1932):

That the ideas of Lenin and Stalin might overcome the resistance the European states are trying to bring against them is beginning to seem possible to those states; and this fills them with terror. But that it might be desirable for those ideas to win out is something they refuse to envisage. There is a great deal of stupidity, a great deal of ignorance, a great deal of stubbornness in their refusal; and also a certain lack of imagination that keeps them from believing that humanity can change, that a society can be built up on different foundations from those they have always known (even though they deplore them), that the future can be anything but a repetition and reproduction of the past.

It is now a little difficult to sense the enthusiasm for the *ethical possibilities* of the Russian Revolution which Gide, freedom-loving individualist that he was, felt, and also the hope for a situation in which it appeared so likely that "humanity can change." But he is surely right that the ideas of Lenin concerning the withering away of the state express a real confidence in the possibility of *the recreation of the natural man* profoundly sympathetic to French ears. For underneath countless layers of opportunism and political realism, there is in Lenin a certain faith, reminiscent of Rousseau, that, freed from economic bondage and political exploitation and from the unceasing pressures of organizational compulsion, there is in man a morality of natural goodness and social participation. "How readily," he says, "people get accustomed to observe *the necessary rules of life in common* if there is no exploitation, if there is nothing that causes indignation, that calls forth protest and revolt and has to be *suppressed*."[48] Only communism renders the state power absolutely unnecessary, for there remains no class to be suppressed. Possibly there will remain occasional individual "excesses," but they will be put down by the people themselves as any crowd of civilized persons "parts a pair of combatants or does not allow a woman to be outraged."

The first phase of communist society will not yet have achieved the final goal, for a society just emerging from capitalism will still bear the birthmarks of the stage from which it sprang. Although the means of production will have been socialized, individuals will still receive compensation according to the socially necessary work which they have performed. Thus at this stage there is still inequality. This is a defect, but in the first phase of socialist society it is unavoidable, for always the old surviving in the new is the great danger.[49] But the factory discipline which the proletariat extends to the whole of society is not the final aim. It is only the foothold necessary for "the radical cleansing of society" of all the dirt and ugliness of capitalist exploitation. When this cleansing is completed, says Lenin, then the Marxist formula ("From each according to his ability, to each according to his need") can be realized. This means a new generation and also a new morality.

It is perhaps unfortunate that Lenin never explicitly examined the presuppositions of this new morality. He nowhere analyzes the humanistic consequences of "the necessary rules of life in common" to which he repeatedly refers. But even without this examination and analysis, it is clear to what final pass this theoretician of violence has been brought.

We set ourselves [he says][50] the ultimate aim of destroying the state, i.e., every organized and systematic violence, every use of violence against man in general. We do not expect the advent of an order of society in which the principle of subordination of minority to majority will not be observed. But, striving for Socialism, we are convinced that it will develop into Communism; that, side by side with this, there will vanish all need for force, for the *subjection* of one man to another, and of one part of the population to another, since people will *grow accustomed* to observing the elementary conditions of social existence *without force and without subjection.*

The Hegelian wheel has come full circle. Violence has posited its contradiction. *State and Revolution,* beginning with the purpose of undermining the moral claims of the liberal-democratic state and providing a justification, therefore, for the most absolute use of revolutionary violence against the concentration of bourgeois power, ends with a utopian vision of what life might be without any violence whatsoever.

But this bifurcation of means and ends, this use of violence to establish peace, this invocation of power in the service of humanism, invites the realistic criticism that it is naive, contradictory, and, in the real world, unworkable. Koestler in *Darkness at Noon* (through Ivanov, Rubashov's first interrogator) suggests the dilemma of this mixture of moral ideologies.[51]

I don't approve of mixing ideologies, Ivanov continued. There are only two conceptions of human ethics, and they are at opposite poles. One of them is Christian and humane, declares the individual to be sacrosanct, and asserts that the rules of arithmetic are not to be applied to human units. The other starts from the basic principle that a collective aim justifies all means, and not only allows, but demands, that the individual should in every way be subordinated and sacrificed to the community—which may dispose of it as an experimentation rabbit or a sacrificial lamb. The first conception could be called anti-vivisection morality, the second, vivisection morality. Humbugs and dilettantes have always tried to mix the two conceptions; in practice, it is impossible. Whoever is burdened with power and responsibility finds out on the first occasion that he has to choose, and he is fatally driven to the second alternative.

State and Revolution is the great Marxist classic on the nature of the state, capitalist democracy, and proletarian revolution. And it pretends to a realism far removed from Sorel's romanticism of violence. But in the end, it too succumbs to the lure of fantasy and becomes a social myth.

4. VEBLEN AND MARX

Lenin, Georges Sorel, and Thorstein Veblen are all social theorists who, in greater or lesser degree, have felt the impress of Marx. All reached maturity toward the end of the nineteenth century, when the Marxist principles were sweeping the continent and pushing their way to the New World. Each lived well into the first quarter of the twentieth century. Sorel died in 1922, Lenin in 1924, Veblen in 1929. Each made his own modification or revaluation of the original Marxist paradigm which has set the pattern for the social criticism of the modern world.

Naturally, their temperaments and their modes of social perception are very different. Lenin is the true heir of Marx and Engels, the realistic practitioner of revolution, the theorist whose theories are eternally counters in some sort of struggle for power. Every line that Lenin wrote, it has been said, was a document in an intra-Party struggle. From an examination of *Materialism and Empirio-Criticism* one could well believe it. It is not that Lenin does not have a grasp of general principles. It is rather that his perception of famine, social distress, police brutality, and the conspiratorial way of life is so immediate that he is never capable of that "aesthetic distance" which constitutes the qualification of an objective and socially rootless intelligentsia.

Sorel is another matter. He was an engineer for twenty-five years, and although this gave him a supreme contempt for the bourgeois class for whose sake he was employed, yet that contact with the machine process which (according to Veblen) should have made him skeptical, materialistic, and matter-of-fact, threw him finally into the arms of Bergsonian mysticism and a romantic theory of social violence. Sorel derived from Marx a framework of class antagonism to which he could willingly subscribe, but his theory of the social myth was designed to overcome Marxist rationalism. Sorel's years of retirement provided him with that social isolation which Lenin was never to experience, and this perhaps (as in the case of Nietzsche also) is what gave him that quasi-academic ferocity which turns toward the theory of violence precisely those who have never experienced it in their own lives.

Sorel begins as an engineer and ends as a philosopher. For Veblen it is just the reverse. He was a graduate student under the influence of C. S. Peirce at Johns Hopkins, and took his doctorate in philosophy at Yale with a thesis on "Ethical Grounds of a Doctrine of Retribution." His first published article was on *Kant's Critique of Judgment*. Certain concepts of Peirce and Kant were to be a permanent influence,[52] but his last major works, *The Engineers and the Price System* (1921) and *Absentee Ownership and Business Enterprise* (1923) are a far cry from Peirce and Kant. The logic of practice and a theory of judgment have here turned into a large-scale critique of the whole system of modern business enterprise. Between these termini lie other influences. Veblen begins as a philosopher, and he ends as protagonist of the engineer mentality and its application to the problems of an industrial society in distress. The shift, in a certain important, if not total, sense is due to Marx.

Of course it is always necessary to distinguish between the tenor of one's social sympathies and the intellectual constructs which constitute one's machinery for theoretical dealings with the world. Veblen's Marxism is perhaps less apparent in his economic theory than in his moderate enthusiasm for the Russian Revolution. Dorfman reports[53] that "Six months before his death in 1929, Veblen said in substance to his neighbor, Mrs. R. H. Fisher: 'Naturally there will be other developments right along, but just now communism offers the best course that I can see'." Some confirmation for this is also to be found in the series of articles which he wrote in *The Dial* in 1919. In his "Bolshevism Is a Menace—To Whom?" he minced no words: "Bolshevism," he said, "is revolutionary. It aims to carry democracy and majority rule over into the domain of industry. Therefore it is a menace to the established order and to those persons whose fortunes are bound up with the established order." Nor did he deny the strife and bloodshed, the horror and distress which accompanied the Russian Revolution. "But," he continued, "it is as well to keep in mind that the original substance and cause of this Bolshevist trouble is a cleavage and antagonism between the vested interests and the common man, and that the whole quarrel turns finally about the vested rights of property and privilege."[54]

What Veblen learned from Marx was to view society in terms of the social cleavages discernible within it. If he did not literally apply the Marxist doctrine of the contradictions within capitalism, he discovered his own set of contradictions (engineering efficiency versus the price system), and his analysis also emphasized modern industrial society as an uneasy conflict of interests. Veblen is a Marxist not in any orthodox sense, but rather in the way in which he makes the European doctrine of the class struggle fit into the somewhat different pattern of the American scene. The language of "bourgeois" and "proletarian" always has an air of foreignness to American ears. This, I think, is because in Europe the emerging class structure of the industrial revolution is grafted upon a set of feudal distinctions which saw the nobility and the serfdom as far apart as the poles. The sharp distinction between capitalist and proletarian classes is but a modernization of one of the ancient clichés of the European mentality—to which the meaning of the middle class is the great stumbling-block. But America has no feudal tradition. In a certain sense, from the very beginning, it is all middle class. Thus the Marxist problem in America has always been to apply those tools of social analysis which originated in the European cultural tradition so as to formalize important cleavages within a large, single, and excessively heterogeneous social class. It is interesting to see in the *Dial* article not only how Veblen does this for America, but how in turn he reads his own concepts back into the Russian Revolution. Veblen's version of the bourgeoisie is "the vested interests," and his version of the proletarian is "the common man;" thus in American terms the Russian Revolution sprang from "a cleavage and antagonism between the vested interests and the common man." Veblen is the clearest of all proofs that when Marxian theory migrates to the New World, the Marxist vocabulary suffers a profound sea-change.

Although Veblen agreed with Marx in saying that "there is no single spot or corner in civilized Europe or America where the underlying population would have anything to lose by such an overturn of the established order as would cancel the vested rights of privilege and property," yet he was at some pains to dissociate himself from the philosophical presuppositions of Marxist theory. He does this by distinguishing between the Marxist and Darwinian approaches to economic behavior.[55]

The neo-Hegelian, romantic Marxian standpoint was wholly personal, whereas the evolutionistic—it may be called Darwinian—standpoint is wholly impersonal. . . . The facts were construed to take such a course as could be established by an appeal to reason between intelligent and fair-minded men. . . . The romantic (Marxian) sequence of theory is essentially an intellectual sequence, and it is therefore of a teleological character. The logical trend of it can be argued out. That is to say, it tends to a goal. On the other hand, in the Darwinian scheme of thought, the continuity sought in and imputed to the facts is a continuity of cause and effect. . . . The sequence is controlled by nothing but the *vis a tergo* of brute causation, and is essentially mechanical. The neo-Hegelian Marxian scheme of development is drawn in the image of the struggling ambitious human spirit; that of Darwinian evolution is of the nature of a mechanical process.

It is clear that Veblen, like Marx, was a product of the historical thinking of the nineteenth century, but that for Marx historical explanation is fashioned after the pattern of Hegel, for Veblen after that of Darwin. Marxists pride themselves on the superiority of materialism to Hegelian idealism; but Veblen finds the Marxists themselves too idealistic. In Veblen's opinion, Marx's view of social causation was not mechanistic enough to entitle his work to be classified as social science. He therefore dismisses the labor theory of value as a mere assumption, and the theory of surplus value as a myth based on little more than the discredited seventeenth-century doctrine of "natural rights."

But even in his criticism of Marx, Veblen shows how much of a Marxist he really is. The heart of Marx's materialism was not the doctrine of dialectical development, but his insistence that the mode of production and the material conditions of life determine the social structure, the ideological biases of men, and the nature of individuals. Veblen appropriates this insight and develops it in one of the most famous essays in the whole body of his work—the chapter on "The Cultural Incidence of the Machine Process" in *The Theory of Business Enterprise*.

The contradiction which Marx discerned in the system of capitalist production was the conflict of interest between the owners of capital and the workers whom they needed. In the end, the combination of workers would eliminate the class which brought them into being. But Veblen's insight into the contradiction is much deeper, much more radical, for it recognizes that those very abstract forces which co-operate to produce the modern industrial system are in the end contradictory and irreconcilable.[56]

The material framework of modern civilization is the industrial system, and the directing force which animates this framework is business enterprise. To a greater extent than any other known phase of culture, modern Christendom takes its complexion from its economic organization. This modern economic organization is the "Capitalistic System" or "Modern Industrial System" so called. Its characteristic features, and at the same time the forces by virtue of which it dominates modern culture, are the machine process and investment for a profit.

The co-operation between "the machine process" (the application of scientific technique to the technical problems of productivity) and "investment for a profit" has created the modern industrial order, but the means (science) and the end (profit) do not form one seamless web. Veblen's entire critique of the system of modern capitalism (as expressed in such works as *The Vested Interests and the Common Man*, *The Engineers and the Price System*, and *Absentee Ownership and Business Enterprise*) is an attempt to pry apart and exhibit as intrinsically incompatible "the machine process" and "investment for a profit."

The disjunction between the machine process and investment for a profit has psychological as well as sociological consequences. It appears at the level of ownership as the conflict between the vested interests and the propertyless common man; at the psychological level it appears as different modes of perception in the human material. The machine process requires "the enforcement of precise mechanical measurements and adjustment and the reduction of all manner of things, purposes and acts, necessities, conveniences, and amenities of life to standard units."[57] The effect of this enforcement upon the mind of the worker and the engineer is to produce the machine mentality. The machine is a strict disciplinarian of intelligence; it demands quantitative precision, and it encourages impersonality of judgment at the same time as it discourages anthropological habits of thought. "What the discipline of the machine industry inculcates, therefore, in the habits of life and of thought of the workman, is regularity of sequence and mechanical precision; and the intellectual outcome is an habitual resort to terms of measurable cause and effect, together with a relative neglect and disparagement of such exercise of the intellectual faculties as does not run on these lines."[58]

On the other hand, the business classes, lawyers, and, in fact, all those with a stake in pecuniary employment, are prone to theological and metaphysical thinking. The natural-rights approach to property, the emphasis upon conventional ritual, and the hospitality to a religious point of view are all characteristic of those whose lives are not lived in the immediate environment of the machine, but in the ambience of investment for a profit. And, as Thurman Arnold has shown, business, politics, and the law are shrouded in that curious incubus of "anthropological habits of mind" which he calls "the folklore of capitalism."[59]

One can now appreciate the irony of Veblen's criticism of Marxist ideology, for what it really states is that Marx, like Hegel, is too metaphysical, too close to the anthropological natural-rights method of thinking, and too far from the skeptical, matter-of-fact, unmoral, unpatriotic, undevout, and *truly* materialistic point of view which a direct acquaintance with the machine process would have given him. In making this criticism, Veblen is employing a social psychology which is completely in the spirit of Marx's attempt to show that bourgeois and proletarian mentality are as radically different as their roles in the process of industrial production.

Veblen's distinction between the business and the engineering mentality has all the appearance of an objective, impersonal sociological fact, but the least acquaintance with the body of his work will indicate that Veblen himself feels a preference. He not only identifies himself with the factual objectivity of scientific (almost icy) withdrawal, but he sees the machine discipline as touching wider and wider circles of the population of Western civilization in an increasingly intimate and coercive way. It is clear that Veblen is by no means in agreement with the sentiment of Bernanos (quoted at the head of this chapter) that mechanization is a vice of man, a nervous disturbance, a defect of the imagination and the will. Living before the Bomb, he is not distressed by the threat of technological barbarism or by any fear of "the dictatorship of a technology in delirium." Rather, like Spengler (although he, in contrast with Spengler, holds to a doctrine of slow evolutionary progress rather than one of inevitable decline), he suggests that ours is the age of the engineer, and he views this with such wry approval as his uncommitted style permits.

As a social reformer of the productive system, Veblen exhibits none of the indignant passion of the classical Marxist statements. But in the end he proposes a formulation which is in some respects not unlike that of Lenin in *State and Revolution*: a system in which the industrial complex is removed from the irresponsibility of private ownership and managed by a bureaucracy of technicians. *The Engineers and the Price System* has prepared us for such an outcome. It recognizes the possibilities of sabotage by business interests who, in their search to maintain profits, may control the rate and volume of output at a level less than that of maximum efficiency. Veblen understands perfectly the technique by which a "conscientious withdrawal of efficiency" may be instrumental to a maximization of private profits. That politics and investment should not be allowed to decide matters of industrial policy best left to "the discretion of the general staff of production engineers driven by no commercial bias" is for him self-evident. So, without any hope for its achievement in the near future, with, so to say, the most exquisitely impartial pessimism, Veblen puts forward the solution.[60]

In short, so far as regards the technical requirements of the case, the situation is ready for a self-selected, but inclusive, Soviet of technicians to take over the economic affairs of the country and to allow and disallow what they may agree on; provided always that they live within the requirements of that state of the industrial arts whose keepers they are, and provided that their pretensions continue to have the support of the industrial rank and file; which comes near saying that their Soviet must consistently and effectually take care of the material welfare of the underlying population.

It is perhaps unfair to Veblen to emphasize his technocratic bent without at the same time recognizing that his drama of the technically competent engineer of good will versus the business representatives of a predatory capitalism is played against the backdrop of a theory of the instincts which is almost Freudian in its dualism. On the one hand is "the instinct of workmanship" (the creative element in man) drawing to itself the "idle curiosity" (which yields the objectivity of scientific inquiry) and "the parental bent" (the source of altruism in man) into one constructive complex. On the other hand is "pugnacity" (the warlike instinct) "the self-regarding disposition," and "the predatory disposition," joining into one complex of destruction.[61] If Freud's cosmic contest of Eros and Thanatos seems simpler and at the same time more metaphysical, Veblen's background of the instinctual struggle sets the stage for the social conflict in such a way as to moralize it as truly as Marx and Lenin, though not by explicit statement. The cold and forbidding suggestion of a Soviet of technicians seems unthinkable until one realizes that in the back of Veblen's mind is again that imagined juncture of creativeness, objectivity, and altruism which (like Plato's philosopher-kings) the engineer-politicians are supposed to sustain.

Beginning with matter-of-fact, Veblen, like Marx and Lenin, ends with utopia. John Dos Passos in his novel *The Big Money* shows his effect upon the rebellious within a society newly self-conscious of its own distress.

> Veblen
> a greyfaced shambling man lolling resentful at his desk with his cheek on his hand, in a low sarcastic mumble of intricate phrases subtly paying out the logical inescapable rope of matteroffact for a society to hang itself by. . . .

The "logical, inescapable rope of matter-of-fact," while it permits a society to hang itself, gives few clues for salvation. But there is a way of salvation in Veblen also, and this, no less than the acid of criticism, touched the generation for whom he lived. Dos Passos continues:[62]

> These were the years he did most of his writing, trying out his ideas on his students, writing slowly at night in violent ink with a pen of his own designing. Whenever he published a book he had to put up a guarantee with the publishers. In *The Theory of Business Enterprise, The Instinct of Workmanship, The Vested Interests and the Common Man,*
> he established a new diagram of a society dominated by monopoly capital, etched in irony
> the sabotage of production by business,
> the sabotage of life by blind need for money profits,
> pointed out the alternatives: a warlike society strangled by the bureaucracies of the monopolies forced by the law of diminishing returns to grind down more and more the common man for profits,
> or a new matteroffact commonsense society dominated by the needs of the men and women who did the work and the incredibly vast possibilities for peace and plenty offered by the progress of technology.

5. THE THEORY OF THE LEISURE CLASS

If Veblen had written only *Absentee Ownership and Business Enterprise, The Vested Interests and the Common Man,* and *The Engineers and the Price System,* he would have still been an important link in the chain of Marxian-inspired critics who have bent their talents to an exposé of the system of modern capitalist production. Such an exposé implies both a theoretical framework for criticism and perhaps also that kind of practical wisdom in the technique of revolution which suggests the strategies of change. Lenin, Kautsky, Bernstein, Bakunin, Sorel, and Veblen all turn their attention to one or both of these modes of social criticism.

But Veblen also wrote in 1899 *The Theory of the Leisure Class*, which finally became the classic by which his reputation is assured. This book, seriously discounted by economists, but hailed by sociologists, marks a new and prophetic phase in the history of social criticism. Its importance is that it registers a profound shift in awareness which the evolution of modern capitalist society has made imperative.

In the history of Western civilization there have been three decisive stages in the development of the economic process. The first is the system of handicraft production which dominated the West from the early Middle Ages to the late Renaissance. The second is the phase of early machine industrialization, emphasizing work and productivity, which lasted roughly from the seventeenth through the nineteenth century. The third is the phase of late industrialization, emphasizing leisure and consumption, and reaching its zenith in the psychology of the middle classes of contemporary America.[63] *The Theory of the Leisure Class* inaugurates the shift of emphasis in social criticism from an economics of production to an economics of consumption.

This perhaps is why the book was disparaged by economists. For the areas of legitimate economic concern as crystallized in so influential a classic as John Stuart Mill's *Principles of Political Economy* (last revised edition, 1865) were production, distribution, and exchange (with, perhaps, some attention to the claims of labor and the functions of government as affecting these three areas). Nor is this merely a matter of a conservative as opposed to a radical view of economic theory. For, in this respect, Marx is at one with Mill; however they disagree upon the ethics of distribution, the nature of capitalist production is central for them both. Marx, the greatest critic of the middle phase of the industrial revolution, is yet the inevitable product of its economic presuppositions. For him too, work and productivity are the pivots of society. In the Marxist works which Veblen wrote, his interest is also in production and distribution, but in *The Theory of the Leisure Class* the focus is altogether different.

The striking difference between Marx and Veblen is perhaps best illustrated in the shift which has taken place in the concept of "commodity." The first chapter of *Das Kapital* contains Marx's metaphysics of the commodity, which, as we have seen, he speaks of as "a mysterious thing." The mystery consists in how the efforts of *living labor* have been transmuted into the objectivity of an exchangeable *thing*. The commodity for Marx is a *product*, the consummation for which labor has been the instrument, and his interest is always introspective toward the process by which it has been produced. But in *The Theory of the Leisure Class*, Veblen regards commodities as *material for consumption;* he is interested in the peculiar ways in which they are consumed, exhibited, and enjoyed.

There is a certain analogy here with the field of aesthetic theory. The total artistic process contains both an act of artistic creation and an act of artistic enjoyment. To the extent that one considers the work of art as a product of creativity, one concentrates upon an aesthetics of the act of making; to the extent that one considers it as a work to be enjoyed, one concentrates upon the act of perception. It is perhaps no accident, that the aesthetics of Greece and the Renaissance is an aesthetics of the creative act, while beginning with Kant and increasingly in the modern world, aesthetic theory has concentrated upon aesthetic perception. The aesthetics of creation is the analogue to an economics of work and productivity. The aesthetics of appreciation is the analogue to an economics of leisure and consumption.

The thesis of *The Theory of the Leisure Class* is at once simple and revolutionary. It is that in the modern world all those who live above the level of bare economic subsistence do not use this surplus primarily for an extension of means and sensory comforts, or for any commonly understood "useful" purpose, but rather as a demonstration of their superiority of status. They demonstrate this superiority not by their capacity to lead, administer, or create, but by their conspicuous wastefulness: by an expenditure of effort, time, and money which is intrinsically reputable in a class-conscious world.

The thesis is revolutionary in two respects. In the first place, it marks a shift in the world of values from biology to the mind. In the second place, it reverses the economic assumption that the motives of men are most realistically conceived as the calculus of gain. Both of these ideas are in some sense outgrowths of Bentham's eighteenth-century utilitarianism. Any moral theory which takes pleasurable feeling as the criterion of value is at least in part biologically grounded, for it implies biological health, the goods of physical functioning, the absence of pain, the feeling of pleasure, a sharpening of sensation, the heightening of awareness, even the addition of physical grace and movement. But the pleasures of "reputation" are based upon the intangibles of esteem and admiration, and they hinge upon symbolic acts and ritual performances. Values here are removed from biology: not the sensory pleasures of an excellent dinner, but satisfaction in the figures in a bankbook with many zeros. In the second place Veblen's theory subordinates the motive of income to the motive of deference in a theory of social action. This is to reverse the classical economic assumption (even in so up-to-date a version as the theory of marginal utility), but it is the inevitable consequence of the shift in emphasis from production to consumption. For if an economics of production hinges upon a *calculus of gain,* an economics of consumption (as every advertiser knows) hinges upon a *calculus of reputation.*

True to his Darwinian presuppositions, Veblen sees the emergence of the modern leisure class as a slow process of evolutionary growth. Though it may reach its height in a feudal society, where the upper classes (whether warriors or priests) are exempt from industrial employment, it is an outgrowth of primitive culture. The primitive distinction between the work of men and the work of women, that is, between "exploit" and "drudgery,"[64] evolves into an important difference in honorific status of the two types of employment. The barbarian culture exalts the exploits of the hunter or the warrior, which are regarded as worthy, honorable, and noble, while manual labor is unworthy, debasing, and ignoble. By an interesting association, the trophies or "property" of the hunter or warrior become the evidence of his prowess. Thus the worthiness of doing is transmuted into a worthiness of having.

The emergence of the leisure class coincides with the beginnings of ownership. But wherever there is private property, there is a competition between men for its possession. Here, in Veblen's opinion, the assumption of the classical economists goes wrong. The struggle for property continues not in order to increase the comforts of life, but because of the intrinsic honorableness of accumulation itself. The possession of wealth confers honor. Property is a trophy in the game of competitive ownership. The real motive of economic acquisition is not the spur of need, but *pecuniary emulation*—the competition for honor in the possession of wealth.

Property now becomes the most easily recognized evidence of a reputable degree of success as distinguished from heroic or signal achievement. It therefore becomes the conventional basis of esteem. Its possession in some amount becomes necessary in order to [have] any reputable standing in the community. It becomes indispensable to accumulate, to acquire property, in order to retain one's good name.[65]

The principle of pecuniary emulation is Veblen's great discovery. With it go hand in hand the principles of *conspicuous leisure* and *conspicuous consumption.* If the end of action in a consumption-oriented society is to rank high in acquisition in comparison with other members of the community, then this motive in turn shapes the actual expenditure of funds for personal comfort, and the forms of activity constituting a decent mode of life. The secondary demand of emulation is abstention from productive work, for this is an obvious demonstration of the possession of wealth. From the earliest times the better classes have felt a repugnance for vulgar labor, and for the gentleman of leisure there have always been substitute forms of activity—war, diplomacy, scholarship, religion, sport, proficiency in dead languages, emphasis upon decorum, manners, and ceremonialization of life. Perhaps the most obvious form which conspicuous leisure takes is the growth of the ménage of personal and domestic servants. Ostensibly to perform household tasks, their ultimate purpose is to manifest "vicarious leisure" on the part of their employers.

In the modern world conspicuous consumption is more important than conspicuous leisure. It demands a certain discrimination in food, clothing, furniture, domestic arrangements, and other specialized forms of consumption. A cultivation of the luxurious and the recondite is at once an evidence of wealth and an evidence of taste, and it is just as important to put the latter on display as the former.[66] The cultivation of taste and of the aesthetic faculty both demand time and effort, and this lies behind both the connoisseurship of the gentleman and the consumer patterns of middle-class good taste. It is, in fact, one of the chief discoveries of Veblen that the distance between the forms of consumption of the various social classes has grown progressively less.

In modern civilized communities the lines of demarcation between social classes have grown vague and transient, and wherever this happens, the norm of reputability imposed by the upper class extends its coercive influence with but slight hindrance down through the social structure to the lowest strata. The result is that the members of each stratum accept as their ideal of decency the scheme of life in vogue in the next higher stratum, and bend their energies to live up to that ideal.[67]

Veblen's treatment of the pecuniary standard of living rests upon an implicit system of valuation represented by his own commitment to "the instinct of workmanship," and his description of the consumer practices of modern society demonstrates the prevalence of its opposite. "From the foregoing survey of the growth of conspicuous leisure and consumption, it appears that the utility of both alike for the purposes of reputability lies in the element of waste that is common to both. In the one case it is a waste of time and effort, in the other it is a waste of goods." The irony implicit in his analysis is thus based upon the contrast between functional efficiency and honorific waste.

That wasteful but honorable expenditure may become more indispensable than subsistence, that the standard of expenditure which guides our efforts is the one just beyond our reach, that with increased industrial efficiency, energies go into higher and higher expenditure rather than a slackening of industrial pace is an indictment of a society in distress, not because of its poverty or injustice, but because of its very prosperity—because of economic habits not confined to one exploiting class, but diffused throughout the society as a whole. Not injustice, but foolishness, has become total. The great originality of Veblen as a social critic is that he has taken the Marxist standpoint, developed in an age which had not yet solved the problem of production and distribution, and projected it into an age where the new distress is related to the problem of consumption.

Veblen's description of pecuniary canons of taste as expressed in devout observances and the higher learning, his analysis of the breeding of animals for uselessness and the dress of women as a symbolism of waste is often hilarious, but it adds little to his major thesis. It documents it, but (except, perhaps, for his demonstration of the meaning of the "conservation of archaic traits") does not expand it. But he has already made his point.

Both poles of Veblen's social criticism are to be understood in terms of his essential functionalism: his espousal of the craft idea in production and of reasonable serviceability in consumption. *The Theory of Business Enterprise* and *Absentee Ownership* contrast acquisition and production, business and industry, exploitation and serviceability in such a way as to reinforce the intuitive insistence of the poetry of Ezra Pound. When Pound contends that "Usury rusts the man and his chisel," that "It destroys the craftsman, destroying craft," he is giving to "usury" and to "craftsmanship" the same roles which Veblen gives to "the profit motive" and "the instinct of workmanship." *The Theory of the Leisure Class* attacks the underpinnings of the consumer society through devices which approach the strategy of "naturalism" as a literary form. The attack and the reform are made by letting the facts speak for themselves, by presenting a detailed image without any evaluation except irony. *The Theory of the Leisure Class* is not a muckraking exposé; but its effect is even greater, for it views the institutions which we take for granted with the genteel detachment of a visiting anthropologist with a purposely cool and objective social science vocabulary. Where Marx and Lenin exhibit outrage and vehemence, Veblen aloofly and almost primly contents himself with detailed description. Of the symbolic significance of objects and acts, he notices almost everything.

It is perhaps a little strange to use the term "naturalism" in connection with Veblen, for it has more traditionally been applied to those who like Zola or Céline have applied the method of objective description to the lower orders of society, to the really seamy side of life. But there is no reason why there should not be a naturalism of the leisure-class way of life, a description illuminating what is meant by pecuniary emulation and conspicuous consumption. In fact I have often thought that Scott Fitzgerald played this role to perfection. Four years before Veblen died, in 1925, Fitzgerald described in *The Great Gatsby* that idolization of the consumer commodity, that consecration to the norms of honorific waste of which Veblen wrote in *The Theory of the Leisure Class*.[68]

Recovering himself in a minute he opened for us two hulking patent cabinets which held his massed suits and dressing-gowns and ties, and his shirts, piled like bricks in stacks a dozen high.

"I've got a man in England who buys me clothes. He sends over a selection of things at the beginning of each season, spring and fall."

He took a pile of shirts and began throwing them, one by one, before us, shirts of sheer linen and thick silk and fine flannel, which lost their folds as they fell and covered the table in many-colored disarray. While we admired he brought more and the soft rich heap mounted higher—shirts with stripes and scrolls and plaids in coral and apple-green and lavender and faint orange, with monograms of Indian blue. Suddenly, with a strained sound, Daisy bent her head into the shirts and began to cry stormily.

"They're such beautiful shirts," she sobbed, her voice muffled in the thick folds. "It makes me sad because I've never seen such—such beautiful shirts before."

VII

Reason in Nature:
The Revolution of Einstein
and Planck

Da gab es draussen diese grosse Welt, die unabhängig von uns Menschen da ist
und vor uns steht wie ein grosses, ewiges Rätsel, wenigstens teilweise zugänglich
unserem Schauen und Denken.

ALBERT EINSTEIN

Each answer which physics imparts concerning the character and the peculiar nature
of its fundamental concepts assumes inevitably for epistemology the form of a question.

ERNST CASSIRER

It is inherent in my theory to maintain the old division between physics and
geometry. Physics is the science of the contingent relations of nature and geometry
expresses its uniform relatedness.

ALFRED NORTH WHITEHEAD

1. SCIENCE AND METAPHYSICS

The interplay between science and metaphysics is one of the enduring features of Western civilization. And the mentality of an epoch
as indicated by the topics which engage its interest (and which lie,
often unconsciously, behind its most cherished beliefs) is partly formed
by the wider conception of Nature to which it adheres. Hence the
peculiar relevance of Darwin (and his implicit emphasis on the irrationality in man) to the mentality of the late nineteenth century, and
hence also the relevance of his influence upon the figures of twentieth-
century thought with whom we have hitherto been concerned. Evolutionary theory forms a background to Bergson's insistence upon the
instrumental role of the intellect and the development of intuition. The
paradigm of organic growth underlies Spengler's delineation of the
birth and death of historic civilizations. Without the general biology
of post-Darwinian central Europe Freud would not have arrived at his
theory of the instincts and of the psychological apparatus through
which they are expressed. Without the Darwinian emphasis upon
instinct theory Veblen could not have provided an underpinning for a
theory of society in effective contrast to the dialectical Marxian picture.

If biological science seems to have dominated the philosophical sources of the late nineteenth century, this was only because the physical assumptions of that age were seething with still dormant possibilities. Continuity and atomicity had not yet broken out into open dialectical mutiny. The concept of the physical field pervasive of space and underlying the theory of electromagnetism (in the form of the differential equations of Clerk Maxwell) had not yet caused physicists to view with uneasiness the prior formulations of post-Newtonian dynamics. It was not quite clear that physical theory was poised between two worlds, one dead, the other as yet powerless to be born.

Physical science has been a basic factor throughout the history of Western civilization. Its developments have contributed the three dominant concepts of nature by which Western man has lived. Three scientific revolutions have been at the foundation of the metaphysics of the Western world.[1] The first was the revolution of the Ionian nature-philosophers, which, in its search to identify the material properties of all natural substances, was led to seek in rational principles the explanation of the multiformities of change. This effort to establish reason in nature culminated not in a single system but in the construction of three great cosmologies: the system of Aristotle, emphasizing form and matter; the system of Democritus, establishing atomism; and the system of Plato, based on mathematical relations. The second revolution was that of the seventeenth-century philosopher-physicists Galileo, Newton, and Descartes, which found the rationality of nature to consist in its susceptibility to mathematical treatment, and which, although it led both to mechanistic exploitation as in Newton and Descartes, and to less materialistic treatment in Leibniz and Spinoza, was dominated by the image of a machine whose parts function harmoniously and regularly with calculable mathematical precision.

The philosophical consequences of the Cartesian revolution and the Newtonian physical synthesis continued up to the last decades of the nineteenth century. But in the early years of the twentieth occurred the latest of the great revolutions in physical science. "Two great theoretical constructions," says Hans Reichenbach, "have shaped the face of modern physics; the theory of relativity and the theory of quanta."[2] The first, although prepared for by many (Fizeau, Michelson, Fitzgerald, Lorentz) has been chiefly the work of one man—Albert Einstein. The second, although developed by many (Max Born, Schrodinger, Bohr, Heisenberg, de Broglie, Dirac) can also be associated with one man—Max Planck. The philosophic consequences of the revolution initiated by Einstein and Planck cannot yet, perhaps, be definitively stated. But even now, after approximately forty years, they have left a profound impress on the philosophizing of the twentieth century. In what sense has this latest scientific revolution provided a new conception of the operation of reason in nature? What have been its logical, metaphysical, and epistemological effects?

The question is comprehensive, and the answer for which it calls is complex, but a brief preliminary summary is in order. The theory of relativity in its widest interpretation is a critique of previous theories of space and time dependent for its validation upon the most minute reconsideration of exactly what is involved in the process of physical measurement. This at once raises questions about our ways of measuring space and time; the availability of alternative systems of geometry; and the epistemological position to which one is committed by his theory of the relationship between geometry and experience. Since the theory of relativity is a theory within the field of mathematical physics, its correction of the Newtonian assumptions still falls within the framework of a conception of science which it shares with the seventeenth century; this means that the problem of reason in nature remains a problem of the interpretation of the role and status of mathematics. If, as Whitehead suggests in the epigraph quoted at the head of this chapter, it is necessary to maintain the Newtonian division between physics and geometry, there remains the serious task of organizing "the contingent relations of nature" (physics) within the manifold of "its uniform relatedness" (geometry).

The quantum theory in its widest interpretation is a critique of previous theories of matter and energy which is also dependent for its validation upon a careful reconsideration of what is involved in the process of physical measurement. But this species of physical measurement is concerned less with the manifold of uniform relatedness than with the meaning of the contingent relations within nature. Where relativity deals with galaxies and nebulae, quantum theory deals with entities so minute that they are far below the threshold of ordinary sensory observation. Hence their postulation raises serious questions about the logical and philosophical status of unobserved objects. Also the infinitely minute character of these energetic entities means that they can be measured only in aggregates, and that their behavior can perhaps be interpreted only in terms of the laws of probability. This idea is not entirely new; Boltzmann had discovered that the second law of thermodynamics needed to be stated in a statistical rather than a causal format, but the generalization of this procedure which quantum mechanics requires implies a transition from causal laws to probability laws and raises issues about physical indeterminacy which are capable of alternative interpretations. This in turn seems to require certain basic changes in the fundamentals of the theory of knowledge.

The most interesting thing about the physical revolution initiated by relativity and quantum theory is that it originates in the problems of physical measurement; hence its intrinsic philosophic interest centers in the implications of scientific methodology for the theory of knowledge. A type of physical theory which would be congruent with both cosmological and sub-atomic measurements seems, therefore, to require a reinterpretation of the categories of time, space, substance, and causality. The necessity for this reinterpretation of basic categories has affected philosophy in a variety of ways.

A revolution in science can be assimilated within the philosophic tradition in different ways. There are, first, those who believe that novelty in physical theory has radical consequences for the theory of knowledge and that *a critical analysis of the meaning* of the new physical theory in itself suggests the necessary revisions in traditional conceptions. These advocates of a critical approach are philosophers of science in the narrower sense, and among those who have performed this service for the theories of relativity and quantum mechanics are Hans Reichenbach, C. D. Broad, and Ernst Cassirer. There are, second, those who understand that something both novel and of great importance has taken place, yet whose efforts do not really lead in the direction of a new metaphysics. Physicists themselves, for example (with the important exception of Einstein), have tended to interpret relativity and quantum theory within the framework of classical idealist doctrine; A. S. Eddington has done this in such lively and persuasive fashion that no account of the philosophic consequences of the new physics can quite neglect his contribution. Thirdly, there are those who are stimulated by the new discoveries to create a new metaphysics sufficiently comprehensive both to incorporate the special scientific theories and to create in the process a new concept of nature. This is what Locke and Leibniz accomplished for the revolution of Newton, and what Russell and particularly Whitehead in his early period have accomplished for the revolution of Einstein and Planck, deriving from the equations of the electromagnetic field a metaphysics of events to supplant the older metaphysics of natural objects simply locatable in a three-dimensional empty space. Finally, there are those, physicists or philosophers, who are stimulated by the problems of methodology presented by the new theories to formulate a novel theory not of metaphysics or epistemology, but of language and meaning. P. W. Bridgman is perhaps the most important representative of this impulse, and his operationalism is a natural logical consequence of the theory of relativity viewed as a crisis of methodological reform.

In what follows, I should like first to present the cardinal features of the theory of relativity and of quantum mechanics, so far as possible in the more simplified statements of Einstein and Planck, utilizing the interpretative suggestions of Reichenbach, Broad, and Cassirer wherever possible. Finally, I should like to suggest briefly the most obvious consequences which have manifested themselves in the philosophy of Russell and Whitehead, the idealistic speculations of Eddington, and the operationalism of Bridgman.[3]

2. RELATIVITY AND QUANTUM THEORY

It is generally assumed that changes in the physical sciences come gradually; that they build upon one another; and that their cumulative effect is without excitement or surprise. In a sense this is true. Viewed in sufficiently broad perspective, the history of science is a continuity. But sometimes the acceleration of the changes is dramatic and unsuspected. This is what permits us to speak of "the Einstein revolution," and its real impact can be discerned in the recollections of the aged Whitehead:[4]

Let me speak personally for a moment. I had a good classical education, and when I went up to Cambridge early in the 1880's my mathematical training was continued under good teachers. Now nearly everything was supposed to be known about physics that could be known—except a few spots, such as electromagnetic phenomena, which remained (or so it was thought) to be co-ordinated with the Newtonian principles. But, for the rest, physics was supposed to be nearly a closed subject. Those investigations to co-ordinate went on through the next dozen years. By the middle of the 1890's there were a few tremors, a slight shiver as of all not being quite secure, but no one sensed what was coming. By 1900 the Newtonian physics were demolished, done for! Still speaking personally, it had a profound effect on me; I have been fooled once, and I'll be damned if I'll be fooled again! Einstein is supposed to have made an epochal discovery. I am respectful and interested, but also sceptical. There is no more reason to suppose that Einstein's relativity is anything final than Newton's *Principia*.

A synthesis of physical theory which for three hundred years had dominated Western culture was suddenly swept aside, and the philosophical consequences are shown in the metaphysics of Whitehead himself.

The ideal in the descriptive analysis of physical science is the formulation of a law of nature, the identification of a relationship between physical quantities which does not depend simply upon the peculiar standpoint of the observer or upon the system of co-ordinates which he adopts for the purposes of his description. Thus a prime criterion of physical theory is *universality*, which may be defined as the ability to formulate equations which are invariant however the system of co-ordinates is transformed. The contrast between Newton's postulation of an absolute time and an absolute space and Einstein's relativizing of the perceptions of duration and of length does not do justice to the formal superiority of Einstein's formulations over those of Newton. For the ultimate consequence of Einstein's work is that it vindicates the objectivity of the laws of nature, and demonstrates that the laws of electrodynamics and optics are independent of the standpoint of the observer.

It was Einstein himself who, on the occasion of Max Planck's sixtieth birthday, stated to the Physical Society of Berlin: "The supreme task of the physicist is to arrive at those universal elementary laws from which the cosmos can be built up by pure deduction." This was the genius of the Newtonian formulations: that through their axioms of space and time and their laws of motion a theoretical mechanics could be set up permitting the future path of a moving body to be charted (and its past also) provided its present state of movement and the forces acting upon it are known. These forces are gravitational forces and are relative to mass and distance. The result of Newtonian mechanics was the generalization for all branches of physics of a mode of explanation utilizing the concept of the mutual attraction between unchangeable particles. The kinetic theory of matter was thus both an explanation of such phenomena as the generation of heat and a more abstract image of the structure of matter itself.

With respect to co-ordinate systems in relative uniform rectilineal motion, classical mechanics succeeded admirably in formulating invariant equations. But from the beginning certain paradoxical problems appeared in optics, and toward the end of the nineteenth century, the situation in electrodynamics grew increasingly uneasy. Einstein in his Inaugural Address to the Prussian Academy of Sciences in 1914—that is, after the publication of the Special Theory of Relativity, but before the formulation of the General Theory—with his usual modesty paid tribute to the revolutionary discoveries of Planck.[5]

About fifteen years ago nobody had yet doubted that a correct account of the electrical, optical and thermal properties was possible on the basis of Galileo-Newtonian mechanics applied to the movement of molecules and of Clerk Maxwell's theory of the electro-magnetic field. Then Planck showed that in order to establish a law of heat radiation consonant with experience, it was necessary to employ a method of calculation the incompatibility of which with the principles of classical physics became clearer and clearer. For with this method of calculation Planck introduced the quantum hypothesis into physics, which has since received brilliant confirmation. With this quantum hypothesis he dethroned classical physics as applied to the case where sufficiently small masses are moved at sufficiently low speeds and high rates of acceleration, so that today the laws of motion propounded by Galileo and Newton can be allowed validity only as limiting laws.

Planck's discoveries are one example of the purely physical arguments which had gradually called the traditional kinematics into question, and which ultimately led to its replacement by the theory of relativity. But of course there were others. According to traditional conceptions, space, time, and matter are separable entities, largely independent of one another; but the concept of electrodynamic phenomena which produced the field theory (which Einstein rightfully calls "the most important invention since Newton's time") challenged this assumption. Not particles, not charges, but the continuous field, electromagnetic or gravitational, is essential to physical description, and here space and matter (and even time) are granted a more intimate union. The theory of relativity arose from problems which first manifested themselves in the interpretation of Clerk Maxwell's field equations. And it was the difficulties in the older formulations which suggested a new definition of the space-time continuum which is the comprehensive matrix of all physical events.

Paul Valéry once said: "Achilles cannot win over the tortoise if he meditates on space and time." This anti-intellectualism may hold in poetics (which was what M. Valéry was discussing), but it is refuted in the evolution of modern physical theories. For it was a meditation upon the nature of space, time, and measurement which produced the special theory of relativity. Great progress in the field of precision measurement (through the interferometer) had enabled Michaelson to obtain a negative result in looking for the optic phenomena which should have resulted from the earth's motion relative to the ether. Lorentz, in examining the way in which the Maxwell equations are transformed when one passes from one frame of reference to a second in uniform rectilineal motion with it, showed that by a special transformation formula these equations could be made invariant. And Fitzgerald, using the Lorentz formulas in his own fashion, explained the curious result of the Michaelson experiment in terms of the longitudinal contraction of every solid (measuring rod or clock) in the direction of its motion. But if the Michaelson-Morley experiment, the Lorentz transformation, and the Fitzgerald contraction were the material grounds for an uneasiness which had beset physical theory, they were at the same time artifices explaining certain properties of the electro-magnetic field without disclosing the revolutionary implications which lay only a few short steps away. It was Einstein who took these few short steps by a meditation on space and time, as Paul Valéry's com-patriot—the famous physicist Louis de Broglie—has pointed out.[6]

Then came Albert Einstein.

With great vigor he attacked this formidable problem, which had already been the object of so much study, by resolutely adopting a new point of view. For him, the Lorentz transformation formulas were not simple mathematical relations defining a change of variables, convenient for studying the equations of electromagnetism; rather they were the expression of the relations which *physically* exist between the spatial and temporal co-ordinates of two Galilean observers.* A daring hypothesis, indeed, before which the perspicacious mind of Lorentz recoiled! It carried in its wake, in fact, an abandonment of the ideas, traditional since Newton, regarding the absolute nature of space and time. . . . It was the distinction of Albert Einstein to succeed in showing, by means of an extremely minute and subtle analysis of the manner in which the physicist is led by his measuring operations to constitute his own scheme of space and time, that the co-ordinates of space and time are really interlocked by the Lorentz formulas. Revealing that the absence of signals which travel at infinite speeds results in the impossibility of verifying the simultaneity of two events occurring at points distant from each other, he analyzed the manner in which observers related to the same Galilean system nevertheless are able, through synchronization of clocks by exchanges of signals, to define a simultaneity within their system of refer-ence; however this simultaneity would be valid only for them, and events which would seem to them to be thus simultaneous would not be so for observers in motion relative to them. Central to this reasoning is the fact that no signal can travel with a speed greater than that of light in a void. . . .

It is, as de Broglie says, from the constitution of the operations of measurement that the system of space and time is constructed, and this construction depends ultimately upon the fact that no signal can surpass the velocity of light. For the special theory of relativity (meant to apply only to systems in which the Newtonian principle of inertia holds) was

* A system of Cartesian co-ordinates is composed of three plane surfaces perpen-dicular to each other and rigidly attached to a rigid body. When this body follows the fundamental law of the Galileo-Newton mechanics (the law of inertia), the system of co-ordinates is called a "Galilean" system or a "Galilean" frame, and an observer located on such a body is called a "Galilean" observer.

based upon two assumptions. The first is that physical laws are the same in all co-ordinate systems moving in uniform relative motion. The second is the absolute constancy of the velocity of light. From these assumptions the properties of moving rods and clocks (the measuring criteria of space and time), such as their changes in length and rate according to velocity, are deduced. The special theory of relativity implies a correction of the laws of classical mechanics, for while the older laws provide adequate predictions in a universe of relatively low velocities, they are invalid in those systems where particles in motion approach the speed of light.

The two assumptions of the special theory of relativity both require a concept of invariance. The basic laws of electrodynamics involve the speed of light, and if the laws of electrodynamics are to be invariant, then the speed of light must be a constant. But this constancy of the speed of light in different inertial systems requires that simultaneity be relative, that moving clocks be retarded, and that moving rods contract. Thus the necessity for objectivity in physical description suggests a relativity in the area of immediate observation. And, as we shall see, it is just this differential character of observational data which opens up the theory of relativity to a series of alternative interpretations.

Hans Reichenbach has insisted that "The theory of relativity shows that space and time are neither ideal objects nor forms of order necessary for the human mind. They constitute *a relational system* expressing certain general features of physical objects and thus are *descriptive of the physical world*."[7] It remains true, however, that the concept of the relational system which underlies the behavior of physical objects has here undergone a simple but profound change. This change involves the substitution of a four-dimensional continuum of space-time (the world of Minkowski) for the separated dimensions of Newtonian physics. One can say that this four-dimensional continuum retains an *a priori* character if one wishes, for distances and elements of volume retain an invariant value for all Galilean observers despite the diversity of space and time co-ordinates which they employ. Each observer "carves out" his own space and time, and the function of the formulas of the Lorentz transformation is to exhibit how these different perspectives are related.

In such a world the notion of a particle in space is represented as a motionless line in space-time, or as a "world line." Nor is the principle of strict causality abandoned. The relativity of simultaneity does not imply an absence of the kind of cross-section through nature which is formed of co-present happenings; it only means that there are plural cross-sections of this sort, and that there is no reason intrinsic to the system for choosing any particular one and calling it "absolute simultaneity." Each observer may, as time passes, discover new cross-sections of nature which appear to him as successive aspects of the material world, and these will be causally related. But the shift in the conception of the space-time continuum has one important metaphysical consequence: it means the abandonment of physical atomism. Not the particle, not the point in space, not the instant in time has physical reality; but only *the event* embedded in its four-dimensional continuum. Of this no one has been more aware than Einstein himself.[8]

In the pre-relativity physics space and time were separate entities. Specifications of time were independent of the choice of the space of reference. . . . One spoke of points of space, as of instants of time, as if they were absolute realities. It was not observed that the true element of the space-time specification was the event specified by the four numbers x_1, x_2, x_3, t [the three dimensions plus time]. The conception of something happening was always that of a four-dimensional continuum; but the recognition of this was obscured by the absolute character of the pre-relativity time. Upon giving up the hypothesis of the absolute character of time, particularly that of simultaneity, the four-dimensionality of the space-time concept was immediately recognized. It is neither the point in space, nor the instant in time, at which something happens that has physical reality, but only the event itself. There is no absolute . . . relation in space, and no absolute relation in time between two events, but there is an absolute . . . relation in space and time. . . . The circumstance that there is no objective rational division of the four-dimensional continuum into a three-dimensional space and a one-dimensional time continuum indicates that the laws of nature will assume a form which is logically most satisfactory when expressed as laws in the four-dimensional space-time continuum. Upon this depends the great advance in method which the theory of relativity owes to Minkowski.

One further consequence of the special theory of relativity ought to be noted: the connection between mass and energy. In the newer dynamics, the energy of a material particle in any Galilean system of reference is equal to the mass which the particle enjoys by virtue of its motion in the given system times the square of the velocity of light. Thus mass and energy enjoy a certain equivalence, and it is now possible to combine the two principles of the conservation of mass and the conservation of energy into a single principle of the conservation of mass-energy. It follows that a radiating body loses mass and an absorbing body gains it. An immediate consequence of this principle of mass-energy is that in virtue of its mass, even a tiny fragment of matter contains an enormous quantity of energy. The mere conception that matter is an immense reservoir of crystallized energy is a principle of fundamental importance in the development of nuclear physics.

The concept of inertial energy leads at once to the General Theory of Relativity, which Einstein had established by 1916, for the consequence of the general theory is that the gravitational attraction between any two bodies is proportional to the product of their inertial masses, and this identity of inertial and gravitational mass (considered in Newtonian theory as merely a strange coincidence) is here shown as essential to the principle of relativity.[9]

The special theory of relativity deals only with Galilean frames. It is therefore incomplete. The general theory attempts to remove this restriction. Obviously it is possible to arrive at general laws of nature only by measuring various observable magnitudes and determining the functional correlations which hold between them. On the one hand there must be innumerable frames of reference for the dating and placing of natural events. But it is also a postulate of simplicity and objectivity that there should be natural laws absolute in the sense of being independent of any particular frame of reference. Thus the laws discovered by observers in particular frames will be but transcriptions of absolute relations in the language of that particular frame.

It would thus be reasonable [as Broad says[10]] to suppose that, on comparing the laws discovered by observers who observe the same phenomenon and use all kinds of different frames of reference, we might be able to extract a kind of "kernel" which should be neutral as between them all. This kernel would be the absolute law of the phenomenon in question, and it is this which the General Theory of Relativity seeks to extract.

The General Theory of Relativity is built upon the idea that the laws of physics may be expressed in "covariant equations"—those which have the same mathematical form whatever reference system of space-time variables is used. But it also provides a more elaborate analysis of the space-time continuum in that it brings the problem of gravitation within the orbit of relativity, and by doing so formulates new structural laws for the gravitational field. And by regarding the equality of inertial and gravitational mass as essential rather than as accidental, it requires a new and revolutionary appraisal of the role of geometry in the description of the physical world.

The analogy between centrifugal and gravitational forces suggests that both may be derived from the metrical form of space-time. In the absence of gravitational forces, space-time may be considered as

Euclidean. On the other hand, in the presence of a gravitational field, events take place as if obeying the principles of Riemann's geometry of curved surfaces. Gravitation is therefore expressible as the curvature of a space-time dependent upon the existence of masses scattered throughout the universe. Thus the structure of the universe (its curvature in a geometric sense) depends upon the disposition of its matter.[11] The General Theory of Relativity thereupon by means of a tensor-calculus develops an interpretation of gravitational phenomena which relies upon a theory of spatial curvature derived from Riemann. The experimental confirmations of the General Theory have come from three sources: (1) the prediction of a more exact value of the rotation of the perihelion of the planet Mercury; (2) the prediction of the deflection of light in a gravitational field (experimentally verified by the Sobral expedition of 1917); and (3) a predicted displacement of spectral lines toward the infra-red pole.

These experiments are neither completely accurate nor conclusive, but even their partial success raises interesting questions about the geometrical interpretation of the concept of force which the General Theory of Relativity implies. If the observed properties of space, and particularly the phenomena of the propagation of light, show that the Minkowski space-time continuum required by relativity theory resembles Riemann's space rather than Euclid's (except in regions of relatively small magnitude), then what of the *a priori* status of our spatial intuitions as asserted by Kant? If nature as a sum total of events can be said to have an intrinsic structure, and if the phenomena of gravitation suggest that this intrinsic structure is best conceived after the pattern of a spherical geometry, then it becomes difficult (in Whitehead's sense) to maintain the old division between physics and geometry. The objectivity of a uniform relatedness is reduced to such validation as is supplied by the contingent relations of nature.

The revolution in the scientific conception of the physical universe which followed from the theory of relativity was profound, although the transformations in our conceptions of space, time, and measurement which it occasioned are not easy to describe. There is an air of strangeness, almost of paradox, about the newer ideas which are forced upon the attention of philosophers, and about whose final meaning physicists themselves are often perplexed. But in the domain of quantum theory the situation is, if anything, even more disturbing, for here the very concepts of *physical description* and *causality* have become problematic and ambiguous. Here, the breakdown of that mechanism which was the presupposition of the seventeenth-century physical synthesis is almost complete. Even in relativity physics, strict causality reigns. Max Born quite correctly says of Einstein:[12] "His conviction seems always to have been, and still is today (1949) that the ultimate laws of nature are causal and deterministic, that probability is used to cover our ignorance if we have to do with numerous particles, and that only the vastness of this ignorance pushes statistics into the fore-front." He adds, with considerable justification: "Most physicists do not share this view today, and the reason for this is the development of quantum theory."

The quantum theory, like the theory of relativity, originated just after the turn of the century, and was also a response to results of physical experiment and measurement which were not in accord with the classical doctrines of optics and the electrodynamics of atomic behavior. The theory of relativity was the product of an uneasiness occasioned by the negative results of the Michaelson-Morley experiment. The quantum theory was a startling hypothesis introduced by Max Planck in 1901 to account both for the sharp spectral lines on a spectrogram (indicating that atomic wave-lengths and frequencies were definite and discontinuous), and for the mysterious behavior of incandescent solids. In the first case the assumptions of electrodynamics were at variance with the spectroscopic result; in the second they were at variance with the observed facts of radiation. In the midst of this embarrassment, Planck put forward the hypothesis (in contradiction to the traditional electrodynamics) that the vibratory properties of electrons within solid bodies which are responsible for the emission and absorption of radiation were such that these electrons could emit radiant energy only in finite quantities (or *quanta*) whose value was proportional to the frequency emitted. Thus the phenomenon of radiation is not continuous, but, like matter, can be envisaged only as individual units or atoms whose aggregate or large-scale behavior can be scientifically dealt with not absolutely, but only in terms of the principles of probability. The units of energy emitted by radiation are not of equal size, but vary with the frequency of the oscillation. In formulating this proportionality Planck was led to introduce the famous constant h, the product of energy and time called *Action*. The details of the earlier formulation of the quantum theory are without philosophic interest. But its general significance is enormous. For it introduces into the world an element of discontinuity or chance which (however unlike the continuities of our habitual experiences) seems to be intrinsic to nature and her underlying processes.

In 1913 Niels Bohr put forward his quantum theory of the atom. Here again the details are unimportant, but what had already emerged from this early stage of development of quantum theory was a dual resolution of the nature of matter and a paradox which affected this resolution. The fields of optics and dynamics were in one sense unified by the quantum theory of radiation. The photon (or quantum of energy) was taken to be the unit of the first, while the electron (or quantum of matter) was taken to be the unit of the second. But physical theory was now involved in a dilemma with respect to the perplexing nature of these elementary units. On the one hand there was abundant evidence that both photons and electrons behave like corpuscles, and on the other that they are waves.[13] It is not a dilemma which can be solved either by an appeal to observation or to logical principle. Nor is the strategy of combination a valid solution, for the wave-like and particle-like properties are not merely different; they are incompatible. The difficulty follows from an attempt to deal with the constructs of physical theory as if they were describable in the imagery of sensory observation. But if electrons and photons are neither particles nor waves, nor for that matter colored nor shaped nor visible, then we shall not expect them to follow the rules of order in the larger world or to be subsumed under the categories of immediate observability. This leads directly to the second stage of the development of quantum theory from 1925 onward and to the work of de Broglie, Heisenberg, and Schrödinger. This is the period of the discovery of the structure of quantum mechanics, a discovery which involves new and dramatic problems about our knowledge of ultimate physical objects, about our knowledge of the position and velocity of elementary particles (the assumption of classical mechanics that position and velocity are compatible is called in question), and about principles of causality (the applicability of predictive measures to individuals and to mass aggregates of individuals).

In 1925 Heisenberg proclaimed a new theory of quantum mechanics based not upon Bohr's model of the planetary orbits of atoms (which cannot be physically observed), but upon the radiation absorbed and emitted by the atom (which can). From the observable magnitudes of the quantities and frequencies of emitted radiation and from the energy levels of the atomic system he established a mathematical formulation in terms of matrices. A year later Schrödinger derived the same results by a system of wave mechanics in which elementary particles are conceived of as wave systems. The two forms of mathematical statement yielded equivalent results, one of which was that from the radiation data, the spatial position of an electron could be placed indiscriminately within its field. It has therefore a certain indeterminacy of position. In 1927 this result was converted into a principle by Heisenberg and developed by Bohr. The former pointed out that our knowledge of the state of an atomic system will always involve a peculiar *indeterminacy*. Thus a measurement of the position of an electron by some device like a high frequency radiation microscope will involve an exchange of momentum between the electron and the agency of measurement which will vary directly with the attempted accuracy of the measurement. Niels Bohr has restated it with reference to the experimental situation as "the impossibility of any sharp separation between the behaviour of atomic objects and the interaction with the measuring instruments which serve to define the conditions under which the phenomena appear."[14]

This formulation, which hinges upon the distinction between the objects under investigation and the scientist's measuring instruments, is not in itself startling or paradoxical. Indeed, while it may be an axiom of a realistic theory of knowledge that the act of awareness or observation is non-transforming or non-affecting with respect to the phenomena observed, this naive assumption is disproved every day not only in physical science, but equally in social science and aesthetic perception. What is of real consequence here is a shift in the mathematical tools of physical "description" and the use of a new and somewhat Pickwickian conception of what an "observable" is. In the classical mechanics, the position of a mass-particle is a quantity shifting in time and space. It is an observable expressed in the language of mathematical functions. But such properties as position, momentum, energy, and velocity in quantum mechanics are not observables in the sense of being establishable in a single act of observation. They have different values in different observations, but at the same time, these values have a unified distribution over a series of observations, and this permits the physicist to consider the scatter as a determinate probability distribution. For this purpose not the mathematical language of "functions" but that of "operators" is employed. It is evident, then, that the concept of a "physical observable" has profoundly altered. It is not an atomic constituent of a physical system, but an object *determined by the physical operation to be performed*. If the operation to be performed yields only a scattered cluster of measurements, then this must not be interpreted as an incomplete description given by a defective theory, but as a result compatible with the nature of the "observables" which the conditions of the experimental matrix presuppose.

Quantum mechanics does not assert that particles *have* position and velocity although both together cannot be observed with accuracy. Nor does it imply the existence of particles with a *real indefiniteness* of position and velocity. Its concern is with experimental arrangements, and in this area, where the expression "velocity of a particle" is relevant, the expression "position of a particle" is intrinsically excluded. Thus, as in Niels Bohr's formulation of 1936, the description of a system in terms of position is *complementary* to the description of a system in terms of momentum. In the language of formal logic the principle of complementarity expresses the uninterpreted fact of mutual exclusiveness in the exactitude of physical quantum measurements.[15]

The uncertainty principle draws its significance from the fact that the state of an atomic system must be related to an aggregate of observations, and, therefore, such prediction as is possible within this area will be a case of statistical inference. Does this mean that there is a new and necessary shift from "causal laws" to "probability laws"? The answer hinges in part upon whether the uncertainty principle is interpreted as a mysterious but practical limitation upon physical measurability or as a fundamental shift in the meaning of physical reality. In either case there are important implications for the philosophy of science. Just as the theory of relativity has re-energized philosophical inquiries concerning the categories of space and time, so the quantum theory has re-introduced speculations about the category of causality. These speculations are the special battleground of the field of scientific epistemology, and upon this battleground great names in the philosophy of science and in the physical sciences themselves contend. For as Cassirer has said: "Each answer which physics imparts concerning the character and the peculiar nature of its fundamental concepts assumes inevitably for epistemology the form of a question."

3. THE INTERPRETIVE EFFORT

It would be a satisfying state of affairs, indeed, if the distinction between philosophy and science were neat and adequate so that theoretical and experimental physicists might concentrate upon the details of their work without having to raise more controversial issues about meaning, significance, and implications. But as Einstein himself has said:[16] "The present difficulties of his science force the physicist to come to grips with philosophical problems to a greater degree than was the case with earlier generations." Problems implicit in the subject matter turn the physicist from the electron microscope and the tensor equations to the interpretive effort. Despite the discipline of the positivistic tradition this is a necessity upon which both physicists and philosophers of science are agreed. "The philosophy of physics," Reichenbach tells us,[17] "should be as neat and clear as physics itself . . . but it should not use the operational form of empiricism as a way to evade problems of the logic of interpretation." And Einstein in a famous note on the theory of knowledge of Bertrand Russell[18] has criticized Hume in such an astonishing way as to suggest that the anti-metaphysical bias is a disease of contemporary thinking:

> By his clear critique Hume did not only advance philosophy in a decisive way but also—through no fault of his—created a danger for philosophy in that, following his critique, a fateful "fear of metaphysics" arose which has come to be a malady of contemporary empiricistic philosophizing; this malady is the counterpart to that earlier philosophizing in the clouds, which thought it could neglect and dispense with what was given by the senses.

In the philosophical speculations of Einstein there is no "fateful fear of metaphysics," but on the other hand there is hardly an abandonment of empiricism either. The position is moderate: science would be empty if the propositions of its conceptual system were not firmly rooted in sensory experiences, but at the same time the conceptual system does not derive from experience and it has its own rules of system, logic, and order. There is a dualism here, which sees mathematics and experience as joint sources of the systematic edifice of science—an almost Kantian attempt to avoid the excesses of both rationalism and empiricism. "Science," Einstein says, "is the attempt to make the chaotic diversity of our sense-experience correspond to a logically uniform system of thought."[19] Very well. So far there is nothing original or startling here, nothing to which Sir Isaac Newton would not heartily agree. But what is the origin of a logically uniform system of thought? What can conceptualization supply independently of sense experience? And what can pure mathematical thought contribute to our understanding of the world of things? The question is as old as Plato or Leibniz or Hegel. Einstein provides his own unique answer.

In his "Autobiographical Notes" Einstein presents simply what he calls *"mein erkenntnistheoretisches Credo"*—my epistemological credo:[20]

> I see on the one side the totality of sense-experiences, and, on the other the totality of the concepts and propositions which are laid down in books. The relations between the concepts and propositions themselves are of a strictly logical nature. . . . The concepts and propositions get "meaning," i.e., "content" only through their connection with sense-experiences. The connection of the latter with the former is purely intuitive. . . . The system of concepts and the rules of syntax which together constitute the conceptual system are a creation of man. . . .
>
> A proposition is correct if it is derived according to the accepted rules within a logical system. . . . A system has truth-value according to the possibility of its coordination to the totality of experience. A correct proposition borrows its truth from the truth of the system to which it belongs. . . .

All concepts, even those closest to experience, are from the logical stand-point, freely chosen conventions, even the concept of causality. . . .

On the surface this passage is a more modern restatement of Leibniz's distinction between truths of reason and truths of fact (although for the former Einstein uses not "truth" but "correctness"), and it seems to simply reaffirm the positivistic insistence upon the crucial difference between analytic and synthetic judgments—those true by definition or by deduction from definitions, and those testable by sense experience. But there are other implications of the passage which are not so clear. What does Einstein mean by the "intuitive" apprehension of the relation between concepts and sense perceptions? Even more ambiguous is the assertion that both concepts and syntactical rules are a creation of man—"freely chosen conventions," Einstein says—and he underlines this by the suggestion that even so basic a concept as causality is also a convention freely accepted; not, as Kant would have maintained, a form of our understanding which we could no more freely accept (or reject) than we could our mind itself.

It would seem that Einstein had fallen under the influence of Poin-caré's conventionalism, and possibly for reasons not unlike Poincaré's own. The nineteenth-century discovery of non-Euclidean geometry had shown that there are alternative geometries, and the fact that some geometries are better suited for application to some parts of the natural world than others reinforced the conventional interpretation. Poincaré himself noted that metric geometry is the geometry of solids while projective geometry is the geometry of light. Considerations of this sort led Poincaré to affirm:[21] "The axioms of geometry are therefore neither synthetic a priori judgments nor experimental facts. They are conventions; our choice among all possible conventions is guided by experimental facts: but it remains free and is limited only by the necessity of avoiding all contradiction. . . . In other words the axioms of geometry . . . are merely disguised definitions." This is the reasoning which Einstein also appears to follow.

It is one thing to say that the axioms of geometry are merely disguised definitions. It would be quite another to say the same about laws of nature. But so close are the interweavings of mathematics and physical interpretation in the equations of mathematical physics that the issue of conventionalism, raised originally with respect to pure geometry, has now become a problem of science also. Even if one holds that the equations of physics (like geometrical axioms) in themselves assert nothing about reality until they are given physical application (the position of

Moritz Schlick), still, the conventional element in their formulation must make them mysterious, if not definitely suspect. Hans Reichenbach has called attention to the conventional character of relativity theory. "The logical basis of the theory of relativity is the discovery that many statements, which were regarded as capable of demonstrable truth or falsity, are mere definitions."[22] That our conventional units of physical measurement (yard, meter, gram, etc.) are defined entities is a commonplace, but Einstein was the first to make clear that the notion of "congruence" (and hence the comparison of distances) is also an affair of definitions. Similar situations hold for time, energy, and gravitation. The special theory of relativity *defines* the simultaneity of events occurring at distant places as relative. One of its important consequences is the *defined* equivalence of mass and energy. The general theory of relativity *defines* inertial and gravitational mass as equivalent. But what is important is to recognize that although the theory of relativity constitutes a *re-definition* of the concepts of space, time, and gravitation rather than an *empirical discovery* of their "true nature" (and that therefore freely chosen conventions play an extraordinarily important role in the domain of natural knowledge), it is not for this reason either lacking in scientific objectivity or unreliable in the sense of expressing a meaningless subjective preference.

To understand this, I think, requires that we recognize and enter into the faith that lies back of Einstein's mathematical rationalism, while at the same time appreciating his rigid distinction between rational and empirical knowledge. "Pure logical thinking" (as he says in his famous essay "On the Method of Theoretical Physics"[23]) "cannot yield us any knowledge of the empirical world; all knowledge of reality starts from experience and ends in it. Propositions arrived at by purely logical means are completely empty as regards reality." But a system of theoretical physics is like Euclid's geometry; it is made up of concepts, fundamental laws relating these concepts, and propositions derived from these laws by logical deduction. It is these deduced propositions which we must examine for their congruence with sensory experience. Just as Euclidean geometry may be regarded as potentially applicable—as the science of the *possible* relations of rigid bodies in space—so theoretical physics in its mathematical form is potentially applicable as an explanation of experimental data.

At this point [says Einstein[24]] an enigma presents itself which in all ages has agitated inquiring minds. How can it be that mathematics, being after all a product of human thought which is independent of experience, is so admirably appropriate to the objects of reality? Is human reason, then, without experience, merely by taking thought, able to fathom the properties of real things?

Now, of course, mathematics cannot by itself "fathom the properties of real things." The external confirmation of a theory of mathematical physics, the intuitive awareness of its applicability, depends upon an empirical effort. Mathematics as such cannot predicate anything about perceptual objects. But real objects can be co-ordinated to this merely conceptual scheme, and when such co-ordination is accomplished, mathematical equations become physical science.

But there is more to it than this. All physical theory, whether that of classical mechanics or of relativity, as a mathematical or logical structure has certain internal demands of "naturalness" or "logical simplicity." This is not a matter of external confirmation but of inner perfection. Because the history of the acceptance and rejection of physical theory shows it to be as much dependent upon the criterion of logical simplicity as upon that of external confirmation, it is here that the mystery becomes acute. The attempt to incorporate wave-optics into the mechanical picture of the world was bound to produce a certain logical incongruity, and the existence of two types of conceptual element in physics—first mass-points functioning through action at a distance and second the electro-dynamic notion of a continuous field—also indicated an intermediate stage in physical theory where maximum uniformity, coherence, and simplicity had not yet been achieved. Einstein's revolution was precipitated by a crisis of non-confirmation of the reigning theory of the behavior of light, but its almost immediate success was the overwhelming triumph of a mathematical unification.

Reichenbach once asked Einstein how he had discovered the theory of relativity; Einstein answered that he arrived at it because he was so strongly convinced of the harmony of the universe. This is the heart of the mystery. The axioms of geometry are free creations of the human mind, and the axiomatic basis of theoretical physics is equally a free creation of the human mind rather than an extraction from experience. But Hegel's faith in the pre-established harmony of reason and the world finds its modern parallel in Einstein's faith in the congruence of mathematical *simplicity* and physical fact.

Our experience hitherto justifies us in believing that nature is the realization of the simplest conceivable mathematical ideas. I am convinced that we can discover by means of purely mathematical constructions the concepts and the laws connecting them with each other, which furnish the key to the understanding of natural phenomena. Experience may suggest the appropriate mathematical concepts, but they most certainly cannot be deduced from it. Experience remains, of course, the sole criterion of the physical utility of a mathematical construction. But the creative principle resides in mathematics. In a certain sense, therefore, I hold it true that pure thought can grasp reality, as the ancients dreamed.[25]

If one represents the world as a four-dimensional continuum measured by the methods of Riemann's geometry of curved surfaces, and seeks the very simplest laws for such a system, one arrives at the laws of gravitation presented by the general theory of relativity. In a certain sense this constitutes a model for all theory construction in the physical sciences. In the mathematically simplest concepts and the simplest links between them lies the theoretician's hope of approximating physical reality. It was for this reason that up to the time of his death Einstein recognized that there existed no fundamental single principle of theoretical physics.[26] In the quantum theory and the theory of relativity the twentieth-century revolution in physics has produced not one, but two theoretical systems which are essentially independent of one another. Although as Einstein noted, the two systems are not in direct contradiction, they do, he said, "seem little adapted to fusion into one unified theory." Such a theoretical unification was nonetheless the dream of his last years. According to his own testimony, "The theory of relativity arose out of efforts to improve, *with reference to logical economy*, the foundation of physics as it existed at the turn of the century."[27] But also by his own admission:

. . . it cannot be claimed that those parts of the general relativity theory which can today (1940) be regarded as final have furnished physics with a complete and satisfactory foundation. In the first place, the total field appears in it to be composed of two logically unconnected parts, the gravitational and the electromagnetic. And in the second place, this theory, like the earlier field theories, has not up till now supplied an explanation of the atomistic structure of matter. This failure has probably some connection with the fact that so far it has contributed nothing to the understanding of quantum phenomena.

Are relativity theory and quantum mechanics capable of unification? If so, what form would their unification take?

The question is highly speculative. Physicists themselves (including Einstein, Planck, Born, and Heisenberg) do not agree upon its answer. But the problems which underlie their disagreement are in no small part philosophical, and they turn upon two issues. The first is the metaphysical issue of whether our direct representation of physical reality in space and time shall ultimately use a model of continuity or of discontinuity. The second is the epistemological issue of whether physics can grasp reality as what actually goes on in nature independent of the act of observation (and thus employs strict causality), or whether it must confine itself to making statistical predictions based upon the results of all measurements which can be carried out upon a physical system. In each case Einstein himself (somewhat quixotically according to his colleagues) favors the first alternative.

If one retained the basic epistemology of classical physics, assuming that there is a physical reality which can be defined as having stable properties, then it would be necessary to extend those field theories in which every element in a four-dimensional continuum is the possessor of qualities (metrical or electrodynamic) which can be expressed in partial differential equations. In this case the idea of continuity would be reinstated, and with appropriate modifications causality as well. The statistical and indeterminate character of contemporary quantum theory would then be seen as a necessary consequence of the incompleteness of contemporary quantum-mechanical description. But if, on the contrary, immediate reality must be assumed for Planck's quanta and if they must be considered an irreducible property of radiation and molecular structure, then classical physics must be left behind, the notion of a "physical state" will be permanently redefined in the mode of quantum-mechanical description, continuity will be abandoned, the rhythmic and periodic nature of physical reality will be assumed, and the predictive power of physical theory will rest upon a frequency theory of probability.[28]

The domain of physical science has traditionally been considered to be an area of factuality and mathematical exactitude. But those who are not themselves workers in this field do not always realize how problematic and how speculative are the conclusions of the contemporary revolution in physics, and, above all, how deeply the interpretive efforts of men like Einstein and Planck are conditioned by assumptions and a philosophical point of view which transcends the sphere of the experimental results themselves. No one who reads much of Einstein can fail to be impressed by the profound influence which mechanistic conceptions have had upon him. He is a realist. He believes in a real physical world in space and time whose phenomena we can represent to ourselves. Time and again one finds him dissatisfied with a physical world which, in Eddington's terms, "has dissolved into a world of shadows" or a quantum-mechanical device interpreted as indicating a universe of *real chance* or contingency. In 1944 he wrote to his old friend Max Born, a strong proponent of the quantum mechanics school of physical interpretation:[29] "In our scientific expectations . we have grown as far apart as the poles. You believe in God playing dice and I in perfect laws in the world of things existing as real objects, which I try to grasp. . . ." This belief conditions Einstein's own interpretation of relativity and quantum theory.

It is clear that Einstein believes in a world of real objects whose relations are expressible in "perfect laws." And it is also clear that he views mathematics as the creative tool whereby theoretical physics can formulate with growing approximation these perfect laws. But there seems to be a problem here. For he has asserted over and over that the axiomatic basis of theoretical physics is independent of experience and that the concepts of mathematics (whether simple integers, differential equations, or a tensor calculus) are "a free creation of the human mind." But this returns us to the question which we have raised before. If mathematical concepts are "freely chosen," that is, arbitrary rather than necessary, then how can they approximate "perfect laws" of nature? The arbitrariness of the instrument seems incongruous with the perfection and necessity of that which it is its function to disclose.

The answer lies in the degree of arbitrariness which Einstein has in mind for the freely chosen axioms of mathematical physics. In one place[30] he suggests that this freedom "is not the freedom of a fiction writer, but rather like that of a person who has to solve a cleverly designed word-puzzle." The analogy is instructive. Many solutions are theoretically available, but probably only one solves the puzzle. The problem is to test by trial and error for that one word which does the trick. In this analogy lies the clue to Einstein's conception of the relation of geometry to experience. He does not agree with Newton that physical theory is a copy of physical reality. One of the crucial ideas of the theory of relativity is that geometry (which Newton regarded as a set of propositions summarizing and *describing* physical experience) is a construct of the intellect, and this holds for any geometry. Alternative geometries (spherical, elliptical, or hyperbolic) are systems of hypothetical propositions founded upon axioms which in themselves make no claim to be founded upon reality. This is the fruit of the axiomatic method of modern mathematics, where the logical-formal structure of mathematical ideas has been cleanly separated from the intuitive content which for Kant was their most important property.

For Kant the axioms of Euclidean geometry were intuitively self-evident. The modern view accepts axioms only as implicit definitions, and denies that Euclidean geometry is more nearly "the natural geometry

of the human mind" than any other. Einstein not only recognized that
mathematics as such cannot predicate anything about perceptual objects, but he saw that the supposed universality of Euclidean geometry
was based upon the *assumption* that there are in the physical universe
absolutely rigid bodies, and that the possible relations between them
can be most simply stated by a Euclidean geometry of three dimensions.[31]
These assumptions are empirical, and they turn geometry into a natural
science. When once this point is clarified, it follows that the question
of whether the geometry of the universe is or is not Euclidean is a valid
one answerable only by experience. For, as Einstein has said:

All linear measurement in physics is practical geometry in this sense, so
too is geodetic and astronomical linear measurement, if we call to our help
the law of experience that light is propagated in a straight line, and indeed
in a straight line in the sense of practical geometry.
I attach special importance to the view of geometry which I have just set
forth, because without it I should have been unable to formulate the theory
of relativity. Without it the following reflection would have been impossible:—In a system of reference rotating relatively to an inert system,
the laws of disposition of rigid bodies do not correspond to the rules of
Euclidean geometry on account of the Lorentz contraction; thus if we admit
non-inert systems we must abandon Euclidean geometry.

The abandonment of Euclidean geometry as a self-evident absolute,
which is required by the general theory of relativity, calls into question
Kant's whole theory of space. In Kant's formulation the three-dimen-
sionality of Euclidean space is the space presupposed by sensory perception—is, in fact, the form of perception by means of which sensation
is organized. When Einstein contends that the question of whether
the structure of the four-dimensional space-time continuum is Euclidean
or Riemannean is *a physical question to be answered by experience*, he
is denying both the conventionalism of Poincaré (which, however, does
in his opinion hold for pure or uninterpreted geometries) and the absolutism of Kant. For the relativity of geometry is simply an analogue of
the relativity of space-time and simultaneity which Einstein's theory
requires.
It may seem that I have dwelt overlong upon the fate of Kant's
philosophy in terms of the revolution in contemporary physics. But the
point is crucial. Modern philosophers are by no means completely
agreed upon the matter. Reichenbach believes that with Einstein and
Planck the "synthetic *a priori*" is forever banished. Cassirer holds that
Kant can be adapted to modern scientific requirements. The consensus,
however, supports Reichenbach. It is generally assumed that modern

physics is the refutation of Kant; that the redefinition of space, time, causality, and matter has made imperative a reassessment of the categories which Kant derived from his predecessors. In a sense this is obvious. For the great physical revolution of the seventeenth century was Newtonian, and Kant's ideas are saturated with the presuppositions of Newtonian dynamics. The counter-revolutions of Einstein and Planck against Newton have inevitably had repercussions upon metaphysics and epistemology proper. The next section will note these as they occur in Russell and the early Whitehead. For what Kant was to the physical science of Newton, Whitehead is to the physics of early quantum theory and relativity. Meanwhile I should like to summarize the interpretive results of the newer physics in the following eight propositions.

1. Time is not a uniform flow independent of an observer and above empirical examination. It is a matter of experimental inquiry and is dependent upon the physical process of the propagation of light.

2. All geometries are hypothetical and in themselves claim no relevance to reality. But when coordinated with propositions of existence (for example, those asserting the existence of rigid measuring rods or curved surfaces), they become physical geometries whose relevance to reality can be determined by observation and experiment.

3. Although the time and space of every observer is local and subjective, scientific theory requires an invariance of physical laws. Objectivity lies within the formal structure of the mathematical theory.

4. At the atomic level accurate simultaneous measurement of conjugated quantities is impossible. It is however possible to calculate the mean values of all measurements performable on the system.

5. The concept of time with its order of before and after derives from the notion of causality. There is no absolute simultaneity because the speed of light is finite; that is, causal transmission requires time.

6. Kant's assumption of the synthetic *a priori* status of space, time, and causality is untenable. The Euclidean geometry which fits so well the intermediate region of the human environment is empirically inapplicable to sub-microscopic and astronomical dimensions.

7. Quantum theory has cast suspicion upon the classical concept of material substance and has suggested that atomic entities have a periodic or rhythmic rather than a continuously enduring character.

8. Relativity theory emphasizes the concept of the "field" which makes the physically real not matter in empty space but lines of force within a field. The concept of substance is abandoned for electrodynamic

activity; to the extent that matter is retained it is simply an outgrowth of the field or a concentration within it.

4. RUSSELL AND WHITEHEAD

It is interesting that the most sustained and influential metaphysical speculations based upon the new physics should center about Cambridge University. Whitehead's *The Concept of Nature*, Russell's *The Analysis of Matter*, and Eddington's *The Philosophy of Physical Science* were all Tarner Lectures delivered in Trinity College during the two decades 1919-1939. The University Press also published Eddington's *Space, Time and Gravitation* and *The Nature of the Physical World* as well as Whitehead's *The Principles of Natural Knowledge* and *The Principle of Relativity*. Eddington is perhaps the most spectacular interpreter of quantum mechanics and relativity theory in the Western world, but it is Russell and Whitehead who have made the solider philosophical contribution, and it is to their work that I should first like to turn. This is not, of course, a consideration of their work as a whole. That will have its place elsewhere in this book. It is my intention to show that certain propositions of relativity physics and quantum theory have been the stimulating causes of their metaphysical constructions, and they are to serve, therefore, not as distinct philosophical types, but as examples of the manner in which the revolution of Einstein and Planck has affected the destiny of contemporary philosophy.

The newer physics poses two questions. The first concerns the status of matter. The second concerns the relations of matter to mind. Because both relativity theory and quantum mechanics originated in problems of physical measurement, and because measurement requires the distinction between the observer and the observed, the second question has seemed of particular importance. This belief has been reinforced by the fact that inferred scientific entities like protons, electrons, and molecules bear no resemblance to the products of raw perception such as sounds, colors, shapes, and their associated cluster into ordinary objects. Almost every philosopher of science has therefore been concerned with the relations between physics and perception.[32]

Now, in dealing with the relation of matter and mind in nature, Russell and Whitehead have come to conclusions which are very much alike. Whitehead has protested against "the bifurcation of nature into two systems of reality," one of which would be the entities like electrons which are the subject-matter of speculative physics, the other "the greenness of the trees, the song of the birds, the warmth of the sun, the hardness of the chairs, and the feel of the velvet."[33] Russell in the formulation of his famous "neutral monism" concurs. "This problem," he says,[34] "has two parts: to assimilate the physical world to the world of perceptions, and to assimilate the world of perception to the physical world. Physics must be interpreted in a way which tends towards idealism, and perception in a way which tends towards materialism. I believe that matter is less material, and mind less mental, than is commonly supposed. . . ." But with this somewhat enigmatic suggestion, I should like for the present to leave the question of the relation of matter and mind, and turn to that of the status of matter. For here we have in both Russell and Whitehead a revolutionary shift indeed—a shift away from the traditional metaphysics of matter in motion and enduring substances to a conception of matter as "energy" or "process," to the notion that "a thing is what it does," in short, to *a metaphysics of events*.

The revolutionary theories of contemporary physics have caused both Russell and Whitehead to ask essentially the same question. Whitehead's question, as formulated in the Preface of *An Enquiry Concerning the Principles of Natural Knowledge*, is "What are the ultimate data of science?" Russell's question, as formulated in the introductory chapter of *The Analysis of Matter*, is "What are the ultimate existents in terms of which physics is true?" Such a question is implicit in the definition of space-time as produced by the theory of relativity, and in the non-causal formulations of quantum mechanics. Russell proceeds at once to answer his own question: "We shall find, if I am not mistaken, that the objects which are mathematically primitive in physics, such as electrons, protons, and points in space-time, are all logically complex structures composed of entities which are metaphysically more primitive, which may be conveniently called 'events.'" The term "event" is not completely without ambiguity—sometimes Russell when he emphasizes the logical constructions implicit in physical theory calls it a "particular" —but its virtue is that it makes an undeniable reference to time. And it is that element in the theory of relativity which merges space and time into a single space-time continuum which has had the most important metaphysical consequences. When classical physics asserted that bodies occupy space and endure through time, it gave a different importance to the two modes of occupancy. The change of position of a natural body in space was crucial, but a difference of situation in time had no physical consequence. For classical physics the passage of time is only accidentally related to the character of material. But in relativity theory, lapse of time is no accident but the very essence of changing events, and quantum theory suggests that nature itself is composed of a plurality of "natural units of historic fact." History and Nature have always been distinguished as two distinct realms of being. It is perhaps ironic that at the very moment when Spengler and Toynbee have been converting History into Nature, Einstein and Planck have been converting Nature into History. For this is the consequence of the time perspective which emphasizes the physical "event."

It is also the consequence of a long development in theoretical physics. During the nineteenth century it was well known that processes occur where there is no "bodily" matter, and that these processes act in accordance with Maxwell's equations. Also Heisenberg's theory in effect reduces the electron to a series of radiations, and nuclear physics has indicated that protons and electrons are no longer strictly indestructible. According to Russell, each of these bits of evidence calls into question the myth of permanent bits of matter and enduring substances.

The argument from physics is reinforced by the argument from perception. We perceive events, not substances. What we perceive "occupies a volume of space-time which is small in all four dimensions ... and what we can primarily infer from precepts, assuming the validity of physics, are groups of events, again not substances."[35] It is a mere linguistic convention to regard a group of events as states of a thing or substance, but by such conventional definition nothing is gained philosophically. Naturally there is qualitative continuity in experience, persisting through change, but this can be accounted for by making a series of events the elements of a single "causal chain" with a certain intrinsic unity. Thus a unity of causal process is substituted for the endurance of an assumed substance with material identity. Nothing is lost, and, in fact, the philosophical picture has been made congruent with the scientific situation.

The concept of time which is implied by the theory of relativity suggests a world of events rather than of substances. A similar result is implied by the discovery of quantum mechanics. The importance of the latter to philosophy lies in its suggestion of periodicity at the heart of nature. The quantum analogy suggests that for nature, lapse of time is no accident, but the very essence of its material, and that this material cannot be itself in any sub-period however short. An object displays an emergent pattern requiring a definite lapse of time, and what we call an enduring object is merely a repetition of pattern sustained by a plurality of successive events. If the discovery of space-time has substituted events rather than substances as the raw material of physics, then, equally, quantum theory with its demand for periodicity has suggested to Russell that "fundamentally, periodicity is constituted by the recurrence of *qualities*."

If the basic terms of metaphysics are to follow upon the basic types of physical occurrence, and if the event is the metaphysical ultimate which must be used in philosophical transcriptions of physical theory, it would then follow that types of events would need to be distinguished which might explain such diverse areas as field theory and quantum mechanics. Metaphysics might then provide the theoretical unification which physics has been unable to establish. Without by any means making so excessive a claim, Russell has nonetheless found it necessary to distinguish species of the more generic "event" which shall do justice to the results of theoretical physics.

I propose [he says] to advocate a division of physical occurrences into three types, which I shall call respectively steady events, rhythms, and transactions. The phrase "steady events" is formed on the analogy of "steady motions," although the events concerned are not supposed to be motions. Rhythms are periodic processes. . . . Transactions are quantum changes, in which energy passes from one system to another. . . .[36]

A steady event is a class of events which have a time-like interval. A rhythm is a recurring cycle of events in which there is qualitative similarity between members of different periods. A transaction is a quantum change in which energy is exchanged between different physical systems. It is, of course, periodic.

The most important consequence of this classification is the way in which it enables Russell to relate perceptions and the entities of physics. Percepts are systems of steady events. They "extend over" the rhythms which are the pulse of physical reality. This suggests to Russell's imagination a cosmological metaphor:[37] "I suggest that the world consists of steady events accompanied by rhythms, like a long note on the violin while arpeggios are played on the piano, or of rhythms alone. Steady events are of various sorts, and many sorts have their appropriate rhythmic accompaniments. Quantum changes consist of transactions, i.e., of the substitution, suddenly, of one rhythm for another." To the ordinary man and to us all, immersed in our perceptions, it is the steady events which provide the apparent reality, but sub speciae naturae, it is the rhythms which provide the true metaphysical clue.

Russell's distinction between steady events and rhythms suggests the mysterious gap between the apparent world and the world of theoretical and experimental physics. It is a gap which Whitehead had also considered, and which he is extremely anxious to bridge. The empirical tradition has always supported the thesis that the subject-matter of physics is the series of entities observed by the senses, or, in the more

elegant formulation: "Natural science is the study of the interconnections of the things forming the apparent world." But Whitehead knows
the hollowness of the pretension:

This profession of the motive of science seems however in sharp contradiction to its actual achievement. The molecular theory, the wave theory of
light, and finally the electromagnetic theory of things in general have, as it
seems, set up for scientific investigation a society of entities such as ether,
molecules, and electrons, which are intrinsically incapable of direct observation. When Sir Ernest Rutherford at Cambridge knocks a molecule to pieces,
he does not see a molecule or an electron. What he observes is a flash of
light. There is at most a parallelism between his observation and the con-
jectural molecular catastrophe.

If we are to avoid this unfortunate bifurcation of a strange world
of molecular interactions on the one hand, and psychological time, external perception, and bodily feeling on the other, it is necessary to
consider our knowledge of the apparent world as something more than
merely personal. For our sensory experiences are themselves included
within nature, and our perceptions are themselves natural events. These
perceptions are of two types: Whitehead distinguishes them as "cognisance by adjective" and "cognisance by relatedness," but the terminology is more formidable than the fact. Cognizance by adjective is the
perception of sensory quality: the patch of redness, or the thunderous
sound. Cognizance by relatedness is based on the knowledge that nature
is an interconnectedness of spatio-temporal relations, a closed system
of related things; and the function of natural science is, indeed, to exhibit this relatedness.[38] Whitehead is not by any means implying Kant's
proposition that space and time are *a priori*, but only that the essential
relatedness of any perceived field of events to all other events presupposes a certain systematic uniformity of relatedness. The homogeneity
of time with space arises from the fact that they share in, and are
abstractions from, "the more fundamental quality of extension which
is a quality belonging exclusively to events." Of course the physical
occurrences are individual and atomic insofar as they are available for
approximate measurement. But when we discriminate in Minkowski's
four-dimensional continuum events with physical characteristics independent of the characteristics pervading other regions of nature, it is
with the recognition that this cutting up and separating off of regions
in space-time is a requirement of measurement rather than a quality
of the natural world.

This doctrine of relatedness which Whitehead develops with special reference to the theories of Einstein in *The Principle of Relativity* (1922) had already been worked out in considerable detail in *The Principles of Natural Knowledge* (1919). In this earlier work Whitehead was concerned to show that the old principles of physical explanation (a time flowing uniformly in measurable intervals; a timeless Euclidean space, empty, and void of activity; a material moving continuously in the empty space or at rest within it) were governed by the idea that extension (whether in space or time) expresses lack of relationship, and that the multiplicity of material bodies were themselves, as extended, diverse and disconnected. And he wished to demonstrate that when the new physical principles of relativity and quantum theory supplanted the old, they required no less a revolution in the philosophy of science, which it was his purpose to explore. In *The Principles of Natural Knowledge* he said:[39]

> The fundamental assumption to be elaborated in the course of this enquiry is that the ultimate facts of nature, in terms of which all physical and biological explanation must be expressed, are events connected by their spatio-temporal relations, and that these relations are in the main reducible to the property of events that they can contain (or extend over) other events which are part of them. In other words, in the place of emphasizing space and time in their capacity of disconnecting, we shall build up an account of their complex essences as derivative from the ultimate ways in which these things, ultimate in science, are interconnected.

The effect of this emphasis upon connection, relatedness—and hence totality—is twofold. On the one hand it shows the artificiality of all atomistic materialism. On the other, it relates the concepts of natural science to the facts of sense awareness. Instants of time, points in space, particles of matter situated at a point on an instant—these are high abstractions and not the stuff of immediate perception. "It needs very little reflection," Whitehead has said elsewhere,[40] "to convince us that a point in time is no direct deliverance of experience. We live in durations and not in points." Instants are derived from durations. Points are derived from volumes.[41] Particles are derived from events.

If we adopt the principle of relativity, we have still to settle the issue of the foundation of geometry, and the starting-point here is not the assumption of geometrical points, but the fashion in which they issue from the immediate data of perception. A similar problem confronts us in the examination of time and space. Much of our difficulty arises out of the conception of "an instant of time" (as though perceptual knowledge were not based on duration), and this leads to the misleading belief in "nature at an instant." The way out is to express the concepts of space, time, and material as derivative from the character of events and the relations between them. For observation confirms that events extend over and are spread through space and time.

If we begin with the fact of relatedness as an immediate datum of perceptual knowledge, then totality is the starting-point rather than the end product artificially constructed out of things and their specified relations. From this initial continuity of events we may abstract or discriminate the various entities of nature. Russell derives these entities directly from the results of theoretical physics; thus his "steady events," "rhythms," and "transactions" do not completely resolve the contradictions between the world of physics and the world of ordinary perception. But since, for Whitehead, nature contains everything, including events of perception, its analysis or breaking up (or, as he says, its "diversification") will include the most ordinary as well as the most scientifically recondite objects. The types of entity which he therefore discriminates are (1) events, (2) percipient objects, (3) sense objects, (4) perceptual objects, (5) scientific objects, and they are alike in that they are all given in our perception of nature. Events are the ultimate facts of actuality and process. They appear as indefinite entities without clear boundaries and with relations of infinite complexity. Percipient objects are centers of awareness, of recollection, and of recognition. Sense objects are the simplest permanences which we recognize in events like "this patch of redness here and now." Perceptual objects are the ordinary objects of common experience: stars and trees, tables and chairs, etc. Scientific objects are the entities which form the subject-matter of theoretical physics: molecules, protons, and electrons. Scientific objects are, of course, not directly perceived, but are inferred by reason of their capacity to express the causal characters of events.

From the current status of scientific objects Whitehead draws conclusions about the nature of physical reality. One of these is based upon the presupposition of relativity theory. It is to the effect that the electrons, which are the ultimate scientific objects for contemporary physical science, are each specially related to each event in nature, and that the events so related constitute a "field" for that object. The relations of the object to different parts of its field are interconnected, and it is on the basis of this connectedness that physical calculations are possible. The other conclusion is the same as that implied in Russell's "rhythms;" it is based upon quantum mechanics:[42]

Such ultimate scientific objects embody what is ultimately permanent in nature. Thus they are the objects whose relations in events are the un-analysable expression of the order of nature. But the recognition in per-ception requires the recurrence of the ways in which events pass. This involves the rhythmic repetition of the characters of events. This permanence of rhythmic repetition is the essential character of molecules. . . . There is no such thing as a molecule at an instant. A molecule requires a minimum of duration in which to display its character. Similarly physical objects are steady complexes of molecules with an average permanence of character throughout certain minimum durations.

The general thesis of *The Principles of Natural Knowledge* would have been unthinkable without the prior results of relativity and quantum theory. It is to the effect that there is a structure of events which pro-vides the framework of nature within which objects are located. The uniformity of this structure is constituted by the quantitative and quali-tative relations of space-time. Space and time as separately conceived are abstractions derivable from this structure and, indeed, many space-time abstractions are possible, each with its own relationship to nature. Time expresses certain qualities of the "passage" or "creative advance" of nature, and no single time system exhausts the fact of "passage." This general thesis is further elaborated in *The Principle of Relativity*. Refined observations (such as those of the Michaelson-Morley experi-ment) indicate that there are alternative time systems, and that the one actually observed is that for which our body (percipient object) is at rest. But the alternative time systems are all interconnected, and this interconnection is the ground of uniformity in nature. Any event is a spatio-temporal happening; every event is significant of others; and there is no such thing as an event in isolation.

Whitehead's organic universe is not stipulated in Einstein's theo-retical advances, but it is a natural consequence of the field theory which is at the heart of the principle of relativity. If his final insight is a uniform spatio-temporal structure of events (whose qualitative char-acter he takes to be the very condition for measurement) which is not exactly consonant with Einstein's beliefs, still his early philosophizing, expressed in the trilogy *The Principles of Natural Knowledge, The Concept of Nature,* and *The Principle of Relativity* (no less than Russell's *The Analysis of Matter*), is saturated with the problems, the principles, and the modes of thought of the new physics. No one has more generously acknowledged this than Whitehead himself.[43]

The course of my argument has led me generally to couple my allusions to Einstein with some criticism. But that does not in any way represent my attitude towards him. My whole course of thought presupposes the magnificent stroke of genius by which Einstein and Minkowski assimilated time and space. It also presupposes the general method of seeking tensor or invariant relations as general expressions for the laws of the physical field, a method due to Einstein. But the worst homage we can pay to genius is to accept uncritically formulations of truths which we owe to it.

5. OPERATIONALISM AND METHOD

Any great revolution in the physical sciences is a new insight into the rationality of nature. But this insight may take either of two forms. It may provide a new frame for the physical universe—a cosmological picture by which the age may live. Or, it may provide a new method: a form of rationality powerful and decisive for the new physical revelation. Any truly important advance will contain them both. The Cartesian-Newtonian revolution of the seventeenth century is a case in point. It produced the Newtonian cosmology, which was the wonder of the European mind for two hundred years, and it sustained an almost obsessive preoccupation with method, not only in Descartes and Leibniz, but also in the British empiricists, who were occupied for more than a century in an attempt to apply Newtonian method to the sciences of man. This dream only came to an end in Bradley's critique of associationism and in the sixth book of Mill's *Logic*.

The revolution of Einstein and Planck has had the same two-fold consequence. My very brief treatment of the repercussions of the new physics on the early philosophical speculations of Russell and Whitehead was an effort to show its substantive effects—in the somewhat quaint epistemology of Russell's "neutral monism," and in Whitehead's concern with metaphysical entities and with nature's uniform relatedness. But if philosophy has both a speculative and a critical branch, then, just as Einstein's cosmology may stimulate speculation, so a meditation upon Einstein's method may stimulate critical philosophy to new discoveries with respect to language and meaning. From the critical standpoint the theory of relativity has precipitated not primarily a metaphysical refreshment, but a crisis of methodological reform.

The heart of the idea underlying this reform can perhaps best be demonstrated by reference to the writing of Einstein himself, and I should like to turn to two passages from *Relativity: The Special and the General Theory*.[44] The first occurs in Chapter II, entitled "The System of Co-Ordinates":

On the basis of the physical interpretation of distance which has been indicated, we are also in a position to establish the distance between two points on a rigid body by means of measurements. For this purpose we require a "distance" (a rod S) which is to be used once and for all, and which we employ as a standard measure. If, now, A and B are two points on a rigid body, we can construct the line joining them according to the rules of geometry; then, starting from A, we can mark off the distance S time after time until we reach B. The number of these *operations* required is the numerical measure of the distance AB. *This is the basis of all measurement of length.*

The second occurs in Chapter VIII, "On the Idea of Time in Physics," where Einstein speaks of lightning striking the rails of a railway embankment at two places A and B, and asks what it means to say that the two lightning flashes occurred simultaneously. To reply that the significance is self-evident does not satisfy him. The issue is: What does the conception *simultaneous* mean when it occurs in any statement of physical science? He proceeds:

We encounter the same difficulty with all physical statements in which the conception "simultaneous" plays a part. The concept does not exist for the physicist until he has the possibility of discovering whether or not it is fulfilled in an actual case. *We thus require a definition of simultaneity such that this definition supplies us with the method by means of which, in the present case, he can decide by experiment whether or not both the lightning strokes occurred simultaneously.* As long as this requirement is not satisfied, I allow myself to be deceived as a physicist (and of course the same applies if I am not a physicist), when I imagine that I am able to attach a meaning to the statement of simultaneity.

In the first passage Einstein has described the operational basis of the physical measurement of length, and thus has demonstrated the operational foundation of all physical measurements. In the second he has stated the principle of the empirical theory of definition. In doing so he has provided the groundwork for the operationalism of P. W. Bridgman[45] and a confirmation of the empirical theory of meaning which has long been one of the cardinal tenets of the philosophical movement which began with Moritz Schlick and which came to maturity in the work of Reichenbach and Carnap.[46]

It is obvious that there is a close relationship between the mode of thought illustrated in Einstein's two passages. It appears, therefore, that there is something intellectually cognate in the operational theory of measurement and in the empirical theory of meaning. If we conceive of "length" as the product of the operations of measurement, and of "simultaneity" as that which is experimentally established, in both cases we invoke the appeal to observation and sensory data in which empiricism is grounded, and we have recourse to the practice, perform-ance, and consequences which are the hallmark of the pragmatic point of view. Indeed, Charles Saunders Peirce, the father of American prag-matism, had already in the last century put forward a similar criterion of clarity of meaning to be applied to ideas and concepts. "Consider," said Peirce,[47] "what effects that might conceivably have practical bear-ing, we conceive the object of our conception to have. Then, our con-ception of these effects is the whole of our conception of the object." Peirce's formulation is suggestive and it comes from the fertile brain of an exact logician. But Einstein's formulation is more impressive. Not only does it have the prestige of the newer physics at its disposal, but one can see how it evolved, not merely as a reflection of abstract logic, but as a methodological requirement—a condition for the rescue of theoretical physics from an impasse in its history.

When Newton distinguished "absolute," "true," and "mathematical" time from the "relative," "apparent," and "common" time which was the way it appeared in the data of ordinary perception, he was stipulat-ing a meaning without reference to empirical considerations. This absolute time which "flows equably without regard to anything external" could not with assurance be identified as having an existence within the domain of nature. A physics, therefore, based on so abstract a con-cept would have the same character as a postulational geometry—inter-nally consistent perhaps, if strictly deduced, but without applicability until anchored in the physical behavior entailed in natural events. It was Einstein's peculiar genius to note that if the concept of Newtonian time is examined in the light of the experimental evidence, nothing with such properties exists in nature. The two passages quoted indicate why. If the physical meaning of "length" consists in a stipulation of the operations of measurement, and if the definition of "simultaneity" requires a method which provides decisive positive or negative evidence of simultaneity in any particular case, then it must follow that we do not really understand the meaning of "absolute time" unless we can determine the absolute time of any actual physical event. But an examination of any of the operations by which the physicist measures time shows that all such operations are relative to the observation of specific observers. To say, therefore, that Newton's definition is physically meaningless is not to assert an alternative doctrine about physical nature; it is merely to make explicit the implications of the current physical operations used in the measurement of time. This is the essence of Einstein's critique of simultaneity which produced the special theory of relativity of 1905.

In dealing with the theory of bodies moving with high velocity, Einstein started with the mathematical equations in which the theory was expressed. But in analyzing the relationship of the equations to the theory, he was led to examine what the physicist actually does in applying the equations in any specific case. One of the variables in the equations was time, and his question was: how is its numerical value derived when the equation is concretely applied? If the equation involves the times of two different spatially separated events, then it is necessary to know how physicists determine the time of such events. Two clocks are read, one at each event, but at this point it is necessary to set up some operation (system of light signals etc.) by means of which the two clock readings can be compared. From an examination of these operations of comparison came Einstein's revolutionary idea: the property of two events, hitherto called simultaneous, can be determined only by a complicated sequence of physical operations involving a specification of who is reading the clocks. Since one result of such comparison is that different observers do not invariably get the same results, it became apparent that "simultaneity" was not an absolute property of two events, but relative to the observational system in which the measurement or time-reading takes place. Thus Einstein's critique of simultaneity, directed toward the functional definition of the meaning of the physical concept, at once demonstrated an experimental inapplicability of the Newtonian conception of absolute time, and suggested a general criterion of empirical determination for the clarification of our general ideas.

It is true, of course, that Einstein's exact formulations were determined largely by the particular area of physics in which he worked: an area of high velocities and enormous distances, where only light signals are adequate devices of comparison. Many of the popular paradoxes of relativity theory are due to somewhat misguided attempts to state the consequences of measuring rods and clocks traveling with speeds approaching those of light and of the geometry of light propagation itself in terms drawn from the more modest range of terrestrial sensory experience. But behind these paradoxes there is, indeed, a problem: one which involves the relationship within physical theory between the mathematical formulations and the kinds of physical operations by means of which values are assigned to their variables.

If it is true that physical laws when expressed in mathematical form are usually differential equations connecting events which appear as measured quantities, then it is obvious that such laws are ultimately verifiable only to the extent that they express relations between *actual magnitudes* derived from the transportation of measuring rods, clock readings, the registration of scales, galvanometers, magnetometers and the like. It is customary to interpret these magnitudes as a certain length, time interval, gravitational force, or magnetic attraction. But it is also possible to ask whether these *de facto* measures do *really* represent actual physical entities. From the standpoint of theoretical physics, the measured quantities are of first importance and the question of physical actuality is secondary. The effect of the special theory of relativity has therefore been to place an extraordinarily heavy emphasis upon the role of "pointer readings" in physical science. Eddington, whose idealistic interpretation of the new physics has led him much further into specula- tive metaphysics than even Russell's neutral monism,[48] has even been persuaded that the primacy of measured quantities symbolically ex- pressed indicates that "the mind has by its selective power fitted the processes of Nature into a frame of law of a pattern largely of its own choosing; and in the discovery of this system of law the mind may be regarded as regaining from Nature that which the mind has put into Nature."[49] This conclusion is in part due to Eddington's recognition that whenever we state the properties of a body as physical magnitudes, we "are imparting knowledge as to the response of various metrical indicators to its presence *and nothing more.*" It is not far from this to the interpretation of the general theory of relativity as a tensor calculus for dealing with enormous schedules of pointer readings, and to the physical atom as also a schedule of pointer readings attached to some unknown background.

But I want to stress not Eddington's idealism, but rather the opera- tionalism which he has derived from Einstein, and particularly that intimacy of concept and operation, of knowledge and procedure, which applies equally to relativity theory and quantum measurement:[50]

Our knowledge of the external world cannot be divorced from the nature of the appliances with which we have obtained the knowledge. The truth of the law of gravitation cannot be regarded as subsisting apart from the experimental procedure by which we have ascertained its truth.

The conception of frames of space and time, and of the non-emptiness of the world described as energy, momentum, etc., is bound up with the survey by gross appliances. When they can no longer be supported by such a survey, the conceptions melt away into meaninglessness. . . . It cannot be too strongly insisted that the terms distance, period of time, mass, energy, momentum, etc., cannot be used in a description of an atom with the same meanings that they have in our gross experience. The atomic physicist who uses these terms must find his own meanings for them—must state the appliances which he requisitions when he imagines them to be measured. . . .

The implication for philosophy of the Einstein revolution in method lies in the generalization of these principles. If "the truth of the law of gravitation cannot be regarded as subsisting apart from the experimental procedure by which we have ascertained its truth," perhaps the truth of any proposition cannot be established except through the empirical evidence which can be brought forward in its substantiation. And if, when concepts like space, time, energy, and momentum are no longer supported by observational procedure, they "melt away into meaninglessness," then perhaps the same is true of all those abstract nouns and general terms in the presence of which so much of our life is lived. This conviction is at the heart of one of the great movements of contemporary philosophy—logical empiricism. To its more extended consideration I shall subsequently return.

VIII

Reason in Society:
John Dewey

Whatever profits man, that is the truth. In him all nature is comprehended, in all nature only he is created, and all nature only for him. He is the measure of all things and his welfare is the sole and single criterion of truth. Any theoretic science which is without practical application to man's salvation is as such without significance and we are commanded to reject it.

Metaphysics is the evil. It is for no purpose but to put to sleep the energy we should apply to the building of the temple of society.

THOMAS MANN, *The Magic Mountain*

A thought which does not result in an action is nothing much, and an action which does not proceed from a thought is nothing at all.

GEORGES BERNANOS

John Dewey is to be classed among those men who have made philosophic thought relevant to the needs of their own day. . . . He has disclosed great ideas relevant to the functioning of the social system. . . .

ALFRED NORTH WHITEHEAD

1. THE FUNCTION OF PHILOSOPHY

John Dewey is the most systematic, and, I think, the most important representative of the American pragmatic movement. Less brilliant perhaps than the intermittently inspired methodologist Charles Saunders Peirce, less metaphysically and religiously oriented than the lovable and neurotic William James, and less restricted in his emphasis than the Darwinian social psychologist George Herbert Mead, Dewey combines James' sense of *Weltanschauung* with Peirce's feeling for method and with Mead's ever-present acknowledgment of the social matrix of all human life. And, as compared with Peirce's eccentricity and isolation, James' delicacy and hypochondria, and Mead's massive reticence, there is a simplicity and a healthy straightforwardness in Dewey which one sensed in the man and recognizes in his work. It is comparable to the situation in modern poetry: after the superb refinement of Wallace Stevens and the hothouse cultivation of Eliot's verse, there is something infinitely refreshing about the open speech of William Carlos Williams and the simplicity of Robert Frost. What Frost is to American verse of this century, Dewey is to American philosophy.

When Hans Reichenbach wrote his appreciative critique of "Dewey's Theory of Science" for *The Philosophy of John Dewey*,[1] intended as a tribute to Dewey on his eightieth birthday, he was at some pains to show the empirical rapprochement between American pragmatism and European logical positivism, and he celebrated generously and with considerable plausibility the *entente cordiale* between two philosophies of knowledge which consider science and the quasi-scientific inferential methods of daily life as the only approach to reality. He concluded with a description of the present state of philosophy which for him was both a program and an accolade:

The early period of empiricism in which an all-round philosopher could dominate at the same time the fields of scientific method, of history of philosophy, of education and social philosophy, has passed. We enter into the second phase in which highly technical investigations form the indispensable instrument of research, splitting the philosophical campus into specialists of its various branches. We should not regret this unavoidable specialization which repeats on philosophical grounds a phenomenon well known from all the other fields of scientific inquiry. Let us hope that in each of these branches of future philosophy we shall be presented with scientific personalities of the seriousness, the effectiveness, and the caliber of John Dewey.

But this is a left-handed compliment, for Dewey himself was an all-round philosopher who dominated the fields of ethics, metaphysics, and methodology, and the content of whose philosophical speculations stressed the unity, the interrelated purposiveness, and the organicity of all forms of philosophical knowledge. Dewey also produced highly technical investigations of scientific method, of the history of philosophy, and of social theory of the kind that Reichenbach demands, but without that technical fragmentation and specialist fanaticism (sometimes associated with the school to which Reichenbach belongs) which redoubles its analytical efforts because it has forgotten its normative aim. In this respect Dewey shows himself *not* to be one of those "minute" philosophers (as Berkeley called them), but deeply under the synthetic spell of Hegel. This he has himself acknowledged:[2]

There were, however, also "subjective" reasons for the appeal that Hegel's thought made to me; it supplied a demand for unification that was doubtless an intense emotional craving, and yet was a hunger that only an intellectualized subject-matter could satisfy. It is more than difficult, it is impossible, to recover that early mood. But the sense of divisions and separations that were, I suppose, borne in upon me as a consequence of a heritage of New England culture, divisions by way of isolation of self from the world, of soul from body, of nature from God, brought a painful oppression—or, rather, they were an inward laceration. My earlier philosophic study had been an intellectual gymnastic. Hegel's synthesis of subject and object, matter and spirit, the divine and the human, was, however, no mere intellectual formula; it operated as an immense release, a liberation. Hegel's treatment of human culture, of institutions and the arts, involved the same dissolution of hard-and-fast dividing walls, and had a special attraction for me.

It is almost like the account of his mental crisis which John Stuart Mill gives in his *Autobiography*. And the healing of the wounds of division which Dewey owed to Hegel, was accomplished for Mill by Wordsworth and Coleridge.

Dewey began as a Hegelian, and although he subsequently drifted away from Hegelianism (as he became more interested in empirical rather than in formal logic, and in a biologically rooted social psychology rather than in ethical idealism),[3] yet he cheerfully admitted "that acquaintance with Hegel has left a permanent deposit in my thinking." The Darwinian picture of man has determined the content of Dewey's instrumentalism as it has of Bergson's, but the Hegelian feeling for totality and context has left its indelible mark upon its form.

In the same passage in which Dewey finds a "greater richness and variety of insight in Hegel than in any other single systematic philosopher," he is at once led to couple Hegel's name with Plato's. The coupling is instructive. For the Plato to whom Dewey admiringly refers is not the Plato of "that all-comprehensive and overriding system which later interpretation has, as it seems to me, conferred upon him as a dubious boon," but rather "the dramatic, restless, cooperatively inquiring Plato of the Dialogues, trying one mode of attack after another to see what it might yield . . . the Plato whose highest flight of metaphysics always terminated with a social and practical turn. . . ." From Hegel Dewey derives the emotion of unity; but from Plato he gets the spirit of continuous inquiry and an ultimate purpose geared to the norms of moral reconstruction.

In a certain sense, it is the last which provides the crucial clue to the pragmatic enterprise. The seventeenth-century scientific revolution had in the work of Descartes and Locke led to the bifurcation of nature: to a distinction between the primary qualities of objects succeptible of measurement and the secondary qualities of sensations subjectively produced in the mind. But in the nineteenth century the bifurcation became a trifurcation. Here the tertiary qualities or "values" were convincingly cut off from any grounding which they might have in natural law or in "the nature of things." Bertrand Russell's adolescent early essay, "A Free Man's Worship," is an expression in purple prose of the consequence which such a separation was to entail for a sensitive late Victorian mentality—a despair turned to defiance at the thought that the whirling concourse of atoms constituting physical nature was an immense and unfeeling abyss, knowing nothing and caring less about the dreams of goodness and beauty which haunt the human mind.

Dewey seems never to have deeply felt the urgencies of religious doubt, but, as he says: "Social interests and problems from an early period had to me the intellectual appeal and provided the intellectual sustenance that many seem to have found primarily in religious questions." The motivating thread behind these interests was the sturdy resolution never to be forced into the nineteenth century's dread dilemma of a choice between an objective science *or* moral values, but rather, like Aristotle, to seek for a method of effective inquiry which would indicate the continuity between a speculative and a practical science, and so provide canons of warranted assertibility for ethical and political not less than physical and biological judgments. Thus he says:[4]

A second point is that as my study and thinking progressed, I became more and more troubled by the intellectual scandal that seemed to me involved in the current (and traditional) dualism in logical standpoint and method between something called "science" on the one hand and something called "morals" on the other. I have long felt that the construction of a logic, that is, a method of effective inquiry, which would apply without abrupt breach of continuity to the fields designated by both of these words, is at once our needed theoretical solvent and the supply of our greatest practical want. This belief has had much more to do with the development of what I termed, for lack of a better word, "instrumentalism," than have most of the reasons that have been assigned.

But "the construction of a logic . . . which would apply without abrupt break of continuity" to both science and morals implies that the realm of values, of human desires, and of the ends of action can be objects of knowledge in the same sense as ordinary physical objects. For if "real things" are at the basis of all experience, and scientific constructions are mere instruments for their manipulation and control, then ethical valuations refer to real properties of things which are analogous to their purely cognitive properties, and it is a mistake to cut off valuations as "subjective" from the objective properties of nature. The unreal division "man *and* nature" is rectified by the insight "man *within* nature," and those values which have been discarded from the real world by the quixotic seventeenth-century preference for the abstractions of physics above the concrete revelations of immediate experience can be restored where they belong.

It is interesting that Reichenbach (in the article previously referred to) bridles at precisely this point. After showing that Dewey's pragmatism and European logical empiricism are alike in their operationalism, in their acceptance of the verifiability theory of meaning, and in their emphasis upon probability rather than truth as the criterion of empirical knowledge, he refuses to admit that ethics or aesthetics might have a validity comparable to physics or that aesthetic or moral judgments could possibly be objectively established. Reichenbach is willing to subscribe to the theory that values are "volitional decisions," and that they may be rooted in our nature as biological and social beings. But he is true to the spirit of contemporary positivism in his denial that the value properties of objects are publicly verifiable, and in his skepticism about the use of scientific method in establishing a normative ethics which should be "binding" and "compulsory" in its claim upon human choice. This has its own irony, because the hopes of an earlier positivism ran parallel to those of Dewey. Auguste Comte in the later portions of his *Système de politique positive* projected a final science in the positive hierarchy which he titled "La Morale," and John Stuart Mill wrote a final book in his *System of Logic* entitled "The Logic of the Moral Sciences" which was to be not only the *raison d'être* but the coping-stone of the whole. It is to this nineteenth-century, humanistically oriented positivism that Dewey's work is akin. In the truest sense he is the heir not only of Hegel, but of John Stuart Mill.

Dewey is the heir of Mill in another sense also. Both are essentially moralists and social philosophers, deeply committed to a program of social reconstruction, who turned toward logic and metaphysics less for their intrinsic interest than because they were the theoretical foundations upon which any adequate social reform must rest. Mill's *Examination of Hamilton* was an enterprise in epistemology which was meant to demolish intuitionism and to establish a sound empirical method for the evaluation of social change, and Dewey's Gifford Lectures, *The Quest for Certainty*, were an analogous attack upon the arrogant rationalism of the pure and separated intellect in order to establish the prestige of the arts of experiment and control. Dewey's *Logic* works with painful thoroughness toward a "Logic of Social Inquiry" as Mill's *System of Logic* works toward a "Logic of the Moral Sciences."[5]

Moreover a similarity of ultimate concern is mirrored in a relative similarity of social outcome. The social thought of the nineteenth century polarized itself about the axes of John Stuart Mill and Karl Marx.

Both were concerned with the misery and dislocation of the industrial revolution, with a social milieu in which it had become apparent that the steam engine had been invented too soon for the happiness of man, and with an age of exploitation which had turned aside from making a just society in order to concentrate upon maximum productivity and profits. Marx met the challenge of a society in distress with a critique of exploitation and a sociology of class antagonisms which found its logical culmination in a theory of social violence. Mill saw many of the same evils, but his criticisms fall well within the liberal-democratic tradition. He supported the claims of equality and social justice, but he emphasized just that application of rationality to which Marxism as a creed is blind: the experimental design of social institutions to abolish the conflicts of interests within society; the foundation of a valid social science which might yield knowledge valuable in the guidance of social policy; a democratic technique of social decision founded upon representative government and the most absolute protection of the civil liberties of the members of every social class.

The social strategies of the nineteenth century have obviously influenced their contemporary analogues. What the opposition between Marx and Mill meant for the men of the nineteenth century, the opposition between Lenin and Dewey means for the social struggles of today. On the one hand, an ardor for vituperative analysis and revolutionary acts; on the other, a stubborn insistence upon the application of the method of intelligence in social affairs. As *The Communist Manifesto* contrasts with Mill's essay *On Liberty,* so Lenin's papers of the *Iskra* period and *State and Revolution* contrast with Dewey's *The Public and Its Problems, Freedom and Culture,* and the devastating criticism of the *Report of the Moscow Trials.*

Actually, within the philosophic context of the modern world there are not two but three methods of social criticism—revolutionary, liberal-democratic, and existentialist. The latter stems partly from Marx, but more largely from the radical individualism of Nietzsche and Kierkegaard. But the point is that within this context pragmatic social theory is a reinforcement of the faith in liberal democracy. Against the ill-disguised rage of Marxism and the often shrill and histrionic existentialism of Sartre and Camus stands the social theory of Dewey—the only major social philosophy which the liberal tradition has produced in the twentieth century.

Essentially, Dewey's philosophy and Marxism have nothing in common. But all social philosophies are, by definition, alike in that they stress the relevance of human acts, products, and ideas to the social situations out of which they spring and the social consequences which they entail. Dewey, in acknowledging the tremendous influence which the Darwinism of William James' psychology had upon him, added that it "led straight to the perception of the importance of distinctive social categories especially communication and participation." He continued: "It is my conviction that a great deal of our philosophizing needs to be done over again from this point of view, and that there will ultimately result an integrated synthesis in a philosophy congruous with modern science and related to actual needs in education, morals, and religion."[6]

At this point there is indeed something common to Dewey and the sociology of knowledge which has been inspired by Marxist theory. Both recognize that in some sense social existence determines consciousness, that thought is the creature of social milieu. Thus all knowledge must be dated and contextualized. It is inherently relational and historic. It must be given a local habitation and a name. Although Dewey's theory does not make the preposterous Marxist leap which denies the objectivity of social science, sees all ideas as weapons, and classifies them according to whether they are friends or enemies of the class struggle, it does insist that ideas have roots and that they are to be tested by their social consequences. This conviction underlies Dewey's approach to the very nature of the philosophic enterprise, and guides him in presenting his principles of philosophic reconstruction.[7]

For G. E. Moore the difficulties of philosophizing arise because philosophers attempt to answer questions without first discovering precisely what question it is which they desire to answer, and what they really ought to do, therefore, is the much-needed work of analysis and distinction. For Henri Bergson, philosophy is the exercise of an intuition which shall make intimate contact with the real, and philosophic reform therefore consists in avoiding the temptation to intellectualize, to conceptualize, and to freeze experience, so that the way of philosophic vision lies open. But for Dewey the error of philosophers lies in being content to construct their edifices and explore their essences without coming to grips with the spotty actualities and ambiguous twists of the human condition. His most barbed shafts are therefore directed at those reasonable metaphysicians who have managed to fish in the great sea of Being without stirring up the waters which might indiscreetly reveal the personal maladies and the social disorders from which we suffer. The disease of philosophy is isolationism, and it is healthiest when it attempts to perform its social function.

Only a profound wrench can dislocate philosophy from its social context, for, as Dewey says: ". . . philosophy, like politics, literature and the plastic arts is itself a phenomenon of human culture. Its connection with social history, with civilization, is intrinsic."[8] No philosophers, least of all those who like Bacon or Descartes believed that they were founding philosophy anew by placing it for the first time upon an exclusively intellectual basis, are cut free from the scientific tendencies and the political aspirations of their times. They are "parts of history, caught in its movement; creators perhaps in some measure of its future, but also assuredly creatures of its past." The notion of timelessness, of placelessness, of abstract purity of conception, is revealed as an illusion. "However it may stand with philosophy as a revelation of eternal truths, it is tremendously significant as a revelation of the predicaments, protests and aspirations of humanity."

The "significance" of predicaments, protests, and aspirations is not merely the clue to the meaning of a tradition arising in a dim and immemorial past; it is also the vector character of a philosophy which arises in the present as an instrument for the transformation of the future. *Reconstruction in Philosophy* insists that "the distinctive office, problems and subject matter of philosophy grow out of stresses and strains in the community life in which a given form of philosophy arises."[9] This basic postulate is as applicable to contemporary efforts as to the massive systems of the past. Yet it is clear that Dewey in enunciating this postulate is not so much describing what contemporary philosophy is, as prescribing what it ought to be. For no one is more cognizant than he of the lack of self-confidence, indeed, of the failure of nerve of contemporary philosophy which is expressed in its minute concern for the improvement of its logical techniques and with its endless comparisons and poring over the dead records of its own past. This is not to say that Dewey himself has not made important technical contributions to logical method, or that his work neglects the materials provided by the history of philosophy.[10] But his technical contributions are thoroughly informed by a sense of moral direction, and he re-assesses traditional materials in the light of current needs. Dewey, like Whitehead, is fundamentally a wholist in a world of specialisms, an interpreter of the ideas of the past only insofar as they contribute to the complex texture of his own thought. No one, therefore, knows better than he the pathos of a philosophy lost in the triviality of "merely professional" concerns, and the remedy for that diminution. "Philosophy," he said,[11] "recovers itself when it ceases to be a device for dealing with the problems of philosophers and becomes a method, cultivated by philosophers, for dealing with the problems of men." A comparison of this ideal with the practice of Bertrand Russell or G. E. Moore,

Carnap or Wittgenstein will reveal more clearly than any other means that conflict over philosophic method which splits the practitioners of philosophy in the modern world.

But how does philosophy go about dealing with the problems of men? Dewey's answer is divided between two solutions: one specific, one general. The first considers philosophy as a social method; the second considers it as a means for widening the human horizon by a vivid illumination of the various forms of human experience.

The function of philosophy is to serve not as mere custodian, but as the creative source of "intelligence": of those "great and ever-growing methods of observation, experiment, and reflective reasoning" which have so successfully revolutionized the natural sciences and the physical conditions of life in the modern world. Philosophy in its methodological aspect ought, therefore, to try to carry over into inquiries into human and moral subjects the same methods which have already proved their worth in physics and biology. The attempt to establish reason in society is analogous to and continuous with the attempt to establish reason in nature. The crises and tensions in the conduct of human affairs are provoked by failures of insight and of instruments. Philosophy in its technical capacity is the originator of instruments, and in its cultural capacity it is the initiator of transformations of awareness.

Some philosophers have, indeed, been immersed in pure speculation concerning logical or epistemological detail, but most have been thoughtful men, reflecting upon what they would like life to be, and presenting a reasoned picture of the ends for which they would have men shape their intelligent activities. To this extent philosophy has been prospective—not a survey of static forms of existence, but a canvassing of future possibilities for the realization of value—and it has conformed to the pragmatic definition of knowledge: an act securing the future (by the procuring or avoiding of consequences) through the exercise of foresight. But the projecting of new and more adequate ends is in itself a liberation of thought from blindness and routine; it is an awakening of the mind to the novel qualities of a future experience, and as such it creates that readiness of the imagination and the will which is the first step in any social transformation. This is how philosophy functions as vision.

It may seem that I have dwelt overlong upon Dewey's conception of the nature of philosophy. But more and more in the modern world the content of any philosophy is the reflection of what its author regards as the philosopher's legitimate task. Therefore when one says that Dewey is, despite the varieties of experience which he has illuminated, primarily a moralist and a social philosopher, this is a logical consequence of his definition of the philosophic enterprise. When Reichenbach praised Dewey's all-round empiricism for the specialized research to which it might lead, the praise was at least incongruous with Dewey's purpose. But when Whitehead said: "John Dewey is to be classed among those men who have made philosophic thought relevant to the needs of their own day. . . . He has disclosed great ideas relevant to the functioning of the social system," it was eminently congruous. It was exactly what Dewey himself would have wished.

2. THE METAPHYSICAL BASE

In 1925 in his Carus Lectures, *Experience and Nature*, and in 1929 in his Gifford Lectures, *The Quest for Certainty*, Dewey nevertheless produced a metaphysics. When Santayana read *Experience and Nature* for the first time, he was impressed. "Here," he said,[12] "is a remarkable re-reading of things with a new and difficult kind of sincerity. For my part I am entirely persuaded of the genuineness and depth of Dewey's views within the limits of his method and taken as he means them." But he professed himself puzzled by the phrase *naturalistic metaphysics* by which Dewey characterized his system. To Santayana these two characteristics seemed contradictory.

Santayana was thinking of metaphysicians like Plato or Hegel or Spinoza, and in their sense a metaphysics of empirical experience would possess a certain paradoxical flavor. But when Dewey toward the end of *Experience and Nature* did come to treat of the relationship of metaphysics to philosophy in general, he defined it, in a fashion which would have been equally acceptable to Aristotle or to Whitehead, as "a statement of the generic traits manifested by existences of all kinds without regard to their differentiation into physical and mental."[13] A discovery or identification of the generic qualities of nature and experience could be both the product of a most scrupulous empiricism—one ardently attentive to the nuances of natural detail—and at the same time the condition for the critical evaluations which were to be the business of philosophy in general.

There is, however, a terminological problem which Santayana did not remark, a difficulty inherent in Dewey's point of view to which he himself initially calls attention.[14] "The title of this volume, Experience and Nature, is intended to signify that the philosophy here presented may be termed either empirical naturalism or naturalistic empiricism; or, taking 'experience' in its usual significance, naturalistic humanism. To many the associating of the two words will seem like talking of a round square, so engrained is the notion of the separation of man and experience from nature." To Santayana the conjunction of metaphysics and empiricism was the stumbling-block. But in Dewey's anticipation it was the conjunction of naturalism and humanism. In my opinion Dewey's is the sounder insight. For *Naturalistic humanism* is the juster designation for Dewey's metaphysics, and it does indeed express an intrinsic tension between the characteristically human and the characteristically natural which it is Dewey's purpose to hold taut and eternally unresolved. When Dewey points out that even imagination and its ideal envisagements are a continuation of natural processes—something man has learned from the world, not something he arbitrarily injects into it—his naturalism is uppermost. But when he is showing how inquiry is a practical instrument whereby the objects and relations of nature are changed, transformed, even created in the potential service of human purposes and valuation, then the humanism has driven out all else. It is this eternal dialectic of natural conditions and human consequences, of experience and nature, of inquiry and its biological matrix, asserted in the rhythmic succession of two modes of perception, which, alternating in his work, gives his naturalistic humanism its resonance and its distinctive flavor.

When one speaks of Dewey's metaphysics, one refers neither to a construction of pure reason comparable to the architecture of Spinoza's *Ethics,* nor to a cosmology organizing the content and conclusions of the special sciences. In this respect, pragmatism as a tradition has a somewhat dubious reputation. Whether in the logic of Peirce or the epistemology of James, it is noted for its preoccupation not with the substantive, but with the procedural. Grounded in the Darwinian picture of man as a sign-making and instrument-using animal, it was fated to dwell upon the supreme importance of "instruments" and of "action," and to interpret intellect (as Bergson and Freud, with the same cultural sources, did also) as an essentially practical faculty of human adaptation. But such a procedural emphasis implies a cosmic setting, and no elaboration of a dependable method of inquiry can obscure the necessity for a theory of existence.[15] Dewey, like other philosophers, conducts his logical, ethical, and political researches within the framework of certain assumptions about man and the natural world. These assumptions color his proposals for logical reconstruction and for the reform of social institutions. *Experience and Nature* and *The Quest For Certainty* are an attempt to render these assumptions articulate, and to make explicit the center from which his convictions radiate. They therefore include the paraphernalia of even a traditionally more conservative metaphysical enterprise: a theory of experience, a theory of natural events, a theory of mind (and what it produces in the acts of scientific knowing), and a theory of values.

The crux of Dewey's empiricism is his appeal to immediate experience, that is, experience saturated with qualities, permeated with aesthetic and moral traits, and gross in its unmediated appeal to the senses and stimulation of the feelings.

> Tilting up his nose,
> He inhaled the rancid rosin, burly smells
> Of dampened lumber, emanations blown
> From warehouse doors, the gustiness of ropes,
> Decays of sacks, and all the arrant stinks
> That helped him round his rude aesthetic out.
> He savored rankness like a sensualist.[16]

Such primary experience is crude and unclassified, untouched by science, unrefined by the regulation of reflective inquiry. It is the original material out of which all knowledge is generated, and the final referent to which all knowledge is returned for validation. The whole complicated mechansim for generating reliable knowledge exists only as an instrument for its purification and enhancement. Experience, therefore, in relation to knowledge is at once the source of its raw material, the test of its truth, and the measure of its value.

The last is particularly important. For the prejudice of cultivated thought is always in favor of the refined products of systematic thinking. Philosophy and science are both instances of this cultivated thought, and the temptation to which both give rise is to judge the results of reflection as having in themselves a reality superior to other and more primitive modes of experience. But the sense of duty may be as indicative of the character of nature as the law of gravitation, and poetry may have a metaphysical import as well as science. Philosophy and science (like all forms of reflective analysis) "take us away, for the time being, from the things had in primary experience as they directly act and are acted upon, used and enjoyed," and this inveterate predilection for abstractions[17] leads to the vice of intellectualism.

By "intellectualism" as an indictment is meant the theory that all experience is a mode of knowing, and that all subject-matter, all nature, is, in principle, to be reduced and transformed till it is defined in terms identical with the characteristics presented by refined objects of science as such. The assumption of intellectualism goes contrary to the facts of what is primarily experienced. For things are objects to be treated, used, acted upon and with, enjoyed, and endured, even more than things to be known. They are things *had* before they are things cognized.[18]

The trouble with intellectualism is that it inverts the normal relation between knowledge and experience. It is, as Vaihinger would have said, a preponderance of the means over the end. But with the elevation of immediacy, knowledge can be valued for what it is: an instrument which contributes "the possibility of intelligent administration of the elements of doing and suffering." Moreover, "when intellectual experience and its material are taken to be primary, the cord that binds experience and nature is cut." For the human organism is involved in the struggle to adapt and utilize resources for the maintainance of its life. Hence the function of cognition must originate within a natural environment which is non-cognitive. The only way to avoid radical separation between the mind, which is the focusing center of experience, and the natural world, which is its ground, is to admit that all modes of experience are processes in which genuine traits of nature are manifested. This is the fruit of a radically empirical approach to experience. For only if "felt" and "willed" as well as "known" objects are granted residence in nature, can the self be repatriated into an otherwise alien world.

This repatriation is a crucial feature of all contemporary "revolts against dualism," and its consequence is the healing of philosophic wounds opened over three hundred years ago, but it exacts a drastic price. By attributing superior reality to what immediate experience reveals, we may restore status to the declarations of poetic insight and to our intuitions of moral and religious value, but in so doing we press the authenticity of the humanistic pole in "man versus nature" to a point where it almost seems to pre-empt nature.[19] Since the seventeenth century relations may have been supreme over qualities in philosophic esteem, but a reversal of this situation, while it redresses the balance, may also create a "naturalism" which is so humanistic as to smack of anthropomorphism. This was, indeed, the gist of Santayana's criticism when he said of Dewey's metaphysics:[20]

Yet in this case how comes it that Dewey has a metaphysics of his own, that cosmology is absent from his system, and that every natural fact becomes in his hands so strangely unseizable and perplexed?

This question, which is the crux of the whole system, may be answered, I think, in a single phrase: *The dominance of the foreground.* In nature there is no foreground or background, no here, no now, no moral cathedra, no center so really central as to reduce all other things to mere margins and mere perspectives. A foreground is by definition relative to some chosen point of view, to the station assumed in the midst of nature by some creature tethered by fortune to a particular time and place. If such a foreground becomes dominant in a philosophy naturalism is abandoned.

It is an axiom with Dewey that only what is immediate is real. But "immediacy" is a category of epistemology, not of physical existence. The standpoint of immediate experience is the standpoint of the human center of experiencing—the panorama which appears, the events which happen within a dominant foreground. Santayana is perhaps extreme when he says that this means the abandonment of naturalism; it only means the abandonment of a neutral naturalism for one predisposed to look upon man with an especial favor.

Dewey himself, I think, would not wish to deny that the human situation is his metaphysical center. He would only wish to insist that

While . . . philosophy has its source not in any special impulse or staked-off section of experience, but in the entire human predicament, *this human situation falls wholly within nature.* It reflects the traits of nature; it gives indisputable evidence that in nature itself qualities and relations, individualities and uniformities, finalities and efficacies, contingencies and necessities are inextricably bound together. . . .[21]

But at the same time he would surely repudiate Santayana's imputation that his system represents "the dominance of the foreground." For this is exactly how he himself might characterize a philosophy which emphasized not experience, but cognition.

What is really "in" experience extends much further than that which at any time is *known.* From the standpoint of knowledge, objects must be distinct; their traits must be explicit; the vague and unrevealed is a limitation. Hence whenever the habit of identifying reality with the object of knowledge as such prevails, the obscure and vague are explained away. It is important for philosophic theory to be aware that the distinct and evident are prized and why they are. But it is equally important to note that the dark and the twilight abound. For in any object of primary experience there are always potentialities which are not explicit; any object that is overt is charged with possible consequences that are hidden; the most overt act has factors which are not explicit.[22]

The claims of cognition demand shape, outline, and definiteness in perception. This is the source of all search for clear and distinct ideas. On the contrary, tolerance of immediate experience emphasizes the vagueness, the inarticulateness, the "soft focus" of the background. It is true that the pragmatic account of knowledge is contextual, that it takes note of the figure in the carpet and the pattern upon its ground.

But it stresses their mutual implication. The virtue of a philosophy of total, rather than merely cognitive, experience (whether Dewey's or Whitehead's) is that it is continually mindful and deeply respectful of the lures for feeling which lie in the dusky twilight of the background. For it is precisely this which, however obscure, is immediate.

Dewey's theory of immediate experience leads at once to a theory of natural events. If our metaphysics is to describe the generic traits of the existential world, we must face unflinchingly the results with which it provides us. This result, obvious on the face of it, but still disquieting to an older metaphysical tradition,[23] is that "the world of empirical things includes the uncertain, unpredictable, uncontrollable and hazardous."[24] However we assert our philosophical safeguards against the dangers of contingency by denying chance, appealing to the universal and necessary, to the existence of natural law and the inherent rationality of the universe, we shall sooner or later come to grips with the facts of reality, and they will show us that although the world permits achievement, continuity, and satisfaction, it also is the home of struggle, transiency, and frustration. Our human needs and desires are themselves a clue to the essence of natural being. The actual and the complete are only culminations of the contingent and the incomplete, and because of this, nature is itself therefore "wistful and pathetic, turbulent and passionate." Nature is a fullness of restless, ongoing processes passing from states of youthful unsettlement to mature settlement and ultimate (though temporary) equilibrium.

There is nothing particularly remarkable in this rather elementary account of a world of nature in process. What is remarkable is the way in which the metaphor of material change becomes for Dewey a paradigm of every type of actuality—moral, social, biological, social, and cognitive. The passage from indeterminateness to stability, from incompleteness to completion, from the restlessness of anxiety and desire to peace and satisfaction, endlessly repeated (and hence always without true finality), is the fate of living organisms, of moral beings, and of social orders. But most remarkable of all, it is the operative mode of the cognitive process.[25]

Empirically, all reflection sets out from the problematic and the confused. Its aim is to clarify and ascertain. When thinking is successful, its career closes in transforming the disordered into the orderly, the mixed-up into the distinguished or placed, the unclear and ambiguous into the defined and unequivocal, the disconnected into the systematized. It is empirically assured that the goal of thinking does not remain a mere ideal, but is attained often enough so as to render reasonable additional efforts to achieve it.

A philosophy which accepts the denotative or empirical method accepts at full value the fact that reflective thinking transforms confusion, ambiguity and discrepancy into illumination, definiteness and consistency. But it also points to the contextual situation in which thinking occurs. It notes that the starting point is the actually *problematic*, and that the problematic phase resides in some actual and specifiable situation.

Man's reflective inquiry, moving from confusion to clarity, is but an instance of the inherent restlessness of nature, and thinking is no different from the use of mechanical tools for the shaping purposes of the human artisan. For a naturalistic metaphysics thought must therefore be "itself a natural event occurring *within* nature because of traits of the latter."[26] Dewey has constantly protested against the hypostatization of the logic of reflection into an ontology of Rational Being, and this has led some of his followers to the dream of a "Logic without Ontology."[27] But however such a protest deplores Platonism and asserts an autonomous logic, it cannot escape *the derivation of logic* from the problematic matrix of nature.

If nature is a process, then every existence is an event, and every structure which appears in nature is a structure of events. Thus the ground of the permanent is to be found in the facts of flux. "Similarly," says Dewey,[28] "what we call matter is that character of natural events which is so tied up with changes that are sufficiently rapid to be perceptible as to give the latter a characteristic rhythmic order, the causal sequence." It sounds like Russell and Whitehead and what they have learned from Einstein and Planck, but Dewey's reasons, I think, are less like Whitehead's than like Bergson's—they derive, that is, less from Einstein than from Darwin. Dewey's choice of events to be his metaphysical units, his notion that they are natural waves or pulsations of being, is less physically than biologically inspired, and, as Santayana has noted, it shows Dewey to have been more under the spell of Aristotle's doctrine of growth, culmination, and mature state of being than he might wish to acknowledge.

The time of nature is not the mechanical, endlessly repetitive "time by the clock." It is "time lived"—the qualitative temporality which bites into material and accumulates as it pursues its directed course. Nature, therefore, is not the locus of mere objects, but of *histories*. These histories have their moments of slow development and their moments of climactic achievement. Every history (human histories too —from which we learn the most) has periods of preparation followed by moments of consummation; this double aspect is at once a fact of nature and of human experience. The instrumental phase of human life appears in labor and the use of tools; the consummatory in the actualities of concrete enjoyment and the ideal transformations of existence generated in the imagination. The industrial arts are the modes of experience which exhibit the causal connections of things, but in every event "there is something obdurate, self-sufficient, wholly immediate, neither a relation nor an element in a relational whole, but terminal and exclusive."[29] This is what Pierce would have referred to as the "firstness" of things.

The immediacy of experience is incommunicable. It can be pointed to but it can be neither described nor defined. Always it is *felt*, and the immediacy of enjoyment and suffering is the conclusive proof that in nature there are finalities as well as connections. Another proof is the contemplative peace of the aesthetic object.

> And for what, except for you, do I feel love?
> Do I press the extremest book of the wisest man
> Close to me, hidden in me day and night?
> In the uncertain light of single, certain truth,
> Equal in living changingness to the light
> In which I meet you, in which we sit at rest,
> For a moment in the central of our being,
> The vivid transparence that you bring is peace.[30]

But the ancient distinction between art and nature should not condition our approach to the qualitative aspects of the latter, nor make us reluctant to admit nature's saturation with value qualities: "Aesthetic quality, immediate, final or self-enclosed indubitably characterizes natural situations as they empirically occur."[31] This is proof that nature literally possesses "ends," "termini," "arrests," and "enclosures." But this is still not quite the Aristotelian theory of a single terminal moment of perfection. For if we acknowledge that nature is a scene of incessant beginning and endings, then "ends" are not ultimate finalities, but "ends-in-view" which exist prior to achievement as regulative ideas for action and which, once achieved, perish, to be superseded by still further ends-in-view. But value qualities are not mere ideas in the mind: "*Things* are beautiful and ugly, lovely and hateful, dull and illuminated, attractive and repulsive. Stir and thrill in us is as much theirs as is length, breadth and thickness."[32]

It should by now be clear what the strategy of this humanistic naturalism is to be. It means to assimilate all qualities to nature, whether primary, secondary, or tertiary. Its metaphysics or theory of existence is forced to view cause and effect, means and ends, qualities and relations, the beginnings and the endings of temporal processes as of equal importance because equally "natural." At this point the traditional difficulties introduced by Locke and Descartes cease to constitute an interpretive problem. For "it is as much a part of the real being of atoms that they give rise in time under increasing complication of relationships, to qualities of blue and sweet, pain and beauty, as that they have at a cross-section of time extension, mass, or weight."[33]

Aesthetics is concerned with intrinsic value. Technology by definition is concerned with things as instrumentalities, rather than as immediate. Tools denote a recognition of the connective bonds in nature. And the sciences were born of the arts.

The distinctively scientific attitude originated in efforts to control persons, things, events, so that their outcomes would be valuable and assured. But from this point of view immediate qualities are forgotten, and those features of things which are indicative and relational—which point to a future and relate to consequences—come into the foreground. Naturally therefore science is stripped of commerce with the immediate and the intrinsically valuable, and grows more and more preoccupied with abstraction. This is not a psychological accident, but the logical turn of an enterprise devoted to predicting and producing the future. This instrumental account of the operation of the natural sciences clearly establishes their practical utility, and clearly cuts off their possession of metaphysical completeness—their claim to give a total account of existence. By the same token it reconciles the asserted incompatibility between "the world of physics" and "the world of sense."

Physical science does not set up another and rival realm of antithetical existence; it reveals the state or order upon which the occurrence of immediate and final qualities depends. It adds to causal having of ends an ability to regulate the date, place and manner of their emergence. Fundamentally, the assertion that this condition of ordered relationships is mathematic, mechanical, is tautology; that is, the meaning of anything which is such that perception and use of it enables us to regulate consequences or attain terminal qualities is a mathematical, mechanical—or if you please—logical order.[34]

There remains, of course, the problem which so concerns Broad and Russell: the attempt to relate the equations of theoretical physics to the data of perception, and to discover what sense data form the basis of our scientific concepts. If the details of such an analysis lie outside of Dewey's metaphysics, he does at least accomplish two results. As opposed to Russell's extreme positivism, which sees the real world as nothing but primitive sense data like "this patch of blue" or "this hot feeling," from which the common world is constructed, Dewey has insisted that atomized sense data are as much abstractions as the variables of differential equations, and that the true immediacy from which both arise is the concrete "thing with qualities." But the real merit of Dewey's instrumental account of science is that it clears away the kind of confusion which besets Eddington[35] when he distinguishes his "ordinary substantial table," which has shape, weight and color, from his "scientific table," which is mostly empty space pervaded by a scattering of electric charges rushing about with great speed. The consequence is that when Eddington reads in Lamb's *Hydrodynamics* the series of equations for the generation of waves against viscosity by forces applied at the surface, and sets them against Rupert Brooke's poem beginning "There are waters blown by changing winds to laughter . . . ," he thinks he is the inhabitant of two worlds, equally "real," and perplexing in their mutual confrontation. Dewey's theory assures us that they are both parts of one world—not metaphysical rivals, but alternative aspects of things viewed (1) as they enhance the immediate qualities of feeling or (2) as they are designated instruments for the direction and guidance of the processes of natural change.

In Dewey's theory, natural events viewed individually are histories exhibiting moments of preparation and culmination, but viewed collectively they are events in process of continual interaction and reciprocal influence. To process and immediacy *interaction* must be added as one of experience's generic traits. From this feature arises the pragmatic doctrine of the emergence of mind and of the self. Mind and the self originate within the matrix of society, and the clue to social nature is to be found in the uses of language.

"Of all affairs," says Dewey, "communication is the most wonderful." This is because the natural fruit of communication is participation and sharing. Where communication exists, the meanings which things acquire through symbolism and representation become agencies of use and management. When in Greek thought meanings under the name of "forms" or "essences" were given a mode of being beyond temporal happenings, this was erroneous yet scarcely surprising. For "ideas" have manipulative power which makes them somehow superior to things. Language, communication, and discourse mediate between *ideas* and the *things* which they control and represent.

Language is the fruit of sociality. Speech arises in the necessities of social interaction, and is domesticated in acts of individual reflection, foresight, and recollection. The private world of romantic revery—

Emily Dickinson's "place where the soul holds converse with itself"—
is a secondary growth. "Soliloquy is the product and reflex of converse
with others. . . . If we had not talked with others and they with us,
we should never talk to and with ourselves."[36] In the dialectic of social
discourse, in the give and take of communication, organic attitudes
become consolidated in "persons." Listening, we learn our own natures,
and answering the demands of others, we become "responsible."
"Through speech a person dramatically identifies himself with potential
acts and deeds; he plays many roles, not in successive stages of life but
in a contemporaneously enacted drama. Thus mind emerges."[37]

The Greeks mistook the structure of discourse for the structure of
things instead of the form which things assume under the pressures of
social intercourse. Since

> This structure of ideas, those ghostly sequences
> Of the mind, result only in disaster. . . ,

they therefore produced a false objectivity. But modern thought, failing
to recognize that the world of inner experience depends upon an appropriation of language, which is through and through a social product,
produces in its turn a falsely individualistic and subjectivistic strain. The
pragmatic solution is to see that language and significance come into
existence not by intent and through mind, but by a social transformation of gesture and of sound; that meaning is not a psychic entity but
is a property of behavior before it becomes a property of objects; and
that intelligence is not a non-natural quality, but the peculiar aptitude
for the conservation of meanings which is a natural consequence of the
forms of human interaction.

The most interesting feature of discourse or communication is that,
like any natural process, it is both instrumental and consummatory. It
is an exchange which leads to the satisfaction of wants. And it is an
immediate enhancement of life, enjoyed for its own sake. From the
pragmatic standpoint "meanings" are not passive universals, they are
"rules for using and interpreting things;" they are methods or plans
of action rather than pictures characterizing reality. But a theory which
would restrict the functions of language to merely instrumental and
"practical" uses would miss the point of fiction and drama, of poetry,
song, and ceremony. Dewey not only recognizes the existence of alternative modes of discourse, but insists upon the importance of literary
and artistic values shared in detachment from the instrumental consequences of mutual assistance and cooperative action. For the sharing
of the arts whereby meanings are enhanced, solidified, and deepened also

creates the sense of community, not as agency but as finality. The social function of the arts of discourse lies in their being themselves. For in being themselves they supply the standard of social value:[38]

> The saying of Matthew Arnold that poetry is a criticism of life sounds harsh to the ears of some persons of strong esthetic bent; it seems to give poetry a moral and instrumental function. But while poetry is not a criticism of life in intent, it is in effect, and so is all art. For art fixes those standards of enjoyment and appreciation with which other things are compared; it selects the objects of future desires; it stimulates effort. This is true of the objects in which a particular person finds his immediate or esthetic values, and it is true of collective man. The level and style of the arts of literature, poetry, ceremony, amusement, and recreation which obtain in a community, furnishing the staple objects of enjoyment in that community, do more than all else to determine the current direction of ideas and endeavors in the community. They supply the meanings in terms of which life is judged, esteemed and criticized.

Language is the fruit of sociality. Personality, subjectivity, *the human self* likewise emerge from the complex of organic and social interactions. Existentialists like to pretend that subjectivity is the original quality of selfhood, and that the individual mind is somehow from the beginning an independent creative source. But pragmatic social psychology is an antidote to the exaggeration of the power of the ego so characteristic of modern life; it insists that selfhood is formed within a system of beliefs and ignorances, acceptances and rejections which have solidified under the influence of custom and crystalized as tradition. The private self grows in an environment of social interactions which defines its limits and mirrors its qualities, so that it finally comes to resemble the image that it sees reflected in the eyes of others. But though the purely private may be looked upon by society as the source of a possibly dangerous eccentricity, as something to be subdued and kept within bounds, it is nevertheless the somewhat quixotic source of the criticism which slowly works to change the given character of customs and institutions. The individuality which is precipitated from the social whole becomes an ego, a subject, a center of will and desire which can deliberately intervene to modify the current standards of social order and desirability.

Thus the self occupies a genuinely intermediate position. It originates within society, but at the same time it becomes an agency through which society may be compelled to undergo a directed reconstruction. For, as the self is "minded," it is possessed of Cartesian freedom—that is to say, the power of independent thought—and freedom of thought means doubting, inquiring, suspending judgment, tentativeness, and experimentation. With independent thought who knows where we shall end, what institutions or traditions will be put in jeopardy? It is, as William Carlos Williams says somewhat metaphorically, "a reply to Greek and Latin with the bare hands." And Dewey puts it in his own simpler fashion:[39] "Every thinker puts some portion of an apparently stable world in peril and no one can wholly predict what will emerge in its place."

Insofar as the self is a central organization of thoughts and energies, it insists upon its independence; even upon its self-origination. But if the stubbornness of bias and of preference points in the direction of subjectivity, the plasticity of attitudes and the pressing of needs toward their satisfactions turns the self outward. Inner and outer are complementary directions of selfhood. "The human individual in his opacity of bias is insofar doomed to a blind solitariness. He hugs himself in his isolation and fights against disclosure, the give and take of communication, as for the very integrity of existence. Even communicable meanings are tinged with color of the uncommunicated; there is a quality of reserve in every publicity."[40] But sociality and communication are traits which are just as immediate, just as primary. Inner and outer are complementary, but they may at the same time point to a real ambiguity.[41]

In some form or other, the dualism erected between the ego and the world of things and persons represents failure to attain solution of the problem set by this ambiguous nature of the self. It is a formulated acceptance of oscillation between surrender to the external and assertion of the inner. In science and in art, especially in the art of intercourse, real solutions occur. Private bias manages in them to manifest itself in innovations and deviations, which reshape the world of objects and institutions, and which eventually facilitate communication and understanding. Thereby the final and efficient, the limiting and the expansive, attain a harmony which they do not possess in other natural events.

But the outcome is not always so happy. Science, art, and harmonious social intercourse are not the solution for every perplexity of selfhood. When Pirandello's unhappy hero, Moscarda, looks at himself one day in the mirror, he is shocked, for he does not recognize what he sees.[42]

Was it really my own, that image glimpsed in a flash? Am I really like that, from the outside, when—all the while living—I do not think of myself? For others then, I am that stranger whom I surprised in a mirror; . . . From that time on, I had one despairing obsession: to go in pursuit of that stranger who was in me and who kept fleeing me; whom I could not halt in front of a mirror, . . . I wanted to see and know him, too, as others saw and knew him. I still believed, I may repeat here, that the stranger in question was a single individual to myself. But my atrocious drama speedily grew more complicated, with the discovery of the hundred-thousand Moscardes that I was, not only to others, but even to myself, all with the single name of Moscarda, a name that was ugly to the point of cruelty, all of them lodged within this poor body . . .

This ambiguous nature of the self to which pragmatic theory calls attention has been prepared by the very theory of selfhood to which pragmatism adheres. For if in his genesis the individual experiences himself not directly, but from the particular standpoints of other members of his social environment, and so becomes an object to himself only by taking toward himself the attitudes which other individuals have taken to him, then there is an inevitable pluralism about the self, and it is the central and organized unity which must be explained. This is what Mead means by asserting that "a multiple personality is in a certain sense normal."[43]

We carry on a whole series of different relationships to different people. We are one thing to one man and another thing to another. There are parts of the self which exist only for the self in relationship to itself. We divide ourselves up in all sorts of different selves with reference to our acquaintances. We discuss politics with one and religion with another. There are all sorts of different selves answering to all sorts of different social reactions. It is the social process itself that is responsible for the appearance of the self; it is not there as a self apart from this type of experience.

Such a theory presents no difficulty so long as the constancy and the unity of selfhood is so pervasive as to be the background of experience without falling into the foreground of attention, when it is as omnipresent and as little noticed as the air we breathe. But when, through the pathology of self-consciousness, the mechanism itself is exposed to view, then the multiple personality which is "in a certain sense normal" has become a disease. Moscarda, the central organization crumbling, begins to experience the world not as a self, but as a social psychologist like Mead. His wife Dida and his friend Quantorzo are sitting in the little drawing-room as he comes in.[44]

"Whom are you looking for?" my wife asked me, upon seeing me turn. I hastened to reply, with a smile, "Ah, no one, my dear, no one. We are all here, aren't we?"

She naturally did not know what I meant by that "no one" whom I had looked for at my side, but believed that my "We are all here, aren't we?" referred to the two of them, being very sure that in that little drawing room, we were three and not nine—or rather, eight, seeing that I, to myself, no longer counted. I mean to say:

1) Dida as she was to herself;
2) Dida as she was to me;
3) Dida as she was to Quantorzo;
4) Quantorzo as he was to himself;
5) Quantorzo as he was to Dida;
6) Quantorzo as he was to me;
7) Dida's dear Genge;
8) Quantorzo's dear Vitangelo.

What a charming conversation there was going to be, here in this drawing room, among these eight who believed themselves three!

Moscarda represents the moment when "the dualism between the ego and the world of things and persons" has become an open wound. But naturally, the intention of Dewey's theory of the self is to reconcile the directions of inwardness and outwardness in a single harmony. In this it but follows the usual pragmatic urge toward reconciliation of subject and object, experience and nature, thought and action. The same urge toward unification which is exemplified in Dewey's theory of mind and of the self is also reflected in his theory of value.

Modern value theory has often (following Plato) erected a "realm of values," objective in its claims upon human choice, containing everything admirable and precious, but set off from the mundane world of temptation and compromise, and therefore isolated from all natural existence. But if the realm of values is to be so distinguished from the realm of factual existence, how are these two worlds to be related? "The problem," says Dewey,[45] "of restoring integration and cooperation between man's beliefs about the world in which he lives and his beliefs about the values and purposes that should direct his conduct is the deepest problem of modern life."

Dewey's solution of this problem is neither to assert a difference in kind between affective-volitional meanings and cognition of material objects, nor to attempt a metaphysical classification of the hierarchy of valuable objects. It is to assimilate values to the act of criticism by which they are appraised. The "realm of values" is forsaken for those principles of action and of choice through which values may be made secure. Values therefore become the ends-in-view of those judgments which terminate the process of *evaluation*.

However an axiological Platonism gives security to values by placing them outside the contingency of temporal events, empirical evidence always shows them to be infinitely diversified in nature, negative and positive (that is to say, some working for, some against human likings and purposes), and above all, fugitive and precarious. Of values *as values* there is nothing to say. They are immediate. They are intrinsically interesting. They are what they are. "All that can be said of them concerns their generative conditions and the consequences to which they give rise." Therefore the important concern is not "a theory of values, but a theory of criticism; a method of discriminating among goods on the basis of the conditions of their appearance and of their consequences."[46] The Platonist may feel a false security by placing "the supreme form of the good" beyond temporality; the romantic poet may express the pathos of a world in which love and pleasure are fleeting and evanescent. But the philosopher is committed to an activity which is more mundane but more *consequential* than either. For his is the problem of *intelligent inquiry* into the conditions for the existence of value objects. Only critical appraisal can secure the possession and enjoyment of the goods which are our aim.

Platonism is not, of course, the only possible theory of value. Other naturalisms have substituted for transcendent values concepts more in harmony with the practices of daily life. But in bringing values down to earth—to "emotional satisfaction" or "pleasure" or "that which is liked and enjoyed" or "any object of any interest"—they have often imported into value a purely subjective character. Thus values are things "liked" or "desired" or "things congruent with personal inclination" and beyond the area of disputation or discussion. But to make value judgments mere statements about our own feelings is to forget that "the fact that something is desired only raises the *question* of its desirability; it does not settle it." Contrary to the adage that there is no disputing about tastes, they are the one thing worth disputing about, if by dispute one means discussion of the results of reflective inquiry. Dewey's emphasis upon evaluation is an attempt to avoid both the extreme of an axiology which in order to save the objectivity of values places them beyond experience and nature, and one which in order to keep them well within the natural world reduces them to mere qualifications of subjective feeling. A pragmatic theory of value must be as prospective and as practical as a pragmatic theory of meaning or of truth, for its aim is to assist us in having beliefs about values adequate to direct our future actions. Thus Dewey is led to his chief proposition:[47] "*Judgments about values are judgments about the conditions and the results of experienced objects: judgments about that which should regulate the formation of our desires, affections and enjoyments.*"

Because of his emphasis upon evaluation as a process of inquiry, because of his constant insistence that enjoyment is not a datum but a problem, it may seem that for Dewey the immediacies of value experience are lost. But I do not think this is really the case. Here again there is the characteristic interplay of the instrumental and the consummatory. Precisely because many values are unstable and mutually exclusive in the act of appropriation, innocent enjoyment needs to give way to cultivated taste if perception of value is to be continuous. Hence criticism becomes an integral part of the enjoyment which is its consummation. Experience of value itself represents a dialectical interplay of "appreciation" and "criticism," the one being whole-hearted involvement in experience, the other a questioning or comparison or an estimate of the future to make subsequent whole-hearted involvement both discreet and possible. Enlightened conscience in morals, cultivated taste in aesthetics, and wise convictions in belief generally are the fruit of that generalized criticism which is called philosophy.

Between the immediate value object and the ulterior value object (the given good and the good reached and justified by reflection) lies the critical process, but the justification of the latter is not intrinsic; it hinges upon its success in securing the terminating value experience. The notion that there are some value properties which carry their justification upon their face is for Dewey the snare and delusion of the whole axiological tradition, for it tends to isolate the operations of the intellect from the realm of values and evaluation. Such isolation produces another malignant dualism: on the one hand a realm of intellectual objects without value, and on the other a realm of value objects without intellect. This is to make the separation between science and the normative disciplines conclusive and final.

But the very nature of philosophy is that it partakes of both the scientific and the normative. "Like literature, it is a comment on nature and life in the interest of a more intense and just appreciation of the meanings present in experience. Its business is reportorial and transcriptive only in the sense in which the drama and poetry have that office. Its primary concern is to clarify, liberate and extend the goods which inhere in the naturally generated functions of experience."[48] But also its purpose "is criticism of beliefs, institutions, customs, policies with respect to their bearing upon good." Interpretation of fact and the underwriting of values is the philosophic task, but this interpretation and underwriting are the results of an activity of unceasing criticism and inquiry.

It is, I think, completely characteristic that our examination of Dewey's metaphysics shows it to arise in an appeal to immediate experience and hence, passing to a theory of natural events, a theory of minds and selves and a theory of values, to culminate in a theory of

philosophy as criticism. For this shows the extent to which his naturalism is dominated by a conception of human concern. When Naphta in
The Magic Mountain says that man's welfare is the criterion of truth,
and that theoretic science without practical application must be rejected, the bombastic Settembrini accuses him of "pragmatism." But
later it is Settembrini himself who complains that a metaphysics which
distracts the mind from its social task is the real evil. Ultimately, therefore, both are agreed. As literary figures they caricature Dewey's position
as a requirement of fiction. But in Mann's extravagance of statement
there is nonetheless much of Dewey's spirit. The idea that "metaphysics
is the evil" may seem a contradiction after the sustained metaphysics
which *Experience and Nature* presents. But Dewey's metaphysics is not
that type with which Settembrini could have had any quarrel. Its purpose is not to put to sleep the energy we should apply to the building
of the temple of society, but to mobilize it.

3. THE LOGIC OF VALUES AND BELIEFS

William James in his *Pragmatism* (A New Name for Some Old Ways
of Thinking) (1907) distinguished between pragmatism as an attitude
or temper of mind, pragmatism as a theory of the nature of ideas and of
truth, and finally pragmatism as a theory about reality. But it was Dewey
who pointed out[49] that what the subtitle emphasized was pragmatism
as a method. Although James seems best remembered for his pragmatic
theory of ideas (the notion that they are intentions or plans with a
prospective reference), Dewey's impulse is always to regard pragmatism
primarily as a method within the wider context of pragmatism as an
attitude or temper of mind. The dominant influence here is the example
of experimental science, the method of treating theories as "working
hypotheses," and this aspect is derivable not from James, but from
Peirce. It is what Peirce himself appropriately called "the laboratory
habit of mind." All of the guiding ideas of Dewey's comprehensive
work in pragmatic method appear in the early *Essays in Experimental
Logic* of 1916. Although they reappear partly developed in *The Quest
for Certainty* of 1929, their culmination comes in *Logic: The Theory of
Inquiry* of 1938. In the preface to this latter work, Dewey indicates his
overwhelming indebtedness to Peirce.

Essays in Experimental Logic announces the theme which underlies
Dewey's fateful early commitment to pragmatism as methodology:
thinking is instrumental to a control of the environment. Man is a
communicating, a tool-using, a language-using animal placed in a natural
environment which he has the power to control for his purposes.

Thought is the chief instrument by which purpose is made effective. Darwin himself could not have stated it more succinctly. Thinking in its successes is intelligence, and success is defined by function: by work done, by consequences effected. For if the assumption of a realistic epistemology is the non-transforming character of awareness, the assumption of pragmatism is the modification by thought of things. "The reorganization, the modification, effected by thinking is, by this hypothesis, a physical one. Thinking ends in experiment and experiment is an *actual* alteration of a physically antecedent situation in those details or respects which called for thought in order to do away with some evil."[50]

Intellect is set within a context which is non-cognitive, immediate, and irrational in this sense: it is dominated by factors of choice and aversion, passion and striving, endeavor and revolt. Within this vague and shifting context, tension focuses the world at one point of immediacy, and a problem is set. Reflection therefore appears as the dominant trait of a situation qualified by trouble, conflict, discord, uneasiness. The situation itself is probably ambiguous—indeed, its very uncertainty requires definition as a first step toward resolution. Intelligence must locate the difficulty before it can devise methods for coping with it. Knowing, therefore, always has a particular purpose, and reflection is a process set in motion by a specific deformation of organic experience requiring composition and reorganization. But the testing of thought must finally be accomplished by the action which, when efficacious, momentarily puts an end to thought. Reflection terminates with a definitive overt act which alleviates the primary tension. Thus value is achieved. It is in this sense that Dewey puts an end to the ancient dichotomy between the speculative and the practical. Cognition and action enjoy a mutual reciprocity and are a mutual requirement. It is in this spirit that Bernanos spoke when he said: "A thought which does not result in an action is nothing much, and an action which does not proceed from a thought is nothing at all."

The consequences of this formulation for logic are immense. For if thinking starts neither from a given rationality attempting to realize itself against all the forces of the irrational (as idealism asserts) nor from a mind whose function is just "to know," to theorize (as Aristotle taught), then logical theory in its usual sense is less the identification of static molds of thought implicit in a given rationality, than a description of actual tools of resolution and processes of inquiry which have been found practically effective. The "forms of mentality" grow less important; the methods of dealing with real objects more so. And although

Aristotle's specific doctrines are denied, his concept of logic as an organon or instrument (not a science but the operative implications of science) is affirmed, and we have the identification of logic and methodology.

These implications, already adumbrated in *Essays in Experimental Logic*, are worked out in classic detail in *Logic: The Theory of Inquiry*. Here it is stated without equivocation "that all logical forms (with their characteristic properties) arise *within* the operation of inquiry and are concerned with control of inquiry so that it may yield warranted assertions."[51] This is a more radical formulation than to assert that logical forms, pre-existent, simply are disclosed in a process of controlled inquiry, for it implies that forms *originate* in such operations, and that inquiry can in its own ongoing course develop the logical standards and forms to which *further* inquiry shall submit. Of course inquiry is related to doubt. Dewey appropriates from Peirce the two propositions which the latter had asserted as far back as 1877 in his famous article on "The Fixation of Belief": "The irritation of doubt is the only immediate motive for the struggle to attain belief" and "The struggle to attain a state of belief is Inquiry, and with the cessation of doubt and the settlement of opinion, it ends."[52] The terminus of inquiry is knowledge. Dewey's phrase for it is "warranted assertibility."

The notion that reason is a power which intuitively apprehends the ultimate first principles of logic is persistent throughout the history of philosophy. According to Dewey it is derived from the axiomatic character of Euclidean geometry. But if (as has happened since the development of nineteenth-century postulational theory) axioms are held to be postulates with meanings determined by the consequences which follow from their implications, then there is more reason to subscribe to the notion that logical forms (the principles of material implication, for example) are instances of a relation between means and consequences in properly controlled inquiry. It is then possible to assert that (1) logic is a progressive discipline: (2) the subject-matter of logic is determined operationally (whether the operations are performed upon existential materials or upon symbols): (3) logical forms are postulational (this does not mean that they are arbitrary, since they involve the assumption of certain logical responsibilities to be met in the course of subsequent inquiry); (4) logic is a naturalistic theory (in the sense that there is no breach of continuity between logical, physical, and biological operations); (5) logic is a social discipline—inquiry is a mode of activity which is socially conditioned and which has cultural consequences and finally, (6) logic is autonomous. Its principles are self-derivative and do not depend either upon an *a priori* intuition or metaphysical or epistemological assumptions. This is the tenet, previously noted, of a "logic without ontology."

It is perhaps necessary to consider (4) and (5) in a little more detail, for these formulations concern what Dewey calls "the existential matrix of inquiry," whether biological or cultural. A biological organism does not strictly speaking live *in* an environment; it lives *by means of* an environment, and in the case of the human animal this means that inquiry provides those transformations of environment which secure values and realize purposes. For doubt and cognitive indeterminacy are themselves functions of the behavior in which an organism and its environment interact. There is no inquiry which does not involve some metamorphosis of antecedent conditions. The serial relations found in the progressive structure of inquiry are rooted in the conditions of life itself.

Also the environment in which human beings live is not simply physical. It is constituted by selves made in the process of human communication and hence able to acquire a fund of meanings consolidated through cultural transmission. Language is the instrument whereby experience may be formalized, and once formalization takes place, experience itself becomes intellectual in character. Thus the experimentation originally possible only in acts or operations upon things is transferred to a realm of artificial signs or symbols, and these symbols introduce into inquiry a dimension other than that of the existential. The passage from sign to object signified provides the pattern of all *inference*. The relation of one sign to another provides the pattern for every *implication*. And in the nexus of symbol and symbol, symbol and thing, or thing and thing is illustrated the pattern out of which all abstract *relations* are generated. The linguistic character of social intercourse is therefore the condition of an extremely valuable form of experiment implying only a limited practical commitment. Biological activity is irrevocable. But an activity which can be rehearsed in purely symbolic terms remains corrigible. Overt activity can be suspended until the symbolic representation indicates an outcome which might be favorable.

Logic is the heart of Dewey's metaphysics, and the notion of "the pattern of inquiry" is at the heart of Dewey's logic. But the search for the pattern of inquiry is obviously a function of the definition of inquiry itself. Here Dewey is as explicit as one might wish: "*Inquiry is the controlled or directed transformation of an indeterminate situation into one that is so determinate in its constituent distinctions and relations as to convert the elements of the original situation into a unified whole.*"[53] We begin, then, with the antecedent conditions of inquiry—

an indeterminate, or, as Dewey more neatly phrases it, a *problematic situation.* Here again is the troubled, the confused, the ambiguous, the *questionable* in experience which we have met with in *Essays in Experimental Logic.* For the uneasiness of the organism in its environment and the conflicting responses which this uneasiness calls out are at once transferred to the cognitive level. At the moment when inquiry is brought to bear upon an organic uneasiness, a problem arises. The first stage of inquiry is the judgment that the situation is indeed problematic. The subsequent stages follow in orderly fashion: the formulation of the problem including the exploration of factors; the anticipation of possibilities; focusing upon the possibilities which are most probably relevant to a solution; reasoning about alternatives; viewing facts in their operational and prospective character; working toward the hypothetical solution which as blueprint for action contains the possible resolution of the original situation.

It is clear that such a transformation utilizes all the resources ordinarily associated with an inductive and a deductive logic: formal reasoning, observation, generalization, estimates of probability. But it also includes a factor of unification not ordinarily associated with the theory of logic or scientific method. This is practical judgment.

The point is crucial, for it provides that intersection of theory and practice, of science and ethics, of the pattern of inquiry and the evaluative element in experience which it is the purpose of Dewey's philosophy to explore and to explicate. The center of importance for one who is at once social philosopher and philosopher of science, methodologist and moralist, is the point at which a generalized logic of inquiry is transformed into a logic of evaluation.

Dewey's most important early treatment of the logic of judgments of practice occurs in the *Essays in Experimental Logic.*[54] By a practical judgment Dewey does not mean one having a different origin or quality from factual judgments, but one which relates to a different subject matter—to things to be done in a situation demanding action. The subject matter of such judgments is an incomplete situation also, and the proposition formulating the judgment is itself an element in the situation carrying it forward to completion. The implication is that with respect to this completion, one outcome is "better" than another. Here "better" does not refer merely to one of a series of alternative means to an end given in advance and with finality. The practical judgment is at once judgment of means and end. For it is obvious that a judgment of what is to be done requires recognition of what the given facts of a situation are, as indicating both the proper course to pursue and the

precise means to be adopted in its pursuit. Practical judgments, therefore, like judgments of fact (from which they are inseparable), are
hypothetical until the course of action suggested has been tried. And
here truth and verification thoroughly coincide. For the conclusion of
the action is the truth or falsity of the judgment.[55] Dewey's motivation
here is the exact inverse of that of the positivist in ethics. The positivist
wishes if possible to reduce ethical propositions to statements of fact
which could be true or false. Dewey's interest, on the contrary, is to
extend to statements of fact the prospective, practical implications of
judgments of practice.

Essays in Experimental Logic introduces early a distinction which
runs through the development of Dewey's value theory like a pervasive
strand: that between *the immediate experience* of a good and *the
judgment* that something is valuable. Finding a thing good apart from
reflective judgment is a mode of organic reaction. But to state that a
thing *is* good is to recognize its relevance to future acceptance-rejection
behavior. *Valuing* (prizing or esteeming) is to be distinguished from
valuation (appraising or estimating). The first is direct and self-sufficient.
The second is an inquiry into consequences. Thus a judgment of value
is simply a case of practical judgment, and, like it, inseparable from
statements of fact which elucidate a situation. Furthermore, judgments
of value are never complete and self-contained. How could they be, since
they also arise in a problematic situation and refer to the course of action
which is to carry such an incomplete situation to its fulfillment? As
Dewey puts it: "Value judged is not existential quality noted, but is
the influence attached by judgment to a given existential quality in
determining judgment."[56] The inference is not that value is subjective,
but that it is practical. Choices, desires, likings, may be original biases
in a given direction, but they are not essentially guides, but that which
is to be guided. Evaluation is *that process of reflection which ends by
instituting a value which shall make a claim upon choice*. Valuation
is, therefore, that mode of inquiry which is relevant to preferential behavior.

When Dewey denies that the means-ends formulation of ethical action
is tenable, he is not by any means denying that we do deliberate about
"aims" or "ends-in-view." His purpose is to make clear that values are
not determined by comparing alternative means with an ideal model,
but by comparing various aims with one another. For the more completely the model is formed outside the specific conditions of the problematic moral situation, the less intelligent, the less truly *deliberative*
is the final moral act. But to the extent that the standard of value is

formed *in* the process of practical judgment, it is a transvaluation of all prior values and a proof that the provisional and self-corrective methods of natural science have ethical application. "It is reasonable to believe," says Dewey, "that what holds moral knowledge back is above all the conception that there are standards of good given to knowledge apart from the work of reflection in constructing methods of action."

The conclusion of *Essays in Experimental Logic* is that, in the last analysis, all judgments of fact are judgments of practice. And the conclusion of *Logic: The Theory of Inquiry* almost a quarter of a century later "is that evaluations as judgments of practice are not a particular kind of judgment in the sense that they can be put over against other kinds, but are *an inherent phase of judgment itself.*"[57] Here Dewey is concerned to show that all inquiry requires deliberation as to what it is better to do. Moral evaluations consider ends as modes of operation which will resolve a doubtful situation, but it is "the situation" which is of paramount importance. The moral judgment is simply that which is logically required when the agent finds himself in a moral predicament. But all scientific inquiry is in some sense a mode of practice, and since all judgments of practice are evaluations, therefore evaluations are intrinsic to scientific inquiry. The net effect of the pragmatic methodology is to show that "fact" and "value" imply one another, and that it is unnecessary to provide a qualitatively independent science of moral evaluation since this can be assimilated without difficulty to a generalized logic of the problematic situation.

The last phase of Dewey's value theory appears in the *Theory of Valuation* of 1939. It adds little which the *Essays in Experimental Logic* and the *Logic* have not already said, but it is interesting because it shows Dewey struggling with the first rumblings of the positivistic avalanche. It is a polemical work, taking its origins in the atmosphere of the ferment occasioned by the writings of Carnap, Ayer, and Stevenson (with their insistence that moral judgments were either merely emotive utterances, the assertion of imperatives, or persuasive definitions—in any case, not factual statements capable of empirical verifiability). Dewey categorically rejects these positivistic assertions. "It cannot be denied," he says,[58] "that propositions having evidential warrant and empirical test are possible in the case of evaluation of things as means. Hence it follows that, if these propositions enter into the formation of the interests and desires which are valuations of ends, the latter are thereby constituted the subject matter of authentic empirical affirmations and denials." This is the heart of the matter for Dewey. But he goes further. For "even if value expressions were ejaculatory and such as to influence the conduct of other persons, genuine propositions about such expressions would be possible." We could inquire whether, indeed, they accomplished the effect intended, in which cases, and how. For even a distinction between linguistic expressions which are "emotive" and those which are "scientific" would imply that the former have conditions and consequences and that they might be objects of inquiry. In short, valuations are empirically observable patterns of behavior and may be studied as such.

But Dewey's point goes beyond the mere assertion that although evaluative and descriptive language may be different, scientific method may be as reasonably available for the control of evaluations as for the control of statements. He indicates why this must be so:[59]

What the foregoing discussion has added to the idea is proof that if, and *only* if, valuation is taken in this sense, are empirically grounded propositions about desires and interests as sources of valuations possible—such propositions being grounded in the degree in which they employ scientific physical generalizations as means of forming propositions about activities which are correlated as means-ends. The resulting general propositions provide rules for valuation of the aims, purposes, plans, and policies that direct intelligent human activity. They are not rules in the sense that they enable us to tell directly, or upon bare inspection the values of given particular ends; . . . they are rules of methodic procedure in the conduct of the investigations that determine the respective conditions and consequences of various modes of behavior. It does not purport to solve the problems of valuation in and of itself; it does claim to state conditions that inquiry must satisfy if these problems are to be resolved, and to serve in this way as a leading principle in conduct of such inquiries.

The position is perhaps a slight modification of the earlier formulations, but not essentially different. Appraisals remain rules of procedure capable of being grounded in and controlled by factual statements, if not quite identical with them. And the whole interpretive effort is, as before, to maintain the continuity of "the scientific" and "the practical," to give value terms meanings which are publicly verifiable in terms of overt behavior, and to give value judgments an empirical status as in some sense factual and descriptive. For only so can the unity of pragmatic methodology be sustained.

But the motivation lies even deeper than this, in a monistic habit of mind which sees that "the hard-and-fast impassible line which is supposed by some to exist between 'emotive' and 'scientific' language is a reflex of the gap which now exists between the intellectual and the emotional in human relations and activities."[60] and which goes on to draw the obvious sociological moral: "The split which exists in present social life between ideas and emotions, especially between ideas that have scientific warrant and uncontrolled emotions that dominate practice, the split between the affectional and the cognitive, is probably one of the chief sources of the maladjustments and unendurable strains from which the world is suffering."

The revolt against dualism in the modern world has many protagonists: Whitehead, who finds "the bifurcation of nature" an epistemological catastrophe; Eliot, who finds "the dissociation of sensibility" a poetic disaster. It is characteristic of Dewey that in the positivistic separation between an "emotive" and a "scientific" language he too should find evidence of the maladjustment, the unendurable strain of modern society.

4. THE RECONSTRUCTED SOCIETY

I have said that despite the importance of his work in logic and metaphysics, Dewey's primary interest lies in ethics and above all in a philosophy of social reconstruction. And yet, when one comes to consider this aspect of his work, there is a certain difficulty in presenting it as a systematic and continuous body of theory. This is due, I believe, to the character of its content, to the fact that its internal constitution denies that very classical schema for social reconstruction which serves as a model for the proposals for institutional reform of a John Stuart Mill or even an Aristotle.

Dewey's emphasis upon "social planning," upon the use of intelligence for conscious intervention within the social process and purposive control of social change, is a pervasive feature of his social philosophy from its earliest stages to its last. Over and over again we are told that "intelligence" is a better method of social guidance than drift or ignorance, authority or caprice, prejudice or passion. Over and over again we are admonished because "we make so little use of the experimental method of forming our ideas and beliefs about the concerns of man in his characteristic social relations."[61] Over and over again we are told that "What is needed is intelligent examination of the consequences that are actually effected by inherited institutions and customs, in order that there may be intelligent consideration of the ways in which they are to be intentionally modified in behalf of generation of different consequences."[62] Dewey's social theory implies the direction of society by ideas and by knowledge. But it is inexplicit to the point of vagueness on the matter of purposes and goals. This is not a matter of incoherence or of oversight. It is a consequence of the very theory of moral action to which Dewey adheres.

The classical schema for social reconstruction is based upon the distinction between "means" and "ends." Social reconstruction is defined as the utilization of knowledge about society to attain the objectives of society. This suggests two difficulties: (1) the moral difficulty of identifying and validating the objective or the end; and (2) the adaptive difficulty of determining the methods or means for achieving it. But the very framework of this formulation implies a theory of action which is rationalistic to the core since it permits the separation of means and ends, and the construction or envisagement of the norms of action quite independently of the proposed chain of events viewed as the vehicle of their achievement. It is this theory of action which Dewey's ethics denies.

Precisely because there are no "ends" fixed and given in advance outside the process of specific moral deliberation; because of the thoroughly reciprocal character of means and ends in the practical judgment; because the end-in-view upon which judgment settles is simply the adequate means of performance of a specified act, there can be no unambiguously formulated and predetermined dominant moral aim in the light of which a society may be politically and economically reconstructed. The abstract clarity of a formulated hierarchy of value gives way to the inventiveness of deliberation and the shifting flux of practice. Everything now depends not on commitment to the proper ends, but *on deliberating in the right way*. The shift in emphasis of such a moral theory is from the substantive to the procedural.

When George Geiger in *The Philosophy of John Dewey* came to write on "Dewey's Social and Political Philosophy," one of the most insistent questions which he raised[63] was that of Dewey's stand on the matter of ultimate values. He wondered "whether Dewey as an instrumentalist is prepared to accept the values of method as final?" or instead, "whether we are not pushed back to some other moral end, say, to happiness or to the complete functioning of the individual which appears to comprise the ethic of liberalism?" For it seemed to him that "Dewey's social philosophy wavers between denying any reliance upon such moral purposes, and assuming unconsciously certain values, characteristically those either of reflective inquiry itself or of the processes of social reform." Geiger's question was much to the point. But its chief value was that it permitted Dewey himself to answer in a fashion which makes his final position abundantly clear.

I am glad to have an opportunity to say something about another question raised in Mr. Geiger's contribution. It concerns what he says about *ultimate* values. I have carried on a polemic against ultimates and finalities because I found them presented as things that are inherently absolute, like "ends-in-themselves" instead of ends-in-relationships. The reason they have been proferred [sic] as absolutes is that they have been taken out of any and all *temporal* context. A thing may be ultimate in the sense of coming last in a given temporal series, so that it is ultimate *for that series*. There are things that come last in reflective valuations and, as terminal, they are ultimate. Now Dr. Geiger is quite right in saying that for me the method of intelligent action is precisely such an ultimate value. It is the last, the final or closing thing we come upon in inquiry into inquiry. But the place it occupies in the *temporal* manifestation of inquiry is what makes it such a value, not some property it possesses in and of itself, in the isolation of non-relatedness. It is ultimate in use and function; it does not claim to be ultimate because of an absolute "inherent nature" making it sacrosanct, a transcendent object of worship.

The first consequence of Dewey's emphasis upon temporality and temporal context is that moral change, whether in the case of the individual or the social group, is to be judged not in terms of whether it is congruent with some end fixed in advance, but by the *direction* in which the movement takes place. Meliorism is thus an inherent quality of this mode of ethical perception. Growth, improvement, and progress as a *process* rather than as an achievement of static outcome become the significant thing. And, as in all inquiry, the end is not a final limit which is reached; it is a process of transforming an existent situation. "Not perfection as a final goal, but the ever-enduring process of perfecting, maturing, refining is the aim in living. Honesty, industry, temperance, justice, like health, wealth and learning, are not goods to be possessed as they would be if they expressed fixed ends to be attained. They are directions of change in the quality of experience. Growth itself is the only moral 'end.' "[64]

The second consequence of a theory of "morality as direction" is the enormous emphasis which it places upon procedure in the individual case. Since all action is "an invasion of the future," and since conflict and uncertainty are pervasive qualities of experience, decision is a question of intelligence or practical wisdom. But however intelligence is concerned with establishing the future so that it may have order and direction, and however it is concerned with principles and criteria of judgment, these principles and criteria somehow resist codification. Since intelligent action proceeds from within a moral situation, it originates an outcome which no rule can determine in advance. In this sense, there is a similarity in pragmatic and existentialist ethics—a certain abstractness in their conception of the seat of moral authority. When Sartre in his little essay *Existentialism Is a Humanism* sets up a very concrete instance of a moral dilemma between responsibility to family and duty to country, he admits that from the existentialist standpoint there is no rule of thumb for its solution. "There are no means of judging. The content is always concrete, and therefore unpredictable; it has always to be invented. The one thing that counts, is to know whether the invention is made in the name of freedom."[65] Change two words and it might be Dewey speaking: "There are no means of judging. The content is always concrete, and therefore unpredictable; it has always to be deliberated. The one thing that counts, is to know whether the deliberation is made in the name of intelligence."

Existentialist and pragmatic ethics are both procedural. The first finds any act moral which springs from an authentically free choice. The second finds any act good to the extent that it is an expression of intelligence in action. But the change in the wording above from "invention" to "deliberation" signifies an important difference. In emphasizing invention Sartre is pointing to a subjectivity inherent in moral choice: a quasi-Bergsonian insistence that in deciding, the individual must look inward to the promptings of the deepest self. Whereas in emphasizing deliberation, Dewey may be denying fixed ends of values, but he is by no means denying the directive validity of information and of knowledge. Although, therefore, choice proceeds from *within* a situation, its guidance is *objective*, for the evidence comes through the agency of scientifically established knowledge. What holds true of the problems of an individual is true also for society, and here above all Dewey shows himself to be deeply under the spell of the liberal tradition. For he ascribes to the conclusions derivable from the social sciences (or, as he calls it "social inquiry") an important function in the improvement of the social structure and the formulation of wise social policy.

I have said that there is a real similarity in the social philosophies of Dewey and of John Stuart Mill. Each believes in the efficacy of knowledge—in the possibility of a valid social science which can yield material for the guidance of social deliberation. And each believes in the necessity for intervention in the course of political and economic behavior —in an experimental design of social institutions which shall mitigate where it cannot abolish the conflicts of interest within society. Both, therefore, make an empirical appeal to the results and the techniques of an experimental social science. If this can be interpreted as a revolution in social method, analogous in its radicalism to the revolution in modern physics, then, at least, the difference in the two revolutions should be recognized. The new attempt to discover reason in nature, to which the work of Planck and Einstein attest, is completed when it is found that nature conforms to, or may be interpreted by, a system of mathematical equations. But the reason which Dewey attempts to introduce into society is a rationality not of relational forms, but of experimental design. It therefore remains to the end true to the presuppositions of his empirical metaphysics.

Dewey's conception of the indeterminacy of the concrete situation feeds the fire of his impatience with a social theory (whether Hegelian, Benthamite, or Marxist) which is committed to a logic of general notions under which specific situations are to be brought. What we want, he insists, is not talk about the individual versus society, obligations toward the state, or the class struggle, but light upon particular groups of individuals, specific economic institutions, definite forms of social arrangements. We need guidance in dealing with particular perplexities in social living, and this is not to be had from general answers which are supposed to cover and dominate all particular cases. Such answers do not assist inquiry; they close it. What Dewey, therefore, has in mind is the substitution of social science for a social philosophy. "Meanwhile, of course, concrete troubles and evils remain. They are not magically waved out of existence because in theory society is organic. The region of concrete difficulties, where the assistance of intelligent method for tentative plans for experimentation is urgently needed, is precisely where intelligence fails to operate."[66]

Dewey is impatient with "the waste of mental energy due to conducting discussion of social affairs in terms of conceptual generalizations." What he would like instead are those "specific inquiries into a multitude of specific structures and interactions" which supply probabilities for the estimate of future behavior. What he does not specify is the way in which the conclusions of an adequate social science might be made available for the makers of social policy, and, indeed, whether science in the pure sense (not oversimplified or propagandistic) could be of any use in the determination of policy by democratic means. Actually, when he wrote *Freedom and Culture* in 1939 he was aware of the general trend toward the increase of public control of private industry and finance in the United States, but he recognized that the consequences of such control were far from consistent. "In fact," he said,[67] "there is one thesis of Herbert Spencer that could now be revived with a good deal of evidence in its support: namely, the economic situation is so complex, so intricate in the interdependence of delicately balanced factors, that planned policies initiated by public authority are sure to have consequences totally unforseeable,—often the contrary of what was intended. . . ."

This passage alone points to one of the difficulties: namely, that there may be no body of scientific information in the social sciences capable of serving as a guide to the making of social policy. Dewey's proposals for the reform of "social inquiry" in the *Logic* were toward the remedy of this situation. Recognizing that in the broad sense the social sciences are branches of natural science, he asked for a reform within the social sciences which should bring together rigorous observational techniques with a conceptual framework also operationally arrived at. His two chief suggestions were (1) that the moralistic approach to social problems in terms of praise and blame should be supplanted by the impartial formulation of these problems and an impersonal inquiry into the conditions of their solution; and (2) that a social science useful in its application must grow out of actual social tensions, needs, and troubles—its subject matter to be determined by that kind of information needed for the resolution of the conflicting social situation. Here was another attempt to assimilate social science and social policy to the generalized format of the problematic situation.

But this suggests a further difficulty—the ambiguities inherent in a problematic situation which is social rather than merely individual. In the individual case the outcome is of primary importance only to the one who faces the problem, and presumably he is at once the subject of the situation and the inquirer into it. But when the situation is social, the problem consists of a conflict of many individual interests, and there is no guarantee whatever that all those whose interests are at stake will participate in the inquiry into causes and consequences. At this point Dewey's commitment to the method of science may lead him to a gross overestimation of the role which scientific knowledge can play in the resolution of conflicts of interest within society.[68]

If social science is taken seriously as the knowledge, produced by social inquiry, which is a potential guide to a policy of social change, this implies a type of society which can control its own actions so as to bring about desirable future consequences providing the conclusions of social scientists are utilized. But for a society to utilize the conclusions of social inquiry, it must understand them, and unless social scientists formulate their doctrines as propaganda to be used manipulatively (or at least "persuasively"), it is doubtful whether society as a whole could understand where "the facts" point, and the weight of probability to be assigned to them.

To reduce issues of social change to the problematic situation as it occurs in exact science or even the area of individual morality is deceptive in two respects. It seems to imply both a single unequivocal formulation of exactly what the problem is, and an unambiguous and scientifically reasonable assessment of the evidence after it is assembled. But the latter, while perhaps possible for experts, is not possible for society at large. This means that planning *for* a society is by no means the same as planning *by* a society. The resulting dilemma seems inescapable. A scientifically constructed plan can probably not be democratically accepted, and a democratically accepted plan will probably not be scientific.[69]

The first difficulty is even more formidable. The formulation of a social problem assumes the kind of agreement upon values and coincidence of interests which a heterogeneous society (however democratic) seems to lack. Rational discussion is possible only with a certain pre-established harmony of social interest. But if democratic society is made up of competing and largely conflicting interests, then the function of the discussion of social policy is as much to define a problem as to solve it scientifically, and the importance of discussion will be rather to create a compromise between conflicting interests than scientifically to weigh evidence and render a purely "rational" decision. To assimilate social problems to the form of scientific inquiry (as Dewey constantly does) is perhaps to overestimate the extent of social rationality, and to underestimate the dilemma of partisanship, political and economic, in a democratic society.

The point is particularly pertinent in its bearing upon the concept of "experimentalism" in social affairs. As early as 1935 Dewey had decided that reliance upon "the method of cooperative experimental intelligence" required a new formulation of the liberal position, that no longer could the accidental convergence of the actions of separate individuals be trusted to further the ends of society.

The ends can now be achieved *only* by reversal of the means to which early liberalism was committed. Organized social planning, put into effect for the creation of an order in which industry and finance are socially directed in behalf of institutions that provide the material basis for the cultural liberation and growth of individuals, is now the sole method of social action by which liberalism can realize its professed aims.[70]

But organized social planning requires two psychological qualities which are difficult to realize simultaneously—an attitude of commitment to the idea of total and coordinated direction, and an open-mindedness which will permit a social experiment to stand or fall with the facts of realized consequences. Just how difficult this is, Dewey himself surely knew. Upon his return from the Soviet Union in 1928, he wrote a series of articles for *The New Republic*, one of which was characteristically entitled "The Great Experiment and the Future." In this he viewed the Russian situation with his typical calmness and common sense. But he pointed out that neither the Marxian fanatics nor the American reactionaries possessed the genuinely experimental temper, since each (although in opposite ways) considered its issue a foregone conclusion. Mr. Hoover found the Russian experiment doomed to failure by "the laws of economics." The Marxists found it bound to succeed by the "laws of the dialectic of history." Dewey commented:[71] "Not being an absolutist of either type, I find it more instructive to regard it as an experiment whose outcome is quite undetermined, but that is, just as an experiment, by all means the most interesting one going on upon our globe—though I am quite frank to say that for selfish reasons I prefer it tried in Russia rather than in my own country." The implications of this comment are instructive. Dewey's own objectivity, he seems to suggest, is only possible at a safe distance. But the most damaging reference concerns the appeal to the concept of "social law," whether that espoused by the Marxists or by Mr. Hoover. For it indicates the profound difficulty of an adequate social science to free itself from a partisan context sufficiently to serve as indisputable knowledge, universally acknowledged and with an objective claim upon the belief of all partisans for the institution of a crucial social experiment.

I have emphasized the problem of social method—the relevance of social inquiry and experimentalism to the intelligent control of social change—because it is the dominant theme of Dewey's social philosophy. But Geiger is right that inextricably bound up with this theme is the proposal of certain values which show Dewey to be *par excellence* the theorist of democracy and the chief proponent of the ethic of a revised liberalism in the twentieth century. These values are not so much asserted as implicit, and they reveal themselves in the two principal objectives of his social theory; the search for the Great Community and the rehabilitation of the Lost Individual. To these dominant (and, of course, co-ordinate) considerations, I should now like to turn.[72]

The liberalism of the nineteenth century opposed the claims of the individual to those of a despotic society. To Dewey this opposition is obstructive and unreal. Not only are the terms "individual" and "social" hopelessly ambiguous, but the individual originates from, and remains rooted within, a social environment which presupposes language and communication. The problem of the individual is not one of politics but of social psychology. The issue which Mill and others treated as that of individual versus society, Dewey transforms into the problem of the realm of "private" action (whether individual or group), where action affects only the actors, versus the realm of "public" action, where the consequences of group behavior extend to persons beyond the group. Whenever these consequences for others are extensive and enduring, we have a situation that concerns the Public. The supervision and regulation of these consequences is political business, exercised by officials. And the Public (the mass of citizens) is organized and defined by those interests in whose behalf officials are presumed to act. This provides a criterion by which to judge a political state: How highly organized is the Public in the expression of its interests? And to what degree are the officials sensitive to their responsibility of caring for "the public interest"? These two questions express the problem of democracy.

Of the two questions, it is the first which most seriously engages Dewey's attention. His concern is with the contemporary failure of an enlightened Public to express its interests, and his analysis digs deep into the causes and the consequences of this failure. The new technology has resulted in a social revolution, and the consequence has been that independent local communities found their affairs conditioned by remote and invisible organizations. The impact of the latter upon face-to-face associations has been destructive of the intimate democracy of the nineteenth century. "The Great Society created by steam and electricity may be a society, but it is no community. The invason of the community by the new and relatively impersonal and mechanical modes of combined human behavior is the outstanding fact of modern life."[73] Every social philosophy in the modern world must take its departure from the facts of industrialization. For Marx this means the de-humanization of the proletariat. For Jaspers and Marcel it means that all have been converted into an assemblage of mere functions, and that therefore man has lost the sense of his own being. For Dewey it means the dissolution of community.

American political democracy was developed out of genuine community life where association, communication, and industry were local. But the machine age has so complicated, enlarged, and impersonalized the social area that the Public, once defined and articulate, is now uncertain and bewildered. If there is a Public, it is discontinuous—a myth, a shadow which comes into reality only at moments of intense social crisis where decision can be put off no longer. Even here there is no guarantee that it is a voice of independent deliberation rather than a Public "made" by the owners of the instruments of public communication in the image of their propagandistic ends. Here is the crux of the situation, and it indicates once again the intimate relation in Dewey's social theory between real democracy, substantive freedom, and the procedures of inquiry and deliberation which alone create an organic democracy.

We have the physical tools of communication as never before. The thoughts and aspirations congruous with them are not communicated, and hence are not common. Without such communication the public will remain shadowy and formless, seeking spasmodically for itself, but seizing and holding its shadow rather than its substance. Till the Great Society is converted into a Great Community, the Public will remain in eclipse. Communication can alone create a great community. Our Babel is not one of tongues but of the signs and symbols without which shared experience is impossible.[74]

It is clear that for Dewey the idea of democracy is defined less by political machinery than by the right of the individual to have a responsible share in forming and directing the activities of the groups to which he belongs, and in participating genuinely in the values which the groups promote. So regarded, "democracy is not an alternative to other principles of associated life. It is the idea of community life itself," and the achievement of democracy is nothing but the achievement of community. From this way of seeing the problem it becomes clear how much of Dewey's criticism of the contemporary scene has been conditioned by his boyhood and youth in the environment of nineteenth-century quasi-rural Vermont. For the deepest and the richest memories of such a past are of a community which is primarily a matter of face-to-face contacts, where neighborliness and family affection are the chief agencies of socialization and growth, and where moral responsibility is meshed with an intimate knowledge of the persons with whom one has to deal.

There is perhaps a certain pathos in Dewey's insistence, for it may well be the case that the intimate community *with roots* is gone for good. But Dewey's conception of the Great Community wavers between a fear that without the re-establishment of face-to-face relations and without the restoration of local communal life, no true democracy is possible, and a hope that through some re-creation of true communication on a broader scale, something approximating democratic quality may infuse the wider area. For even the Great Community may have a *res publica*—a field of participation, interaction, and shared ideas and sentiments. Dewey does not prophesy the forms which this communication will take, but he returns to the themes of his prior logical interests. He is sure that there can be no Public without full publicity. He knows that the prime condition of a democratically organized Public is a kind of knowledge and insight which does not yet exist. And he is sure that the condition of this insight is absolute freedom of social inquiry and the widest possible distribution of its conclusions. His vision is of the formation of a public opinion congruent with the attitudes and the methods of experimental science.

We have but touched lightly and in passing upon the conditions which must be fulfilled if the Great Society is to become a Great Community; a society in which the ever-expanding and intricately ramifying consequences of associated activities shall be known in the full sense of that word, so that an organized, articulate Public comes into being. The highest and most difficult kind of inquiry and a subtle, delicate, vivid and responsive art of communication must take possession of the physical machinery of transmission and circulation and breathe life into it. When the machine age has thus perfected its machinery it will be a means of life and not its despotic master. Democracy will come into its own, for democracy is a name for a life of free and enriching communion. It had its seer in Walt Whitman. It will have its consummation when free social inquiry is indissolubly wedded to the art of full and moving communication.[75]

Dewey's proposal for the re-establishment of the Great Community is the most positive, the most constructive of his social suggestions. Its coordinate doctrine, the rehabilitation of the Lost Individual, is more negative and more critical of older and more traditional views of the relationship of the individual to society. The first expresses his conception of democracy; in the second is to be found his relationship to the great liberal tradition. While the first is treated in political and even more importantly in social terms, the latter is given a primarily economic reference.

Individualism Old and New is, perhaps, of all Dewey's works the one most saturated with the sense of economic crisis, the most socialistic of all his writings—not at all in the strident Marxist sense, but in its criticism of the evils of a primarily acquisitive society. In this society Dewey discerns a gross perversion of the whole ideal of individualism to conform to the practices of a pecuniary culture—a perversion which had become the source and justification of inequality and oppression. But above all, he saw that the real eclipse of individuality was its most serious consequence. Speaking in accents which might have been drawn from R. H. Tawney's *The Acquisitive Society*, he asserted that a stable individuality is dependent upon stable objects of social allegiance, and that an assured and integrated individualism is the product of definite social responsibilities and publicly acknowledged functions. The "tragedy of the 'lost individual' is due to the fact that while individuals are now caught up into a vast complex of associations, there is no harmonious and coherent reflection of the import of these connections into the imaginative and emotional outlook on life." And "the chief obstacle to the creation of a type of individual whose pattern of thought and desire is enduringly marked by consensus with others, and in whom sociability is one with cooperation in all regular human associations, is the persistence of that feature of the earlier individualism which defines industry and commerce by ideas of private pecuniary profit."[76] This reference to the persistence of an earlier individualism suggests the necessity of a reformulation of all that is best in the social theory of the liberal tradition with a critical analysis of its historic roots. It was to this task that Dewey turned in his Page-Barbour Lectures, *Liberalism and Social Action*.

The history of liberalism, Dewey asserts, reveals an inner split which developed as the claims of an artificial individual were placed against the encroachments of a power-hungry society. Beginning with Locke and the doctrine of natural rights, it was asserted that individual reason and individual rights existed prior to the formation of society, and that they remained as an ultimate check upon its illegitimate powers. In Adam Smith liberty becomes economic, with self-interest assumed as the primary human motive, and to this concept of self-interest Bentham adds a social criterion, although he still conceives that customs and institutions are to be judged by their consequences upon the happiness of individuals. John Stuart Mill is the great transitional figure who stands midway between the old atomistic individualism of the utilitarian tradition and the newer organic individualism of T. H. Green and the idealists, for whom relations rather than atomic entities (whether physical, mental, or social) constitute nature, mind, and society. The crucial split is therefore between the old laissez-faire liberalism and the new social welfare liberalism: between those who still protest the encroachment of government upon all individual initiative whether economic or social, and those who "are committed to the principle that organized society must use its powers to establish the conditions under which the mass of individuals can possess actual as distinct from merely legal liberty."[77]

In this split lies the crisis of Liberalism. There were, indeed, enduring values for which the earlier liberalism stood. They are the values which

Mill's essay *On Liberty* celebrates: freedom to develop the inherent capacities of individuals, and freedom to exercise intelligence in the formulation of social policy through inquiry, thought, and discussion. But where these values are most sympathetic, they are not to be found as qualities or rights of individuals, but as a procedural openness within the context of associated living. Effective liberty (and here Dewey and Marx are at one) is a function of social conditions, and the control of these conditions lacks effectiveness without an intelligent attempt to intervene in the direction of economic forces. The application of intelligence in social action (the cooperative use of experimental method) requires direct social intervention, and this means that the function of a newer and more responsive liberalism is to mediate such social transitions so that change will be effective without the gross impairment of liberty to which alternative forms of social organization so often give rise.

What Dewey was asking for was that liberalism should now become "radical," and what he meant by this was that it should assert and organize its perception of the necessity for drastic social change. Although he was by no means innocent of a knowledge of the extent to which physical force and coercion have attended the process of social transformation in time of crisis, his faith remained firm that intelligence rather than force could be built into the procedures of the social system. But his conception of the way in which intelligence expressed itself in social affairs marked a clear break with the competitive, market-place theory of discussion which characterized the older liberalism. There it was assumed that the conflict of parties might be resolved by a public discussion which should bring out necessary truths and effect a synthesis of oppositions. But this social dialectic has little in common with the social inquiry which Dewey conceived as resting upon the most rigorous of scientific procedures. The difference between *On Liberty* and *Liberalism and Social Action* is, therefore, a difference between the judicial and the engineering mentality.

Needless to say, Dewey's identification of the spirit of democracy with the attitude of an adventuresome and freely inquiring natural science has nothing in common with similar scientific pretensions of totalitarian social theories. When Dewey in *Freedom and Culture* undertook his sharp comparison of totalitarian economics and democracy,[78] he attacked the Marxian notion of class warfare as the channel of progress and social change, as well as Marx's denial of the moving power of human valuations, on the ground that such sweeping generalizations were unscientific. He found Marxism "outdated" precisely in the matter of its scientific claim. For the search for a single all-comprehensive law for society, and the *necessity* of all else once this law is established, marks the intellectual climate of the social science of the nineteenth-century. *Pluralism* and *probability* are the characteristics of the science of today. Dewey rightly exposed the Russian ideology (with its rigid control of communication, and its belief that dissent from "the Truth" indicates an evil and a dangerous will) not as science but as theology, and he soberly laid waste a doctrine which claims to be scientific while violating every principle of scientific method.

The form of the criticism is characteristic, for it uses a new weapon to enforce an old claim. The permanent and strategic freedoms of the liberal tradition are freedom of inquiry, toleration of diverse views, and freedom of communication. What we may learn from them is the potential alliance between science and democracy—for they are the presuppositions upon which both science and democracy rest.

IX

The Passion for Logic:
Bertrand Russell and
Rudolph Carnap

The only proper task of Philosophy is Logical Analysis.
RUDOLPH CARNAP

An end must come in a merciless triumph
An end of evil in a profounder logic.
WALLACE STEVENS

I like precision. I like sharp outlines. I hate misty vagueness.
BERTRAND RUSSELL

Victor Serge said, "I followed his argument
With the blank uneasiness which one might feel
In the presence of a logical lunatic."
WALLACE STEVENS

1. THE POSITIVISTIC AVALANCHE

It has taken three hundred years to prepare the positivistic avalanche. The seventeenth century contained the poetry of Milton and the sermons of John Donne and Lancelot Andrewes, but the true custodians of its spirit were Galileo, Newton, and Descartes. The philosophy of this period is scientific; it is dominated by mathematical physics, but it raises the problems appropriate to the philosophy of science in an idiom inherited from a previous metaphysical age. Descartes's meditations upon the immediacies of mathematical knowledge owe much to the speculations of St. Augustine. The revival of atomism in Galileo and Hobbes is a reversion to Democritus.

But the mediaeval and the Greek sources of seventeenth-century philosophy are not the chief point. What is important is that the overwhelming successes of seventeenth-century science bequeathed to its philosophical successors the unsolved problems of the foundations of mathematics and of observational science. Implicit in Descartes and Leibniz is a concern to establish the axioms of mathematics and the principles of deductive inference. Implicit in Bacon and Locke is the enterprise of placing beyond question the empirical procedures of experimental science through a really convincing justification of the principle of induction.

The seventeenth century held that the axioms of mathematics were not discontinuous either with the constitution of the human mind or with the purposes and intentions of the divine agency. It believed, too, that the justification of induction required some real connections in nature, a form of quasi-necessity between the immediate occasion of experience and the past from which it sprang and the future to which it was linked. It believed this (with Eliot):

> Because the past is irremediable,
> Because the future can only be built
> Upon the real past. . . .

The moral is clear for both of the areas of science. The prediction of a particular future from the known characteristics of a particular past is one strand in a matrix of connectedness. The future can be "built" upon the past because nature possesses an antecedent structure. The ultimate justification of induction is therefore simply the rational perception of the order of nature. The justification of mathematical axioms and deductive inference is similarly grounded. For these are implicit in the structure of mind, and from Leibniz to Berkeley the faith is unwavering that a pre-established harmony divinely given guarantees the adequacy of mathematical conceptions in ordering the sense-perceptions upon which observation rests.

The philosophy of the seventeenth century is scientific. It wrestles with the ultimate clarification of induction and deduction. But it insists that both induction and deduction presuppose metaphysics, and it therefore rests upon an antecedent rationalism. The philosophy of the seventeenth century is scientific, but it is not positivism.

The philosophic tradition from Descartes to Kant is an analysis of the origin, extent, and validity of human knowledge. This analysis was made necessary by the novelties of Renaissance science. It is therefore far more critical than speculative, and its conclusions are dictated far less by a cosmological hunger than by an inner necessity to construct an epistemology adequate to the going concern of Newtonian physics. That it should thereupon separate into two divergent streams, the rationalism of Descartes, Spinoza, and Leibniz and the empiricism of Bacon, Locke, Berkeley, and Hume is no accident. Rational propositions and empirical propositions are both components of the structure of a general science, and they attest to the equal fruitfulness of mathematical and observational method. Moreover there is during this period a natural relationship between scientific training and epistemological bias. Bacon is a naturalist who makes crude physical and biological experiments. Locke is trained as a physician. On the other hand Descartes and Leibniz are among the greatest mathematicians of the age.

But if rationalists minimize the importance of sensory data and turn away from the images of corporeal things, while empiricists deny primacy to innate ideas and the axioms of mathematics, this is a difference of emphasis, not a contradiction. The empiricist account of mathematics may be weak, and the rationalist interest in sense perception may be wavering and half-hearted, but both (being conversant with science) acknowledge that there are truths of reason and that they differ from truths of fact. Leibniz distinguishes between "necessary" and "contingent" truths—between essential propositions whose certainty hinges upon the meaning of their terms and whose opposites are contradictory, and existential propositions not capable of strict demonstration but true of what actually exists at a certain time.[1] Hume similarly divides all propositions into those which, in his words, concern "relations of ideas" and those which relate to "matters of fact." From this distinction, the essential frame of reference of seventeenth and eighteenth-century thought, contemporary positivism derives its program.

But Hume goes further. Rationalists and empiricists both would have admitted that the classification of propositions into necessary and contingent, the *a priori* statements of logic and pure mathematics as opposed to those concerning perceptual matters of fact (or, in the post-Kantian terminology, *analytic* and *synthetic*), was mutually exclusive. It remained for Hume to assert that from the standpoint of reliable knowledge and firmly grounded meaning, the classification was mutually exhaustive as well. His *Enquiry Concerning Human Understanding* concludes with the famous and prophetic words:

If we take in hand any volume of divinity or school metaphysics, for instance; let us ask, *Does it contain any abstract reasoning concerning quantity?* No. *Does it contain any experimental reasoning concerning matter of fact and existence?* No. Commit it then to the flames: for it can contain nothing but sophistry and illusion.

From the distinction between analytic and synthetic judgments contemporary positivism derives its program. But from Hume's contraction of the area of significant discourse it derives its most passionate and its most controversial principle—a demand for the elimination of metaphysics.

No merely rhetorical appeal of Hume's would have done the trick. The development of the rationalistic, metaphysically oriented philosophy of science of the seventeenth century into the fully mature positivism of Schlick and Reichenbach, of the later Russell and Carnap, is the consequence of two acts of radical criticism in philosophy and in mathematics. The first was Hume's own attack upon a rational theory of causal inference. The second was the implicit denial of "a natural geometry of the human mind" through the discovery of non-Euclidean geometry by Riemann, Lobachevski, and Gauss in the first half of the nineteenth century.

The metaphysical theory of causality assumes that inductive generalization is possible because there is an order of nature expressing real relations which hold between the real things which compose the natural world. Such identities of pattern as disclose themselves in these mutual relations are the laws of nature, and from these uniformities or necessary connections we are entitled to our trust in inductive inference.[2] But Hume shifted the locus of his analysis from the necessary connections of things to the connection of ideas in the mind. He finds that although between such ideas there is "constant conjunction" there is no necessary connection, and that constant conjunction itself is a habit of belief and not a necessity imposed by the texture of nature's connectedness. Thus originates the positivistic doctrine of scientific "explanation." Laws of nature are the observed identities of pattern disclosed in the course of a series of comparative observations, but the pattern is a mere *description* wholly uninterpreted and without metaphysical implication. The doctrine is attractively simple, and it gives to scientific methodology imperatives admirable in their clarity: "Keep to things observed" and "Aim at descriptive simplicity." But it leaves induction suspended in mid-air, cut off from its roots in the natural world.

As Hume's critique of causality prepared the positivistic account of scientific method, so the work of Gauss and Reimann began the positivistic revaluation of mathematics and formal logic. Until the discovery of non-Euclidean geometry, geometry was universally assumed to be the science of existent space, with the implication that the axioms applicable to space are in some sense given *a priori*. But if there are a plurality of abstract geometries, then they must be viewed as a branch of pure mathematics which deals merely with types of relations. Each system of geometry is then investigated, not to determine if its axioms are true but for its internal consistency as a deductive system. To recognize that the relation between axioms and theorems is merely analytic, and that axioms have metaphysically only the status of postulates, is to suggest that even the principles of formal logic themselves are rules of procedure rather than general descriptions of fact. The principles of deductive inference can no longer be regarded as the ultimate *a priori* axioms of logic, intuitively apprehended by reason because they are the natural furniture of the human mind. Logical forms are postulational, that is, assumptions chosen for their fruitfulness, and their systematic arrangement depends upon criteria of clarity and elegance and not of congruence with actuality.

All this leads straight in the direction of the great *Principia Mathematica* of Russell and Whitehead, one of the sacred texts of modern positivism. And it leads directly away from that metaphysical rationalism which grounds logic in the science of *being* and which is prone to interpret it as itself descriptive of some general properties of the world.

The ultimate consequence of Hume's theory of causality and the discovery of non-Euclidean geometry is the rampantly anti-metaphysical bias of the scientific philosophy of contemporary positivism. This bias is all-pervasive, even axiomatic, and it leads on the one hand to the dream of a "logic without ontology" and on the other to the fantasy of "scientific method without metaphysical presuppositions."[3]

Ernest Nagel, a characteristic representative of the first position, specifically dissents both from the Aristotelian view that the axioms of logic are rooted in the nature of being and from the more formalistic position of Leibniz, whose ontological interpretation of logical principles requires the conception of logical relations as the invariants of all possible worlds. Denying that logical validity is grounded in natural fact and that the laws of logic need be considered as either similar in form or identical with certain structural and functional invariants of nature, Nagel calls rather for the examination of logical formulae as they function in specific contexts. He leans heavily toward the syntactical interpretation put forward by Carnap, that logical principles always occur within a system of symbols and operations and are therefore to be judged according to the complicated uses to which they are subject. Within such a context logical principles are obviously less *descriptive* of the structure of the world than *prescriptive* for the use of scientific language.

No one seriously doubts [says Nagel[4]] that logic and mathematics are used in specific contexts in identifiable ways, however difficult it may be to ascertain those ways in any detail. Does it not therefore seem reasonable to attempt to understand the significance of logico-mathematical concepts and principles in terms of the operations associated with them in those contexts, and to reject interpretations of their "ultimate meaning" which appear gratuitous and irrelevant in the light of such an analysis?

To account for logic and mathematics within the context of syntactical operations (that is, as merely the manipulation of symbols) is a strategy common to both contemporary positivism and contemporary pragmatism. To reject all interpretation of philosophical concepts in the light of their ultimate meaning is the heritage of positivism alone.

Herbert Feigl is a characteristic representative of the second position, for he contends "that there are no philosophical postulates of science, i.e., that the scientific method can be explicated and justified without metaphysical presuppositions about the order or structure of nature." He supports this contention with an argument analogous to that which Nagel uses to account for the structures of formal logic. This is to the effect that the invariant character of the basic rules of scientific method hinges entirely upon the aims of scientific inquiry. The consequence is, not precisely that the principle of the uniformity of nature is abandoned, but that it is assimilated in non-metaphysical terms. (Carnap absorbs it in a definition of inductive probability; Kneale sees it as a feature of the "policy" of induction; Reichenbach formulates it as "a rule of procedure.") Feigl's own position is stated thus:[5]

The principle of induction when interpreted as a rule of procedure, and not as a postulate regarding the order of nature, is of course not subject to confirmation or disconfirmation. Its adoption depends merely on our purpose: to discover and generalize, tentatively and self-correctively, whatever type or degree of uniformity the accumulating observational evidence suggests. It was perhaps the dim recognition of the implicit functioning of this most basic rule of all empirical knowledge that led so many philosophers to mistake it for a genuinely synthetic truth concerning the universe that could be known on the basis of pure reason.

There is something appealing, something disarmingly reasonable, and yet something shockingly infirm about this conventionalism and contextualism in the principles of logic and scientific method. To interpret the principle of contradiction as a prescription for the use of language and the principle of probable inference merely as a rule of procedure for drawing up laboratory reports is to suggest an almost unbridgeable gap between an ordering interest of the mind and an extensive continuum which exists independently of it. It comes perilously close to propounding the paradox of a natural science which is at the same time *not* a science of Nature.

If a philosopher of science of the seventeenth century should return today to inspect the work of Carnap or Reichenbach he would experience a profound sense of alienation and of insubstantiality. It would be the same if Mozart should return to inspect the work of Webern or Schoenberg. Gone are the old anchorages of tonality, the old dynamic laws of tonic to dominant to tonic; instead there are the shifting sands of the equipotentiality of the twelve tones of the chromatic scale, and a method of composition perhaps self-conscious and surely artificial. For contemporary positivism has abandoned the solid anchorage of Nature and has increasingly turned to the artificiality of purely logical construction.

I have dwelt upon the contrast between the seventeenth century and the contemporary point of view because I wished to show the gradual preparation necessary for the maturation of a new and indeed a radical stance in the history of philosophy. What is particularly important here is not merely the shift in the content of philosophic doctrines which characterizes any age, but the profound alteration in the interpretation of the role which must be played by philosophy itself. We face not simply a difference in belief but a transformation of attitude deeply grounded in conviction and feeling. Behind the cool and lucid exposition of positivistic method lies a passion for logic and a rage for order and clarification. It was Ludwig Wittgenstein who in his *Tractatus Logico-Philosophicus* of 1921 first provided the program for the modern movement:[6]

> The object of philosophy is the logical clarification of thoughts.
> Philosophy is not a theory but an activity.
> A philosophical work consists essentially of elucidations.
> The result of philosophy is not a number of "philosophical propositions," but to make propositions clear.
> Philosophy should make clear and delimit sharply the thoughts which otherwise are, as it were, opaque and blurred.

But it is Hans Reichenbach who understands that what this demands is not simply a new technique, but a rigid intellectual self-discipline and a stern check upon the ever-present dangers of metaphysical self-indulgence. "What is required," he says, "for a scientific philosophy is a reorientation of philosophic desires." The new logical empiricism has therefore not merely a politics, but also a "morality," and its categorical imperative demands the most absolute suppression of the metaphysical impulse and its consequence—speculative licentiousness.

Logical empiricism also has a theory of the history of philosophy (not unconnected with its morality). Reichenbach has presented it in the preface of his *The Rise of Scientific Philosophy*:[7]

Philosophy is regarded by many as inseparable from speculation. They believe that the philosopher cannot use methods which establish knowledge, be it knowledge of facts or of logical relations; that he must speak a language which is not accessible to verification—in short, that philosophy is not a science. The present book is intended to establish the contrary thesis. It maintains that philosophic speculation is a passing stage, occurring when philosophic problems are raised at a time which does not possess the logical means to solve them. It claims that there is, and always has been, a scientific approach to philosophy. And it wishes to show that from this ground has sprung a scientific philosophy which, in the science of our time, has found the tools to solve those problems that in earlier times have been the subject of guesswork only. To put it briefly: this book is written with the intention of showing that philosophy has proceeded from speculation to science.

Now this is only an appropriation of the optimistic positivism of the nineteenth century, when Auguste Comte asserted that human thought begins with religious naïveté, proceeds to metaphysical abstraction, and finally arrives at scientific accuracy. It permits a reading of the intellectual history of the West which conforms to this "law of the three stages:" first mediaeval philosophy as the handmaiden of theology; then modern philosophy as an intermediate stage facing the problems of Renaissance science with the primitive tools inherited from the Middle Ages; finally contemporary logical analysis with the glossy instruments of an established relational logic, a mature axiomatic theory, a sophisticated syntactics, and a modernized postulational theory of induction—indeed a fit ancillary to science itself in the age of quantum theory and an advanced nuclear physics.

But there is an alternative interpretation of the same facts of intellectual history. Whitehead has distinguished between "speculation" and "scholarship," which alternate in historical periods and which distinguish the metaphysical brilliance of post-Periclean Athens from the technical proficiency and scientific specialization of Hellenistic Alexandria.[8] Spengler, deeply moved as we have seen by the example of the downfall of the classical culture, has erected the polarity of the "cultural" springtime and the winter of "civilization" into an ultimate principle of historical interpretation. According to him it is the hard cold facts of a *late* life with which our epoch has to reckon. Ours is an Alexandrian age: cosmopolitan, imperialistic, *technical*. The engineer supplants the poet, the physicist supplants the craftsman, and epistemology itself becomes a branch of technics. This does not deny the fact of the rise of a scientific philosophy as cited by Reichenbach, or his demonstration of the movement of philosophy from speculation to science, but it gives to these facts and to this demonstration an ironic twist. It suggests that if Thomas Aquinas and Duns Scotus are the philosophers of our Western springtime, Descartes and Leibniz of our philosophical summer, Kant and Hegel of the great terminal systems of our autumn, then Wittgenstein and Carnap are the dry and leafless trunks of our wintry conclusion.

I have not meant to urge either the optimistic or the pessimistic view of contemporary positivism, for it is a vexatious point, and hinges too closely upon ultimate philosophic commitments to make the pretense of a settlement by empirical evidence. But I think it is true that philosophy in our time has passed largely into the hands of the technicians, and that this drying up of speculation at its source has had a certain inhibiting effect. I think also that this is recognized, perhaps sometimes a little wistfully, even by those who are most in sympathy with the positivistic direction.

One of the most brilliant minds of the last generation was that of Frank Plumpton Ramsey, a follower and critic of Russell and Wittgenstein, who died in 1929 at the age of twenty-six. His collected papers up to that time have been published under the title *The Foundations of Mathematics*. They deal with such formidable matters as a critique of the logical methods of Frege, Russell, and Whitehead and of Wittgenstein's *Tractatus*. But tucked away at the end is a wholly non-technical and very revealing essay. Ramsey had been invited to give a paper to a philosophical discussion club at Cambridge. He ended quixotically with a dissertation on the thesis that there is really no philosophic subject which is suitable for discussion. As he puts it:[9]

I conclude that there is really nothing to discuss; and this conclusion corresponds to a feeling I have about ordinary conversation also. It is a relatively new phenomenon, which has arisen from two causes which have operated gradually through the nineteenth century. One is the advance of science, the other the decay of religion; which have resulted in all the old general questions becoming either technical or ridiculous. This process in the development of civilization we have each of us to repeat in ourselves.

The development of civilization to which Ramsey refers, the decay of religion and the advance of science, has produced the positivistic avalanche. It has supplanted the philosophies of human concern, the *Lebensphilosophie* of the nineteenth century, with methodological considerations as rigorous and as earnest as those of Kant. It is these methodological considerations, impossible to ignore, although surely not established beyond question, which have provided all the old general questions with the unhappy option of becoming "either technical or ridiculous." To the genesis of these methodological considerations and the curiously constricted *Weltanschauung* to which they give rise I should now like to turn.

Contemporary positivism (*logical positivism* as it was originally called, or *logical empiricism* as its adherents now seem to prefer) originated in two great centers of European culture, Cambridge University and the University of Vienna. Cambridge contributed an astonishingly rigorous new logical method. Vienna contributed a resolute impulse to review the philosophical problems of the natural sciences in such a fashion that the empirical foundations of physical science should be made explicit and that philosophy should be made scientific. Out of the marriage between the two logical empiricism was born.

The time was the first three decades of the century. In 1903 Bertrand Russell produced a pioneer work, *The Principles of Mathematics*, which attempted to show how all pure mathematics might be reduced to formal logic. The program here envisaged was explicitly carried out in the three volumes of *Principia Mathematica*, which he produced in collaboration with Whitehead between 1910 and 1913. The essence of this work is an effort to demonstrate how the concept of natural numbers, the theory of manifolds, and notions like continuity and derivation can be strictly deduced from a handful of primitive notions and about the same number of logical axioms. But the special significance of *Principia Mathematica* for positivism lay in its logic of propositions: the theory of logical types originated by Russell, the logical division of all statements into true, false, and meaningless, and the distinction between atomic and molecular propositions—particularly that class of the latter termed "truth-functions," whose truth value depends not upon the meaning of the statements which compose them, but upon their formal properties as conditionals, negations, conjunctions, or disjunctions.

Ten years later came the remarkable *Tractatus Logico-philosophicus* of Wittgenstein. Wittgenstein had been a pupil of Russell's at Cambridge before the first World War, but he returned to Austria, where the *Tractatus* was published in 1921. This work deeply impressed Moritz Schlick and the entire Vienna Circle, and although Wittgenstein returned to Cambridge in the middle twenties, and occupied G. E. Moore's chair in philosophy after the latter retired in 1939, it is difficult to say whether his influence was more profoundly felt in Cambridge or Vienna. Indeed, Wittgenstein is one of those protean figures who transcends place and doctrinal classification. He has contributed largely both to logical empiricism and to "the philosophy of ordinary language," and if I have chosen to treat him primarily as the ally of G. E. Moore in instituting the latter, it is not without recognition of his services to the former. Here the position which he represents is almost identical in import with that of Bertrand Russell.

What Wittgenstein contributes to positivism is a sense of the profound importance of the problem of intelligibility for any critique of knowledge or of science; an intimation of the way in which an understanding of the logic of language is essential for an exposition of scientific method; and the suggestion that perhaps after all philosophy is fundamentally a critique of language. In effect this is largely to reinforce the logistic argument of *Principia Mathematica*. For such "semantic" investigations show us that the propositions of logic are tautologies, that equally important with considerations of "sense" and empirical meaning are the prescriptions of our rules of symbolic manipulation, and that therefore "if we know the logical syntax of any sign language, then all the propositions of logic are already given."[10] If logical empiricism derives its logic from Cambridge and its empiricism from Vienna, it derives its syntactical dimension from Wittgenstein, the child of both.

Meanwhile there was the "Vienna Circle,"[11] which originated in 1923 in a seminar given by Moritz Schlick at the University of Vienna, and developed many of the views which Schlick had already advanced in his *Allgemeine Erkenntnislehre* of 1918. Its great period began in 1926 when Carnap joined the faculty of the university. During that year the Circle studied both Wittgenstein's *Tractatus* and Carnap's *Der logische Aufbau der Welt*. The publication of its manifesto of 1929, *Wissenschaftliche Weltauffassung: Der Wiener Kreis* marked its self-consciousness as a philosophical movement, and the appearance a year later of its periodical, *Erkenntnis*, under the joint editorship of Reichenbach and Carnap announced this solidarity to the world. Although Carnap left for Prague in the same year, discussions in the Vienna Circle continued until the tragic death of Schlick in 1936. After the fall of Austria in 1938, the remaining members of the group scattered to the four corners of the globe.

I have suggested that contemporary positivism originated in Cambridge and Vienna, and that the impulses which fed this development stemmed from Hume and from non-Euclidean geometry. But in each case this is to omit a crucial connecting link. Between non-Euclidean geometry and *Principia Mathematica* lies the work of Gottlieb Frege; and between Hume and the Vienna Circle lies the work of Ernst Mach.

Frege's work grew out of an attempt to make sense out of the concept of a natural number. He did this by means of a demonstration that the concept is derivable from logical axioms through a series of logical operations. The details (such as the symbolic formulation of a theory of order and the presentation of a set of axioms for a restricted calculus of propositional functions) need not concern us here. What is important is the conclusion which Frege himself states, for example at the end of his brief but now profoundly influential *Die Grundlagen der Arithmetik*:[12] "I hope I may claim in the present work to have made it probable that the laws of arithmetic are analytic judgments and consequently a priori. Arithmetic thus becomes simply a development of logic, and every proposition of arithmetic a law of logic, albeit a derivative one. To apply arithmetic to the physical sciences is to bring logic to bear on observed facts; calculation becomes deduction." In Frege lies the germ of *Principia Mathematica*, that is to say, the formalization of the principles of logic and particularly of the logic of relations which will become the ultimate source of the methodology of logical empiricism.

Frege was a mathematician; Mach was a physicist and philosopher who taught the theory of the natural sciences at the University of Vienna until his retirement around the turn of the century. His importance is that he combined an expert knowledge of late nineteenth-century science with the kind of reductionistic empiricism which informs the more primitive labors of Locke, Berkeley, and Hume. His purpose is to purify science of all metaphysical concepts or unobservable entities, and if, in the end, he finds is necessary to retain "substantives" for their pragmatic value, he does so without seriously compromising his own commitment to the primacy of complexes of sensory atoms and their spatio-temporal relationships. His important *The Analysis of Sensations (and the Relation of the Physical to the Mental)*, with its revealing "Preliminary Anti-metaphysical Remarks,"[13] presents the details of his reduction. The data of physical science are not "things" but more or less stable complexes of qualities which are identical with our sensations, and it is these elements out of which organized scientific knowledge is constructed. Natural laws are therefore simply a formulation of the functional relationships between these sensory elements in a variety of contexts. There is no denial here that the language of physics does require certain concepts like "vectors of forces," "ionization," or "wave movements;" the only requirement is that these technical concepts should in the end be reducible to the language of elementary sensation, to experiences like "blue," "moving," "there."

Mach is a relentless empiricist; for him, as for all those within the tradition of Hume, the function of science is to describe and predict the observable relations between phenomena. With his reiteration that sensations alone are the "given" elements, the "matter" of knowledge, he has provided the problem of conceptual analysis which science at every stage of its progress must undertake anew. It was in the spirit of Mach that Einstein began the re-examination of time which produced the theory of relativity, that Broad undertook to examine the sensational and perceptual basis of the concepts of relativity physics, and that Reichenbach attempted to account for those "unobservable entities" which the newer quantum mechanics presupposes. And when Russell in Part II of the *Analysis of Matter* exhibits the relation between physics and perception or in Lecture IV of *Our Knowledge of the External World* shows the transitional logical operations necessary to pass from the world of physics to the world of sense, or when Carnap in *Der Logische Aufbau der Welt* attempts to show even more systematically how all the objects of perception and the secondary concepts of science may be derived by forming logical constructions out of elementary experiences, we feel ever more clearly the distinctive preoccupation of the positivism of today: the attempt to solve Mach's problem with the aid of a logical method which derives from Frege.

Logical empiricism is one of the most powerful influences in contemporary philosophy. As in the case of any philosophical school, the earlier period of fiery partisanship with its quest for doctrinal unity has given way to a diffusion of belief and a constant effort toward the purification of fundamentals. At first the Vienna Circle, like the Freudian circle, seemed to present a united front, or rather a united affront to the outside world. To a proper and half-unaware society Freudianism was an outrage, and to an academic community steeped in the atmosphere of *fin-de-siècle* idealistic metaphysics logical positivism was a scandal. The society and the academic community were not slow to counterattack, and this, together with the removal of both groups from Vienna, meant that an original raw simplicity of doctrine gave way to various forms of revisionism.[14] Today among the logical empiricists there are probably as many slightly different formulations of the famous "principle of verifiability" as among the followers of Freud there are slightly divergent interpretations of the significance of the Oedipus complex.[15] This makes it somewhat difficult to present an authentic account of either position, but it remains true, I think, that their essential features are obvious.

The essence of the philosophical revolution which logical empiricism has accomplished lies in its assertion of six doctrinal theses. They are not perhaps all on the same level of generality or importance, nor will they be formulated identically by all the chief adherents of this school.

It is even possible that one or another of them may be repudiated as belonging to an earlier period of development. But in the general philosophic community they represent the center of the insights, and also of the challenges, which contemporary positivism contributes to thought in the modern world.

1. *The function of philosophy is logical analysis.* It is no longer appropriate that the philosopher should search for first principles of reason, form judgments about the validity of our moral beliefs, or attempt the construction of a system of speculative truths. Instead the function of philosophy is wholly critical. It should analyze all pretensions to knowledge so as to clarify the meaning of terms and the logical relationships between ideas. In the end this will mean that philosophy has become the logical analysis of science through the syntactical analysis of scientific language.

2. *All cognitively significant (meaningful) discourse is divisible without remainder into analytic or synthetic propositions.* This thesis permits a crucial distinction between (1) the formal sentences of logic and pure mathematics, which produce propositions that are "necessary" or "certain" and cannot be refuted by experience but formulate our decision to use symbols in a certain fashion whether as stipulated definitions, designation rules, or syntactical commitments, and (2) the factual sciences, where propositions may be judged probably true or probably false according to a principle of verifiability.

3. *Any proposition that purports to be factual or empirical has meaning only if it is possible in principle to describe a method for its verification.* This is closely related to the "operationalism" of the Einstein revolution, to the belief that the meaningfulness of concepts is established by the observational procedures which support them. The criterion of actual testability was progressively softened to that of the logical possibility of verification. And since empirical statements can be confirmed or disconfirmed only probably, the notion of degree of confirmation has supplanted that of verifiability. Factual meaningfulness thus depends upon the possible utilization of a method which could yield confirming or disconfirming empirical evidence.

4. *All metaphysical assertions, being neither analytic nor synthetic propositions, are meaningless.* Metaphysical assertions are not synthetic since there is no empirical method for determining their truth. Nor are they postulated rules of syntax or stipulated definitions. As nonempirical propositions with supposed existential import they are "pseudo-propositions." This may be indicated by showing that they are not

reducible to elementary propositions verifiable in experience, and that they have been produced by errors in logical syntax.

5. *There is a single language for all science; it is similar in form to the language of physics, and all synthetic propositions are reducible to elementary experiences expressible in this language.* Any empirical science should rest on a base of sensory perception and should be intersubjectively verifiable. To meet these requirements and to unify the various special sciences requires the formation of a universal language of science in which propositions from the most various sciences might be combined in a single body. Such a language would be a thing-language consisting of definite quantity-quality descriptions for definite space-time values.

6. *All normative assertions, whether positing moral, aesthetic, or religious values, are scientifically unverifiable, and are therefore to be classified as forms of non-cognitive discourse.* Normative judgments, being neither tautologies nor factually testable, cannot be said to have validity as logical or informative modes of speech. An analysis of such statements will always reveal them to be either sociological descriptions of moral phenomena, psychological descriptions of moral beliefs, emotion-laden expressions of moral sentiment, or imperative statements seeking to compel activity. From this it follows that no value assertion can possibly be judged as true.

Philosophy as logical analysis, analytic and synthetic propositions, the principle of verifiability, the elimination of metaphysics, radical physicalism and the unity of science, and the non-cognitive character of value judgments: these are the heart of logical empiricism, and while it might be of value to pursue each systematically, I should prefer in what follows to present two case studies in positivism rather than to deal with theses and problems as such. For basic philosophic solutions are the product of individual men. Contemporary positivism numbers many able adherents, but two philosophers of genius display the originality of the positivistic temper at its best. I refer to Bertrand Russell and Rudolph Carnap.

Russell represents Cambridge, and no one has done more than he toward the formalization of logic and mathematics. Carnap represents Vienna, and no one has contributed more to the logic of empirical knowledge. But Russell has had a lifelong interest in sense data and the mechanisms of perception, and Carnap's interest in logical syntax is legendary. All logical empiricists are interested in three basic themes: logic, perceptions, and language. One might say that Russell begins with logic, turns to perception, and ends with language, while Carnap begins with perception, turns to language, and ends with logic.[16] Russell writes with a dash and brilliance that are almost breath-taking. Carnap is admirable in a different way. He is painstaking, thorough, exact, and his clarity, not intuitive like Russell's, is a victory, not a gift.

In the sections which follow I shall briefly treat (1) the positivism of Russell, (2) the contribution of Carnap, and (3) the peculiar problem of the positivistic theory of value.

2. BERTRAND RUSSELL: A FOUNDER

Without Russell's early book, *The Principles of Mathematics*, and the great *Principia Mathematica* which he wrote in collaboration with Whitehead, modern logical empiricism would not have been possible. For Russell is responsible for a series of technical innovations in the formalization of logic and mathematics which have had widespread and productive consequences. Among these are the discovery of propositional functions, the invention of the theory of types, the introduction of the theory of descriptions, and by no means least, the invention of a symbolism for the expression of the logic of relations, of an extensional logic of material implication, and of a logical definition of cardinal numbers.[17] The discovery of propositional functions makes clear certain truths about quantification generally obscured by the ambiguities of ordinary language. The theory of types indicates how a language system, in order to be workable and free of internal contradiction, must be governed by certain syntactical rules (one might even say that the more semantical theories of Carnap and Tarski distinguishing different language levels are a continuation of Russell's strictly logical discovery). The theory of descriptions, by equating the reference of definite descriptions and proper names, illuminates the nature of elementary propositions and the existential import of propositions in general.

The technical contributions to formal logic are impressive, but they are not the chief contributions which Russell has made to the positivistic tradition. These come, I think, rather in his conception of what philosophy is, of the kind of business in which the philosopher ought to engage, and in his own brilliant engagements in this kind of business. In his writing all purely formalistic interests are somehow qualified by what he calls "that feeling for reality which ought to be preserved even in the most abstract studies." Russell's passion for logic, his involvement with structure, his fanatical struggle for formalization are accompanied by some sixth sense that is always concentrated on empirical matter of fact. Hence his logic is never quite a logic without ontology (not quite mere conventionalism), and he remains well within the tradition of

Locke and Hume. In insisting that confusions about unreal entities originate in confusions about groups of symbols which have no significance
(one of the major consequences of his theory of descriptions), he makes
this clear:[18]

The sense of reality is vital in logic, and whoever juggles with it by pretend-
ing that Hamlet has another kind of reality is doing a disservice to thought.
A robust sense of reality is very necessary in framing a correct analysis of
propositions about unicorns, golden mountains, round squares, and other
such pseudo-objects. . . . Logic, I should maintain, must no more admit a
unicorn than zoology can; for logic is concerned with the real world just as
truly as zoology, although with its more abstract and general features.

To say that logic is concerned with the real world just as truly as
zoology seems to deny, or at least to obscure, the crucial distinction
between analytic and synthetic propositions upon which logical positivism insists, and to find revealed in formal logic the "more abstract and
general features" of the world seems to be a recurrence to that type
of seventeenth-century metaphysical interpretation of mathematics illustrated in Descartes, Leibniz, and Newton. Indeed, this is one of the
characteristics of the doctrine of "logical atomism" which Russell has
made famous, and to which both he and Wittgenstein adhered in the
period immediately following the first World War.[19] Despite the anti-
metaphysical bias found in sections of Wittgenstein's *Tractatus,* logical
atomism is less an attack on metaphysics than an attempt to supply
a metaphysics that is adequate to the newer formulations of relational
logic and to the theory of language which the analysis of descriptions
seemed to imply.

Logical atomism is, in fact, a metaphysics founded upon logic: it is
a description of what follows if the universe has a structure identical or
at least similar in form to that of *Principia Mathematica. Principia
Mathematica* develops in an elegant symbolic language (artificial but
lucid and unambiguous as compared with the misleading natural languages) a compact deductive system in which principles and secondary
propositions are derived from a few primitive notions.

These primitive notions are the irreducible surd and the not further
referrable primes from which the total system is serially constructed.
But when Russell deals with such "atoms" metaphysically, he is not
unwilling to include elements which are sensory as well as strictly logical.

The reason [he says[20]] why I call my doctrine *logical* atomism is because
the atoms that I wish to arrive at as the sort of last residue in analysis are
logical atoms and not physical atoms. Some of them will be what I call

'particulars'—such things as little patches of colour or sounds, momentary things—and some of them will be predicates or relations and so on. The point is that the atom I wish to arrive at is the atom of logical analysis, not the atom of physical analysis.

The important thing is that the logical atoms are represented by an exact symbolism comparable to that of *Principia Mathematica*. This means not merely (as it did likewise to Descartes and Leibniz) that what is complex and logically posterior will be composed of simples which are logically prior, but also that the exact symbolism in which these elements are expressed should approximate an "ideal language." And through such an ideal language Russell paradoxically expects to establish *a limited number* of propositions about the real world.

Behind this expectation is an uneasy awareness that throughout history the influence of natural language upon philosophy has been profound, almost unrecognized, and frequently disastrous. To repair these metaphysical disasters is the function of an ideal language:

The purpose of the foregoing discussion of an ideal logical language (which would of course be wholly useless for daily life) is twofold: first, to prevent inferences from the nature of language to the nature of the world, which are fallacious because they depend upon the logical defects of language; secondly, to suggest by inquiring what logic requires of a language which is to avoid contradiction, what sort of a structure we may reasonably suppose the world to have.[21]

With a later and more developed logical empiricism (say, that of Carnap) Russell shares the semanticist's mistrust of the logical inaccuracies of natural language. He seeks a logically perfect language having syntactical rules that prevent nonsense and giving to each symbol a logically definite and unique meaning, but he also hopes (with a faith far in excess of any that Carnap might have) that the elimination of internal inconsistency will in itself provide a clue to the structure of the world.

The metaphysical presupposition which underlies the doctrine of logical atomism is the simultaneous existence of two worlds: a world of logical discourse and a world of facts, with the implication that the function of the former is to "mirror" or "picture" the latter. Such mirroring is possible only because the two realms are structurally isomorphic. In the universe of fact there are hierarchies of organization which are matched by hierarchies in the universe of logical discourse; there are atomic facts which are matched by the atomic propositions which they render true, and there are molecular facts matched by the existence of molecular propositions. In the world of facts the atomic facts are conceived of as being either particulars having characteristics or the relations between two or more particulars. Particulars are in a certain sense the metaphysically privileged entities in the universe of facts, for they are self-subsistent; each stands alone without logical dependence upon any other particular. Particulars are defined as "the terms of the relations in atomic facts," and in the world of logical discourse particulars are designated by proper names.

It might seem as if this elevation of particulars were simply a reinterpretation of Aristotelian logic, but this is precisely what Russell wishes to guard against. He is careful to say that the real world consists not of mere particulars but of atomic facts. This implies not merely that relations are external to particulars, but that the *existence* of relations is no less secure than that of particulars. It is this anti-idealist insistence upon the real existence of relations and their crucial structural role in the real world which guarantees that the relational logic of *Principia Mathematica* shall correspond to the architecture of the universe.

In some respects Russell's logical atomism is similar to classical continental rationalism, for it begins with indubitable concepts and proceeds by deduction from them. Russell himself says:[22] "The things we have got to take as premises in any kind of work of analysis are the things which appear to *us* undeniable—to us here and now as we are —and I think on the whole that the sort of method adopted by Descartes is right: that you should set to work to doubt things and retain only what you cannot doubt because of its clearness and distinctness. . . ." Clearly and distinctly for Russell the world contains *facts*. It also contains *beliefs* whose linguistic expressions are *propositions*. A fact is the kind of thing that makes a proposition true or false. Facts belong to the objective world, and the truth of a proposition depends upon the adequacy with which it corresponds to reality.

The method of logical atomism is designed to reveal the "simples" of logical experience:[23]

One purpose that has run through all that I have said, has been the justification of analysis, i.e., the justification of logical atomism, of the view that you can get down in theory, if not in practice, to ultimate simples, out of which the world is built, and that those simples have a kind of reality not belonging to anything else. Simples, as I tried to explain, are of an infinite number of sorts. There are particulars and qualities and relations of various orders, a whole hierarchy of different sorts of simples, but all of them, if we were right, have in their various ways some kind of reality that does not belong to anything else. The only other sort of objects you come across in the world is what we call *facts*, and facts are the sort of things that are asserted or denied by propositions, and are not properly entities at all in the same sense in which their constituents are . . . although in another sense it is true that you cannot know the world unless you know the facts that make up the truths of the world; but the knowing of facts is a different sort of thing from the knowing of simples.

Logical atomism did not deny that the question of whether a given atomic proposition corresponds to a given atomic fact was a matter to be settled by extra-logical, empirical methods. It only hoped that the structural identity between verbal statement and concrete fact could be accomplished by the method of analysis. Its chief ingredients remain therefore a structural identity theory of ideal language, a correspondence theory of truth, and the method of reductive analysis.

Of these three, the last is undoubtedly of greatest significance both for Russell's philosophy as a whole and for its contribution to logical empiricism. Contemporary positivism, for all its commitment to the search for an ideal language, views the structural identity theory as a piece of illegitimate metaphysics, and a simple verification theory of truth seems much too rude and unworkable. But positivists agree with Russell in insisting that the proper method for philosophy is the method of logical analysis. It must be admitted, however, that on this point Russell is somewhat ambiguous. In the statement of his credo in *Contemporary British Philosophy* he was more precise. "The business of philosophy, as I conceive it," he said, "is essentially that of logical analysis, followed by logical synthesis." This is, of course, the classic method of Descartes: first an analysis which reduces complex propositions to simples, followed by the step-by-step reconstruction of complexes out of the simples isolated.[24] This is the only way to reconcile analytic method with the famous methodological maxim which also appears in the above credo: "Wherever possible, substitute constructions out of known entities for inferences to unknown entities."[25] The method of "construction out of known entities" is simply the obverse of analysis narrowly conceived, but is *a part of it* as a generalized method. It is the use of this method to establish the foundations of empirical knowledge which marks the transition of Russell's interest from formal logic to perception.

The principle that all "inferred" entities should be replaced by logical constructions had served Russell well in *Principia Mathematica*, for it had made possible the definition of classes, descriptions, and cardinal numbers. Also Whitehead had used it to construct points and instants out of sets of events with finite extent and duration. Why then should it not serve equally the interests of an ardent empiricism? Why should it not make possible a similar construction of material objects and the entities of physics? To this task *Our Knowledge of the External World* (1914) and much of *Mysticism and Logic* (1918) and *The Analysis of Matter* (1927) are devoted.

Logical atomism is a metaphysical doctrine which finds a correspondence between mathematical logic and the structure of the world. The construction of material objects and the entities of physics involves a reference to the knowing mind and hence to epistemology. If this construction is to be empirically reliable, it depends upon an anterior critique of the immediacy of sensory knowledge. This is somewhat summarily provided by Russell's famous distinction between "knowledge by acquaintance" and "knowledge by description."[26]

We shall say that we have *acquaintance* with anything of which we are directly aware, without the intermediary of any process of inference or any knowledge of truths. Thus in the presence of my table I am acquainted with the sense-data that make up the appearance of my table—its colour, shape, hardness, smoothness, etc.; all these are things of which I am immediately conscious when I am seeing and touching my table. . . .

My knowledge of the table as a physical object, on the contrary, is not direct knowledge. Such as it is, it is obtained through acquaintance with the sense-data that make up the appearance of the table. We have seen that it is possible, without absurdity, to doubt whether there is a table at all, whereas it is not possible to doubt the sense-data. My knowledge of the table is of the kind which we shall call "knowledge by description." The table is "the physical object which causes such-and-such sense-data." This describes the table by means of the sense-data.

In his formal analysis of descriptions Russell had concluded that "Every proposition which we can understand must be composed wholly of constituents with which we are acquainted." Now he generalizes the principle: "All our knowledge, both knowledge of things and knowledge of truths, rests upon acquaintance as its foundation."[27] By "acquaintance" Russell means a direct cognitive relation in which the knower is confronted by the presentational immediacy of his experience; the "object" of such experience is in its most obvious example "sense-data." We are acquainted not with the table as a physical object, but with the sense-data which that object "causes." We proceed from the sense-data to the object (from acquaintance to description), whether we are dealing with material objects or with the entities of physics. Despite Russell's methodological similarity to Descartes, he remains the heir of Locke, Berkeley, and Hume, for he wishes to show that whether we are dealing with material objects or with propositions concerning them, we can provide a reduction that ends in the sensory experience of the individual. The atomic facts are the facts of sense perception.

When, says Russell, we apply the logical-analytic method to one of the oldest problems of philosophy, the problem of our knowledge of the external world, our first result is a distinction between that in our common knowledge which is primitive and that which is derivative. Although the immediate facts perceived by sense are completely self-evident, yet because of the confusions of inference and interpretation, the discovery of what is really given by sense is full of difficulty. Reflection upon this kind of difficulty leads Russell to a somewhat vague distinction between what he calls "hard" data and "soft" data. "I mean by 'hard' data those which resist the solvent influence of critical reflection, and by 'soft' data those which, under the operation of this process, become to our minds more or less doubtful. The hardest of hard data are of two sorts: the particular facts of sense, and the general truths of logic."[28] Thus the positivistic distinction between analytic and synthetic propositions is paralleled by the distinction between two types of primitive data. If we confine ourselves to these hard data, what sort of world can be constructed by their means alone? The quality of spatial externality, for example, can be thus constructed (as Berkeley has shown) by the correlation of touch and sight sensations. Russell generalizes this association of sensations into a principle of scientific verification. "I think it may be laid down quite generally that, *in so far* as physics or common sense is verifiable, it must be capable of interpretation in terms of actual sense-data alone. The reason for this is simple. Verification consists always in the occurrence of an expected sense-datum."[29]

There is, in fact, a certain regularity or law-like character about the occurrence of sense-data, and the simplest interpretation of their connection is the construction or "logical fiction" of a "real object:" a quasi-permanent entity providing a series of possible sense-data of which only some represent actual perception. Statements about sensible objects may thus be replaced by statements about the *effects* of sensible objects, and the "reality" of objects becomes a function of the kind of connections between various sense-data which repeated experience has led us to regard as normal. This is, of course, phenomenalism with a vengeance.

But there is another way to approach the creation of objectivity. If we begin with radical subjectivism, and assume that each mind looks out upon the world from a point of view peculiarly its own, then we can construct a system consisting of all views of the universe, perceived and unperceived; this would be the system of total perspectives. Since it is frequently possible to establish a correlation by similarity between the entities in one perspective and many of those in another, when the similarity is very great, we speak of the two perspectives as near together in space. (The space in which they are near together is of course not the space inside either one of them. It is a *relation* between perspectives and is hence not perceived but inferred.) Moreover, between any two perceived perspectives which are similar it is possible to imagine a whole series even more similar, and in this way the space relating all possible perspectives can be rendered both continuous and three-dimensional. The construction of "permanent objects" follows the rule for a uniform space: correlation of minutely similar entities in different perspectives identifies the common-sense "thing." The thing is but the composite of its perspectives; its "aspects" are "real" (i.e., given as sense-data) but "it" is a mere logical construction.

It remains to explain precisely how the private space of a single perspective is located with reference to the single all-embracing perspective space. This requires an explanation of what is meant by the phrase "the place (in perspective space) where a thing is." The answer can almost be supplied in the exact language of projective geometry. A straight line represents the class of perspectives in which the object has the same geometric form. There are an infinite number of such straight lines representing the multiple types of perspective of the object. The point at which all of these lines intersect is "the place where the thing is." Thus perceptual place is a function of the intersection of perspectives, and the place where an object is located is the point where all perspectives meet. It is obvious that this resolution maintains the old distinction between subject and object, for the former refers to the perspective of which a given aspect of the thing is a member, while the latter refers to a plurality of aspects only one of which appears in any given perspective. Any aspect may therefore be classified in two ways with respect to space; we may distinguish the place *at* which, or the place *from* which the aspect appears. The virtue of this hypothetical construction is that it permits the reconciliation of the claims of physics and the claims of psychology. And it exemplifies that same "neutral monism" which Russell was later to develop out of the philosophical challenge of relativity and quantum theory.

In Russell's philosophy the acceptance of logical analysis is an ultimate methodological commitment. In the formalization of logic and mathematics it worked well. But with empirical subject-matter its powers are tried to the utmost. In the simple constructions of material objects as they appear to ordinary common sense this is not so evident, but in the area of mathematical physics we meet a crucial case. The revolution of Einstein and Planck challenged Russell as it did White-head for many reasons, but chiefly because its doctrine of time and gravitation and its theory of unobservable entities require a re-interpre-tation of the empirical point of view. This re-interpretation culminates in *The Analysis of Matter* with its doctrine of neutral monism and its causal theory of perception,[30] but neither of these additions seriously qualifies the need to employ the method of logical constructions. This method as applied to the entities of physics is exhibited even more purely in *Our Knowledge of the External World* and *Mysticism and Logic*.

The important essay, "The Relation of Sense-Data to Physics," in the latter states the problem:[31]

Physics is said to be an empirical science, based upon observation and experiment.

It is supposed to be verifiable, i.e., capable of calculating beforehand results subsequently confirmed by observation and experiment.

What can we learn by observation and experiment?

Nothing, so far as physics is concerned, except immediate data of sense: certain patches of colour, sounds, tastes, smells, etc., with certain spatio-temporal relations.

The supposed contents of the physical world are *prima facie* very different from these: molecules have no colour, atoms make no noise, electrons have no taste, and corpuscles do not even smell.

If such objects are to be verified, it must be solely through their relation to sense-data; they must have some kind of correlation with sense-data, and must be verifiable through their correlation *alone*.

But how is such correlation managed? Essentially for Russell by two devices. The first is actually to define the entities of physics as *functions* of sense-data. The second is to regard both *sensibilia* and sense-data (a *sensibile* becomes a sense-datum by entering into the relation of ac-quaintance) not as mental, but as part of the actual subject-matter of physics.

The application of the method of constructions has indicated that the "object" of common sense is identical with the entire class of its appearances. A complete application of the method of substituting con-structions for inferences in physics would involve three steps: (1) the construction of a single space, (2) the construction of a single time, and (3) the construction of "permanent" objects or "matter." The all-embracing perspective space which has been sketched for ordinary objects will do as well for the objects of physics. The device for the construction of time is similar. The primitive notions of "before" and "after" provide a means for defining a "biography" (a biography is everything earlier than or later than or simultaneous with a given "*sensibile*"); there exist a number of mutually exclusive biographies; and through the correlation of times in different biographies (according to relativity principles) a generalized concept of simultaneity may be established. Russell admits that there is no direct means of correlating the time in one biography with the time in another. In consequence any temporal grouping of the sense-data constituting "a given thing at a given moment" is largely conventional; its motive is to secure convenience in the formulation of causal laws.

The construction of "matter" offers difficulties which are not so apparent in the case of space and time, for the inferred entities of physics shift with the refinements of theory; thus the physics of rigid and permanent bodies was replaced by electromagnetic theory, which has, since Heisenberg and de Broglie, dissolved the atom into a system of wave motions or radiations originating at that point at which the atom was formerly supposed to be. Still, even with periodicity and field theory, the definition of points, instants, and particles retains a certain relevance. A physical entity may still be defined as "a certain series of appearances connected with each other by continuity and by certain causal laws." The things of physics are still *those series of aspects which obey the laws of physics.*[32]

If the world be conceived of as a multitude of "particulars" or "events" arranged in a certain pattern, then the arrangement or pattern is a sum of relations among particulars, and certain classes or series of events collected together "on account of some property which makes it convenient to be able to speak of them as wholes" are just those persistent particles of mathematical physics which Russell regards as the "logical constructions or symbolic fictions enabling us to express compendiously very complicated assemblages of facts." But to effect the logical construction of the persistent particle means for Russell simply to employ that method of "extensive abstraction" which had worked so well for Whitehead in the case of points and instants. An entity in physics fluctuates according to the context of its perceptual status, and perceptual status refers to such elementary notions as "near," "center," "distance," "far off." Thus a provisional definition becomes: "The *matter* of a given thing is the limit of its appearances as their distance from the thing diminishes."[33] Russell admits that this definition is far from satisfactory (because empirically there is no such limit to be obtained from sense-data), and he admits that it must be supplemented by further definitions and constructions, but it does throw light upon the relation of matter to sense-data and hence of the status of unobservable entities in physics. Our knowledge of matter empirically derived is always seriously limited by our inability to observe at very small distances, but we may make approximate inferences by means of the sense-data which are available, and our determination of hidden structure can sometimes be effected by means of elaborate dynamical inferences. But this, of course, is to admit a certain failure in the constructionist program for the materials of physics and perception.[34]

In the end Russell's analysis of empirical knowledge reduces on the one hand to the individual's momentary perceptual experience and on the other to the particulars or events which are the basic metaphysical entities upon which all constructions must be built. But there is never a systematic attempt to relate the two in such a way that a comprehensive derivation of all empirical knowledge might be attempted. This would have required a new *Principia Mathematica* with sense-data replacing logical concepts as primitives, and it is the recurrent dream of logical empiricism in it constructionist mood. Russell's piecemeal investigations of the relation of sense-data to physics and of the construction of material objects represent its initial phase. Carnap's *Der Logische Aufbau der Welt*, infinitely more systematic but still programmatic and incomplete, represents its second.

The development of Russell's thought is, as I have suggested, from formal logic to perceptions to the logic of language, but in this development it is the interest in perceptions that dominates. To the end Russell remains an epistemologist, and in *An Inquiry into Meaning and Truth* (1940), perhaps his last significant work, he brings to bear the resources of a semantic climate of opinion upon the eternal problems of empirical knowledge. Since in a perfected epistemology propositions are ordered in such a way that what comes later is known because of what comes earlier, special attention is devoted to "what comes earlier"—to those "basic propositions" which appear credible independently of argument and on the basis of immediate experience. But at the same time Russell explicitly denies that his enterprise is similar to that of Carnap's *The Logical Syntax of Language*, for empirical propositions are not linguistically validated, and the question of empirical truth is concerned with a relation between linguistic and non-linguistic events.[35] It is clear that

An Inquiry into Meaning and Truth is to be an enterprise in "semantics" rather than "syntactics."

Russell is concerned with such questions as: What is a word? What are the relations between sentences, syntax, and the parts of speech? When we use sentences describing experiences, how do we distinguish, for example, between "experiencing," "knowing," "noticing," "attending to," etc.? But the central apparatus which he employs is the insight that the words "true" and "false" as applied to the sentences of a given language always require another language of higher order for their definition. This conception of a hierarchy of languages, implied in Russell's own theory of types and suggested in his introduction to Wittgenstein's *Tractatus*, plays an important role in the work of Carnap and Tarski. In *An Inquiry into Meaning and Truth* its validity is assumed. The consequence is clear. In any hierarchy of languages there must be one of lowest type which would be the "primary language" or "object-language." Russell's first task therefore is to identify the primary or "object-words" of which such a language must wholly consist. They must obviously exclude such "logical words" as "and," "or," "some," "all," "not;" they must be capable of having meaning in isolation (without the context of a completed language structure); and, psychologically speaking, their meaning must first be indicated through ostensive definition, i.e., we must point out their intended objects: "This is a dog," etc.

A consideration of object-words leads naturally to a general classification of names, and here Russell distinguishes between ordinary proper names, denoting particular individuals,* and a special class of words such as "I," "you," "here," "this," "that," which have an egocentric definition. These latter, which Russell terms "egocentric particulars," have a special significance in the relation of raw perception to formulated knowledge, for, at the primitive level, they make the relation possible. But if in its primitive use every object-word has an implicit egocentricity, still Russell's theory of proper names provides that all knowledge stated by means of egocentric particulars can be stated also without employing them. This device obviates the inconvenient conclusion that since all empirical words are, strictly speaking, defined in terms of egocentric particulars, no intersubjective observational knowledge is possible.

The consideration of "object-words" leads naturally to the fundamental epistemological premises or "basic propositions" in which they

---

* Common nouns like dog and book do not strictly belong in an object language, since they denote classes, which we do not actually perceive. They are, however, derived from the object language.

are ingredients. Basic propositions for Russell are those propositions immediately caused by perceptual experience (which is the evidence for their truth), and of such a form that no two propositions having this form can be mutually contradictory if derived from different percepts. They are the equivalent of what the Vienna Circle called *Protokollsätze* (I am cold; this is blue), but to the assertion of positivists like Neurath or Hempel that no set of such propositions can be singled out as primitive epistemological premises for the remainder, Russell offers vigorous denial. Maintaining to the end a correspondence theory of truth and the particular kind of empiricism which it implies, he rejects any syntactical conception of truth which attempts to define truth as consistency within a closed system of self-contained propositions. Russell opposes both the attempt to show that any basic proposition is in the end adopted by a "decision," and the attempt to make the linguistic world self-sufficing.[36] His own contention is that the basic propositions are factual premises of our empirical knowledge; the reflection of that momentary perception which is the least questionable thing in our entire experience, and which is therefore "the criterion and touchstone of all other certainties."

In denying an extreme syntactical position, Russell is by no means abandoning the usefulness of linguistic analysis. What he wants to do is to use it in such a way as to make clear the "psychological" elements involved in any treatment of the significance of sentences and propositions. Here a distinction between alternative functions of language becomes crucially important. Russell recognizes that sentences are of three sorts—true, false, and nonsensical—and that in the case of the first two it is possible to construct rules of syntax which, given the meaning of the separate words (established by the perceptual experiences, real or imagined, which are their sufficient criterion of significance), shall insure that every combination of words which obeys the rules shall be significant. But he sees that "significance" is not a syntactical concept, but, on the contrary, belongs to a non-tautologous sentence in virtue of some relation that it has to certain states of the person using the sentence. This is to "psychologize" the logic of language.

Russell is aware that language is multivalent, that it serves three purposes: (1) to *indicate* facts, (2) to *express* the state of the speaker, (3) to *alter* the state of the hearer. Although this suggests that every proposition has both indicative and expressive aspects, Russell wishes to explore the relation between syntax and significance primarily from the point of view of indication:[37]

In the present section [says Russell] I propose to consider the possibility of constructing a logical language in which the psychological conditions of significance, considered in the previous section, are translated into precise syntactical rules.

Starting from a vocabulary derived from perception, and from sentences expressing judgments of perception, I shall give a definition of an assemblage of significant sentences defined by their syntactical relation to the initial vocabulary and to judgments of perception. When this assemblage has been defined, we can consider whether, in an adequate language, it can contain *all* significant sentences and no others.

The initial object-vocabulary consists of names, predicates, and relations, all having ostensive definitions. . . .

This is a program for a complete syntactical construction on empirical grounds, but unfortunately Russell never achieves its completion. After a brief discussion of the atomistic hierarchy of sentences—the assemblage of sentences obtained from atomic judgments of perception through the operations of substitution, combination, and generalization —he passes on to the last subject of his major concern: the relation of verifiability to meaning and truth.

The theory of truth to which Russell adheres makes the truth of "basic propositions" dependent upon their relation to perceptual experience, and the truth of other propositions dependent upon their syntactical relations to basic propositions. Similarly for "meaning," Russell takes seriously Hume's principle "no idea without an antecedent impression" for the definition of words in the object-language. But he goes further. Even "logical words" like those expressing negation or alteration must derive from actual experiences of rejection or of hesitation. The empiricism is comprehensive: "Thus no essential word in our vocabulary can have a meaning independent of experience. Indeed, any word that I can understand has a meaning derived from *my* experience."[38] With respect to the "verifiability theory of meaning" Russell's position is very close to Carnap's. Like Carnap he rejects Schlick's older formulation: *The meaning of a proposition is the method of its verification.* And like Carnap he rejects the notion of ineffable knowledge. But the thrust of his atomistic empiricism makes his starting-point somewhat different.[39]

Between the method that I advocate in theory of knowledge and that advocated by Carnap (in company with many others), there is a difference in starting-point which is very important and (I think) insufficiently realized. I start from sentences about particular occurrences, such as "this is red," "that is bright," "I now am hot." The evidence in favour of such a sentence is not other sentences, but a non-verbal occurrence. . . .

In the end this reduces to a difference concerning the primacy of merely syntactical considerations. Russell's passion for logic never completely dominates his inheritance from Hume—his sensory atomism—and, essentially good logical empiricist that he is,[40] when he criticizes other logical empiricists, it is chiefly on the ground that they are not empirical enough, that they are blinded by what he takes to be "verbalistic theories."

In the preface to *An Inquiry into Meaning and Truth* Russell had said:

As will be evident to the reader, I am, as regards method, more in sympathy with the logical positivists than with any other existing school. I differ from them, however, in attaching more importance than they do to the work of Berkeley and Hume. This book results from an attempt to combine a general outlook akin to Hume's with the methods that have grown out of modern logic.

The last sentence is surely ironic. For it is precisely the way in which more orthodox or more doctrinaire logical empiricists would describe their own efforts. For this reason, if for no other, although Russell might be reluctant to subscribe to all the classic theses of the positivistic position, and although his structuralist thesis suggests a metaphysics which Schlick or Reichenbach or Carnap would be unwilling to share, in the doctrinal battles of philosophy in the modern world they occupy a common ground.

3. RUDOLPH CARNAP: A CLASSIC

The logical empiricism of Russell is true to the British tradition in philosophy although it has been touched by his wit and purely personal bias. The logical empiricism of Rudolph Carnap is more continental, and at the same time more representative of an entire school which has become far-flung and widely proliferate. Russell's work is seminal. Carnap's is the fruit of organizational genius and a mature articulation. The relationship between them is for modern positivism almost precisely that of Bach and Mozart for Baroque music. Bach and Russell are the *founders*. Mozart and Carnap are the *classics*.

While Russell has often been accused of great inconstancy in his successive philosophic positions, Carnap's development has been assumed to be cumulative and consistent. But an excellent case could be made for the exact reverse. In Russell's case, it is not merely that the unity of his work revolves about his method; more important I think, is the fact that even his passion for logic is dominated by his empiricism. The primacy of perceptions qualifies both his exact logic and his theory of language. Whereas the work of Carnap can be cut in two. *Der Logische Aufbau der Welt* of 1928 is a heroic attempt to demonstrate the empirical premise, to show how the solipsism of the sensational present can build up a conceptual structure which not only establishes the private world, but also makes possible the intersubjective language presupposed by the special sciences. But sometime between 1928 and the publication of *Die Logische Syntax der Sprache* in 1934 the climate changed. A devotion to the sensory foundations of empirical science turned into a special interest in artificial sign systems. A conception of verification akin to Russell's in which scientific propositions within a system of discourse are compared with *sensory facts lying outside of discourse* was transformed into a process in which secondary statements to be verified were derived from other primitive or "protocol" *statements.*

The consequence was, as Hempel has pointed out,[41] that a correspondence theory of verification was transformed into a coherence theory. Protocol statements were no longer considered as basic because they were the product of *direct observation,* but rather as propositions to be adopted or rejected by *decision.* Carnap did not deny that sensory observation is essential for science, but he held that a study of the relation of observation to the propositions it produces was the business of science proper and not of philosophy. Philosophy thus becomes the logical analysis of scientific propositions. The method of verifying propositions is defined by the syntactical principles of a given language system, and since no proposition is significant in isolation, there is no longer any verification of singular propositions by reference to an indubitable atomic fact.

There are then two Carnaps:[42] the Carnap of the *Aufbau* and the Carnap of *Logical Syntax,* for in a sense all the work he produced subsequent to the latter (such as *Meaning and Necessity,* 1947, and *Introduction to Semantics,* 1948), whether devoted to new methods for analyzing and describing the meanings of linguistic expressions, or to a reinterpretation of the signifying function of language, is a realization of the syntactical program. I should like now to turn to the first Carnap, still under the spell of Russell and Wittgenstein, and mindful of Mach's empirical vision.

The task of logical construction is recondite, seemingly foolish, almost repugnant to common sense. Everyone knows that solidly and with our five senses we build the universe around us. But it is a task which every empiricism seriously worthy of the name assumes: to reduplicate this feat logically in the form of a deductive system, and therefore to prove (with an inverse and redundant logic) that what is actual is also possible. So it was with Locke and Hume, and so it is with Russell and Carnap. There are, however, differences. Carnap does not begin, as the British empiricists do, with "simple ideas of sensation" or "impressions" or Russell's sensory atoms. His primitives are "moments of experience" —*Elementarerlebnisse*, as he calls them—and although they are indeed the thinnest possible temporal slices of the streaming continuity of experience, they have a certain vertical fullness of content. Carnap does not choose them because they are further unanalyzable, but because they do seem to represent the epistemologically "given"—that which comes as close as possible to the unprocessed or the unedited in perception.

Like those of Locke, Hume, and Russell, Carnap's is a phenomenalist system, but unlike them he does not completely insist upon the primacy of the epistemological elements with which he begins. This already portends the struggle between the epistemological and the merely logical concerns which dominates this work.[43] In Locke and Hume the aim is nothing less than a natural history of the cognitive process. Carnap's claims are much more modest, for he considered his efforts merely as a *logical reconstruction* of that process—not the actual derivation of knowledge from the given, but the demonstration of its logical possibility. Here Carnap shows himself almost more under the logical spell of *Principia Mathematica* than is Russell himself in his epistemological investigations. When Russell chooses his perceptual primitives, he is subtly under the influence of the genetic approach. But in Carnap this is qualified by the effort to reveal concepts less in their origins than in their connectedness; his interest lies in the creation of an elegant, an integrated, and a comprehensive system.

This is indicated in the briefest and most condensed manner by Carnap himself in his introduction to *Der Logische Aufbau der Welt*, where he states the essence of the book: "the aim: to construct a system of concepts—the means: an analysis of reality with the help of the theory of relations."[44] Carnap's purpose is to provide a system of objects and their relations in which all of the fundamental concepts of the natural and humanistic sciences can be "constituted" through their reducibility to, and definition in terms of, elementary experiences. Such a program of constitution, if successful, accomplishes two important tasks.

In the first place, it makes it possible to test all scientific propositions for meaningfulness through the criterion of their reducibility to originally empirical components. It is an axiom of intelligibility for empiricism that factual propositions must be grounded in experience. The construction of a constitutional system indicates how the "objects" of science may be interpreted so that scientific statements about them may be grounded in the more primitive propositions of the total system. Thus the empirically meaningful can be distinguished from the empirically meaningless. In the second place, the system of constitution establishes the unity of science, for the principle of reducibility operates in such a way as to make higher-level concepts such as those of "other minds" and "non-material objects" dependent upon "physical objects," and these latter in turn dependent upon original perceptual experience (*eigenpsychische Gegenstände*). There is thus finally only a single domain of "objects," and consequently only a single comprehensive science.[45] There are special sciences, of course, but they take their place within the single system according to the genealogy of the objects with which they deal.

The analogy with *Principia Mathematica* is clear. As Russell and Whitehead proposed the reduction of all mathematical notions to those concepts which are most logically primitive, so Carnap in *Der Logische Aufbau der Welt* proposes a reduction of all the concepts of the empirical sciences, natural or social, to the primitives of perceptual experience. That the enterprise is carried out only partially and in outline does not diminish its brilliance.

The purpose of the *Aufbau* is to produce a conceptual structure, and since the classical components of structure are terms or elements and the relationships through which they are hierarchically and derivatively ordered, Carnap's system begins with a plurality of basic units (*Grundelemente*) and a single fundamental relation (*Grundbeziehung*).[46] The basic units are the "elementary experiences" or cross-sections of experience, and they are chosen not because they are not further analyzable, but because they have a priority in the order of knowledge which seems to place them close to the epistemologically "given." Since Carnap wishes to conceive the entire system of constitution as "a rational reconstruction of the formation of reality, a construction which in the actual process of knowing is made intuitively,"[47] the consideration of epistemic primacy is decisive for the choice of basic elements. The single fundamental relation which Carnap chooses is "recognition of similarity" (*die Ähnlichkeitserinnerung*). Its superiority to the relation of "part-similarity," which is a rival candidate, is that it provides a means for the temporal ordering of elementary experiences which the former symmetrical relation does not. The superiority of "recognition of similarity" is that its asymmetrical nature permits the construction of temporal order and at the same time the relation of "part-similarity" can be derived from it.

It is not possible to follow the argument in detail, but the order of conceptual derivation may be briefly indicated. From elementary experiences in the relation of recollection of similarity, part-similarity is defined. Then "a region of similarity" is defined as the maximal class of qualities between which part-similarity holds, and "a quality-class" is derived as that which expresses the common quality of elementary experiences. After quality classes comes the derivation of sense classes, the visual sense, temporal order, places in the visual field, the spatial order of the visual field, the order of colors, and finally sensations themselves as the ordered couples of an elementary experience and the quality class to which it belongs. This concludes the lowest level of the system as Carnap sees it: the construction of the private psychical realm from the original elementary experiences.

The next set of definitions in the hierarchy makes possible the construction of the space-time world which is the locus of physical objects. Carnap defines the space-time world as the class of world-points to which can be assigned the multiple sense qualities of experience. In theory such a construction presupposes the establishment of the modalities of all of the senses, whereas the lower-level analysis has only deduced the properties of the visual field, but since the present construction is admittedly exemplary rather than complete, Carnap is content to construct the space-time world from the temporal series of visual fields which occur in experience. With the ascription of visual qualities to world-points, physical objects are produced. The determination of shape, size, position in space and time, plus the ascription of qualities, constitutes the physical object, and once visual objects are constituted, it is possible to derive that epistemologically very special visual object *my own body*. With the aid of this last, tactual-visual objects and the remainder of the sensory qualities are defined.

With the attribution of sensory qualities to world-points the entire world of perception comes into being, and it is completed by analogy in a way which utilizes partly a "postulate of causality" and partly a "postulate of substance." But the important thing is this: that between the perceptual world and the physical world there is a significant difference. Whereas the former is characterized by the attribution of sense qualities, the latter is made by the attribution of physical quantities or numbers. This permits for the physical world the mathematical formulation of determinate laws and the achievement of "a unique, contradiction-free, intersubjectivity."[48] Within this physical world the next step is the constitution of biological objects including human beings and their expressive characteristics (*Ausdrucksbeziehung*), and these expressive characteristics serve to define the highest level of the system of constitution: that of other minds and cultural objects.

The expressive relation defines certain correspondences between my own body and my own mind, and the mind of another can then be constituted by the attribution of similar mental components to similar bodily manifestations. Communication together with its symbolization is a further step toward the constitution of the world of the other person, and once this has been established, it may be correlated with my own observational world in such a way as to produce that *intersubjective world* which is the proper locus of the objects of science. The creation of the intersubjective world is important in two respects. In the first place, as the world of intersubjective agreement between various world-views (Russell would have called them "perspectives"), from it can be derived systems of human relations, dispositional behavior, and experiences of value. In the second place, it seems to make possible an ultimate avoidance of the epistemological solipsism with which the system of the *Aufbau* presumably begins. Carnap speaks of this as a merely "methodological" solipsism, and he insists that his system of constitution does not psychologize either perceptions, or physical objects, or values. "Indeed, the theory of constitution does not speak this realistic language, but is neutral with respect to the metaphysical components of realistic statements."[49] But this is one of the claims of the *Aufbau* which has been the subject of widespread dispute.

From elementary experiences to quality classes to sensations to physical objects to my own body to other minds to social systems and values— the development is impressive. Partial and incomplete though it is, it represents the furthest efforts of an empiricism taking advantage of all the resources of modern relational logic. For on the one hand it attempts to show how all the statements of the special sciences may be verified or falsified according to the success of the effort to reduce them to the level of immediate experience, and on the other it seeks to afford a final justification for Hume's contention that it is unnecessary to assume any sources of knowledge other than logic and immediate experience. As such it is the culmination of the first stage of logical empiricism's development.

The program of logical empiricism's second stage is defined by Carnap in *The Logical Syntax of Language*, and the posture which it adopts

with respect to the formulation of linguistic problems is inseparable
from the attitude of the Vienna Circle toward the role and function of
philosophical activity.

In our "Vienna Circle" [says Carnap[50]] ". . . the conviction has grown,
and is steadily increasing, that metaphysics can make no claim to possessing
a scientific character. That part of the work of philosophers which may be
held to be scientific in its nature—excluding the empirical questions which
can be referred to empirical science—consists of logical analysis. The aim
of logical syntax is to provide a system of concepts, a language, by the help
of which the results of logical analysis will be exactly formulable.

Philosophy is to be replaced by the logic of science—that is to say, by
the logical analysis of the concepts and sentences of the sciences, for *the
logic of science is nothing other than the logical syntax of the language of
science.*

The conviction that metaphysics can make no claim to possessing a
scientific character has been prepared for by the positivistic distinction
between the "representative" and the "expressive" function of language.
Some linguistic utterances express a feeling, present a mood, indicate
a disposition. Others represent a certain state of affairs, predicate something, assert something about the factual world. Whereas the latter are
in some sense capable of verification or falsification, the former are
not; they simply *are*. The positivistic rejection of metaphysics therefore
hinges upon a prior consideration of "expressive" language.

The meaning of our anti-metaphysical thesis may now be more clearly
explained. This thesis asserts that metaphysical propositions—like lyrical
verses—have only an expressive function, but no representative function.
Metaphysical propositions are neither true nor false, because they assert
nothing, they contain neither knowledge nor error, they lie completely outside the field of knowledge, of theory, outside the discussion of truth or
falsity. But they are, like laughing, lyrics, and music, expressive. They express not so much temporary feelings as permanent emotional or volitional
dispositions. . . . Thus we find a great similarity between metaphysics and
lyrics. But there is one decisive difference between them. Both have no
representative function, no theoretical content. A metaphysical proposition,
however—as distinguished from a lyrical verse—*seems* to have some, and by
this not only is the reader deceived, but the metaphysician himself. . . .[51]

The danger of metaphysics lies in the illusion that it gives of being
knowledge, which actually it is not. Logical positivists, with their passion
for logic and their almost obsessive attachment to the single-minded
pursuit of clarity, therefore reject it. To the positivist, metaphysics is
neither the truth which soars above mere science nor the harmless ex-

pressiveness of the lyrical spirit in philosophy; it is a malignant disease of language.

The Logical Syntax of Language seeks both to lay bare the roots of this disease and to lay the syntactical foundation for the logical analysis of the language of science. It does this through an insistence that any examination of the logic of science can dispense with an analysis of the meaning content of terms and confine itself to the formal rules of the linguistic expressions which science employs. Indeed, it goes so far as to suggest that the formal rules of any language whatsoever may be conventionally instituted, and that the statements which the language generates are functionally dependent upon the kind of logical syntax thus presupposed.

> By the *logical syntax* of a language we mean the formal theory of the linguistic forms of that language—the systematic statement of the formal rules which govern it together with the development of the consequences which follow from these rules. A theory, a rule, a definition, or the like is to be called *formal* when no reference is made in it either to the meaning of the symbols . . . or to the sense of the expressions . . . but simply and solely to the kinds and order of the symbols from which the expressions are constructed.[52]

Carnap draws heavily upon the metamathematical researches of Hilbert and the Polish logicians in holding that any language system consists of two kinds of syntactical rules: (1) formation rules and (2) transformation rules.[53] Formation rules state how sentences may be constructed out of different kinds of symbols. Transformation rules state how statements may be derived from or translated into other statements. They are, in short, (1) the principles of derivation or (2) the rules of inference. Any natural language is so rich and so ambiguous that it is impossible to state its formation rules with completeness, but for any "artificial" language (such as that of *Principia Mathematica*) it is possible to state exhaustively both its grammatical rules of sentence-formation and its operational rules of derivation. This possibility of completeness (with the clarity which it entails) is at the root of Carnap's constant preoccupation with the syntax of formalized languages.

The longer one ponders the philosophical strategy of Carnap's theories of logical syntax, the clearer it becomes how they all hinge on a dualistic mode of logical analysis. He distinguishes (1) between analytic and synthetic judgments, (2) between the "object-questions" and the "logical questions" (which together exhaust any theoretical field), (3) between the physical P-rules and the logical L-rules (which together exhaust the transformation rules of a given language), and (4) between the quasi-syntactical sentences which he terms "the material mode of speech" and their correlated syntactical sentences which he terms "the formal mode of speech." These distinctions are designed to further the tactics of elimination. By eliminating everything except object-sentences and syntactical sentences Carnap is able to reject the "pseudo-object-sentences" of metaphysics. Thus he is able to destroy metaphysics' claim to legitimacy as an independent sovereign beside the dual monarchy of logical analysis and empirical science. I should like to dwell on this strategy a little further.

The distinction between object-questions and logical questions, which occurs in any theoretical field, marks the difference between those which are factual, having to do with the properties and relations of objects, and those which are at second remove, dealing with sentences, theories, and terms which are the symbolic vehicles for the expression of knowledge about objects. Object-questions are the principal preoccupation of the empirical sciences, logical questions of traditional logic and epistemology. But a logical analysis of philosophical problems shows them to contain what seems to be object-questions but are, in fact, only pseudo-problems. Further considerations of these supposed object-problems in philosophy will show that they do not belong with any of the empirical sciences, but are actually logical questions in disguise. And once philosophy is purified of "unscientific elements," only the logic of science remains.

It is the distinction between "object-sentences" and "syntactical sentences" which permits this purification. An object-sentence deals directly with an entity, for example, "The rose is red" or "Five is a prime number." A syntactical sentence is a statement about language, for example, "The word 'rose' is a thing-word" or "Five is not a thing-word, but a number-word." Between these two clear alternatives there falls the troublesome class of "pseudo-object-sentences," for example, "A rose is a thing" or "Five is not a thing, but a number." These are the kinds of sentences which so often occur in traditional philosophy and which lend color to its contention that it in some sense deals with empirical entities. But the hollowness of this contention is revealed by the fact that although philosophical sentences of this type *seem* to concern the objects mentioned, in reality they concern only the form of linguistic expression. Thus, as Carnap says,[54] "we shall see that these pseudo-object-sentences are simply *quasi-syntactical sentences of the material mode of speech.*"

The analysis of pseudo-object-sentences requires the distinction between the "material" and the "formal" mode of speech. All sentences of empirical science, all propositions asserting matters of fact, are real object-sentences and employ the material mode of speech. All syntactical sentences refer to matters of logical or grammatical form and are therefore to be assigned to the formal mode of speech. The pseudo-object-sentences, although they occur in the material mode of speech, are really syntactical sentences. In other words, the so-called philosophical problems of the foundations of science are really only questions of the logic of science, which are at heart formal, that is to say, syntactical questions.

The use of the material mode of speech produces ambiguity because it employs absolute concepts rather than syntactical concepts. Hence, to dispel this ambiguity, it is advisable to translate all pseudo-object-sentences in the material mode of speech into sentences in the formal mode. This is a methodological precaution; it does not mean that Carnap believes that the material mode of speech should be entirely eliminated.

If a sentence of the material mode of speech is given, or, more generally, a sentence which is not a genuine object-sentence, then the translation into the formal mode of speech need not always be undertaken, but it must always be possible. *Translatability into the formal mode of speech constitutes the touchstone for all philosophical sentences*, or, more generally, for all sentences which do not belong to the language of any of the empirical sciences. . . . Sentences which do not, at least to a certain extent, univocally determine their translation are thereby shown to be ambiguous and obscure. Sentences which do not give even a slight indication to determine their translation are outside the realm of the language of science and therefore incapable of discussion, no matter what depths or heights of feeling they may stir.[55]

The distinction between the formal and the material mode of speech is not meant to refer to genuine object-sentences and so not to the propositions of the empirical sciences. It is simply a device which the logic of science has at its disposal for the elimination of the moribund propositions of metaphysics.

The Logical Syntax of Language is a work of considerable subtlety and complication, but its chief result for the philosophy of logical empiricism is to sustain the distinction between analytic and synthetic judgments (upon which positivism has always rested its case) through an appeal to linguistic considerations. Once again it seeks to divide all significant questions making valid cognitive claims into two exhaustive classes: (1) questions which concern factual knowledge and the extralinguistic objects of experience, and (2) questions which depend upon the various symbolic mechanisms through which these objects may be represented in discourse. Thus it follows that *every* indicative meaningful sentence is either an object-sentence falling somewhere within the range of the special empirical sciences, or a syntactical sentence belonging to logic, mathematics, or philosophy. For philosophy is now purged of all of its "dangerous" traditional elements and defined simply as the sum of the true syntactical sentences explicating the languages of the various sciences.

The consequence of this exhaustive division between the two realms of empirical science and logical analysis is a division in the methods by which their respective issues may be resolved. The appeal to experience is decisive for empirical science. The appeal to linguistic convention is decisive for logical analysis. Thus the position which Carnap takes upon the duality of cognitively meaningful propositions commits him to the further consideration of two criteria of the greatest importance: the criterion of *symbolic conventionalism,* used for logical analysis, and the criterion of *confirmability,* used for empirical science.

Suppose that we raise the question of the logical analysis of physics. We shall have to formulate rules of formation for sentences in the physical language and we shall have to lay down both L-rules (logical) and P-rules (physical) as transformation rules of this language. Also, syntactical rules will have to be stated for the form which the basic propositions expressing observations (the *protocol-sentences*) must take. What principles must govern the establishment of these rules? We must first recognize, says Carnap,[56] that no rules are fixed once and for all. "No rule of the physical language is definitive; all rules are laid down with the reservation that they may be altered as soon as it seems expedient to do so. This applies not only to the P-rules (physical rules) but also to the L-rules (logical rules), including those of mathematics."

This conclusion is startling. For it makes the principles of inference and even the system of mathematical expression for the propositions of physics a matter not of truth, but of apparently arbitrary *decision.*

The construction of the physical system is not effected in accordance with fixed rules, but by means of conventions. These conventions, namely, the rules of formation, the L-rules, and the P-rules (hypotheses), are, however, not arbitrary. The choice of them is influenced, in the first place, by certain practical methodological considerations (for instance, whether they make for simplicity, expedience, and fruitfulness in certain tasks). This is the case for all conventions, including, for example, definitions.[57]

The conclusion is indeed startling, for we had been accustomed to believe that acts of choice do not create knowledge, and that the foundations of science are not to be found in what are, from the more rigid vantage point of truth, mere arbitrary postulates. It is, however, a logical conclusion, given Carnap's assumptions.

The symbolic conventionalism of *The Logical Syntax of Language* is one of the most prominent and enduring features of Carnap's system. What was implicit in its treatment of the construction of a physical language is stated explicitly in connection with the problem of abstract entities which he raised fifteen years later in the article "Empiricism, Semantics, and Ontology." Are there such things as properties, classes, propositions, and numbers? What is their ontological status? The answer to these questions lies in the recognition that all such entities are ingredients in a particular linguistic framework. Within such a framework one can ask certain questions about truth and falsity or empirical confirmability or disconfirmability. The "reality" of the entities like classes or numbers is a function of their place and function within the total linguistic structure. "To be real in the scientific sense means to be an element of the system."

When we ask, however, "external" questions about the "truth" of the system as a whole, the situation is completely different. Here questions of "truth" are meaningless; it is the issue of utility which we ought to raise. When we, like Russell for example, raise questions about the reality of the external world, this is not a theoretical question as Russell seems to suppose. It is a practical decision whether we will or will not accept the structure of a particular "thing-language" within which observations can be empirically tested and propositions about descriptive characteristics can be formulated. The acceptance of this "thing-language" depends upon certain practical considerations such as its efficiency and fruitfulness for the communication of factual knowledge. But to inquire about the "reality" of the thing-world is not a proper theoretical question; as a question it cannot even be legitimately formulated within the limits of the thing-language. Given a practical commitment to such a language, the "reality" of things is a "truth" by postulation and convention. To raise the question of theoretical truth is essentially meaningless.[58]

An alleged statement of the reality of the system of entities is a pseudo-statement without cognitive content. To be sure, we have to face at this point an important question; but it is a practical, not a theoretical question; it is the question of whether or not to accept the new linguistic forms. The acceptance cannot be judged as being either true or false because it is not an assertion. It can only be judged as being more or less expedient, fruitful, conducive to the aim for which the language is intended. Judgments of this kind supply the motivation for the decision of accepting or rejecting the kind of entities.

In short, the alleged ontological question of the existence of abstract entities is no question at all. The real question concerns the expediency of adopting certain abstract linguistic forms in the construction of the language of science. The effect of this linguistic restatement is to shift the ordinary problem of conceptual truth to the higher level of linguistic utility. Thus the ultimate conclusion of "Empiricism, Semantics, and Ontology" merely restates the famous Principle of Tolerance ("It is not our business to set up prohibitions, but to arrive at conventions") which Carnap had arrived at fifteen years before. In *The Logical Syntax of Language* he had said: "*In logic, there are no morals. Everyone is at liberty to build up his own logic, i.e., his own form of language, as he wishes. All that is required of him is that, if he wishes to discuss it, he must state his methods clearly, and give syntactical rules instead of philosophical arguments.*"[59] Now, in "Empiricism, Semantics, and Ontology" the language is slightly different, but the linguistic morality is the same. "Let us grant to those who work in any special field of investigation the freedom to use any form of expression which seems useful to them; the work in the field will sooner or later lead to the elimination of those forms which have no useful function. *Let us be cautious in making assertions, and critical in examining them, but tolerant in permitting linguistic forms.*"[60]

The "truth" of analytic statements is thus a matter of stipulated definition, and the introduction of abstract entities into the language of science depends upon a decision to accept the general linguistic frameworks within which they appear. But what of "empirical" propositions? What of those object-sentences which fall within the domain of observational and experimental science? From its very earliest days logical empiricism has dealt with this problem by a strategy which seeks the most intimate relation between the concept of "meaning" and that of "truth." The strategy originated with Wittgenstein, but has been given a late classic expression by Moritz Schlick:[61]

Whenever we ask about a sentence, "What does it mean?", what we expect is instruction as to the circumstances in which the sentence is to be used; we want a description of the conditions under which the sentence will form a *true* proposition and of those which will make it *false*. . . . Stating the meaning of a sentence amounts to stating the rules according to which the sentence is to be used, and this is the same as stating the way in which it can be verified or falsified. *The meaning of a proposition is the method of its verification.*

The early positivistic identification of meaning and verification, with its implication that object-sentences which cannot be verified or falsified are meaningless, at once ran into serious theoretical difficulties. Even protocol-sentences could never be established with certainty, and empirical generalizations of a higher order, whose proof depends upon citing a necessarily limited number of instances from an almost infinite number of possible instances, caused even greater difficulty. Revision was clearly in order, and as usual it was Carnap whose clarity and sustained thought provided the new direction. As early as 1935 he had urged the necessity for a distinction between "truth" and "confirmation,"[62] and in his important article on "Testability and Meaning" (1936-37) he worked out this line of thought in detail. But the essential positivistic position is not abandoned: confirmation and testing are substituted for verification, but the analytic relation between empirical criteria and meaning remains.

Two chief problems of the theory of knowledge [says Carnap[63]] are the question of meaning and the question of verification. The first question asks under what conditions a sentence has meaning, in the sense of cognitive, factual meaning. The second one asks how we get to know something, how we can find out whether a given sentence is true or false. The second question presupposes the first one. Obviously we must understand a sentence, i.e., we must know its meaning, before we can try to find out whether it is true or not. But, from the point of view of empiricism, there is a still closer connection between the two problems. In a certain sense, there is only one answer to the two questions. If we knew what it would be for a given sentence to be found true then we would know what its meaning is. And if for two sentences the conditions under which we would have to take them as true are the same, then they have the same meaning. Thus the meaning of a sentence is in a certain sense identical with the way we determine its truth or falsehood; and a sentence has meaning only if such a determination is possible.

Carnap distinguishes the testing of a sentence from its confirmation. A sentence is *testable* if we know a method for testing it; it is *confirmable* if we know under what conditions the sentence would be confirmed. The purpose of the distinction is, of course, to formulate the principle of empiricism in such a way that *degree of confirmabilty or testability* supplants verification as a criterion of meaning. Since no complete verification is ever possible for universal sentences, a process of gradually increasing confirmation must take its place. Whether for general or particular propositions, it is completely in the positivistic spirit that every synthetic proposition is a hypothesis, and that the reducibility of physical object-names to perception predicates (qualities immediately given in sensation) is always a matter of approximation and degree.

In the actual operations of science the chief methods of confirmation and testing are observation and the production of phenomena. Therefore the concepts of confirmation and testing must be logically defined in terms of the latter. A sentence S is called confirmable (completely or incompletely) if its confirmation is reducible (completely or incompletely) to that of a class of perception predicates. If a predicate is either observable or introduced by a test chain the last link of which is observable, it is testable. This type of definition associates the newer theory of confirmability with the older positivistic thesis of physicalism (which holds that every term in the language of science can be reduced to terms of the language of physical entities). It makes possible a statement of testability and confirmability in physicalistic terms:[64]

1. *Thesis of Physicalistic Testability*: Every descriptive predicate of the language of science is testable on the basis of observable thing-predicates.
2. *Thesis of Physicalistic Confirmability*: Every descriptive predicate of the language of science is confirmable on the basis of observable thing-predicates.

Positivism has always asserted that the class of perception terms is a sufficient basis for the language of science; physicalism now asserts the same for the class of observable thing-predicates. Carnap's syntactical reservations prevent him from formulating the principle of empiricism any longer as an assertion; he now thinks of it as a "proposal" or a "requirement." But it is a proposal that the language of science shall be so restricted that descriptive predicates (and hence synthetic propositions) shall not be admitted unless they can be connected with possible observations. There are now, therefore, four possible formulations of the empirical position.[65]

Requirement of Complete Testability: Every synthetic sentence must be completely testable. I.e., if any synthetic sentence S is given, we must know a method of testing for every descriptive predicate occurring in S. . . .
Requirement of Complete Confirmability: Every synthetic sentence must be completely confirmable. I.e., if any synthetic sentence S is given, there must be for every descriptive predicate occurring in S the possibility of our finding out for suitable points whether or not they have the property designated by the predicate in question. . . .

Requirement of Testability: Every synthetic sentence must be testable. This formulation admits incompletely testable sentences—these are chiefly universal sentences to be confirmed incompletely by their instances. . . .

Requirement of Confirmability: Every synthetic sentence must be confirmable. This is the most liberal formulation of the four. Predicates which are confirmable but not testable are admitted as are generalized sentences. This enlargement leads to a confirmable generalized language, but it suffices to exclude all non-empirical sentences. It is, in Carnap's opinion, a sufficient formulation of the principle of empiricism.

The logical empiricism of Carnap is a classic statement of the consequences of dividing all significant assertions into syntactical and empirical sentences, and it eventuates in the appeal to two governing principles, "the principle of symbolic conventionalism" and "the principle of confirmability," which control respectively the domains of logical analysis and empirical science. But if we ponder over these two principles sufficiently, we shall arrive, I think, at a paradox. The peculiar mentality of positivism accepts no level of experience on its own terms. Nothing is its own justification. It must be analyzed, reduced, transformed. In Russell and in the Carnap of the *Aufbau* this meant reducing the higher levels of experience to the lower—physics to sense-data, or other minds and cultural objects to the elementary relation of "recognition of similarity." But in the Carnap of *The Logical Syntax of Language* and after, this process of dependence is neatly and exactly reversed. Now each clear-cut philosophical category must be referred to the level that lies just above. Thus the ultimate wisdom of the positivists comes very close to that of the pragmatists.

Suppose we admit that the great and perennial problems of philosophy are the problems of meaning, of truth, and of value, and that correspondingly, the tests of any proposition are of its intelligibility, its probability, and its utility. Now, what for Carnap is the criterion of the intelligibility of an empirical sentence? It is the principle of confirmability. Intelligibility is a function of confirmability, in short, questions of meaning are in an important sense referrable to considerations concerning truth. Secondly, what for Carnap is the criterion of the "truth" of philosophical principles? It is the principle of symbolic conventionalism. This tells us that whether or not we employ abstract entities, admit the existence of natural numbers, reduce experience to sense data, or accept the world of physical objects, is not a matter of assertion but of convention adopted out of fruitfulness, expediency, utility. What we had thought were questions of truth are really questions of value. But if meaning reduces to truth, and if truth is really a matter of value, then the categories of philosophical analysis no longer retain their pristine purity, and the positivistic avalanche gives promise of succumbing to the broadening pragmatic stream.

4. THE POSITIVISTIC TEMPER IN ETHICS

Neither Russell nor Carnap has produced a general theory of value. The passion for logic which expresses itself so well in constructions from sense data and the creation of artificial languages is less comfortably at home with religious intuition, problems of the fine arts, and the complex facts of the moral life. There is, perhaps, even some native blindness (on both sides, of course) in the practitioners of the sciences and the humanities which has traditionally made humanists contemptuous of science and which now takes its revenge in the insistence of the positivistic philosophers of science that the "sentences" of art, religion, and morality cannot possibly claim to stand as reliable knowledge. For logical empiricism, although it does not have a positive theory of values, does implicitly propose a negative one, and the basis of this proposal is an analysis of the functions of ordinary language.

A rarely acknowledged source of contemporary positivism, particularly relevant here, is the analysis of the symbolizing function of language presented by C. K. Ogden and I. A. Richards in their *The Meaning of Meaning* of 1923. This work is both primitive in its theory and diffuse in its development, but it presents and elaborates one basic distinction, that between the "emotive" and the "referential" use of language. Language has two primary uses: to designate and to express. A sentence may be used with the purpose of making a reference which is in the nature of the case either true or false; this use of language is scientific. Or it may be used to express feelings or to arouse them; this is not scientific, but emotive. The distinction between these two uses coupled with a preference for the former is the essence of *semantic positivism*. It provides a strategic focus in terms of which the language of science may be vindicated, while the "assertions" of religion, poetry, metaphysics, and the arts, although allowed their expressive virtue, are condemned to the status of being *cognitively meaningless*. Carnap has never explicitly acknowledged the debt which his theory owes to the suggestive remarks of Ogden and Richards, but his treatment of object-questions, and particularly those object-questions whose "objects" are not the materials for the natural sciences shows him to be deeply under their spell. He has said:[66]

The logical analysis of philosophical problems shows them to vary greatly in character. As regards those object-questions whose objects do not occur in the exact sciences, critical analysis has revealed that they are pseudo-problems. The supposititious sentences of metaphysics, of the philosophy of values, of ethics (in so far as it is treated as a normative discipline and not as a psycho-sociological investigation of facts) are pseudo-sentences; they have no logical content, but are only expressions of feeling which in their turn stimulate feelings and volitional tendencies on the part of the hearer.

The heart of the positivistic theory of value is the denial of cognitive content to religious, poetic, and ethical assertions. Being essentially unverifiable, they are meaningless; being meaningless, they cannot possibly be true; being incapable of being true, they cannot pretend to make a rational or logical claim upon human choice. They are non-logical, and therefore essentially arbitrary, for as expressions of emotion and of volitions, they are incapable of that type of symbolic formalization to which the authentic contents of science lend themselves. Falling outside of science, they represent a certain irrational surd which may puzzle us, or dismay us, or even charm us, but which as subject-matter lies upon the periphery of logic and therefore outside the circle of authentic philosophical concern.

It is clear that the implications of semantic positivism are multiple and widespread, and that they are still the subject of profound controversy in metaphysics, aesthetics, and the philosophy of religion. But it is in the field of ethics that logical empiricism has most conclusively expressed its axiological theory. I should like therefore briefly to examine the development of the positivistic temper in contemporary ethics.

This development consists of three stages. The first is proto-positivism, which does not really depend upon the emotive theory of language, but uses the general positivistic framework of analytic and synthetic judgments to deal with the traditional ethical issues bequeathed by the nineteenth century. This first stage is represented by the *Fragen der Ethik* (1930) of Moritz Schlick. The second stage presents the emotive theory in embryo. It is based upon a few undeveloped remarks of Carnap, the widely influential currency which they received in Ayer's *Language, Truth and Logic* (1936), and a series of articles in *Erkenntnis* and elsewhere between 1934 and 1939 which showed that the emotive theory was very much in the air.[67] The third stage is the semantically sophisticated and persuasively argued theses of Stevenson's *Ethics and Language* (1945).

The chief burden of Schlick's argument is to show that there can be no such thing as a "normative" science, since any attempt to establish ultimate or intrinsic values is to leave the solid ground of the empirically verifiable:[68]

The question of the justification of the higher norms or the ultimate values is senseless, because there is nothing higher to which these could be referred. Since modern ethics . . . often speaks of this absolute justification as *the* fundamental problem of ethics, it must be said, unfortunately, that the formulation of the question from which it proceeds is simply meaningless. . . . If I say of a thing that it is desirable, and mean that one must desire it as a means if one desires a certain end, then everything is perfectly clear. If, however, I assert that a thing is desirable simply in itself, I cannot say what I mean by this statement; it is not verifiable and it is therefore meaningless. A thing can be desirable only with respect to something else, not in itself.

The purpose here is twofold: on the one hand, to deny the intelligibility of the conception of *intrinsic* value, and on the other to indicate that a statement of *instrumental* value as a hypothetical imperative expressing a maxim of prudence is possible in the form of a factually verifiable proposition. Schlick's fundamental question is: Granting the positivistic assumptions, how much of traditional ethics is salvageable as scientific assertion? He is able to retain more than one might expect by a kind of naturalism which sees even the ultimate norms as somehow derivable from human nature and the facts of life, but more importantly by the belief that "the central problem of ethics concerns the causal explanation of moral behavior." The consequence is that ethics by his explicit intention becomes a part of psychology.

Our moral conduct is derived from our natural inclinations; the content of a community's moral precepts is seen to depend upon its form of life, and the word "moral" merely denotes what according to the prevailing opinion in society is advantageous. Pleasure can easily be taken as an empirical criterion of value ("the sense of every proposition concerning the value of an object consists in the fact that this object . . . produces a feeling of pleasure or pain in some feeling subject"), and, with this understood, the meaning of any value proposition is that it seeks to be an empirical statement of the conditions under which value is achievable. The form of Schlick's ethics is much like that of John Dewey; it is dominated by attention to empirical conditions and consequences, but its content is a traditional hedonism made congruent with the demands of positivistic method.

Carnap's remarks and Ayer's expansion of them are much more radical. Carnap, like Schlick, distinguishes between the two senses of moral philosophy: between ethics as psychological and sociological inquiry into the actions of human beings, which belongs to empirical science rather than to philosophy, and ethics as a philosophy of values or of moral norms. The difficulty with the latter is that what are supposedly value judgments are in reality only disguised imperatives.[69]

The rule, "Do not kill," has grammatically the imperative form and will therefore not be regarded as an assertion. But the value statement, "Killing is evil," although, like the rule, it is merely an expression of a certain wish, has the grammatical form of an assertive proposition. Most philosophers have been deceived by this form into thinking that a value statement is really an assertive proposition, and must be either true or false. Therefore they give reasons for their own value statements and try to disprove those of their opponents. But actually a value statement is nothing else than a command in a misleading grammatical form. It may have effects upon the actions of men, and these effects may either be in accordance with our wishes or not; but it is neither true nor false. It does not assert anything and can neither be proved nor disproved.

This is revealed as soon as we apply to such statements our method of logical analysis. From the statement "Killing is evil" we cannot deduce any proposition about future experiences. Thus this statement is not verifiable and has no theoretical sense, and the same thing is true of all other value statements.

Carnap's analysis is important because it calls attention to the imperative character of value statements, to the dynamic intention which lies behind them, to their function in discourse as motivational instruments. To this insight Ayer adds a note concerning their emotive flavor, and a more extensive classification of the statements customarily found in moral discourse. Acknowledging the positivist thesis that all propositions are either tautologies, hypotheses, or nonsensical, he then examines the kind of statements which are actually contained in ethical systems, and finds them to be of the following four types: (1) definitions of ethical terms or criticisms of such definitions (tautologies), (2) descriptions of moral experience and its causes (sociological and psychological hypotheses), (3) exhortations to moral virtue (Carnap's imperatives disguised or undisguised and hence cognitively nonsense), and (4) ethical judgments proper, which are simply *the expression of moral emotion* or personal feeling (and hence also cognitively meaningless).[70] Statements of types (1) and (2) are clearly cognitively significant and as such are a part of science or logical analysis; statements of types (3) and (4) are normative in the invidious sense—they can be neither true nor false but merely expressive or motivational. It follows that the fundamental ethical concepts in this latter sense are unanalyzable, inasmuch as there is no logical criterion by which one can test the validity of the judgments in which they occur.

The considerable merit of Ayer's brief account lies in his recognition of how ethical statements actually vary in their assertoric weight, of the increasing strength of command in statements like the following: "It is good to tell the truth," "You ought to tell the truth," "It is your duty to tell the truth." But his recognition is, of course, only therapeutic. Ayer himself believes that if there is any excuse for moral philosophy it lies in the analytic definition of ethical terms, and, like Schlick, he is convinced that empirical argument is possible on moral questions only if some system of ultimate value is presupposed.

C. L. Stevenson's *Ethics and Language* incorporates in its account of moral argumentation both Carnap's description of its motivational character and Ayer's belief as to its emotive properties. Its greater subtlety lies in its recognition that the positivistic disjunction between the cognitive and the non-cognitive in moral discourse is too sharply drawn. "When ethical issues become controversial, they involve disagreement that is of a *dual* nature. There is almost inevitably *disagreement in belief*, which requires detailed, sensitive attention, but there is also *disagreement in attitude*." Disagreement in belief represents a cognitive issue; disagreement in attitude does not. "Moral judgments are concerned with recommending something for approval or disapproval; and this involves something more than a disinterested description, or a cold debate. . . . That a moralist is so often a reformer is scarcely an accident. His judgments plead and advise, and open the way to counter-advice. In this way moral judgments go beyond cognition, speaking to the conative-affective natures of men."[71] Ethical statements have a threefold nature: they have an imperative function, an expressive function, and a descriptive function.

Stevenson's conclusions about the two kinds of ethical disagreement prepare the way for the "working models" of his definitions for ethical terms: "This is wrong" means I *disapprove of this; do so as well.* "He ought to do this" means I *disapprove of his leaving this undone; do so as well.* "This is good" means I *approve of this; do so as well.* Thus "rightness," "oughtness," "goodness" imply the same expression of moral sentiment and the same imperative recommendation. This is the element which relates ethical terms to agreement and disagreement in attitude, and which places moral controversy beyond the pale of rational solution. "If any ethical dispute is rooted in disagreement in belief, it may be settled by reasoning and inquiry to whatever extent the beliefs may be so settled. But if any ethical dispute is *not* rooted in disagreement in belief, then no reasoned solution of any sort is possible."[72] It is of course true that such disagreements in attitude may be settled—by rhetoric, by persuasion, by various obviously non-rational devices—but such solutions are completely *ad hoc*, and in this area no question can be asked about the *validity* of the solution.

Stevenson's analysis of moral statements concentrates upon the emotive power implicit within them, of their capacity to move the hearer, to establish his moral acquiescence. This leads him to describe the role of emotive or what he calls "persuasive definitions" in ethics. Definitions are usually taken to be a logical device for the clarification of common notions and as such to be impersonal, emotively neutral. But in moral philosophy this is rarely the case. "Ethical definitions involve a wedding of descriptive and emotive meaning, and accordingly have a frequent use in redirecting and intensifying attitudes. To choose a definition is to plead a cause, so long as the word defined is strongly emotive."[73] Thus the struggle for the alteration of ethical attitudes uses every dynamic weapon available; it may be done at the level of pseudo-assertion by a moral judgment, and it may be done at the level of meaning in the form of a persuasive definition. At any rate, what we have here is not the logic but the rhetoric of the moral life.

What all the positivistic ethical theorists have in common is their insistence that ethical sentences are essentially non-descriptive, that ethical terms do not designate any unique moral quality other than the emotive involvement of those upon whose lips they appear. This postulation of a non-cognitive ethics is matched by the postulation of an equally non-cognitive theory of poetry, of metaphysics, and of religion. But any theory of language which pushes its interests relentlessly toward clarity, unique designation, and scientific exactitude, and away from the depth, the fullness, but also the complication and ambiguity of metaphysics, religion, and poetry, may, in the end, pay a heavy price. The values of the scientific mentality are great, but a logic of science which admits only analytic and synthetic propositions, and finds the statements of religion, poetry, and metaphysics to be neither, has consigned the better half of human culture to the domain of "nonsense." Whitehead, speaking in quite another context, has seen this well:[74]

Every age produces people with clear logical intellects, and with the most praiseworthy grasp of the importance of some sphere of human experience, who have elaborated, or inherited, a scheme of thought which exactly fits those experiences which claim their interest. Such people are apt resolutely to ignore, or to explain away, all evidence which confuses their scheme with contradictory instances. What they cannot fit in is for them nonsense. An unflinching determination to take the whole evidence into account is the only method of preservation against the fluctuating extremes of fashionable opinion.

The passion for logic is an ambiguous emotion—ambiguous in its sources and in its effects. It can create the world, and it can destroy it, and it is sometimes not quite clear which has really been accomplished. Russell has shown us how the world of physics can be constructed out of sense data alone, and Carnap is the architect of the syntactical structures of an admirable number of formalized languages, but the logical empiricism in whose name these constructions have been made has, at the same time, done much in spirit to undermine the religious consciousness and to undercut the poetic vision of the world. This is why the two opposing sentiments of Wallace Stevens (quoted at the head of this chapter) seem to me to formulate so well the perplexity of any impersonal spectator who views the impact of logical empiricism upon the modern world. From one point of view it has scored a merciless triumph; it has brought an end of the evil of ambiguity and confusion through a profounder logic. But as we follow its argument with respect to values, as we ponder its consequences for art, for poetry, and for metaphysics, then, indeed, we must from time to time experience that "blank uneasiness which one might feel in the presence of a logical lunatic."

X

The Drama of Choice:
Karl Jaspers and Jean-Paul Sartre

But philosophy is, after all, perhaps only the recognition of the abysses which lie on each side of the footpath that the vulgar follow with the serenity of somnambulists.

GEORGES SOREL

The only drama which really interests me and that I should always be willing to depict anew is the debate of the individual with whatever keeps him from being authentic, with whatever is opposed to his integrity.

ANDRÉ GIDE

There are crimes of passion and crimes of logic. The line that divides them is not clear. But the Penal Code distinguishes between them by the useful concept of premeditation. We are living in the era of premeditation and perfect crimes. Our criminals are no longer those helpless children who pleaded love as their excuse. On the contrary, they are adults, and they have a perfect alibi: philosophy, which can be used for anything, even for transforming murderers into judges.

ALBERT CAMUS

1. EXISTENTIALISM: SOURCES, METHOD, AMBIENCE

Jean-Paul Sartre's finest play, *The Flies*, follows an old literary tradition. He takes an ancient theme, a plot well known to the Greek dramatists, reworks it, and adapts it to the modern uses of his own crystalline intentions. It is the theme of matricide, of the *Oresteia*, of the dark complicity of Orestes and Electra in a deed of revenge so just and at the same time so revolting, so disgusting to the moral sentiments, so ethically equivocal and even ritually ambiguous, that it required the utmost resources (religious in Aeschylus, humanistic in Sophocles, and psychological in Euripides) to fit it to the dramatic requirements of ancient Greek sensibility. Sartre selects and combines elements of plot and character from Aeschylus' *Choephoroi* and from the *Electras* of Sophocles and Euripides, but what he has managed to produce is not another Greek tragedy but an existentialist manifesto. The irony of the performance is that by a complete inversion of the philosophical presuppositions of the Greek mind, he has managed to set forth brilliantly the prevailing atmosphere of existentialist thought.

383

In this respect Freud and Sartre are at opposite poles. Freud has taken the dreams and the case histories of Faustian man, and interpreted them in the spirit of Greek tragedy. Sartre has done just the reverse: he has utilized the plot and the outward trappings of Greek tragedy to exhibit the inmost nature of the existential hero. What is involved here is a complete re-evaluation of the meaning of Greek tragedy, and if we follow this re-evaluation more closely, if we explore the stages by which it reveals itself in *The Flies*, we shall see at once both the chief ingredients of the existentialist position, and the historic sources in the philosophy of the nineteenth century whose ancestry has made it possible.

The Flies begins, like the *Electra* of Sophocles, with Orestes and his Tutor arriving in the land of Mycenae. For Aeschylus and Sophocles he comes with a purpose, determined to avenge his father's death and win his rightful kingdom, blessed by the Gods in this venture and urged on by the Tutor. But in Sartre's play he comes to visit the land of his birth as a sight-seer, without interest in its internal affairs and encouraged by the Tutor in his role of mere spectator. He returns a stranger to his native land, a young man with no home, no roots, no memories. As the play continues we see that this has been his Tutor's intention.[1]

ORESTES: . . . Why, an old mangy dog, warming himself at the hearth, and struggling to his feet with a little whimper to welcome his master home— why, that dog has more memories than I! At least he recognizes his master. *His* master. But what can I call mine?

THE TUTOR: And what of your culture, Lord Orestes? What of that? All that wise lore I culled for you with loving care, like a bouquet, matching the fruits of my knowledge with the finest flowers of my experience? Did I not, from the very first, set you a-reading all the books there are, so as to make clear to you the infinite diversity of men's opinions? And did I not remind you, time and again, how variable are human creeds and customs? So, along with youth, good looks, and wealth, you have the wisdom of far riper years; your mind is free from prejudice and superstition; you have no family ties, no religion, and no calling; you are free to turn your hand to anything. But you know better than to commit yourself—and there lies your strength. So, in a word, you stand head and shoulders above the ruck and, what's more, you could hold a chair of philosophy or architecture in a great university. And yet you cavil at your lot!

ORESTES: No, I do not cavil. What should I cavil at? You've left me free as the strands torn by the wind from spiders' webs that one sees floating ten feet above the ground. I'm light as gossamer and walk on air. I know I'm favored. I appreciate my lot at its full value. (*A pause.*) Some men are born bespoken; a certain path has been assigned them, and at its end there is something they *must* do, a deed allotted. . . . When I was seven, I knew I had no home, no roots. . . .

Here is Orestes at the beginning of the play, and the chief point which it makes dramatically is Orestes' slow transformation. To the Tutor's dismay, in the face of Jupiter's expressed displeasure, even with Electra's warning, he sees that he must remain in Argos, that he must take revenge for his father's death as the means for establishing his own identity, that he must murder Clytemnestra and Aegisthus if for no other reason than to fill up the empty rooms of his memory. After the bloody act is performed, there is an exultant scene between Orestes and Electra. She asks if he is afraid. He has a strange air.

ORESTES: I am free, Electra. Freedom has crashed down on me like a thunderbolt.

ELECTRA: Free? But I—I don't feel free. And you—can you undo what has been done? Something has happened and we are no longer free to blot it out. Can you prevent our being the murderers of our mother—for all time?

ORESTES: Do you think I'd wish to prevent it? I have done *my* deed, Electra, and that deed was good. I shall bear it on my shoulders as a carrier at a ferry carries the traveler to the further bank. And when I have brought it to the further bank I shall take stock of it. The heavier it is to carry, the better pleased I shall be: for that burden is my freedom. Only yesterday I walked the earth haphazard; thousands of roads I tramped that brought me nowhere, for they were other men's roads. . . . Today I have one path only, and heaven knows where it leads. But it is *my* path. . . .

The transformation of Orestes in the course of the play is striking. Before the decisive act, he walked a thousand roads; now he walks one. Before, he was empty and light as air; now he is heavy with the burden of his freedom. Before, he enjoyed the doubtful pleasures of aesthetic disengagement; now he experiences the dense reality of moral choice. To put it this way is to recognize the debt which Sartre (and with him the whole existentialist position) owes to Kierkegaard. Before Kierkegaard *The Flies* would not have been possible.

The center of the contribution which Kierkegaard has made to existentialism is *the significance of the act of choice*, the baptism of the will which lifts up the act of choice into the realm of the ethical, the distinction between the aesthetical and the ethical in the composition of personality.[2] What is important is that one shall stand "at the crossroads" where decision is called for, and that one shall "make the choice with real earnestness." The choiceless man exploits the tactics of defense; his occupation consists in preserving his hiding-place. But in the end the circle of defense becomes the circle of confinement; he dissolves into multiplicity. He who cannot reveal himself cannot love. "For me," says Kierkegaard, "the instant of choice is very serious, not so much on account of the rigorous cogitation involved in weighing the alternatives . . . but rather because there is danger afoot, danger that the next instant it may not be equally in my power to choose, that something already has been lived which must be lived over again." The consequence of this doctrine is that what is really morally relevant is not the outcome of the choice but the exercise of will which makes the choice possible. "As soon as one can get a man to stand at the crossroads in such a position that there is no recourse but to choose, he will choose the right." This is what Sartre means when he has Orestes say: "I have accomplished *my* act, Electra, and this act was good." It is not a celebration of the ethical virtues of matricide; it is an assertion of the intrinsic value of free choice.

It was the Tutor's wish that Orestes should be rootless and reflective, and in the end for Kierkegaard these two are the same. Reflection has the remarkable property of being infinite, but the moral life asks not for reflection but for a *resolve*. What is necessary for a man is not that he shall be a logical thinker, but that he be conscious of himself as *an existing individual*, and what this means is essentially a shift from the intellect to the will. "It is from this side in the first instance," says Kierkegaard,[3] "that objection must be made to modern philosophy; not that it has a mistaken presupposition, but that it has a comical presupposition, occasioned by its having forgotten, in a sort of world-historical absent-mindedness, what it means to be a human being." From Descartes to Kant modern philosophy has taken epistemology as its central concern. What it ought to have done was to produce a phenomenology of moral experience.

But what does it mean to be conscious of oneself as an existing individual? Sartre answers the question in the spirit of Kierkegaard. It means to be free ("I am neither master nor slave, Jupiter," says Orestes, "I *am* my freedom") but it also means loneliness, dread, and despair. "Suddenly," says Orestes, "freedom crashed down upon me and knocked me over. Nature sprang back, my youth was gone, and I knew myself alone, utterly alone in the midst of this benign little world, like someone who has lost his shadow, and there was no longer anything in heaven, no good nor evil, nor anyone to give me orders." Toward the end of the play there appears a brief dialogue between Orestes and Jupiter. It concerns Orestes' duty to bring freedom to his subjects, the people of Argos. It, too, is reminiscent of Kierkegaard, although there is more than a hint of Dostoievsky's Grand Inquisitor.

ORESTES: . . . You are God and I am free; each of us is alone, and our anguish is akin. . . .

ZEUS: What do you propose to do?

ORESTES: The folk of Argos are my folk. I must open their eyes.

ZEUS: Poor people! Your gift to them will be a sad one; of loneliness and shame. You will tear from their eyes the veils I had laid on them, and they will see their lives as they are, foul and futile, a barren boon.

ORESTES: Why, since it is their lot, should I deny them the despair I have in me?

ZEUS: What will they make of it?

ORESTES: What they choose. They're free; and human life begins on the far side of despair.

If we examine this short exchange, we cannot, I think, but be struck by its *extreme*, indeed, by its un-Greek flavor. It is not merely the catastrophic character of freedom, but the implication that in the end God and man are in the same situation of insight and power. But this means not that man is thoroughly alive, but that *the Gods are dead*. In Aeschylus' *Choephoroi* the deed lies under the blessings of the Delphic oracle; both Orestes and Electra pray reverently for success to a benign Hermes. But in *The Flies* Jupiter first slyly and then menacingly attempts to dissuade Orestes from the fatal act. And the reason becomes slowly clear. Sartre's Jupiter is not an Olympian Greek, he is a Christian Machiavelli, that is to say, the Christian God projected on the retina of an atheist. *The Flies* begins in a public square in Argos dominated by a statue of Jupiter, "*dieu des mouches et de la mort*" (God of death and of remorse), a statue with white staring eyes and blood-smeared cheeks. The statue is symbolic. The flies are attracted to Argos as to a corpse. Every year the people of Argos celebrate a holiday of the dead on the day of Agamemnon's death. It has been ritualized; on this day they even have someone scream in the palace of the dead king. Aegisthus his murderer still reigns. Jupiter has not seen fit to punish him, instead he has "turned the tumult to the profit of the moral order." He has sent instead the flies of remorse. Black mourning has become the costume in Argos, all are penitent, all are crushed under the heavy burden of complicity in crime, of the sense of original sin. When Orestes demurs, Jupiter tells him to go and leave these people undisturbed, for "their fear and their bad consciences are as perfume in the nostrils of the Gods." The climax of this line of reasoning occurs in the second act, where Jupiter actually comes to warn the tyrant Aegisthus that he is in danger from Electra and Orestes. Aegisthus asks why he wishes to prevent this crime, since he did not prevent the death of Agamemnon, and Jupiter replies that Aegisthus' crime served his purposes; he likes the kind of crimes that pay off; for one dead man, twenty thousand others plunged into repentance—that's a balance sheet for you! But the point is that the tyrant of earth and the tyrant of heaven are accomplices, joint conspirators for the maintenance of human bondage.

ZEUS: Look at me. (*A long silence.*) I told you you were made in my image. Each keeps order; you in Argos, I in heaven and on earth—and you and I harbor the same dark secret in our hearts.

AEGISTHUS: I have no secret.

ZEUS: You have. The same as mine. The bane of gods and kings. The bitterness of knowing men are free. Yes, Aegisthus, they are free. But your subjects do not know it, and you do. . . . So you see we are alike.

AEGISTHUS: Alike? A god likening himself to me—what freak of irony is this? Since I came to the throne, all I said, all my acts, have been aimed at building up an image of myself. I wish each of my subjects to keep that image in the foreground of his mind, and to feel, even when alone, that my eyes are on him, severely judging his most private thoughts. But I have been trapped in my own net. I have come to see myself only as they see me. I peer into the dark pit of their souls, and there, deep down, I see the image that I have built up. I shudder, but I cannot take my eyes off it. Almighty Zeus, who am I? Am I anything more than the dread that others have of me?

ZEUS: And I—who do you think *I* am? . . .

For Sartre God is dead, and all that remains is the ancient paraphernalia of remorse, guilt, and bad conscience, which is but dust in the eyes of those who are too weak, too poverty-stricken in spirit, too ignorant to see. To put it this way is to recognize the debt which Sartre (and much of existentialism with him) owes to Nietzsche.

Nietzsche's principal contribution to existentialism is the concept of *the transvaluation of all values*. Naturally this transvaluation is a function of the cultural condition, and since the structure of evaluation of

Western man is founded upon the Christian tradition, the chief task is to assess the implications of the total loss of a supernatural guarantee for the hierarchy of values. One moment of religious doubt and the foundations of customary morality crumble. What if our moral judgments are but moral prejudices? What if man's perception of good and evil is not a discovery of laws implicit in the universe, but a human invention? What if our moral sentiments in reality lead only to the distress, impoverishment, and degeneration of man? What if the imposition of the moral code results chiefly in inhibiting the maximum power and splendor of the human species? To answer these questions is the program which Nietzsche sets for himself in *The Genealogy of Morals.*[4]

The program is brilliantly accomplished. The chief terms of our moral vocabulary are found to originate in the accidents of class structure and social status, in the knightly and aristocratic natures of joyful men or in the morbidity and neurasthenia of priests. Bad (*schlecht*) is how the noble and heroic view the low, the inferior, and the vulgar. Evil (*böse*) is how the beloved of Christianity—the meek, the patient, and the altruistic—envisage the selfish, the overbearing, and the proud. But this appeal to history and philology has devastating axiological consequences. For it shows through the meshes of its naturalistic method the ultimate self-deception of the Christian mind: the interpretation of weakness as freedom. And for a philosophy of history it suggests an implicit preference for Rome over Judea, the Renaissance over the Reformation, the age of Richelieu and Racine over that of Robespierre and Rousseau.

But this is not all. All religions are at bottom systems of cruelty. It is their function to maim the instincts of freedom, internalize them, and by turning them against man, produce their final triumph, the bad conscience. The bad conscience is nothing but the serious illness of having to live in a maimed and thwarted society. It is the will toward self-laceration and self-persecution which provides the necessary conditions for the existence of altruism as a value. And as the foundation of that form of self-torture which Christianity has finally perfected as the sense of sin, it is the same penalty which Jupiter exacted of the people of Argos (a proper levy of remorse) and the "mild" price which, even after the murder of Clytemnestra and Aegisthus, he wished to exact of Orestes and Electra in order to install them on the throne of Argos (it's almost nothing, he says; you can give it to me easily—just a little repentance). Electra is too weak, too "Christian" perhaps, and she is unable to support the consequences of her crime. But Orestes defies Jupiter. Like Nietzsche's ideal—the superman of the truly independent will—he looks upon himself as free in that he is competent to promise and to guarantee his responsibility strictly from his own nature. It is his moral pride which inspires his contempt for the imitative social morality of the herd. Only such a man—inner-directed, finding the standard of value in his own moral commitment—can resist the terrible power of mediocrity, can summon the courage to be self-sustainingly different. Promethean defiance is very close to Nietzsche's heart, and much of it enters into the composition of Sartre's existential hero.

Nietzsche's criticism of the religious consciousness also requires an analysis of the meaning of ascetic ideals, and it is here above all that questions of mere philosophic doctrine are transformed into questions of attitude and psychological atmosphere. For the aescetic ideal, long celebrated in the images of Christian saintliness, is converted by Nietzsche's transvaluation of values into a nihilistic flight from life, a demand for Nothingness which denies the health of human Existence. The great danger to man is not the powerful or the ethically ruthless, it is rather to be found in the sickness of self-contempt, in the *nausea with man* which follows from the consistent application of the Christian view of the world. In the end the ascetic ideal means that all of human suffering has been brought under the perspective of human guilt, and that a hatred of the intrinsically human and an almost animal horror of the senses expresses a diseased will for Nothingness.

Nothingness, nausea, the sickness of self-contempt, guilt, bad conscience: these terms reappear over and over in the Nietzschean analysis of the transvaluation of all values. They are histrionic, and they suggest a definite psychological condition. When we note the similarity to the labors of Kierkegaard, three of whose most important works are entitled respectively *Fear and Trembling, The Concept of Dread,* and *The Sickness Unto Death,* it is impossible to escape the conviction that the peculiar atmosphere of contemporary existentialism has been prepared not merely by a series of doctrinal convictions, but by a new sensitivity to the *feeling-tone* of modern perception. Kierkegaard's emphasis on the significance of the act of choice and Nietzsche's doctrine of the transvaluation of all values are crucial, but they are no more fundamental than the former's infinitely patient exploration of despair and the latter's recognition of modern Man's emotional plight: "I have got lost, I am everything that has got lost."[5]

Karl Jaspers has given an exhaustive analysis of what he calls "the origin of the contemporary philosophical situation."[6] He sums it up thus: "We can no longer tranquilly proceed in the continuity of a traditional, intellectual education. For through Kierkegaard and Nietzsche a mode of existential experience has become effective, whose consequences on all sides have not yet come to light. They posed a question which is not yet clear but which one can feel: this question is still open. Through them we have become aware that for us there is no longer any self-evident foundation. There is no longer any secure background for our thought." Kierkegaard's subordination of the infinite train of intellectual deliberation to the act of decision and Nietzsche's suggestion that the ascetic ideal and science are allied (since the objectivity of the latter is a form of cowardice—a retreat from the resolute assertion of values) tend to undermine the "traditional intellectual education;" and the attack which both mount against Christianity as an institutionalized source of values has helped to undermine "any secure background for our thought." What remains? According to Jaspers it is "a mode of existential experience" to which both Kierkegaard and Nietzsche were the first to call attention.[7] What is the nature of "the existential experience" and where is it to be found?

In a sense it is any experience "lived at the limits" of the feelings, the intellect, and the will; it is the quality of all perceptions which arise within the confines of "extreme situations." It is therefore to be found in its purest state wherever there is dread, despair, death, nausea, self-contempt, guilt, bad-conscience, anxiety, disgust, and the confrontation with "nothingness." This means that its native habitat is less where it can be connotatively defined than where it can be emotively shown forth. This, of course, means literature. We have already experienced it in Orestes of The Flies. It is also to be found in Sartre (if less purely and effectively portrayed) in Garcin of No Exit, Hugo of Dirty Hands and Antoine Roquentin of the short novel Nausea. It appears classically in Dostoievsky's Ivan, Raskolnikov, and Stavrogin, and in the poems of Rilke. More recently it is found in the novels of Kafka and Camus, and in general in the novel of anxiety, ambiguity, and disgust.

But to say that the existential experience is the stuff of modern literature is to raise the question of how this immediate content can be rendered through philosophic treatment and granted a philosophic form. This suggests that existentialism has need not only of the type of content dramatized by Kierkegaard and Nietzsche, but of the suggestions with respect to form and method which spring from the point of view of Husserl.[8] We have already seen how through a kind of pre-established harmony the temporal disquisitions of Bergson have found a natural analogue in the literary work of Proust. The two sides of Sartre, not unnaturally, express a similar congruence. Sartre, the philosopher, is interested in the manifestations and the structure of Being; his chef d'oeuvre *L'être et le néant* he subtitles *Essai d'ontologie phénoménologique*,[9] and in his analysis of the phenomenon he says:

The appearance is not supported by any existent different from itself; it has its own being. The first being which we meet in our ontological inquiry is the being of the appearance. . . . Thus there must be for it a phenomenon of being, an appearance of being capable of description as such. Being will be disclosed to us by some kind of immediate access—boredom, nausea, etc., and ontology will be the description of the phenomenon of being as it manifests itself; that is, without intermediary.

The description of the phenomenon of being is a triumph of the phenomenological method, and in this passage as throughout *L'être et le néant* Sartre must constantly attest his debt to Husserl. But the immediate disclosure of being receives its only possible symbolic rehearsal in the forms of literature. Here it is necessary to turn to Sartre, the literary artist.

The thing which was waiting [says Roquentin in *Nausea*[10]] was on the alert, it has pounced on me, it flows through me, I am filled with it. It's nothing: I am the Thing. Existence, liberated, detached, floods over me. I exist. I exist. It's sweet, so sweet, so slow. And light: you'd think it floated all by itself. It stirs. It brushes by me, melts and vanishes. Gently, gently. There is bubbling water in my mouth. I swallow. It slides down my throat, it caresses me—and now it comes up again into my mouth. For ever I shall have a little pool of whitish water in my mouth—lying low—grazing my tongue. And this pool is still me. And the tongue. And the throat is me. . . . I see my hand spread out on the table. It lives—it is me. . . . How serpentine is this feeling of existing—I unwind it, slowly. . . . My thought is *me*: that's why I can't stop. I exist because I think . . . and I can't stop myself from thinking. At this very moment—it's frightful—if I exist, it is because I am horrified at existing. *I am the one* who pulls myself from the nothingness to which I aspire: the hatred, the disgust of existing, there are so many ways to *make* myself exist, to thrust myself into existence. . . .

As exemplified in this passage, the existential emotions lack structure, lack magnification, lack essence. To supply this quality is the aim of the phenomenological method which Sartre (and certainly Heidegger as well) has learned from Husserl. For in phenomenological analysis is revealed "the objective correlative" of the subjective immediacy of literature.

The science of "Pure Phenomenology" founded by Edmund Husserl claims to "be nothing beyond a Theory of Essential Being developed within a medium of pure intuition."[11] The claim is formidable, and even the formulation is reminiscent of Kant, but what is important for the existential enterprise is not the theory but the method. Phenomenology attempts a descriptive account of the essence of pure experience, but its material is phenomena in their givenness; it therefore neither attempts to idealize that which is presented nor to work back to the assumed substructure of what lies behind. Phenomenology denies the validity of the distinction between appearance and reality, and is concerned exclusively with the descriptive aspects of the appearances. This means neither the type of positivistic concern which Russell and Carnap might have with sense-data nor the analysis of the data of consciousness as these might present themselves to the inspection of a naturalistic psychology. With phenomenology, says Husserl,[12] "we meet a science—of whose extraordinary extent our contemporaries have as yet no concept—which, it is true, is a science of consciousness and still not psychology, a *phenomenology of consciousness as opposed* to a *natural science about consciousness.*" What Husserl has in mind is clearly what is anathema to the naturalistic imagination—an absolutely strict science which is at the same time not empirical analysis.

Phenomenological analysis is possible only after the natural standpoint has been abandoned, for what is at stake here is not the individual experience in its particularity but *the structure of experience,* its *logic,* the *essence* which is objectively manifest when more subjective involvement has been relaxed. Upon reflection it seems that there is a certain paradox here, a certain tension of opposites within the existentialist ambience. The content of Kierkegaard stresses the passionate inwardness of the subjective thinker; Husserl's phenomenological method requires the employment of logic and objectivity. In a sense, the problem of *an existential philosophy* (as contrasted with the immediacy of an existential experience) is to preserve a sense of the absolute uniqueness of individual existence without forcing the abandonment (as Kierkegaard actually tried to do) of the philosophical enterprise.

Husserl is interested in everything in consciousness which can be made transparent without recourse to the discipline of logic in the ordinary sense or to the empirical disciplines, and his proposals for a descriptive phenomenology which is independent of these resources require a special methodological device. This is the famous self-suspension of the experiencing subject from the natural world, to which it remains none the less in fact connected, and a similar fictional disconnection of the object from the larger cosmological context within which it appears. As Descartes employed the device of universal doubt (not naively, but as a device of method, as a demonstration that from the standpoint of the intellect we exist in a realm of perfect freedom), so Husserl employs the device of "disconnection" or "bracketing." By "bracketing" the object, we suspend the phenomenon from all existential judgments, all valuational concern, and we systematically make no use of our "lived experience" in order that the object may reveal itself without the accompanying distortion of our cognitive attitudes. In relation to every purely natural predisposition we employ the *"epoche"* of the Greek skeptics, but this "suspension," like that of the Cartesian doubt, is not directed toward the intrinsic annihilation of the self, but toward the discovery of a new scientific domain, that of *the object as it reveals itself*. As Heidegger, quoting Husserl, sums it up in *Sein und Zeit*:[13] "The word 'phenomenology' carries with it a formula which can be stated thus: 'to the facts themselves.' "

The appeal "to the facts themselves," the decision to permit experience to declare its own intentions and exhibit its own nature, requires as method what Husserl calls respectively a "phenomenological" and an "eidetic" reduction. The first means the resolute abandonment of the natural standpoint; the second means that the framework of formal logic may be rejected for a descriptive analysis based upon pure intuition.[14] The details are not important, for they are not followed by existentialists like Heidegger and Sartre; what counts is the ultimate purpose. Husserl is really interested in the possibility of achieving that state of receptivity in the knowing subject where the intelligibility of the logico-formal structure of experience becomes transparent. Positivists, who are committed to a method which demands freedom from metaphysical presuppositions, are nevertheless totally unsympathetic to reliance upon pure intuition, and the existentialists are by no means convinced that it is possible to carry through the phenomenological reduction, but they have adopted the framework of a method which permits some degree of formalization of the immediately elusive existential experience. If dread, anxiety, bad faith, nausea, and guilt can somehow be rescued from their evanescence in the stream of mere experience, if it can be shown that their qualitative force can also be handled by giving them a generalized frame of reference in some situational context, then the more primitive insights of Nietzsche and Kierkegaard are available for development within a generalized ontology of the human situation. This is what Sartre and Heidegger, and perhaps even Jaspers, owe to Husserl's phenomenology.

The first few pages of Sartre's chief work introduce the theme, *à la recherche de l'être*—in pursuit of Being. The first article of faith is the assumption that the being of an existent is exactly what it appears— that a phenomenon can be studied and described not for what lies behind it, but for its self-indicative character. "This is why," says Sartre,[15] "we can equally well reject the dualism of appearance and essence. The appearance does not hide the essence, it reveals it; it *is* the essence. The essence of an existent is no longer a property sunk in the cavity of the existent; it is the manifest law which presides over the succession of its appearances, it is the principle of the series." In short, as both Kant and Husserl might have said, *the object shows itself as the structure of its appearance.*

The quest for Being in Heidegger is both an attempt to re-establish metaphysics, and an inquiry into the nature of human existence. As he puts it:[16] "The understanding of Being is itself a defining quality of human existence." But the reverse is also true, for only out of an existial analysis of human existence is it possible to establish a basic ontology. This seems self-evident, yet it sets a problem of ultimate aim for the existential enterprise—a problem which we have already seen in other terms as the existential *experience* versus the existential *philosophy*—and in each case it grows out of the assimilation in one existentialist cadre of two influences which are strong, but not entirely compatible—that of Kierkegaard and that of Husserl.

Existentialism is oriented about two major themes: *the analysis of Being* and *the centrality of human choice.* This means that its theoretical energies may be devoted alternately to *ontology* and *decision.* For any "existentialist" philosopher, it is of interest to inquire whether his chief concern is metaphysics or a phenomenology of moral experience. If, like Heidegger, he answers "Both" (and, indeed, it seems eminently reasonable to do so), then one must examine the system in its totality to see if the practice is congruent with the intention, for existentialist systems are deceptive in this respect.

Sartre's *L'Etre et le néant* and Heidegger's *Sein und Zeit* start identically with great respect for Husserl and the phenomenological method,[17] with the promise of an equal interest in ontology and the human predicament. But as we reach the end it becomes clear that the outcome is essentially different in the two cases.

Sartre's examination of the problem of Nothingness and his analysis of the ontology of temporality are a necessary preliminary for his phenomenological investigations of mind and body, social relations, the conditions of freedom and responsibility. And in the end the metaphysical implications pale into insignificance before the promise of the future construction of a concrete ethics and a social philosophy.

The analysis of Being has therefore served as an instrument for the assertion of the centrality of human choice. But in Heidegger, the movement of thought is reversed. He is concerned with "our being" and "our being in the world" and that "care" which constitutes the being of our human existence, and he has also expressed with a new vividness the importance which a recognition of death has for the authenticity of the human person and the peculiar poignancy of our "dread in the face of Nothingness." But although all this seems profoundly relevant to the phenomenology of the human condition, it is not because this is Heidegger's primary interest. For he is an ontologist, almost (if not quite) within the classical tradition, and his basic concern is with the explication of Being. At the heart of Heidegger's philosophy there is a paradox which a positivist might describe as the pathetic fallacy raised to the dignity of an ontological method. Its strategy is to produce a metaphysics through the ontologizing of human emotional experience.

Thus far I have tried to show the philosophical sources of existentialism in the recent past: Kierkegaard's emphasis upon the existing individual and the significance of the act of choice; Nietzsche's transvaluation of all values in which God is dead, leaving a residue of the existential emotions: guilt, bad conscience, self-contempt, disgust with man; and finally Husserl's phenomenology, which provided a new method for structuralizing these emotions, for exhibiting the essence of the human experience, and for permitting the nature of Being to reveal itself. I have suggested, too, how Kierkegaard's radical individualism is somewhat at variance with Husserl's ontological concerns, leaving existentialists like Heidegger and Sartre with two themes—the analysis of Being, and the centrality of human choice—not completely reconciled in practice. They are obviously both legitimate philosophical concerns, but if in defining the existential enterprise, a choice between them were required, it would have, I think, to rest with the latter. This is what is new in existentialism. There are already traditional and classical views of Being which treat it as a transcendental, show that its predication is always analogically related to a ground of experience, or (as in the case of St. Thomas) make of it the unity of essence and existence. If the Thomistic solution is not final, it at least indicates the necessity of relating the two poles of the distinction: an "essence" which is rich in abstractness and generality, and an "existence" which overflows with particularity and immediacy. Always throughout the history of philosophy there are the two versions: a view of Being which sees it as the anchorage of essence in existence, and a view of existence which places it at a certain point in the exhaustive continuity of the scale of essences. One might say that the more modern metaphysics of Kierkegaard and Heidegger cannot avoid a stand on just such traditional matters. But whereas Heidegger's is really a philosophy of Being, that of Kierkegaard and Sartre is really a philosophy of human existence. It was Kierkegaard's genuine originality to demand a strict separation of essence and existence, to recognize that emotion expresses existence, and, like Sartre, who follows him in this respect, to insist that *existence precedes essence*.[18]

Kierkegaard's extreme emphasis upon individuality serves to reinforce two impulses which lie close to the spiritual situation of our time. One is the loss of religious faith which since the beginning of the nineteenth century has undermined the confidence in cosmic values, and has made the decisions of the isolated individual the last stand of a desperate humanism. The other, operating since the rise of modern industry, is the encroachment of mass society upon the domain of personal privacy and authentic selfhood, giving to the ideal of private self-determination a holiness hitherto accorded only to prayer. Existentialism, as a cultural phenomenon (rather than as a philosophy) is, then, half protest, half refuge, and where (as in Sartre, for example) it is defiant, this defiance shields its devotees against a coercive society and against a universe denuded of intrinsic value. Thus both the religious crisis and the social predicament have served to bring out in existentialist thought that very emphasis upon personal decision and the isolated individual which the philosophy of Kierkegaard projects. This is why I have chosen to interpret it not simply as "the recognition of the abysses which lie on each side of the footpath that the vulgar follow with the serenity of somnambulists" which Georges Sorel finds all philosophy to be, but rather as that philosophical position in the modern world which takes as central the drama of human choice.

It is impossible to find a simple definition for existentialism.[19] Let us say that it is that indeterminate central point around which the eccentric orbits of Karl Jaspers, Martin Heidegger, Jean-Paul Sartre, and Gabriel Marcel revolve like some irregular planets in a constellation visible but not finally known. Let us say further that in the end existentialism is to be judged by the merit of four basic texts: Jaspers' *Philosophie*, Heidegger's *Sein und Zeit*, Sartre's *L'Etre et le néant*, and Marcel's *Journal métaphysique*. In what follows I shall not attempt the complete interplanetary journey, but shall take as central (1) the *Existenzphilosophie* of Karl Jaspers, (2) the philosophy of the self in Sartre, and (3) the composite existentialist critique of society to be found not only in Jaspers and Sartre, but in Marcel, Simone de Beauvoir, and Merleau-Ponty as well.

2. THE "EXISTENZPHILOSOPHIE" OF JASPERS

The classic dilemmas of the philosophic life are found in the opposition between the theoretical and the practical, between thinking and existing, between contemplating and doing. The deepest philosophic problems are concerned with the resolution of these oppositions, which are somehow intolerable to the mediating and unifying philosophic mind. Bergson distinguishes sharply between the method of philosophy and the method of science, but at the cost of maintaining that the intellect which we have adjudged a speculative instrument is in reality a practical device. Carnap, on the contrary, insists that the method of philosophy and the method of science are the same, but at the cost of maintaining that metaphysics is meaningless, and that there can be no cognitive foundations for the moral life. An even more interesting contrast is provided by the work of Dewey and of Karl Jaspers. For Dewey science and philosophy alike are members of the continuum of inquiry, and the division of theoretical and practical is overcome by showing that there is no type of speculative science which does not involve practical judgment, just as there is no type of practical problem to whose solution theoretical knowledge cannot contribute. For Jaspers, on the contrary, the employment of knowledge as a means of exploring possibilities which relate to a finite objective is a technical, not a philosophic, activity, and philosophic meditation is anything but impartial. For both Dewey and Jaspers the aim of the philosophic impulse is "practical," but where for Dewey philosophy is the promotion of human *doing*, for Jaspers it is the achievement of man's *being*.

We philosophize not to arrange the conclusions of the special sciences, or to establish beyond question a method of knowledge, or to master the systems and the texts of the history of philosophy, but rather because, finding ourselves in the midst of life, philosophic meditation is the practical activity through which we attain Being and become fully conscious of our selfhood. Philosophizing is not the formulation of countless propositions; it is the activity of thought by which the individual man realizes the essence of all men, and this activity originates not at the surface level of finite purposes and narrowly individual projects, but in the depths of perplexity and crisis where decision is not a mere matter of the next moment, but of a total life, and where the atoms of Time somehow seem to intersect with the demands of Eternity.

Philosophizing, therefore, is an inner action by which I become myself, and in this sense it is *a revelation of Being.*

This does not mean that philosophizing is unrelated to science, to epistemology, and to the philosophic tradition. Since the basic philosophic questions spring from the conditions of life, and since life at any moment is embedded in a specific historical situation, temporality itself originates the fundamental questions. In our age science has achieved an overwhelming importance; "By its consequences," as Jaspers says, "it has become the fate of the world." But if science cannot be avoided, we experience it as much at the limits of its ability to know as at the center of its practical accomplishment. What Carnap takes as an axiom of method Jaspers takes as an index of failure: "the knowledge of science fails in the face of all ultimate questions." Our infinite desire for knowledge and for truth brings us to the acknowledgment of the limitations of science, and this acknowledgment forces us beyond the confines of an imperfect naturalism to the self-reliance which is the last stand of a desperate humanism. Sartre's Orestes puts it melodramatically in his reply to Jupiter:

Foreign to myself—I know it. Outside nature, against nature, without excuse, without any recourse except what I find within myself. But I shall not return under your law. I am condemned to have no other law but my own. Nor shall I return to nature. . . .

Jaspers asserts the same humanistic consequence more calmly, less defiantly, and perhaps more optimistically:[20]

In the world *man* alone is the reality which is accessible to me. Here is presence, nearness, fullness, life. Man is the place at which and through which everything that is real exists for us at all. To fail to be human would mean to slip into nothingness. What man is and can become is a fundamental question for man.

Philosophizing is therefore the attempt to answer the question of "what man is and what he can become," but it would be a mistake to believe that this question is answerable by using the type of scientific knowledge which can be proved in order to fortify the convictions by which we live. One espouses the sciences, but only in the course of working out a methodology which points toward a universal consciousness of Being, and illuminates it. Philosophy is wholly unlike science; it is the activity of thought through the inwardness of which I become aware of the deepest levels of Being.

But it would also be a mistake to confuse inwardness with mere subjectivity. Man is not isolated or alone in his being. He "is constituted by the things which he makes his own. In every form of his being man is related to something other than himself: as a being to his world, as consciousness to objects, as spirit to the idea of whatever constitutes totality, as Existenz to Transcendence."[21] The human is developed through its encounter with and devotion to "the other," and this other, whether the deepest reaches of internality or the furthest boundaries of the surrounding spiritual environment (and whether termed "the Encompassing," "Transcendence," or "Deity"), serves as the "limits" for the definition of individual existence. In this sense the metaphysics of Jaspers is not unlike that of Dewey or Whitehead. The individual as the focus of experience is the figure set against a wider background. When this configuration is set within the context of consciousness rather than of atomistic objects in some impersonal Nature, the quality of human existence becomes a function of its "sense of the horizon."

It is the exceptional accomplishment of Kierkegaard and Nietzsche that they demonstrate the way in which isolation and radical loneliness can engulf the human person,[22] for their lives express the perils of the human condition: "We are so exposed that we constantly find ourselves facing nothingness. Our wounds are so deep that in our weak moments we wonder if we are not, in fact, dying from them."[23] At one level these wounds are healed by the "will to communication," by the successful establishment of that spiritual "conversation" or "dialectic" which is manifested within the atmosphere of social reciprocity. In an autobiographical moment Jaspers indicates how central this is for his whole position.[24]

No urge seemed stronger to me than that for communication with others. If the never-completed movement of communication succeeds with but a single human being, everything is achieved. It is a criterion of this success that there be a readiness to communicate with every human being encountered and that grief is felt whenever communication fails. Not merely an exchange of words, nor friendliness and sociability, but only the constant urge towards total revelation reaches the path of communication.

One major existential source of philosophizing is the gnawing uneasiness of insufficient communication. Solitude in nature may be a temporary replenishment of the sources of selfhood, but to remain solitary is an invitation to impoverishment. Nature as "the other" is therefore questionable when it does not lead back to humanity, to community, and to language. Jaspers, like Dewey, is profoundly aware of the consequences for the modern world of the loss of the sense of real community, and like Dewey also he finds the genesis of authentic selfhood to arise within the matrix of interaction and participation. When Dewey interrogates experience for its intimations of value, he asks: Is it the way of stagnation or of interactive growth? And when Jaspers passes in review thoughts, subject matters, and possibilities, his question is: Are they tempters to solitude or heralds of communication? At bottom the questions are the same. Says Jaspers:[24a]

> The thesis of my philosophizing is: The individual cannot become human by himself. Self-being is only real in communication with another self-being. Alone, I sink into gloomy isolation—only in community with others can I be revealed in the act of mutual discovery. My own freedom can only exist if the other is also free. Isolated or self-isolating Being remains mere potentiality or disappears into nothingness.

As the individual cannot become human by himself, so the thinking man cannot become philosophic without the resources of the philosophic tradition. It is true of course that our apprehension of truth is conditioned by our situation within the historical tradition, and that the specific content of *our* truth depends upon the type of appropriation of the philosophic past which we make. But on the other hand any philosophizing which is authentic must originate within our own problematic situation; hence "all appropriation of tradition must proceed from the intentness of our own life." There is here a double recognition: first, that the philosophic quest arises out of personal urgencies which cannot be ignored; second, that in the realm of the spirit men become contemporaries across the boundaries of time, become "occasions for each other to find the way to truth from their own source."

> Everything depends therefore on encountering thought at its source. Such thought is the reality of man's being, which achieved consciousness and understanding of itself through it. Though one needs knowledge of the concepts that emerge in the history of philosophy, the purpose of such knowledge remains to gain entrance to the exalted living practice of those past thoughts. My own being can be judged by the depths I reach in making these historical origins my own. . . . Such true thinking goes through history as a mystery which can reveal itself . . . for this hidden thinking was once reality. Having been written down, it can be rediscovered; at any time it can spark a new blaze.[25]

Jaspers' evaluation of the availability of the philosophy of the past for the solution of the problems of the present rests upon his belief both that philosophy has no institutional reality and that the history of philosophy constitutes one vast unity. Philosophizing is an individual and not a social activity. Hence any objectification of its message, any formation of schools or sects, any premature crystallization of its doctrine constitutes its ruin. But at the same time philosophers across the ages form one secret, limited community (perhaps like the Pythagoreans of old) joined by the ties of speculative brotherhood and mutually committed to "the penetration without limit into the unity of the revelation of Being."

Jaspers' own "penetration into the revelation of being" occurs primarily in his great work *Philosophie,* published in three volumes in 1932.[26] Since it is Jaspers' belief that philosophic truth is infinitely more than mere scientific correctness, the impulse behind his philosophical communication is to stimulate a "knowing" which shall be less the acquisition of fixed content than an inner act of illumination and awakening. The condition of the philosophic act is *a leap of transcending thought,* beyond psychology, beyond the objective and the determinate, toward *the limits* of the being which confronts us.

Jaspers' *Philosophie* is divided into three parts: "Philosophical World-Orientation," "The Illumination of Existence," and "Metaphysics." In each volume the attempt is made to show how transcendence is possible. The ultimate outcome of philosophical world-orientation indicates how the individual, originally deeply embedded in the world and its conditions of natural existence, reaches the freedom of his own selfhood. The ultimate outcome of the illumination of existence is to awaken man to what he really is: to make self-evident (and therefore negotiable) "the abysses which lie on each side of the footpath that the vulgar follow with the serenity of somnambulists." The ultimate outcome of metaphysics is to give some intimation of those final limits which man faces if he pushes the dimensions of his destiny past the world, past even the conditions of selfhood, to what might lie beyond.[27]

World-orientation presents us with the concept of objectivity, with what it means to be of and in the world, but as a knowledge of the things within the world, it is not quite the same as the analysis of the conditions of human existence. As orientation, it remains a perpetual experiment, an exploration which can never come to an end because its terrain is incapable of closure. Objective knowledge derivable from the empirical sciences is indispensable here; without it no philosophical world-orientation is possible, but at the same time it aims at a unification of empirical experience of which the natural sciences by their very natures are incapable. Philosophical world-orientation seeks to break through the limitations which the natural sciences impose.[28] By world-orientation Jaspers hopes to treat in his own distinctive way the problems which have been the enduring concerns of a more traditional epistemology: the relations between the "I" and the "not I," the dialectical interplay between subjective existence and objective reality and the kind of world projected by each, the clashes and reconciliations between the viewpoints which consider the world in its givenness and the world as an artifact of human construction. Implied also are the more traditional problems of methodology: the principles and divisions of reality, the distinction between nature and spirit and the separation between the natural and the cultural sciences which is its consequence, the ordering of the sciences and the setting of their limits of relevance for the total philosophic enterprise. Finally, world-orientation contrasts the insights of positivism and idealism, shows their mutual inadequacy as systems which claim a monopoly upon all knowledge, but indicates rather how philosophy, being identical neither with science, religion, nor art, yet has need of all three and must be for all three a final recall to order.

Metaphysics is the analysis of ultimate objectivity, of experience as a cryptogram of transcendence. It is an attempt to seek all existential roots in that which lies beyond existence. As such it is clothed in darkness from beginning to end, and it is full of danger. Metaphysics turns to the transcendent for the source and the confirmation of existence, and in this quest it is willing to make use of such resources as are available. It invokes a logic of transcendence where this is possible. More characteristically it utilizes art, poetry, and myth as revelations of transcendence. It employs not only a logic of discovery, but also a system of creation, and if its concepts and elements seek a rational intelligibility, they are nevertheless allied to mythical structures. Metaphysics in Jaspers' sense is not identical with religion; nevertheless it is closer to the impulse of St. John of the Cross than to that of Aristotle's *Metaphysics*. It asserts not that philosophy is analysis but that philosophy is vision.

Jaspers attempts an analysis of the nature and method of metaphysics, provides an account of the logical structure of transcendence (in which existence figures as the form of its historical appearance) and a formal description in which the classical categories of being and nothingness, unity and duality, form and matter, possibility and necessity, individuality and universality, time, space, substance, and freedom all appear as its qualifications. He concludes with a treatment of light and darkness, the one and the many, the world of symbolism and of human speech.

If from one point of view Jaspers' world-orientation is merely the traditional epistemology wrapped in a more romantic package, and his metaphysics is the customary ontology transliterated in the special vocabulary of transcendence, it is his illumination of existence (*Existenzerhellung*) which constitutes his chief claim to originality and the bridge between his form of existentialism and that of Heidegger and Sartre.

"That being which—appearing in the guise of empirical existence—*is not, but can be and ought to be,* determines in time if it shall be eternal. This Being I myself am in the form of Existenz." So begins the illumination of existence.[29] "Thus, not my empirical existence is Existenz, but *man in his empirical existence* is a possible Existenz. Empirical existence is actually given; but 'Existenz' appears only as freedom." The reference is obscure, but its development in Jaspers is not difficult to follow. The self realizes its own nature in its communication and its historicity. But its essence lies in its freedom, and this freedom is a characteristic of the will. The truth of our being is not an intellectual truth, but if it is founded upon the Existenz which we can become, what counts is that our life is guided by an absolute and unconditional necessity which flowers in the fact of our *decisions.* "Decision makes Existenz real, forms life, and changes it in its inner action." We are here in the presence of the same awareness of the drama of choice which has informed the philosophy of Kierkegaard. The decisive act is the agency for the consolidation of personality; it is the chief instrumentality in the process of self-creation.

Freedom is exclusively the possession of the realm of Existenz. In world-orientation Being is a state or condition; there is knowledge here, but no freedom. In transcendence there is no longer freedom; it has been left behind. But existential freedom, hanging upon the fact of choice, illumines the sphere of the characteristically human. In one sense freedom is always mediated; it is mediated by knowledge, by preference, by law, by moral requirement. But in another sense it is absolute. For it is the definitive quality of selfhood. We are here in the last stages of the philosophical revolution which has been initiated by Kierkegaard, the ultimate triumph of voluntarism as a mode of thought. For the sources of our existential reassurance are no longer cognitive, but moral. "*Cogito ergo sum*" was the assertion of Descartes. But "*Indem ich wähle, bin ich*" (I choose, therefore I am) is the assertion of Jaspers.[30]

In ethics, freedom is a formal structure, the over-all relationships of a situation in which action may be accomplished. In politics freedom is the factual absence of pressures, the intersection of obligation and response where opportunities remain for the development of a self which is pre-political. Thus the necessity for distinguishing between social and metaphysical freedom. By localizing freedom in the realm of Existenz, and by making it the defining quality of selfhood, Jaspers is treating freedom in its metaphysical rather than its ethical or political aspects. But by qualifying its absoluteness by the facts of man's immediate situation, and by recognizing the essentially limiting characteristics of the human condition, he avoids the predicament of Sartre, who is hard put to reconcile the absoluteness of freedom with the obvious limitations which situation-in-the-world imposes. Rather he approaches the position of Merleau-Ponty that there is never complete determinism and never absolute choice, and that it is impossible to separate the parts played by "freedom" and "situation" respectively. The fact is that Jaspers' great contribution to the phenomenology[31] of the human condition is the recognition and elaboration of the *Grenzsituation*, the "boundary" or "limiting" or "extreme" or perhaps best of all "inescapable" situations within whose absolute limits the necessities of human life are set.

That we are dealing here less with scientific description than with phenomenology is clear. "Situation" is not merely a naturalistic concept, but a reality in the realm of human meaning; not merely the possible object of the special sciences, but more.[32] Actual empirical existence *means* "being in a situation." It is impossible to escape from one situation without moving into another. Thus, that we are always placed within the confines of situation, that we cannot live without struggle and without suffering, that we experience unavoidable guilt, and that in the end we must die, are the "inescapables" of our being, but they are at the same time the agencies of tragic knowledge and the source of that unique intuition which informs us of the reality of our own existence. At this point we reach the essential formula which lies at the root of Jaspers' philosophy of existence: "*Grenzsituationen erfahren und Existieren ist dasselbe*"—"to experience inescapable situations and to exist are the same thing."[33]

Jaspers' treatment of the phenomenology of the human condition is brilliant. He deals in detail with the way in which inescapable situations constitute the historical determination of Existence in its four forms of death, suffering, conflict, and guilt. He indicates the impact of death upon life in the form of the death of those nearest me and the consciousness of my own death in all of its frightening unbearability. In his treatment of the anxieties of natural existence and existential dread (*Daseinsangst und Existenzangst*) he approaches the poetry as he equals the depth of a similar analysis which Heidegger makes in *Sein und Zeit*. The fearfulness of death appears in two forms: (1) as the fear of an existence which is inauthentic, (which might continue end-lessly without possibilities, means, or consequences), and (2) as the dread of radical non-Being which constitutes our real confrontation with Nothingness. But the analysis is not one-sided. For there is also a treatment of death as security, not so much in the sense of final peace as of fulfillment. Death is therefore friend as well as foe; when it is considered "less than life" it produces anxiety, but when it is considered "more than life" it breeds security. But friend or foe, Jaspers' treat-ment of death intimately relates it to life. It is not death and life in immediate opposition, but death and life as mutually implicated, as brothers, as having with one another that peculiar "commerce" (*Wandel*) which defines the human situation.

It is impossible, I think, to read Jaspers' account of the boundary situations—guilt, conflict, suffering, and death—without feeling his kinship with the spirit of Greek tragedy. There is the same sense of universal fate and of inevitability. This shows that existentialism need not have but one possible outcome. Sartre in *The Flies*, as we have seen, uses the outward trappings of Greek tragedy to propound an exis-tential moral which is as un-Christian as it is un-Greek. Jaspers, without explicit appeal to the Greeks, provides a situational analysis which is completely in their spirit. In this respect he is like Freud. But between Freud and Jaspers there is perhaps one crucial difference. By projecting the human condition within the setting of a naturalistic metaphysics, Freud leaves the terrors of existence unresolved. They are starkly there, and if he fortuitously adds on an afterthought of stoic resignation, this is a philosophical accident in a position which should have eventuated in a logic of despair. We must remember that the essence of the tragic drama is its purgation of pity and fear, and that this is accomplished in the work of art by the formalization of its material. This also is the outcome of the phenomenological method. If Jaspers is right in his belief that philosophy begins only where reason has suffered shipwreck, nevertheless there is a formal power of reason in its second coming, which deals with conflict and suffering, guilt and death, by exhibiting the logic of their relational structure. To anatomize anxiety and dread is to domesticate their immediate quality. This is what both Jaspers and Heidegger have learned from Husserl. To see in our "being-in-the-world," in our "being-with-others," and our "being-in-inescapable-situations" the essence of the human condition is an ac-tivity analogous to Greek tragedy. For it too is *to formalize the terrors of existence*.

A naturalistic account of guilt, conflict, suffering, and death can

leave no room for further metaphysical resources, for the world of
nature is finite, and the positivistic temper shrinks from any theorizing
beyond the self-enclosure of empirical method. But the existential point
of view as exemplified in Jaspers has this speculative advantage, that it
can see the human as a cryptogram of that which lies beyond; it can
utilize even the human experience of inescapable limits as a symbol of
the possibility of transcendence. "In the experience of inescapable
situations originates the path to Nothingness or the path to Being.
If inescapable situations as such are experienced, there are two possibilities—the road to Nothingness and the road to authentic Being; and
it can even be that the one lies hidden in the other."[34] But this possible
movement toward Being or Nothingness indicates the metaphysical
boundaries between which existence oscillates, and it serves to introduce
Jaspers' ultimate doctrine of relational being: the concept of *the Encompassing*.[35]

"What I actually am is the Encompassing of self-being. Self-being
means Existenz."[36] The problem of the Encompassing arises out of
the philosophical quest for a glimpse of the ultimate horizon, and this
ultimate horizon as it conditions all our experience has two forms:
"Being for us" (*Sein-für-uns*) and "Being-in-itself" (*Sein-an-sich*).
Being-in-itself is like Hegel's absolute: it is that which shows itself in
an infinite number of appearances, and provides the ground for endless
inquiries, although it is always shadowy and recessive, manifesting itself
in empirical existence but recalcitrant to final formulation. We call
it the World, or Nature, or Spinoza's God. But the Encompassing,
which we ourselves are, expresses itself in three specific modes: empirical
existence, consciousness in general, and Spirit.[37]

Everything which I experience as matter, life, or mind appears as
a part of my being in its perceptible relations to my body, which is
the emblem of my empirical existence. Once I am concerned with
this mode of inquiry, I become absorbed in that other form of the
Encompassing, Nature. The second form of the Encompassing which
I am is consciousness. What is not given to my consciousness, is for
me nothing. But to see that consciousness is not merely mine, but a
universal form in which all humanity participates, is to pass beyond the
empirical to its condition. Spirit is the third mode of the Encompassing
which we are. It is the urge for comprehensiveness and totality which
attempts to complete and to unify empirical existence; the drive toward
relatedness and intelligibility. Empirical existence, consciousness in
general, and Spirit are not separable facts. They are simply three as-

pects through which we experience our own Being and through which all the objects of our consciousness appear.

These three modes of the Encompassing present a limitless possibility, too vast to be genuinely known, where "each individual in his deepest inwardness seems to have disappeared." It is therefore not here, but in the awareness of possible Existenz, that the central point of all philosophizing is reached. "Existenz is the Encompassing, not in the sense of the vastness of a horizon of all horizons, but rather in the sense of a fundamental origin, the condition of selfhood, without which all the vastness of Being becomes a desert. Existenz, although never itself becoming an object or form, carries the meaning of every mode of the Encompassing."[38] Existenz is the concentration of Being in which the spaciousness of the Encompassing has been contracted into the uniqueness of the individual self. For here alone is the historicity, the expression of Being in time. Only as Existenz can the Self become genuinely certain of its Being. Thus Existenz is the particularity which serves as counterpart to Spirit. Spirit sees individuality as part of a whole, but Existenz is the decision by which individuality in itself is secured. "Spirit is the will to become *whole*; potential Existenz is the will to be *authentic*."[39] The Encompassing is the realm of possibility, but it is only Existenz which gives to human life its invincible actuality. "Existenz is the dark ground of selfhood, the concealment out of which I come to encounter myself, and for which Transcendence first becomes real."

Curiously bound to Existenz, but essentially different from it, is reason. Reason is a demand, not merely for objective thinking (which would be "understanding"), or for totality (which would be "spirit"), but for the primacy of thought in all modes of the Encompassing. Reason is not itself a source of Being, but it is the unrest which will remain satisfied with nothing less than complete order. It is the inextinguishable impulse to philosophize which binds together all modes of the Encompassing, and which drives fatefully toward a law and an order which it can never finally reach.

Reason and Existenz are thus the two great poles of our being, but they are less opposites than inseparable. Reason without Existenz would be form without substantial reality. Existenz without reason would be isolation without the resources of communication. Each without the other loses the genuine continuity of Being.

Thus reason and Existenz are not two opposed powers which struggle with one another for victory. Each exists only through the other. They mutually develop one another and find through one another clarity and reality.

Although they never combine into an ultimate whole, every genuine accomplishment is whole only through them.

Reason without Existenz even in the richest possible field finally passes into an indifferent thinking, a merely intellectual movement of consciousness as such, or into a dialectic of the spirit. And as it slips away into universality without the binding root of its historicity, it ceases to be reason.

Irrational Existenz which rests upon feeling, experiencing, unquestioned impulse, instinct, or whim, ends up as blind violence, and therewith falls under the empirical laws which govern these actual forces. Without historicity, lost in the mere particularities of contingent empirical existence in a self-assertion unrelated to Transcendence, it ceases to be Existenz.[40]

It is interesting, I think, that in this moderate synthesis Jaspers provides his own quiet clue to the solution of the problem which, as we have seen, haunts the background of our age: the conflict of rationality and the irrational. But he offers the solution to that problem not at that point of its moral emergence where it requires an opposition between deliberation and the act of resolute choice, but rather in terms of metaphysics. The classical tradition of Plato and Aristotle elevates essence over existence and form over empirical actuality. Sartre's defiant counterclaim is that existence logically precedes essence. But Jaspers' reconciliation of the polarity of reason and Existenz is to see them as mutually implying each other.

The distinction between reason and Existenz, of course, is only one level upon which the nature of the Encompassing is revealed. In the end even the question of rationality and the irrational assumes for Jaspers merely its subordinate place in the hierarchy which has the Encompassing at its apex. For Jaspers' whole mode of perception is dominated by the ambiguity of the notion of "limit" which finds its classic expression in the conflict of the transcendental ideas detailed in Kant's First Antinomy. The existential limit is *the boundary within which* human life is set. But it is at the same time *the point beyond which* transcendence is a fact. Jaspers' thought, whether in the phenomenology of "inescapable human situation" or in the metaphysics of "*Grenzen überhaupt*" (limits in general) and the Encompassing, hinges upon the shifting sands of contextual analysis, but in such a way as to give it stability and metaphysical anchorage. The idea of the Encompassing is a subversive, indeed a profoundly unsettling, notion, for it removes us from the objectivity of our momentary preoccupations and our scientific inquiries back into the domain of ourselves. It turns us from the

questions to the questioner. And, indeed, I am not authentically myself
if I am only that which I know myself to be. But here we return to Jaspers' conception of philosophy, with which we began. "The purpose and
therefore the meaning of a philosophical idea is not the cognition of an
object, but rather an alteration of our consciousness of Being and of
our inner attitude toward things." To explore the meaning of the
Encompassing is not to assert propositions, but to *create possibilities*.
Therefore the moral consequence of the *Existenz-philosophie* which
has been Jaspers' life work is less the construction of a system than a
dialectical prologue after which the assertion of a few simple imperatives
seems neither fatuous nor arrogant. Do not lose yourself in what is
merely here and now. Preserve the openness of the Encompassing. In
your decisiveness do not succumb to the factuality which might cut
you off from the unlimited ranges of Being.

3. SELF AND FREEDOM IN SARTRE

It is impossible, I think, to view the philosophy of Sartre without a
certain distaste. Not because he is an expert in the emotion of nausea
or because (as Gabriel Marcel has said) in his literary work his preoccupation is with the experience of the viscous secretions. Nor is it his
self-consciousness, which, projected upon his heroes, gives them the
feeling that the eyes of the world are upon them and that this is "an
alien gaze." Nor is it because of his obvious resentment of social order
and his denial of God. Nausea may be an existential fact. The invasion
of privacy may be a democratic tyranny. God and social order may be
invoked in acts of extreme cruelty. Rather it is because Sartre's philosophy is a cool demonstration that destructiveness is no accident but
an ontological necessity and that all human experience is founded upon
nothingness. Heidegger saw before Sartre our dread before the general
threat of nothingness, but even he has not shown the nihilating activity
of the human consciousness at the very center of the self.

Sartre's initial pursuit of Being begins characteristically enough with a
modification of Husserl and the payment of a debt to Heidegger. If
the distinction between appearance and reality no longer holds because
the phenomenon manifests its essence and its existence together, the
immediacy of the given is expressed equally in the qualities of the
object and in the meaning which it contains. But this does not mean
that it may be interpreted indifferently as either "in the world" or "in
the mind" as a Cartesian dualism requires. The object is a thing, a
dense focal point for consciousness ("*un centre d'opacité pour la conscience.*"), and the first procedure of philosophy ought to be to expel

things from consciousness so that consciousness itself may be seen as a plenum of existence, self-activated, the cause of its own way of being. But this only leads to a further dualism: of the appearances which present themselves only "in profile" but are in themselves fully being, and the consciousness of man, which, as Husserl proclaimed, is always intentional, always *of* something, always supported by a being not itself. Such a conception implies that there are two modalities of being, two absolutely separated regions: on the one hand the being-in-itself (*l'être-en-soi*) of phenomena, and on the other the being-for-itself (*l'être-pour-soi*) of consciousness, which functions as a "prereflective" *cogito* in the Cartesian sense. Are we condemned to regard these two modes of being as two closed totalities without possible communication? This is the ontological question which haunts Sartre's philosophy. For we are obliged to say of the being-in-itself that it is underivative, without explanation. Being is. Being is in-itself. Being is what it is. It is what Roquentin experiences as he gazes dumbfounded at the roots of the chestnut tree. The same emotion which he experiences here of being—that it is too much, in the way, *de trop*—Sartre retains for the more logical description which he has presented of being-in-itself in *Being and Nothingness*: "Uncreated, without reason for being, without any connection with another being, being-in-itself is *de trop* for eternity."[41] But what is the ultimate meaning of this theoretical disconnectedness? Why are the in-itself of independent things and the for-itself of consciousness so inexplicable in fact both by an idealistic and by a realistic ontology? "It is to attempt to reply to these questions," says Sartre, "that I have written the present work."

Sartre's first effort is to repudiate the idealistic implications of Husserl's phenomenology; his second is to acknowledge the relevance of Heidegger's analysis of Nothingness and of the way in which Nothingness is revealed to us in the anguish of our own possible non-Being and of the non-Being which we therefore project into the world. Consciousness as such is an abstraction. What is concrete is man within the world, that specific character of human situationality which Heidegger calls "being-in-the-world." It is only through this immediate connectedness with the world that it is possible for the human consciousness to assume the posture of interrogation, to question being, understanding all the while that we are surrounded by nothingness. This nothingness has two dimensions, an inner and an outer. Nothingness as outer we encounter in raising the question of the origin of negation as an existential experience. Nothingness as inner, as constituting consciousness, we encounter as we investigate the mechanisms of what Sartre calls "bad faith" (self-deception.)

The first question can be put as a problem of the primacy of logic or of ontology: Is negation only the structure of those negative propositions by which we make judgments? Or on the contrary is nothingness an actual characteristic of reality upon which our negative judgments are founded? At this point Sartre opposes the position of Bergson; he chooses the second possibility. Man is a fragile being. He is fragile because non-being lies perpetually in wait for him, and because he is the agent of a perpetual destructiveness. Non-being is a perpetual presence in us and outside us, and it follows that man adopts different types of conduct in the presence of being and in the presence of Nothingness. Nothingness haunts being, and this means not (as the Greeks thought) that nothingness is an original abyss out of which being arose, but that there is a constant, almost a dialectical, interplay between them. Human reality springs forth invested with being and finds itself in being, but there are also numerous attitudes of human reality which show that they partake of nothingness, like hate, repression, regret. And *in extremis* (as Jaspers and Heidegger would both maintain) there is always the possibility of human existence coming face to face with Nothingness and experiencing this confrontation with anguish. The fact is, there are an infinite number of realities which not only appear in negative logical judgments, but which are experienced, opposed, and dreaded by human beings because it is their inner nature to express nothingness. Thus for Sartre ontology reveals the radical negativity of existence, and this is why it is impossible to view the philosophy of Sartre without a certain distaste. For the metaphors of his ontological imagination are the images of disgust: *"Le néant . . . c'est au sein même de l'être, en son coeur, comme un ver"*—nothingness lies coiled in the heart of being, like a worm.[42]

Still, where does Nothingness come from? Sartre's answer is paradoxical, and it is the clue to his entire system. Nothingness originates in that "delicate, exquisite region of Being" where the human being is infected and infecting. For man as the for-itself, the empty, is afflicted with non-being in his very source and therefore "Man is the Being through whom nothingness comes into the world." We owe this insight to Descartes. Not that he used Sartre's language. Descartes called it "freedom," but the Cartesian freedom is simply "this possibility which human reality has to secrete a nothingness which isolates it." Human freedom is inseparable from the human essence. It precedes it in order to make it possible. Man does not exist first in order to realize a subsequent freedom, but his "being" is his "being free." The implications are indeed curious. For, in the first place, consciousness continually experiences itself as the "nihilation" of the claims of its own past being in order to secure the decisiveness, that is, the freedom, of its own present choices. In the second place, such consciousness of freedom as we are capable of is given in the form of anguish. "Kierkegaard describing anguish in the face of what one lacks characterizes it as anguish in the face of freedom. But Heidegger, whom we know to have been greatly influenced by Kierkegaard, considers anguish instead as the apprehension of nothingness. These two descriptions of anguish do not appear to us contradictory; on the contrary the one implies the other."[43] A situation provokes fear if I am threatened from without. But anguish ensues if I am threatened by my freedom from within.

The threat of freedom from within mobilizes all those defenses which arise to protect the individual against his own authenticity, and it is these defenses, protean in their infinite shapes and forms, which constitute *mauvaise foi*—that "bad faith" in the form of self-deception which constitutes the nothingness of our interior life. There are many men whose social function or mode of perception is expressed in the act of negation. Caretakers, overseers, gaolers are negations imbedded in the social structure, and irony as a mode of seeing the world takes pleasure in asserting and denying values at the same moment. But bad faith is an attitude of the very essence of human reality which directs its negation not outward upon the world, but inward upon the self. To be in bad faith is to hide from myself the truth of my inescapable freedom. It may take the form of a conventional mode of life, a bourgeois acquiescence in the forms of bad faith around me practically unrelieved by cynicism or bad conscience. Or it may consist in more sophisticated theories like the Freudian "unconscious," which, cutting the psyche in two, gives over to a powerful but mysterious part of my psychic being the ability to determine my conduct in such a way that I can deny rational responsibility for its consequences. Sartre's critique of Freud hinges on this point: that in the end the authority which the ego is unable to exercise is delegated to a censorship which within itself combines the duality of rationality and the irrational. "By separating consciousness from the unconscious by means of the censor, psychoanalysis has not succeeded in dissociating the two phases of the act, since the libido is a blind conatus toward conscious expression and since the conscious phenomenon is a passive, faked result. Psychoanalysis has merely localized this double activity of repulsion and attraction on the level of the censor."[44]

If we should examine more closely the patterns of bad faith—attempt, that is to say, a phenomenology of bad faith—we should say that it feeds upon duality—"It is a certain art of forming contradictory concepts which unite in themselves both an idea and the negation of that idea."[45] On one level this duality (or duplicity) arises socially, when my being-for-itself also appears as a being-for-others, when, in short, my conduct is the subject of two "looks," my own and that of another. It is not here simply a question of the sincerity which should make my being and my appearance congruent or at one, nor is it a question of the inward glance being the authentic one cut off from the look of the other as is a solid object from its deformed image. It is that however sincerity presents itself as a demand, I am by nature condemned to that form of instability which suggests a perpetual oscillation between the alternate roles. "The equal dignity of being possessed by my being-for-others and by my being-for-myself permits a perpetually disintegrating synthesis and a perpetual game of escape from the for-itself to the for-others and from the for-others to the for-itself."[46] Appearance and reality are not therefore the question. The bad faith is less an achievement than a built-in quality of the social genesis of the self.

Still, this built-in quality is augmented and reinforced by social demand. Sartre, like Jaspers and like Gabriel Marcel, is well aware of that misplacement of the sense of being which has come about through the apotheosis of social functionality.

Let us consider this waiter in the café. His movement is quick and forward, a little too precise, a little too rapid. He comes toward the patrons with a step a little too quick. He bends forward a little too eagerly; his voice, his eyes express an interest a little too solicitous for the order of the customer. Finally there he returns, trying to imitate in his walk the inflexible stiffness of some kind of automation while carrying his tray with the recklessness of a tight-rope walker by putting it in a perpetually unstable, perpetually broken equilibrium which he perpetually reestablishes by a light movement of the arm and hand. All his behavior seems to us a game. He applies himself to chaining his movements as if they were mechanisms, the one regulating the other; his gestures and even his voice seem to be mechanisms; he gives himself the quickness and pitiless rapidity of things. He is playing, he is amusing himself. But what is he playing? We need not watch long before we can explain it: he is playing at being a waiter in a café. There is nothing here to surprise us. . . . This obligation is not different from that which is imposed on all tradesmen. Their condition is wholly one of ceremony. The public demands of them that they realize it as a ceremony; there is the dance of the grocer, of the tailor, of the auctioneer, by which they endeavor to persuade their clientele that they are nothing but a grocer, an auctioneer, a tailor. A grocer who dreams is offensive to the buyer, because such a grocer is not wholly a grocer. Society demands that he limit himself to his function as a grocer. . . . There are indeed many precautions to imprison man in what he is, as if we lived in perpetual fear that he might escape from it, that he might break away and suddenly elude his condition.[47]

Thus society by imposing upon the individual the concept of his function, by attempting to imprison him within the limits of his condition, only stimulates those impulses toward bad faith which already reside within the human individual. If the waiter neutralizes his selfhood by mechanizing the gestures through which his function becomes a matter of almost histrionic display, this is by way of converting his function into the solidity of a visible thing. He pretends to forget that there is at his core a self which not only voluntarily sustains the role but which in addition transcends it a thousand times on every side. The role-playing is thus in some sense deceptive, for it is an exhibition of the mode of being which at the same time he is not.

But in this pervasiveness of social ambiguity, in this consciousness of the other as what he is not, what can be the meaning of any attempt to achieve "sincerity?" For must it not be a meaning in contradiction with the very structure of my consciousness? "How then can we blame another for not being sincere, or rejoice in our own sincerity since this sincerity appears to us at the same time to be impossible? How can we in conversation, in confession, in introspection even attempt sincerity, since the effort will by its very nature be doomed to failure, and since at the very time when we announce it, we have a prejudicative comprehension of its futility?"[48] The question is rhetorical. Obviously in Sartre's system we cannot. And no pragmatic criterion of congruence between conduct and assertion will solve the problem either. For man is not finally known, and human reality is ultimately no more given in the pattern of conduct than in the plausibility of verbal assertion. Thus the essential structure of sincerity does not differ from that of bad faith. One can even fall into bad faith by the very strenuousness of the effort to be sincere. So it was with Stendhal, and with Hamlet.

To take constant inventory of the self in the name of sincerity is to assume an objectivity which is self-denying, therefore also in bad faith. For it is to convert oneself into a pure, objective consciousness. And this too (since it is a disengagement of my activity) is to put myself out of reach; it is an escape. The forms of bad faith are infinite. I may deny the qualities which I possess. I may fail to see (almost by magic) the sort of being which I am. Or I may attempt to pass myself off as being what I am not. The more of Sartre one reads, the more one sees how he is obsessed by this matter of bad faith. And if one finds in his plays, novels, and short stories a preoccupation with the neurotic and the abnormal, it is not (as with Céline) *la nostalgie de la boue*, but rather the literary expression of an almost clinical phenomenology, an effort to explore without the delicacy of an undue reticence the protean disguises of bad faith. Consider the collection of short stories published under the title of *La Mur*. "Intimacy" is the story of a woman content neither in her life with an impotent husband nor with a quasi-animal lover because her narcisscism seeks satisfaction in the fiction of her frigidity. "Erostratus" is the story of a madman who believes himself as impregnable as the Eiffel Tower (but faints at the sight of blood) who murders a man he has never seen before on the Boulevard Edgar-Quinet and then, unable to pull the trigger with the barrel in his own mouth, surrenders abjectly from a public toilet. "The Room" is the story of a wife who lives with her insane husband on the sixth floor of an old building, refusing to let him be put in a sanatorium, trying, out of her love and sympathy to be like him, to actually experience the flavor of his madness, but failing, and therefore existing in the twilight zone which is neither madness nor health. "The Wall" tells of a man, waiting to be shot by Spanish insurgents during the civil war, who pretends hardness but is paralyzed by fear and whose normal attitudes disintegrate in the face of this extreme situation. "The Childhood of a Leader" is the story of a weak, futile and dependent youth whose anguish at the recognition of his own insignificance and nothingness is finally assuaged by the anti-Semitism and assumed Fascist stance which permits him the uncertain arrogance of a model bourgeois and a leader of men. Each story is a case history in self-deception. Sexual derangement, insubstantial paranoia, twilight zones, the steel armor around the interior quaking like jelly, the arrogant facade for abject weakness: these are the multitude of shapes which *mauvaise foi* assumes in the phenomenal world. Each occasion is extreme, but in its essence it is not atypical. Like the more dramatic illustrations of neurosis in Freud, these are but exaggerations of the mechanisms which are inseparable from normal life. But this is only to say that for Sartre the pathology of bad faith is an inherent quality of human reality. "Bad faith is a type of being-in-the-world, like waking or dreaming."

With bad faith a method of thinking appears, a type of truth which is patterned not upon the infinite malleability of consciousness, but upon the solidity and opacity of objects. The confidence of the waiter depends upon seeing himself as a mechanical object. The safety of the frigid woman lies in viewing her frigidity as "physiological"—that is, as inherent in nature, in the object which is her body. But it is in Sartre's brilliant presentation of the anti-Semite[49] that the essence of this method appears.

And this is what the antisemite chooses first of all. But how can one choose to reason falsely? Because one feels the nostalgia of impermability. The rational man seeks the truth gropingly, he knows that his reasoning is only probable, that other considerations will arise to make it doubtful; he never knows too well where he's going, he is open, he may even appear hesitant. But there are people who are attracted by the durability of stone. They want to be massive and impenetrable, they do not want to change: where would change lead them? This is an original fear of oneself and a fear of truth. And what frightens them is not the content of truth which they do not even suspect, but the very form of truth—that thing of indefinite approximation. . . .

Bad faith seeks for the self the permanence and the impenetrability of rock, and this search is the self's first attempt to flee from what it really is. But "the very project of flight reveals to bad faith an inner disintegration in the heart of being," and so we are back again at the ontological foundations of human experience. As nothingness is the worm coiled in the heart of being, so the permanent risk of bad faith is the worm coiled in the heart of human consciousness.

Sartre's conception of bad faith is crucial, I think, for an understanding of his doctrine of the self, and of the provisional ethics which he now holds, and which he has promised to expand into a complete moral philosophy. For the same reason it is possible to neglect those parts of Sartre's ontology which do not directly contribute to the theory of decision implicit in his work. The basis of Sartre's system as expounded in *L'Etre et le néant* is the distinction between a being-in-itself which *is* everything and *does* nothing, and the human being-for-itself which *is* nothing and which has everything to do. The in-itself is the presented objectivity (the *toujours-déjà-donné*), the structure of the related sum of appearances which may be progressively known. It is obvious that the problem of the in-itself is the traditional problem of epistemology—how the in-itself is given to the for-itself, temporality as it appears in knowledge and as it qualifies the world, the categories of quantity, quality, potentiality, instrumentality, and the way in which reflection is determined by the presuppositions of knowledge. All this is dealt with in the second part of Sartre's chief work. But before turning to the last and in my opinion most significant section of the work (the explication of Sartre's doctrine of human freedom), I should like to mention the conclusions of Part Three of *L'Etre et le néant*, "being-for-others." For this section too throws light upon the human self, and will of necessity be the foundation for the kind of social philosophy which Sartre ultimately produces.

The classical forms of idealist epistemology founder upon "the reef of solipsism." The problem of "others" has never seriously disturbed the realists. Therefore between a solution whose sophistication violates common sense, and a naïveté which sees no problem at all, reality is lost. For Sartre the problem of the existence of others is real, and its solution adds one more dimension to the despair of nothingness and bad faith. The existence of the other is posited not (as Jaspers might have seen it) in the total communication of love, but in the phenomenology of "shame," and the power of the other is attested not by the warmth of his benevolent gaze but by the annihilating and alienating malevolence of his "look." The mechanism here is the same as in the case of the waiter or the anti-Semite. My self-deception is to turn myself into an object. But my feeling of shame is the recognition of how I am an object for others, and the potency of "an alien gaze" is precisely that, as the head of Medusa turned men to stone, it transforms me into the recalcitrant solidity of rock.

In fact no matter what results one can obtain in solitude by the religious practice of shame, it is in its primary structure shame before somebody. I have just made an awkward or vulgar gesture. This gesture clings to me; I neither judge it or blame it. I simply live it. I realize it in the mode of for-itself. But now suddenly I raise my head. Somebody was there and has seen me. I suddenly realize the vulgarity of my gesture, and I am ashamed.[50]

That I am ashamed implies that I am conscious of myself as being looked at, conscious of the Other looking at me. Thus shame is possible only through the Other. The Other is the indispensable creator of my "objectness," for my shame is by nature the recognition that I am as the Other sees me. If shame is shame of oneself before the Other, then it is clear that I need the Other to realize fully the various aspects of my being. And in turn I must therefore admit that the Other is a real existent being, independent of my existence, and possessing the same intrinsic freedom and subjectivity which I experience directly in myself.

The interesting consequence of the phenomenology of shame is that it reveals to us through the medium of a socio-psychological intuition the existence of that same "kingdom of ends" or "society of subjects" which Kant was forced to postulate as a moral requirement. For the nature of the "subject" is that it can look at objects, transform other subjects into objects by its "look," and preserve its own subjectivity against the object-making look of the Other by its own reciprocal annihilating looking back. Our experience of the objects in nature shows that they may be looked at, but our "fundamental apprehension of the Other in which he will not be revealed to me as an object but as a presence in person" is due to his ability to look back. There is something fundamental for Sartre in this relation of "being-seen-by-another." And "if the Other is on principle the one who looks at me, then we must be able to explain the meaning of the Other's look."[51] That meaning is at once clear and terrifying. It is the aggressiveness by which the Other alienates my freedom by turning me into an object, and suddenly, that alienation of myself which is the act of being looked at involves the total alienation of the world which I in my subjectivity organize. It is not merely that I lose my freedom by becoming a *thing*; my nature, first experienced in my lived freedom, has now become an attribute external to myself, a quality of the being which I am for the Other. Here again, as in the case of *mauvaise foi*, the work of Sartre is saturated with this "terror of the Other's look." And again, what on the surface seems to be merely neurotic hypersensitiveness is revealed as the consequences of an ontological principle. Aegisthus in *The Flies* maintains his power through this terror: "I want each of my subjects . . . to feel that even when alone my stern gaze is upon him, weighing his most secret thoughts. . . ." And Sartre speaks of the morbid demophobia of Baudelaire in similar terms:

Was not the function of the Other's look to transform him into a thing? . . . Baudelaire had a horror of feeling that he was a quarry. It was a torture for him to go into a cafe, into a public place, because in this case the looks of everyone there converged on the person who just came in; while the new arrival, taken aback and not accustomed to the place, could not defend himself by staring back at the people who were staring at him.[52]

But the *locus classicus* is, of course the denouement of *No Exit*, where Garcin, condemned for ever to inhabit the same room with Estelle and Inez, suffering the weight of their eternal gaze, recognizes at last that he is in hell:[53]

GARCIN: . . . Yes, now's the moment . . . and I understand that I'm in hell. I tell you, everything's been thought out before hand . . . with all those eyes intent on me. Devouring me. (He swings round abruptly.) What? Only two of you? I thought there were more, many more. (Laughs.) So this is hell. I'd never have believed it. You remember all we were told about the torture chambers, the fire and brimstone. . . . Old wives' tales! There's no need for red-hot pokers. Hell is—other people!

Hell is other people for Sartre because in his quaint universe of appropriation and domination (a kind of Hobbesian state of nature where the stakes are not the externals of wealth and deference but purely internal states of consciousness like nausea, shame, pride, and alienation) all contact with the Other implies a latent contest. Shame reduces me to the state of mere object and establishes me as a thing for the Other. Similarly, my body, which is for-me, is, at the same time, the-known-by-the-Other. But this implies a further alienation. Lulu in "Intimacy" daydreams about her lover: ". . . it must be funny to go up a stairway when you're naked; I'd make him go up ahead of me so that he wouldn't look at me; or else I wouldn't be able to move a foot, I'd stay motionless, wishing with all my heart he'd go blind. . . ." To be seen from behind, to be seen naked; these are the symbols of powerlessness in the encounters of the body.

The experience of my alienation is made in and through affective structures such as, for example, shyness. To "feel oneself blushing," to "feel oneself sweating," etc., are inaccurate expressions which the shy person uses to describe his state; what he really means is that he is vividly and constantly conscious of his body not as it is for him but as it is for the Other. This constant uneasiness, which is the apprehension of my body's alienation as irremediable, can determine psychoses . . . these are nothing but the horrified metaphysical apprehension of the existence of my body for the Others.[54]

Thus all concrete relations with the Other reduce to some form of conflict. All these relations are governed by my attitudes toward that object which I am for the Other. What then are the possible attitudes which I can assume in his presence? I can attempt to alienate the freedom of the Other through love; such enslavement is the lesson we have learned from Proust (either through Odette's effect upon Swann, or Albertine's upon Marcel, or Morel's upon Charlus—and Sartre appears to be very familiar with Proust's work). Or I can make conquest of the Other's body through the appropriation of desire, or I can indirectly destroy him through my hate. Love fails for Sartre because it is impossible to provide an intimacy which permits both subjectivities to relinquish the claim to domination and at the same time retain the freedom of subjectivity itself. It is therefore no accident that (as in Freud's account) love and hate exhibit a certain reciprocity, and that the failures of communicative love slide easily into the twin surrogates of sadism and masochism. Here again the conclusion of Sartre's ontology is the tragic failure of human existence. Every human act seems an act of attempted appropriation where the self tries to surround, take in, encompass Being. But the more we acquire, the less we "possess." Human reality may be a passion for Being, but its expression is a longing for identification with the in-itself doomed to end in failure. And because the Other, too, is inaccessible to this longing for identification, the concrete relations with Others must be pathological, provisional, *faute de mieux*. There is no place in Sartre's system for the transcendent values of an optimistic sociology: the felicities of genuine communal feeling, or the transports of a selfless love.

With such a tragic outcome for the ontology, what of the famous existential emphasis upon choice and human freedom? The insistence upon freedom remains, but it is a freedom which is limitless, gratuitous, and unanchored—a quality of consciousness in itself shut off from the world and the conditions of social action. Sartre's freedom is too absolute to be realistic and too desperate to be believed. It is his counterattack against determinism and against science, but because it claims everything, it can persuade nobody. The "indispensable and fundamental condition of all action is the freedom of the acting being" but since we must admit the continuity of past, present, and future in the moral economy, since "the present is the upsurge of the act," and since the act projects itself into the future, the problem of a position which wishes to deny determinism is the problem of abolishing the past. For, since it is *the act* which decides its own ends and motives, I am indeed an existent being who learns his freedom from his acts, and my freedom is perpetually in question in the very nature of my being. Human reality escapes from causation by its very existence. "I am condemned to exist forever beyond my essence, beyond the causes and motives of my act. I am condemned to be free. This means that no limits to my freedom can be found except freedom itself or, if you prefer, that we are not free to cease being free."[55] This follows from the fact that freedom in its foundation coincides with the nothingness which is at the heart of man, and which forces man *to make himself*. This making is never partial. It is either total or it is not at all. But this is only to express Sartre's desperation in the form of a moral absurdity. For Sartre there are only two solutions. Man is either wholly determined or he is wholly free. And since "human reality in and through its very upsurge decides to define its own being by its ends, it is therefore the positing of my ultimate ends which characterizes my being and which is identical with the sudden thrust of the freedom which is mine."[56] Thus I am totally free.

The heart of Sartre's strategy for freedom is an attempt to destroy the decisiveness of the past. Here the previous identification of human consciousness with the activity of negation stands him in good stead. There must be for consciousness "the permanent possibility of effecting a rupture with its own past, of wrenching itself away from its past so as to be able to consider it in the light of a non-being. . . ." Only so can the urge toward "that which is not yet, but can be" make itself felt. Human reality must always hold its own past indefinitely in suspense because the indeterminacy of the future keeps continually fluid the right which I have to consider any actual revelation of my past as definitive. It is the same point which Eliot in "East Coker" has made so well:[57]

> There is, it seems to us,
> At best, only a limited value
> In the knowledge derived from experience.
> The knowledge imposes a pattern, and falsifies.
> For the pattern is new in every moment
> And every moment is a new and shocking
> Valuation of all we have been. . . .

The imposition of a pattern is a falsification because the future is not yet, and it is the future's retrospective gaze which continually remakes the past. Human reality is condemned to make itself past and hence to wait forever for the confirmation which it expects from the future. Thus the past is in indefinite suspense because the future is a perpetual expectation. Any force of compulsion in my past is therefore borrowed from my free, reflecting choice. For I am a "progressive project" and this "involves in relation to my past a series of uprootings."[58] My past is simply a passive object for moral evaluation and judgment. It exists precisely because I can dissociate myself from it, and this dissociation is the assertion of my freedom. Determinism plays its game as if there were "an ossification of motives" and tries to assert that they are "things" as if they were not perpetually modified by the growth of my insight and the fact of my perpetual evaluation. Determinism forgets (as Wallace Stevens has it) that:[59]

> Freedom is like a man who kills himself
> Each night, an incessant butcher, whose knife
> Grows sharp in blood. . . .

Freedom is what time is for Whitehead: a "perpetual perishing," a "perpetual becoming," and if it cannot be defined, or described except in the acts which it produces, this is because it creates itself incessantly.

The difficulty with Sartre's freedom is that it is "ontological" freedom, a "freedom by definition" implicit in the concept of the for-itself, and that all of its counterfeit characteristics become obvious when it is passed off as good coinage in the realm of moral action. Jaspers too asserts the primacy of freedom, but he qualifies it through human situationality in such a way as to exhibit the human condition as a kind of tragic dialectic. Sartre also, in the existential manner of both Jaspers and Heidegger, gives attention to "facticity"—the series of obstacles which freedom has to face in "the givens" of my *place*, my *past*, my *environment*, my *fellowmen*, and my *death*[60]—but it is a sometimes brilliant *tour de force* which will persuade no one. What he wants to show is that these are not really obstacles; either they constitute opportunities for my free behavior, or I acquiesce in their requirements by the decision of my own free will. Only so can he guarantee in its acutest form the inescapability of the individual's moral responsibility. "The essential consequence of our earlier remarks is that man being condemned to be free carries the weight of the whole world on his shoulders; he is responsible for the world and for himself as a way of being."[61] But this is a requirement which no reasonable moral philosophy could possibly sustain. To demand that the self (the for-itself) "must wholly assume [any] situation with its peculiar coefficient of adversity, even though it be insupportable"[62] is to reduce even Stoicism to an absurdity. It may be possible to maintain that absolute responsibility is a *logical* requirement of our freedom *ontologically defined*, but it is impossible to maintain it as a principle *axiologically* observed. And if the ultimate consequence of this total responsibility is an anguish before the dreadfulness of freedom, then this is less the consequence of an intrinsic human condition than of a philosophy which traffics with the absurd. It is an anguish not in the face of suffering, but of senselessness.

But this is hardly surprising. Sartre's entire philosophy is haunted by this "senselessness." As "the principle of radical contingency" it can even be said to be its cornerstone. "Nothingness is prior to being." "Being is without reason, without cause, and without necessity." "Man is a useless passion." "Everything happens as if the world, man, and man-in-the-world succeeded in realizing only a missing God." "Thus it amounts to the same thing whether one gets drunk alone or is a leader of nations." These maxims of hopelessness scattered through Sartre's writings are capable of infinite multiplication, and they are at different times ontologically, ethically, or sociologically inspired. Behind it all is a veritable lust after nothingness. Perhaps it is even a sickness unto death.

L'Etre et le néant was published in 1943. It is clear from its last few pages that Sartre projected an ethics which should supplement and complete his ontology. Naturally ontology cannot formulate ethical precepts. One cannot derive imperatives from the analysis of that which is. But if, as ontology makes clear, human reality is always situational, then an ethics which raises the question whether absolute freedom can escape its situationality by constituting itself the sole end of moral action must come to grips with a problem which has been ontologically prepared. Thus far no definitive ethics has yet appeared, but in 1946, in response to the challenges of the times, Sartre delivered the lecture "L'Existentialisme est un humanisme"[63] which is not only a brilliant minor statement of his position, but also a provisional ethics which indicates the lines along which a more extended moral treatise might be constructed.

Sartre begins with an attempt to defend existentialism against the criticisms of both the Marxist Left and the Catholic Right, the former contending that existentialism denies human solidarity, the latter that it emphasizes all that is sordid and base in the human condition. In a kind of left-handed way Sartre admits the truth of both charges but turns the force of their moral disapproval. For at bottom, Sartre himself concedes, existentialism *is* alarming; it confronts the individual with that necessity of moral choice which Dostoievsky's Grand Inquisitor insisted men could not endure. Atheistic existentialism does maintain that existence comes before essence, that man exists, encounters himself, and is condemned to be precisely what he makes of himself. Man is a "project" propelling himself toward a future in full awareness and therefore in full responsibility; what he is and will be rests squarely upon his own shoulders. But here Sartre adds a curious and not completely consistent corollary. In being responsible for his own individuality he is, at the same time, responsible for all men: "As we fashion our image, that image is valid for all and for the entire epoch in which we find ourselves. Our responsibility is thus much greater than we had supposed, for it concerns mankind as a whole." This recalls Kant's requirement that one ought to act by a maxim capable of being accepted by all. "But in truth, one ought always to ask oneself what would happen if everyone did as one is doing; nor can one escape from that disturbing thought except by a kind of bad faith."[64] But there is also here something of the histrionic self-consciousness of the object of the "look," of the actor before the unseen audience sitting in moral judgment. "Nevertheless I also am obliged at every instant to perform actions which are examples. Everything happens to every man as though the whole human race had its eyes fixed upon what he is doing and regulated its conduct accordingly." From this sense of responsibility arises the existential anguish.

From Nietzsche we have learned that the existential emotions are the outgrowth of a cosmological commitment. From Sartre we learn that they are implicit in the moral situation of man. Because each man must choose for all as if the eyes of the world were upon him, he is in *anguish*. Because God does not exist, because we are left alone, "without excuse" (i.e., without the excuse that someone else is responsible for us), condemned to be free, we suffer *abandonment*. Because we must rely only upon ourselves, because I cannot count on other men, because I must act without illusion (and therefore without much hope), my normal condition is *despair*. The existential emotions are not, therefore, the indications of a specific and atypical neurosis; they are the symptoms of a universal pathology. They are the proof that human life is cut off from natural foundation and supernatural guarantee, that value has no anchorage in natural law or divine command, that man in his dreadful freedom and total responsibility stands completely alone.

If there is a moral philosophy to be derived from this predicament, it is clear what it must be. Such an ethics can be neither naturalistic nor teleological. For (1) there are no *natural* qualities which are intrinsically valuable, and therefore (2) there are no obligations immediately entailed by a specific theory of value. Man is nothing but his purposes. He exists only insofar as he realizes what he is. His life is nothing but the sum of his actions. We have then an ethics of action and of self-commitment where the moral agent "draws his own portrait," but for action there are no guideposts outside the situation itself, and for self-commitment there are no patterns of value authoritatively established. There is much of Kant here, and even something of Dewey, for what existentialism proposes is, clearly, not a *substantive*, but a *procedural* ethics. The dilemmas of the moral life yield to no abstract principles, for how in any perplexity of moral choice can decision be definitively established? "There are no means of judging," says Sartre. "The content is always concrete, and therefore unpredictable; it has always to be invented. The thing that counts, is to know whether the invention is made in the name of freedom."[65] What is significant to the existentialist is not the consequences of the act, but the quality of the moral agent, and this means neither the happiness produced in his life, nor the goodness of his will, but *the authenticity of his existence*. The authenticity of his existence is a function of the way he assumes total responsibility for his acts and always in his acts *wills freedom for freedom's sake*. We are back once again to the structure of Sartre's ontology, for it can now be seen that the moral judgments which we may legitimately form upon our fellows are governed by our intuition of the absolute evil of bad faith.

Sartre's Inferno (unlike Dante's) possesses only two circles. "Those who hide from this total freedom, in a guise of solemnity or with deterministic excuses, I shall call cowards. Others, who try to show that their existence is necessary, when it is merely an accident of the appearance of the human race on earth—I shall call scum. *But neither cowards nor scum can be identified except upon the plane of strict authenticity.*"[66]

It is now clear that the drama which interested Gide in 1930, "the debate of the individual with whatever keeps him from being authentic, with whatever is opposed to his integrity" (as cited in the epigraph) was a foretaste of existentialist ethics. For Jaspers, *Existenz* is the dark ground of selfhood out of which I become authentic; for Heidegger, authenticity is that *Sein zum Tode* (that genuine existence which dares to face death) which is to be distinguished from the frittering away of one's freedom in the trivial cares of everyday life. For Sartre, genuine existence is that subjectivity or immediate sense of one's self which acknowledges the absolute character of the free commitment and understands that freedom is the foundation of all values. Thus for Jaspers, Heidegger, and Sartre alike, authenticity is a kind of courage, or clarity of vision, or honesty in the confrontation with the self. It is the successful outcome of the debate of the individual with whatever is opposed to his integrity.

It is clear that this position has certain limitations as a comprehensive moral philosophy. Authenticity is a quality of persons, not of acts, and therefore it is not itself the end toward which acts aim, but a by-product of their successful completion. As a moral quality it is therefore almost epiphenomenal in character. But there is a further difficulty. In his rebellion against the bourgeois mentality, capitalist exploitation, and the forms of social order, Sartre almost seems to suggest that the ethics of authenticity can truly flourish only within the crisis situations of extreme oppression. Never more than here does he reveal the bondage of his thought to the atmosphere of the French Resistance. His work is rich in literary demonstrations of bad faith, which fall almost without exception in the everyday ambience of the bourgeois conventions. But if he must paint a picture of *good* faith, if he must sketch the features of authenticity, he can produce but a single example—that of *La République du silence*, which begins:[67]

We were never more free than during the German occupation. We had lost all our rights, beginning with the right to talk. Every day we were insulted to our faces and had to take it in silence. Under one pretext or another, as workers, Jews, or political prisoners, we were deported en masse. Everywhere, on billboards, in the newspapers, on the screen, we encountered the revolting and insipid picture of ourselves that our oppressors wanted us to accept. And because of all this, we were free.

Exile, captivity, and especially death (which we usually shrink from facing at all in happier times) became for us the habitual objects of our concern. We learned that they were neither inevitable accidents, nor even constant and exterior dangers, but that they must be considered as our lot itself, our destiny, the profound source of our reality as men. At every instant we lived up to the full sense of this commonplace little phrase: "Man is mortal!" And the choice that each of us made of his life and of his being was an authentic choice because it was made face to face with death. . . .

Thus the basic question of liberty was posed, and we were brought to the verge of the deepest knowledge that man can have of himself. For the secret of a man is not his Oedipus complex or his inferiority complex: it is the limit of his own liberty, his capacity for resisting torture and death. . . .

The insight is hard-won, and we must respect the suffering out of which it grew. But we may perhaps also question whether an adequate moral philosophy can be constructed upon the paradox that only where we are outwardly in chains can we be authentically and inwardly free. That men require obstacles to develop the power of moral decision we already know. And the experienced conclusion of *The Republic of Silence* has already appeared in the presentation of the existential hero in *The Flies*. Orestes discovers himself in a land weighed down under the bondage of remorse. He is brought to the acknowledgment that freedom is the foundation of all values only by his opposition to that compact for man's slavery in which Jupiter and Aegisthus are accomplices. But if the play of feeling is formed by the deeds that one does, it is still true that others beside Prometheus can draw their own portraits. The inescapable situations are there even where the religious, economic, or political despots are not, and any man, whether day laborer, banker, or clerk can experience the need to find himself again, and can understand that in the end nothing can save him from himself.

4. EXISTENTIALIST SOCIAL PHILOSOPHY

There is a certain embarrassment in attempting to identify the "social philosophy" of existentialism, for the essence of the doctrine is that it has exalted the category of "the individual" to an almost exclusive position in its ethical and ontological concern. Sartre's egocentric treatment of actual relations with others (*"les relations concrètes avec autrui"*) is not an auspicious vantage point for the development of closeness of social relations, and even Jaspers' emphasis upon communication is abstract and formalistic in the extreme. Nonetheless, existentialism has a certain eccentric social philosophy, which mirrors its sources in the nineteenth century. Mill and Marx polarized the socially constructive attempts of their generation, and they have, as we have seen, produced in Dewey and Lenin their contemporary analogues. But Nietzsche and Kierkegaard are also in a somewhat bizarre fashion "social philosophers," for they are the great critics of their age, and their greatest effort was to recall the individual to himself "against the system" conceived either as passionless institutionalized religion or the vulgar morality of the herd. Dewey's liberal-democratic social philosophy and Lenin's Marxism are constructive, forward-looking, *utopian,* for whether one advocates the reestablishment of community through a scientific social reconstruction, or the establishment of solidarity through the complete proletarization of the class structure, a pattern is given, and the evaluation of the present is a function of the claims of the future. But contemporary existentialism is true to its sources in Nietzsche and Kierkegaard; *it is a social philosophy by virtue of its criticism.* It has no plan for the future as such, and in those moments when a vague impulse toward the constructive sneaks up on it from behind, as it were, it looks uneasily to the dreams of the United States or to the blatant promises of the U.S.S.R.

But although existential social philosophy is social criticism, not all existentialists are the same kind of critic. The field seems to me to be divided in two, and I should like to distinguish the "tender-minded" existentialist social philosophers of the "spiritual Right" (men like Karl Jaspers and Gabriel Marcel) from the "tough-minded" existentialist social philosophers of the "revolutionary Left" (Sartre, Merleau-Ponty, Simone de Beauvoir, and perhaps Camus). It is the kind of distinction which one would make in literature between the mind of Gide and Thomas Mann on the one hand, and that of Céline and Genêt on the other. Marcel and Jaspers (like Mann and Gide) are tender-minded in that their social criticism belongs to the great tradition of European humanism founded by Goethe. Sartre, Merleau-Ponty, and Beauvoir (like Céline and Gênet) are tough-minded in that their social criticism is "hard-boiled" in a fashion which could have been nurtured only upon the naturalistic revolt of the nineteenth century.

The contrast between the two mentalities comes to dramatic focus in the antagonism between Gabriel Marcel and Simone de Beauvoir. "Simone de Beauvoir," says Marcel,[68] "wrote a few years ago that crimes against the common law—crimes, that is, against person and property— ought not to be judged with too much severity; but that political crimes,

on the other hand, are inexpiable." He adds with the proper horror:
"Such an assertion, as soon as one reflects on it a little, opens out gulfs
beneath one's feet. . . ." It is the revolutionary ardor against the conservative function, the claims of security and status against personal violence and a fanatical political loyalty. Marcel in the preface to *Man
against Mass Society* admits his hostility toward "the spirit of abstraction," and confesses the innate horror of violence, disorder, and cruelty
which reading about the French Revolution inspires in him. Simone de
Beauvoir in *The Ethics of Ambiguity* coolly estimates the practical consequences of the "criminal violence assumed by Stalinist politics," and
abstractly considers in terms of Russian population figures "the numerical coefficient of the injustices committed."[69] It is as if we were living
again in the century of Burke and Bentham.

The heart of the "tender-minded" critique goes back to Marx nevertheless, to the alienation of the person in mechanical and "rationalized"
work, and the transformation of the individual into a "thing" (*Verdinglichung*) through the commodity orientation of modern industrial
society. Marcel sees the degradation of modern man in the misplacement of the idea of "function," in the bondage to the time-table and
the schedule which subordinates the emotional necessities of "time
lived" to the mechanical necessities of "time by the clock," and he
wishes to recall the human person from a social situation riddled with
"problems" to the lost domain of his sense of Being where to be involved
is the fundamental fact, where what matters most is the "encounter"
with the selfhood of the other, leaving deep and lasting traces, and
where birth, love, and death are not a set of vital statistics, but the
"mystery" in which we are all involved.[70] The burden of Jaspers' argument is similar. Like Marcel and like Ortega he is obsessed by the undesirable tension between technical mass-order and the requirements of
genuine human life, and to the humanistic mode of criticism of Dilthey
and Simmel he adds the fear of mechanical organization and bureaucracy which he learned from Max Weber. "Control and organization are
supreme. The matter-of-factness of the technical realm makes its
familiars skilled in their dealings with all things; the ease with which
ideas about such matters are communicated, standardises knowledge;
hygiene and comfort schematise bodily and erotic life. Daily affairs are
carried on in conformity with fixed rules. . . ."[71] Today the "hero" is no
longer visible. The man who stands fast against the impalpable masses
(who use their overwhelming power to enforce their blind will against
the lonely doer) is a silent and inconspicuous martyr. Still it is possible

to engage in a last stand for man's nobility. We may perhaps rescue "the reality of the best." "When men are huddled together like dust in a heap, reality and certainty exist where friends are true friends in the factual communication of their manifestations and in the solidarity of personal loyalty."[72] The only gift which the contemporary world can give is this proximity of self-existent human beings, and they are the guarantee that Being exists. True nobility thus survives in the interlinkage of independent human beings, widely scattered but interacting—a dispersed élite which forms an Invisible Church, a *corpus mysticum* in the anonymous mass of mechanized social relationships.

It is astonishing how much alike are the ideology and even the imagery of Jaspers and Marcel, in diagnosis and in outcome. Marcel assails "the depersonalization of human relationships" and calls for "the reintegration of honor." Jaspers assails "the degradation of consciousness during an era of advanced technique" and asks for "a reinstatement of man's nobility." In each case the community envisaged is one *outside* of politics and the formal organization of society. Marcel looks to the spiritual fellowship of creative fidelity, Jaspers to the spiritual fellowship of exceptional men. But there is something archaic about Marcel's "honor" and Jaspers' "nobility," something which suggests the Stoicism of the noble Roman during the time of Maximinus or Valerian, proud in his isolation, and cognizant of the impotence of his class, but conscious of a certain personal grandeur in the midst of the general disaster. The tender-minded variety of existentialist social philosophy criticizes the failures of Western industrial civilization in an idiom which has become a commonplace, almost a cliché of contemporary thought, but its only solution is a retreat from the domain of the political altogether, and a dependence (without essential inventiveness) upon the traditional resources of the good man in the bad society.

In what would pass as an existentialist social philosophy, there is something at once rhetorical and thin. This holds as much for the "tough-minded" existentialism of the materialistic Left as for the "tender-minded" existentialism of the spiritual Right. To be sure, the former is, as Sartre would have wished it, *engagé*; it is "political" through and through, but this political engagement seems strangely "journalistic," that is to say, cut off from the deeper level of ontological analysis and axiological justification. In a certain sense this disjunction is the consequence of the absolute theory of freedom which appears in Sartre's own philosophy. In ontology, as we have seen, freedom is a formal structure, the total relatedness of a situation in which action may be accomplished. In politics freedom is the factual absence of pressures, the intersection of obligation and response where opportunity remains for the development of aspects of a self which is pre-political. Thus the necessity for distinguishing between social and ontological freedom. But if ontological freedom is absolute, then any sociological qualification which it may need is compromising indeed, and the subconscious desire to preserve the ontology intact may forestall the risk which any deep consideration of political principle might entail. So far this has inhibited Sartre in the presentation of a positive social philosophy, although it has not interfered with his criticism of orthodox Marxism as a speculative system. This criticism is most conclusively accomplished in his famous article of 1949, *"Matérialisme et Révolution."*[73]

Sartre first attacks the false Marxist claim that one must choose between materialism or idealism because there is nothing in between; he then indicates his reasons for believing that materialism as a metaphysics is false. Materialism is a metaphysics which hides behind the skirts of positivistic method. But man is no object, no objective beholder, and thus the world can produce no ideas in him without the epistemic freedom of his undertermined consciousness. Determined reason is no reason. And precisely how did the external world set mathematics and logic inside us as the modes of our perception?

Dogmatic when it asserts that the universe produces thought, materialism immediately passes into idealistic scepticism. It lays down the inalienable rights of Reason with one hand, and takes them away with the other. It destroys positivism with a dogmatic rationalism. It destroys both of them by the metaphysical affirmation that man is a material object, and it destroys this affirmation by the radical negation of all metaphysics. It sets science against metaphysics and unknowingly a metaphysics against science. Nothing is left but ruins. How then can I be a materialist?

Sartre's attack upon materialism is studied and persuasive. In the end he finds its function in the total structure of Marxism neither that of a metaphysics nor of a method, but rather of an intellectual orientation, perhaps even "a style of living." Materialism is a religion: "the subjectivity of those who are ashamed of their subjectivity" and also "the irritation of those who suffer physically and who are familiar with the reality of hunger, illness, manual work, and everything which can undermine a man's strength."[74] Thus it has become clear that the "truth" of materialism is merely pragmatic; it now shelters and preserves a revolutionary attitude as previously it has served as a revolutionary stimulus.

Unfortunately in Sartre's opinion this is not enough. Materialism may be the only "myth" which meets revolutionary requirements, but the revolution needs *not a myth, but the truth*. Materialism as "the epic of the factual" has served its purpose, for historically it has denied all those fictions of status and divine right for which the oppressing class stands, but in decomposing man into his mere behavior patterns, it plays into the very hands which it wishes to destroy, for it assumes the perspective of that same oppressor who sees the proletarian as rightful slave of the machine and of the unappeasable thirst for profits.

Sartre's strategy is clear. He is not in opposition to the proletarian revolution, but only to its false materialistic justification, and he wishes to effect their separation in order that existentialism may be substituted as the true philosophy of proletarian violence. Determinism may be the law of the natural world, but freedom is the structure of human action, and it appears always in that resolute commitment of which every revolutionary impulse should be an example. But if we should ask of Sartre, What is the existentialist moral justification for proletarian violence?, no explicit answer would be forthcoming. For him, the facts of capitalist exploitation, of bourgeois hypocrisy and bad faith, and of despotic political oppression are assumed to be obvious, and the revolutionary conclusion necessarily follows. We have already seen that the existentialist theory of value provides no very explicit criteria for judging alternative forms of society. The achievement of a value is a leap in the dark (or, as Sartre has it, "values leap up before our acts, like partridges"); thus political preference is an intuitive choice which permits very little in the way of rational justification. Perhaps for this reason Sartre has left to Simone de Beauvoir the less ethically rewarding preoccupation with a "calculus of violence;" in his own writing it does not specifically appear.

The work of Simone de Beauvoir, on the other hand, is haunted by the notion that the ambiguity of freedom implies the outrage of violence. She too is forced to admit that whenever the good of a group of individuals is taken as an absolute end of political action, we are philosophically unauthorized to decide upon this end *a priori*. Still, good causes do make an *a priori* claim upon our sympathies, and the method which we use to judge the necessity for their acts of violence is a calculus of means and ends which finally supplies a judgment of their political good faith:

We repudiate all idealisms, mysticisms, etc. etc. which prefer a Form to man himself. But the matter becomes really agonizing when it is a question of a Cause which genuinely serves man. That is why the question of Stalinist

politics, the problem of the relationship of the Party to the masses which
it uses in order to serve them, is in the forefront of the preoccupations of all
men of good will. However, there are very few who raise it without dishonesty. . . .[75]

But as we note the form which Beauvoir's own casuistry assumes, we may
perhaps wonder at the subconscious dishonesty which is at work here also.

> One can no more judge the means without the end which gives it its
> meaning than he can detach the end from the means which defines it.
> Lynching a negro or suppressing a hundred members of the opposition are
> two analogous acts. Lynching is an absolute evil; it represents the survival
> of an obsolete civilization, the perpetuation of a struggle of races which
> has to disappear; it is a fault without justification or excuse. Suppressing
> a hundred opponents is surely an outrage, but it may have meaning and a
> reason; it is a matter of maintaining a regime which brings to an immense
> mass of men a bettering of their lot. Perhaps this measure could have been
> avoided; perhaps it merely represents that necessary element of failure which
> is involved in any positive construction. It can be judged only by being
> replaced in the ensemble of the cause it serves.

There is something enormously opportunistic here, but at the same time
something exceedingly abstract, and if we ponder over it long enough
we may perhaps begin to understand Gabriel Marcel's instinctive hostility toward the spirit of abstraction as the ally of war and violence,
and the similar insight which is perhaps the ultimate political moral
of Dostoievsky's *The Possessed*. It is not therefore surprising when in
conclusion Beauvoir states explicitly the perverse dialectic which underlies the entire "tough-minded" existential social philosophy of the revolutionary Left: "Indeed, on the one hand it would be absurd to oppose
a liberating action with the pretext that it implies crime and tyranny;
for without crime and tyranny there could be no liberation of man;
one cannot escape that dialectic which goes from freedom to freedom
through dictatorship and oppression."[76] This may be mere political
"realism," ideologically innocent as it views the course of history, or it
may be just one of those "crimes of logic" to which Camus referred
in the epigraph given at the head of this chapter. For if he is right that
our political criminals are no longer those helpless children who pleaded
love as their excuse, but are, on the contrary, adults with the perfect
alibi of philosophy, here is an instance of that perfect alibi. Philosophy,
as Camus says, can be used for anything, even for transforming murderers into judges. Or, as we might add, in its existentialist guise, for
transforming absolute freedom into absolute tyranny.

The presuppositions of Sartre and Simone de Beauvoir with respect to the existential philosophy of the revolutionary Left are shared by Maurice Merleau-Ponty. In his paradoxical *Humanisme et terreur* he attempts to provide for "terror" a "humanistic" justification. He sees the problem as the dilemma set by Arthur Koestler—the alternatives of the spiritual Yogi, to whom any immoral means are abominable, and the opportunistic Commissar, for whom the revolutionary end justifies all means—and he tries to go between its horns by the expedient of *l'humanisme marxiste*. In any case he maintains that violence is inevitable. Politically speaking, it is the human condition. What matters is that it shall be meaningful violence, and that it shall be relevant to the establishment of the perfected future. In a certain sense this means practically that no presently available political position is possible. Merleau-Ponty's words have become famous in France: "*On ne peut pas être communiste, on ne peut pas être anti-communiste*" (one cannot be Communist, one cannot be anti-Communist). This does not mean that Merleau-Ponty is ever even neutral toward the liberal-democratic position. His position toward the democracies, as well as that of Sartre and de Beauvoir, reminds one of the words of Louis Aragon: "I have never looked for anything except scandal, and I have looked for it for its own sake. . . ." Thus his "a plague upon both your houses" is weighted much like the "calculus" of Simone de Beauvoir: "In the Soviet Union violence and trickery are official, while daily life is humane; in the democracies, on the contrary, the principles are humane, but daily life is full of trickery and violence."[77]

What then is the role of the dedicated existentialist in the political mélange? The answer is clear. "Our role," says Merleau-Ponty, "is to make clear the ideological situation . . . to recall the Marxists to their proper humanist inspiration, to recall to the democracies their basic hypocrisy, and to maintain intact against the propagandists whatever chance History may still have to illuminate its own meaning." Existentialism is relevant to politics not merely because it has originated an ontology which purports to illuminate the political necessities of violence, but because the emotions to which it has called attention are those which are generated within the political arenas of our time. "One cannot," says Merleau-Ponty,[78] "be an existentialist merely at will, and there is more existentialism—in the sense of paradox, discord, anguish, and determination—in the stenographic reports of the Moscow Trials than in all the works of Heidegger."

Existentialism is the political philosophy *par excellence* because it demands commitment, because it is the philosophical correlative of displacement and ruin in the domain of political order, and it is perhaps this above all which gives it authenticity as a philosophy. Merleau-Ponty's last comment applies as much to existentialism in general as to its distinctly political focus. "This philosophy, they say, is the expression of a world which is out of joint. Most assuredly, and this is precisely what makes it true!"

XI

The Lure of the Part:
G. E. Moore and Ludwig Wittgenstein

I do not think that the world or the sciences would ever have suggested to me any philosophical problems. What has suggested philosophical problems to me is things which other philosophers have said about the world or the sciences.

G. E. MOORE

I wonder at the outlay of subtlety on the part of those who . . . exhaust the unrest of their strong minds in the examination and critical analysis of the works of others.

ANDRÉ GIDE

Every ambiguity, every misunderstanding, lead to death; clear language and simple words are the only salvation from it.

ALBERT CAMUS

Our language can be seen as an ancient city: a maze of little streets and squares, of old and new houses, and of houses with additions from various periods; and this surrounded by a multitude of new boroughs with straight regular streets and uniform houses.

LUDWIG WITTGENSTEIN

1. LANGUAGE AND COMMUNICATION

Plato's *Cratylus* is a passport into the Hellenistic age. It is obsessed with the problem of communication; it prefigures an epoch in which literature has passed into the hands of the grammarians, and in which semantics has dethroned metaphysics as the chief claimant to philosophic attention.

But it has a modern ring also. The Platonic dialogue opens with an argument between Cratylus and Hermogenes. Do names signify in accordance with some natural property (so that there is always some intrinsic appropriateness between the verbal sign and the thing which it signifies), as Cratylus maintains? Or are names only significant by convention, by stipulated definition, by arbitrary imposition, as Hermogenes asserts? Change the terminology slightly and it might be Cassirer arguing that there is a certain native congruence between the language of poetry and myth and the emotional experience which it illuminates, or

436

perhaps Wittgenstein insisting that "The proposition is a picture of reality" and that "The propositions *show* the logical form of reality." For both Cassirer and Wittgenstein, different as are their linguistic perspectives, suggest modern variants upon the position of Cratylus. And each might be opposed by the later Carnap (assuming the position of a modern Hermogenes), asserting his principle of tolerance: that anyone shall be free to introduce his own linguistic framework, and to stipulate his own linguistic rules, and the meaning of his terms, provided that such stipulation is both unambiguous and practically useful.

The intervention of Socrates does not resolve the dispute. Instead he uses his irony to further confound it. First he pretends to show that considerations from language support the philosophy of Heracleitus, only to turn around the next moment and show how they equally support that of Parmenides. The whole thing is a satire on any attempt to reach an adequate metaphysics by way of philology. The same is true of the lengthy presentation of the fantastic and far-fetched etymologies which follow. But for all its playfulness the intention of the *Cratylus* is serious. The real purpose of the dialogue is to consider not the origin of language, but its use and function. Language, it is asserted, is a social activity—an instrument of communication. If language is to be adequate, it must (as Wittgenstein also maintained in the *Tractatus*) conform to certain structural principles. Statements are true if they speak of realities as they really are. Or, in the language of Logical Atomism originated by Wittgenstein and the early Russell: A proposition is made true by its correspondence with fact, and the world consists of an indefinitely large number of atomic facts to which the true atomic proposition will correspond.

Plato, of course, employs not the terminology of "propositions" but of "names." A name is an instrument by which we inform one another about realities and discriminate between them. But in a certain sense this is ultimately to take the side of Cratylus against Hermogenes, of Wittgenstein against Carnap. Since the function of language is the accurate communication of knowledge about things, the vocabulary of "social usage" or of "arbitrary imposition" will be satisfactory only when it supplies a nomenclature which corresponds to the real agreements and differences between the things named. This is only a passport into the Hellenistic age; it is not the Hellenistic age itself, for Plato is still primarily interested not in words but in things, and his willingness to deal with linguistic foundations is always subject to his major axiom of intelligibility that semantics is the handmaiden of metaphysics, not its master. But it is the hallmark of an Alexandrian age that this relationship should be reversed. An Alexandrian age is accompanied by a crisis of communication, and in such a crisis of communication philosophy falls into the hands of the grammarians. We feel, says Wittgenstein,[1]

as if we had to *penetrate* phenomena: our investigation, however, is directed not towards phenomena, but, as one might say, towards the '*possibilities*' of phenomena. We remind ourselves, that is to say, of the *kind of statement* that we make about phenomena. Our investigation is therefore a grammatical one. Such an investigation sheds light on our problem by clearing misunderstandings away. Misunderstandings concerning the use of words, caused, among other things, by certain analogies between the forms of expression in different regions of language. . . .

An age which is concerned less to penetrate phenomena than to examine the kinds of statements that we make about phenomena, which wishes to clear away misunderstandings by pointing out systematic ambiguities, has been motivated by the realities of the contact of peoples and the confrontation of diverse cultures with one another. With the rise of the Sophists in Greece, the days of simplicity and innocence are over—not because of their extreme sensitivity to problems of language or because they initiated complicated linguistic and rhetorical analyses, but because they were the first true cosmopolites in Greece. Given their cosmopolitanism, then their intellectuality, their interest in the instruments of communication, and even their moral relativism are inevitable consequences. Plato's *Cratylus* celebrates a typical controversy of the Sophists, the issue of nature versus convention as applied to language, and it therefore reflects the type of interest which is to flourish not only among the grammarians of ancient Alexandria, but also among the philosophical grammarians of contemporary Oxford.

Professor McKeon has put it excellently:[2] "The problems of an age arise in what is said—in the communications of the age—and they cannot be formulated accurately, intelligibly, or effectively without taking into account how they arise and in what context they are stated. The vogue of 'communication' today is no accident, but rather a response to the problems we face." These problems involve new contacts of diverse cultural values, the uneasy confrontation of alternative ways of life, the enormous development of the instruments of mass communication. This carries with it new perplexities about the possibility of mutual understanding, the modes of functioning of our linguistic currency, the preconditions which are necessary for the guarantee of responsible speech. The consequences of concentrating upon the details of verbal behavior, upon the functioning of the instrument rather than upon the content for which it is only the vehicle, are a new stance for a certain type of philosophy in the modern world.

For the last three decades contemporary philosophy has been more than usually concerned with problems of language, symbolism, and communication. In this it shares a point of view with *avant-garde* literature, which has been just as interested in the discovery and creation of new modes of expression and techniques of narrative as in the qualities of experiences expressed or stories told. In philosophy there is a new self-consciousness about the instrumental function of language which has obscured, or at least diverted attention from, the ontology which Plato would have said it is the business of language to illuminate. The customary transparency of language has given way to an opaqueness which has transformed it from something to be seen through into something to be looked at—like a pair of binoculars which one takes to the races, finds dirty, and has to clean while the horses gallop past unwatched. There is a tendency within the linguistic ambience of contemporary philosophy to stress "the language of morals," "the language of politics," or "the language of aesthetics" and to neglect the materials of morals, politics, and aesthetics in such a way as to suggest that the binoculars are so fascinating that it is unprofitable to follow the race.

If this seems to imply irresponsibility, the inference is, I think, mistaken. If other ages have been able to pursue the search for the formulation of reality, or the systematic derivation of our concepts and ideas, it was because society was at once more provincial and more orderly. Although it may well be that some philosophers have attempted to bypass the intricacies of metaphysics and to avoid the pitfalls of epistemology through an exclusive reliance upon semantics and the instrumentalities of communication, it is also true that in the end even the exhaustive analysis of symbolic systems and syntactical rules is fated to lead to the inescapable cul-de-sac of ontological deliberation and epistemological commitment. Any inquiry which is motivated by the desire to separate the real from the meaningless questions and to perform linguistic therapy upon the confusions of a recalcitrant metaphysics (a metaphysics indistinguishable from a virulent disease of language) is morally one in spirit with the efforts of the most responsible of the modern poets: their intense preoccupation with the preservation of linguistic purity, and their attempts to refine the tools of their craft so that language, whether as communication or expression, is exquisite, honest, and exact.

No poet is more aware than Eliot of how

> Words strain,
> Crack and sometimes break, under the burden,
> Under the tension, slip, slide, perish,
> Decay with imprecision . . .[3]

and no one is more aware of the purificatory function which the poet may exercise on the speech of his generation. In Eliot the battle against imprecision is a battle to maintain the standards of the poetic craft, to preserve an art against the dangers of technical deterioration. But Wallace Stevens sees the matter somewhat differently:[4]

> The soldier is poor without the poet's lines.

> His petty syllabi, the sounds that stick,
> Inevitably modulating, in the blood.
> And war for war, each has its gallant kind.

> How simply the fictive hero becomes the real;
> How gladly with proper words the soldier dies,
> If he must, or lives on the bread of faithful speech.

To see that we live upon "the bread of faithful speech" is to appreciate the crucial relation between linguistic purity and the conditions of social life. Faithfulness and decency in the motives with which we employ language and accuracy in the communication which language undertakes are the preconditions for life in an honest society. But to see this is to pass from a conception of the poet as artist to that of the poet as society's trustee. And it is to pass from the point of view of Eliot to that of Ezra Pound, for it is Pound among all modern poets who has been most passionate against the perversions of language, not simply with the outrage of an artist but also with the outrage of a moralist.[5]

Language is not a mere cabinet curio or museum exhibit. It does definitely function in all human life from the tribal state onward. You cannot govern without it, you cannot make laws without it. That is you make laws and they become mere mare's nests for graft and discussion. . . . Printed word or drum telegraph are neither without bearing on the aggregate life of the folk. As language becomes the most powerful instrument of perfidy, so language alone can riddle and cut through the meshes. Used to conceal meaning, used to blur meaning, to produce the complete and utter inferno of the past century . . . against which SOLELY a care for language, for accurate registration by language avails. And if men too long neglect it, their children will find themselves begging and their offspring betrayed. . . .

Pound's language is extreme, but it suggests a problem which has its analogues in every area of modern life. This is why I have appealed to the example of modern poetry. For it too registers a concern analogous to that of present-day linguistic philosophy. When Eliot indicates how words decay with imprecision, when Stevens asserts that we must all live upon the bread of faithful speech, and when Pound points to the possibility of language as an instrument of perfidy, they indicate a moral dimension of the problem of communication. But there is an intellectual dimension also, and this is reducible less to the motives of men than to the intrinsic nature of the instrument through which they express their meanings and their motives alike. What therefore if "perfidy" is not the extraneous evil which men bring to language when they pervert it, but the intrinsic evil which they find *in* their language when they use it? This uneasiness, elevated into a canon of method, marks the revolution which Wittgenstein has introduced into philosophy. "The problems arising through a misinterpretation of our forms of language have the character of *depth*. They are deep disquietudes; their roots are as deep in us as the forms of our language and their significance is as great as the importance of our language."[6] When Pound emphasizes the role of the writer in preventing the use of language as an instrument of perfidy, this is connected with his belief that poets exercise a definite social function. "Good writers are those who keep the language efficient. That is to say, keep it accurate, keep it clear." And although Wittgenstein does not speak in the idiom of social function, his conception of philosophic responsibility depends upon the same moral concern applied in the domain of the intellect. "Philosophy is a battle against the bewitchment of our intelligence by means of language."

Such a conception of philosophy is not altogether new. We have seen it in embryo in Russell's formulation of "the logical-analytic method in philosophy," and more developed in Carnap's "logical syntax of language." To find the essence of philosophy in logical analysis of the sentences of science and in inquiry into the formal rules of the linguistic expressions which science employs is, as Carnap said, to be preoccupied with the kinds and orders of symbols, not with their content. And to allocate to philosophy the formal mode of speech in which logical questions may be posed, in contrast to the material mode of speech which is appropriate to object questions (and is hence the proper domain of the special sciences), means that logical empiricism has already implicitly assumed the theoretical framework which was not made completely explicit until Wittgenstein did so in *Philosophical Investigations*. Already in 1936 Ayer had made this clear:[7]

But, actually, the validity of the analytic method is not dependent on any empirical, much less any metaphysical presupposition about the nature of things. For the philosopher, as an analyst, is not directly concerned with the physical properties of things. He is concerned only with the way in which we speak about them.

In other words, the propositions of philosophy are not factual, but linguistic in character—that is, they do not describe the behaviour of physical, or even mental objects; they express definitions, or the formal consequences of definitions. Accordingly, we may say that philosophy is a department of logic. . . .

To say that the propositions of philosophy are linguistic in character, and at the same time that philosophy is a department of logic, is to speak ambiguously. For this program seems to conform to Wittgenstein's maxim that "philosophy is a battle against the bewitchment of our intelligence by means of language," but in reality it does not. The difference lies in alternative assessments of, and therefore alternative logical strategies with respect to, ordinary language.

The strategy of Russell and Carnap grew out of a faith that the logical notation of *Principia Mathematica* was a model of clarity and philosophical expressiveness. Implicit in this faith was the belief that the grammatical requirement of the subject-predicate form in ordinary language was the source of a dangerous assumption as to the adequacy of the subject-predicate formulation of the Aristotelian logic. Carnap believed that ordinary language was the source of much metaphysical nonsense which was dissolved once we turned to the crystalline notation of a constructed artificial language. Russell still believed that even from the study of syntax we might arrive at considerable knowledge concerning the structure of the world, but he concurred as to the pitfalls implicit in our use of ordinary language. Therefore the program was the use of symbolic logic to remake ordinary language into an artificial language which should be adequate to the scientific requirement of unambiguously stated and empirically verifiable propositions.

It is clear that a price had to be paid for this program of reform. The logical empiricism of Russell and Carnap stemmed from an ultimate concern with scientific precision, but its criterion of meaningfulness excluded serious consideration of the greater number of the ways in which ordinary language behaves. Its interest was in the informative statements of "cognitive" discourse—with factual propositions, hypotheses, scientific laws, mathematical and logical statements, axioms, definitions, theorems. It would have been willing to admit that there were additional functions of language—practical, expressive, poetic, ceremonial, and the like—but while it viewed them as perhaps socially interesting modes of linguistic behavior falling within the special sciences of anthropology, psychology, or linguistics, it held that they were without cognitive significance and therefore without philosophic interest. The positivism of Russell and Carnap is a form of Philosophical Analysis, but it is that type of analysis which is in revolt against the expressive ambiguities of natural languages. It is therefore to be distinguished from the form of Philosophical Analysis with which we are here concerned[8]—that of G. E. Moore and Wittgenstein, which also conceives the philosophic task as a struggle against ambiguity, but finds its natural battleground not in the rarefied atmosphere of the peaks of symbolic logic, but upon the rolling uplands, the great broad plains, and the occasional soggy marshes of ordinary language which we all inhabit. If, in the opinion of Moore and Wittgenstein, the philosopher pursued a special task, it was that of serving as a guide over the sometimes ambiguous and rocky terrain, sustained by his somewhat greater powers of common sense, analytical skill, and linguistic knowledge.

In one sense this second form of Philosophical Analysis represents an expansion of the area of philosophic interest. For, in Wittgenstein's phrase, it concentrates on "the multiplicity of the tools in language and the ways they are used." By analyzing the significant and important things which we do when we tell a story, solve a practical problem, make a contract, pray, greet one another, construct and test a hypothesis, curse, translate from one language into another, apologize, make a poem, promise our help, report a factual event, or take a role in a play, it passes beyond the limited semantics of logical empiricism to the possibility of a generalized philosophic reconstruction. There is, as Gilbert Ryle suggests,[9] a certain merit in this idiom.

Where we can speak of managing, handling, and employing [terms] we can speak of mismanaging, mishandling and misemploying. There are rules to keep or break, codes to observe or flout. Learning to use expressions, like learning to use coins, stamps, checques and hockey sticks, involves learning to do certain things with them and not others; when to do certain things with them and when not to do them. Among the things that we learn in the process of learning to use linguistic expressions are what we may vaguely call "rules of logic". . . .

By the extraction of the logical rules implicitly governing the way of operating with a type of expression, we may gain insight into the limitations and the failures of philosophical investigations in the past. We may find, for example, that "the language of morals" has patterned itself upon the language of reporting a factual event instead of on that of solving a practical problem or making a contract, and that "the language of aesthetics" has gone astray because it does not sufficiently distinguish between the criteria of meaning involved in telling a story and making a poem.[10]

This type of philosophical criticism is broader than logical empiricism in the area which it admits into the legitimate sphere of philosophic consideration, but its formulation of the essence of a philosophic problem indicates a restrictive narrowness unsurpassed since the Hellenistic grammarians. For what does a preoccupation with the informal logic of the employment of expressions do when it confronts for example the problem of perception—that classical challenge which haunts the history of philosophy? Gilbert Ryle again provides the characteristic and disquieting answer.

If we are enquiring into problems of perception, i.e., discussing questions about the concepts of seeing, hearing and smelling, we may be taken to be tackling the questions of opticians, neurophysiologists or psychologists, and even fall into this mistake ourselves. It is then salutary to keep on reminding ourselves and one another that what we are after is accounts of how certain words work, namely words like "see," "look," "overlook," "blind," "visualize" and lots of other affiliated expressions."[11]

Logical empiricists also would wish to avoid confusing the proper task of philosophers with that of opticians, neurophysiologists, or psychologists, but even they would hold that to give an account of how words like "see," "look," or "visualize" work is the task of the philologist or dictionary-maker rather than that of the philosopher.

When we view the philosophic fashions of the last five decades, we must be struck, I think, by the urgency with which the question of what philosophers ought to do and what philosophy is, has itself been put forward as one of the chief questions for philosophic debate. Nor is this simply the defensive strategy of strong-minded men who disagree. Aristotle disagreed with Plato with love and regret and did not find it necessary to deny that Platonism was a philosophy. Locke disagreed with Descartes as to the origin of our ideas, but he did not maintain that the use of a rational method inspired by the successes of mathematics disqualified a man from the practice of philosophy. Kant proclaimed his "Copernican Revolution" with deep sincerity and assurance, but this did not prevent him from paying his intellectual debt to "the celebrated Leibniz" and "the estimable Mr. Locke," with both of whom he significantly differed. But the philosophic movements of the recent past are to be viewed as waves of successive reform beating upon an infinite shore, with each group of partisans committed to a conception of philosophy which assures them a virtual monopoly of its legitimate practice. To the pragmatist, to philosophize is to give aid and comfort in the resolution of problematic situations. To the logical empiricist, to philosophize is to engage in the investigation of the logic of science. To the linguistic analysts, to philosophize means to extract the rules which govern the behavior of linguistic expressions. And to pragmatists, logical empiricists, and linguistic analysts alike, any alternative conception of what philosophy is rests upon a tragic mistake.

But despite the differences between logical empiricism and linguistic analysis, they both reflect what is perhaps the dominant characteristic of the philosophical revolution of our time—the statement of philosophic problems as questions intrinsic to symbolic manipulations and the characteristics of words. Philosophically the ancient world is dominated by the requirements of a reality external to the mind. Plato and Aristotle both are deeply committed to an examination of the realms of being, to an exploration of the modes of existence, to a classification and description of entities. Philosophy from the Renaissance to Hegel is dominated by the subjectivist principle. It speaks of the genesis of ideas, the connection of concepts, the structure of appearances. Hume transforms the problem of causality from the productive action of one substance upon another to the habitual association of ideas in the mind, and Kant announces his Copernican revolution in epistemology to the effect that henceforth it is not our modes of thought that must conform to things, but things that must conform to our modes of thought.

But contemporary philosophy is dominated by the symbolic instrumentalities of language. Here knowledge must conform neither to the properties of things nor to the necessary pattern of our ideas but to the canons of linguistic utility. Language is a curious mixture of the cultural deposit of the ages and the requirements of an autonomous reason, but whatever its substance, it is the inescapable medium through which our social and our intellectual lives are lived. Like the water to the fish and the air to the bird, it seems often transparent and impalpable, but it has marked quality nonetheless, and its peculiar properties support the possibilities of life and locomotion. Therefore it is a tenet of Philosophical Analysis that we have philosophic knowledge in the deepest sense when we "know" the medium with that specific intimacy which guarantees, or at least facilitates, a frictionless navigability. To know for Plato meant to have intimations of the forms from which particular things derive their reality; to know for Kant meant to respect the synthesis which the mind creates within the molds of the understanding. To know in the newer forms of Philosophical Analysis is to have mastered

the machinery of discourse, to have subjugated the recalcitrance of grammar to the requirements of a facile use.[12]

Thus far I have treated the innovations of the schools of Philosophical
Analysis as though they were rooted exclusively in the problems of
language. But in another respect also they have created a revolution in
philosophical method. This is due partly to the piecemeal character
which they attribute to the act of analysis and partly to the increasingly
technical quality which British and American philosophy has assumed
since the turn of the century. Men like John Stuart Mill and William
James were public philosophers, publishing in the popular reviews of
the day, and speaking a language intelligible to any intelligent and
educated man. But Bradley and Peirce were largely "philosopher's philosophers," concerned with the more technical problems of logic and
epistemology, and speaking a language dialectically subtle and analytically rigorous, but hardly suitable to the tastes of a general audience.
To be sure, Bradley was much more than a minute dialectician and
Peirce much more than an exact logician, but the organic tendency of
the former and the latter's preoccupation with metaphysics have been
neglected in favor of their logical precision. With Bradley and Peirce
philosophy grew technical, but it is perhaps to Russell that we owe the
formulation of the philosophic task as an attack upon a series of limited
objectives, as a concentration (essentially like that of the natural scientist or mathematician) on separate technical problems rather than upon
a general synthesis of the sciences or an unlimited cosmology. With
Russell, philosophy succumbed to the lure of the part, to the temptations of the exactitude of small-scale analysis rather than large-scale construction. His characteristic themes—What is a cause? What are
descriptions? What is continuity? What is the relation of sense-data to
physics? What is infinity?—although generally set by problems in natural
science or mathematics, yet served as pattern for the more linguistic
orientation of the followers of the later Wittgenstein and their concern
with such issues as proper names, negative terms, "Know" and "Think,"
Tense Usage and Propositions, Subjunctive Conditionals, "Saying" and
"Asserting," and the like.

The chief influence here is neither the subtlety of Bradley, nor the
limited themes of Russell, but the minute analytic practice of G. E.
Moore. When Moore writes in his autobiography[13] of the influence of
one of his English public-school classical masters upon himself he says:
"And I was also, no doubt, impressed by the pains he took to be accurate
—to get everything *exactly* right." The impression was prophetic, for
the profoundly influential effect which Moore has had upon the entire

field of Philosophical Analysis, including the Oxford school of Ryle and Austin, lies in the infinite pains which he himself has taken "to be accurate—to get everything *exactly* right." In a certain respect this influence (like that of John Stuart Mill upon his own generation) is as much moral as substantive. G. E. Moore has perhaps produced little philosophical theory which will live, but his method has borne many offspring, and in his passion for clarity and understanding, he was the keeper of the philosophical conscience of his generation.

An analytic philosopher is one who settles upon limited and definite issues, whose intent (in Broad's sense) is "critical" rather than "speculative," who tries to untangle the twisted strands of meaning and the verbal ambiguities which lie at the heart of any philosophical problem. Moore, Russell, Carnap, and Wittgenstein have instituted the discipline, and of the four it is probably Moore who has had the greatest methodological influence. At a time when the positivistic attack upon the traditional metaphysics was in high gear, Moore's analytic method was a standing reminder of what philosophy could and ought to be. Here was a philosopher who had in no sense trespassed upon the empirical domain of the natural sciences, yet was practicing a mode of investigation with obviously high standards of strictness and logical rigor. At the same time, at a period when Wittgenstein was still caught in the web of the logical atomism which he and Russell had spun, Moore was insisting that philosophical problems might be solved by a closer attention to the uses of language, and was employing what was undreamed of even by the authors of the *Principia Mathematica*: a technical analysis which was framed in the untechnical sentences of ordinary language.

There is a certain irony in this developmental twist in the history of the Philosophy of Ordinary Language. Although this movement originated with Moore and Wittgenstein, these men were the products and finally the chief Professors of Philosophy at Cambridge, whereas the present development of the philosophy is so associated with Oxford that it is sometimes simply called "Oxford Philosophy."[14] It is said that Cambridge University owes its foundation to a thirteenth-century migration of dissatisfied students from Oxford. If so the debt has now been repaid. For contemporary Oxford philosophy owes its foundation to a migration of the ideas of Moore and Wittgenstein from Cambridge. In a sense the migration is culturally appropriate. For Cambridge is traditionally the home of scientific thought, and therefore Russell, Whitehead, and Eddington with their orientation to mathematics and exact science reflect the Cambridge spirit in philosophy more exactly than Wittgenstein and Moore. But Moore, unlike Russell, was the product of a strict classical education and Wittgenstein, although scientifically trained, was an Austrian, to whom English was a second language and who remained throughout his entire life aware of the pitfalls of "translation" and sensitive to the nuances of ordinary language which such pitfalls display.[15] Therefore their preoccupation with ordinary language was consistent with the generally linguistic and humanistic bent of Oxford, and when Moore was invited to lecture there for a term in 1939, it was like the welcome of a relative with whom the ties of natural election are even stronger than those of blood.

It remains, perhaps, to say that this little drama of withdrawals and advances, of philosophical "alarums and excursions" between Oxford and Cambridge in the matter of the philosophy of ordinary language is a country masque, an expression of the simple playfulness of an island province. The passion for logic (positivism) was an international movement, and the drama of choice (existentialism) has permeated the entire European mind, but the lure of the part (linguistic analysis), except for its corruption of a few American universities, is the exclusive possession of the territory just south of Ely and east of the Cotswolds. Whatever the importance of the philosophy of ordinary language, in this matter, as in that of the storm clouds and the weather, as the British say, "The continent has been isolated."

I should now like to investigate the lure of the part as it originates and flowers (1) in the analytical method and deeply impressive philosophic seriousness of G. E. Moore, (2) in the early logical preoccupations and later linguistic originality of Ludwig Wittgenstein, and (3) in the culminating Oxford formulations of such men as Austin and particularly Gilbert Ryle.

2. THE METHOD OF MOORE

The philosophy of G. E. Moore presents a curiously meager and fragmented surface. For what is there? A refutation of idealism. A criticism of ethical naturalism. An argument for the existence of intrinsic value. A defense of common sense. A proof of an external world. And a series of systematic but generally partial and inconclusive analyses of sense perception. On the one hand there is in Moore an assertiveness verging upon dogmatism, on the other a modesty, humility, and love of truth unsurpassed in his generation. The paradox is pointed up by the testimony of the brilliant companions of his youth at Cambridge. Lord Keynes, whose own early beliefs were simply a mirror of Moore's *Principia Ethica*, speaks of the temper of their philosophical arguments:[16]

In practice, victory was with those who could speak with the greatest appearance of clear, undoubting conviction and could best use the accents of infallibility. Moore at this time was a master of this method—greeting one's remarks with a gasp of incredulity—Do you *really* think *that*, an expression of face as if to hear such a thing said reduced him to a state of wonder verging on imbecility, with his mouth wide open and wagging his head in the negative so violently that his hair shook. *Oh!* he would say, goggling at you as if either you or he must be mad; and no reply was possible.

But Earl Russell, never one to be gentle with his adversaries, tells a different story:[17]

For a long time I supposed that somewhere in the University there were really clever people whom I had not yet met, and whom I should at once recognize as my intellectual superiors, but during my second year I discovered that I already knew all the cleverest people in the University. In my third year, however, I met G. E. Moore, who was then a freshman, and for some years he fulfilled my ideal of a genius. He was in those days beautiful and slim, with a look almost of inspiration, and with an intellect as deeply passionate as Spinoza's. He had a kind of exquisite purity. I have never but once succeeded in making him tell a lie, and that was by a subterfuge. "Moore," I said, "do you *always* speak the truth?" "No," he replied. I believe this to be the only lie he has ever told.

The different views of Keynes and Russell are perhaps not really contradictory, for to "use the accents of infallibility" is not necessarily incompatible with "an intellect as deeply passionate as Spinoza's." The thought of G. E. Moore has in fact a double quality. On the side of substance there is an almost obstinate realism and a hardy common sense; on the side of method Moore takes infinite pains to ask precisely the right questions and stops at nothing until they are given exact, relevant, and unambiguous answers. The accents of infallibility appear in Moore only when he has encountered some provoking example of philosophic insincerity or clear nonsense. The intellect as deeply passionate as Spinoza's is revealed in the searching and minute analyses of epistemological problems and ethical theories for which he has become famous. Even Keynes, I think, recognized the primacy of the method:[18]

It was all under the influence of Moore's method, according to which you could hope to make essentially vague notions clear by using precise language about them and asking exact questions. It was a method of discovery by the instrument of impeccable grammar and an unambiguous dictionary. 'What *exactly* do you mean?' was the phrase most frequently on our lips. If it appeared under cross-examination that you did not mean *exactly* anything, you lay under a strong suspicion of meaning nothing whatever.

Moore did not hesitate to apply this method not only to the brash young intellectuals of the Keynesian circle, but to the most mature work of Mill, Hume, Russell, Bradley, or McTaggert. From the time when Moore heard McTaggert express his belief in the view that "Time is unreal," which seemed to him then and throughout his life "a perfectly monstrous proposition," and which he never ceased indignantly to refute, his method seemed best adapted not to the exploration of *things*, but to the examination of the *assertions* of other men. Such a method is linguistic and redolent of scholasticism; as Moore said, philosophical problems were suggested to him not by "the world or the sciences," but by the "things which other philosophers have said about the world or the sciences." Gide's "wonder at the outlay of subtlety on the part of those who . . . exhaust the unrest of their strong minds in the examination and critical analysis of the works of others," although the natural response of the creative man to the display of a merely critical intelligence, has been directed by others toward Moore himself in disapproval of the practice of directing all one's critical energies to the mistakes of one's immediate philosophical predecessors. If this is a fault, it is endemic to the entire enterprise of linguistic analysis, and it is from Moore that they have learned it.

After candidly admitting the sources of his usual motives for philosophizing, Moore continues:[19]

> In many problems suggested in this way I have been (and still am) very keenly interested—the problems in question being mainly of two sorts, namely, first, the problem of trying to get really clear as to what on earth a given philosopher *meant* by something which he said, and, secondly, the problem of discovering what really satisfactory reasons there are for supposing that what he meant was true, or alternatively, was false. I think I have been trying to solve problems of this sort all my life, and I certainly have not been nearly so successful in solving them as I should have liked to be.

There are two questions here—"What did he mean?" and "What is the evidence that what he meant is either true or false?"—and they require alternatively a theory of meaning and a theory of truth, or rather, a theory of evidence which defines both what is a reason for a belief and what ought to have been a reason for a belief, so that the work of *inference* directed toward the establishment of meaning is supplemented by an act of *judgment* in which normative considerations play a determining part. The inference of meaning in Moore's analyses, therefore, is always preliminary to the assessment of an argument on the grounds of its validity. Each act is part of an essentially Socratic enterprise—"the steady pursuit of methodical questioning."

Moore's emphasis upon questioning the words of others is supplemented by an insistence that the proper method for philosophy lies first of all in the initial asking of the proper questions. His *Principia Ethica* opens with a famous passage asserting this simple doctrine:[20]

It appears to me that in Ethics, as in all other philosophical studies, the difficulties and disagreements, of which its history is full, are mainly due to a very simple cause: namely to the attempt to answer questions, without first discovering precisely *what* question it is which you desire to answer. I do not know how far this source of error would be done away with, if philosophers would *try* to discover what question they were asking, before they set about to answer it, for the work of analysis and distinction is often very difficult; we may often fail to make the necessary discovery, even though we make a definite attempt to do so. But I am inclined to think that in many cases a resolute attempt would be sufficient to ensure success; so that, if only this attempt were made, many of the most glaring difficulties and disagreements in philosophy would disappear.

Philosophers often seem to be asking a single question when in reality they are asking several, and to distinguish the different questions which a philosopher has confusedly been attempting to answer as a single question often clarifies the issue sufficiently to dissolve the problem. If one notes the persistence with which Moore seeks to apply this canon of method throughout the body of his work, it is perhaps possible to discern the unifying cement which holds together the limited mosaic of his philosophic themes.

The subjects of his attention are ethics and epistemology; the mode of his thought is realistic and commonsensical; the instrument of his philosophizing is a precise and closely applied analytic method. Thus the same distaste for subjectivism which appears as a "refutation of idealism" through the application of an analysis which can distinguish between the "object" and the "content" of a sensation, appears also in epistemology as the sturdy "proof of an external world" and in ethics as a closely reasoned defense of "the objectivity of moral judgments." But the method is central, and if we attempt to follow it in the articles "A Defense of Common Sense," "Proof of an External World," "The Refutation of Idealism," and more cursorily in *Principia Ethica*, we shall see the activity of Philosophical Analysis at its best.

In "A Defense of Common Sense" Moore attempts to indicate some of the most important points in his philosophical position by indicating a series of propositions which he says he knows with certainty to be true.[21] These are:

There exists at present a living human body, which is *my* body. This body was born at a certain time in the past, and has existed continuously ever since. . . . Ever since it was born it has been in contact with or not far from the surface of the earth and at every moment since it was born there have also existed many other things having shape and size in three dimensions from which it has been at various distances. . . . Among the things which have, in this sense formed part of its environment have been large numbers of other living human bodies. . . . Finally I am a human being and I have had many different experiences e.g. I have often perceived my own body and other things which formed part of its environment including other human bodies.

Moore then goes on to state that surely ". . . very many of the human beings belonging in this class . . . have frequently during the life of their bodies known with regard to themselves or their bodies propositions corresponding to each of the propositions which I have written down about myself or my body." Thus common sense suggests not only that I exist and have experiences, but that I am not alone in being in this situation; there are others too. But there are philosophers whose subtlety of conception seems to make these statements doubtful, and it is this kind of subtlety which Moore takes to be questionable and confusing, for it violates the intelligibility of ordinary language:[22]

In what I have just said, I have assumed that there is some meaning which is *the* ordinary or popular meaning of such expressions as "The earth has existed for many years past." And this, I am afraid, is an assumption which some philosophers are capable of disputing. They seem to think that the question . . . is not a plain question such as should be met either by a plain "Yes" or "No," . . . but is the sort of question which can be properly met by: "It all depends on what you mean by "the earth" and "exists" and "years". . . . It seems to me that such a view is as profoundly mistaken as any view can be. Such an expression as "The earth has existed for many years past" is the very type of an unambiguous expression, the meaning of which we all understand. Any one who takes a contrary view must, I suppose, be confusing the question whether we understand its meaning (which we all certainly do) with the entirely different question whether we *know what it means,* in the sense that we are able to *give a correct analysis* of its meaning. . . .

Moore's insistence that we may understand a meaning without being able to give a correct analysis of it is related to the doctrine which appears in his *Philosophical Studies*[23] that we may know certain facts about the external world through the evidence of direct observation and in this sense have a reason although not a *logically conclusive* reason for believing them. Its effect is to call attention to that type of philosophical insincerity (characterizing Russell no less than the subjective idealists, according to Moore) which permits one to hold on speculative grounds a doctrine which every part of his practical conduct and everyday behavior refutes. The above propositions about my body and the earth and the nearness of my body to the earth in a certain sense imply that material things are real and that space is real and that time is real and that the self is real, and therefore to assert (as some philosophers have) that "Material things are not real" or that "Time is not real" is to express a position which no philosopher has been able consistently to hold. They have betrayed this inconsistency by referring to the existence of other philosophers, to the human race, to the beliefs of other people, and

In holding views incompatible with the proposition that propositions of all these classes are true, they have, therefore, been holding views inconsistent with propositions which they themselves *knew* to be true; and it was, therefore, only to be expected that they should sometimes betray their knowledge of such propositions. The strange thing is that philosophers should have been able to hold sincerely, as part of their philosophical creed, propositions inconsistent with what they themselves *knew* to be true, and yet, so far as I can make out, this has really frequently happened.[24]

The beliefs about our existence and the existence of other minds and other bodies are beliefs of common sense, and *because* they are such beliefs, they must be true. All philosophers without exception have agreed in holding such beliefs, and Moore thinks that if we know such beliefs to be features in the common-sense view of the world, it follows that they are true, for it would be self-contradictory to hold otherwise.

In direct contrast to the certainty about the truth of propositions which assert the existence of material things is the difficulty of giving a correct analysis of such propositions. The assertion of a proposition like "Material things exist" depends upon a prior analysis of the propositions of immediate perception, such as "At this moment I am perceiving a pen and a sheet of paper," for this seems to be a deduction from a pair of still simpler propositions, "I am perceiving *this*" and "*This* is a pen." It is surprising to Moore that so many philosophers have had things to say about what material things *are* without concerning themselves with a clear account of what precisely they *know* when they know or judge that "This is a pen" or "This is a hand." He himself was convinced of two things about the analysis of such propositions: (1) that there is always some sense-datum about which the proposition is a proposition and (2) that nonetheless what one judges true about this sense-datum is *not* that it itself is a pen, a hand, or a sheet of paper. In short, without adhering to the type of constructionism held by Russell and the early Carnap, Moore did believe that in some sense the analysis of sense contents was more primitive than the analysis of physical objects. "In other words, to put my view in terms of the phrase 'theory of representative perception,' I hold it to be quite certain that I do not *directly* perceive *my hand;* and that when I am said to 'perceive' it, that I 'perceive' it means that I perceive something which is *representative* of it, namely, a certain part of its surface."[25] But still, when I know that *this* is part of the surface of a human hand, just what do I know about the *sense-datum?* (1) Is the sense-datum itself part of the surface of a human hand? (2) Or is it in such a relation to the surface of the hand that it might be said to be an appearance or manifestation of it? (3) Or is the sense-datum only related to other sense-data in such a way as would imply the type of phenomenalism expressed in Mill's statement that a material thing is simply "a permanent possibility of sensation"? Moore's response to these three alternatives is very tentative. The first he thinks may just possibly be true. To the second there seem to him to be grave objections. The third again he thinks may just possibly be true. But I have presented his analysis not because it is a conclusive epistemology (which it obviously is not), but to show how he believes that the pronouncements of common sense which we know to be certainly true do not exhaust the subject, but specifically call for an epistemological analysis requiring all the resources of our analytical skill.

In the "Proof of an External World," the Annual Philosophical Lecture of the British Academy for 1939,[26] Moore once again combines his trust in the certainty of those things which we can know without being able to *prove* with his meticulous analysis of the situation in which this trust becomes a reasonable presupposition. Taking his text from the *Critique of Pure Reason,* where Kant calls it a philosophical scandal that the existence of things outside us must be accepted merely on faith, Moore concurs that "it is a matter of some importance and also a matter which falls properly within the province of philosophy, to discuss the question what sort of proof, if any, can be given of the existence of things outside of us."

Moore begins with an analysis of the phrase "things outside of us" which he finds "an odd expression, and an expression the meaning of

which is certainly not perfectly clear." He considers three possibilities
for replacement by expressions less odd, the candidates being (1) "external things," (2) "things external to *our minds*," and (3) "things
external to *us*," finally choosing the second as the clearest. But even
the expression "things external to our *minds*" will not do. Kant himself
points out the ambiguity between external things in the transcendental
sense and empirically external objects. To make clear that it is the
latter which are here relevant, he agrees to call them "things which are
to be met with in space." This suggests things like my body, the bodies
of other men, stones, houses, planets, in short the standard "physical
objects," "material things," or "bodies" of philosophic discourse. But
Kant also uses the phrase "things *to be met with in* space" as equivalent
to the expression "things *presented in* space," and Moore proceeds to
demonstrate why this equivalence is untenable and misleading. After-
images (the kind which come from looking at a four-pointed white
paper star on a dark ground), double images, bodily sensations of pain
can be classified as "things presented in space" although they are surely
not the kind of things which are "to be met with in space." They are in
fact typical examples of the kind of thing which most philosophers
would agree are *not external* to our minds, but *within* them. Thus it
is clear that from the fact that a thing is *presented in* space, it by no
means follows that it is *to be met with in* space. And with respect to
things described as "to be met with in space," it is clear "that there is
no absurdity in supposing with regard to any one of them which *is*, at
a given time, perceived, both (1) that it might have existed at that
very time, without being perceived; (2) that it might have existed at
another time, without being perceived at that other time; and (3) that
during the whole period of its existence it need not have been perceived at any time at all."[27]

Moore's purpose in this analysis is not merely to show that "things
presented in space" fall outside the conception of "things external to
our *minds*," but also to underline the doctrine of a realistic epistemology
that "there is no contradiction in supposing that there have been and
are to be met with in space things which never have been, are not now,
and never will be perceived." But his primary purpose, of course, is to
so relate the phrase "things to be met with in space" with the meaning
"things external to our minds" that it will be possible through one
intermediate step finally to assert the "proof of an external world."
Thus, there are objects like the bodies of men and animals, and houses
and chairs and stars, and Moore wants to use the expression "things
to be met with in space" in such a way that from the proposition that

there *are* houses and chairs and stars, it *follows* that there are things to be met with in space. Therefore, from the proposition "at least two chairs *exist* at the present moment" *it follows* that "at least two chairs are to be *met with in space* at the present moment." But Moore's interest in the identification of externality and spatial location is not the only question. We have been speaking of Kant and his usage as one focus of the problem. Therefore, even in the consideration of a simple epistemological problem we are implicated both in the inference of Kant's meaning and also in an appeal to the usages of ordinary language.[28]

Have philosophers, in fact, ever used 'external' as a mere synonym for 'to be met with in space'? Does he himself do so? I do not think they have, nor that he does himself; and in order to explain how they have used it, and how the two conceptions 'external to our minds' and 'to be met with in space' are related to one another, I think it is important expressly to call attention to a fact which hitherto I have only referred to incidentally: namely the fact that those who talk of certain things as external to our minds, do, in general, as we should expect, talk of other 'things,' with which they wish to contrast the first, as 'in' our minds.

Moore points out the obvious fact that "in" one's mind is a metaphorical usage, and that such phrases as "I had you in mind when I made that arrangement" are usages which "occur in common speech, and which we all understand quite well," but he also asserts that this is not the meaning which philosophers use when they contrast what is "in" the mind with what is "external" to it. For here it is a matter of physical objects on the one hand and such things as bodily pain, after-images, or dream-images on the other.

It should, I think, be noted, first of all, that the use of the word 'mind' which is being adopted when it is said that any bodily pains which I feel are 'in the mind,' is one which is not quite in accordance with any usage common in ordinary speech, although we are very familiar with it in philosophy. Nobody, I think, would say that bodily pains which I feel are 'in my mind,' unless he was also prepared to say that it is *with* my mind that I feel bodily pains, and to say this latter is, I think, not quite in accordance with common non-philosophic usage. . . .

Ordinary language permits us to say that we think, imagine, remember, and feel mental pain "with" the mind, but in the case of *bodily* pains such as a headache or a toothache, or even in the case of the usual stimulation of the organs of sensation, the "mental" idiom is far from customary. One source of confusion lies, therefore, in the difference

between the habits of ordinary discourse and the more esoteric philosophical vocabulary.[29]

There is, however, a well-established philosophical usage according to
which seeing, hearing, smelling, tasting, and having a bodily pain are just
as much mental occurrences or processes as are remembering or thinking,
or imagining. This usage was, I think, adopted by philosophers, because
they saw a real resemblance between such statements as 'I saw a cat,' 'I heard
a clap of thunder,' 'I smelt a strong smell of onions,' 'My finger smarted
horribly,' on the one hand, and such statements as 'I remembered having
seen him,' 'I was thinking out a plan of action,' 'I pictured the scene to
myself,' 'I felt bitterly disappointed,' on the other—a resemblance which
puts all these statements in one class together, as contrasted with other
statements in which 'I' or 'my' is used, such as, e.g., 'I was less than four feet
high,' 'I was lying on my back,' 'My hair was very long.' What is the resemblance in question? It is a resemblance which might be expressed by
saying that all the first eight statements are the sort of statements which
furnish data for psychology, while the latter three are not.

But the first eight statements referred to are important for a philosophic
reason in addition to their furnishing data for psychology, for they all
indicate that the subject was *having an experience*. This is not the case
with the last three. And the difference between bodily pain which we
feel, or after-images which we see, and the body as such, is that whereas
there is no contradiction in supposing my body to exist at a time when
I am not having an experience, to have a bodily pain which I feel or
to see an after-image at a time when I am not having an experience is,
indeed, contradictory.

The upshot is that although the phrase "external to our minds" is
not a mere synonym for the phrase "to be met with in space," the two
are related, and they are related in such a way, Moore believes, that if
it is true that "There is one star," it follows not only that "There is one
thing to be met with in space" but also that "There is one external
thing." Moore also believes that from any proposition of the form
"There's a star" there does really *follow* the propositions: "There's an
external object" and "There's an object external to *all* our minds."
Thus, if there is a pair of things that are to be met with in space, then
one can prove *ipso facto* that there are at least two things outside of us.[30]

I can prove now, for instance, that two human hands exist. How? By
holding up my two hands and saying, as I make a certain gesture with
the right hand, 'Here is one hand,' and adding, as I make a certain gesture
with the left, 'and here is another.' And if, by doing this, I have proved

ipso facto the existence of external things, you will all see that I can also do it now in numbers of other ways: There is no need to multiply examples.

The "proof of an external world" has now been completed, and can anyone fail to be dumbfounded by the result? Not since Dr. Johnson's "refutation" of Berkeley has anyone had the temerity to put forward such a "proof." In Moore's case the result is even more astounding when we compare the naïveté of the conclusion with the ponderous apparatus of its preparation. Naturally we ask, "But what is the proof that 'here is a hand'?" or of "and here is another?" For these propositions Moore has given no proof, and indeed his own defense of "Common Sense" commits him to the position that *no proof can be given*. Proof that "Here's one hand, and here's another"? "This, of course," says Moore, "I haven't given; and I do not believe it can be given: if this is what is meant by proof of the existence of external things, I do not believe that any proof of the existence of external things is possible." But *this is just what Kant was* maintaining in holding that we have no proof of the existence of external things, which must be accepted therefore merely upon faith. Moore's position returns to the claims put forward in "A Defense of Common Sense." We can *know* things which *we cannot prove*. And the basis of all our experience is not the secondary propositions of our systems, but the immediacies of our knowledge.

It is true, I think, that one often has the frustrating experience in reading Moore of feeling that here is a fine, infinitely sharp instrument engaged in grinding out almost precisely nothing. Perhaps this (as well as Moore's intention) has the effect of giving primacy to the influence of his method. His method is to take the statement of a philosopher (that of Kant on the external world in the analysis above), list, analyze, and compare the meanings which might possibly be given to the central concepts, and then test these philosophic concepts against the usages of ordinary language. The meticulousness of this procedure has impressed Wisdom,[31] Ryle, Austin, and the Oxford philosophers. But the doctrinal results are always the same: dogmatic assertion of the deliverances of "common sense," constant attack upon idealist presuppositions in the name of a realistic epistemology, and a resultant insistence upon objectivity in judgments of fact and of value.

If there is any area in which the doctrine of Moore is important in itself, that area is ethics, and if any single work can bear the burden of Moore's reputation, it is the *Principia Ethica* of 1903. Here a stringent method of analysis is combined with a solid body of positive doctrine in a single constructive enterprise. Subsequent disciples of Moore have accepted the method while rejecting the positive doctrine. This is ironic in view of the enthusiasm of his early Cambridge followers for the positive doctrine above all. Modern ethics has taken its point of departure from Moore's celebrated critique of "the naturalistic fallacy" (*Principia Ethica*, Chapter II) and has forgotten his discussion of "The Ideal" (*Principia Ethica*, Chapter VI). This marks the turning-point in ethical theory away from concern with substance and toward the pursuit of merely logical analysis. An age takes what it needs, but it would be interesting to speculate on what might have been the history of modern ethical theory if it had turned in the other direction.

Principia Ethica attempts to distinguish clearly between two kinds of question which, in Moore's opinion, moral philosophers have frequently confused: questions concerned with *intrinsic value,* and questions concerned with *duty.* From this distinction follows naturally the question of *the nature of moral evidence,* of what reasons can be considered relevant for the establishment of either type of proposition. We have therefore three issues which dominate the subject matter of ethics: (1) What kind of things ought to exist for their own sakes?, (2) What kind of actions ought we to perform?, and (3) What is the nature of the evidence by which alone any ethical proposition can be proved or disproved, confirmed or rendered doubtful?[32] The net result of the argument and critical inquiry of *Principia Ethica* is to assert (1) that for assertions about what kind of things ought to exist for their own sakes "no relevant evidence whatsoever can be adduced: from no other truth except themselves alone, can it be inferred that they are either true or false"; (2) that for assertions about what kind of actions we ought to perform evidence is possible but "so many different considerations are relevant to their truth or falsity, as to make the attainment of probability very difficult, and the attainment of certainty impossible."

Evidence for propositions about the "rightness" of acts must consist of two kinds of "knowledge"—*causal* knowledge about *the consequences of acts,* and *ethical* knowledge about *the nature of intrinsic value.* Moore's efforts are directed in large part to examination of the recent history of moral theory in an effort to show that these two kinds of knowledge have often been confused. Although in Chapter VI he has attempted to present his own conclusions as to what kind of things are intrinsically valuable, the chief purpose of *Principia Ethica* is "to discover what are the fundamental principles of ethical reasoning." Moore adds characteristically, "the establishment of these principles, rather than of any conclusions which may be attained by their use, may be regarded as my main object." This objective he believes he has achieved in presenting two principles which, although they may be stated separately, are really aspects of a single doctrine; (1) the Intuitionist principle and (2) the Naturalistic Fallacy. The intuitionist principle holds that statements of intrinsic value are incapable of proof, that whatever is the manner of our cognition of them, they cannot be deduced from more ultimate propositions. The strategy here is, again, that of the "Proof of an External World" and "A Defense of Common Sense." Ethically as well as epistemologically, we can know things which we cannot prove. Indeed, such things are the most crucial and the most indispensable aspects of the structure of our knowledge.

The exposition of the naturalistic fallacy comes as a necessary by-product of Moore's attention to "the most fundamental question in all Ethics"—the question of how "good" is to be defined.[33]

What, then, is good? How is good to be defined? Now, it may be thought that this is a verbal question. A definition does indeed often mean the expressing of one word's meaning in other words. But this is not the sort of definition I am asking for. Such a definition can never be of ultimate importance in any study except lexicography. If I wanted that kind of definition I should have to consider in the first place how people generally use the word 'good'; but my business is not with its proper usage, as established by custom. . . . My business is solely with that object or idea, which I hold, rightly or wrongly, that the word is generally used to stand for. What I want to discover is the nature of that object or idea, and about this I am extremely anxious to arrive at an agreement.

To this question what is Moore's answer? As disappointing as that given in the "Proof of an External World," and for the same reason: "If I am asked 'What is good?' my answer is that good is good, and that is the end of the matter." The answer is trite, but it is not trivial. For to say, as Moore does, that "good" is *indefinable*, that it is a simple, unanalyzable, notion like yellow or any immediate sensory quality implies that it is nonsense to say, as certain moralists do, that "Pleasure is the only good" or "The good is that which is desired" or "The good is that which is commanded by God." Indeed, this mistake is what Moore terms "the naturalistic fallacy." *Good* is indefinable because there is no other concept which can be substituted for it, because definition is customarily of what is complex and has parts, because the really simple objects of thought are themselves the ultimate terms by which all other notions are defined. Therefore to propose that pleasure, or that which is desired, or growth, or free activity are the *same* as goodness, to confuse "good," which is not really a natural object, with any natural property whatsoever constitutes the "naturalistic fallacy."

Three-quarters of *Principia Ethica* is devoted to showing the havoc worked by this fallacy upon the validity of nineteenth-century moral theory. Herbert Spencer, Mill, Bentham, the "metaphysical" ethics of Kant and Bradley, each in turn falls under the application of Moore's critical method, and if Sidgwick escapes on these grounds, he is attacked on others equally fatal to his system. All this prepares the way for Moore's famous last chapter on "The Ideal." In speaking of the ideal, says Moore, we may mean any one of three things: (1) the *best* state of things *conceivable*, (2) the best *possible* state of things in this world, or (3) that which is itself good in a high degree. Moore chooses the last and most modest of the meanings and goes on to attempt a positive solution to the question "What things are goods or ends in themselves?" Indeed, says Moore,[34]

once the meaning of the question is clearly understood, the answer to it, in its main outlines, appears to be so obvious, that it runs the risk of seeming to be a platitude. By far the most valuable things which we know or can imagine, are certain states of consciousness, which may be roughly described as the pleasures of human intercourse and the enjoyment of beautiful objects. No one, probably, who has asked himself the question, has ever doubted that personal affection and the appreciation of what is beautiful in Art or Nature are good in themselves; . . . I regard it as indubitable . . . that [the] mere existence of what is beautiful has value, so small as to be negligible in comparison with that which attaches to the *consciousness* of beauty. This simple truth may, indeed, be said to be universally recognized. What has *not* been recognized is that it is the ultimate and fundamental truth of Moral Philosophy.

If we attend to the rhetoric by which the problem of evidence is bypassed: the claim of "obviousness," "of seeming to be a platitude," of "indubitability," then we are back again to the dogmatism of the "common-sense" view of philosophic truth. But if we attend to its content, we are transported to a world of great clarity and great purity. Lord Keynes has observed:

The New Testament is a handbook for politicians compared with the unworldliness of Moore's chapter on 'The Ideal.' I know no equal to it in literature since Plato. And it is better than Plato because it is quite free from *fancy*. It conveys the beauty of the literalness of Moore's mind, the pure and passionate intensity of his vision, *un*fanciful and *un*dressed-up. Moore had a nightmare once in which he was unable to distinguish propositions from tables. But even when he was awake, he could not distinguish love and beauty and truth from the furniture. They took on the same definition of outline, the same stable, solid, objective qualities and common-sense reality.[35]

Moore's value theory is, in the end, of one piece with the stringent method of analysis which testifies to the influence which the lure of the part has had upon him. It culminates in a philosophical attitude of search, of attentiveness, of infinite *care* in the pursuit of clarity or of an idea. It is an attitude which Proust describes as that "of those who are engaged in thought, and whose whole body waits on their thinking . . . as though thinking nobly and deeply were summed up in thinking so attentively that one allows no part of the thought to escape." It is this attitude which Moore has bequeathed to the tradition of Philosophical Analysis.

3. THE WISDOM OF WITTGENSTEIN

Two months before Moore delivered his British Academy Lecture on "Proof of an External World," he gave up his professorship at Cambridge. His successor was Ludwig Wittgenstein. Moore had known Wittgenstein since 1912; between this time and the outbreak of the First World War, Wittgenstein attended Moore's lectures in Cambridge, but he then left for Austria and did not return to Cambridge until 1929. Of Wittgenstein Moore has said:[36] "When I did get to know him, I soon came to feel that he was much cleverer at philosophy than I was, and not only cleverer, but also much more profound, and with a much better insight into the sort of inquiry which was really important and best worth pursuing, and into the best method of pursuing such inquiries. . . . I am glad to think that he is my successor in the Professorship at Cambridge." It is Moore's usual and genuine modesty at work, but it also expresses a certain bafflement about a difference in philosophic method which sharply distinguishes the two men. Moore's method is meticulous, concentrated, but prosaic. He says everything. He spells it out in detail. He leaves nothing to mere inference or implication. But Wittgenstein's method is terse, glancing, and aphoristic. He says only enough to begin the process of illumination. The gaps in his argument (like the rests in music) work even more powerfully than the statements. He supplies only so much in the way of premises as permit the flash of insight to draw the conclusion.

Moore and Wittgenstein are alike in their attentiveness to the "puzzling" issues in philosophy, and in their reliance upon the resources of ordinary language to cope with these puzzles. Their difference stems perhaps from a profound difference in what they take to be the source of philosophic confusion. For Moore it is always in something which lies *hidden*, but for Wittgenstein it is in something which is *overlooked*. Moore considers confusion to be the result of a real failure of the sense of vision or of attention. The remedy is to search with care, to contract the straining mind to a fine point, to *look*. Wittgenstein considers it to be the result of seeing too well; the important things escape because they are always before our eyes. It is like the difference between the meticulous botanist and the distorting painter of floral still-lifes. Both are interested in a correction of the sense of sight. The botanist works with a concentration of descriptive attention which leaves no detail unnamed, which *forces us to see everything*. This is the technique of Moore. But the artist uses shocking color and distortion not to describe, but to rearrange and to *transform* reality. He *forces us to see things differently*. This is the technique of Wittgenstein.

In a sense it is somewhat misleading to speak simply of "*the* technique of Wittgenstein." For just as there were two Carnaps—the Carnap of *Der Logische Aufbau der Welt* and the later Carnap of *The Logical Syntax of Language*—so there are two Wittgensteins—the early Wittgenstein of the *Tractatus Logico-Philosophicus* and the later Wittgenstein of the *Philosophical Investigations*. It is no accident that the Vienna Circle read Carnap's *Aufbau* and Wittgenstein's *Tractatus* simultaneously, for, different as are their styles and intentions, they are both heavily under the influence of *Principia Mathematica*, and they hope to deal even with sense contents in a fashion which will make them structurally congruent with a rigorously constructed artificial language. It is a moment in the history of contemporary philosophy when Carnap, Wittgenstein, and Russell are almost as one. The subsequent divergence represents almost opposite interpretations of the supposed "failure" of the early work. Carnap became convinced not that the method of *Principia Mathematica* was wrong, but that it was a mistake to use this method for the elaboration of a language of sense-contents. Hence, purging his work progressively of every empirical reference, he turned more and more to logical syntax, to the "language of science," to a constructed, artificial language. Wittgenstein's revulsion was more radical, for he became skeptical of the very foundations of the *Principia Mathematica* itself, of the view of mathematics which it espoused, of its comprehensiveness as a deductive system, and of its value as a philosophical enterprise. This skepticism led him on the one hand to re-examine the problem of the foundations of mathematics and logic, and on the other to abandon artificial language and to transform philosophy into a critique of ordinary, natural language. This latter and most influential aspect of his work is expressed in the *Philosophical Investigations*. But anyone who reads attentively between the lines of Wittgenstein's transitional *Remarks on the Foundations of Mathe-*

matics will surely feel that it was Goedel's theorem concerning the existence of true but *unprovable* propositions in the system of *Principia Mathematica* which is primarily responsible for the drastic shift from the *Tractatus* to the *Investigations*.[37]

Although the techniques and the intentions of the *Tractatus* and the *Investigations* are different, there remains a similarity of cryptic statement and aphoristic manner. While it has become fashionable to see them as entirely different enterprises, yet a case can still be made for the unity of Wittgenstein's thought. He never departed from the conviction that actuality can be approached only through a consideration of symbols. Metaphysics must always begin with symbolic forms, and the essence of "being," "existing," "changing," and "enduring" is always bound up with the operations of "designating," "saying," "describing," "representing," "showing," "elucidating," and "clarifying." Thus even in the *Tractatus* are intimations and suggestions of the centrality of language (even ordinary language), which is to become the major theme of the *Philosophical Investigations*.

The two most striking and at the same time most controversial features of the *Tractatus* are (1) its logical atomism and (2) its picture theory of meaning. The first is illustrated in the following:[38]

1.1	The world is the totality of facts, not of things.
1.13	The facts in logical space are the world.
2.01	An atomic fact is a combination of objects.
2.013	Every thing is, as it were, in a space of possible atomic facts. . . .
2.014	Objects contain the possibility of all states of affairs.
2.0201	Every statement about complexes can be analysed into a statement about their constituent parts. . . .
2.0231	The substance of the world *can* only determine a form and not any material properties. For these are first presented by the propositions—first formed by the configuration of the objects.
2.0271	The object is the fixed, the existent; the configuration is the changing, the variable.
2.0272	The configuration of the objects forms the atomic fact.
2.061	Atomic facts are independent of one another.

The second is illustrated in the following:

2.1	We make to ourselves pictures of facts.
2.12	The picture is a model of reality.
2.131	The elements of the picture stand, in the picture, for the objects.
2.1514	The representing relation consists of the coordinations of the elements of the picture and the things.
2.18	What every picture, of whatever form, must have in common with

reality in order to be able to represent it at all—rightly or falsely—
is the logical form, that is, the form of reality.

2.223   In order to discover whether the picture is true or false we must
compare it with reality.

The world of the *Tractatus* is divided into entities of two kinds:
objects, which are formal but not materially characterized, and *facts*,
which are the individuated elements. So quixotic is this usage that it is
not always easy to remember that Wittgenstein is not talking about a
material but a logical space, and that his universe has more in common
with Leibniz' universe of logical possibilities than with a Newtonian
universe of spatio-temporal actualities. Only such a distinction permits
us to recognize that the efforts of the *Tractatus* are not directed toward
the establishment of specifications for an adequate ordinary language,
but for an artificial language analogous to that of *Principia Mathematica*. The picture theory of meaning is not immediately available
for the solution of the problems of ordinary language, and even within
Wittgenstein's universe of discourse it seems to hold only for elementary
propositions and not for the simple notations of which they are composed or the molecular propositions which they generate. Also the theory
of "objects" in the *Tractatus* is ambiguous, and yields no clear analogues
to traditional metaphysical conceptions.[39]

Nonetheless there are some references to ordinary language in the
Tractatus, although these are almost always negative. The sign for
Wittgenstein is arbitrary; this means (1) that the purpose of a sign
is to indicate logical form and (2) that the real meaning of the sign
lies in the *necessity* of its syntactical application. In an artificial language,
the specification of exact meaning for every sign itself determines the
rules of logical syntax to be followed. But just here lie the pitfalls of
ordinary language.[40]

3.323   In the language of everyday life it very often happens that the same
word signifies in two different ways—and therefore belongs to
two different symbols—or that two words, which signify in different
ways, are apparently applied in the same way in the proposition.
Thus the word "is" appears as the copula, as the sign of equality,
and as the expression of existence. . . .

3.324   Thus there easily arise the most fundamental confusions (of which
the whole of philosophy is full).

3.325   In order to avoid these errors, we must employ a symbolism which
excludes them, by not applying the same sign in different symbols
and by not applying signs in the same way which signify in dif-

ferent ways. A symbolism, that is to say, which obeys the rules of *logical* grammar—of logical syntax.

But the logical rules for a reasonable and successful syntactics lie outside of all natural languages, not because such languages are by nature irrational, but because of the tropes and metaphorical complications implicit in their use. Thereby are introduced the illusions and the mere appearances, the mystifications and the disguises which are inseparable from the natural languages.

4.002   Man possesses the capacity of constructing languages, in which every sense can be expressed, without having an idea how and what each word means—just as one speaks without knowing how the single sounds are produced. Colloquial language is a part of the human organism and is not less complicated than it. From it it is humanly impossible to gather immediately the logic of language. Language disguises the thought; so that from the external form of the clothes one cannot infer the form of the thought they clothe, because the external form of the clothes is constructed with quite another object than to let the form of the body be recognized. *The silent adjustments to understand colloquial language are enormously complicated.*

4.003   Most propositions and questions, that have been written about philosophical matters are not false, but senseless. . . . Most questions and propositions of the philosophers result from the fact that *we do not understand the logic of our language.*

4.0031 All philosophy is "Critique of language". . . .[41]

Already Wittgenstein is well aware of the problems of ordinary language, and in the assertion that "all philosophy is critique of language" and the emphasis upon the complication of the "adjustments to understand colloquial language" lies the latent program of the *Philosophical Investigations.*

For Wittgenstein the essential characteristic of logical propositions is that one can by an inspection of the symbols alone perceive that they are true, and in this basic "contentlessness" they differ from the sentences of ordinary language. But even these latter must in some sense have a logic, and perhaps in some sense also illuminate the world. For just as the gramophone record, the score, the sound waves, the musical thought all share in some pattern of order, so the modes of ordinary language also refer to or interpenetrate the world. As the musician can read the symphony from the score, and as the poet can in the verse adapt the music to the sense, so all the projective possibilities of language, wherein its richness lies, seem to inhere in a complicated logic of representation. In this lies all possibility of similes and metaphors, all the imagery of our language.

It is essential to the propositions of logic and also to ordinary sentences that they can communicate novel meanings, and yet "empirical reality is limited by the totality of objects." Logic fills the world, but it has limits, and these are illustrated by the limits of language itself. "*The limits of my language* mean the limits of my world." But this leads to a proposition of the *Tractatus* which is as difficult to understand as any to be found there: "All propositions of our colloquial language are actually, just as they are, logically completely in order." If this were to be taken literally, it would deny the necessity for the kind of linguistic therapy which the *Philosophical Investigations* undertakes. But it is, I think, implicitly denied by a later statement: "In philosophy the question 'Why do we really use that word, that proposition?' constantly leads to valuable results." To ask the "why" of linguistic use is to focus attention upon the mechanism of the use, and this attentiveness to use is the clue to the puzzles of philosophy.

Wittgenstein's *Philosophical Investigations* does not attempt to reform linguistic usage. It attempts to understand it. For it sees in this understanding a clue both to the solution of prior philosophic puzzles and to the proper practice of philosophy. It is a puzzling work: disjointed, thematically rambling, occasionally repetitive, often brilliant, but lacking, as Wittgenstein himself noted, in system and fundamental unity. He himself called it "only philosophical remarks," and compared it to a number of landscape sketches made in the course of long and involved philosophical journeys (over a period of sixteen years), constantly redrawn and augmented and rearranged.

It is perhaps inevitable that such a work should be the subject of sometimes conflicting judgments of worth.[42] The book is now probably at the high water mark of its influence, and its message, like that of the work of Aristotle and Kant before it, is worthy of attention not only for its intrinsic merit, but for an understanding of the scholasticism which has followed in its wake. In the case of Aristotle it was a scholasticism of the *thing*. In the case of Kant it was a scholasticism of the *idea*. In the case of Wittgenstein it is a scholasticism of the *word*.

But despite its fragmentary appearance certain themes keep recurring in Wittgenstein's work: the contrasting nature of the series of "language games;" an attempt to discover or suggest how language is related to inner experience; the attack upon the primacy of a private language which seems to be presupposed in every attempt to "infer" philosophically the existence of other minds or of an external world; the intimate connection between the language of sensation and the forms of behavior which are its expression; the relation of "form of life" to linguistic usage and the natural context of experience which surrounds the words with which we express our natures; the limitations of a merely labeling or reportorial theory of language; analyses of such crucial logical and epistemological expressions as "seeing," "imagining," "thinking," "understanding," "naming," "intending," and the like.

Wittgenstein begins with a famous passage from the *Confessions* of St. Augustine which advances a theory that "bodily movements . . . are the natural language of all peoples." From this primitive concept of "language as gesture" Wittgenstein branches out into a criticism of the simple theories of linguistic meaning which "surround the working of language with a haze which makes clear vision impossible." It is useful to us to say that naming is like attaching a label to a thing, but to see this act as arbitrary (as, indeed, it is in the case of the symbolism of chemistry or the notation of the infinitesimal calculus or in any constructed artificial language) is only to describe the suburbs, forgetting that language is not an artificial edifice, but a form of life. Wittgenstein uses the phrase "language-game" to indicate that the speaking of language is, indeed, a form of life, and his emphasis is upon the multiplicity of our language games. We give orders, describe objects, speculate about causes, make jokes, sing words, solve problems, greet, thank, and pray, and our "commanding, questioning, recounting, chatting, are as much a part of our natural history as walking, eating, drinking, playing." But where, from this natural ease in the playing of the language games, do the perplexities of philosophy arise?

They arise when the philosopher treats names as simples, when like Russell he searches for the unanalyzable elements of language, naming those objects that can be named by ostensive definition (i.e. by pointing them out), and hoping eventually to reach elements like "this" and "here" beyond which one cannot go. "And here we may indeed fancy naming to be some remarkable act of mind, as it were a baptism of an object." Thus, in Wittgenstein's now famous phrase: *"Denn die philosophischen Probleme entstehen, wenn die Sprache* feiert"—when language is *idle*, then philosophical problems arise. Naming is only one of the functions of language, and many words (adverbs, prepositions, conjunctions) which are not names can be defined only by their *use* in the language. Thus that "lure of the part" which hopes to reduce the elements of meaning to "particulars" (like Russell) or "objects" (like Wittgenstein himself in the *Tractatus*) is here abandoned. Names, propositions, descriptions have no privileged status: their role is given by the *rules* of the language game and their function is expressed in the technique of using the language. But here is a further difficulty. To speak of *the* rules and of *the* language game is to disguise the fact of multiplicity.

65. Here we come up against the great question that lies behind all these considerations.—For someone might object against me: "You take the easy way out! You talk about all sorts of language-games, but have nowhere said what the essence of a language game, and hence of language, is: what is common to all these activities, and what makes them into language or parts of language. . . . And this is true.—Instead of producing something common to all that we call language, I am saying that these phenomena have no one thing in common which makes us use the same word for all—but that they are *related* to one another in many ways. And it is because of . . . these relationships that we call them all "language."

66. Consider for example the proceedings that we call "games." . . . What is common to them all?—Don't say: "There *must* be something common, or they would not be called 'games' "—but *look and see* whether there is anything common to all.—For if you look at them you will not see something that is common to *all*, but similarities, relationships, and a whole series of them at that. . . . And the result of this examination is: we see a complicated network of similarities overlapping and criss-crossing. . . .

67. I can think of no better expression to characterize these similarities than "family resemblances"; for the various resemblances between members of a family: build, features, color of eyes, gait, temperament, etc. etc. overlap and criss-cross in the same way.—And I shall say: "games" form a family.[43]

The moral is distrust of *exactitude* and contentment with only so much certainty as the subject matter will bear. If you look for exact definitions of our concepts in ethics or aesthetics you will have to ask genetic questions. How did we learn the meaning of this word "good"? From what sort of examples has our concept of "beautiful" arisen? In which types of language-games are these "pieces" or "counters"? For to know and to say are by no means equivalent. We may say the height of Mont Blanc without really knowing. We may know how a clarinet sounds without being able to say. But to believe that knowledge conforms to the requirements of an exact logic, that whenever anyone utters a sentence he is operating a calculus according to a single set of fixed rules, is to invite misunderstanding. The rule by which anyone proceeds linguistically is the hypothesis which satisfactorily describes his use of words. "One person might say 'A proposition is the most ordinary thing in the world' and another: 'A proposition—that's something very queer.'—And the latter is unable simply to look and see how propositions really work. The forms that we use in expressing ourselves about propositions and thought stand in his way."[44] When we believe that we must discover an *ideal* order in our language, then we become dissatisfied with our concepts of "word," "symbol," "proposition," for the more narrowly we examine actual language, the sharper becomes the conflict between it and our requirement. Then the question rightly becomes not "What is the essence of a word?" but "How do our words function?" In the attempt to answer this last question lies the mission of philosophy.

Such a mission involves *guidance* but not reform. It is a contemplative therapy, not a linguistic transformation.

123. A philosophical problem has the form: "I don't know my way about."
124. Philosophy may in no way interfere with the actual use of language; it can in the end only describe it.
For it cannot give it any foundation either. It leaves everything as it is.[45]

It leaves everything "as it is" with respect to language, but not with respect to philosophy. We may indeed institute improvements in our terminology which will prevent the more obvious misunderstandings, but when we aim at complete clarity, we *ipso facto* aim at the complete elimination of philosophy.

The real discovery is the one that makes me capable of stopping to philosophize when I want to.—The one that gives philosophy peace, so that it is no longer tormented by questions which bring *itself* in question.—Instead, we now demonstrate a method, by examples; and the series of examples can be broken off.—Problems are solved (difficulties eliminated), not a *single* problem. There is not *a* philosophical method, though there are indeed methods, like different therapies.[46]

Kant had discovered the philosophical torments of a pure reason which asked questions which by its very nature it was unable to answer. Wittgenstein transforms this ideational into essentially linguistic perplexity. But the *Critique of Pure Reason*, like the *Philosophical Investigations*, ends at that point where the ground of the perplexity has been demonstrated. They are alike in their assumption that this demonstration itself constitutes a philosophical therapy.

One of the most important areas of the therapy lies in the relation of our language to the intrinsic nature of our inner experiences, in the question of how we "attach" words to the emotions, feelings, sensations which are ours in the purest privacy. There is a philosophic prejudice in favor of the primacy of the private, in favor of the doctrine that genetically experience begins with privacy, and only later, through a labeling activity of language, attaches public words to private meanings. The consequence is indeed philosophically perplexing, for it leads to the belief that common meanings are not *implied* by common words, but must be *inferred* from them; moreover, it also suggests the characteristic philosophical problems entailed by an instinctive solipsism— the problem of the existence of other minds and the problem of the proof of an external world. The time which Russell has devoted to the first, and Moore to the second, is itself evidence of the prevalence of such perplexities. Wittgenstein's solution of the difficulty is in effect the denial of a purely "private" language, and the abandonment of a labeling theory of naming for a theory which conceives of an infinitely more intimate relation between language and experience. The serious question is not: How do words refer to sensations? It is: How does a human being learn the meaning of the names of sensations? The answer is a species of pragmatic functionalism. Language is not the *mirror* of sensation behavior; it is itself a *kind* of sensation behavior.

Here is one possibility: words are connected with the primitive, the natural expressions of the sensation and used in their place. A child has hurt himself and he cries; and then adults talk to him and teach him exclamations and, later, sentences. They teach the child new pain-behaviour. 'So you are saying that the word "pain" really means crying?'—On the contrary: the verbal expression of pain replaces crying and does not describe it.[47]

In a sense, therefore, the proposition "Sensations are private" is false, for they cannot be *merely* private. Even with a completely private language rules would be needed, rules of memory, of identity, of criteria for similarity, and such rules could never be themselves a purely private matter if the concept of "a rule" or of "a criterion" is to have any fixity of meaning.[48] Sensations are from one point of view universals as well as particulars and this is indicated by the very non-particularity of (for example) color adjectives. "What am I to say about the word 'red'? —that it means something 'confronting us all' and that everyone should really have another word, besides this one, to mean his *own* sensation of red? Or is it like this: the word 'red' means something known to everyone; and in addition, for each person, it means something known only to him? . . ."[49] The question is rhetorical, for what is really important is the notion "confronting us all"—a notion given by the very existence of color adjectives in our language. For when we "think," it is not that "meanings" run through our minds in addition to words, but rather that the linguistic expression is itself the vehicle of thought. This causes Wittgenstein to say that "*Essence* is expressed by grammar" and that "Grammar tells what kind of object anything is."[50] Suppose that we should ask: How do I know that this color is red? Russell would say "Because I am at this moment experiencing a sense-datum of red." Moore would say "I see it and I am not color-blind." But Wittgenstein asserts: "It would be an answer to say: 'I have learnt English.'" Just so, with respect to the immediacies of pain and pleasure: "You learned the *concept* 'pain', says Wittgenstein, "when you learned language."

The clue, therefore, to linguistic intelligibility is attention to *use*. "Look at the sentence as an instrument, and at its sense as its employment." This is to pass far beyond a theory of meaning which identifies meaning with the connotation and denotation of names. The significance of an expression is like the *powers* and the *functions* of a knight or a rook in chess; to understand the piece, you must understand its utility for the game. It follows that there are plural pieces with plural utilities.

I say "I am afraid"; someone else asks me: "What was that? A cry of fear; or do you want to tell me how you feel, or is it a reflection on your present state?"—Could I always give him a clear answer? Could I never give him one?

We can imagine all sorts of things here, for example:

"No, no! I am afraid!"

"I am afraid. I am sorry to have to confess it."

"I am still a bit afraid, but no longer as much as before."

"At bottom I am still afraid, though I won't confess it to myself."

"I torment myself with all sorts of fears."

"Now, just when I should be fearless, I am afraid!"

To each of these sentences a special tone of voice is appropriate, and a different context. . . .

We ask "What does 'I am frightened' really mean, what am I referring to when I say it?" And of course we find no answer, or one that is inadequate. The question is: "In what sort of context does it occur?"[51]

The functions of language are multiple, and to see in what sense meaning is contextual is to pass beyond linguistic atomism to a position which recognizes the structure and texture of the whole. Camus may be right in his extreme diagnosis: "Every ambiguity, every misunderstanding, lead to death," but his remedy, "clear language and simple words are the only salvation from it," is naïve and unrealistic from Wittgenstein's point of view. When Wittgenstein says,[52] "Here it is easy to get into that dead-end in philosophy, where one believes that the difficulty of the task consists in . . . our having to describe phenomena that are hard to get hold of. . . . ," in one sentence he disposes of the method of G. E. Moore. And when he says,[53] "It is like the relation physical object—sense–impressions. Here we have two different language-games and a complicated relation between them.—If you try to reduce their relations to a *simple* formula you go wrong," he lays waste to the whole enterprise of Russell's *Our Knowledge of the External World*. Wittgenstein's conception of language, as we have seen, is that of the ancient city, the maze of little streets and squares, the houses with additions from various periods, the surrounding boroughs of science with regular streets and uniform houses. Here nothing is simple. It is complicated, archaic, maze-like. But a philosophy which is respectful of its nature, which sees the differences between its parts, and does not pretend that the inner city possesses the geometrical simplicity of the suburbs, is the only one which can keep us from getting lost.

4. THE OXFORD CULMINATION

The fruits of Moore's method and of Wittgenstein's linguistic emphasis are found in the "Oxford Philosophy" of the last two decades. It is concerned almost exclusively with the elucidation of certain important philosophical concepts and with the "informal logic" of the expressions of "ordinary language." But for a movement which has spoken to the world for over twenty years, its voice is curiously muted and inbred. With one exception, it has produced nothing which remotely resembles a philosophical masterpiece, and its major contributions have been delivered within the confines of the periodical *Mind* and the *Proceedings of the Aristotelian Society*. Within the last few years some twenty of these articles have been republished in two slim volumes by Anthony Flew (*Logic and Language*, First and Second Series), but they present nothing which might be called either systematic doctrine or clear unity of method. Two of them are, I think, of real interest: H. L. A. Hart's "The Ascription of Responsibility and Rights" with its analysis of action and its concept of "defeating claims" and J. L. Austin's "Other Minds" with its attention to the actual usages of the verb "to know" and its concept of "performatory utterances," both published in the *Proceedings of the Aristotelian Society* between 1940-1947. But two swallows do not make a summer (even an Oxford summer) and these twenty or so verbalists of the Oxford springtime may disperse like so many sparrows when the winter winds compel a stouter substance and a broader wing-spread.

There is one striking exception to this charge of triviality and thinness of substance. That is Gilbert Ryle, Waynflete Professor of Metaphysical Philosophy in Oxford University. Ryle has written one undoubted classic, *The Concept of Mind*. If, in what follows, I seem to neglect this book, with its valuable distinction between "knowing how" and "knowing that," its analysis of sensation, observation, and imagination, and its ultimate program for a behavioristic psychology, it is because I have taken as central in Ryle not his treatment of the perplexities of epistemology, but the technique of linguistic analysis which he has pressed from intuitive flabbiness into the mold of a systematic discipline.

For the last twenty-five years Ryle has systematically developed the linguistic program which had been little more than announced by Wittgenstein's *Philosophical Investigations*. What was in Wittgenstein only a hope and an intimation has been transformed by Ryle into a general logic for promoting the intelligibility of ordinary language and philosophic discourse. This general logic has three facets, three aspects, three general stages in its development, which may be stated as (1) the analysis of "systematically misleading expressions," (2) the concept of "categories" and of "category-mistakes," and (3) the analysis of "inter-theory questions" or "dilemmas."[54]

In his "Systematically Misleading Expressions" of 1932 Ryle attempts to exhibit the function which philosophy may perform in the clarification of meanings. The crux of what he wishes to establish is that:[55]

There are many expressions which occur in non-philosophical discourse which, though they are perfectly clearly understood by those who use them and those who hear and read them, are nevertheless couched in grammatical or syntactical forms which are in a demonstrable way *improper* to the states of affairs which they record. . . . Such expressions can be reformulated and for philosophy but *not* for non-philosophical discourse must be reformulated into expressions of which the syntactical form is proper to the facts recorded. . . . When an expression is of such a syntactical form that it is improper to the fact recorded, it is systematically misleading in that it naturally suggests to some people . . . that the state of affairs recorded is quite a different sort of state of affairs from that which it in fact is. . . .

Ryle proceeds to distinguish three types of statement that are systematically misleading, which he labels respectively (1) quasi-ontological statements, (2) quasi-Platonic statements (statements seemingly about universals), and (3) quasi-descriptions. Quasi-ontological statements are those in which the grammatical form of the statement *suggests* the existence of the entity which serves as its subject although in fact it may not or in some cases clearly does not exist at all. Ever since Kant disclosed that "existence" is not a predicate, we have been suspicious of the type of proposition "God exists." Ryle points out that propositions of the form "Satan does not exist" or "Carnivorous cows do not exist" or "Mr. Pickwick is not a substance" are systematically misleading for essentially the same reason. But if we transform them into "Satan is not the proper name for anything" or "Nothing is both a cow and carnivorous" or "There is no substance named Mr. Pickwick" the misleading clue of the grammar has been removed and the proper denial of existence is made clear. None of the first statements is really *about* anything, for there is no "Satan" or "carnivorous cow" or "Mr. Pickwick" for them to be about. In these statements the *appearance of existence* "is a purely grammatical one, and what the statements really record can be stated in statements embodying no such quasi-ontological predicates."[56]

Statements seemingly about universals or quasi-Platonic statements are also systematically misleading. When we say "Unpunctuality is reprehensible" or "Virtue is its own reward," Ryle observes, it almost seems as if we were saying something like "Jones merits reproof" or "Smith has given himself the prize" and so "philosophers, taking it that what is meant by such statements as the former is precisely analogous to what is meant by such statements as the latter, have accepted the consequence that the world contains at least two sorts of objects, namely, particulars like Jones and Smith and 'Universals' like Unpunctuality and Virtue."[57] But this is obviously absurd. It is nonsense to speak of a universal "meriting reproof" or "having a reward," for, of course, what we really mean in the first expressions is "Whoever is unpunctual deserves that other people should reprove him for being unpunctual" and "Whoever is good, gains something by being good." By transforming "unpunctuality" into "Unpunctual men" and "Virtue" into "virtuous persons" we avoid the pitfalls of a Platonic realism and make unambiguously clear that general terms are never really the names of subjects to which qualities may be attributed. Of course the plain man who uses these quasi-Platonic expressions is not making a philosophical mistake. Being concerned with the content, he is not misled by the form. It is only the philosopher who, generalizing about *sorts* and *kinds,* may mistake the grammatical forms of the sentences before their eyes for the logical structures of which they are in search.

To use an expression of the form "the so-and-so" is not generally misleading, for it is meant to describe some uniquely designatable individual. Thus to say "The president of the United States has a farm at

Gettysburg" is not ambiguous, for it is clear that the descriptive phrase refers to the unique individual Eisenhower. What can be misleading are "the" phrases which behave grammatically as if they were unique descriptions, when in fact they are not referential phrases at all. Already a proposition like "The president of the United States lives in the White House" has lost its unique designation and refers to "any" president, but the serious cases are those like "the top of the tree" or "the center of the bush" which may lead philosophers and those who generalize to believe that such phrases are used referentially.

Ryle concludes:[58]

I have chosen these three main types of systematically misleading expressions because all alike are misleading in a certain direction . . . . they are all temptations to us to multiply entities . . . . In each of them, the quasi-ontological, the quasi-Platonic, and the quasi-descriptive expressions, an expression is misconstrued as a denoting expression which in fact does not denote . . . . Occam's prescription was therefore in my view, 'Do not treat all expressions which are grammatically like proper names or referentially used "the"-phrases, as if they were therefore proper names or referentially used "the"-phrases.'

The danger of systematically misleading expressions is that they lead to theses which are metaphysically unreliable, to paradoxes, contradictions, and mistakes, and it is the function of philosophy to deal with them through "the exercise of systematic restatement."

Ryle's paper "Categories" of 1937 deals ostensibly with Aristotle's forms of predication and Kant's forms of judgment, but its purpose is to show the close connection between theories of categories and theories of types, and how philosophical arguments are therefore acts in which, by exhibiting the logical properties of statements, we show the categories or types of significant or absurd expressions. "The matter is of some importance," says Ryle,[59] "for not only is it the case that category-propositions [namely assertions that terms belong to certain categories or types] are always philosopher's propositions, but, I believe the converse is also true. So we are in the dark about the nature of philosophical problems and methods if we are in the dark about types or categories." Now, any sentence can be cut up into sub-expressions or "sentence-factors" and the way in which these sentence-factors are co-significant is strictly limited by categorial considerations. Any sentence-factor with its completion left open is a "sentence-frame." (Examples would be: "Socrates is . . ." or "I am the man who . . ." or ". . . implies that tomorrow is Saturday.") Such sentence-frames can be completed by filling in the appropriate *type* of expression. (Thus ". . . ugly" would complete the first, ". . . visited London yesterday" the second, and "Today being Friday . . ." the third.) If, however, we should begin with the sentence-frame ". . . is in bed" and complete it with "Saturday . . . ," the result, although grammatically correct, would be in meaning absurd. Thus the compatibility of sentence-factors is a matter of category membership, and to say "that a given proposition-factor is of a certain category or type, is to say that its expression could complete certain sentence-frames without absurdity." When a sentence is nonsensical or absurd (although its vocabulary is conventional and its grammar regular) its absurdity lies in a lack of co-significance of its member parts.

In ordinary discourse we seldom fall into absurdities of this sort, but in philosophical discourse it frequently happens, and it follows that our conception of philosophical analysis is mistaken if it involves merely the attempt at a clarifying paraphrase of a philosophically perplexing expression. Absurdities result not from the improper coupling of mere expressions, but from what the expressions signify. Therefore categorial or type analysis is crucial for a proper approach to those logical properties which permit us to understand the intelligible functioning of expressions. Expressions fall into different categories; the error of Locke's terminology of "ideas" and Meinong's terminology of "objects" was the assumption that the *significata* of expressions could all be of one and the same type. Category-propositions are those which assert something about the logical type of a sentence-factor. They are asserted by philosophers, and indeed, they are the chief instruments in the achievement of philosophic clarity.

The doctrine of categories which is introduced in the paper of 1937 finds its full-scale development and application in *The Concept of Mind* of 1949. That work offers "a theory" of the mind, not by providing new information or experimental results, but through a re-interpretation of psychological language: of the concepts of "intellect," "intelligence," "understanding," "feeling," "emotion," "sensing," "willing," and the like. The purpose of its philosophical arguments is, therefore, to set right the logic of the subject, to exhibit the proper use of "mental-conduct concepts," to "rectify the logical geography of the knowledge which we already possess." To determine the logical geography of concepts is to discover the logical type or category to which they belong, and this is the essential aim of philosophy. "Philosophy," says Ryle,[60] "is the replacement of category-habits by category-disciplines," and the chief strategy of *The Concept of Mind* is to enforce a category-discipline which shows that the "official doctrine" of modern epistemology since Descartes rests upon what is essentially a *category-mistake.*

The tenets of Cartesian dualism are well known. Human bodies exist in space and are subject to mechanical laws. But minds are not in space nor are they subject to mechanical laws. The one realm is private and inner; the other is public and outer, and the relation between the two is hedged with theoretical difficulties, for between "physical existence," which is one type of thing, and "mental existence," which is quite another, the causal link is highly recondite and mysterious. We observe the external world, and we introspect the stream of our own consciousness. During life the body and the mind are somehow harnessed together, but when the body dies, the mind may somehow continue to exist and to function. One of the chief purposes of *The Concept of Mind* is to show the absurdity of "the official doctrine," to overthrow the powerful reign of the Cartesian myth. But what is crucial is the use of the categorial therapy to accomplish this purpose. Ryle says:[61]

I shall often speak of it [the "official theory"], with deliberate abusiveness, as 'the dogma of the Ghost in the Machine.' I hope to prove that it is entirely false, and false not in detail but in principle. It is not merely an assemblage of particular mistakes. It is one big mistake and a mistake of a special kind. It is, namely, a category-mistake. It represents the facts of mental life as if they belonged to one logical type or category . . . when they actually belong to another. The dogma is therefore a philosopher's myth. In attempting to explode the myth . . . I aim at doing nothing more than rectify the logic of mental-conduct concepts. . . .

But what exactly is a category-mistake? Ryle provides a simple ex-- ample. If a visitor to Oxford, after having been shown over the place, were to say: "I have now seen your colleges, libraries, administrative offices, and so on, but I have not yet seen your University. Where is your University?" he would be the victim of a category-mistake. He would have thought that the University was some other physical entity, some collateral institution *in the same category as* Christ Church, Balliol, or the Bodleian, whereas it is in reality simply the totality, the principle of organization, the co-ordinating power of everything which he had in fact seen. His mistake was in believing the University to be simply another member of that class to which each of the individual colleges belongs. The implication is, of course, that Cartesian dualism sees the mind as another substance beside the body, whereas it is (as Aristotle long ago noted) simply the form or organizing principle of the body. A category-mistake indicates an inability to understand, to wield, to properly operate with a concept. It can occur with the concept of mind, or of substance, or of moral action. But wherever it occurs, it is the function of the philosopher to show that it generates puzzles which arise out of an inability to use certain items of the English language, and to bring to bear his own powers of linguistic analysis as a powerful solvent against what is essentially philosophical nonsense.

In his *Dilemmas* of 1954 Ryle comes very close to realizing the hope which was implicit in Wittgenstein's *Philosophical Investigations*. He rejects as a "baseless dream" the hope "that philosophical problems can be, by some stereotyped operations, reduced to standard problems in Formal Logic."[62] Instead he utilizes a technique of informal logic which draws on his earlier notions of "category-mistakes."

A dilemma for Ryle is a quarrel which arises "between theories, or, more generally, between lines of thought, which are not rival solutions of the same problem, but rather solutions or would-be solutions of different problems, and which, none the less, seem to be irreconcilable with one another."[63] They are embarrassments which arise because theorists of one kind "may unwittingly commit themselves to propositions belonging to quite another province of thinking." Dilemmas arise then as *inter-theory questions*—when the language of physics confronts the language of common sense, or when the language of mathematics confronts the language of ordinary events. The vocabularies of the law, of physics, of art criticism, of theology, of mathematics are quaint and infinitely diversified, and each has its own method, its own *logic*, in the employment of concepts. When different thinkers are in conflict, it may be less because they really disagree on a single issue, than because they are basing their arguments upon concepts derivable from different categories. Here once again category differences appear as the crux of unintelligibility in the supposed antagonisms within pure theory. Ryle's "solution" of dilemmas always has the form of an untangling of what are essentially "verbal issues." This follows naturally from his belief that all inter-theory questions are not technical but philosophical questions, and that they are therefore to be settled not by more information or additional scientific researches, but by linguistic inquiries.

Ryle's earlier technique of elucidation of "Systematically Misleading Expressions" came perilously close to being an operation in ordinary language which could better have been performed with the symbolism of *Principia Mathematica*. But for the solution of his dilemmas Ryle (without ever saying so explicitly) has recourse to Wittgenstein's ancient insight into "the plurality of language games" and the confusions which arise when we assume that there is only one.

It is perhaps instructive to look at one of them. Ryle's first dilemma he calls that of "It was to be." It is the dilemma of fatalism vs. contingency, and it goes like this: "For anything which takes place, it was antecedently true that it was going to take place, and since it was always true that it would in fact take place, it is foolish to do anything to prevent its taking place. But this fatalistic argument that nothing can be helped goes directly counter to our common belief that some things are indeed our own fault, that some disasters can be foreseen and prevented, and that there is therefore real sense in deliberation, planning, precautions." This is the dilemma, and it is important because it is not a mere riddle or joke, but a live intellectual trouble which perplexes most of us. Ryle's solution is detailed and cannot be given completely, but it rests upon a series of linguistic insights. The adjectives "true" and "false" which we apply to propositions about the future do not function like the adjectives "white" or "sweet" which we attribute to objects. Therefore "trueness" or "fulfilledness" is not really an enduring property of propositions or prophecies. Also, in thinking of a predecessor making its successor necessary, we unwittingly import into the idea of merely "logical" necessity (of antecedent to consequent) the idea of *causal* necessitation; we think, that is, (mistakenly) of the anterior truths as "causes" of the happenings of which they are true. But logical implication is not causal necessitation. The menacing statement "It was to be" tells us only the cliché that a proposition once true is always true and not that whatever happens is inevitable or doomed to occur. The root error of the fatalist theory is that it "tries to endue happenings with the inescapability of the conclusions of valid arguments."[64]

The dilemma "It was to be" is resolved when we see that it involves a confusion in the meaning of the word "necessity" due to a confusion between *the language of logic* and *the language of events*. But it is not merely the word "necessity" which causes the trouble, but also the words "event," "before and after," "cause," "fault," and "responsibility" —in short, *a family of interrelated terms*. The issue is tricky, because it is not a matter merely of professional terminology, and because it concerns a complicated knot which cannot be untied one strand at a time. The kind of philosophizing or conceptual analysis which can deal with it requires an over-all grasp of the interlocking functioning of words. Ryle says:[65]

I have no special objection to or any special liking for the fashion of describing as 'analysis' the sort or sorts of conceptual examination which constitutes philosophizing. But the idea is totally false that this examination is a sort of garage inspection of one conceptual vehicle at a time. On the contrary, to put it dogmatically, it is always a traffic-inspector's examination of a conceptual traffic-block, involving at least two streams of vehicles hailing from the theories, or points of view or platitudes which are at cross-purposes with one another.

Such "traffic-blocks" are also at the heart of the other dilemmas which Ryle considers: the confusion between mathematical method and the method of events which underlies the paradox of "Achilles and the Tortoise," the wrong allegation of parity of concepts like "enjoying" and "disliking" on the one hand and "having a pain" on the other which is at the heart of the dilemma of "Pleasure," or, finally, the lack of comparability of the language of theoretical physics and the language of ordinary experience which constitutes the dilemma of the "World of Science and the Everyday World." It seems to be a paradox of our language that different teams of ideas interfere with one another. And the confusions, paradoxes, and dilemmas which result can be dissipated only by the philosophical discipline which devotes itself to the "informal logic" of our ordinary and our technical concepts.

XII

The Vision of the Whole:
Alfred North Whitehead

since feeling is first . . .
                    E. E. CUMMINGS

The force that through the green fuse drives the flower
Drives my green age . . .
                    DYLAN THOMAS

The detail of the pattern is movement . . .
                    T. S. ELIOT

1. THE PHILOSOPHY OF SYNTHESIS

When in 1941, as a man already mellow with age, Whitehead composed the brief and modest "Autobiographical Notes" which introduced the volume in "The Library of Living Philosophers" dealing
with his work, he ventured one final remark. "Philosophy," he said, "is
an attempt to express the infinity of the universe in terms of the limitations of language." The remark is characteristic, for it combines the
setting of a generous intellectual task with recognition of its inevitable
failure. The two themes, "the infinity of the universe" and "the limitations of language," are recurrent in Whitehead's work, but what is
important here is the conception of philosophy as an attempt to survey
the world with some large generality of understanding. Ultimate notions
have intrinsic relevance to all aspects of experience—to daily life, to
physical science, to social organization, to literature—and they are a
vital concern to civilized beings. Therefore, since philosophy is the
entertainment of notions of large, adequate generality, "such a habit of
mind is the very essence of civilization." Philosophy is indispensable,
and it can exclude nothing.

The conception is formidable. And it has a quaint ring, faintly
redolent of the flavor of nineteenth-century idealism and the ghost
of Hegel or Spinoza. For, as we have seen, philosophically ours is an
age of limited ambitions and partial solutions, mirroring in its analytic

methods and specialist aims the general fragmentation of our culture and the various multiplications and divisions of the learned world. Logical empiricism implies a philosophy of nature, but it is weak in its treatment of human values. Existentialism has an elaborate philosophy of man, but it has no philosophy of nature. Linguistic analysis has a philosophy of human expressiveness, but it contains no substantive theory either of nature or of man. In the modern world, in addition to Whitehead, perhaps only Bergson and Dewey have been able to resist the lure of the part in the attempt to gain some painstaking, if fleeting, vision of the whole.

Whitehead's, like Dewey's, is a philosophy of synthesis in which a natural effort is made to combine insights from the most diverse sciences, to reconcile the testimony of common sense and ordinary sense-perception with the most recondite conceptions of physical theory, and to show how all the dualisms of seventeenth-century science and of nineteenth-century value theory can be overcome by the construction of an adequate metaphysics. But Dewey's and Whitehead's sources are very different. The early Dewey was deeply under the spell of Hegel; as a young man Whitehead "nearly knew by heart parts of Kant's *Critique of Pure Reason*," but he adds: "I have never been able to read Hegel: I initiated my attempt by studying some remarks of his own on mathematics which struck me as complete nonsense."[1] Also, insofar as the concepts of the natural sciences have been influential, Dewey (like Bergson) has assimilated the atmosphere of a Darwinian biology, whereas Whitehead has been learned in the development of mathematical physics. Finally, while the spirit behind almost everything which Dewey has written is the practical motivation of the social engineer, Whitehead's work breathes the quiet speculative passion of the abstract mathematician.

But I would not wish to press these differences to the point where they obscure the fundamental similarity. What Dewey has himself spoken of as "a demand for unification that was doubtless an intense emotional craving" is characteristic of them both. In Dewey it produced an all-embracing concept of experience. In Whitehead it has produced what is perhaps the culminating unification of the entire Western tradition.

It has become customary to divide Whitehead's development into three periods, roughly equivalent to his residence at Trinity College, Cambridge, at the University of London, and at Harvard, and to characterize them respectively as the period of the philosophy of mathematics, the period of interest in the foundations of natural science, and the period of the ultimate metaphysics.[2] But the transition from mathematics to the science of nature, and from mathematical physics to cosmology, is continuous, and the background of that continuity is unremitting warfare against "incoherence," against the multiplication and disconnection of first principles which expresses at once the mathematician's quest for "elegance" and the philosopher's interest in a unity of interpretation. In every period Whitehead is concerned with the "ultimate notions," the widest generalities, the integrating mechanisms of a universal synthesis. This intuitive feeling for maximum generality expressed itself for mathematics in *Universal Algebra* (1898) and *Principia Mathematica* (1910-1913), for natural science in *An Enquiry Concerning the Principles of Natural Knowledge* of 1919, and for metaphysics in *Process and Reality* of 1929.

When Dewey presented his final evaluation of Whitehead's philosophy,[3] he found that they were alike in attributing central importance

to the idea that experience is a manifestation of the energies of the organism; that these energies are in such intimate continuity with the rest of nature that the traits of experience provide clews for forming "generalized descriptions" of nature—the especial business of philosophy according to Whitehead—and that what is discovered about the rest of nature (constituting the conclusions of the natural sciences) provides the organs for analyzing and understanding what is otherwise obscure and ambiguous in experiences directly had . . . .

This similarity expresses not only a confidence in the validity of immediate experience, but in its ability to serve as a clue to nature in its more comprehensive aspects. Such a theory implies a reconciliation of the customary dualisms between man and nature, minds and objects, quantities and qualities. The germ of this reconciliation is to be found in the famous Chapter II of Whitehead's early *The Concept of Nature* ("Theories of the Bifurcation of Nature"). What Whitehead was there registering was a protest against the seventeenth-century doctrine of secondary qualities; against a fiction of quantitative entities completely disconnected from those features of our experience which are disclosed in sense awareness, and against the "metaphysical" habit of bringing in something *beyond* nature (the mind) to explain that which is located *within* nature (such as the transmission of light waves through the ether).

The recourse to metaphysics is like throwing a match into the powder magazine. It blows up the whole arena. This is exactly what scientific philosophers do when they are driven into a corner and convicted of incoherence. They at once drag in the mind and talk of entities in the mind or out of the mind as the case may be. For natural philosophy everything perceived is in nature. We may not pick and choose. For us the red glow of the sunset should be as much a part of nature as are the molecules and electric waves by which men of science would explain the phenomenon. It is for natural philosophy to analyze how these various elements of nature are connected.[4]

In asserting that the red glow of the sunset is as much a part of nature as the molecules by which physics explains it, Whitehead initiates from the standpoint of natural science alone a unification which is to be given later metaphysical expression in the doctrine that all actual existences are to be conceived as "occasions of experience." In refusing to countenance the theory of "psychic additions" (the notion that the immediate qualities of experience are additions furnished by the perceiving mind), he requires from science itself a coherence adequate for the totality of the facts. For a science which insisted upon the distinction between a nature of causal relations and a nature of sensory appearance (the "nature" apprehended in awareness as opposed to the "nature" which is the cause of awareness)[5] would be a fairy tale "decking out unknowable entities with arbitrary and fantastic properties."

I have cited Whitehead's polemic against theories of the bifurcation of nature in order to illustrate a generic property of his philosophic temperament—the revolt against dualism. In a certain sense the dualistic mode of perception is endemic to philosophy: it sets the problems and it gives the impetus to philosophic work—spontaneity and order, the the public and the private, quantity and quality, mind and matter, atomicity and continuity, fact and value, permanence and change, subject and object—these are the givens upon which the speculative intellect may operate. It is even possible to define the special fields of philosophic research in terms of such presented oppositions. Epistemology is the persistent attempt to determine the spatial location of sense data, to so adjust the "internal" and the "external" aspects of the perceptual process that the poles of "geometry" and of "feeling" may be given their proper status. Ethics since Aristotle is the study of the rational will, or of the question to what extent our decisions to act can be influenced by rational deliberation. Aesthetics studies the quaint development by which form issues into feeling, by which the most austere complexities of structure within the work of art produce a contagion of bare emotion. In each case it is an original opposition which sets the problem, and it is an unusual philosophy in whose dialectic it is dissolved. But it is the peculiar quality of Whitehead that seemingly antagonistic perspectives can be overcome. This is the consequence of a belief that philosophy expresses the infinity of the universe and that it can exclude nothing.

This is why the "philosophy of organism" (which is what Whitehead calls his mature metaphysics) so quixotically suggests the synthesis of incompatibles. It is Bergson's sympathy with a universe of dynamic process presented within the mold of Russell's scientific analysis. It is the vivid emotional world of the lyric poet presented according to the axioms, postulates, and primitive notions of symbolic logic. It is the psychologized cosmos of James's "drops of pure experience" assimilated to the mentality of projective geometry. Sentience within an extensive continuum, the massive structures of feeling, the novel creations produced by the ingression of forms*—these are the preoccupations of Whitehead's philosophy.

From what foundations in experience did such preoccupations arise in Whitehead's mind? The questions he asks are such as might readily occur to a mathematical physicist contaminated by the reading of philosophy or by common sense. How can the concepts of theoretical physics account for the status of life in nature?[6] To what *in our immediate experience* can we appeal to substantiate our belief in induction? What metaphysical entities must be presupposed if the revolutionary concepts of contemporary physics are to make sense? Probably, however, something much more common-place, yet more miraculous, was responsible for the quality of Whitehead's thought—something akin to his vague uneasiness when he read to the Royal Society of London his memoir "On Mathematical Concepts of the Material World" while haunted by memories of the shoals that run northward from the Straits of Dover and the treacherous tides of the Goodwin Sands.[7] Or the curious coincidence that the Cambridge mathematician who by day was systematizing the axioms of projective and descriptive geometry was obsessed with the poetry of Wordsworth, and "would read *The Prelude* as if it were the Bible, poring over the meaning of various passages"[8] by night.

But this is fact embroidered with fancy. More massive and more obvious is the internal evidence of the primary sources which helped to form Whitehead's philosophy. These are, I think, (1) a cluster of concepts from contemporary physics, (2) the philosophy of Plato, and (3) a conception of nature best epitomized in the poetry of Wordsworth. To these three germ-motifs I should like briefly to turn.

We have already called attention to certain interpretive results of the revolution initiated by Einstein and Planck. Quantum theory had

---

* Whitehead believes that things become definite when forms "ingress" or "enter into" the process of the world.

cast suspicion upon the classical concept of material substance and had suggested that atomic entities have a periodic or rhythmic rather than a continuously enduring character. Relativity theory emphasizes the earlier concept of the physical field, which defines the physically real not as particles at a point in empty space, but as vectors or lines of force (directed magnitudes) within a field. The slow development of Whitehead's philosophy from the early philosophy of mathematical physics to the fully developed metaphysics of *Process and Reality* represents the transformation of the physical concepts of "atomic vibratory entity," "vector," and "physical field" into the metaphysical concepts of "actual entity," "prehension," and "the community of actual occasions within the extensive continuum."[9]

Whitehead's discussion of the Maxwell equations in *The Principles of Natural Knowledge* makes clear why the vector concept was of such importance for his thinking. The Maxwell equations require for each point in space and each instant of time the vector quantities representing electric and magnetic forces and the velocity of the charge of electricity. "Now a vector involves direction; and direction is not concerned with what is merely at that point. It is impossible to define direction without reference to the rest of space; namely *it involves some relation to the whole of space*."[10] The ultimate facts expressed in the Maxwell equations are thus certain events which are occurring throughout all space; the vector concept provides the first bridge from the physics of isolated particles located at a point to the field physics of general interconnectedness. It is this latter which is the suggestive progenitor of Whitehead's metaphysics.

That the theory of relativity implies field theory, and that this in turn requires a physics of "events" rather than a physics of "objects," was the conclusion of *The Concept of Nature*. "Our knowledge of nature," says Whitehead, "is an experience of activity or passage. The things previously observed are active entities, the 'events'. They are chunks in the life of nature." He continues:[11]

The objects with which we are here concerned in the formulation of physical laws are material objects, such as bits of matter, molecules and electrons. An object of one of these types has relations to events other than those belonging to the stream of its situations. The fact of its situations within this stream has impressed on all other events certain modifications of their characters. In truth the object in its completeness may be conceived as a specific set of correlated modifications of the characters of all events, with the property that these modifications attain to a certain focal property for those events which belong to the stream of its situations. The total assemblage of the modifications of the characters of events due to the existence of an object in a stream of situations is what I call the 'physical field' due to the object. But the object cannot really be separated from the field. *The object is in fact nothing else than the systematically adjusted set of modifications of the field.* The conventional limitation of the object to the focal stream of events in which it is said to be 'situated' is convenient for some purposes, but it obscures the ultimate fact of nature.

Field theory provides the first assault upon a Newtonian doctrine of the independent existence of material particles, for by defining an "object" as the systematic modifications of its "field," it asserts a cosmological interdependence.

The second attack upon a static universe comes from the side of quantum theory. There is reason to believe that the physical revolution introduced by Planck had profound effect upon Whitehead's mentality. In the end it was to provide a clue to the nature of process which underlies the whole of Whitehead's metaphysics. The last chapter of *The Principles of Natural Knowledge*[12] translates quantum phenomena into a pervasive characteristic of nature through the concept of *rhythms.* "The physical object as apparent, is a material object, and as such is uniform; but when we turn to the causal components of such an object, the apparent character of the whole situation is thereby superseded by the rhythmic quasi-periodic characters of a multitude of parts which are the situations of molecules." This leads in turn to a characteristic Whitehead twist, namely, first the identification of "rhythm" with "life" and then the treatment of rhythm itself as a problem of aesthetic contrast.[13]

This suggests a closer identification of rhythm as the causal counterpart of life; namely, that wherever there is some rhythm, there is some life, only perceptible to us when the analogies are sufficiently close. The rhythm is then the life, in the sense in which it can be said to be included within nature. . . . The essence of rhythm is the fusion of sameness and novelty; so that the whole never loses the essential unity of the pattern, while the parts exhibit the contrast arising from the novelty of their detail. A mere recurrence kills rhythm as surely as does a mere confusion of differences. A crystal lacks rhythm from excess of pattern, while a fog is unrhythmic in that it exhibits a patternless confusion of detail. . . .

That such a passage should occur in a work attempting to rationalize the conclusions of contemporary mathematical physics is ample evidence of the continuity of Whitehead's philosophy; between the mentality which conceived "On Mathematical Concepts of the Material World" and that which wrote the chapter on "Beauty" in *Adventures of Ideas*, there is no disjunction whatsoever.

Science and the Modern World takes up the concept of quantum theory where *The Principles of Natural Knowledge* had left it and develops it further in the direction of a general theory of time.[14] If the steady endurance of matter is to be conceived as "a vibratory ebb and flow of an underlying energy or activity," then the system forming the primordial element is nothing at any instant. It requires a whole period or duration in which to manifest itself. This means (in contrast to the classical Newtonian theory, where the passage of time is only an accidental qualification of material particles) that lapse of time is no accident but rather of the very essence of material. Material cannot be fully itself in any subperiod, however short, and thus the endurance of objects requires the display of an emergent pattern. Endurance is the repetition of pattern in successive events. And time is "sheer succession of epochal durations."

It was the quantum theory which suggested to Whitehead the epochal theory of time, and thus permitted him to escape the necessity of all static space-time and physical forms of order. It was the stimulus from physical theory which suggested to him that process is the fundamental actuality, and that each separate individual "matter of fact" must somehow be describable in terms of process. A decade after *Process and Reality* had been written, Whitehead summed it all up in a single elegant sentence:[15] "There is a rhythm of process whereby creation produces natural pulsation, each pulsation forming a natural unit of historic fact." The phrase "a pulsation forming a natural unit of historic fact" can apply with equal suitability to Planck's quantum vibrations or to Whitehead's "actual entities." This is a measure of Whitehead's debt to contemporary physics.

A cluster of concepts from contemporary physics set the problem for Whitehead's thought, but the philosophy of Plato served as a permanent and inexhaustible background. His is a natural Platonism, nurtured by temperament and ancestral piety, but also by the mathematical mode of perception. All mathematicians and aestheticians are unconscious Platonists, for they investigate the most powerful techniques for the understanding of pattern and the multiple ingredients which constitute pattern; but in Whitehead the affinity is intuitive and deeply personal. Thus as Socrates is himself the hero of the Platonic Dialogues, so more and more Plato becomes the protagonist of *Process and Reality*. In this work[16] Whitehead makes his oft-repeated remark: "The safest general characterization of the European philosophical tradition is that it consists of a series of footnotes to Plato," and adds, "my belief [is] that the train of thought in these lectures is Platonic."

He indicates that the philosophy of organism is merely Plato's general point of view rewritten to accommodate the changes made necessary by two thousand years of scientific and mathematical development. Moreover, he characterizes the affinity of Platonism and the philosophy of organism in a few brief sentences:[17]

In such a philosophy the actualities constituting the process of the world are conceived as exemplifying the ingression (or 'participation') of other things which constitute the potentialities of definiteness for any actual existence. The things which are temporal arise by their participation in the things which are eternal.

These "other things" which are eternal and which constitute the potentialities of definiteness for any actual existence Whitehead calls "eternal objects." They are the Platonic "ideas" in modern dress, and their inclusion in his philosophy constitutes his most dramatic debt to Platonism. But they also counterbalance and supplement the emphasis upon "process" derivable from modern mathematical physics. In *The Principles of Natural Knowledge* Whitehead had distinguished between "events" and "objects," the former the indefinite entities expressing the fluency of the world, and the latter the ultimately permanent characteristics of nature which perception recognizes as the recurring character of events. Any Platonism seeks to disentangle the permanent elements from the flux. Whitehead's "eternal objects" are those forms of definiteness or recurrent types of uniformity which constitute the elements of the pattern of nature.

The "eternal objects" are Whitehead's most dramatic debt to Platonism, but they are only one strand in a texture of infinitely greater breadth. And it is the full breadth of Platonism with its shadowy, dialectical, and fragmentary nuances which haunts Whitehead's pages. For the expression of this plenitude one must turn not to *Process and Reality* but to *Adventures of Ideas*.[18]

No one could be perplexed over Aristotle's classifications; whereas Plato moves about amid a fragmentary system like a man dazed by his own penetration.

A few main doctrines stand out and they are of priceless importance for science, in the largest sense of that term. . . . His later thought circles round the interweaving of seven main notions namely, The Ideas, The Physical Elements, The Psyche, The Eros, The Harmony, The Mathematical Relations, The Receptacle. These notions are as important for us now, as they were then at the dawn of the modern world. . . .

The seven Platonic notions constantly recur in Whitehead's philosophy,[19] although naturally with a subtle difference, for Whitehead's vocabulary is tinged with individual flavor, and reflects the impress of a tradition, scientific and religious, of which Plato never dreamed. Yet for all the differences it was Whitehead's conviction that there are strictly analogous elements in the composition of nature. Of the Platonic concepts he commented: "I mention them because I hold that all philosophy is in fact an endeavour to obtain a coherent system out of some modification of these notions."

To obtain such coherence is indeed the problem of a philosophy of synthesis, for the Platonic notions suggest the radical dualisms of philosophic thought—The Ideas versus The Physical Elements, The Psyche versus The Mathematical Relations; "the intelligent activities of indwelling souls, and the geometric necessities of the indwelling shapes." And for any philosopher who holds (as does Whitehead) that the very nature of existence is exemplified in "the acquisition of pattern by feeling," the Platonic opposition of The Eros and The Mathematical Relations and its final reconciliation in The Harmony must have provided a climactic foretaste of the metaphysical drama.

Still, it is perhaps not The Ideas, nor The Eros, nor even The Harmony which plays the predominant role in Whitehead's thought, but The Receptacle, that difficult notion which Whitehead explained as "the conception of the essential unity of the Universe conceived as an actuality." In Whitehead there is a constant appeal to the individual Dialogues: to *The Laws* for its sociology, to the *Symposium* for the conception of the urge toward ideal perfection, to the *Sophist* for its definition of being as power. But the *Timaeus* in its quaint Pythagorean symbolism is the most systematic Platonic expression of the doctrines of space, time, and material to which Whitehead is committed. His whole notion of "personal identity" is a transcription of the doctrine of the Receptacle.[20]

Three comprehensive metaphysical constructions, three cosmologies, have dominated Western philosophy: the *Physics* of Aristotle, the *Timaeus* of Plato, and the system of Democritus transmitted by Epicurus and finally adumbrated in Lucretius' epic.[21] The first assumes the qualitative hierarchy of substances composed of form and matter; the second proposes the ingression of ideal forms into a receptacle of becoming through the agency of a divine artisan; the third postulates atoms and the void, the former moving regularly but without teleology in finite measurable arcs. If one assumes the exhaustiveness of this classification, then it is apparent that the cosmology of Whitehead sides with Plato as against Aristotle and Democritus. The notion of a medium connecting the eternity of being with the process of becoming is common to both accounts; in Whitehead it is "creativity;" in Plato "The Receptacle." But there is another consequence of this identification also. The assumptions of Democritus became the postulates of Newtonian physics. It is therefore possible for Whitehead to affirm that the modern wave-theory of the atom sustains Plato rather than Democritus, while the Newtonian physics sustains Democritus against Plato. "Newton," says Whitehead, "would have been surprised at the modern quantum theory and at the dissolution of quanta into vibrations; Plato would have expected it." The consequence is that in *Process and Reality* (Part II, Chapter III, Section III) Whitehead can use the contrast of doctrine between Plato's *Timaeus* and the Scholium of Newton's *Principia* both to advance the philosophy of organism and to vindicate the ultimate claims of Plato's cosmology. This is but the strategy of scholarship for a confirmed Platonist.

One of the last lectures which Whitehead gave was one entitled "Mathematics and the Good"[22] in emulation and in explication of the famous lecture which Plato delivered in antiquity to an audience which included Aristotle and Xenophon. Plato's lecture was notoriously a failure. Whether Whitehead's was is a moot question. But in that lecture he paid his last respects to Plato. "The abiding interest of Plato's Dialogues," he said, "does not lie in their enunciation of abstract doctrines. They are suffused with the implicit suggestion of the concrete unity of experience, whereby every abstract topic obtains its interest." As usual, in characterizing Plato's writings, he is unconsciously characterizing his own.

There may be in Plato a harmonious inter-weaving of abstract topics with the concrete unity of experience, but it is more usual in science and philosophy to witness their separation. And in science generally there is a neglect of concreteness in favor of the abstract. To redress the balance, the symbolic logician turned to the Romantic poets, and particularly to Wordsworth. The record of this influence is detailed richly in the famous Chapter V ("The Romantic Reaction") of *Science and the Modern World* and more theoretically in the second of the Chicago lectures entitled "Nature Alive."[23]

In discussing Wordsworth's *Excursion*, Whitehead said:[24] "Wordsworth in his whole being expresses a conscious reaction against the mentality of the eighteenth century. This mentality means nothing else than the acceptance of the scientific ideas at their full value. Wordsworth was not bothered by any intellectual antagonism. What moved him was moral repulsion. He felt that something had been left out, and that what had been left out comprised everything that was most important." What had been left out, of course, was life itself with its absolute self-enjoyment, its creative activity, its aim. The eighteenth century was rigorously materialistic, but the legacy which it left was "the discrepancy between the materialistic mechanism of science and the moral intuitions which are presupposed in the concrete affairs of life." Wordsworth's genius was to express this moral intuition as a truth about living nature. He was passionately absorbed in nature, and passionately mistrustful of science. Whitehead's comment is characteristic. "It is important therefore," he says, "to ask, what Wordsworth found in nature that failed to receive expression in science. *I ask this question in the interest of science itself.*" The answer indicates how the naive experience formalized in poetry provides an evidence which no science can afford to neglect. It is to be found in Wordsworth's greatest poem, *The Prelude:* "It is the brooding presence of the hills which haunts him. His theme is nature *in solido,* that is to say, he dwells on that mysterious presence of surrounding things, which imposes itself on any separate element that we set up as an individual for its own sake. He always grasps the whole of nature as involved in the totality of the particular instance." This means not only that nature is a unity, but also that it is an *organism,* that it is *alive.*

The reaction of the Romantic poets to the rationalism of the eighteenth century is the reaction of organism to mechanism, of full concrete emotional experience to the abstract analysis of science, of nature alive to nature dead. In expressing the discord between the aesthetic intuitions of mankind and the mechanism of science, the poetry of Wordsworth recalls to us "how strained and paradoxical is the view of nature which modern science imposes on our thoughts." "Remembering the poetic rendering of our concrete experience, we see that the element of value, of being valuable, of being an end in itself . . . must not be omitted in any account of an event as the most concrete actual something. . . . Value is an element which permeates through and through the poetic view of nature. . . . This is the secret of Wordsworth's worship of nature." Romantic poetry taught Whitehead that the concept of nature cannot be divorced from aesthetic values, that these values are in large part derivable from the organic wholeness of the natural world, and that "the brooding presence of the whole" is immanent in the various parts. From the poets, if not from Planck or from Plato, he derived the insight that a philosophy of nature cannot dispense with the notions of value, of motion, of feeling, of immediate quality, and of life.

What *Science and the Modern World* presents within the context of poetic intuition, "Nature and Life" asserts in the condensed accents of ultimate theory. "The doctrine that I am maintaining," says Whitehead,[25] "is that neither physical nature nor life can be understood unless we fuse them together as essential factors in the composition of 'really real' things whose inter-connections and individual characters constitute the universe." Like Wordsworth, he protests against a science whose data are derived solely from sense-perception and therefore omit all reference to "danger or desire," "triumph and delight," "hope and fear." such a mechanistic science is not so much mistaken as one-eyed, for it sees only half of what is there. "Science can find no individual enjoyment in nature: Science can find no aim in nature: Science can find no creativity in nature: it finds mere rules of succession. These negations are true of Natural Science. They are inherent in its methodology. The reason for this blindness of Physical Science lies in the fact that such Science only deals with half the evidence provided by human experience."[26] But the full evidence must enter into any cosmological theory. There is a life which lies below the grade of mentality, and in its quality is to be discerned the principle of the interconnectedness of nature. This was what caused Whitehead early in *Science and the Modern World*[27] to quote with approval from Francis Bacon's *Silva Silvarum:* "It is certain that all bodies whatsoever, though they have no sense, yet they have perception; for when one body is applied to another, there is a kind of election to embrace that which is agreeable, and to exclude or expel that which is ingrate. . . ." The "perception" of all bodies whatsoever, below the level of ideas consciously entertained, is the enjoyment of emotion, derived from the past and aimed at the future. It is the "prehension" of *Process and Reality,* "the enjoyment of emotion which was then, is now, and which will be then." Under the influence of the poetic intuition of Wordsworth, the electromagnetic vectors of Clerk Maxwell have become vectors of feeling, characterizing each actual entity whose process constitutes the world.

It has been my purpose to show that many diverse strands of interest have entered the philosophy of Whitehead: from relativity and quantum theory the concepts of the vibratory entity and the physical field; from Plato the establishment of a permanence in contrast to process, the reconciliation of the notions of The Eros and The Mathematical Relations, and the cosmology of the *Timaeus;* from Wordsworth and the Romantic poets the truth that fact is instinct with feeling and the intuition of a living nature. Thus, in turn, natural science, traditional philosophy, and poetry each makes its contribution to this philosophy of synthesis. How these strands unite in the great trilogy *Science and the Modern World, Process and Reality,* and *Adventures of Ideas* will be the subject of our next inquiry.

2. THE CONNECTED UNIVERSE

Toward the end of the first chapter of *Science and the Modern World* Whitehead makes explicit the rationalism which is ultimately the foundation upon which his metaphysics rests.[28] "Faith in reason," he says, "is the trust that the ultimate natures of things lie together in a harmony which excludes mere arbitrariness. It is the faith that at the base of things we shall not find arbitrary mystery." And a moment later: ". . . the harmony of logic lies upon the universe as an iron necessity. . . ." It is clear that Whitehead thinks of nature as a coherent logical system; faith in the order of nature has made possible the expansion of scientific theory. But there is a problem here. The symbolic logician who jointly with Russell produced the *Principia Mathematica* must naturally have been concerned with the internal coherence of his axiomatic system. Was the metaphysician who produced the categorial schema of *Process and Reality* any more than a mathematical logician in disguise? The answer lies in the recognition that the metaphysical situation has two dimensions: one constituted by the requirement of a logical framework of order, the other by the intrinsic nature of the temporal process of the world. In Whitehead neither is neglected, although there is a constant attempt to fit the second to the first, and to insist that the second by its own nature requires the first. Order is an intrinsic property of events, although if we are required to justify this insight from our experience we can only say (with Leibniz): It is because factuality is so infinitely patient of mathematical interpretation. If the harmony of logic lies upon the universe like an iron necessity, it is not a tyrannical imposition of the mind, but a necessity implicit in the facts themselves.

Whitehead's later work is haunted by the doctrine of essential relevance. "There is no entity," he says in *Mathematics and the Good,* "which enjoys an isolated, self-sufficiency of existence. In other words, finitude is not self-supporting. . . . Even in arithmetic you cannot get rid of a subconscious reference to the unbounded universe. You are abstracting details from a totality, and are imposing limitations on your abstractions." "It will be presupposed," he says in *Immortality,*"[29] that all entities or factors in the universe are essentially relevant to each other's existence. . . . any one finite perspective does not enable an entity to shake off its essential connection with totality. The infinite background always remains as the unanalysed reason why that finite perspective of that entity has the special character that it does have." "A single fact in isolation," he says in *Modes of Thought*, "is the primary myth required for finite thought. . . . This mythological character arises because there is no such fact. Connectedness is of the essence of all things of all types. . . . It follows that in every consideration of a single fact there is the suppressed presupposition of the environmental co-ordination requisite for its existence."

If the primary efforts of the logician are directed against irrelevance, those of the metaphysician are directed against disconnectedness. In Whitehead the concept of "connectedness" is so much an intrinsic mode of his perception that the mere distinction between philosophic fields fades into insignificance. There is the *relevance* of propositions; there is the *order* of nature; there is the *connectedness* of occasions of experience; all are exemplifications of one *relatedness* which rules the world. Thus what is immediately qualitative is ultimately relational, what is concrete is imbedded and contextual, and what seems self-sufficient is found upon closer analysis to be the product of abstraction. The clear blue expanse of the sky is supported by its infinite atmospheric depth; the Beethoven crescendo stems from the dynamics of its instrumental source; and the "mere object" which G. E. Moore perceives in space is but the abstracted item of his strained attention.

Such a conception of relatedness has equal applicability in mathematics and aesthetics, in ontology and epistemology, in biology and in physics. It permits the connection of the moment of experience with its past and with its future, of the organism with its environment, of the mathematical series with its members, of the sense perception with its antecedent data and its direction, of the actual entity with its spatial context. It suggests therefore that, whether metaphysically or mathematically conceived, a general science of ordered relationship must constitute the clue to our understanding of the world. The *Principia Mathematica* and "On Mathematical Concepts of the Material World" represent such a general science in its mathematical aspects; the famous second chapter of *The Principle of Relativity* ("The Relatedness of Nature") shows how this can be applied to the spatio-temporal continuum of the natural world; and Part IV of *Process and Reality* ("The Theory of Extension") gives to the spatio-temporal continuum of the early works on natural science a metaphysically generalized status as derivative from a more ultimate extensive connection. The development of Whitehead's philosophy can be seen, therefore, as successive periods of attentiveness to the logico-mathematical, the physical, and the metaphysical relatedness of the world.

In the early works on the foundations of mathematical physics, the strategy is almost wholly negative. By "negative strategy" I mean, of course, not the assertion of interconnectedness, but the attack upon its opposite. In *Science and the Modern World* the clearing away of the metaphysical debris is a dramatic preparation for the act of systematic construction. And in *Process and Reality* the act of systematic construction overshadows any backward glance at the details of philosophical error.

The whole point of *The Principles of Natural Knowledge* was the assertion of a doctrine of "significance," namely the doctrine of the relatedness of things in nature. This led to an examination of perception, since "the relatedness which is the subject of natural knowledge cannot be understood without reference to the general characteristics of perception." The examination of perception led in turn to the establishment of a matrix theory of space and time. "The fundamental assumption," said Whitehead,[30]

to be elaborated in the course of this inquiry is that the ultimate facts of nature, in terms of which all physical and biological explanation must be expressed, are events connected by their spatio-temporal relations, and that these relations are in the main reducible to the property of events that they can contain (or extend over) other events which are parts of them. In other words, in the place of emphasizing space and time in their capacity of disconnecting, we shall build up an account of their complex essences as derivative from the ultimate ways in which those things, ultimate in science, are interconnected.

This is, indeed, the positive doctrine, but the chief energies are directed toward the demolition of the philosophical presupposition of Newtonian physics, the possibility of atomistic and self-sufficient entities. This is accomplished primarily by an attack upon the atomistic theory of time. The great enemy here is the mistaken assumption of the experiential reality of the "instant" of time.

The *Concept of Nature* also addresses itself to a demolition of the materialism of the Newtonian world-view, to the belief that nature is an aggregate of material uniquely designatable in space and time. The central concept of this physics is the notion of "a particle" at "a point in space" at "an instant." But the "trinity of this natural materialism" cannot be granted the luxury of perceptual validation. Points, instants, and particles (the atomistic notions of the seventeenth-century view of physical nature) may be the necessities of an earlier theory of dynamics, but "there is a wide gap between these presuppositions of the intellectual theory of materialism and the immediate deliverances of sense-awareness."[31] Quantum theory has indicated that "There is no such thing as a molecule at an instant. A molecule requires a minimum duration in which to display its character. Similarly physical objects are steady complexes of molecules with an average permanence of character throughout certain minimum durations." Biological science has indicated that "there is no such thing as life 'at an instant'; life is too obstinately concrete to be located in an extensive element of an instantaneous space." If there is no molecule at an instant, no such thing as life at an instant, then it is possible to draw the obvious conclusion that "there is no nature at an instant." From the standpoint of a rigorous empiricism, "points," "particles," and "instants" are fictions. This is not to say that they are the product of imagination, but only that they are reached by a process of abstraction from the concrete givenness of experience. We do not live at "instants" but in "durations." We do not perceive "particles" but simply "volumes." We do not experience "points" but only "extensive magnitudes."[32] Thus a point or an instant or a particle may be a set of natural properties, but it is a set which is reached by a route of approximation. Far from the least of Whitehead's technical accomplishments is that he has invented a Method of Extensive Abstraction which exhibits the route of approximation to be followed in the derivation of atomic properties from the background of connectedness given in sense perception.

Whitehead's attack upon Newtonian atomism is in essence metaphysical, for it denies the real existence in nature of the entities which Newtonian science presupposes, but it has also important epistemological consequences. In the first place, to deny the real existence of points, instants, and particles requires some reference to the process of sense perception by whose authority they are denied. At this point "relatedness" is identified with immediate sense perception and atomism with the intellectual act of abstraction. In the second place, the physical atomism of Newton found subsequent and analogous expression in the sensory atomism of Hume, leaving the same problematic disconnectedness in the process of human knowledge as Newton had left in nature. Knowledge at an instant, Whitehead maintained, is no more valid than a particle at an instant, for it cuts off the continuity of the funded past with the pregnant future, turns memory into a mystery, and makes the inductive inference upon which natural science rests into an arbitrary and reasonless act.

In *Science and the Modern World* Whitehead's attack upon Newtonian atomism reaches its high point, for it is here formalized as the Fallacy of Misplaced Concreteness. Newtonism is a doctrine of *simple location,* for to hold that the universe is a succession of instantaneous configurations of material is to suggest that they may be given conceptual definiteness through the assignment to them of specific spatial and temporal coordinates. A particle at a point at a specific instant is the basic model for this physical doctrine; it envisages the possibility of such simple location as *"This* particle *here now."* It would seem that there is no greater immediacy of sense perception than this. But this is precisely what Whitehead denies:[33]

To say that a bit of matter has *simple location* means that, in expressing its spatio-temporal relations, it is adequate to state that it is where it is, in a definite region of space and throughout a definite finite duration of time, apart from any essential reference of the relations of that bit of matter to other regions of space and to other durations of time. . . . This idea is the very foundation of the seventeenth century scheme of nature. . . . I shall argue that among the primary elements of nature as apprehended in our immediate experience, there is no element whatsoever which possesses this character of simple location. . . . I hold that by a process of constructive abstraction we can arrive at abstractions which are the simply-located bits of material, and at other abstractions which are the minds included in the scientific scheme. Accordingly, the real error is an example of what I have termed: The Fallacy of Misplaced Concreteness.

The fallacy of misplaced concreteness is that error which results from mistaking the abstract for the concrete, which takes very abstract logical constructions as the rudimentary elements of our concrete experience, and therefore as the ultimate constituents of reality. Points, particles, and instants are extremely useful for physical science, which cannot dispense with abstractions. The fallacy becomes "vicious" only when such scientific abstractions are taken as the clue to the most fundamental existential properties of the world. At the conclusion of the chapter on "Objects" in *The Concept of Nature* Whitehead said: "The aim of science is to seek the simplest explanations of complex facts. We are apt to fall into the error of thinking that the facts are simple because simplicity is the goal of our quest. The guiding motto in the life of every natural philosopher should be, Seek simplicity and distrust it." It is now possible to see what he meant. He had in mind the necessary separation of the scientific and the philosophic functions.

The scientist cannot live without abstractions. But the philosopher must be vigilant in their critical revision. "It is here that philosophy finds its niche as essential to the healthy progress of society. It is the critic of abstractions."

Whitehead's critique of abstractions extends not only to the dominant philosophy of science of the seventeenth century, but also to Hume's epistemology, which was its eighteenth-century consequence. As the Newtonian dynamics presupposes the successive but instantaneous existence of physical particles, so Hume's theory of the mind presupposes successive, instantaneous, and unrelated moments of perception. Since causes and effects are also for Hume mental contents, they are separate, distinct, and without internal relatedness. Since the present perception discloses no information as to its future successors, the cause also discloses no information about its effect. Between the present and the future (and therefore the cause and its effect) any connection must be entirely arbitrary. This denies an Order of Nature and an Order of Mentality; and it makes impossible the rational justification of the method of induction. How can the philosophy of science be extricated from this impasse? Whitehead's solution lies in seeing that the immediate occasion of experience as set before us in direct cognition, in its full concreteness, suggests a general character of relatedness beyond itself.

Either there is something about the immediate occasion which affords knowledge of the past and the future, or we are reduced to utter scepticism as to memory and induction. It is impossible to overemphasize the point that the key to the process of induction, as used either in science or in our ordinary life, is to be found in the right understanding of the immediate occasion of knowledge in its full concreteness. . . . We find ourselves amid insoluble difficulties when we substitute for this concrete occasion a mere abstract in which we only consider material objects in a flux of configurations in time and space. . . .[34]

As the quantum theory makes permanently obsolete the Newtonian notion of "nature at an instant," so the solution of the problem of induction renders untenable Hume's assumption of an isolated "perception at an instant." Both lead back to a conclusion which Whitehead had established in The Principle of Relativity:[35] "Thus an entity is an abstraction from the concrete, which in its fullest sense means totality. . . . It is therefore impossible to find anything finite, that is to say, any entity for cognition, which does not in its apprehension by consciousness disclose relationships to other entities, and therefore disclose some systematic structure of factors within fact. . . ." Any present occasion of experience implies a community of such occasions unified by their mutual relatedness and by their mutual implication in one another's natures. What we speak of as the space-time continuum is therefore the general system of order which we abstract from the general relatedness perceptually apparent.

Whitehead's critique of Newtonian atomism is a preliminary, but crucial, enterprise. Once its tenets are established, the field is open for the explicit introduction of his own alternative organic metaphysics to supplant the materialism "with which, since the seventeenth century, science has saddled philosophy." The important thing is that an organic philosophy of nature must start at the opposite end. The starting-point of materialism is the fact of independence: the independent existence of matter and of minds, and the simple location of bits of matter in space and time. On the contrary, says Whitehead: "The organic starting point is from the analysis of process as the realization of events disposed in an interlocked community. The event is the unit of things real. The emergent enduring pattern is the stabilization of the emergent achievement so as to become a fact which retains its identity throughout the process."[36] All of the important concepts are here: "process," "interlocked community," "event," "emergent pattern," "retention of identity," "achievement." The way in which Whitehead effects the transition is through the concept of *prehensive unification*.

A "prehension" is a grasping together into unity by which an organism appropriates what it needs from the characteristics of its environment. It is the act of experience by which the subject experiences its many objects in a movement of feeling which "feels what is *there* and transforms it into what is *here*." It is thus a growing together or a becoming in which a pattern emerges and thereby an occasion of experiences realizes itself against the background of the world of total possibilities of what it might and could have been. It is a "concrescence" which culminates in the concrete pattern, with the "ingression" of certain possibilities becoming ingredient or actual, and it therefore represents a "decision" in the sense of cutting off alternative possibilities. This is the terminology of the more mature doctrine of *Process and Reality*. In *Science and the Modern World* it is restricted to the concepts of "prehension," "actual entity," "eternal object" and "the inheritance of pattern." To these concepts I should like briefly to turn.

The most concrete fact is process, and process itself may be analyzed into the underlying activity of prehension and realized prehensive events. Each event is thus an individual matter of fact issuing from this underlying activity, but to say that it is individual is not to say that it is independent. It depends for its being upon other individuals, and the way in which we specify its relation to space-time is only a more abstract characterization of the mutual ordering of events. "For space and time are simply abstractions from the totality of prehensive unifications as mutually patterned in each other." We have therefore in the concept of "prehension" the clue to an alternative account of nature in which unification and totality constitute what essentially there is. We can be content, says Whitehead,[37]

with a provisional realism in which nature is conceived as a complex of prehensive unifications. Space and time exhibit the general scheme of interlocked relations of these prehensions. You cannot tear any one of them out of its context. Yet each one of them within its context has all the reality that attaches to the whole complex. . . . A prehension is a process of expansive development, necessarily transitional from prehension to prehension. What is achieved is thereby passed beyond, but it is also retained as having aspects of itself present to prehensions which lie beyond it.

Thus nature is a structure of evolving processes. The reality is the process. It is nonsense to ask if the colour red is real. The colour red is ingredient in the process of realization. The realities of nature are the prehensions in nature, that is to say, the events in nature.

It is interesting to note that the process of nature requires forms of definiteness or "eternal objects." The things which occur are therefore in some sense dependent upon the things which endure. Although the "event" or "actual entity" or "actual occasion" is the ultimate unit of natural occurrence, the interrelation of events is accomplished through those eternal objects such as colors, geometrical shapes, sounds, or quantities which are the prerequisites of nature and not emergent from it. Such eternal objects will be the ingredients in events which contribute the aspect of form. The primary organisms of becoming are actual entities, and their "realization" is the emergence of some particular pattern as grasped into the unity of the real event. Such an actual event is constituted by the real togetherness of diverse eternal objects in that pattern to the exclusion of other eternal objects. Thus reality involves not only achieved togetherness, but also exclusion.

Eternal objects are those "possibilities" whose self-identity is not dependent upon the flux of things. They have "ingression" into the flux just as the Platonic "ideas" have ingression into the Platonic "Receptacle" in the *Timaeus*, and they "interpret events each to the other," but they belong to a realm which transcends the actual course of realization however much they are relevant to it. Whitehead says:[38] "It is the foundation of the metaphysical position which I am maintaining that the understanding of actuality requires a reference to ideality. The two realms are intrinsically inherent in the total metaphysical situation." Eternal objects are in their nature "abstract;" they are universals or "possibilities" which define any actual occasion by the specific way in which their actualization occurs. For "actualization" is a selection among possibilities, and these "possibilities" sustain certain purely abstract relations to one another. Accordingly, says Whitehead, "there is a general fact of systematic mutual relatedness which is inherent in the character of possibility. The realm of eternal objects is properly described as a 'realm,' because each eternal object has its status in this general systematic complex of mutual relatedness."[39] The realm of eternal objects is the ghost of Platonism which haunts the speculation of this mathematically-oriented metaphysician. But it is a useful ghost, whose presence is due not merely to ancestral piety. Eternal objects inform actual occasions with hierarchic patterns. They are therefore a preservative against the persistent danger of the anonymous flux, namely, formlessness. The process of the world is an energy that needs the rationale of pattern. In Whitehead's system this pattern is illustrated in two examples. One is the extensive continuum whose exemplifications are the complex of spatio-temporal relations. The other is the ideal arrangement of the realm of eternal objects.

Pattern is important, but "the final real entity is *an organizing* activity, fusing ingredients into a unity, so that this unity is the reality." This individual entity has a life-history which is a part within the life-history of some larger, deeper, and more complete pattern of the world. The larger pattern dominates the individual, and the individual in turn makes the larger pattern different from what it would otherwise be. Thus Whitehead's picture of the world envisages both atomicity and continuity, and it avoids the dangers of both the Hegelian and the Leibnizian alternatives. It skirts the dangers of both a world of individuals so hermetically sealed and autonomous that they are practically relationless, and of a world of unity so wholistic and so organically interrelated that real individuality is swallowed up in the mist of totality.

But there is a problem. Prehensions are the threads of process. They are the puffs of experience constituting actual occasions. Where in the evanescence of this flux lies endurance? An Aristotelian substance may be successively qualified by diverse adjectives but *it* endures. A Leibnizian monad undergoes internal development but *it* retains its self-identity. A Newtonian particle may shift its successive locations in space, but *it* is the same particle. But where in the shifting succession of "occasions of experience" lies the permanence which we have learned to attribute to the "object" of an older physics? The answer lies in understanding how the pattern of ingression of eternal objects is sustained by the flow of time. Enduring things are the outcome of a temporal process. For example, a molecule is a pattern exhibited in an event of two minutes or of any subdivision of that two minutes. The enduring pattern is wholly derived from the various temporal sections of the event, and it expresses a certain unity of character uniting the underlying individualized activities. "There is then an enduring object with a certain unity for itself and for the rest of nature. Let us use the term physical endurance to express endurance of this type. Then physical endurance is the process of *continuously inheriting* a certain identity of character transmitted throughout a historical route of events."[40]

What is involved in the endurance of emergent objects is the display of a pattern marked by *the reiteration* of selected characters. Such reiteration requires a duration involving a definite lapse of time and not merely an instant. Here the Newtonian theory of time is abandoned, and an "epochal theory" of time (or process) more congruent with the requirements of quantum mechanics makes its appearance. Time, as Bergson has previously insisted, is not to be assimilated to the model of a homogeneous space. It is not another form of extension, but the "sheer succession of epochal duration," and temporalization is not a continuous process, but a form of atomic succession. This is the final rejection of the doctrine of "simple location." Newtonian absolute time flows equably; it is the general matrix within which natural motion occurs; but it is external to, and fundamentally irrelevant to, the nature of the matter which can be located within it. Whitehead's time, like Bergson's time, is real. It can "bite into" and transform the character of matter. The very nature of the enduring entity is dependent upon the lapse of time required for the exhibition of the pattern which constitutes its nature.

In the epochal theory of time is revealed, I think, the elementary strategy of a metaphysics of process. Process is the becoming of actual entities. Actual entities are the real concrescence of many potentials. Concrescence as the achievement of the satisfaction of complete actuality implies the atomic lapse of time. The heart of the matter lies in Whitehead's ninth category of explanation as stated in *Process and Reality: How* an actual entity *becomes* constitutes *what* that actual entity *is*. Here the genetic account is generalized as a method of metaphysical explanation so that, no longer a mere historical accident, it becomes the lever for the determination of actuality. It is evident that the requirements of physical theory first put forward by Planck suggest an outcome very similar to that of the epochal theory of time. For just as the corpuscular organisms at the base of the physical field are conceptualized as vibratory entities, so the societies of actual occasions exhibit endurance in the sense of a reiteration of their relational pattern. Endurance in a philosophy of process cannot be a brute fact. It must be capable of analysis into types of "social" and "personal" order. Thus an enduring object becomes a "nexus" of actual occasions with an inheritance of near-identical pattern through time.

Whitehead's criticism of Newtonian materialism is not merely that this physical theory should have more intimately related material and time. It is also the larger cosmological criticism that any doctrine of simple location and the isolated self-sufficiency of material bodies renders unintelligible an interconnected world of real individuals. If the Newtonian doctrine has served admirably for an earlier stage of scientific development, it has nonetheless produced two types of disconnectedness—one within the individual entity, the other between diverse individuals—for it has failed to show what for each individual is its binding actuality, and it has failed to disclose in what sense the cosmos is a universe. In the end, this deficiency is important for an understanding of Whitehead himself: it sets the program for his own metaphysical construction. On the one hand he must show how an actual occasion is an achievement in its own right—"a grasping of diverse entities into a value by reason of their real togetherness in that pattern"—while at the same time indicating that this is not a mere "logical" togetherness of diversified eternal objects. On the other hand, he must show that the "passage" of nature itself constitutes an extensive continuum which provides the real communication between ultimate realities. A consciousness of this double requirement leads Whitehead to the discovery of two kinds of fluency, and thus sets the program for his greatest work, *Process and Reality*.

Whitehead's philosophy is indeed "a vision of the whole," and I have tried to indicate the principal aspects under which this philosophy of process reveals itself. These are: (1) a theory of time in which time enters into the essence of materiality, (2) a theory of relatedness in which the world enters into the constitution of each actuality, and (3) a theory of inheritance whereby endurance is explained as conformal inheritance of pattern. Essential temporality, total relatedness, and conformal inheritance are the chief qualities of Whitehead's philosophy of process. They are the means whereby he can outline the metaphysical requirements of the Connected Universe.

3. THE METAPHYSICS OF FEELING

Process and Reality opens with a famous and magnificent defense of speculative philosophy. Whitehead's purpose is to present a positive doctrine of "the becoming, the being, and the relatedness of actual entities," a total scheme of cosmological ideas by which all aspects of experience may be rendered intelligible. This means both that the traditional philosophical problems of space-time, perception, and causality should find their solution in the epistemology of the interconnected universe, and that the humanistic aspects of experience should not be found incompatible with the results of an advanced mathematical physics. "It must be one of the motives of a complete cosmology to construct a system of ideas which bring the aesthetic, moral, and religious interests into relation with those concepts of the world which have their origin in natural science."

"Speculative philosophy," says Whitehead,[41] "is the endeavour to frame a coherent, logical, necessary system of general ideas in terms of which every element of our experience can be interpreted." Its coherence lies in its presupposition that no entity can be conceived in complete abstraction from the system of the universe. Its logical quality lies both in its internal consistency and in its applicability to empirical matters of fact. Its necessity lies in the universality of its application. "The metaphysical first principles can never fail of exemplification. We can never catch the actual world taking a holiday from their sway."

There is something Promethean about this conception of the scope of speculative philosophy, and this rationalistic dream of a completed metaphysics would smack of *hubris*, of overwhelming pride, if its ambitions were not so thoughtfully qualified by a profound sense of limitation. This sense of limitation lies in a recognition of the impossibility of metaphysical finality, of the basic inadequacy of linguistic expression, and of the pitiful achievement of even the best of philosophical abstractions. Any voyage toward the larger generalities must bear in mind that "first principles" change and develop from age to age, in philosophy no less than in natural science. A mathematical physicist, who in 1880 thought that physics was nearly a closed subject, only to be rudely awakened from his dogmatic slumbers twenty years later by the first rumblings of the special theory of relativity, was not likely to succumb to a Cartesian romance with clear and distinct ideas or to the Aristotelian faith in the immutability of philosophic first principles. The history of culture is strewn with the rise and fall of "supreme generalities." Philosophy, like science, adheres to the method of successive approximation. "Metaphysical categories are not dogmatic statements of the obvious; they are *tentative* formulations of the ultimate generalities."[42]

Also there are the inadequacies of language. Words, phrases, sentences are concrete in their ordinary employment; as philosophical instruments they must be stretched toward a generality foreign to their common usage, and "however such elements of language be stabilized as technicalities, they remain metaphors mutely appealing for an imaginative leap." The difficulty here is twofold. On the one hand any single form of expression (as Wittgenstein also saw) is elliptical, since it belongs to a universe of discourse, and since it requires some systematic background of fact and linguistic structure to give it determinate status. Wittgenstein turned to language as a storehouse of human experience, as if the essence of culture were distilled in the variety of our language games. He distrusted not language, but its "idle," that is to say, its "philosophic" use. Whitehead holds a similar idea, but draws a different conclusion. It is true that the language of ordinary discourse and of literature breaks down at the point where it seeks to express the larger generalities. This, however, is not an edict against metaphysics, but only a caution in the formulation of its method. If it is impossible to tear any proposition from its systematic context in the actual world, then the method of imaginative rationalization will yield only an approximately accurate approach to a system of principles. Such a system must continually measure itself by the degree to which it does, indeed, provide an elucidation of immediate experience. Philosophy begins with matters of fact, in particular topics of human interest like physics or aesthetics or sociology, and it works toward those concepts which shall explain all experience whatsoever.

It was this aspect of Whitehead's conception of philosophy which particularly appealed to Dewey: that in seeing all actual existences as occasions of experience, nothing natural or human is to be omitted. In the chapter on "Philosophic Method" in *Adventures of Ideas*, Whitehead said:[43]

In order to discover some of the major categories under which we can classify the infinitely various components of experience, we must appeal to evidence relating to every variety of occasion. Nothing can be omitted, experience drunk and experience sober, experience sleeping and experience waking, experience drowsy and experience wide-awake, experience self-conscious and experience self-forgetful, experience intellectual and experience physical, experience religious and experience sceptical, experience anxious and experience carefree, experience anticipatory and experience retrospective, experience happy and experience grieving, experience dominated by emotion and experience under self-restraint, experience in the light and experience in the dark, experience normal and experience abnormal.

In commenting on this passage, Dewey remarked:[44] "Those who profess belief in empirical philosophy can hardly be other than grateful for emancipation from chains which after all were self-imposed. Artists, poets, prophets may be drawn to a philosophy that sees 'experience' to be rich beyond the possibility of exhaustion and subtle beyond the reach of human wit."

In holding that experience is rich beyond exhaustion and subtle beyond the reach of human wit, Whitehead expresses his mistrust in any simple set of philosophic abstractions—those, for example, arrived at through conscious introspective analysis, or through a sensationalist doctrine of perception, or through exclusive reliance upon a subject-predicate logic. And yet, from the passage above it is clear that White-head wants to "discover some of the major categories under which we can classify the infinitely various components of experience." In *Process and Reality* he explicitly said: "Philosophy will not regain its proper status until the gradual elaboration of categoreal schemes, definitely stated at each stage of progress, is recognized as its proper objective." *Science and the Modern World* had already presented the general outline of such a categoreal scheme in the concepts of "prehension," "actual occasion," and "eternal object." In *Process and Reality* the categoreal scheme receives extended attention.[45]

In the three notions—actual entity, prehension, nexus—[says Whitehead[46]] an endeavour has been made to base philosophical thought upon the most concrete elements in our experience. 'Actual entities'—also termed 'actual occasions'—are the final real things of which the world is made up. There is no going behind actual entities to find anything more real. They differ among themselves: God is an actual entity, and so is the most trivial puff of existence in far-off empty space. But, though there are gradations of importance, and diversities of function, yet in the principles which actuality exemplifies all are on the same level. The final facts are, all alike, actual entities; and these actual entities are drops of experience, complex and interdependent.

Each actual entity may be analyzed in many different ways, but to analyze it in terms of "prehensions" shows the most concrete elements. In one sense a prehension or occasion of feeling is only a subordinate element in an actual entity, but it always has a "vector" character; that is, it involves emotion and purpose and valuation and a causal principle. Actual entities involve each other by reason of their prehensions of each other. They therefore point to the real individual facts of the togetherness of actual entities. Such an individual fact of together-ness Whitehead calls a "nexus."

It is impossible to deal exhaustively with the richness and complexity of Whitehead's terminology. But the mere citation of his Category of the Ultimate, and a few selections from his Categories of Explanation, will give some indication of the philosophic atmosphere of *Process and Reality*. It will show not only the emphasis upon relatedness which we already know, but also the slow emergence into major prominence of the concept of "feeling."

The Category of the Ultimate: 'Creativity,' 'many,' 'one' are the ultimate notions involved in the meaning of the synonymous terms 'thing,' 'being,' 'entity' .... 'Creativity' ... is that ultimate principle by which the many, which are the universe disjunctively, become the one actual occasion, which is the universe conjunctively. It lies in the nature of things that the many enter into complex unity. ... Creativity is the principle of novelty. ... The ultimate metaphysical principle is the advance from disjunction to conjunction, creating a novel entity other than the entities given in disjunction. ... Thus the 'production of novel togetherness' is the ultimate notion embodied in the term 'concrescence.' ...

Process: The actual world is a process and ... the process is the becoming of actual entities. Thus actual entities are creatures. ... How an actual entity becomes constitutes what that actual entity is. ... Its being is constituted by its becoming. This is the principle of process. ...

Prehension: The first analysis of an actual entity, into its most concrete elements, discloses it to be a concrescence of prehensions, which have originated in its process of becoming. ... Every prehension consists of three factors: (a) the 'subject' which is prehending, namely, the actual entity in which that prehension is a concrete element; (b) the 'datum' which is prehended; (c) the 'subjective form' which is *how* that subject prehends that datum. ... There are two species of prehensions: (a) 'positive prehensions' which are termed 'feelings' and (b) 'negative prehensions' which are said to 'eliminate from feeling.' ... There are many species of subjective forms such as emotions, valuations, purposes, adversions, consciousness, etc. ... Whatever is a datum for a feeling has a unity as *felt*. ...

Eternal Objects: The fundamental types of entities are actual entities and eternal objects, and ... the other types of entities only express how all entities of the two fundamental types are in community with each other in the actual world. ... The functioning of one actual entity in the self-creation of another actual entity is the 'objectification' of the former for the latter actual entity. The functioning of an eternal object in the self-creation of an actual entity is the 'ingression' of the eternal object in the actual entity. ... The final phase in the process of concrescence, constituting an actual entity is one complex, fully determinate feeling. This final phase is termed the 'satisfaction'. It is fully determinate (a) as to its genesis, (b) as to its objective character for the transcendent creativity, and (c) as to its prehension—positive or negative—of every item in its universe. ...[47]

There are several other "derivative notions" which are important in Whitehead's system. One is the concept of "God." But since the fundamental types of things are actual entities and eternal objects, even God's definition is in some sense relevant to them, and his twofold nature is to be understood accordingly. The primordial created fact is the "conceptual valuation of the entire multiplicity of eternal objects," and this whole, which might be translated as "the total knowledge of the realm of possibility," Whitehead calls "the primordial nature of God." But God also prehends or "feels" the totality of the creatively advancing world of actual entities, and this togetherness of all actual things in "the mind of God" Whitehead calls "the consequent nature of God." Whitehead's God is (like Aristotle's) a metaphysical rather than a theological necessity, but he has managed nonetheless to assimilate in one conception two ideas which have, in the history of theology, been constantly at war. God's primordial nature expresses the entire transcendence of a Platonized Christianity. His consequent nature is but the total immanence of Spinoza's pantheism.

A second important "derivative notion" concerns what we have previously treated as a theory of inheritance. It consists of the notions of "personal order" and "social order." A "society" for Whitehead is a nexus with social order; and an "enduring object" is a society whose social order has taken the form of "personal order." In the philosophy of organism it is not substance which is permanent, but "form." Social order characterizes a nexus wherever there is some common element of form in the actual entities which compose it, when this common element of form is prehended by each actual occasion, and when these prehensions impose the condition of reproduction. Thus a society possesses a form which is its defining characteristic in space. A nexus enjoys personal order when it is a society whose members are related serially in time. When the nexus forms a single line of inheritance of its defining characteristic, it endures. Thus an enduring object, as has already been maintained in Science and the Modern World, is a nexus of actual occasions with an inheritance of near-identical pattern through time.

The concepts of social order and personal order are extremely important in Whitehead's metaphysics, since they permit the construction of the objects of our grosser world of sensory perception out of elements which are at once more metaphysically atomistic and more concrete. From this point of view, and in the light of Whitehead's own insistence that the failure of Hume's doctrine of sense perception lies in the fact that it is simply not empirical enough, it is interesting to note the way in which the philosophy of organism can account for the more ordinary furniture of the worlds of science and of common sense. First a molecule:[48]

It is sufficient to say that a molecule in the sense of a moving body with a history of local change is not an actual occasion; it must therefore be some kind of nexus of actual occasions. In this sense it is an event. . . .

This [the doctrine of actual entities] is a theory of monads; but it differs from Leibniz's in that his monads change. In the organic theory, they merely *become*. Each monadic creature is a mode of the process of 'feeling' the world, of housing the world in one unit of complex feeling in every way determinate. Such a unit is an 'actual occasion'; it is the ultimate creature derivative from the creative process. . . . The term 'event' is used in a more general sense. An event is a nexus of actual occasions inter-related in some determinate fashion. . . . The most general sense of the meaning of change is 'the difference between actual occasions in one event.' For example, a molecule is a historic route of actual occasions; and such a route is an 'event.' Now the motion of the molecule is nothing else than the differences between the successive occasions of its life-history . . . and the changes in the molecule are the consequential differences in the actual occasions. . . .

Then a real chair (as opposed to a "chair-image" given in sense perception):[49]

If there be a 'real chair,' there will be another historical route of objectifications from nexus to nexus in this environment. The members of each nexus will be mutually contemporaries. Also the historical route will lead up to the nexus which is the chair image. The complete nexus, composed of this historical route and the chair image, will form a 'corpuscular' society. This society is the 'real chair.'

These are far from ordinary accounts of the "ordinary" worlds of science and common sense, but the purpose of a metaphysics in Whitehead's sense is not descriptive simplicity, but generality of application and concreteness of conception. Concreteness here means not what is perceptually apparent through the senses, but what is more immediately apparent through the agencies of feeling. Whitehead's notion of the concrete is bound up with the notion of "feeling," whether expressed externally in the constitution of actual entities or internally in human modes of awareness other than those of sensory perception. To this doctrine of feeling I should now like to turn.

Each actual entity is conceived as an act of experience arising out of data, out of a "given" world. It is therefore a process of "feeling" the many aspects of this given world so as to absorb them into the unity of one individual satisfaction. "Feeling" here refers to the basic historical operation of passing from the objectivity of the data to the subjectivity of the actual entity. An actual entity has a perfectly definite bond with each item in the universe, and this bond is the way in which it prehends or feels each item. Some feelings are inclusive. Some are exclusive. Some items are definitely included in such a way as to make a positive contribution to the subject's real internal constitution. Others are felt more vaguely. But only a selection of eternal objects or possibilities can be positively felt by a given subject. The precise configuration of these feelings constitutes the "decision" of the actual entity: that is, its actuality. The word "decision" does not imply conscious judgment. It is used in its Latin sense of "cutting off." Actuality is the product of a decision among alternative potentialities, and the real internal constitution of an actual entity progressively becomes a decision conditioning the general creativity of the world. Decision is the source of all particular things.

Each actual entity includes the universe by virtue of its determinate attitude toward every element in the universe. "It belongs to the nature of every being that it is a potentiality for every becoming." This is what Whitehead terms "the principle of relativity."[50]

The principle of universal relativity directly traverses Aristotle's dictum, '(A substance) is not present in a subject.' On the contrary, according to this principle an actual entity *is* present in other actual entities. In fact if we allow for degrees of relevance, and for negligible relevance, we must say that every actual entity is present in every other actual entity. The philosophy of organism is mainly devoted to the task of making clear the notion of 'being present in another entity.'

Whitehead's term for "being present in another entity" is "objectification." It means that actual entities enter into one another by the way in which they are felt. This is the meaning of the entire doctrine of prehension, and it explains how through the concrescence or "integration of feelings" the universe itself becomes one vast complex unity of feeling. Every actual entity is an "object" for another, thus entering into the creation of another and enjoying an "objective immortality;" at the same time each actual entity is a "subject," gathering its content and prehending the universe (like Leibniz's monads) from its own point of view. But to be an "object" means to be an entity which is a potentiality for becoming a component in feeling. And to be a "subject" means to be an entity which is constituted by the process of feeling and includes this process. In this multifarious interweaving of subjects and objects lies the solidarity of the world.[51]

The chief ground of order in the universe is the gradation of intensity in the satisfactions of actual entities. The heightening of this intensity depends upon an aesthetic principle: that the multiplicity of components in feeling can enter as contrasts rather than as incompatibilities. Every actual entity reaches an attainment of being. This is its "satisfaction" —the notion of its concreteness abstracted from the process of concrescence which constitutes its becoming. The intensity of the satisfaction is promoted by the orderliness of its process of becoming, or enfeebled by its disorderliness. But the subjective aim or internal purposiveness of the actual entity is always toward a maximal intensity of satisfaction. "This subjective aim is not primarily intellectual; it is the lure for feeling. This lure for feeling is the germ of mind."[52]

Satisfactions may be classified as to "triviality," "vividness," "vagueness," "massiveness," "narrowness," "width." Triviality arises when the mutual factors are not sufficiently coordinated so as to reinforce one another. Vagueness arises out of insufficient contrast in the components of feeling. Intensity, on the other hand, is the reward of narrowness. The principles of the harmonious resolution of feeling are multiple, but these few serve to make the central point. When a cosmology based upon the concepts of mathematical physics is transformed into a metaphysics of feeling, then the scheme of systematic order which renders it uniform must be found in the structure of a pure aesthetics. This is no more than Whitehead himself recognized. The philosophy of organism, he said,[53]

aspires to construct a critique of pure feeling, in the philosophical position in which Kant put his *Critique of Pure Reason*. . . . Thus in the organic philosophy Kant's 'Transcendental Aesthetic' becomes a distorted fragment of what should have been his main topic. The datum includes its own interconnections, and the first stage of the process of feeling is the reception into the responsive conformity of feeling whereby the datum which is mere potentiality, becomes the individualized basis for a complex unity of realization.

To substitute a critique of pure feeling for a critique of pure reason has other implications also. It assumes an epistemology in which the primary emphasis is not placed upon the cognitive outcome of knowledge. This in turn requires a diminution of the role of sensory perception. Modes of perception are types of feeling, and there are two primary kinds: "perception in the mode of causal efficacy" and "perception in the mode of presentational immediacy." The first is direct, through intuitive awareness of the feeling-tone of particularity, and it includes memory, the direct awareness of the immediate past, and the vague feeling of underlying bodily processes. The second is the issuing into clarity of a contemporary spatial region through the sense perceptions of perspective and spatial shape. It is the classic form of perception to which the entire empirical tradition has ultimate recourse. This reliance is the basis of Whitehead's critique of the sensationalist empiricism of Locke and Hume, for from such an epistemology both the sensory atomism of Hume and the material atomism of Newton follow inevitably. "It is evident that 'perception in the mode of causal efficacy' is not that sort of perception which has received chief attention in the philosophical tradition. Philosophers have disdained the information about the universe obtained through their visceral feelings, and have concentrated on visual feelings."[54] Such concentration has prevented the construction of an adequately concrete metaphysics. For we prehend other actual entities most primitively by direct mediation of emotional tone, and only vaguely and inconstantly through sense perception. Hume and Locke, with the over-intellectualist bias prevalent among philosophers, assume that emotional feelings necessarily derive from sensations. It would be closer to the truth, thinks Whitehead, to assume precisely the opposite.

All actual entities enter into each others' constitutions under limitations imposed by the incompatibilities of feeling, for "process" is but "the rush of feelings" whereby the givenness of the antecedent world attains subjective immediacy. Thus any treatment of physical nature which stresses material atoms, and any treatment of knowledge which sees it as the composition of atomistic intellectual concepts, is a high abstraction.

The primitive form of physical experience is emotional—blind emotion —received as felt elsewhere in another occasion and conformally appropriated as a subjective passion. In the language appropriate to the higher stages of experience, the primitive element is *sympathy*, that is, feeling the feeling *in* another and feeling conformally *with* another. We are so used to considering the high abstraction, 'the stone as green,' that we have difficulty in eliciting into consciousness the notion of 'green' as the qualifying character of an emotion. Yet, the aesthetic feelings, whereby there is pictorial art, are nothing else than products of the contrasts latent in a variety of colours qualifying emotion, contrasts which are made possible by their patterned relevance to each other. The separation of the emotional experience from the presentational intuition is a high abstraction of thought. Thus the primitive experience is emotional feelings, felt in its relevance to a world beyond. The feeling is blind, and the relevance is vague.[55]

Of course, emotion in human experience is not *mere* emotion: it is emotion interpreted, integrated, and transformed into higher and more complex categories of feeling. But the mistake lies in taking the higher grades of consciousness as the dominating and the genetically prior. Nicolai Hartmann in his *Ethics* has proposed a law of valuation in which he asserts that the "higher" values are at the same time the "weaker." Whitehead suggests an analogous principle for the realm of perceptual feelings.

It is clear then to what this reinterpretation of the role of feeling must lead: on the one hand to a reformulation of the nature of physical science, and on the other to a reformulation of the intrinsic meaning of the operations of the intellect in human life. "Physical science is the science investigating spatio-temporal and quantitative characteristics of simple physical feelings. The actual entities of the actual world are bound together in a nexus of these feelings."[56] But the investigation is itself guided by considerations which grow out of the objects of investigation. The effects of an actual entity are its interventions in processes of becoming other than its own. Thus Berkeley was wrong; the truth is not *esse est percipi* (to be is to be perceived) but *esse est sentiri* (to be is to be felt). This holds for operations of mentality no less than for ultimate organisms. The primary function of theory is as a lure for feeling, thereby providing immediacy of enjoyment and purpose; truth is the aesthetic quality of the conformation of appearance to reality; a judgment is a decision of feeling in the "process" of the judging subject.[57] But this is to propose a revolutionary conception of the nature of logic.

It is true, of course, that the virtues of intellectuality consist in a gain in the power of abstraction. An irrelevant multiplicity of detail is eliminated, and it is thereupon possible to emphasize the elements of systematic order in the actual world. But this emphasis is itself in the service of promotion of intensity of feeling, and is ruled by aesthetic considerations.

It is the mark of a high-grade organism to eliminate by negative prehension the irrelevant accidents in its environment, and to elicit massive attention to every variety of systematic order. . . . In this way the organism in question suppresses the mere multiplicities of things, and designs its own contrasts. The canons of art are merely the expression in specialized forms of the requisites for depth of experience. The principles of morality are allied to the canons of art, in that they also express, in another connection the same requisites.[58]

Precisely the same is true of the principles of logic.

The strict separation between the cognitive and the emotive functions of language is, as we have seen, one of the cornerstones of the positivistic mentality, and it leads, even among non-positivists, to a conception of logical statements which finds them to be essentially informative in nature. They may be informative about the meaning of a word, in which case they are definitions, or about the nature of the world, in which case they are factual propositions which must be either true or false. But the emphasis is upon cognitive content, and the obvious preference is for true propositions. It is this account of propositions which Whitehead's theory opposes. A proposition shares with an eternal object the general character of indeterminateness, but it does refer to definite logical subjects. It is not itself a feeling, but its whole importance is the relation which it bears to feeling. "A proposition has neither the particularity of a feeling, nor the reality of a nexus. It is a datum for feeling, awaiting a subject feeling it. Its relevance to the actual world by means of its logical subjects makes it a *lure for feeling*. In fact many subjects may feel it with diverse feelings and with diverse sorts of feelings."[59] A moment later the obvious, but unusual conclusion is drawn: ". . . in the real world it is more important that a proposition be interesting than that it be true. The importance of truth is, that it adds to interest."

The later Wittgenstein had seen that the positivistic logical interest was too narrow, and that non-cognitive functions of language merited the closest attention, but even he did not require the invasion of logic by emotion. For Whitehead even the judgmental functions of the affirmation, negation, and entertainment of propositions are emotive: affirmation is composed of "feelings in the yes-form," negation of "feelings in the no-form," and entertainment of "feelings in the suspense-form." The truth of the matter is that for Whitehead the cognitive acts of mentality are inseparable from the requirements of feeling, and they are therefore subject to all of the aesthetic criteria to which feelings lend themselves. Intellectual feelings are a concentration of attention which permits both increase of importance and the act of criticism, but they are the tool of physical purposes more primitive than themselves. This is why "affirmation or negation," "belief," or "truth" are not the exclusively cognitive operations of an older logical tradition.

But the main function of intellectual feelings is neither belief, nor disbelief, nor even suspension of judgment. The main function of these feelings is to heighten the emotional intensity accompanying the valuations in the conceptual feelings involved, and in the more physical purposes which are more primitive than any intellectual feelings. . . . In so far as these logical subjects by reason of other prehensions, are topics of interest, the proposition becomes a lure for the conditioning of creative action. . . .[60]

So we are back once again to aesthetics. Whether in the case of physical feelings or intellectual feelings, of conceptual feelings or simple causal feelings, of perception in the mode of causal efficacy or perception in the mode of presentational immediacy, we cannot escape the demands of massiveness and depth, and of intensity by reason of studied contrast. The subjective aim of every actual entity is in the direction of a balanced complexity (where complexity means the power of contrasts, and balance the absence of mutually inhibiting factors). All actual entities seek such a disposition of emphasis as to maximize the intensities of feeling, and insofar as there is cosmic coordination of actual entities in their various processes of becoming, there is an aim toward order in the universe. This "aim toward order" is nothing but the creation of a "society" of actual occasions expressing a patterned intensity of feeling arising from the adjusted contrasts of the individual items. Whitehead sometimes calls it "God" or "the principle of concretion."

It is an interesting journey when one begins with Newton's laws of motion and Maxwell's equations and arrives at the conclusion that an intense experience is an aesthetic fact, and that *any* actual fact is a fact of aesthetic experience.[61] But the stages of its progress are continuous. If the concept of a particle at an instant is abandoned, if the doctrine of simple location gives way to the doctrine of the connected universe, then the model of reality is not a mechanism, but an organism. If actual occasions are organisms, then their process and their realization must occur according to the laws of conformal feeling. And if there is to be an order of conformal feelings reducible to law-like statement, then such a statement will be an expression of aesthetic principle.

There is a passage here from physics to psychology to aesthetics, illustrated conceptually in the passage from an actual occasion of experience, to the prehensions in terms of which it may be analyzed, to the principles of order which are illustrated in the coordination of these prehensions. We are reminded again of the strategy which underlies the *Dialogues* of Plato. Platonism does indeed deal with the "likely story" of the structure of the universe; with The Physical Elements and with The Mathematical Relations. But it cannot grant that such a universe is thinkable without the characteristics of "life and motion." Emotion and purpose are intrinsic to natural existence, and therefore

The Physical Elements and The Mathematical Relations are supplemented by The Eros and The Psyche. But The Eros and The Psyche, in turn, introduce problems of measure and balance and coordination. So we arrive finally at the aesthetic culmination of The Harmony. This is Platonism, and it is also the philosophy of Whitehead.

The consequence of Whitehead's metaphysics of feeling is not only that it permits a unification where before there were only bifurcations and disjunctions. It effects this unification in such a way as to return to the intuitions of Romantic poetry without participating in its blind attack upon the intellect. The assertion of the primacy of feeling is there: in the recognition that the primitive form of physical experience is blind emotion; in the epistemological elevation of causal efficacy above presentational immediacy; in the reinterpretation of the logical proposition as a "lure for feeling." But the claims of the higher grades of mentality are not forgotten. Science and philosophy are both attempts at understanding, and they function by abstraction, by the attempt at generality.

4. PHILOSOPHY OF HISTORY AND CULTURE

Science and the Modern World is Whitehead's attack upon atomism and his substitution of the notion of the connected universe. *Process and Reality* is the presentation of his metaphysics of feeling. *Adventures of Ideas* is the application of the metaphysics to the philosophy of history and of culture.

To his early mathematical and physical interests Whitehead adds a deep humanistic concern with the course of history and the intellectual factors in the development of Western civilization. Moreover, his metaphysics, having taken the quality of immediate human experience as a clue to the functioning of nature, is especially applicable to the areas of sociological structure and historical occurrence. That there can be "adventures" of "ideas" implies not only that certain ideas promote the "slow drift of mankind towards civilization," but also that it is of the very nature of ideas that they shall be "forces" founded upon feeling. If, as Whitehead puts it in *Modes of Thought*,[62] "a thought is a tremendous mode of excitement," and if, as he also believes, "History is the record of the expressions of feelings peculiar to humanity," then the history of ideas must be the life of ideas as energizing factors in the development of history. In his charming "Memories" Whitehead has said,[63] "in abstraction from the atmosphere of feeling, one behaviour pattern is as good as another; and they are all equally uninteresting." His attitude toward history is suffused with "the atmosphere of feeling," which springs from the deepest memories of his youth. "Canterbury Cathedral," he wrote as a man of eighty, "with its splendour and its memories was sixteen miles distant [from home]. As I now write I can visualize the very spot where Becket fell A.D. 1170, and can recall my reconstruction of the incident in my young imagination. . . ." He went to school at Sherborne in Dorsetshire, which "dates from St. Ald-helm, and claims Alfred the Great as a pupil" and where "we worked under the sound of the Abbey bells, brought from the Field of The Cloth of Gold by Henry VIII." These living contacts with history, conscious strands in the texture of his youth, are no less important for their influence upon Whitehead's general conception of history and civilization than the specific debt to Gibbons's *Decline and Fall*, Sarpi's *History of the Council of Trent*, Osborn Taylor's *The Mediaeval Mind*, and Leslie Stephen's *English Thought in the Eighteenth Century* which the Preface to *Adventures of Ideas* details.

But, once again, the greatest influence was Plato. In the first place, the very meaning of "Adventures of Ideas"—the critical consideration of the sort of history which *ideas* can have in the life of humanity— is that it must be a species of "Platonic history." In the second place, the peculiar dialectic of ideas which Whitehead takes as his clue to the understanding of the driving forces of civilization is but a specifi-cation of the cosmology of the *Timaeus*. It is the idea that "Men are driven by their thoughts as well as by the molecules in their bodies, by intelligence and by senseless forces."[64]

Two conceptions of physics have dominated the writing of history in the Western world: the theory of Aristotle's *Physics* and the theory of Plato's *Timeaus*; and from these two have sprung a tradition of "Aristotelian" and of "Platonic" history. According to Aristotle's *Physics*, change is always to be explained as the succession of contraries quali-fying an enduring matter, the world being composed of a multitude of essentially independent substances. In such a universe relations are not necessary, but accidental, while such necessity as holds depends on the essential nature of individuals. But in such a world temporal and efficient causes are real and the laws of physics are in fact just such laws of necessary connection. According to Plato's *Timaeus*, on the other hand, change is always the flux of an eternal pattern of forms, and the elements of change are therefore the pattern of forms, the process of becoming, and the "Receptacle" in which process occurs. Here the universe is, indeed, a single complete organism within which change is always the mere alteration of relational elements. Physics for Plato is a "science of opinion;" for Aristotle it is a "necessary, theoretical science." This distinction has particular relevance for the theory of history.

For Plato, history, sociology, and cosmology are each analogical aspects of a single study in the realm of "opinion;" they are each "likely stories." For Aristotle, science and history are clearly distinguished; science is concerned with universals, but history always presents an account of specific change in a particular individual or train of individuals. Aristotelian history is partial in that it attempts to chart the unilinear thread of a particular change; Platonic history hopes to analyze the rich complexity of an entire historical period. The literary method of Aristotelian history is literal statement; that of Platonic history is analogy or metaphor. The proximate aim of Aristotelian history is the *narration* of change; that of Platonic history the *characterization* of an age or epoch. The ultimate aim of Aristotelian history is *description*; that of Platonic history is *interpretation* or *understanding*. The Aristotelian tradition in historiography is that of Thucydides, Polybius, and Von Ranke. The Platonic tradition is that of Augustine, Vico, and in our own time Spengler, Toynbee, and Whitehead.

I have tried to suggest what is implicit in Whitehead himself: that our history of ideas is derived from our ideas of history, and that our ideas of history are a function of our cosmological outlook. "This notion," says Whitehead,[65] "of historians devoid of aesthetic prejudice, of history devoid of any reliance on metaphysical principles and cosmological generalizations, is a figment of the imagination." This means that for Plato and for Whitehead alike, the history of ideas requires a record of the ingression of forms into the flux of history—into the process of the real world. Platonic history has three tasks: the diagnosis of historical epochs, the classification of historical periods, and the comparison of such periods with one another. The first task, the diagnosis of a historical epoch, is completed when the "Platonic idea" of that age is isolated, and this Platonic idea is the pattern of eternal objects ingressing at that point. In this type of analysis the concept of *pattern* or *order* is preeminent. "Civilization," says Whitehead,[66] "is constituted out of four elements, (1) Patterns of Behaviour, (2) Patterns of Emotion, (3) Patterns of Belief, and (4) Technologies. We can at once dismiss Technologies as beyond our topic, though all four constitutive elements interact upon each other. All patterns of behaviour are in the long run sustained or modified by patterns of emotion and patterns of belief. . . ." The important concept here is *pattern*. The pattern of a culture, like that of a society of actual entities, is the arrangement of elements which through mutual immanence share a common social order, and which individually reflect the general pattern that dominates the age. Since there are "types of order dominating vast epochs" (whether the mediaeval concept of "coordination" or the nineteenth-century concept of "competition"), these types of order will find their reflection in the multiplicity of subordinate cultural elements. The conclusion of this Platonic emphasis upon pattern is a profound rationalism with respect to the assessment of the role which ideas may play in the drama of cultural history.

"The impact of aesthetic, religious and moral notions," said Whitehead, "is inescapable. They are the disrupting and the energizing forces of civilization." Thus the intellectual agencies involved in the modification of historical epochs are the real subject of *Adventures of Ideas*. This assumed that certain ideas of high generality, expressing the nature of things and the final aim which should guide the conduct of individual men, were at the root of the behavior of each cultural epoch. "In each age of the world distinguished by high activity there will be found at its culmination, and among the agencies leading to that culmination, some profound cosmological outlook, implicitly accepted, impressing its own type upon the current springs of action."[67] The ages of Pericles, Alexander the Great, Cicero, and Tiberius were very different, yet they all agreed on one fundamental idea which lay at the base of their political theory—the legitimacy of slavery in a society which was unable to be self-sustaining. On the other hand, the liberal humanitarianism of eighteenth-century Europe is unintelligible without some understanding of the religious ideas of the Quakers and the political philosophy of John Locke. This is almost to say that in ethical ideals are exemplified those consciously formulated ideas which act as driving forces effecting transitions from social state to social state, and that metaphysical understanding guides imagination and justifies purpose. This is what Whitehead would like to maintain, but his own metaphysics will not permit him to draw the completely moralized conclusion.

Whitehead's philosophy of history is the "Platonic" history which follows from the *Timaeus*, since it reads the structure of any epoch as the pattern of the ingression of eternal objects in time. But if this is the case, no rationale intrinsic to the historical process can be assigned to history as its "meaning." Whitehead himself saw this clearly. It is the way he used "the ontological principle" in *Process and Reality*:[68]

The evolution of history can be rationalized by the consideration of the determination of successors by antecedents. But, on the other hand, the evolution of history is incapable of rationalization because it exhibits a selected flux of participating forms. *No reason, internal to history, can be assigned why that flux of forms, rather than another flux, should have been illustrated. . . .* The actual flux presents itself with the character of the merely 'given.' It does not disclose any peculiar character of 'perfection.'

This passage illustrates perfectly that peculiar moral relativity characteristic of the epochal theory of culture, which we have already encountered in Spengler. It is the denial of a theory of progress as that term is usually understood, for it denies that there is a single ideal order to which all history approximates. "The notion of one ideal arises from the disastrous overmoralization of thought under the influence of fanaticism or pedantry. The notion of a dominant ideal peculiar to each actual entity is Platonic."[69] It might be Spengler speaking of the plurality of civilizations.

Yet Whitehead manages to avoid the cold disenchantment of Spengler's relativism. He does so, strangely enough, by a further appeal to the *Timaeus* of Plato. If it is impossible to justify history by an appeal to an autonomous moral theory, perhaps it will be possible by an appeal to aesthetic principle. A non-moralized content will yield to an orderly form, and that form will be the form of ideas themselves, of the only ultimate rationality in a Platonic universe.[70]

The history of ideas is dominated by a dichotomy which is illustrated by this comparison of Steam and Democracy in recent times to Barbarians and Christians in the classical civilization. Steam and Barbarians, each in their own age, were the senseless agencies driving their respective civilizations away from inherited modes of order. These senseless agencies are what Greek writers sometimes (e.g. in the *Timaeus* of Plato) . . . call 'compulsion' . . . and sometimes 'violence' . . . . It is one task of history to display the types of compulsion and of violence characteristic of each age. On the other hand, Democracy in modern times, and Christianity in the Roman Empire, exemplified articulated beliefs issuing from aspirations, and issuing into aspirations. . . .

The *Timaeus* presents a cosmology in which the forms of order are in eternal conflict with the compulsion or necessity implicit in the brute givenness of the materials of nature. Whitehead projects this cosmological Manicheanism into the facts of the history of ideas. Steam vs. Democracy, Barbarians vs. the Christian Ideal, Classical Slavery vs. Modern Freedom, the pedantic force of conservatism vs. the claims of novelty and adventure—these are the senseless agencies and formulated aspirations whose dialectic constitutes the history of ideas and of culture. Now, imperceptibly, into this neutral dialectic creeps a doctrine of progress which only a Platonist tinged with the liberal humanitarianism of Victorian England could manage to evoke.[71]

The history of ideas is a history of mistakes. But through all mistakes it is also the history of the gradual purification of conduct. When there is progress in the development of favorable order, we find conduct protected from relapse into brutalization by the increasing agency of ideas consciously entertained. In this way Plato is justified in his saying, The creation of the world—that is to say, the world of civilized order—is the victory of persuasion over force.

Whitehead has repudiated the positivism which is the theoretical foundation of Jeremy Bentham's Utilitarian Principle and of Auguste Comte's Religion of Humanity, but as working principles, Whitehead, as well as the whole nineteenth century, has fallen deeply under their spell. Only such humanitarian magic could transform the cosmology of the *Timaeus* into "the history of the gradual purification of conduct."

Whitehead's philosophy of history, detailed in the first or "sociological" part of *Adventures of Ideas,* views history as an "enlightenment," as a progressive revelation of what it means to be civilized, to be human.[72]

In each age of the world, the actions of men and their interpretations of feelings, motives, and purposes, throw light upon the recesses of their experience. In this elucidation of what it means to live, to act, and feel, age differs from age. . . . Each age deposits its message as to the secret character of the nature of things. Civilizations can only be understood by those who are civilized. And they have this property, that the appropriation of them in the understanding unveils truths concerning our own nature. It has been said that the great dramatic tragedies in their representations before audiences act as a purification of the passions. In the same way, the great periods of history act as an enlightenment. They reveal ourselves to ourselves.

Thus, in showing throughout the development of Western civilization the conflict between "senseless agencies" and "the increasing agency of ideas consciously entertained," Whitehead chooses in particular to dwell upon the Greek and Hebrew contributions to cosmology and sociology, and to treat in detail the Platonic and Christian contributions to the ideas of freedom and equality. The "co-ordination" of mediaeval culture is contrasted with the "competition" of modern capitalism only to illustrate the slow emergence of the humanitarian ideal even in the face of a predominantly commercial culture. The idea of freedom is traced from Akhnaton and the Hebrew prophets to Erasmus, the Dutch Republic, the Quakers, and the ideas of John Locke, only that it may emerge anew in the self-determination of the independent professions and the quest for inner freedom of modern man. Thus, although "no reason internal to history can be assigned why that flux of forms rather than another flux should have been illustrated," Whitehead's appeal to history is indeed authoritarian. It is what a gentle but confirmed liberal would find in a history tenderly conceived and admitting of some measure of "rational" interpretation.

As the first part of *Adventures of Ideas* contains Whitehead's Platonic philosophy of history, so the last part contains his Platonic philosophy of civilization. The two topics are intimately related. The dialectic of ideas in history reveals the victory of persuasion over force. Thus the worth of men consists in their liability to persuasion, in their sensitivity to the disclosure of alternatives, the better and the worse. But by the same token "Civilization is the maintenance of social order, by its own inherent persuasiveness as embodying the nobler alternative." This nobler alternative can be expressed by the interrelated harmony of five Platonic "ideas."

"I put forward as a general definition of civilization," says Whitehead,[73] "that a civilized society is exhibiting the five qualities of Truth, Beauty, Adventure, Art, Peace." Truth is the conformation of appearance to reality. Beauty is the mutual adaptation of the several factors in an occasion of experience. Adventure is the search for novel perfections. Art is the artificial transformation of nature, bearing the mark of a finite creative effort. Peace is a quality of mind steady in its reliance that fine action is treasured in the nature of things. But in a certain sense the greatest of these is Beauty. Beauty is a wider and more fundamental notion than Truth. Unlike that of Art, its relevance is both to the intrinsic constitution of nature and to the products of a man-made society. As "the internal conformation of the various items of experience with each other for the production of maximum effectiveness," its ideality of structure goes to the very heart of Reality. "The teleology of the Universe is directed to the production of Beauty. Thus any system of things which in any wide sense is beautiful is to that extent justified in its existence."[74] Thus, through a consideration of civilization, Whitehead arrives at the same conclusion which his metaphysics of feeling had reached through a consideration of the order of nature. Platonically, history, civilization, and nature present analogical aspects of a single system of metaphysical principles. For Whitehead, as for Plato and Bergson before him, everything culminates in aesthetics.

As the mutual adaptation of the several factors in an occasion of experience, Beauty qualifies actual entities. This means that it requires the absence of mutual inhibition among the various prehensions so that the various intensities of subjective form may be expressed. Thus the parts of an experience "contribute to the massive feeling of the whole, and the whole contributes to the intensity of feeling of the parts." The subjective forms of prehensions are thus jointly interwoven in patterned contrasts, and this interweaving may be spoken of alternatively as the "perfection of Beauty" or as "Harmony." Harmony may involve a delicacy of detail, but the ultimate outcome is strength of feeling. This strength is the product of the "variety of detail with effective contrast which is Massiveness" and Intensity Proper, which is comparative magnitude.

For Whitehead the chief barrier to all types of perfection is the "mutual inhibition" of the elements of an experience. This inhibition may be the mere exclusion of alternatives (which is "anaesthesia"); or it may be the active co-presence of mutually discordant feelings, which is the truest sense of mutual destructiveness, and the real meaning of "evil" in the world. Whitehead terms it "aesthetic destruction." Whether in the form of physical pain or of mental dislocation such as grief, horror, or hate, the fact of evil lies in the production of discordant feelings. Still, it must be remembered that the intermingling of Beauty and Evil lies in the nature of things; it grows out of the conjoint operation of three metaphysical principles, namely, the principle that all actualization is finite, the principle that finitude involves the exclusion of alternative possibilities, and the principle that the mind envisages perfections which are excluded from the completeness of physical realization. The concerns of the actual world, and of any actual civilization, are deflected from complete harmony by the natural existence of incompatible alternatives and by the unrealizable visions of the mind.

The continuum of evil stretches between the poles of anaesthesia and conflict, between that lukewarmness of feeling which is the denial of life and the bitter clash of antagonistic feelings which can end only in death. Yet, of the two, it seems that for Whitehead anaesthesia is the more lethal. Whatever his Platonic preference for Harmony, he is at the same time quick to acknowledge the more romantic virtues of discord. Progress is founded upon the experience of discordant feelings. The social value of liberty lies in its production of discords. The disease fatal to all dominant civilizations is that perfection once attained, the inspiration withers, repetition sets in, and freshness gradually vanishes. A consideration of ancient Greek civilization illustrates the value of discordance:[75]

The race was awakened into progress by a great ideal of perfection. This ideal was an immense advance upon the ideals which the surrounding civilization had produced. It was effective and realized in a civilization which attained its proper beauty in human lives to an extent not surpassed before or since. . . . With repetition in successive generations, freshness gradually vanished. Learning and learned taste replaced the ardour of adventure. Hellenism was replaced by the Hellenistic epoch in which genius was stifled by repetition. We can imagine the fate of the Mediterranean civilization if it had been spared the irruptions of Barbarians and the rise of two new religions, Christianity and Mahometanism:—For two thousand years the Greek art-forms lifelessly repeated: The Greek schools of philosophy . . . arguing with barren formulae: Conventional histories: A stabilized Government with the sanctity of ancient ceremony, supported by habitual pieties: Literature without depth: Science elaborating detail by deductions from unquestioned premises: Delicacies of feeling without robustness of adventure.

It is Spengler's society in its old age of civilization, but it is founded upon an analogy not from biology, but from aesthetics. The ambience of a Hellenistic age, the Byzantine mentality, late Buddhism, the last stages of Confucian China—these are the cultural expressions of an *aesthetic* failure; of societies suffering from the tedium of infinite repetition, and of insufficient contrasts in the character of their component parts. They demonstrate how the demand for Harmony must be supplemented by a recognition of the necessity for Adventure.

A recognition of the necessity for Adventure (that no static maintenance of perfection is possible) is the foundation of all theories of man and of society. In art it requires that conventional training be supplemented by novel experiment; in sociology it requires the Hellenic mentality rather than the Byzantine; in the learned world it requires the precedence of speculation over scholarship. But ultimately it too is based upon a metaphysical principle: the principle of *process*. Each actual thing can be understood only in terms of its becoming and its perishing. There is no halt in which the actuality is just its static self. Thus "Advance or Decadence are the only choices offered to mankind. The pure conservative is fighting against the essence of the universe."[76] This principle is a commonplace in the field of the fine arts; but it should also be a commonplace in political philosophy and the theory of civilization. Naturally, since there are types of order dominating historical epochs, there may well be in every civilization at its culmination some large measure of realization of the perfections appropriate to its nature. But no culmination can maintain itself long at its height. Without fresh experimentation the minor variations are exhausted. There is a lowering of the vividness of experience in individuals. Convention dominates the usages of society. A learned orthodoxy suppresses adventure in religion and in the university. "A race," says Whitehead,[77] "preserves its vigour so long as it harbours a real contrast between what has been and what may be; and so long as it is nerved by the vigour to adventure beyond the safeties of the past. Without adventure civilization is in full decay."

Finally, among those essential qualities whose joint realization in social life constitutes civilization comes Peace. It is a difficult notion. "Habitually it is lurking on the edge of consciousness, a modifying agency. It clings to our notion of the Platonic 'Harmony' as a sort of atmosphere." The notions of "tenderness" and "love" are too narrow. "Impersonality" is too dead. What Whitehead means is "a broadening of feeling due to the emergence of some metaphysical insight, unverbalized and yet momentous in its coordination of values."[78] It is a trust in the efficacy of Beauty. It is self-control at its widest. It is the understanding of tragedy in nature and in human life as it expresses itself in the inevitability of transformation, decay, and loss. For beneath the immediacy of the flux lies the Harmony of Nature as a fluid, flexible support.

Amid the passing of so much beauty, so much heroism, so much daring, Peace is then the intuition of permanence. It keeps vivid the sensitiveness to the tragedy; and it sees the tragedy as a living agent persuading the world to aim at fineness beyond the faded level of surrounding fact. Each tragedy is the disclosure of an ideal:—What might have been, and was not: What can be. The tragedy was not in vain. This survival power in motive force, by reason of appeal to reserves of Beauty, marks the difference between the tragic evil and the gross evil. The inner feeling belonging to this grasp of the service of tragedy is Peace—the purification of the emotions.[79]

5. ULTIMATE WISDOM

Aristotle, says Whitehead, was the last great European philosopher to consider dispassionately the metaphysical character of God. His Prime Mover is not a moral personality, but a requirement of his physics. After Aristotle, ethical and religious interests dominated metaphysical necessity. The implication is that Whitehead's own treatment of God will eschew the pitfalls of the religious mentality. It is not altogether clear that he has managed this difficult feat. We have already seen that Whitehead's God is in some sense patterned upon the metaphysical primacy of actual entities and eternal objects, so that God's "primordial nature" is the total knowledge of the realm of possibility, while his "consequent nature" is the feeling of the total togetherness of the creatively advancing world. But behind this twofold nature lies a single principle. God is the Principle of Concretion. This means that he is the principle of reality, the ultimate reason why each thing should be exactly as it is. This, in a metaphysics which constitutes actual entities out of the selected ingression of eternal objects, also suggests that to call God the Principle of Concretion is equivalent to calling him the Principle of Limitation. Eternal objects inform actual occasions with acquired patterns, and every actual occasion is therefore a limitation imposed upon possibility. It is by virtue of this limitation that "the shaped togetherness of things" emerges. There is always some particular "how" of actualization and some particular "what" which is realized, but for this "how" and this "what," the ultimate "why" is God.[80] If we do not simply deny the existence of actual entities, then

we must provide a ground for limitation which stands among the attributes of the substantial activity. This attribute provides the limitation for which no reason can be given: for all reason flows from it. God is the ultimate limitation, and His existence is the ultimate irrationality. For no reason can be given for just that limitation which it stands in His nature to impose. God is not concrete, but He is the ground for concrete actuality. No reason can be given for the nature of God, because that nature is the ground of rationality.

God is then "the actual entity in virtue of which the *entire* multiplicity of eternal objects obtains its graded relevance to each stage of concrescence. Apart from God, there could be no relevant novelty." This suggests that it lies in God's nature that evil shall qualify the world. Among mediaeval and modern philosophers anxious to establish the religious significance of God, "an unfortunate habit has prevailed of paying to Him metaphysical compliments." Although the creator of all, he is yet not responsible for the evil in the world. But if God be conceived of as the principle of limitation, then it is God's very nature to "divide the Good from the Evil."

There is in Whitehead a profound effort to save his own God from the qualities of a previous theology. The early Church gave to God the attributes which belonged exclusively to Caesar. Whitehead's God is neither the ruling Caesar of the early Church, the ruthless moralist of the Hebrew prophets, nor the Prime Mover of Aristotle. Nevertheless, as he describes God's nature, Whitehead's God imperceptibly takes on the quality of the loving and compassionate Christ. This seems actually to follow from Whitehead's insistence that "God is not to be treated as an exception to all metaphysical principles to save their collapse. He is their chief exemplification."[81]

A metaphysics of feeling has its own necessities. As Whitehead proceeds, the abstract Principle of Concretion is more and more tinged with the concrete qualities of feeling. God's purpose in the creative advance is said to be the evocation of novel intensities. He is also said to be the lure for feeling, the eternal urge of desire establishing the purposes of all creatures. But this is very like the use which the early Church made of Aristotle's theology. And in the end God's nature also embraces "the tender care that nothing be lost" and "an infinite patience."[82]

> The consequent nature of God is his judgment on the world. He saves the world as it passes into the immediacy of his own life. It is the judgment of a tenderness which loses nothing that can be saved. It is also the judgment of a wisdom which uses what in the temporal world is mere wreckage. . . . God's role is not the combat of productive force with productive force, of destructive force with destructive force; it lies in the patient operation of the over-powering rationality of his conceptual harmonization. He does not create the world, he saves it: or, more accurately, he is the poet of the world, with tender patience leading it by his vision of truth, beauty, and goodness.

God is one of the most important concepts in Whitehead's delineation of final metaphysical truth, but his importance consists, I think, not in the unconscious similarities with the inescapable God of Christian theology, but in the almost Platonic way in which he becomes the central fixture uniting a profound insight into the nature of evil with a truly Greek faith in the potency of an ultimate harmony and order. It is not by accident that God is the principle of limitation, for by this ascription it is possible to show how the process of the temporal world passes into the formation of other actualities in an order where limitation does not result in *mere* loss. The ultimate evil in the temporal world, as Whitehead has already shown, is deeper than any specific evil such as hatred, suffering, or death. It lies in the fact that time is a perpetual perishing and that being actual involves elimination. The nature of evil may be epitomized therefore in two simple but ultimate metaphysical propositions: "Things fade" and "Alternatives exclude." In the temporal world it is an empirical fact that the passage of time entails loss, and that the characteristics of many things are mutually obstructive. But if selection is the measure of evil, why may it not also be the means of its evasion? The struggle with evil may require a method for the utilization of its consequences in the creation of a new and more complex harmony. *Adventures of Ideas* has already indicated that beauty requires contrast, and that discord is itself fundamental in the creation of new intensities of feeling. Whitehead's image—and it is no more than this—of a God who uses what in the temporal world is merely ship-wreck for the introduction of needed contrast (as joy and sorrow, free-dom and necessity, good and evil) is a reinterpretation of God in the light of the Platonic Harmony. It shows how important to the very end, in this philosophy of the connected universe, remains the dialectical significance of those metaphysical fugitives from some Hegelian after-world—"The Ideal Opposites."

The philosophy of Whitehead, like that of Plato, is haunted by prin-ciples of division expressed as "ideal opposites:" joy and sorrow, good and evil, clarity and vagueness, conjunction and disjunction, permanence and flux, the one and the many, freedom and necessity, greatness and triviality, order and disorder, God and the World. Ideals group them-selves about these oppositions, and the world is the victim of the para-doxes which they present. Beauty demands order, but cannot exist with-out the disorder which discords introduce. The clarity of definition of a foreground demands the vagueness of the background against which it is presented. The world craves novelty, but is terrified at the loss of the past. Any one concept requires the plurality of its exemplifications. The good of actualization requires the evil of limitation. God and the World "stand over against each other, expressing the final metaphysical truth that appetitive vision and physical enjoyment have equal claim to priority in creation."[83] Between some of these terms there is a natural affinity. There can be no excellence without some principle of order, and the order which is discoverable in nature is not the result of brute compulsion, but represents an effort at the harmonious adjustment of complex detail.

The task of the creative advance is the reconciliation of these opposi-tions. "God and the World are the contrasted opposites in terms of which Creativity achieves its supreme task of transforming disjoined multiplicity, with its diversities in opposition, into concrescent unity with its diversities of contrast."[84] The opposed elements of the universe stand in the relation of mutual implication. But more important: existen-tially, they require one another. Thus the universe is the active expression of its own variety of oppositions. The analogy with Hegel is, therefore, not completely apt. The dialectical opposition of thesis and antithesis which always in Hegel receives its logical resolution in such a way as to override and therefore nullify the discrepancy, in Whitehead is com-pletely different. In Hegel, opposition disappears in mid-air by an act of dialectical magic. Whitehead is too existentially oriented for such theatrical illusion. His opposites are elements in the nature of things. They are incorrigibly *there*.

The ultimate wisdom of Whitehead's philosophy lies, therefore, where one might expect it to lie in any enterprise motivated by the attempt, amid a milieu of partial concerns and fragmentary solutions, to gain some vision of the whole. It is not primarily in seeing that God is the principle of concretion, or that evil is implicated in the very nature of actuality, or even that all goodness lies in the imposition of modes of order. Its ultimate wisdom lies in the perception that the solemnity and the grandeur of the world arises out of the slow process of unification in which the diversities of existence are utilized, although they are never lost.

NOTES

CHAPTER I

1. T.S. Eliot, *Collected Poems: 1909-1935* (New York: Harcourt, Brace, 1936). Reprinted by permission of the publishers.

2. Alfred Zimmern, *The Greek Commonwealth* (4th ed., rev.; Oxford: Clarendon Press, 1924), p. 58. Reprinted by permission of the publishers.

3. Maurice DeWulf, *Philosophy and Civilization in the Middle Ages* (Princeton: Princeton University Press, 1922), p. 103 f. This and the following reprinted by permission of the publishers.

4. *Ibid.*, p. 130 f.

5. I am referring here only to organization and not to method. Newton distinguishes geometry and mechanics as rational and practical sciences, respectively. By practical is meant that which has reference to existence. Practical mechanics is observational in the sense that its concern is with applicability. Theory is rationally elaborated and then tested for applicability. Thus the first two books of the *Principia* are rational, while the third is a treatment of empirical application. However, Newton insists on the real priority of experience. Observation comes before theory, since the very constructions involved in geometry are prior to demonstrations concerning these constructions. See *Mathematical Principles,* etc., ed. C. Cajori (Berkeley: University of California Press, 1934), Newton's and Cotes's Prefaces.

6. David Hume, *A Treatise of Human Nature,* ed. Selby-Bigge (Oxford: Clarendon Press, 1928), p. 252 f. Note also in this connection what Whitehead says about Hume's implication. Alfred North Whitehead, *Adventures of Ideas* (New York: Macmillan, 1933), p. 36 f. Quotations from this work by permission of the publishers.

7. Luigi Pirandello, *One, None and A Hundred Thousand,* trans. Samuel Putnam (New York: E.P. Dutton, 1933), pp. 106-108. I have made slight alterations where the present English translation is awkward. Reprinted by permission of the heirs of the Pirandello estate.

8. The classic statement of this position is in the preface and first few chapters of Abraham Kardiner's *The Psychological Frontiers of Society* (New York: Columbia University Press, 1947).

9. David Riesman, *The Lonely Crowd: A Study of the Changing American Charter* (New Haven: Yale University Press, 1950).

10. F. Scott Fitzgerald, "Handle with Care," *Esquire Magazine,* March, 1936.

11. A. S. Eddington, *The Nature of the Physical World* (New York: Macmillan, 1929), p. 40.

12. See Zimmern, *The Greek Commonwealth,* p. 59 f. "The Greek has never known what it is to be in the common sense of the word either in his habits or his ideals an economic man. The Greek word for unemployment is 'schole' which means 'leisure': while for business he has no better word than the negative 'ascholia,' which means 'absence of leisure.' The hours and weeks of unemployment he regards as the best and most natural part of his life."

13. Karl Jaspers, *Man in the Modern Age* (New York: Holt, 1933), p. 51.

14. *Ibid.*, p. 67.

15. Gabriel Marcel, *The Philosophy of Existence* (New York: Philosophical Library, 1949), p. 2 f. Reprinted by permission of the publisher.

16. See Michael Rostovtzeff, *The Social and Economic History of the Hellenistic World* (Oxford: Clarendon Press, 1941).

17. Karl Mannheim, *Ideology and Utopia* (New York: Harcourt, Brace, 1936), p. 9. Reprinted by permission of the publisher.

18. *Ibid.*, p. 10.

19. For a brief but excellent account of these matters see Henri Pirenne, *Mediaeval Cities: Their Origins and the Revival of Trade* (Princeton: Princeton University Press, 1925).

20. F. Dostoyevski, *The Brothers Karamazov* (New York: Random House, 1929), p. 310 ff.

21. The contrast between open and closed societies is presented by Henri Bergson in *The Two Sources of Morality and Religion* (New York: Holt, 1935) in a sense slightly different from its use here. He probably derived it from Durkheim.

22. The analysis of the plurality of elites in modern society, and a description of their nature and selection, are presented in Karl Mannheim, *Man and Society in an Age of Reconstruction* (New York: Harcourt, Brace, 1938), p. 86 ff.

23. Whitehead, *Adventures of Ideas*, p 133.

24. The way in which movements of thought are causally related to movements in art and literature will be treated in greater detail subsequently. Another example of such treatment is Edward F. Rothschild, *The Meaning of Unintelligibility in Modern Art* (Chicago: University of Chicago Press, 1934).

25. This is clearly stated by David Daiches in *The Novel and the Modern World* (Chicago: University of Chicago Press, 1939), pp. 7-9. See also Chapter XII, "Fiction and Civilization." A treatment of the same problem which is more original and less direct is that of Paul Goodman, "Advance-Guard Writing; 1900-1950," *Kenyon Review*, Summer, 1951.

26. Wallace Stevens, *The Necessary Angel: Essays on Reality and the Imagination* (New York: Alfred Knopf, 1951), p. 170 f.

27. See for example the discussion of Edwin Berry Burgum, "Thomas Mann and the Present," *Antioch Review*, Fall, 1942.

28. "The subject is so equivocal, the limits so fluctuating. We make bold to laugh at the idea. Is it not well done that our language has but one word for all kinds of love, from the holiest to the most lustfully fleshly? All ambiguity is therein resolved: love cannot but be physical, at its furthest reach of holiness: it cannot be impious in its utterest fleshliness. It is always itself as the height of shrewd 'geniality' as in the depth of passion; it is organic sympathy, the touching sense-embrace of that which is doomed to decay. In the most raging as in the most reverent passion, there must be *caritas*. The meaning of the word varies? In God's name, then, let it vary. That it does so makes it living, makes it human; it would be a regrettable lack of 'depth' to trouble over the fact." Thomas Mann, *The Magic Mountain* (New York: Random House, 1927), p. 756.

CHAPTER II

1. The connection between Aeschylus and Plato is made by F.M. Cornford, in the Epilogue to *Plato's Cosmology* (London: Routledge and Kegan Paul; New York: Humanities Press, 1952).

2. René Descartes, *Discourse on Method* (Chicago: Open Court Publishing Co., 1938), p. 35 f. One could have cited also Pascal's famous characterization of man as a "thinking reed." But there is an irrational strain in Pascal. Descartes' rationalism is purer.

3. Charles Darwin, *The Descent of Man* (New York: Random House, n.d.), p. 445 f.

4. In the thought of Descartes there is frequent confusion between the passions and the intellect. In some places "thinking" is taken to include "feeling" and even "willing." But I am interested here less in the details of the Cartesian philosophy than in its implications and its effects.

5. Galileo's *Dialogue Concerning Two New Sciences*, Henry Crew and Alfonso de Salvio, eds. (New York: Macmillan, 1933), p. 276.

6. Descartes, *Discourse on Method*, p. 7.

7. The relationship between metropolitan living and rationality, calculability and a money economy, has been interestingly dealt with by Georg Simmel in his "Die Grosstädte und das Geistesleben," trans. Gerth and Mills as "The Metropolis and Mental Life" and reprinted in Kurt Wolff, *The Sociology of Georg Simmel* (Glencoe, Ill., Free Press, 1950), pp. 409-424.

8. T.K. Abbott, *Kant's Theory of Ethics* (London: Longmans, Green, 1883), p. 47.

9. Descartes, *Discourse on Method*, p. 29.

10. *The Confession of J.J. Rousseau* (New York: Tudor, 1936), p. 418.

11. *Ibid.*, p. 165.

12. I have in mind here, for example, a section like *The World as Will and Idea*, II, 27. In such a section alone are to be found striking anticipations both of Bergson's *Creative Evolution* and Dewey's *Experience and Nature*.

13. These ideas are developed in *The World as Will and Idea*, particularly in Bk. I and the first part of Bk. II.

14. *The Philosophy of Schopenhauer*, ed. Irwin Edman (New York: Random House, 1928), p. 63 ff. Reprinted by permission of the publishers.

15. Friedrich Nietzsche, *The Will to Power*, trans. Ludovici (London: Allen and Unwin, 1924), II, 394.

16. Erich Heller, *The Disinherited Mind* (Philadelphia: Farrar, Straus and Cudahy, 1952), p. 140.

17. This is expressed in Soren Kierkegaard, *Either/Or*, trans. Swenson and Lowrie (Princeton: Princeton University Press, 1944), Vol. II.

18. This occurs in the section on "The Teleological Suspension of the Ethical," in *Fear and Trembling*, but its classic statement is in the *Concluding Unscientific Postscript*, "The Subjective Truth."

19. Robert Bretall, *A Kierkegaard Anthology* (Princeton: Princeton University Press, 1951), p. 214. Reprinted by permission of the publishers.

20. Karl Mannheim says: "German sociology has placed the concepts 'rational' and 'irrational' at the very center of its interests." *Man and Society in an Age of Reconstruction* (New York: Harcourt, Brace, 1940), p. 52, footnote. Max Lerner believes that "The intellectual revolution of the twentieth century is likely to prove the charting of the terra incognita of the irrational and the extraction of its implications for every area of human thought." *Ideas Are Weapons* (New York: Viking, 1939), p. 4.

21. This question has been raised (although not in terms of the Cartesian-Dar-

winian contrast used here) by Charner M. Perry. See his "Knowledge as a Basis for Social Reform," *International Journal of Ethics*, April, 1935.

22. Thurman Arnold, *The Folklore of Capitalism* (New Haven: Yale University Press, 1937). Reprinted by permission of the publishers.

23. There is one seeming exception in which the rancor, caprice, and irresponsibility of the artist is a matter of general acknowledgment. This is the Dadaist school flourishing from 1916 to 1922 in Paris, Berlin, New York, and Zurich. For details consult Georges Hugnet's article "Dada," in *Fantastic Art Dada Surrealism*, ed. Alfred H. Barr, Jr. (New York: Museum of Modern Art, 1936). But it can be maintained that these artists were facing not the artistic problems of form or subject matter, but a simple problem of existence—how to continue at all, being artists.

24. See Alfred H. Barr, Jr., *Cubism and Abstract Art* (New York: Museum of Modern Art, 1936), p. 18, footnote.

25. Plato, *Philebus* (Loeb Classical Library Edition, Cambridge: Harvard University Press, 1925), p. 343 f. Reprinted by permission of the publishers.

26. The passage following is quoted from this former work in André Breton, *What Is Surrealism?* (London: Faber and Faber, 1936). Reprinted by permission of the publishers.

27. Introduction to Cincinnati Art Museum Catalogue of 1949.

28. *Art News*, Vol. 51, No. 8.

29. Sigmund Freud, *Civilization and Its Discontents* (London: Hogarth Press, 1946), p. 23 f. Quotations from this book by permission of the publishers.

30. *Ibid.*, p. 42.

31. From T. S. Eliot, *Four Quartets* (New York: Harcourt, Brace, 1943). Reprinted by permission of the publishers.

32. Herbert Feigl, "Logical Empiricism," in *Twentieth Century Philosophy*, ed. D. D. Runes (New York: Philosophical Library, 1943). Reprinted by permission of the publishers.

33. Henri Bergson, *The Two Sources of Morality and Religion* (New York: Holt, 1935), p. 92. Reprinted by permission of the publishers.

34. *Ibid.*, p. 112.

35. Hans Vaihinger, *The Philosophy of As If* (New York: Harcourt, Brace, 1925), p. viii.

36. Nietzsche, *The Will to Power*, Sec. 605.

CHAPTER III

1. Oswald Spengler, *The Decline of the West* (New York: Knopf, 1939), I, 373.

2. Henri Bergson, *Creative Evolution* (New York: Holt, 1931), p. xiii. Quotations from this work by permission of the publishers.

3. Bergson, *An Introduction to Metaphysics*, trans. T. E. Hulme (London: G. P. Putnam, 1912), p. 1. Quotations from this work by permission of the publishers.

4. *Ibid.*, p. 7. It is interesting that Bergson, having laid the foundations for a complete doctrine of aesthetic intuition, never presents a comprehensive system of aesthetics. In the first few pages of *Time and Free Will* he presents certain theories of art and aesthetic empathy, but they are soon dropped. When he returns to art it is but fitfully. *Laughter*, Part III, contains some reflections upon art, as does more briefly an essay like "The Perception of Change." But all this is unsystematic. It is curious that the aesthetic promise of *Time and Free Will* is never fulfilled. In this

respect Bergson reminds one greatly of Whitehead. Both developed philosophies congenial to aesthetics; neither developed an aesthetics as explicit doctrine. One might say in both cases that men whose philosophy as a whole depends so much upon the categories of feeling and creativity had no need to develop a special aesthetics since their metaphysics was itself but aesthetics generalized.

5. Bergson, *Laughter* (New York: Macmillan, 1911), p. 156 f. This work has been reprinted as *Comedy* by Doubleday, and the quotations from it which appear in this chapter are by permission of them as publishers.

6. *Ibid.*, p. 159 f.

7. Bergson, *An Introduction to Metaphysics*, p. 9.

8. The evidences are at hand for any reader of the two men and have been continuously exploited by critics. I will mention only two: the first a brief summary of the critical treatment by Fernand Vial, *Le Symbolisme Bergsonian du temps dans l'oeuvre de Proust* (PMLA, Vol. LV, No. 4, p. 1191); the second F. C. Green's *The Mind of Proust* (Cambridge: Cambridge University Press, 1949), p. 399. This is the most comprehensive summary of Proust's work in English.

9. Bergson, *Time and Free Will*, trans. Pogson (London: George Allen, 1912), p. 7 f. All quotations from this work reprinted by permission of Allen and Unwin, Ltd.

10. *Ibid.*, p. 130.

11. *Ibid.*, p. 172.

12. *Ibid.*, p. 169 f.

13. This doctrine of crisis situations, or *Grenzsituationen*, had been most completely developed by Karl Jaspers in his *Psychologie der Weltanschaungen*, and *Philosophie*. He also treats it in *Man in the Modern Age*, cited in Chapter I. I shall deal with it more explicitly in Chapter X.

14. Bergson, *Time and Free Will*, p. 231 f.

15. Marcel Proust, *The Past Recaptured*, trans. F. Blossom (New York: Albert and Charles Boni, 1932), p. 36. All quotations from this and other volumes of *Remembrance of Things Past* are reprinted by permission of Random House.

16. *Ibid.*, p. 198.

17. Proust, *Swann's Way*, trans. Moncrieff (New York: Random House, 1928).

18. Proust, *The Past Recaptured*, p. 206.

19. See the account of the errors of empirical and rational psychology in *An Introduction to Metaphysics*, p. 30 ff.

20. Bergson's "inverted Kantianism" has been remarked by Maritain, Laird, Lindsey, and, in fact, almost all who have devoted attention to his philosophy.

21. Bergson, *Matter and Memory*, trans. Paul and Palmer (London: Allen and Unwin, 1929), p. xvi f. Reprinted by permission of the publishers.

22. I have mentioned Dewey rather than James here because the doctrine of instrumentalism is the best pragmatic doctrine to compare with Bergson. Actually it was James for whom Bergson felt real affection and kinship of spirit. They corresponded for many years. Some of this correspondence is to be found in *The Letters of William James* (Boston: Little, Brown, 1920), and in R. B. Perry's *The Thought and Character of William James* (Boston: Little, Brown, 1935). Bergson himself wrote a gracious preface to the French translation of James's *Pragmatism*. It is reprinted as "*Sur le pragmatisme de William James: Verité et réalité*," in *La Pensée et le mouvant* (Paris: Libraire Félix Alcan, 1934).

23. Bergson, *Matter and Memory*, p. 8. Bergson's theory of matter as "the aggre-

gate of images" has much in common with the epistemological theory of Bertrand Russell at the time he delivered the Lowell Lectures in 1914. He viewed the world then as a "system of perspectives" and objects as composites of possible perspectives. See Bertrand Russell, *Our Knowledge of the External World* (New York: W. W. Norton, 1929), p. 93 ff. It is ironic that in the first chapter of this book he criticizes Bergson severely, yet at some points later in the book comes to conclusions much like Bergson's own. I shall deal with this more completely in the chapter on Russell.

24. Bergson, *Matter and Memory*, p. 30.

25. *Ibid.*, p. 71.

26. *Ibid.*, p. 94.

27. Bergson, *Creative Evolution*, p. ix. Reprinted by permission of Henry Holt and Company.

28. *Ibid.*, p. 6 f.

29. I have borrowed here the phrase of Whitehead. See his *Science and the Modern World* (New York: Macmillan, 1923), pp. 69, 81, *et passim*.

30. Bergson, *Creative Evolution*, p. 8.

31. *Ibid.*, p. 16.

32. *Ibid.*, p. 39. That this appeal to the nature of "real time" is the heart of Bergson's system cannot be doubted by any who have worked through the details of his thought. But there is external evidence as well. In May, 1908, William James delivered the Hibbert Lectures at Oxford. One of them was devoted to Bergson exclusively. But before delivering it he wrote to Bergson asking for biographical data and an account of his philosophic experiences. Bergson answered from Paris in a remarkable letter (May 9, 1908) which says in part: "Now as to events worthy of note, there have been none in the course of my career,—at least nothing objectively remarkable. On the subjective side, however, I cannot but attribute great importance to the change which took place in my thinking during the two years which followed my leaving the Ecole Normale, from 1881 to 1883. I had remained up to that time wholly imbued with mechanistic theories, to which I had been led at an early date by the reading of Herbert Spencer, a philosopher to whom I adhered almost unreservedly. It was my intention to devote myself to what was then called the philosophy of the sciences, and to examine some of the fundamental scientific notions. It was the analysis of the notion of time, as that enters into mechanics and physics, which overturned all my ideas. I saw, to my great astonishment, that scientific time does not *endure*, that it would involve no change in our scientific knowledge if the totality of the real were unfolded all at once, instantaneously, and that positive science consists essentially in the elimination of duration. This was the point of departure of a series of reflections which brought me by gradual steps to reject almost all of what I had previously accepted and to change my point of view completely. . . ." Perry, *The Thought and Character of William James*, Vol. II, p. 623. Permission to reprint granted by Paul R. Reynolds and Son, 599 Fifth Avenue, New York.

33. Bergson, *Creative Evolution*, p. 45.

34. Bergson's refutation of mechanism is based upon two distinct forms of proof: (1) the intuitive appeal to the nature of real time, and (2) an empirical appeal to the biological evidence. For the second he reasons thus: If we can prove that life can manufacture a like organ in different biological forms although the external environments of the two forms are different, then this similarity must not come

from adaptation to environment alone, but from an inner directing principle. Bergson appeals to a comparison between the eye of the vertebrate and that of the mollusc (the Pecten) to make this point, as well as to the researches of a number of theoretical biologists (De Vries, Wolff, Bateson, Silensky, etc.). It is not necessary to dwell upon the details of this demonstration. They are given in *Creative Evolution,* pp. 53-84.

35. *Ibid.,* p. 98.

36. *Ibid.,* p. 161. It is clear from this quotation that Bergson believes that the intellect is hypnotized by the power of inert matter, but this belief might be seriously criticized by questioning two concepts which Bergson employs here: the first is the concept of "a natural geometry of the human mind"; the second is the concept of "mere inert matter." One should remember that Kant's philosophy of nature largely derived its validity from the assumption of the ultimate trustworthiness of Newtonian cosmology and the innate applicability of Euclidean geometry to the structure of the world. Kant's derivation of the forms of perception and the categories of the understanding depended upon the adequacy of Newtonian and Euclidean ideas. But the development of non-Euclidean geometry in the nineteenth century and the growth of the logistic and formalistic schools of mathematical interpretation in the early decades of the twentieth have served to call into question Kant's postulates. If the arguments against Kant have any validity, they hold also against Bergson's assumption of "a natural geometry of the human mind." I have taken up this matter in further detail in Chapter VII.

The other concept is equally questionable. That there is a natural geometry of the human mind depends, according to Bergson, upon the properties of solids. Geometry and logic are the product of an intellect which patterns itself upon "inert matter." But if non-Euclidean geometry undermines the metaphysical foundations of Kant's forms of perception, what do the developments of modern theoretical physics do to Bergson's conception of *inert* matter? As Planck, Eddington, and Whitehead have admirably shown, the emphasis of modern physics upon quanta, centers of force, electrical charges, and radiant energy has completely transformed our conception of matter. It has, in fact, removed from "inert matter" both its *inertness* and its *materiality*. We are forced, then, to conclude that if Bergson's attack is aimed against a logic patterned upon a conception of "inert matter," then this *logic* is itself merely a historical accident, and Bergson's point (completely valid against the naive mechanistic materialism commonly held during the nineteenth century) cannot be urged against what he calls "the natural geometry of the human mind." I will treat this also in greater detail in the chapter dealing with Einstein and Planck.

37. "La pensée la plus vivante se glacera dans la formule qui l'exprime. Le mot se retourne contre l'idée. La lettre tue l'esprit." *L'Evolution créatrice* (Paris: Libraire Félix Alcan, 1912), p. 138.

38. Piet Mondrian makes the point relative to art. "Art is not a manifestation of instinctive faculties but arises through intuitive capacity. . . . instinctive faculties are of animal nature while intuitive capabilities are human." *American Abstract Artists* (New York: Ram Press, 1946).

39. Bergson, *Creative Evolution,* p. 267 f.

40. Bergson, *An Introduction to Metaphysics,* p. 65 f.

41. Bergson, *Creative Evolution,* p. 301.

42. *Ibid.,* p. 302.

43. *Ibid.,* pp. 304-306.

44. *Ibid.*, p. 369 f.

45. A somewhat similar point is made by R. G. Collingwood, *The Idea of Nature* (London: Oxford University Press, 1945), p. 137.

46. I believe that this is essentially the contention of H. R. Pritchard's *Mind* article of 1912, "Does Moral Philosophy Rest on a Mistake?" It was his belief that the sense of obligation is absolutely un-derivative and immediate, and that the mistake lies in our asking for proof of obligation through moral argument or reasoning.

47. Bergson, *The Two Sources of Morality and Religion* (New York: Holt, 1935), pp. 42, 71. This and the following quotations reprinted by permission of the publishers.

48. *Ibid.*, p. 59.

49. T. S. Eliot, *Four Quartets* (New York: Harcourt, Brace, 1943). Copyright 1943 by T. S. Eliot. Reprinted by permission of Harcourt, Brace and Co.

50. Bergson, *The Two Sources of Morality and Religion*, p. 209.

51. Eliot, *Four Quartets.*

52. Bergson, *Laughter*, pp. 151-55.

53. Bergson, "The Perception of Change," from *The Creative Mind* (New York: Philosophical Library, 1946), p. 185 f. Permission to reprint by the publishers.

54. Bergson, *The Two Sources of Morality and Religion*, p. 222.

55. Eliot, *Four Quartets.*

56. Bergson, "Philosophical Intuition," in *The Creative Mind*, p. 132.

CHAPTER IV

1. H. A. L. Fisher, *A History of Europe* (Boston: Houghton, Mifflin, 1935), I, vii. Reprinted by permission of the publishers.

2. This matter is taken up in the context of an extended consideration of the philosophy of history dealing chiefly with Plato and Marx in his two-volume work, *The Open Society and Its Enemies* (London: J. Routledge and Sons, 1945). Popper's conclusions are stated in Vol. II, Ch. 25, "Has History Any Meaning?" The two following quotations are from this work: II, 254, and II, 265.

3. Karl Löwith, *Meaning in History: The Theological Implications of the Philosophy of History* (Chicago: University of Chicago Press, 1949), p. 191. Löwith's treatment is original in form (he works back historically from Burckhardt and Marx to Orosius and Augustine) and extremely suggestive in its classification of philosophies of history.

4. Jacob Burckhardt, *Force and Freedom: Reflections on History* (New York: Pantheon, 1943), pp. 80, 82. Although Burckhardt is not a philosopher of history in the strict sense, he is a philosophically-minded historian, and his reflections indicate a climate in which a philosophy of history can flourish.

5. G. W. F. Hegel, *Philosophy of History*, trans. J. Sibree (New York: P. F. Collier, 1901), p. 48 f.

6. Alfred North Whitehead, *Adventures of Ideas* (New York: Macmillan, 1933), p. 139. All of Ch. VII deals illuminatingly with this most important question in the philosophy of science. Reprinted by permission of the publishers.

7. This is clear from a study of the nature of calendars. The Christian calendar dates forward and backward from such a single epoch-making event. The Romans count *"ab urbe condita"*—"from the founding of the city of Rome." But the Greeks

count by 4-5 year periods from one Olympiad to another. Even their calendar has a "periodic" basis.

8. R. G. Collingwood, *The Idea of History* (London: Oxford University Press, 1946), p. 49.

9. Löwith, *Meaning in History*, p. 19.

10. Burckhart, *Force and Freedom*, p. 90.

11. Oswald Spengler, *The Decline of the West*, trans. C. F. Atkinson (New York: Knopf, 1939). Quotations reprinted by permission of the publishers.

12. There is no absolute evidence here. Spengler told a close friend that, not having read Bergson before the publication of *Der Untergang* in 1918, upon publication he was accused of borrowing. So in the fall of 1918 he read as much Bergson as he could to see if they were really so similar. See August Albers, "Oswald Spengler," *Preussische Jahrbucher*, CLXXXXII, May 2, 1923, p. 133. I have not compared the first and second editions for Bergson's additions.

13. This thesis deals specifically with the concepts of pure process (*die Reine Bewegung*); the strife of opposites (*Der Kampf der Gegensätze*); and the concept of unity and necessity (*die Idee der Einheit und Notwendigkeit*), in Heracleitus. But in the course of it Spengler refers to doctrines of relativism, of eternal recurrence, of cultural organicity and of fate—precisely the ideas which were to dominate *The Decline of the West*. This work deserves to be better known. The thesis has not been translated into English but can be found in Oswald Spengler, *Reden und Aufsätze* (Munich, 1937) pp. 1-47.

14. Spengler, *The Decline of the West*, I, 48.

15. *Ibid.*, I, 6.

16. *Ibid.*, I, 49, footnote.

17. *Ibid.*, I, 6.

18. Immanuel Kant, *The Idea of a Universal History*, Prop. VIII.

19. Spengler, *The Decline of the West*, I, 18.

20. *Ibid.*, I, 20.

21. *Ibid.*, I, 112. It is perhaps appropriate at this point to ask if this does not modify the sharpness of Spengler's distinction between the world-as-nature and the world-as-history, between a world cognized according to a principle of necessity imposed by law and a world felt in its pure becoming. On the one hand Spengler wishes to preserve Bergson's distinction between the dead concept and the vital flux, but on the other hand he wishes to assert for every great historical culture a strict correspondence of internal structure. Is it really possible to distinguish between the systematic method of science, which deals with the morphology of the mechanical and the extended through the technique of laws of nature and causal relations, and the physiognomic method of Spenglerian history, which tries to chart the morphology of that which has direction in time? To be sure, a technique of causal explanations differs from a technique of analogy. An analogy is an assertion of resemblance. A law is an assertion of constant co-variation. But the resemblance of analogy approaches identity as to an ideal limit. And if analogy is raised to the status of a *technique*—if, that is, the resemblances which are asserted are essential rather than accidental— then the fact of essential resemblance, although the product of perception (intuition, even) is important only insofar as it is the exemplification of a historical or sociological law. Spengler may rely heavily upon intuition and a physiognomic method which produces spiritual portraiture (so that an Oedipus, a Hamlet, a Don Quixote, a Faust, or a Julian Sorel become epochal symbols as well as fictive beings), but his

final outcome would still seem to be a synchronic and diachronic study of cultural entities as envisaged by the positivist tradition to which Comte, Durkheim, and Levy-Bruhl belong.

22. *Ibid.*, I, 118.

23. *Ibid.*, II, 30 f.

24. *Ibid.*, II, 57.

25. *Ibid.*, I, 21. Spengler's identification of eight cultures was anticipated by the work of N. I. Danilevsky (originally published in 1869 but later translated into German, *Russland und Europa* [Berlin, 1920]) who identified ten. Spengler's work preceded the discovery of Ur and the Chaldean culture. And he was confused about the Mycenean-Minoan problem. But these are the shortcomings of an armchair historian insulated from certain empirical details. They hardly affect his theory.

26. Spengler, *The Decline of the West*, I, 106.

27. *Ibid.*, I, 32 f.

28. *Ibid.*, II, 99 f.

29. *Ibid.*, I, 359.

30. *Ibid.*, I, 353.

31. *Ibid.*, II, 507.

32. *Ibid.*, I, 37 f.

33. ". . . dass ich von der Kunst als der höchsten Aufgabe und der eigentlich metaphysischen Tätigkeit dieses Leben. . . . überzeugt bin. . . ." Nietzsche, *Die Geburt der Tragödie* (Leipzig: C. G. Naumann, 1894), Foreword to Richard Wagner, p. 18.

34. Spengler, *The Decline of the West*, I, 40 f.

35. Erich Heller, "Oswald Spengler and the Predicament of the Historical Imagination," in *The Disinherited Mind* (Philadelphia: Farrar, Straus, and Cudahy, 1952), p. 152. Reprinted by permission of the publishers.

36. Spengler, *The Decline of the West*, I, 345.

37. *Ibid.*, I, 23.

38. Arnold J. Toynbee, *A Study of History* (New York: Oxford University Press, 1934-54), Vols. I, II, III (1934), Vols. IV, V, VI (1939), Vols. VII, VIII, IX, X (1954). Quotations by permission of the publishers.

39. *Ibid.*, X, I.

40. Toynbee, *Civilization on Trial* (New York: Oxford University Press, 1948) p. 9 ff. Quotations by permission of the publishers.

41. Toynbee, *A Study of History*, I, 51.

42. These are Egyptian, Andean, Sinic, Minoan, Sumeric, Mayan, Yucatic, Mexic, Hittite, Syriac, Babylonic, Iranic, Arabic, Far Eastern, Far Eastern Japanese Branch, Indic, Hindu, Hellenic, Orthodox Christian, Orthodox Christian Russian Branch, Western. (*Ibid.*, I, 129 ff.)

43. *Ibid.*, IV, 11 f.

44. This is illustrated very interestingly in an essay, "History," which Toynbee contributed to *The Legacy of Greece*, ed. R. W. Livingstone (Oxford: Clarendon Press, 1921). In the first few pages of this essay he himself uses Spengler's analogy: "This description of the relationship between ancient Greece and the Modern Western world may be something more than a metaphor, for, societies like individuals are living creatures, and may therefore be expected to exhibit the same phenomena." And he goes on (p. 290) to speak of Western society "in the body of Greek society like a child in the womb," of its birth, childhood, puberty. But six pages later he has

produced the metaphor of "the plot of civilization." "Students of the drama, from Aristotle onwards, seem to agree that nearly all the great tragedies of history—that is, the great civilizations that have been created by the spirit of man—may all reveal the same plot, if we analyze them rightly" (p. 297). And he goes on to develop the metaphor in detail showing the *"katharsis"* of our study of the Greeks, and even (p. 303) outlining the "Three Acts of the tragedy of the Greek Civilization."

45. Toynbee, A *Study of History*, I, 271.

46. Toynbee, *Civilization on Trial*, pp. 10-12.

47. Toynbee, A *Study of History*, III, 112 ff.

48. *Ibid.*, III, 118, 125.

49. *Ibid.*, III, 243.

50. *Ibid.*, IV, 120.

51. Burckhardt, *Force and Freedom*, p. 103.

52. Toynbee, A *Study of History*, V, 35-375.

53. *Ibid.*, V, 376-569; VI, 1-174.

54. *Ibid.*, IV, 245 ff.

55. *Ibid.*, IV, 258 f. I have transliterated the Greek.

56. Toynbee, A *Study of History*, Vols. I-VI, published before the beginning of the Second World War, really completes the Spenglerian task of an examination of the genesis, growth, breakdown, and decay of civilizations. But the year 1939 ushers in a period which marks a profound break with Toynbee's previous angle of vision. Henceforth (at the age of fifty) he shifts the focus of his concern from "civilizations" to "the higher religions." Vols. VII-X, published only in 1954, are almost entirely a new work, and they press Toynbee's relentless religiosity to burdensome lengths. His pedantry also increases and, in my opinion, there is a marked decline in Toynbee's powers as a creative philosopher of history exhibited in these last volumes. Volume VIII, for example, is mostly a rehash of the commonplaces of contemporary sociology, and the section of Volume IX on the prospects of Western Civilization is pedestrian and bitterly disappointing. Toynbee since the war is more oracular, and as he approaches the end of his "monumental task" more and more awed by it and self-intrusive into it. There is also a falling off of style and imagery and an increase of reference, much of it purely pedantic. Sometimes Toynbee broaches a subject and piles up quotation upon quotation as if marking time before he knows what he really wants to say. The entire ten volumes (but the last four particularly) would have profited greatly by rigorous pruning and condensation. Toynbee's erudition (for which he has been universally praised) is impressive, but there are many occasions when its parade is imperceptive and merely self-indulgent. For all my admiration of his work, I think this needs to be said.

57. Toynbee, A *Study of History*, VI, 49-169.

58. *Ibid.*, VI, 174.

59. As announced in *ibid.*, VII, I.

60. *Ibid.*, VII, 392-420.

61. *Ibid.*, VII, 422. Also see VII, 444, 526.

62. T. S. Eliot, *Collected Poems: 1909-1935* (New York: Harcourt, Brace, 1936). Reprinted by permission of the publishers.

63. Toynbee, A *Study of History*, VII, 425.

64. *Ibid.*, VII, 428.

65. *Ibid.*, IX, 167-395.

66. *Ibid.*, IX, 168.

67. *Ibid.*, IX, 288 f.
68. Toynbee, *Civilization on Trial*, p. 12.
69. Toynbee, *A Study of History*, IX, 173 f.
70. *Ibid.*, IX, 338 f.
71. *Ibid.*, IX, 347.
72. *Ibid.*, IX, 395-405.
73. *Ibid.*, IX, 406.
74. *Ibid.*, 406-641.
75. *Ibid.*, IX, 643. Elsewhere Toynbee is more specific about the path to salvation: "What shall we do to be saved? In politics, establish a constitutional co-operative system of world government. In economics, find working compromises (varying according to the practical requirements of different places and times) between free enterprise and socialism. In the life of the spirit, put the secular super-structure back onto religious foundations." *Civilization on Trial*, p. 39.
76. Professionally neither Toynbee nor Spengler was a strict historian. Spengler taught many subjects as a secondary-school teacher and, after his fame, declined further teaching. A few months after the publication of *Der Untergang* he was approached in connection with a chair in philosophy at Göttingen. Fourteen years later he received a formal offer to a Professorship of History (Karl Lamprecht's chair) at Leipzig. He refused both offers. Toynbee was originally Professor of Byzantine and Modern Greek and is now Research Professor of International History at the University of London.
77. Collingwood, *The Idea of History*, p. 164. Reprinted by permission of Oxford University Press.
78. Toynbee, *Civilization on Trial*, pp. 158-59.
79. Toynbee, *A Study of History*, X, 213-42.

CHAPTER V

1. Freud himself says of this early period: ". . . the theories of Darwin which were then of topical interest, strongly attracted me, for they held out hopes of an extraordinary advance in our understanding of the world; and it was hearing Goethe's beautiful essay on Nature read aloud at a popular lecture by Professor Carl Bruhl just before I left school that decided me to become a medical student." Sigmund Freud, *An Autobiographical Study* (London: Hogarth Press, 1948), p. 14. Quotations from this work are by permission of W. W. Norton and Company, New York.
2. Quoted by Ernst Simmel, "Sigmund Freud: The Man and His Work," *Psychoanalytic Quarterly* (1940), IX, 167.
3. D. H. Lawrence, *Psychoanalysis and the Unconscious* (New York: T. Seltzer, 1921). Forsaking Freudian rationalism, Lawrence developed his own implications of the unconscious in *Fantasia of the Unconscious* (New York: T. Seltzer, 1922). The more complete story of Lawrence's quarrel with Freud is detailed in Frederick J. Hoffman, *Freudianism and the Literary Mind* (Baton Rouge: Louisiana State University Press, 1945), Ch. VI.
4. Freud, *New Introductory Lectures on Psychoanalysis* (New York: W. W. Norton, 1933), p. 216. Lecture XXXV, "A Philosophy of Life," contains some of the most interesting materials for an assessment of Freud's philosophical position. All quotations from this work reprinted by permission of the publishers.

5. *Ibid.*, p. 219.

6. *Ibid.*, p. 233.

7. These two courses of lectures by Freud (forming 28 in all) have been published as *A General Introduction to Psychoanalysis* (New York: Garden City Publishing Co., 1938). Brilliant in their clarity and persuasiveness (it is uncanny the way Freud anticipates objections and answers criticisms just as they come to mind), they are the best leisurely introduction to his system as a whole. The material which follows is from Lecture I. Quotations from this work are by permission of Liveright Publishing Co.

8. The difficulty of bridging the gap between the psychological and physiological remains a root difficulty. It has cropped up most recently in discussions of the "logical" status of psychoanalysis. These came to a head in a series of papers by Toulmin, Flew, and Peters published in *Analysis*, Vol. 9, 10 (1948-50). They are reprinted in Margaret MacDonald, *Philosophy and Analysis* (New York: Philosophical Library, 1954), pp. 132-56). Toulmin and Flew argue that Freud did not discover the *causes* of mental illness, but only the *motives* for it, and that successful therapy therefore results not from the *eradication of a cause* but from *the purification of a motive*. The distinction is suggestive and, I think, true, but probably less fatal to Freudian theory than its authors believe. For it only distinguishes two types of explanation relevant to different levels of scientific advance. It is an appropriate irony that Freud, insistent upon the scientific character of his own work, should have been so frequently challenged concerning the subjectivity of the psychoanalyst's work and the lack of controlled experimental check of his therapeutic successes. See for example R. R. Sears, *Survey of Objective Studies of Psychoanalytic Concepts* (New York: Social Science Research Council Bulletin No. 51); and G. S. Blum, *Psychoanalytic Theories of Personality* (New York: McGraw-Hill, 1953). The latest attempt in this direction is Herbert Feigl and Michael Scriven, Minnesota Studies in the Philosophy of Science, Volume I: *The Foundations of Science and the Concepts of Psychology and Psychoanalysis*. See particularly the contributions of B. F. Skinner, "Critique of Psychoanalytic Concepts and Theories;" Albert Ellis, "An Operational Reformulation of Some of the Basic Principles of Psychoanalysis;" and Antony Flew, "Motives and the Unconscious" (this latter a further paper in the *Analysis* series).

9. Freud, *A General Introduction to Psychoanalysis*, p. 27.

10. *Ibid.*, pp. 60, 68.

11. *A General Introduction to Psychoanalysis* consists of four lectures on the psychology of errors (covering in condensed fashion the material included in *The Psychopathology of Everyday Life*), eleven lectures on dreams (from the larger work *The Interpretation of Dreams*), and thirteen lectures on the theory of the neuroses (containing material previously published in separate papers and in *Three Contributions to the Theory of Sex*). The three more complete works are available in *The Basic Writings of Sigmund Freud* (New York: Random House, 1938).

12. Some interesting suggestions concerning psychoanalysis and the more poetic conception of "rhythm" and "pace" have been made by Kenneth Burke. See his "Freud—and the Analysis of Poetry," *The American Journal of Sociology*, Vol. XLV, No. 3 (November, 1939).

13. Freud, *A General Introduction to Psychoanalysis*, p. 252.

14. *Ibid.*, p. 246 f.

15. Freud, *An Outline of Psychoanalysis* (New York: W. W. Norton, 1949) p. 105 f. Quotations from this work by permission of the publishers.

16. In a short but illuminating article, Jerome Brunner, "Freud and the Image of Man," *Partisan Review* (Summer, 1956).

17. Freud's definition of metapsychology is not completely satisfactory. He seems to mean by the term a psychology which is completely descriptive in the sense of including "economic," "dynamic," and "topographical" factors of explanation. Cf. *Beyond the Pleasure Principle* (New York and London: International Psychoanalytical Press, 1950), p. 1. In what follows I shall deal with Freud's metapsychology in this order: (1) the economics of personality (pleasure and reality principles), (2) the dynamics of motivation (love and death), and (3) the topography of the self (ego, id, super-ego).

18. Freud, *A General Introduction To Psychoanalysis*, p. 311. The classic sources for Freud's treatment of the economic principles of personality are *Beyond the Pleasure Principle*, pp. 1-8; and "Formulations Regarding the Two Principles in Mental Functioning," in *Collected Papers* (New York and London: International Psycho-analytical Press, 1925), IV, 13-21.

19. In using the word "instinct" to render the German *Trieb*, I bow to the usage of Freud's translators. The word does not imply immutability—obviously, since the whole Freudian theory is a commentary upon their mutability. It means rather "drive" or "impulse"—the oldest remnant of the psychical apparatus. In his 1915 paper, "Instincts and Their Vicissitudes," Freud defines an instinct as a source of stimulation originating within an organism, one against which no actions of flight avail. The classic sources for Freud's theory of the instincts are *Beyond the Pleasure Principle; The Ego and the Id* (London: Hogarth Press, 1927), pp. 54-66; *Collected Papers*, Vol. IV, pp. 60-83. A brief summary is in *An Outline of Psychoanalysis*, Ch. II.

20. *Collected Papers*, IV, 67.

21. *Ibid.*, IV, 81.

22. Freud, *Beyond the Pleasure Principle*, p. 46 f. Quotations from this work by permission of the Liveright Publishing Corporation.

23. *Ibid.*, p. 51.

24. *Ibid.*, p. 54.

25. *Ibid.*, p. 67.

26. See for example W. Bischler, "Schopenhauer and Freud: A Comparison," *The Psychoanalytic Quarterly*, Vol. VIII (1939), p. 88 ff.

27. Herbert Marcuse, *Eros and Civilization: A Philosophical Inquiry into Freud* (Boston: Beacon, 1955), p. 17.

28. In this brief account of the tragic I follow the suggestive papers in Henry Alonzo Myers, *Tragedy: A View of Life* (Ithaca: Cornell University Press, 1956). A more complicated (and romantic) doctrine is put forward in Karl Jaspers, *Tragedy Is Not Enough* (Boston: Beacon, 1952).

29. The classic sources for Freud's topology of the self are *The Ego and the Id*, and "The Anatomy of the Mental Personality," Ch. III of *New Introductory Lectures on Psychoanalysis*.

30. Freud, *New Introductory Lectures*, p. 103 f.

31. Freud, *The Ego and the Id*, p. 87.

32. It is, however, as Freud notes, a remarkable thing that the superego often develops a severity for which no example has been given by the real parents. His explanation is that actually the superego is the heir of the Oedipus complex. This means that the original guilt-ridden incestuous love of the child for its parent of the

opposite sex is sublimated and transformed into a mere identification with the father as ideal figure. This is, of course, not the complete story. See *The Ego and the Id*, p. 44 ff.

33. Freud, *An Outline of Psychoanalysis*, p. 62 ff.

34. Literary efforts to depict the analytic situation have grown by leaps and bounds over the past three decades. The one by Anais Nin (*Winter of Artifice*) is sensitive, if a trifle florid. A more ironical one occurs in Mary McCarthy's *The Company She Keeps*, and a more philosophical one in Arthur Koestler's *Arrival and Departure*.

35. Freud, *New Introductory Lectures*, p. 111 f.

36. Freud, *An Autobiographical Study*, p. 133 f.

37. Freud, *Civilization and Its Discontents* (London: Hogarth Press, 1946), p. 34. All quotations from this work by permission of the publishers.

38. It is interesting that Freud relegates these insights on work to a footnote, and also that he never returns to a more extended consideration of the psychology and sociology of work, for this is one of the most vulnerable spots in the whole of psychoanalytic theory. To say that work "has a greater effect than any other technique of living in the direction of binding the individual more closely to reality," seems to assume that this "reality" is good. But what if the reality principle at any particular time refers to only a historical, changing reality? Then Freudian theory would be in the position of Hegelian metaphysics, and its identification of rationality with the current reality would justify whatever was socially given. Current social reality of whatever sort would always be the representative of the reality principle, and attachment to the current institutional structure would be beyond question. I do not believe this was Freud's intention. But it is the consequence of his purely psychological approach to social alienation. At this level, not only Marx, but Adler and the revisionists and Herbert Marcuse have been more perceptive.

39. Freud, *Civilization and Its Discontents*, p. 46.

40. *The Journals of André Gide*, trans. Justin O'Brien (New York: Knopf, 1948), I, 24.

41. Freud, *The Future of an Illusion* (New York: Liveright, 1949), p. 9.

42. Freud, *Civilization and Its Discontents*, p. 59.

43. That Freud has Hobbes in mind is clear. In *The Future of an Illusion* (p. 25) occurs a perfect Freudian description of the state of nature with an outcome of Hobbesian despotism.

44. Freud's original treatment of this primal crime comes as an explanation of totemism in *Totem and Taboo* (see *The Basic Writings of Sigmund Freud*, particularly pp. 915-30). He himself summarizes his position in *Moses and Monotheism* (New York: Knopf, 1947), pp. 127-32, and it is upon this that I have chiefly drawn.

45. Thus Herbert Marcuse (*Eros and Civilization*, p. 60) says: "We use Freud's anthropological speculation only in this sense: for its *symbolic* value." Even more striking is the case of A. L. Kroeber, who, having demolished *Totem and Taboo* in 1920 in *The American Anthropologist*, twenty years later ("Totem and Taboo in Retrospect," *The American Journal of Sociology*, November, 1939) makes *amende honorable* by treating it now finally not as "historic truth" but as "abstract truth expressed through intuitive imagination."

46. Freud, *Civilization and Its Discontents*, p. 118.

47. *The Basic Writings of Sigmund Freud*, p. 927.

48. Freud, *Civilization and Its Discontents*, p. 85.

49. *Ibid.*, p. 102 f.

50. *Ibid.*, p. 136.

51. *Ibid.*, p. 138.

52. "The gift of the rings had a certain symbolical significance; it reminded us that our mutual relation had the same center of gravity. It made us feel that we belonged to a group within the group. . . ." Hanns Sachs, *Freud: Master and Friend* (Cambridge: Harvard University Press, 1946), p. 153.

53. Two very useful books dealing with the development and comparative aspects of the Freudian revolution are Gerald S. Blum, *Psychoanalytic Theories of Personality* (New York: McGraw-Hill, 1953); and Ruth Munroe, *Schools of Psychoanalytic Thought* (New York: Dryden Press, 1956).

54. Freud, *The Future of an Illusion*, p. 86.

55. *Ibid.*, p. 93.

56. My treatment is based largely upon Otto Rank, *Will Therapy and Truth and Reality* (New York: Knopf, 1950), Chs. XVIII and XIX.

57. *Ibid.*, p. 250.

58. *Ibid.*

59. *Ibid.*

60. *Ibid.*, p. 252.

61. *Ibid.*, p. 239.

62. Rank, *Beyond Psychology* (privately printed, 1941), p. 52. The entire essay in which this subject is discussed, "Psychology and Social Change," is of the greatest importance. Rank's distinction between the standpoint of theory and that of therapy needs much fuller consideration. Certainly the Freudian therapy assumes free will for the ego. In discussing the problem of therapeutic success (*The Ego and the Id*, footnote, p. 72), Freud makes this abundantly clear. "Perhaps it may depend, too, on whether the personality of the analyst allows of the patient's putting him in the place of his ego-ideal, and this involves a temptation for the analyst to play the part of prophet, saviour, and redeemer to the patient. Since the rules of analysis are diametrically opposed to the physician's making use of his personality in any such manner, it must be honestly confessed that here we have another limitation to the effectiveness of analysis; after all, analysis does not set out to abolish the possibility of morbid reactions, but to give the patient's ego *freedom* to choose one way or the other." But Rank is also correct that the phrase "to give the patient's ego *freedom* to choose one way or the other" accords ill with the weakness of the ego emphasized on pp. 78-82 of the same work.

63. My brief account of the revisionists comes primarily from the following: Karen Horney, *The Neurotic Personality of Our Time* (New York: W. W. Norton, 1937) and *New Ways in Psychoanalysis* (New York: W. W. Norton, 1942); and Erich Fromm, *Escape from Freedom* (New York: Farrar and Rinehart, 1941), and *Man for Himself* (New York: Rinehart, 1947). The most original criticism of the revisionists has come from a little-known article by Paul Goodman, "The Political Meaning of Some Recent Revisions of Freud," *Politics*, July, 1945. Many of the same points, more extensively treated, appear in Herbert Marcuse, *Eros and Civilization*, "Epilogue: Critique of Neo-Freudian Revisionism."

64. Arthur Koestler, *Arrival and Departure* (New York: Macmillan, 1944), p. 107. Quotations by permission of the publishers.

65. *Ibid.*, p. 177 f.

66. Freud, *An Autobiographical Study.*

67. Wallace Stevens, *The Collected Poems of Wallace Stevens* (New York: Knopf, 1954). Quoted by permission of the publisher.

68. Freud, *New Introductory Lectures*, p. 228 f.

CHAPTER VI

1. Jean-Paul Sartre, "Cartesian Freedom," in *Literary and Philosophical Essays*, trans. Annette Michelson (New York: Criterion Books, 1955), p. 169. Reprinted by permission of the publishers.

2. The ones referred to are: R. H. Tawney, *The Acquisitive Society* (New York: Harcourt, Brace, 1921); John Dewey, *Liberalism and Social Action* (New York: Putnam's, 1935); Georges Sorel, *Reflections on Violence* (New York: P. Smith, 1941); Karl Jaspers, *Man in the Modern Age* (London: Hogarth Press, 1933); José Ortega y Gasset, *The Revolt of the Masses* (New York: W. W. Norton, 1932); Gabriel Marcel, *The Philosophy of Existence* (London: Harvill Press, 1948).

3. Dewey, *Liberalism and Social Action*.

4. V. I. Lenin, *Marx, Engels, Marxism: A Collection of Articles* (New York: International Publishers, 1931), p. 50. This article, "The Three Sources and Three Component Parts of Marxism," is also translated by Max Eastman as part of the Introduction to his Modern Library edition of *Capital, The Communist Manifesto and Other Writings by Karl Marx* (New York: Random House, 1932). I prefer the International translation. Quotations from this book by permission of the publishers.

5. *Ibid*. My italics.

6. This essay appears in the *Marx-Engels Gesamtausgabe*, Bd. I, Abt. 3 (Berlin: Marx-Engels Institut, 1932). I have used the first English translation by Ria Stone (mimeographed, 1947) as a foundation; but because of the unavailability of the German edition, I have corrected it by reference to the French translation of J. Molitor (Karl Marx, *Oeuvres Philosophiques* [Paris, 1953], Tome VI, pp 47-49).

7. Karl Marx, *Capital* (Chicago: C. H. Kerr, 1909), Vol. I, p. 25. References are to this edition, and quotations are reprinted by permission of Random House.

8. *Ibid*., I, 787.

9. The entire subject is brilliantly treated in an essay of 1844, "Alienated Labor," which appears with the other early writings in Marx, *Gesamtausgabe*, I, 3. I quote a characteristic passage from that essay (also in the translation of Ria Stone): "The devaluation of the world of men proceeds in direct proportion to the increased utilization of the world of things. Work produces not only commodities: it produces itself and the worker as a commodity. . . . The object which labor produces, its product, is opposed to it as an alien essence, as a power independent of the producer. . . . In this economic condition the realization of labor appears as the loss of reality of the worker . . . as alienation, estrangement. . . . The realization of Labor appears so much as loss of reality that the worker is depersonalized even to the point of starvation."

10. Marx, *Capital*, I, 83.

11. Marx, *Capital, The Communist Manifesto*, etc., p. 323 f. References to *The Communist Manifesto* are from this edition.

12. This problem is dealt with exhaustively by Vernon Venable in *Human Nature: The Marxian View* (New York: Knopf, 1946). That Marx held to any concept of "a permanent, absolute, single, and changeless entity that is man" is categorically denied (p. 19 f).

13. Marx, *The Critique of Political Economy* (Chicago: C. H. Kerr, 1911), p. 11.

14. *The Communist Manifesto*, p. 338.

15. The treatment of objectivity and the social grounding of ideas is the essence of "*Wissenssoziologie*," developed in Germany since the turn of the century largely under the influence of Marx. Important and characteristic works in the tradition are Max Weber, *Aus den Schriften zur Religionssoziologie* (Frankfurt: G. K. Schauer, 1948); Georg Simmel, *Philosophische Kultur* (Leipzig: A. Kröner, 1919); and Max Scheler, *Die Wissensformen und die Gesellschaft* (Leipzig, 1926). In English the best known work is Karl Mannheim, *Ideology and Utopia* (New York: Harcourt, Brace, 1936).

16. Mannheim, *Ideology and Utopia*, pp. 35, 36. Reprinted by permission of Harcourt, Brace.

17. *The Communist Manifesto*.

18. *The Last Essays of Georges Bernanos*, trans. Joan and Barry Ulanov (Chicago: Henry Regnery, 1955), p. 7. Reprinted by permission of the publishers.

19. The details of Marx's economic philosophy have been excellently treated in two articles by Abram L. Harris: "The Social Philosophy of Karl Marx" (*Ethics*, April, 1948); and "Utopian Elements in Marx's Thought" (*Ethics*, January, 1950).

20. *The Communist Manifesto*, p. 328.

21. *Ibid.*, p. 333 f.

22. Dewey, *Freedom and Culture* (New York: Putnam's, 1936), p. 78.

23. Quoted in Edmund Wilson, *To the Finland Station: A Study in the Writing and Acting of History* (New York: Doubleday, 1955), p. 384. Wilson's book is a classic literary treatment of the lives and writings of Marx, Engels, Lenin, and Trotsky, as well as their immediate predecessors. Further biographical and historical material is provided in the excellent book by Bertram D. Wolfe, *Three Who Made a Revolution: A Biographical History* (Boston: Beacon, 1955).

24. Lenin, *Materialism and Empirio-Criticism: Critical Notes Concerning a Reactionary Philosophy* (Vol. XIII of *The Collected Works of V. I. Lenin* [New York: International Publishers, 1927], p. 2). All references to this work are to this edition, referred to as *Materialism*.

25. Lenin, *Materialism*, pp. 113, 114.

26. An excellent account of the background of *Materialism and Empirio-Criticism* and the Machiavellian opportunism expressed by the date of its publication is given in Wolfe, *Three Who Made a Revolution*, Ch. XXIX, "Lenin as Philosopher." This title is slightly misleading, as little is said of the content of the work itself. It cannot be claimed, surely, that *Materialism and Empirio-Criticism* is philosophically original, and everything which Wolfe asserts about its authoritarianism and its use of epithet and invective is true. But in my opinion he underestimates the importance for Marxism of the epistemology which Lenin defends. This in itself is worth attention.

27. F. Engels, *Ludwig Feuerbach and the Outcome of Classical German Philosophy* (New York: International Publishers, 1941), p. 20 ff.

28. Lenin, *Materialism*, pp. 8, 9, 23, 69, 77, *et passim*.

29. *Ibid.*, p. 31.

30. *Ibid.*, p. 47.

31. Some of the problems raised here are interestingly handled by G. A. Paul, "Lenin's Theory of Perception," *Analysis*, Vol. V, No. 5 (1938). His purpose is not to deny that Lenin's theory of perception is a correct description, but only that it plays the part in ordinary life and science which Lenin thinks it does.

32. Lenin, *Materialism*, pp. 125, 143, 153.

33. What A. S. Eddington frankly calls "the idealistic tinge of my convictions of the physical world" (*The Nature of the Physical World* [London: Cambridge University Press, 1929], Preface) and what Ernest Nagel refers to as "views . . . according to which the laws of nature can be deduced from the constitution of the human mind" (*Logic without Metaphysics* [Glencoe, Ill.: Free Press, 1957], p. 318) have been subjected to a sharp and clear-headed criticism by L. Susan Stebbing in *Philosophy and the Physicists* (London: Methuen, 1937). In her preface Miss Stebbing instances Lenin's criticism of the idealistic slant of "the new physics" of his time, and her work three decades later is in the spirit of what he accomplished in Ch. V of *Materialism and Empirio-Criticism*. In other respects also one is frequently astonished at the modernity of many of Lenin's strictures. He criticizes Avenarius' treatment of the body-mind problem (*Materialism*, p. 66) in terms which exactly parallel present naturalistic criticisms of Whitehead, and he criticizes Avenarius' *Kritik der reinen Erfahrung* (*Materialism*, p. 66) in terms which are almost exactly those of modern critics of Dewey.

34. Lenin, *Materialism*, p. 221.

35. *Ibid.*, p. 311.

36. Georges Sorel, *Reflections on Violence*, trans. T. E. Hulme (Glencoe, Ill. Free Press, 1950), p. 32. The following quotations from this work reprinted by permission of the publishers.

37. *Ibid.*, p. 130 f.

38. *Ibid.*, p. 297.

39. *Ibid.*, p. 164.

40. *Ibid.*, p. 295.

41. Georges Sorel, *Réflexions sur la violence* (Paris: Libraire Marcel Rivière, 1946), p. 442. There is no real evidence as to Lenin's opinion of Sorel. It is true that in the only discoverable reference (*Materialism*, p. 249) Lenin calls him "the notorious muddlehead, Georges Sorel," but the context of the reference is Sorel's book *Les Métaphysiques des physiciens modernes*, and not *Reflections on Violence*. Lenin is annoyed that Sorel has found some ground of reconciliation between Abel Rey (with whom Lenin agrees) and Poincaré (whom he attacks). This alone was enough to call out his usual intemperate invective.

42. Lenin, *State and Revolution* (New York: International Publishers, 1932), p. 8. Quotations from this work by permission of the publishers.

43. *Ibid.*, p. 17.

44. *Ibid.*, p. 23 f.

45. From Arthur Koestler, *Darkness At Noon* (New York: Macmillan, 1941). Reprinted by permission of the publishers.

46. Lenin, *State and Revolution*, p. 43.

47. *Ibid.*, p. 74.

48. *Ibid.*

49. This notion of "the dangerous survival of the old in the new" which Lenin presents in *State and Revolution* has become an institutionalized Soviet attitude. The generalization of suspicion, the idea that each individual carries within him a whole set of potentially dangerous attitudes with a capacity for complete betrayal, and that the masses may still be corrupted by lingering vestiges of the bourgeois way of life are probably due to anxiety because the revolution has never completely succeeded.

Cf. Margaret Mead *et al.*, *Soviet Attitudes toward Authority* (New York: McGraw-Hill, 1951).

The old surviving in the new has another slant, also. Gide, who in 1931-32 had such high hopes for the U.S.S.R., in 1936 paid it a visit and returned to France a disillusioned man (*Journal*, September 3, 1936); *The Journals of André Gide*, trans. Justin O'Brien (New York: Knopf, 1948). In his *Journal*, Summer, 1937, he refers to *State and Revolution*, to the sentence where Lenin says, "Until now there has not been a revolution that in the long run has not led to a strengthening of the administrative mechanism." This, says Gide, is as true in 1937 as it was in 1917 when it was written!

50. Lenin, *State and Revolution*, p. 68.

51. Koestler, *Darkness at Noon*.

52. This is brought out clearly in S. M. Daugert, *The Philosophy of Thorstein Veblen* (New York: Columbia University Press, 1950). The indispensable work on Veblen is Joseph Dorfman, *Thorstein Veblen and His America* (New York: Viking, 1934). A recent contribution is David Riesman, *Thorstein Veblen: A Critical Interpretation* (New York: Scribner's, 1953). Riesman is interesting on Veblen's work, but his somewhat hostile psychoanalysis of the man is unconvincing. The periodical literature is enormous, but the following are valuable: Joseph Dorfman, "The Satire of Thorstein Veblen's Theory of the Leisure Class," *Political Science Quarterly* (1932); T. W. Adorno, "Veblen's Attacks on Culture," *Studies in Philosophy and Social Science* (1941); Abram L. Harris, "Veblen as Social Philosopher: A Reappraisal," *Ethics* (1953).

53. Dorfman, *Thorstein Veblen and His America*, p. 500.

54. Thorstein Veblen, *Essays in Our Changing Order*, ed. L. Ardzrooni (New York: Viking, 1934), p. 403.

55. Veblen's calm and aloof exposition of Marxism appears in two lectures which he delivered at Harvard in April, 1906, entitled, "The Socialist Economics of Karl Marx." They have been reprinted in Veblen, *The Place of Science in Modern Civilization* (New York: Viking, 1919). The passage cited is on pp. 436-37. Reprinted by permission of the publishers.

56. Veblen, *The Theory of Business Enterprise* (New York: Scribner's, 1935), p. 1. Reprinted by permission of the publishers.

57. *Ibid.*, p. 306.

58. *Ibid.*, p. 309.

59. The more one reads Veblen, the more one is impressed by certain similarities between his position and Comte's, particularly the later Comte of *Positive Polity*. The distinction between the scientific and the animistic mentality, the social power of a Soviet of technicians, the reading of the curve of societal movement from war to industry and from the predatory to the altruistic (in Veblen the "parental bent") are held in common. The influence of Herbert Spencer upon Veblen is acknowledged (he is supposed to have derived this in part from W. G. Sumner, at Yale) and, of course, most of Spencer's ideas are derived from Comte. But it would be interesting to know in detail whether Veblen knew Comte directly, whether he learned about him also from Sumner, or whether his sole source of Comte's ideas is Spencer.

60. Veblen, *The Engineers and the Price System* (New York: Viking, 1921), p. 166. Reprinted by permission of the publishers.

61. The details of Veblen's instinct theory run through his works like a tangled

but ubiquitous thread. Its most straightforward (but incomplete) presentation occurs in *The Instinct of Workmanship* (New York: Viking, 1922).

62. From John Dos Passos, *The Big Money* (Boston: Houghton, Mifflin, 1936). Reprinted by permission of the publishers.

63. See, for example, Leo Lowenthal, "Biographies in Popular Magazines," *Radio Research* (1943). In an experiment in content analysis of *The Saturday Evening Post* and *Collier's* from 1901-41, Lowenthal discovered that the interest in biographical studies has increased markedly and that the older interest in Ford, Rockefeller, and the other "heroes of production" has shifted to headliners of the movies, the ball park, and the night clubs; in short to the "heroes of consumption."

64. Veblen, *The Theory of the Leisure Class* (New York: Random House, 1934), p. 13 f.

65. *Ibid.*, pp. 28, 29.

66. This is especially stressed by David Riesman in *The Lonely Crowd* (New Haven: Yale University Press, 1950). Although Riesman in his book on Veblen expresses certain reservations about Veblen, the fact is that without Veblen *The Lonely Crowd* would have been impossible. Although it is psychological in orientation and interested in types of character socially produced, in so far as it explores a society in an age of consumption, it is hardly more than a series of important, valuable, and imaginative footnotes to *The Theory of the Leisure Class*.

67. Veblen, *The Theory of the Leisure Class*, p. 84.

68. F. Scott Fitzgerald, *The Great Gatsby* (New York: Scribner's, 1925). Reprinted by permission of the publishers.

CHAPTER VII

1. These advances in science and their philosophical implications have produced a vast literature. Of particular interest to philosophers are the following classic treatments: E. A. Burtt, *The Metaphysical Foundations of Modern Physical Science* (New York: Harcourt, Brace, 1932); A. N. Whitehead, *Science and the Modern World* (New York: Macmillan, 1923); R. G. Collingwood, *The Idea of Nature* (London: Oxford University Press, 1945).

2. Hans Reichenbach, *Philosophical Foundations of Quantum Mechanics* (Berkeley: University of California Press, 1949).

3. For Einstein see his *Relativity: The Special and the General Theory* (London: Methuen, 1920); *The Meaning of Relativity* (Princeton: Princeton University Press, 1953); with Leopold Infeld, *The Evolution of Physics* (New York: Simon and Schuster, 1938); *Essays in Science* (New York: Philosophical Library, 1934); *Albert Einstein: Philosopher-Scientist*, ed. P. A. Schilpp (New York: Tudor, 1941; hereafter cited as Schilpp); Max Born, *Einstein's Theory of Relativity* (London: Methuen, 1924); A. S. Eddington, *Space, Time and Gravitation* (Cambridge: Cambridge University Press, 1929); C. D. Broad, *Scientific Thought* (New York: Harcourt, Brace, 1952); Ernst Cassirer, *Einstein's Theory of Relativity* (Chicago: Open Court, 1923). See also Reichenbach, *Philosophic Foundations of Quantum Mechanics*; Bertrand Russell, *The Analysis of Matter* (New York: Dover, 1954); A. N. Whitehead, *The Principle of Relativity: With Applications to Physical Science* (London: Cambridge University Press, 1922); A. S. Eddington, *The Nature of the Physical World* (London: Cambridge University Press, 1929); P. W. Bridgman, *The Logic of Modern Physics* (New York: Macmillan, 1927).

4. Lucien Price, *Dialogues of Alfred North Whitehead* (Boston: Little, Brown, 1956), p. 277. Reprinted by permission of the publishers.

5. Einstein, *Essays in Science*, p. 8. All quotations from this work are reprinted by permission of the estate of Albert Einstein. A simple authoritative account of the slow emergence of difficulties in the Newtonian picture occurs in Einstein and Infeld, *The Evolution of Physics*, Part II, "The Decline of the Mechanical View." See also Born, *Einstein's Theory of Relativity*, Chs. IV, V.

6. Louis de Broglie, "A General Survey of the Scientific Work of Albert Einstein," in Schilpp, pp. 112, 113. P. A. Schilpp (Editor of The Library of Living Philosophers) has given permission for the quotations.

7. Hans Reichenbach, "The Philosophical Significance of the Theory of Relativity," Schilpp, p. 302.

8. Einstein, *The Meaning of Relativity*, pp. 30 f. Reprinted by permission of Princeton University Press.

9. A closely reasoned account of the two kinds of mass, gravitational and inertial, and of their roles, both in the traditional kinematics and in the general theory of relativity, can be found in Broad, *Scientific Thought*, pp. 169 ff. Broad's account is more informing (because less metaphorical) than that given by Einstein and Infeld, *The Evolution of Physics*, Ch. III.

10. Broad, *Scientific Thought*, p. 186.

11. Thus Einstein says: "According to the general theory of relativity the geometrical properties of space are not independent, but they are determined by matter. Thus we can draw conclusions about the geometrical structure of the universe only if we base our considerations on the state of the matter as being something that is known." *Relativity: The Special and the General Theory*, p. 113.

12. Schilpp, p. 166. Werner Heisenberg makes the same point: "Although the theory of relativity makes the greatest of demands on the ability for abstract thought, still it fulfills the traditional requirements of science in so far as it permits a division of the world into subject and object (observer and observed) and hence a clear formulation of the law of causality. This is the very point at which the difficulties of the quantum theory begin." *The Physical Principles of the Quantum Theory* (New York: Dover, 1950), p. 2.

13. The evidence for both views is briefly and clearly summarized in Henry Margenau, *The Nature of Physical Reality: A Philosophy of Modern Physics* (New York: McGraw-Hill, 1950), pp. 313-20.

14. Schilpp, p. 210. Excellent statements of the nature and results of quantum mechanics are to be found in Reichenbach, *Philosophical Foundations of Quantum Mechanics*; Heisenberg, *The Physical Principles of the Quantum Theory*; and Margenau, *The Nature of Physical Reality*, Chs. 17, 18.

15. Although the principle of complementarity is appealed to in each of the above treatments of quantum mechanics, a clear and simple treatment occurs in Philipp Frank, *Between Physics and Philosophy* (Cambridge: Harvard University Press, 1941), Ch. VII, "Philosophical Misinterpretations of the Quantum Theory."

16. Einstein, "Remarks on Bertrand Russell's Theory of Knowledge" in Paul Arthur Schilpp, ed., *The Philosophy of Bertrand Russell* (New York: Tudor, 1951). Quotations by permission of P. A. Schilpp, Editor, The Library of Living Philosophers.

17. Reichenbach, *Philosophical Foundations of Quantum Mechanics*.

18. Einstein, "Remarks on Bertrand Russell's Theory of Knowledge."

19. Einstein, *Essays in Science*.

20. Schilpp, pp. 11, 12.

21. Henri Poincaré, *Science and Hypothesis* (New York: Science Press, 1905), Ch. V. Reprinted in *Readings in the Philosophy of Science*, ed. Herbert Feigl and May Broadbeck (New York: Appleton-Century-Crofts, 1953).

22. Reichenbach, "The Philosophical Significance of the Theory of Relativity," Schilpp, p. 293 ff.

23. Einstein, *Essays in Science*, p. 14.

24. Einstein, "Geometry and Experience," in *Sidelights of Relativity* (New York: E. P. Dutton, 1923), p. 27. Reprinted by permission of the publishers.

25. Einstein, *Essays in Science*, pp. 17, 18. A similar faith has been expressed by Max Planck: "The fact which led me to my science and filled me with enthusiasm for it, from my youth onwards, and which is by no means self-evident is that our laws of thinking coincide with the lawfulness in the course of the impressions which we receive from the external world, so that man is enabled to obtain enlightenment on this lawfulness by means of pure thinking. . . ." *Wissenschaftliche Selbstbiographie* (Leipzig, 1948).

26. See Einstein, "The Fundaments of Theoretical Physics," *Nature*, 1940. Reprinted in Feigl and Broadbeck, *Readings in the Philosophy of Science*.

27. This and the following quotation are from Feigl and Broadbeck, *Readings in the Philosophy of Science*, pp. 257, 258. Italics mine.

28. It is interesting that Einstein equates the "objective reality" of physical things with the idea of strict causal prediction. In "On the Method of Theoretical Physics" he said: "I still believe in the possibility of a model of reality—that is to say, of a theory which represents things themselves and not merely the probability of their occurrence." *Essays in Science*, p. 20. The matter is stated more accurately in a famous article: A. Einstein, B. Podolsky, N. Rosen, "Can Quantum Mechanical Description of Physical Reality Be Considered Complete?," *Physical Review*, Vol. 47 (1935), p. 777. The authors say: "The elements of the physical reality cannot be determined by a priori philosophical considerations, but must be found by an appeal to results of experiments and measurements. A comprehensive definition of reality, is, however, unnecessary for our purpose. We shall be satisfied with the following criterion, which we regard as reasonable. *If, without in any way disturbing a system, we can predict with certainty (i.e. with probability equal to unity) the value of a physical quantity, then there exists an element of physical reality corresponding to this physical quantity.*" It is a little like Planck's neat formulation: "Whatever can be measured exists."

29. Schilpp, p. 176.

30. Einstein, *Essays in Science*.

31. These matters are treated in the brief but very important article, "Geometry and Experience," cited above. The quotation which follows is from this article and is reprinted by permission of E. P. Dutton and Co.

32. Russell devotes the whole of Part II of *The Analysis of Matter* to "Physics and Perception," and Broad takes well over half of *Scientific Thought* to deal with "The Sensational and Perceptual Basis of Our Scientific Concepts."

33. Whitehead, "Theories of the Bifurcation of Nature," Ch. II of *The Concept of Nature* (London: Cambridge University Press, 1955).

34. Russell, *The Analysis of Matter*, p. 7. See especially Ch. XXXVII, "Physics and Neutral Monism." All quotations by permission of Dover Publications.

35. *Ibid.*, p. 284. Elsewhere Russell is seriously concerned over the differences between our perceptions of space and the properties which relativity theory assigns to physical space. This causes him to say, "If physics is correct, the relation of a percept to a physical object is very remote and mysterious." *Ibid.*, pp. 338, 339.

36. *Ibid.*, p. 355.

37. *Ibid.*, p. 402.

38. Whitehead, *The Principle of Relativity*, Ch. IV. The important early chapters of this work (now out of print) appear in *Alfred North Whitehead: An Anthology*, selected by F. S. C. Northrop and Mason W. Gross (New York: Cambridge University Press, 1953) and it is to this volume that I will refer. Reprinted by permission of the publishers.

39. Whitehead, *An Enquiry Concerning the Principles of Natural Knowledge* (London: Cambridge University Press, 1955), p. 4. Reprinted by permission of the publishers.

40. In his essay, "Space, Time and Relativity," appearing in Whitehead, *The Aims of Education* (New York: Mentor, 1956), p. 159.

41. One of Whitehead's most notable mathematical and philosophical achievements is the discovery of a method whereby the accurate concepts of science are defined in terms of perceptible objects and their relations. He calls it the method of *extensive abstraction*. It operates in such a way that points, straight lines, etc., are defined as series of converging volumes. For the details, see *An Enquiry Concerning the Principles of Natural Knowledge*, Part III, and *The Concept of Nature*, Ch. IV. Quotations from these books by permission of Cambridge University Press.

42. Whitehead, *Principles of Natural Knowledge*, pp. 98, 99. Ch. XVIII of this work, entitled "Rhythms," develops the theme further and applies it to percipient objects and living things.

43. Whitehead, *The Principle of Relativity*, p. 357.

44. Einstein, *Relativity: The Special and the General Theory*, pp. 5, 22. Italics mine. Reprinted by permission of Methuen and Co., Ltd.

45. This well-known point of view is expounded in Bridgman, *The Logic of Modern Physics*, and in *The Nature of Physical Theory* (Princeton: Princeton University Press, 1936).

46. See for example Rudolph Carnap, "Testability and Meaning," and Reichenbach, "The Verifiability Theory of Meaning," both reprinted in Feigl and Broadbeck, *Readings in the Philosophy of Science*. The entire movement is examined in Chapter IX below.

47. Charles S. Peirce, "How to Make Our Ideas Clear," *Popular Science Monthly*, 1878.

48. See A. S. Eddington, *The Nature of the Physical World*, Ch. XI ("World Building"), and Ch. XIV ("Causation"). Also instructive are Ch. XII ("Pointer Readings"), and Ch. XIII ("Reality"). Quotations from this work by permission of Cambridge University Press.

49. Eddington, *The Nature of the Physical World*, p. 244.

50. *Ibid.*, pp. 154, 155.

CHAPTER VIII

1. *The Philosophy of John Dewey*, in The Library of Living Philosophers, ed. Paul Arthur Schilpp (New York: Tudor, 1951), henceforth referred to as Schilpp. The

following quotation of Reichenbach is from p. 192. All quotations from this work reprinted by permission of P. A. Schilpp.

2. John Dewey, "From Absolutism to Experimentalism," in Vol. II of *Contemporary American Philosophy*, ed. G. P. Adams and W. P. Montague (New York: Macmillan, 1930), p. 19. Quotations by permission of George Allen and Unwin, Ltd.

3. Dewey's shift from idealism to instrumentalism has been charted interestingly and in detail by Morton G. White in *The Origins of Dewey's Instrumentalism* (New York: Columbia University Press, 1943).

4. Dewey, "From Absolutism to Experimentalism," p. 23. The brief quotations which precede this one are also from this autobiographical article.

5. This is not to say that the logical Dewey always approves of the logical Mill. Dewey's *Logic* is full of references to and criticisms of Mill's *Logic*. But, although critical, Dewey is essentially sympathetic, and for a very obvious reason. For Mill, like Dewey, is one of the very few who identify logic with methodology. Cf. Dewey, *Logic: The Theory of Inquiry* (New York: Holt, 1938), p. 5. This book will henceforth be referred to as *Logic*.

6. Dewey, "From Absolutism to Experimentalism."

7. The need for philosophic reconstruction is a theme developed throughout the body of Dewey's writings. The most succinct statements come in the title essay of *Philosophy and Civilization* (New York: Minton, Balch, 1931); "The Need for a Recovery of Philosophy," in *Creative Intelligence: Essays in the Pragmatic Attitude* (New York: Holt, 1917); and *Reconstruction in Philosophy* (Boston: Beacon, 1953), Chs. I, II, VIII. Quotations from *Reconstruction in Philosophy* by permission of the publishers.

8. Dewey, *Philosophy and Civilization*, p. 3. The other brief quotations in this paragraph are also from this work.

9. Dewey, *Reconstruction in Philosophy*, p. 8.

10. An interesting examination of this aspect of Dewey is provided by John Herman Randall, Jr., in "Dewey's Interpretation of the History of Philosophy," in Schilpp, pp. 77-102.

11. Dewey, *Creative Intelligence*, p. 65.

12. George Santayana, "Dewey's Naturalistic Metaphysics," Schilpp, p. 243.

13. Dewey, *Experience and Nature* (New York: W. W. Norton, 1929), p. 412.

14. *Ibid.*, p. 1a.

15. This has been stressed by two of Dewey's most important followers: Sidney Hook, in his excellent *The Metaphysics of Pragmatism* (Chicago: Open Court, 1927), p. 6; and Ernest Nagel, in his presidential address to the Eastern Division of the American Philosophical Association in 1954, "Naturalism Reconsidered," reprinted in his *Logic Without Metaphysics* (Glencoe, Ill.: Free Press, 1956). Nagel says (p. 6): "It is . . . unfortunate that in recent years naturalists in philosophy have so frequently permitted their allegiance to a . . . method of inquiry to obscure their substantive views on things in general. For it is the inclusive intellectual image of nature and man which naturalism supplies, that sets it off from other comprehensive philosophies. In my opinion of it, at any rate, naturalism embraces a generalized account of the cosmic scheme and of man's place in it as well as a logic of inquiry."

16. Wallace Stevens, *The Collected Poems of Wallace Stevens* (New York: Knopf, 1954). Reprinted by permission of the publisher.

17. This is the chief respect in which the philosophies of Dewey and Whitehead are alike. Both depend upon an appeal to immediate experience and a somewhat

obvious mistrust of abstractions viewed as prime realities. Therefore Whitehead's "fallacy of misplaced concreteness" (*Science and the Modern World*, p. 72) is the exact counterpart of Dewey's "fallacy of selective emphasis" (*Experience and Nature*, p. 27).

18. Dewey, *Experience and Nature*, p. 21. The following brief quotations are from pp. 22-23 of this work.

19. This is the kind of criticism which Arthur Murphy makes. See his "Dewey's Epistemology and Metaphysics," Schilpp, p. 223: "To take concreteness in this sense as the measure of individual reality, and abstractness as evidence of relational or instrumental character *in nature* is to make the special conditions under which a sentient organism gets into connection with things the measure of their reality. It is the basis of every sort of panpsychism and animism, but hardly for an empirical naturalism." Murphy's remarks would have applied equally to Whitehead.

20. Santayana, "Dewey's Naturalistic Metaphysics," p. 251.

21. Dewey, *Experience and Nature*, p. 421. Italics mine.

22. *Ibid.*, pp. 20, 21.

23. This point, briefly mentioned in *Experience and Nature*, becomes the starting-point of *The Quest for Certainty* (New York: Minton, Balch, 1929), written four years later. *The Quest for Certainty* begins with the distinction between two ways of achieving security in a world of hazards—the method of religion and the method of the arts and sciences—and it shows how ancient philosophy (particularly Plato and Aristotle) threw its weight against the latter in its "search for the immutable," through its invidious distinction between the changing world and the realm of true being, its enthronement of pure knowing as opposed to its depreciation of practice. The burden of the work is an emphasis upon techniques for the control of nature, and a proposal for "the naturalization of intelligence" in the service of "the construction of good." What is particularly interesting in the first few chapters of this book is the dependence upon the ideas of Veblen. Dewey's treatment of ancient philosophy is conditioned by his division of Greek society into an artisan and a leisure class, and he derives the distinction between matters of fact and essences, and the Greek preference for knowing over doing, from the characteristic preoccupation of a leisured aristocracy. *The Quest for Certainty* is excellent evidence that Dewey's stature as a social philosopher is due not only to his specific treatments of social problems, but also to the way in which sociological considerations keep cropping up in even the most theoretical treatments of metaphysics and the history of philosophy.

24. Dewey, *Experience and Nature*, p. 42.

25. *Ibid.*, pp. 65-67.

26. *Ibid.*, p. 68.

27. See Nagel's essay of this title in his *Logic Without Metaphysics*.

28. Dewey, *Experience and Nature*, p. 73.

29. *Ibid.*, p. 85.

30. *The Collected Poems of Wallace Stevens*.

31. Dewey, *Experience and Nature*, p. 96.

32. *Ibid.*, p. 108.

33. *Ibid.*, pp. 109, 110.

34. *Ibid.*, p. 146.

35. Eddington, *The Nature of the Physical World*, pp. ix f. and 316 f.

36. Dewey, *Experience and Nature*, p. 170.

37. *Ibid.* It is clear that the account of personality as a resultant of social interaction, of the self as a social emergent, and of the emergence of mind in the "role
playing" which speech permits (as outlined in *Experience and Nature*, Chs. V, VI)
is closely related to the more detailed and extensive social behaviorism of George
Herbert Mead, Dewey's close friend and colleague, as presented in his posthumous
Mind, Self and Society, edited by Charles W. Morris (Chicago: University of
Chicago Press, 1934). Quotations by permission of the publisher. Mead's insistence
that "the self as that which can be an object to itself is essentially a social structure,
and it arises in social experience" (p. 140), and his constant reminder that "the
language process is essential for the development of the self" (p. 135) are identical
with Dewey's position. Both are Darwinian in finding the social to emerge from a
process of interacting biological organisms; both are behavioristic in tracing the
genesis of mind and self to the internalization of vocal gestures become language.
The full pragmatic flowering is to be found in Mead. But it is fair to say that the
entire framework of the position is contained in *Experience and Nature*.

38. Dewey, *Experience and Nature*, p. 204.

39. *Ibid.*, p. 222.

40. *Ibid.*, p. 242 f.

41. *Ibid.*, p. 244.

42. From Luigi Pirandello, *One, None and A Hundred Thousand* (New York:
E. P. Dutton, 1933). Quotations by permission of the heirs of the Pirandello estate.

43. Mead, *Mind, Self and Society*, p. 142.

44. Pirandello, *One, None and A Hundred Thousand*.

45. Dewey, *The Quest for Certainty*, p. 255.

46. Dewey, *Experience and Nature*, p. 396.

47. Dewey, *The Quest for Certainty*, p. 265.

48. Dewey, *Experience and Nature*, p. 407.

49. In the essay "What Pragmatism Means by Practical," Dewey, *Essays in Experimental Logic* (New York: Dover, n.d.), p. 203.

50. Dewey, *Essays in Experimental Logic*, p. 31.

51. Dewey, *Logic*, pp. 3, 4.

52. Charles Sanders Peirce, "The Fixation of Belief," *Popular Science Monthly*
(1877).

53. *Logic*, p. 104. Russell says wickedly: "I cannot but think that this definition
does not adequately express Dr. Dewey's meaning, since it would apply, for instance,
to the operations of a drill sergeant in transforming a collection of raw recruits into
a regiment, or of a bricklayer transforming a heap of bricks into a house, and yet
it would be impossible to say that the drill sergeant is 'inquiring' into the recruits,
or the bricklayer into the bricks." The simple addition of the word "cognitive" would
do the trick, for once the conversion of recruits or bricks was seen as a problem in
the mind of the sergeant or bricklayer, no difficulty would remain. Russell's remarks
do point up that the problematic aspect is necessarily cognitively perceived if "inquiry" is to be used in the usual sense.

54. The development of Dewey's value theory can be found in a series of stages:
(1) "The Logic of Judgments of Practice," *Essays in Experimental Logic*; (2) *Logic*,
Ch. IX, "Judgments of Practice: Evaluation;" (3) *Theory of Valuation* (Chicago:
University of Chicago Press, 1939); (4) "Some Questions About Value," *The
Journal of Philosophy*, XLI (1944). Also relevant are articles in the latter: "Valu-
ation, Judgments and Immediate Quality," and "Further as to Valuation as Judg-

ment." These last two and cognate material constitute Part III of Dewey's *Problems of Men* (New York: Philosophical Library, 1946). Permission to quote from Dewey's *Theory of Valuation* has been given by the publishers.

55. Dewey, *Essays in Experimental Logic*, p. 346.

56. *Ibid.*, p. 364.

57. Dewey, *Logic*, p. 179. My italics.

58. Dewey, *Theory of Valuation*, p. 30.

59. *Ibid.*, pp. 57, 58.

60. *Ibid.*, pp. 64, 65.

61. Dewey, *The Quest for Certainty*, p. 271.

62. *Ibid.*, p. 273.

63. Schilpp, pp. 366-67. The subsequent reply of Dewey is on p. 594 f.

64. Dewey, *Reconstruction in Philosophy*, p. 141. The same point runs through Dewey's moral theory. See *Ethics* with J. F. Tufts; (New York: Holt, 1932), Ch. XV, "The Moral Self;" and *Human Nature and Conduct* (New York: Random House, 1930), III, 6, "The Nature of Aims," and IV, 1, "The Good of Activity." Chapter VII of *Reconstruction in Philosophy* is perhaps the most succinct treatment.

65. Jean-Paul Sartre, *Existentialism and Humanism*, trans. Philip Mairet (London: Methuen, 1948), p. 52 f.

66. Dewey, *Reconstruction in Philosophy*, p. 151.

67. Dewey, *Freedom and Culture* (New York: Putnam's, 1939), p. 62. Reprinted by permission of the publishers.

68. This whole question has been subtly considered in an article previously cited in Chapter II: Charner Perry, "Knowledge as a Basis for Social Reform," *The International Journal of Ethics* (April, 1935). Most of the crucial questions are raised here, although they are somewhat encumbered by historical reference to doctrines of "natural rights" and "natural law."

69. Dewey himself has not been unaware of these difficulties. He does, for example, specifically consider the matter of management by trained technicians as opposed to the apparatus of political consent. (*The Public and Its Problems* [New York: Holt, 1927], pp. 124, 125. Quotations from this work by permission of the publisher.) But the issue remains unsolved.

70. Dewey, *Liberalism and Social Action* (New York: Putnam's, 1935), pp. 54, 55. Reprinted by permission of the publishers.

71. From *The New Republic* (Dec. 19, 1928). Reprinted in *Characters and Events* (New York: Holt, 1929), Vol. I, p. 424.

72. Dewey's chief works in social philosophy are: *The Public and Its Problems; Individualism, Old and New* (New York: Minton, Balch, 1930); *Liberalism and Social Action;* and *Freedom and Culture*. The first was produced when he was 68, the last in his eightieth year. Reading them over, one has the sense that the last three are more dated than the first—more *ad hoc. Individualism, Old and New* arose out of the economic crisis of the great depression. *Liberalism and Social Action* was occasioned by conservative attacks upon the New Deal in America. *Freedom and Culture* was the democratic answer to the joint totalitarian threats of Fascism and Communism just prior to the Second World War. It is my belief that *The Public and Its Problems* remains Dewey's most comprehensive work in the field, and it is upon it, therefore, that I shall chiefly rely.

73. Dewey, *The Public and Its Problems*, p. 98.

74. *Ibid.*, p. 142.

75. *Ibid.*, p. 184. But even here Dewey remains somehow deeply committed to the face-to-face community of inquiry. He says (*ibid.*, p. 218): "Systematic and continuous inquiry into all the conditions which affect association and their dissemination in print is a precondition of the creation of a true public. But it and its results are but tools after all. Their final actuality is accomplished in face-to-face relationships by means of direct give and take. Logic in its fulfillment recurs to the primitive sense of the word: dialogue. Ideas which are not communicated, shared, and reborn in expression are but soliloquy, and soliloquy is but broken and imperfect thought."

76. Dewey, *Individualism, Old and New*, pp. 82, 89, 90.

77. Dewey, *Liberalism and Social Action*, p. 27.

78. Dewey, *Freedom and Culture*, pp. 74-102.

CHAPTER IX

1. See *Opuscules et fragments inédits de Leibniz*, ed. Couturat (Paris: Félix Alcan, 1903), pp. 16 ff.

2. The metaphysical presuppositions which underlie the principle of induction, as well as the role which they played in the philosophy of the seventeenth century, has been interestingly, if briefly, treated by Whitehead. See *Science and the Modern World* (New York: Macmillan, 1925) Ch. III, and *Adventures of Ideas* (New York: Macmillan, 1933), Ch. VII.

3. These phrases are the titles of two articles: "Logic without Ontology," by Ernest Nagel (reprinted in *Logic without Metaphysics*, Glencoe, Ill.: Free Press, 1956, p. 55 ff.), and "Scientific Method without Metaphysical Presuppositions," by Herbert Feigl, *Philosophical Studies*, V, 2 (February, 1954). The literature is enormous, but the following selection is especially valuable. On logic: R. Carnap, *Meaning and Necessity* (Chicago: University of Chicago Press, 1947); *Foundations of Logic and Mathematics* (Chicago: University of Chicago Press, 1939); and the following articles: W. C. Kneale, "Are Necessary Truths True by Convention?," *Aristotelian Society, Supplement to the Proceedings* (1947); W. V. Quine, "Truth by Convention," in *Philosophical Essays for A. N. Whitehead* (London and New York: Longmans, Green, 1936). On induction: R. Carnap, *Logical Foundations of Probability* (Chicago: University of Chicago Press, 1950); W. Kneale, *Probability and Induction* (New York: Oxford University Press, 1949); and the following articles by H. Reichenbach: "On the Justification of Induction," *Journal of Philosophy* (1940); "The Logical Foundations of the Concept of Probability," in Herbert Feigl and May Broadbeck, *Readings in the Philosophy of Science* (New York: Appleton-Century-Crofts, 1953).

4. Nagel, *Logic without Metaphysics*, p. 57. Quotations from this work by permission of The Free Press, Glencoe, Ill.

5. *Philosophical Studies* (February, 1954), p. 25. Reprinted by permission of the University of Minnesota Press.

6. Wittgenstein, *Tractatus Logico-Philosophicus* (London: Routledge and Kegan Paul; New York: Humanities Press, 1955), p. 77 (4.112). Reprinted by permission of the publisher.

7. Hans Reichenbach, *The Rise of Scientific Philosophy* (Berkeley: University of California Press, 1956), p. vii. Reprinted by permission of the publishers.

8. "The progress of mankind proceeds by devious paths. The shift from the bright

Hellenic age, whose final period centered in Athens, to the Hellenistic age, with Alexandria as its intellectual capital, corresponds to a new direction of constructive genius. The special sciences were founded. Their principles were defined, their methods were determined, appropriate deductions were solicited. Learning was stabilized. It was furnished with methodologies, and was handed over to University professors of the modern type. Doctors of Medicine, Mathematicians, Astronomers, Grammarians, Theologians, for more than six hundred years dominated the schools of Alexandria, issuing text-books, treatises, controversies, and dogmatic definitions. Literature was replaced by Grammar, and Speculation by the Learned Tradition." Whitehead, *Adventures of Ideas*, p. 133.

9. Frank P. Ramsey, *The Foundations of Mathematics and Other Logical Essays* (London: Routledge and Kegan Paul; New York: Humanities Press, 1950), p. 290. Reprinted by permission of the publishers.

10. Wittgenstein, *Tractatus*, 6.124. Compare the many suggestions along the same line in p. 157-71 of this work.

11. The best historical accounts of the Vienna Circle are: Jørgen Jørgensen, *The Development of Logical Empiricism* (Chicago: University of Chicago Press, 1951); Victor Kraft, *The Vienna Circle: The Origin of Neo-Positivism* (New York: Philosophical Library, 1953); Herbert Feigl, "Logical Empiricism," in *Twentieth Century Philosophy* (New York: Philosophical Library, 1943); and Otto Neurath, *Le Développement du cercle de Vienne et l'avenir de l'empirisme logique* (Paris, 1935). For developments at Cambridge, see C. D. Broad, "The Local Historical Background of Contemporary Cambridge Philosophy," in *British Philosophy in the Mid-Century* (New York: Macmillan, 1957); J. O. Urmson, *Philosophical Analysis: Its Development between the Two World Wars* (London: Oxford University Press, 1956). General elementary treatments of logical empiricism abound. Typical are: A. J. Ayer, *Language, Truth and Logic* (London: Victor Gollancz, 1936); Richard von Mises, *Positivism: A Study in Human Understanding* (New York: Braziller, 1956); and Hans Reichenbach, *The Rise of Scientific Philosophy* (Berkeley: University of California Press, 1956). A more advanced although somewhat dated critical study is Julius R. Weinberg, *An Examination of Logical Positivism* (New York: Harcourt, Brace, 1936).

12. G. Frege, *The Foundations of Arithmetic*, English trans. J. L. Austin, with German text (London: Oxford University Press, 1953), p. 99e. More of Frege in English is *Translations from the Philosophical Writings of Gottlieb Frege*, by Peter Geach and Max Black (London: Oxford University Press, 1952).

13. Ernst Mach, *Die Analyse der Empfindungen* (Jena: G. Fisher, 1922), pp. 1-31.

14. Attacks upon the foundations of logical empiricism are continual. The most recent to flutter the dovecotes of positivism was the 1950 article of W. V. Quine, "Two Dogmas of Empiricism," read to the Eastern Division of the American Philosophical Association at Toronto in December of that year. It was an assault upon the distinction between analytic and synthetic truths. Positivists were not slow to answer. Characteristic were Gustav Bergmann's "Two Cornerstones of Empiricism" (1951), reprinted in his *The Metaphysics of Logical Positivism* (New York: Scribner's, 1954) and Herbert Feigl's "The Philosophy of Science of Logical Empiricism," read at the International Congress for Philosophy of Science, held in Zurich, August, 1954.

15. A reconsideration and modification of the principle of verifiability formed the

basis of an American Philosophical Association presidential address as late as December 1956. See David Rynin, "Vindication of Logical Positivism," in *Proceedings of the American Philosophical Association*, Vol. XXX (1956-57).

16. I have in mind here nothing more exact than such a sequence of works as: for Russell, *Principia Mathematica* (1910-13), *Our Knowledge of the External World* (1929), *An Inquiry into Meaning and Truth* (1940); and for Carnap, *Der Logische Aufbau der Welt* (1928), *The Logical Syntax of Language* (1937), *Foundations of Logic and Mathematics* (1939).

17. See Russell, *The Principles of Mathematics* (London: Cambridge University Press, 1903); and with A. N. Whitehead, *Principia Mathematica* (London: Cambridge University Press, 1910-13). An interesting treatment throwing light on the logical-empiricist interpretation of this latter work is Hans Reichenbach, "Bertrand Russell's Logic," in *The Philosophy of Bertrand Russell*, ed. P. A. Schilpp (New York: Tudor, 1951).

18. Russell, *Introduction to Mathematical Philosophy* (New York: Macmillan, 1930), pp. 169-70. Reprinted by permission of the publishers.

19. See Russell's lectures of 1918, "The Philosophy of Logical Atomism," first printed in three consecutive issues of *The Monist* and reprinted in R. C. Marsh, ed., *Logic and Knowledge* (London: Macmillan, 1956), pp. 177-281. Also relevant is Russell's Introduction to Wittgenstein's *Tractatus*, and the essay "Logical Atomism" in *Contemporary British Philosophy*, First Series (London: Macmillan, 1924). Valuable also is J. O. Urmson, *Philosophical Analysis*, pp. 1-98.

20. Russell, "The Philosophy of Logical Atomism," in March, *Logic and Knowledge*, p. 179. Quotations from this book by permission of The Macmillan Co.

21. *Contemporary British Philosophy*, pp. 376-77. Quotations from this book by permission of The Macmillan Co.

22. Russell, "The Philosophy of Logical Atomism," p. 181.

23. *Ibid.*, p. 270.

24. See in this connection Harold H. Joachim, *Descartes' Rules for the Direction of the Mind* (London: Allen and Unwin, 1957).

25. *Contemporary British Philosophy*, p. 363.

26. As made in Russell, *The Problems of Philosophy* (New York: Oxford University Press, 1912), Ch. V, and in *Mysticism and Logic* (New York: W. W. Norton, 1929), Ch. X. The following quotation is from *The Problems of Philosophy*, pp. 73-74. Reprinted by permission of the publishers.

27. *Ibid.*, p. 75.

28. Russell, *Our Knowledge of the External World* (New York: W. W. Norton, 1929), p. 75.

29. *Ibid.*, p. 86.

30. See Russell, *The Analysis of Matter* (New York: Dover, 1954), especially Chs. XX and XXXVII.

31. Russell, *Mysticism and Logic*, p. 145. Reprinted by permission of W. W. Norton & Co. The following is drawn from this essay, from *Our Knowledge of the External World*, Ch. IV, and from *The Analysis of Matter*, Chs. XXV, XXVII.

32. Russell, *Our Knowledge of the External World*, p. 117.

33. Russell, *Mysticism and Logic*, p. 165.

34. An excellent critique of Russell's constructionism occurs in Charles A. Fritz, Jr., *Bertrand Russell's Construction of the External World* (London: Routledge and Kegan Paul, 1952), Ch. V.

35. "When we are considering empirical knowledge, the earliest propositions in the hierarchy, which give the grounds for all the others, are not deduced from other propositions, and yet are not mere arbitrary assumptions. They have grounds, though their grounds are not propositions, but observed occurrences. Such propositions, as observed above, I shall call 'basic' propositions; they fulfill the function assigned by the logical positivists to what they call 'protocol propositions.' It is, to my mind, one of the defects of the logical positivists that their linguistic bias makes their theory of protocol propositions vague and unsatisfactory." Russell, *An Inquiry into Meaning and Truth* (New York: W. W. Norton, 1940), pp. 21-22. Quotations from this book by permission of the publishers.

36. *Ibid.*, Ch. X.

37. *Ibid.*, pp. 243-44.

38. *Ibid.*, p. 368.

39. *Ibid.*, p. 390.

40. This is not to say that Russell does not provide sharp criticism of the logical empiricists when occasion demands. As we have seen, *An Inquiry into Meaning and Truth* rejects both the identification of truth with verification and the identification of meaning and verifiability. Other works repeat these criticisms. Cf. *Human Knowledge: Its Scope and Limits* (New York: Simon and Schuster, 1948), p. 75 ff., 363 ff., 447 ff., etc.; and the 1950 article "Logical Positivism" reprinted in Marsh's *Logic and Knowledge*, p. 367-82.

41. Carl G. Hempel, "On the Logical Positivist's Theory of Truth," *Analysis*, II, 4 (January, 1935).

42. Of the two Carnaps, it is the second who is almost universally followed by logical empiricists. A significant exception is Nelson Goodman. See particularly his "The Revision of Philosophy," *American Philosophers at Work*, ed. Sidney Hook (New York: Criterion Books, 1956). See also his *The Structure of Appearance* (Cambridge: Harvard University Press, 1951).

43. Compare, for example, Sec. 50 ("Logischer Wert und Erkenntniswert") with Sec. 54 ("Erkenntnismässige Primatität") of the *Aufbau*, and particularly in the former: "Umformung einer Aussage . . . bleibt der logische Wert stets unverändert, aber nicht immer der Erkenntniswert," with "Die Systemform, die hier dem Entwurf des Konstitutionssystems gegeben werden soll, ist dadurch characterisiert, dass sie nicht nur, wie jede Systemform, die Ordnung der Gegenstände in bezug auf ihre Zurückführbarkeit zur Darstellung bringen will, sondern auch die Ordnung in bezug auf die erkenntnismässige Primarität." Rudolph Carnap, *Der Logische Aufbau der Welt* (Berlin: Meiner Verlag, 1928), pp. 69, 74. All quotations from this work reprinted by permission of Professor Rudolph Carnap.

44. "Das Ziel: Konstitutionssystem der Begriffe—Der Weg: Wirklichkeitisanalyse mit Hilfe der Relationstheorie." *Der Logische Aufbau der Welt*, pp. 1, 3.

45. *Ibid.*, p. 4. "Wenn ein Konstitutionssystem der Begriffe oder der Gegenstände . . . in der angedeuteten Art möglich ist, so folgt daraus: die Gegenstände zerfallen nicht in verschiedene, unzusammenhängende Gebiete, sondern es gibt nur ein Gebiet von Gegenständen und daher nur eine Wissenschaft."

46. The following is worked out in *Der Logische Aufbau der Welt*: the detailed account, pp. 83-132; and the brief, more elegant formalization on pp. 150-162.

47. *Ibid.*, p. 139: "Das Konstitutionssystem ist eine rationale Nachkonstruktion des gesamten, in der Erkenntnis vorwiegend intuitiv vollzogenen Aufbaues der Wirklichkeit."

48. *Ibid.*, p. 181.

49. *Ibid.*, p. 204: "Allerdings spricht die Konstitutionstheorie nicht diese realistische Sprache, sondern ist neutral gegenüber der metaphysischen Komponente der realistischen Aussage."

50. Carnap, *The Logical Syntax of Language* (London: Routledge and Kegan Paul; New York: Humanities Press, 1937), p. xiii. All quotations from this work are reprinted by permission of Routledge and Kegan Paul, Ltd. In *Philosophy and Logical Syntax* (London: Psyche Miniatures, 1937) Carnap is even more absolute. "The *only proper* task of Philosophy is Logical Analysis" (p. 35); and "The method of logical syntax, that is, the analysis of the formal structure of language as a system of rules, is the *only method* of philosophy" (p. 99). The italics are mine and they serve, I think, to indicate the paradoxical nature of these sentences; for they obviously are not factual propositions but rather expressive or practical statements. This is curious in one whose theory denigrates these usages. The sentences are in fact what Stevenson calls "persuasive definitions" and they belong not to the "logic" of logical empiricism but to its "rhetoric."

51. Carnap, *Philosophy and Logical Syntax*, pp. 29-30. Reprinted by permission of Professor Rudolph Carnap.

52. Carnap, *The Logical Syntax of Language*, p. 1.

53. Carnap, *Philosophy and Logical Syntax*, pp. 41-47.

54. Carnap, *The Logical Syntax of Language*, p. 285. It is interesting that Carnap's treatment of object sentences in *Philosophy and Logical Syntax* tends to consider them as empirical entities, whereas in *The Logical Syntax of Language* their objects are *entia rationis*. The example "The rose is red" comes from the former, while "5 is a prime number" comes from the latter.

55. *Ibid.*, p. 313.

56. *Ibid.*, p. 318.

57. *Ibid.*, p. 320.

58. Carnap, "Empiricism, Logic, and Ontology," *Revue Internationale de Philosophie* (1950), reprinted in J. L. Jarrett and S. M. McMurrin, *Contemporary Philosophy* (New York: Holt, 1954), p. 384. Reprinted by permission of *Revue Internationale de Philosophie*, Brussels.

59. Carnap, *The Logical Syntax of Language*, p. 52.

60. Carnap, "Empiricism, Logic, and Ontology," pp. 389-90.

61. Moritz Schlick, "Meaning and Verification," *The Philosophical Review*, Vol. 45 (1936). Reprinted by permission of the publishers.

62. Carnap, "Wahrheit und Bewährung," *Actes du congrès international de philosophie scientifique* (Paris, 1936), IV.

63. Carnap, "Testability and Meaning," *Philosophy of Science* (Baltimore: Williams and Wilkins, 1936), Vol. III, p. 420. Reprinted by permission of the publishers.

64. *Ibid.*, p. 468.

65. Carnap, "Testability and Meaning," *Philosophy of Science*, Vol. IV, pp. 33-34.

66. Carnap, *The Logical Syntax of Language*, p. 278.

67. I have in mind such articles as the following: J. A. Irving, "Toward Radical Empiricism in Ethics," in *American Philosophy Today and Tomorrow* (New York, 1935); H. B. Acton, "The Expletive Theory of Morals," *Analysis*, IV, 3 (1936); Jørgen Jørgensen, "Imperatives and Logic," *Erkenntnis*, VII, 4 (1937-38).

68. Schlick, *Problems of Ethics*, trans. D. Rynin (New York: Prentice-Hall, 1939), pp. 18-19. Reprinted by permission of the publisher.

69. Carnap, *Philosophy and Logical Syntax*, pp. 24-25. Reprinted by permission of Professor Rudolph Carnap. Professor Carnap now feels that these formulations are somewhat less than adequate in the light of his later views. They should therefore be understood in the context of additional remarks which he wrote in 1943 for R. L. Lepley's *Verifiability of Value* (New York: Columbia University Press, 1944, p. 187 f., n. 14) and which occur in his reply to Abraham Kaplan, and will be included in the Carnap volume of The Library of Living Philosophers.

70. A. J. Ayer, *Language, Truth and Logic*, pp. 149-71.

71. C. L. Stevenson, *Ethics and Language* (New Haven: Yale University Press, 1946), p. 13. Reprinted by permission of the publishers.

72. *Ibid.*, p. 138.

73. *Ibid.*, p. 210.

74. Whitehead, *Science and the Modern World*, p. 261. Reprinted by permission of The Macmillan Co.

CHAPTER X

1. Jean-Paul Sartre, *No Exit and Three Other Plays*, trans. Stuart Gilbert (New York: Knopf, 1958). The passages from "The Flies" which I have quoted in this chapter are from pp. 61-62, 108, 122, 103, respectively, and are reprinted by permission of Alfred A. Knopf, Inc.

2. Søren Kierkegaard, "Equilibrium between the Aesthetical and the Ethical in the Composition of Personality," in *Either/Or: A Fragment of Life*, trans. Walter Lowrie, Vol. II (Princeton: Princeton University Press, 1944).

3. Kierkegaard, *Concluding Unscientific Postscript* (Princeton: Princeton University Press, 1941), p. 109.

4. Friedrich Nietzsche, *Zur Genealogie der Moral* (1887). English trans. Horace Samuel, *The Genealogy of Morals* (New York: Random House, 1927).

5. Nietzsche, *Der Antichrist* (1895), Sec. 1.

6. Karl Jaspers, *Reason and Existenz*, trans. William Earle (New York: Noonday Press, 1955), Lecture 1, "The Origin of the Contemporary Philosophical Situation," p. 47. Reprinted by permission of the publishers.

7. Kierkegaard and Nietzsche were the first in an essential and perhaps conscious sense. But other ancestors have been appealed to by Heidegger and Marcel as well as by Jaspers. These others are the pre-Socratics (particularly Heracleitus and Parmenides), Socrates (who is the existential hero of Kierkegaard himself), St. Augustine, and, particularly, Pascal. Personal experience, the exploration of Being, and the reasons of the heart: these seem to be the elements of such a choice.

8. The most rewarding translation in English is Edmund Husserl, *Ideas: General Introduction to Pure Phenomenology*, trans. W. R. Boyce Gibson (New York: Macmillan, 1952). The *Logische Untersuchungen* (Halle, 1901) is, of course, classic, the *Cartesianische Meditationen und Pariser Vorträge* (The Hague, 1950) of the greatest interest. The best in English on Husserl are Marvin Farber, *The Foundation of Phenomenology* (Cambridge: Harvard University Press, 1943), and E. P. Welch, *The Philosophy of Edmund Husserl* (New York: Columbia University Press, 1941).

9. Sartre, *L'Etre et le néant: Essai d'ontologie phénoménologique*, 43rd ed. (Paris, 1955). This has been translated by Hazel Barnes as *Being and Nothingness* (New

York: Philosophical Library, 1956). Quotations are from the translated edition, and are reprinted by permission of the publishers. The present quotation is from p. 1.

10. Sartre, *Nausea*, trans. Lloyd Alexander (New York: New Directions, 1949). The quotation is a composite from pp. 134-36, and is reprinted by permission of the publishers.

11. Husserl, *Ideas*, p. 192.

12. This quotation first appeared in Husserl's famous article, "Philosophie als strenge Wissenschaft," *Logos*, No. I (1910-11).

13. Martin Heidegger, *Sein und Zeit* (Halle, 1935), p. 27.

14. The details of the two reductions may be found briefly stated in Husserl, *Ideas*, pp. 171-84, and more systematically in the *Logische Untersuchungen*.

15. Sartre, *Being and Nothingness*, p. xlviii.

16. Heidegger, *Sein und Zeit*, p. 12.

17. "We find ourselves at present on the ground of the phenomenology of Husserl. . . ." (*Being and Nothingness*, p. lix). The whole of Sartre's Introduction to this work is a sustained tribute to Husserl. And Heidegger says: "Ontologie und Phänomenologie sind nicht zwei verschiedene Disziplinen neben anderen zur Philosophie gehörigen. Die beiden Titel characterisieren die Philosophie selbst nach Gegenstand und Behandlungsart. Philosophie ist universale phänomenologische Ontologie ausgehend von der hermeneutik des Daseins, die als Analytik der Existenz das Ende des Leitfadens alles philosophischen Fragens dort festgemacht hat, woraus es entspringt und wohin es zuruckschlägt. . . . Die folgenden Untersuchungen sind nur möglich geworden auf den Boden, den E. Husserl gelegt, mit dessen 'Logischen Untersuchungen' die Phänomenologie zum Durchbruch kam." (*Sein und Zeit*, p. 38.)

18. Sartre, *Existentialism*, trans. Bernard Frechtman (New York: Philosophical Library, 1947), p. 15.

19. The literature here is enormous, but much of it is of little value. Useful, unpretentious, and generally accurate in English are: John Wild, *The Challenge of Existentialism* (Bloomington: Indiana University Press, 1955), good in exposition but with a "Realist" axe to grind; and James Collins, *The Existentialists: A Critical Study* (Chicago: Henry Regnery, 1952), clear and imaginative criticism presupposing both "Theism" and "Realism." Excellent in German is Leo Gabriel, *Existenzphilosophie: Von Kierkegaard bis Sartre* (Vienna: Verlag Herold, 1951). Outstanding in French is Regis Jolivet, *Les Doctrines existentialistes de Kierkegaard à Sartre* (Paris: Editions de Fontenelle, 1948). Translated from French into English is Jean Wahl, *A Short History of Existentialism* (New York: Philosophical Library, 1949).

20. "In der Welt ist der *Mensch* allein die Wirklichkeit die mir zugänglich ist. Hier ist Gegenwärtigkeit, Näche, Fülle, Leben. Der Mensch ist die Stätte, an der und durch die alles wirklich ist, was für uns überhaupt ist. Das Menschensein versäumen würde für bedeuten, ins Nichts zu sinken. Was der Mensch sei und sein könne, ist eine Grundfrage für den Menschen." Karl Jaspers, *Rechenschaft und Ausblick (Reden und Aufsätze)* (Munich: Piper Verlag, 1951), p. 344. The translation in the text is by Felix Kaufman and appears in *Existentialism from Dostoevsky to Sartre*, ed. Walter Kaufman (New York: Meridian Books, 1956), p. 141.

21. *Ibid.*

22. Jaspers is much concerned with both Kierkegaard and Nietzsche although in a somewhat different connection. The first lecture of his *Reason and Existenz* is taken up with his treatment of their importance for the contemporary philosophical

situation. He finds alike, and crucial in their thinking, the questioning of reason, a suspicion of science, their criticism of the institutional system, their ambiguity and disordering influence. In his treatment of them as "exceptions" is also involved the idea of their loneliness.

23. Jaspers, *Rechenschaft und Ausblick*, p. 340; Kaufmann, *Existentialism from Dostoevsky to Sartre*, p. 138. Reprinted by permission of Piper Verlag and Meridian Books.

24. Quotations below from Kaufmann, *Existentialism from Dostoevsky to Sartre*, pp. 146, 147.

25. *Ibid.*, p. 134.

26. Karl Jaspers, *Philosophie*. I, *Philosophische Weltorientierung*; II, *Existenzerhellung*; III, *Metaphysik* (Berlin: Julius Springer Verlag, 1932). Jaspers has written many books developing and repeating his chief insights. In my opinion *Philosophie* is his greatest achievement, but to be mentioned in addition are the valuable *Reason and Existenz*, originally published in 1935, and the massive late book, *Von der Wahrheit: Philosophische Logik* I (Munich: Piper Verlag, 1947). This latter repeats much that has gone before but also contains many newly developed ideas.

27. Jaspers, *Philosophie*, I, vii.

28. *Ibid.*, I, 27, 53.

29. *Ibid.*, II, 1.

30. *Ibid.*, II, 182.

31. Although Jaspers, unlike Heidegger, does not make explicit acknowledgment of Husserl's influence upon him, he did attend the latter's lectures about 1909. And he speaks of him in "Mein Weg zur Philosophie" (1951): "Was in mir schon wirkte fand ich bestätigt: den Drang zu den Sachen selbst. . . . Aber Husserl als Philosoph enttäuschte mich. . . ." *Rechenschaft und Ausblick*, pp. 323-33. It is interesting that Heidegger's attitude is not too dissimilar. Husserl's emphasis "to the facts themselves" meets with universal approval. There is not, however, agreement as to what these facts are.

32. Jaspers, *Philosophie*, II, 202: "Situation heisst eine nicht nur naturgesetzliche, vielmehr eine *sinnbezogene Wirklichkeit*, die weder psychisch noch physisch, sondern beides zugleich als die konkrete Wirklichkeit ist. . . ."

33. Jaspers, *Philosophie*, II, 204. In my opinion the climax and the heart of Jaspers' existentialism comes in *Philosophie*, II, 201-55.

34. Jaspers, *Von der Wahrheit*, p. 880.

35. The encompassing *(Das Umgreifende)* is treated best in two places: (1) in the second lecture of *Reason and Existenz*, and (2) more completely in *Von der Wahrheit*, pp. 47-222.

36. *Von der Wahrheit*, p. 76.

37. *Ibid.*, p. 47: "Das umgreifende ist entweder das Sein das *alles ist*, in dem und durch das wir sind. Oder es ist das Sein, das *wir selbst* sind, und worin uns jede bestimmte Seinsweise, auch alles Weltsein, verkommt. . . . wir sind aber in dreifacher Weise umgreifendes Sein . . . als *Dasein, Bewusstsein überhaupt, Geist*." The systematic account of the Encompassing which Jaspers proposes is thus the following: The Encompassing of Being Itself is *World* or *Transcendence*. The Encompassing which we are is *Empirical Existence, Consciousness in general*, and *Spirit*. The ground and binding tie of the characteristics of the Encompassing are *Existenz* and *reason*.

38. Jaspers, *Reason and Existenz*, pp. 60-61.

39. *Ibid.*, p. 62.

40. *Ibid.*, p. 68.

41. "Incréé, sans raison d'être, sans rapport aucun avec un autre être, l'être-en-soi est de trop pour l'éternité." *L'Etre et le néant*, p. 34; *Being and Nothingness* (trans. Barnes), p. lxviii.

42. *L'Etre et le néant*, p. 57. It is interesting that Jaspers, who finds that the tragic to some extent consists in negativity, yet denies this is ontological in its reference. "Die Tragik wird in das *Sein* als solche gelegt. . . . Das Sein ist brüchig." But this is just what Jaspers denies. On the contrary he asserts: "Vom Seinsgrund zu sagen, er sei tragisch, das aber scheint uns absurd. . . . Die Tragik wird in die Welt gelegt. . . ." *Von der Wahrheit*, p. 955.

43. Sartre, *Being and Nothingness*, p. 29.

44. *Ibid.*, p. 53.

45. *Ibid.*, p. 56.

46. *Ibid.*, p. 58.

47. *Ibid.*, p. 59.

48. *Ibid.*, pp. 62-63. It is interesting in this connection that Sartre, who criticizes the Freudian mechanism of the unconscious as a device of bad faith, yet cannot himself produce an example of real sincerity. Freud's invention of dream analysis through free association was just such a technique for ensuring frankness; or, we might say, "sincerity in spite of the unconscious."

49. Sartre, "Portrait of the Antisemite," trans. Mary Guggenheim, *Partisan Review* (Spring, 1946), pp. 166-67. Reprinted by permission of Libraire Gallimard, Paris. All rights reserved.

50. Sartre, *Being and Nothingness*, p. 221.

51. *Ibid.*, p. 257.

52. Sartre, *Baudelaire* (London, 1948), pp. 119, 148.

53. Sartre, *No Exit and Three Other Plays*, pp. 46-47.

54. Sartre, *Being and Nothingness*, p. 353.

55. *Ibid.*, p. 439.

56. *Ibid.*, p. 443.

57. From T. S. Eliot, *Four Quartets* (New York: Harcourt, Brace, 1943). Reprinted by permission of the publishers.

58. Sartre, *Being and Nothingness*, p. 503.

59. Wallace Stevens, "Dutch Graves in Bucks County," in *The Collected Poems of Wallace Stevens* (New York: Knopf, 1954). Reprinted by permission of the publishers.

60. Sartre's treatment of situationality and facticity appears in *L'Etre et le néant*, pp. 561-638; *Being and Nothingness*, pp. 481-553.

61. Sartre, *Being and Nothingness*, p. 553.

62. *Ibid.*, p. 553 f.

63. Sartre, *L'Existentialisme est un humanisme* (Paris: Nagel, 1946). There are two English translations, one by Bernard Frechtman for the Philosophical Library, the other by Philip Mairet, published by Methuen and Company. All short quotations are taken from the latter.

64. *Ibid.*

65. *Ibid.*

66. The status of "authenticity" in the existentialist moral philosophy has been interestingly if briefly discussed by Marjorie Grene in "Authenticity: An Existential Virtue," *Ethics* (July, 1952).

67. Sartre. *Situations*, III (Paris: Libraire Gallimard, 1949), pp. 11-14. I have

used the English translation by Ramon Guthrie in *The Republic of Silence*, ed. A. J. Liebling (New York: Harcourt, Brace, 1947), pp. 498-500. Quotations by permission of Libraire Gallimard.

68. Gabriel Marcel, *Man Against Mass Society* (Chicago: Henry Regnery, 1952), p. 5.

69. Simone de Beauvoir, *The Ethics of Ambiguity* (New York: Philosophical Library, 1948). All quotations from this work by permission of the publishers.

70. Gabriel Marcel, *The Philosophy of Existence* (New York: Philosophical Library, 1949). See the first essay, "On the Ontological Mystery."

71. Jaspers, *Man in the Modern Age*, trans. Eden and Cedar Paul (London: Routledge, 1951), p. 49. Quotations by permission of the publishers.

72. *Ibid.*, p. 188.

73. *Situations*, III, pp. 135-225. The brief passage following which I have translated is from pp. 143-44.

74. *Ibid.*

75. De Beauvoir, *The Ethics of Ambiguity*, p. 145.

76. *Ibid.*, p. 155. Sartre expresses much the same thing in the play *Dirty Hands*. Hoederer, the ruthless and opportunistic Communist leader, says: "How you cling to your purity, young man! How afraid you are to soil your hands! All right, stay pure! What good will it do? Why did you join us? Purity is an idea for a yogi or a monk. You intellectuals and bourgeois anarchists use it as a pretext for doing nothing. To do nothing, to remain motionless, arms at your sides, wearing kid gloves. Well, I have dirty hands. Right up to the elbows. I've plunged them in filth and blood. But what do you hope? Do you think you can govern innocently?" *No Exit and Three Other Plays*, pp. 223-24.

77. M. Merleau-Ponty, *Humanisme et Terreur* (Paris: Libraire Gallimard, 1947), p. 197. The next quotation which I have translated is from p. 196. This statement about Merleau-Ponty's bias holds only for the writings of 1946-47. For it is true that the Korean War worked a certain change in his partisanship for the Soviet Union. His new neutrality appears in his later *Les Aventures de la dialectique* (Paris: Libraire Gallimard, 1955). In its epilogue he attempts to explain his change of view, and, indeed, the bulk of the book is a critique of Sartre's flirtation with Marxism ("Sartre et l'ultrabolshevisme"). Still, nothing in this work suggests a need for modifying the basic point that the social criticism of existentialism is pseudo-Marxist, journalistic, and unoriginal.

78. *Ibid.*, p. 205.

CHAPTER XI

1. Ludwig Wittgenstein, *Philosophical Investigations*, trans. G. E. M. Anscombe (New York: Macmillan, 1953), Sec. 90. Quotations by permission of the publishers.

2. Richard McKeon, "Communication, Truth, and Society," *Ethics* (January, 1957). This brief article is an admirable statement of the role of the problem of communication in contemporary society and merits close attention.

3. T. S. Eliot, *The Collected Poems 1909-1935* (New York: Harcourt, Brace, 1936). Reprinted by permission of the publishers.

4. Wallace Stevens, *The Collected Poems of Wallace Stevens* (New York: Knopf, 1954). Reprinted by permission of the publishers.

5. Ezra Pound, in *Literary Essays of Ezra Pound*, ed. T. S. Eliot (New York: New Directions, 1954), pp. 76, 77. Reprinted by permission of the publishers.

6. Wittgenstein, *Philosophical Investigations*, Sec. 111.

7. A. J. Ayer, *Language, Truth and Logic* (London: Victor Gollancz, 1936), pp. 61, 62. Reprinted by permission of the publishers.

8. The two forms of philosophical analysis have been distinguished and their antecedents traced and chief doctrines explicated in two recent books: J. O. Urmson, *Philosophical Analysis: Its Development between the Two World Wars* (Oxford: Clarendon Press, 1956) and Gilbert Ryle, ed., *The Revolution in Philosophy* (London: Macmillan, 1956).

9. Ryle, "Ordinary Language," *The Philosophical Review*, Vol. LXII (April, 1953), p. 173. Reprinted by permission of the publishers.

10. There are suggestions of this kind in R. M. Hare, *The Language of Morals* (Oxford: Clarendon Press, 1952); and in *Aesthetics and Language*, ed. with an introduction by William Elton (New York: Philosophical Library, 1954).

11. Ryle, "Ordinary Language," p. 185.

12. See for example G. J. Warnock, "Verification and Use of Language," *Revue internationale de philosophie*, No. 17-18 (1951): "To know the meaning of a sentence is to know how to use it, to know in what circumstances its use is correct or incorrect. . . . A sentence is meaningful if it *has* a use; we know its meaning if we *know* its use."

13. G. E. Moore, "An Autobiography," in *The Philosophy of G. E. Moore*, ed. P. A. Schilpp (Evanston and Chicago: Tudor, 1942), p. 8. All quotations by permission of P. A. Schilpp, Editor, The Library of Living Philosophers.

14. See for example the long and generally informative summary of Morris Weitz, "Oxford Philosophy," *The Philosophical Review*, Vol. LXII (April, 1953).

15. Wittgenstein was always eccentric. He wished that each of his three published works—*Tractatus Logico-Philosophicus* (London: Routledge, 1955), *Philosophical Investigations*, and *Remarks on the Foundations of Mathematics* (New York: Macmillan, 1956)—should appear with facing pages of original German text and English translation. Supreme care for the "word" shows itself here also.

16. John Maynard Keynes, *Two Memoirs* (New York: Augustus M. Kelley, 1949), p. 85. Quotations by permission of Rupert Hart-Davis, Ltd.

17. Bertrand Russell, *Portraits from Memory and Other Essays* (London: Allen and Unwin, 1956), p. 68. Reprinted by permission of the publishers.

18. Keynes, *Two Memoirs*, p. 88.

19. Moore, "An Autobiography," p. 14.

20. Moore, *Principia Ethica* (Cambridge: Cambridge University Press, 1929), p. vii. All quotations by permission of the publishers.

21. Moore, "A Defense of Common Sense," in *Contemporary British Philosophy*, Second Series, ed. J. H. Muirhead (London: Allen and Unwin, 1925), p. 194 f. Quotations by permission of the publishers.

22. *Ibid.*, p. 198.

23. Moore, *Philosophical Studies* (New York: Humanities Press, 1951), pp. 159-61.

24. Moore, "A Defense of Common Sense," p. 205.

25. *Ibid.*, pp. 218-19.

26. Moore, "Proof of an External World," in *Proceedings of the British Academy*, Vol. XXV (1939). All quotations by permission of the British Academy.

27. *Ibid.*, p. 13.

28. *Ibid.*, p. 18.

29. *Ibid.*, p. 20.

30. *Ibid.*, p. 25.

31. In the Foreword to *Some Main Problems of Philosophy*, Moore's lectures of 1910-11, first published in 1953, Wisdom says: "For in these lectures philosophy is done with a directness and honesty and incisiveness which at once gives hope that we may, working with Moore, soon cut a way out of the jungle into the light. It is the same hope we felt when we read what we still read—Moore's *Principia Ethica* and his *Philosophical Studies.* That hope was justified." Moore, *Some Main Problems of Philosophy* (London: Allen and Unwin, 1953), p. ix.

32. Moore, *Principia Ethica*, p. viii.

33. *Ibid.*, p. 6.

34. *Ibid.*, pp. 188-89.

35. Keynes, *Two Memoirs*, p. 94.

36. *The Philosophy of G. E. Moore*, p. 33.

37. Wittgenstein's three published works are the *Tractatus* (1922), the *Philosophical Investigations* (1953), and the *Remarks on the Foundations of Mathematics* (1956). The last two works are posthumous, and the order of publication does not represent the order of writing. Part I of the *Investigations* was complete by 1945; Part II was written in 1947-49. The *Remarks* contains material written between 1937 and 1944. There are two longish sections here referring to Goedel's theorem, an Appendix to Part I going back to 1937, and the specific remarks (pp. 174-77) going back to 1941. The *Remarks* are valuable as presenting the transitional atmosphere between the *Tractatus* and the *Investigations*, and for the special subject of the logical foundations of mathematics. But for the general philosophy the *Tractatus* and the *Investigations* are sufficient. The latter is now in great vogue for doctrinal reasons, but in my opinion the former is still Wittgenstein's greatest work. I should say the same for Carnap's *Logischer Aufbau* in comparison with his later works. It is a sign of the shifting winds of doctrine that both Wittgenstein and Carnap should have been the first to repudiate their own "first-born," and I think time will show each repudiation to have been a mistake.

38. Wittgenstein, *Tractatus Logico-Philosophicus.* The following propositions appear on pp. 31-43.

39. Perhaps taking the cue from Russell, most commentators agree that Wittgenstein's "objects" are *particulars* rather than simple properties or relations, but "bare particulars" which have formal but no material properties. But what is their metaphysical status? Urmson (*Philosophical Analysis*, p. 57) says: ". . . it would seem that Wittgenstein's objects are very like the Aristotelian first substance as it appears in the *Categories.*" But Irving M. Copi ("Objects, Properties and Relations in the *Tractatus*," in *Mind*, April, 1958) believes that "Wittgenstein's objects correspond more closely to Aristotle's prime matter than to his primary substance."

40. Wittgenstein, *Tractatus*, p. 55.

41. *Ibid.*, p. 62.

42. Compare Norman Malcolm's "Wittgenstein's *Philosophical Investigations*," in the *Philosophical Review* (October, 1954), with P. F. Strawson's "Critical Notice: *Philosophical Investigations*," in *Mind* (January, 1954). Malcolm sees Wittgenstein's subjects as "presented with the passion and profundity of genius, in language of never-failing force." Strawson's language is very different. He finds in Wittgenstein

the "obsession with the expression of pain" and a "prejudice against the inner," and numerous errors of analysis and interpretation. Malcolm's notice follows Strawson's, refers to it, and attempts to set right Strawson's "misunderstandings."

43. Wittgenstein, *Philosophical Investigations*, p. 31e f. Miss Anscombe's translation is in general sound, but contains some unbearably British idioms. *"Philosophieren,"* for example, is given a provincial twist when it is translated "to *do* philosophy."

44. *Ibid.*, p. 43e.

45. *Ibid.*, p. 49e.

46. *Ibid.*, p. 51e.

47. *Ibid.*, p. 89e.

48. These matters are treated in *ibid.*, pp. 89e-105e and *infra*.

49. *Ibid.*, p. 95e.

50. *Ibid.*, p. 116e.

51. *Ibid.*, pp. 187e, 188e.

52. *Ibid.*, p. 129e.

53. *Ibid.*, p. 180e.

54. The chronological development is as follows: (1) "Systematically Misleading Expressions," *Proceedings of the Aristotelian Society*, Vol. XXXII (1931-32), pp. 139-70 (reprinted in *Logic and Language*, First Series, ed. Antony Flew [Oxford: Basil Blackwell, 1952]); (2) "Categories," *Proceedings of the Aristotelian Society*, Vol. XXXVIII (1937-38), pp. 189-206 (reprinted in *Logic and Language*, Second Series, ed. Antony Flew [Oxford: Basil Blackwell, 1953]); and *The Concept of Mind* (London: Hutchinson, 1949); and (3) *Dilemmas* (London: Cambridge University Press, 1954). In what follows my quotations from the "Systematically Misleading Expressions" and the "Categories" will be taken from the Flew volumes, which are generally more accessible than the Aristotelian Society *Proceedings*. Quotations are by permission of Basil Blackwell, Publishers.

55. *Logic and Language*, First Series, pp. 13, 14.

56. *Ibid.*, p. 18.

57. *Ibid.*, p. 20.

58. *Ibid.*, p. 32.

59. *Logic and Language*, Second Series, p. 65.

60. Ryle, *The Concept of Mind* (London: Hutchinson, 1949). Quotations by permission of the publishers.

61. *Ibid.*, pp. 15-16.

62. Ryle, *Dilemmas*, p. 126.

63. *Ibid.*, p. 1.

64. *Ibid.*, p. 24.

65. *Ibid.*, pp. 31-32.

CHAPTER XII

1. "Autobiographical Notes," in *The Philosophy of Alfred North Whitehead*, ed. P. A. Schilpp (New York: Tudor, 1951), p. 7. Quotations by permission of the editor.

2. Whitehead was at Cambridge from 1884 to 1910, at London from 1910 to 1924, and at Harvard from 1924 to 1947. The chief works of each period are: (1) A *Treatise on Universal Algebra* (1898), *Principia Mathematica* (1910-13); (2) *An*

Enquiry Concerning the Principles of Natural Knowledge (1919), *The Concept of Nature* (1920), *The Principle of Relativity* (1922); (3) *Science and the Modern World* (1925), *Process and Reality* (1929), *Adventures of Ideas* (1933), *Modes of Thought* (1938).

3. John Dewey, "The Philosophy of Whitehead," in *The Philosophy of Alfred North Whitehead*, p. 645.

4. Whitehead, *The Concept of Nature* (Cambridge: Cambridge University Press, 1955), p. 29. Reprinted by permission of the publishers.

5. *Ibid.*, p. 31.

6. This topic has been of persistent interest to Whitehead. Two lectures on "Nature and Life" were delivered at the University of Chicago in 1934. In the second of these he said: "The status of life in nature . . . is the modern problem of philosophy and science. Indeed it is the central meeting point of all the strains of systematic thought, humanistic, naturalistic, philosophic." *Modes of Thought* (New York: Macmillan, 1938), p. 202.

7. See the remarkable "England and the Narrow Seas," reprinted in Whitehead, *Essays in Science and Philosophy* (New York: Philosophical Library, 1948), pp. 34-43.

8. So said Whitehead's daughter, Jessie. See Mary A. Wyman, "Whitehead's Philosophy of Science in the Light of Wordsworth's Poetry," *Philosophy of Science*, Vol. 23, No. 4 (October, 1956), p. 283.

9. I do not, of course, mean that the translation is literal or exact, but there is undoubted similarity. The "fluency of concrescence" which characterizes all actual entities has been constructed on the vibratory atomic model. The notion of "prehension" is almost defined in vector terms, and the vector concept appears with constant regularity in *Process and Reality* (New York: Macmillan, 1929; cf. pp. 228, 324). The idea of the physical field has two exemplifications: one with the extensive continuum alone, the other with the community of actual occasions within it, sometimes analogized to "the consequent nature of God."

10. Whitehead, *An Enquiry Concerning the Principles of Natural Knowledge* (London: Cambridge University Press, 1955), p. 24. My italics.

11. Whitehead, *The Concept of Nature*, pp. 189-90.

12. Whitehead, *Principles of Natural Knowledge*, pp. 196-97.

13. *Ibid.*, pp. 197-98.

14. Whitehead, *Science and the Modern World* (New York: Macmillan, 1925). The relevant passages are pp. 50-53 and Chapter VIII. The conclusion with respect to time is drawn on pp. 174-80. All quotations by permission of the publishers.

15. Whitehead, *Modes of Thought* (New York: Macmillan, 1938), p. 120.

16. Whtehead, *Process and Reality*, p. 63. Quotations from this work by permission of the publishers.

17. *Ibid.*

18. Whitehead, *Adventures of Ideas* (New York: Macmillan, 1933), p. 188. All quotations by permission of the publishers.

19. Here again, as in the case of ideas from modern physics, exact translation is impossible. But it would surely be possible to conceive *Process and Reality* as somehow including all seven of the Platonic "notions." My tentative dictionary would be: The Ideas—"eternal objects;" The Physical Elements—"selected actual entities" or "actual occasions;" The Psyche—"the mental pole of every actual occasion," "conceptual feelings;" The Eros—"God as the lure for feeling," "the sub-

jective aim of each actual occasion;" The Harmony—"the consequent nature of God;" The Mathematical Relations—"the extensive continuum," "modes of extensive connection;" The Receptacle—"creativity."

20. Whitehead, *Adventures of Ideas*, pp. 240-41.

21. *Ibid.*, Chapters VII, VIII.

22. Reprinted in *The Philosophy of Alfred North Whitehead*, pp. 666-81.

23. Whitehead, *Nature and Life* (Chicago: University of Chicago Press, 1934).

24. This and the following quotations are from *Science and the Modern World*, pp. 108-31.

25. Whitehead, *Nature and Life*, reprinted in *Modes of Thought*, p. 205.

26. *Ibid.*, p. 211.

27. *Science and the Modern World*, p. 58.

28. *Ibid.*, pp. 26-27.

29. *The Philosophy of Alfred North Whitehead*, p. 682.

30. Whitehead, *Principles of Natural Knowledge*, p. 4.

31. Whitehead, *The Concept of Nature*, p. 71.

32. The relevant passages here are to be found in *Principles of Natural Knowledge*, pp. 99, 196, and *The Concept of Nature*, pp. 57, 62.

33. Whitehead, *Science and the Modern World*, pp. 81-82.

34. *Ibid.*, p. 62. The same line of argument, though it is more comprehensive and better illustrated by example, occurs in the brief and very interesting paper, "Uniformity and Contingency," given in 1922 (*Proceedings of the Aristotelian Society*, Vol. 23).

35. *Alfred North Whitehead: An Anthology*, selected by F. S. C. Northrop and Mason W. Gross (New York: Macmillan, 1953), p. 308.

36. Whitehead, *Science and the Modern World*, p. 212.

37. *Ibid.*, pp. 101-102.

38. *Ibid.*, p. 221.

39. *Ibid.*, p. 224.

40. *Ibid.*, p. 153.

41. Whitehead, *Process and Reality*, p. 4.

42. *Ibid.*, p. 12.

43. Whitehead, *Adventures of Ideas*, pp. 290-91.

44. Dewey in *The Philosophy of Alfred North Whitehead*, p. 646.

45. Part I, Chapter II. In a sense the whole of Whitehead's metaphysics is given in this condensed twenty-page account. But it requires the remainder of the book to explain, apply, and make explicit the historical affiliations of these few notions. Thus Part II, "Discussions and Applications," deals with the scheme in terms of the philosophies of the seventeenth and eighteenth centuries and of Plato and Aristotle. Whitehead shows his tremendous interest in Descartes, Locke, Hume, and Plato. But historians of philosophy will find here a notable example of how a great philosopher uses other philosophers in the tradition for his own purposes, rather than for theirs. The account of Hume is very one-sided. The account of Locke is very sympathetic and, for this very reason, almost unrecognizable. Part III, "The Theory of Prehension," is Whitehead's account of "the genetic theory of actuality;" Part IV, "The Theory of Extension," is his account of "the morphological theory of actuality." That is to say, Parts III and IV supplement each other, as do the basic ideas of "feeling" and of "form." Part V contains a "Final Interpretation."

46. Whitehead, *Process and Reality*, pp. 27-28.

47. These composite quotations are taken from *Process and Reality*, pp. 31-38.

48. *Ibid.*, pp. 114, 124-25.

49. *Ibid.*, pp. 98-99.

50. *Ibid.*, pp. 79-80.

51. In the famous Chapter XI of *Adventures of Ideas* ("Objects and Subjects") Whitehead says "the subject-object relation is the fundamental structural pattern of experience;" and a moment later, "The basis of experience is emotional." The further development of the chapter is an attempt to show how these two statements say essentially the same thing.

52. Whitehead, *Process and Reality*, p. 130.

53. *Ibid.*, pp. 172-73.

54. *Ibid.*, p. 184. The entire doctrine of "causal efficacy," "presentational immediacy," and "symbolic reference" is treated in *Process and Reality*, Part II, Chapter VIII, and in *Symbolism, Its Meaning and Effect* (New York: Macmillan, 1927). But I have not thought fit to expound it in detail. Whitehead is primarily a metaphysician and not an epistemologist, and the current emphasis upon the latter rather than the former aspect of his philosophy distorts its total character. Even so competent an expounder of Whitehead as Victor Lowe, after having made the same point, himself proceeds largely to deal with Whitehead in epistemological terms. See Lowe, "Whitehead's Philosophical Development," in *The Philosophy of Alfred North Whitehead*, p. 52 ff.

55. Whitehead, *Process and Reality*, pp. 246-47.

56. *Ibid.*, p. 364.

57. See *Process and Reality*, Part II, Chapter IX, "Propositions," and Part III, Chapter IV, "Propositions and Feelings."

58. *Ibid.*, p. 483.

59. *Ibid.*, p. 395.

60. *Ibid.*, p. 416.

61. *Ibid.*, p. 427.

62. Whitehead, *Modes of Thought*, pp. 37, 50.

63. *Atlantic Monthly* (June, 1936). Reprinted in *Essays in Science and Philosophy*, p. 16. The brief quotations following are from "Autobiographical Notes," *ibid.*, p. 8.

64. Whitehead, *Adventures of Ideas*, p. 58.

65. *Ibid.*, p. 4.

66. *Ibid.*, pp. 219-20.

67. *Ibid.*, pp. 13-14.

68. Whitehead, *Process and Reality*, p. 74.

69. *Ibid.*, p. 128.

70. Whitehead, *Adventures of Ideas*, p. 6.

71. *Ibid.*, pp. 30-41.

72. *Ibid.*, pp. 210-11.

73. *Ibid.*, p. 353.

74. *Ibid.*, p. 341.

75. *Ibid.*, p. 331.

76. *Ibid.*, p. 354.

77. *Ibid.*, p. 360.

78. *Ibid.*, p. 367.

79. *Ibid.*, p. 369.

80. Whitehead, *Science and the Modern World*, pp. 249-50. See also *Process and Reality*, p. 248. The chief sources for Whitehead's metaphysical treatment of God are *Science and the Modern World*, Chapter XI, and *Process and Reality*, Part V, Chapter II.

81. Whitehead, *Process and Reality*, p. 521.

82. *Ibid.*, pp. 525-26.

83. *Ibid.*, p. 529.

84. *Ibid.*, p. 528.

INDEX

Index